D0879513

A Day in the Life

*Career Options in Library
and Information Science*

Edited by PRISCILLA K. SHONTZ
and
RICHARD A. MURRAY

LIBRARIES
U N L I M I T E D
A Member of the Greenwood Publishing Group

Westport, Connecticut • London

Library of Congress Cataloging-in-Publication Data

A day in the life : career options in library and information science / edited by Priscilla K. Shontz and Richard A. Murray.
     p. cm.
Includes bibliographical references and index.
ISBN-13: 978-1-59158-364-6 (alk. paper)
ISBN-10: 1-59158-364-0 (alk. paper)
1. Librarians—Vocational guidance—United States. 2. Library education—United States.
3. Librarians—Employment—United States. 4. Library science—Vocational guidance—
United States. 5. Information science—Vocational guidance—United States. 6. Librarians—Vocational
guidance. 7. Library education 8. Career development. 9. Librarians—Anecdotes. I. Shontz, Priscilla K.,
1965– II. Murray, Richard A. (Richard Allen), 1973–
Z682.35.V62D39 2007
020.23'73–dc22   2006102804

British Library Cataloguing in Publication Data is available.

Library of Congress Catalog Card Number: 2006102804
ISBN-10: 978-1-59158-364-6

First published in 2007

Libraries Unlimited, 88 Post Road West, Westport, CT 06881
A Member of the Greenwood Publishing Group, Inc.
www.lu.com

Printed in the United States of America

The paper used in this book complies with the
Permanent Paper Standard issued by the National
Information Standards Organization (Z39.48-1984).

10 9 8 7 6 5 4 3 2 1

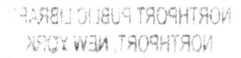

For David. –P.K.S.

For my mom and dad. –R.A.M.

Contents

PART III: SCHOOL LIBRARIES

PART IV: SPECIAL LIBRARIES

PART V: CONSORTIA

PART VI: LIS FACULTY

PART VII: LIBRARY VENDORS

Preface

What do you want to do when you grow up?

Is the grass *really* greener on the other side of the fence?

Are you considering a career in library and information science? Are you curious about the options available to you? Are you currently working in the information field, wondering what it would be like to try another type of job? Do you wonder what else you might do with your master's degree in library or information science?

Many people, whether new to the library field or not, would like to know what career options they have. This book provides a glimpse into the wide variety of jobs available to information professionals. In this book, we asked ninety-six contributors to describe a typical workday or work routine (most replied, "There *is* no typical day in my job!"). We also asked them to point out advantages and disadvantages of their positions and offer advice to job seekers interested in following their career paths. Authors candidly share their experiences to offer readers a sense of what it's really like to work in a job like theirs.

The book covers a wide variety of traditional and nontraditional jobs. Obviously, even with the large number of jobs that we did include, we couldn't include all the ways people are using their LIS degrees. In fact, we had to turn down more than 300 people who offered to write about their fascinating jobs (we hope they will consider sharing their job experiences at LIScareer.com)! In addition to public, academic, school, and special libraries, the authors also represent consortia, associations, LIS programs, vendors, publishers, consultants, and nonlibrary fields.

Though the book is primarily aimed at information professionals working in the United States and Canada, a few authors have written about their experiences working around the world, including Australia, Bolivia, England, Germany, Hungary, Nigeria, Norway, the Philippines, Qatar, and Scotland.

We'd love to hear your comments and suggestions. Please visit LIScareer online at www.liscareer.com and let us know if you'd like to share your career advice with others.

We hope that this book will help you discover new possibilities.

Priscilla K. Shontz
Richard A. Murray

Acknowledgments

We'd like to thank all the authors who contributed their stories. We hope you enjoy reading them as much as we did. Special thanks go to Ellen Symons and Anne Brûlé for indexing the book and Jessamyn West for writing the introduction.

When Ann Snoeyenbos suggested that a "day in the life" might make an interesting LIScareer series, Priscilla thought that sounded like a great topic for a book. This is the second time Ann has inspired Priscilla to write a book. Thanks, Ann, for being such a great muse!

Our acquisitions editor, Sue Easun, not only guided us good-naturedly through the publication process but also contributed the epilogue. We're also grateful to Sue Stewart, Emma Bailey, Sue Wilson, and Laura Poole for helping make this book a reality.

Thanks to Tiffany Eatman Allen, Bea Caraway, Clint Chamberlain, Wayne Jones, Ali Poffinberger, and Lisa Smith for offering opinions when we asked for fresh perspectives.

Rich thanks his colleagues at Duke University as well as the terrific people he has worked with in the past at Vanderbilt University and the University of North Carolina at Chapel Hill. The opportunity to work with such entertaining and amazing colleagues is one of his favorite things about each day in the life of a cataloger.

Priscilla thanks colleagues and friends too numerous to mention for enhancing her life by sharing time, expertise, experience, advice, opinions, and most of all, friendship. As a work-from-home mother, she cherishes the ability to network around the world. She is also grateful to her incredibly patient husband, David, for his love and support, and to her daughters, Laura and Sophie, for distracting her from work most of the time.

Introduction: What Do Librarians Do All Day?

JESSAMYN WEST

Work. For many of us, the job is what lets us call ourselves librarians or information professionals, and allows others to see us as that. (I say librarian, you can say information professional. I mean all of us.) However, librarianship is much more than a job. We're drawn to the information professions by a desire to help, a desire to serve, a desire to teach and to *know*. We stay in the profession despite decreasing funding, ever-changing job descriptions, and uncertain futures.

Librarianship is a magic trick, a perfect profession for someone who likes to fiddle behind the scenes or pull a deftly Googled or indexed rabbit out of a deep and foreboding hat. It is a rare librarian who achieves status outside of the profession; it usually takes a superhero movie or a particularly heinous arrest to put a librarian in the newspapers. This has been changing. Librarians have been noticed as defenders of freedom and privacy, discoverers of hidden histories, and even creators of certain fashion trends. I've had the pleasure of meeting hundreds of librarians over the past decade and when I ask about the work they do, they often explain it by talking about a problem they solved or one they are trying to solve.

Librarianship is a process. We are the translators between our resources and our patrons, each constantly changing and evolving. This can mean amplifying the dusty whispers of almost-forgotten books or toning down the steady cacophonous drone of a frequently updated RSS feed.

At the end, the results are like a gift: "I found this, for you." The work is never done, and yet for many of us, we would be doing it anyhow, without the job, without the position. One of the constant refrains you'll read from the nearly one hundred library workers in this collection—each one motivated enough to take the time to tell us about the work they do—is how much they enjoy what they do:

"I consider myself extremely lucky."
"I thoroughly enjoy my job."
"My library patrons charm me."
"My work is passion-driven."
"I'm making a living off daydreams."

We're used to hearing these statements from the long-suffering public service librarians—you'd have to love a job like that to stay with it, right? But these librarians, many of whom don't even use the L word, come from all manner of library and information-wrangling professions.

Librarianship is not what you think it is. You can't read the job descriptions in this book and think the same way about librarians, or possibly even yourself, ever again. I now have several more descriptions to add to my dream jobs list—an index card that currently hangs above my desk and says:

> 1. Live-in librarian
> 2. Turn barn into library

Among the contenders are: Kevin Kelly's (of *Wired* magazine fame) personal librarian; territorial librarian in the Northwest Territories (1.17 million square km, 40,000 people, 9 libraries); visiting instructor of library and information science in Hungary; and the intriguingly titled "editor, publisher, author, speaker" position that sounds a lot like what I'm doing now.

My current job is actually a hodgepodge of jobs stuck together like a giant Katamari, and almost as unwieldy to maneuver. I work for a regional vocational high school, staffing drop-in computer lab time and teaching evening adult education classes on technology-related topics. The lab time is mostly working with seniors who have technology projects but find it helpful to have someone around to ask questions of if they get stuck. When people ask what I do and they seem pressed for time, I say "I teach e-mail to old people. It's the best job there is." Because many of the people I work with are women, and because they also swim in the community pool where I swim, I am in the odd position of having seen most of my students naked, which I think helps, though I can't describe exactly why.

This job also includes community outreach, working with librarians in the towns that send kids to the school. I help them learn to use their technology, often Gates Foundation computers with some sort of homegrown networking set up. I work with seven small rural libraries that serve populations of between five hundred and three thousand people; I do everything from building little Web sites to teaching classes about eBay to swapping out Ethernet cards. All of the librarians I work with are part-time—some of the libraries are only open sixteen hours a week—and none of the libraries have any technical staff.

That job is, believe it or not, part-time. In the other part of my time, I am a moderator for an online community called MetaFilter. The site has over forty thousand users, maybe a few thousand of whom are active in any given week. I spend the bulk of my time maintaining the part of the site called Ask MetaFilter, where users of the site can ask other users questions. These questions can range from reference types of questions like, "Where is a good place to find good barbecue in Austin, Texas?" to technical questions like, "Why can't I browse/ping/tracert to tikiwiki.org?" to relationship questions like, "I am head over heels in love with someone who is draining my life from me ... please help me." I'm the level-headed person who keeps questions and answers on track, fixes broken HTML, answers user e-mail, and if I have some free time, maintains the site FAQ and wiki. MetaFilter is an online job that I can do from anywhere; the first job is intensely local and I'd have a hard time doing it anyplace else.

In the *other* part of my time, I travel around the country, and sometimes to Australia, to talk about the digital divide and technology and politics and libraries. That's more sporadic work, but because of my modest lifestyle (read: low-paying jobs) it's the only way I get to travel, which is right up there on my to do list, along with eating and sleeping. Then there's my unpaid professional work, like maintaining my blog at librarian.net, writing book chapters and introductions, writing book reviews, and serving in various library professional organization capacities. I'm busy, but I have a lot of leisure time. Since library school, I've never had just one job.

Interestingly, this level of involvement in the things that make up a librarian life is not at all unusual. Sure, there are library professionals who clock in and clock out and then spend the rest of their time doing something completely unrelated, but I find them to be the exception, not the rule. This group of stories is not so much the tale of a typical day in the life, but a meta-story about the reality that there *is* no typical day just as there is no typical librarian. Sure, everyone checks e-mail (almost), and everyone goes to meetings (mostly), and we all work with various sorts of information . . .

What sort of a hazy designation is "information," anyhow? Is it accurate to say that we simply "work with" it? Wouldn't it be more on the mark to say that we swim in it, we inhale it, we dream of it at night? Is there a person in these pages who cannot say they've felt information tickling at their ankles when they work on the computer in the early morning, or heard information murmuring last-minute reminders in their ears when they turn the laptop off in the evening? I know I have. Like the nuns with their wedding rings, we have a lifelong commitment to information. L is for librarian. It is also for love.

PART I

Public Libraries

CHAPTER 1

Adult Services Librarian

KATIE DUNNEBACK

The adult services librarian in a public library is responsible for responding to the information needs of the adult members of the community the library serves. High school students are often included in this population if there is not a separate teen services librarian position. Typically, the primary duty of this position is staffing the reference desk. Secondary duties, depending on the size of the library staff, may include developing bibliographic instruction materials, teaching classes on the use of library resources (including computers), collection management, reader's advisory, interlibrary loan management, serials management, Web site management, and other duties as assigned.

A TYPICAL WORKDAY

There's "typical" and then there are public libraries. You have questions that become routine and tasks that require specific procedures every time you perform them, but every day is unique because you're dealing with the public.

The questions you will be dealing with—in person, via telephone, e-mail, live chat, or some other person-to-person technology—cover a wide range of topics. In one hour of a day, you may deal with a variety of questions such as: How do I attach the photo that I am holding in my hand to the e-mail I am trying to send to my friend? What is the square mileage of Venice, Italy, not including the barrier islands? How can I find articles to help me write my term paper on childhood immunizations?

A typical day in my job here at the Westchester (Illinois) Public Library begins when I come in at my scheduled time. I work two night shifts a week, so I start work at noon during summer hours and 1 p.m. during the school year on those days. In a library with a larger staff, you may be required to work only one night shift per week or none at all.

When I work mornings, I have desk duty until the other librarian comes in, and then I go to lunch. If the desk is quiet, I will work on projects such as bibliographic instruction materials, interlibrary loan, and collection development. I always try to stop what I am doing to smile at and make eye contact with a patron walking by to let them know that I'm not so engrossed in my work that I can't assist them.

When I do get questions, they cover a very wide range of topics, as I mentioned. We have recently seen an increase in reader's advisory inquiries as we have more actively marketed the service to both patrons and staff. Always work with the staff in other departments to let them know what you do so they know what type of questions they can send your way.

When I work away from the desk, I complete tasks that I may have started while at the desk, such as calling patrons regarding interlibrary loan requests, calling other libraries about interlibrary loan, approving the processing of books for which I'm responsible for purchasing, taking a self-directed online continuing education course, discussing patron issues with other members of the staff, or going to meetings. I generally attend meetings that are related to interlibrary loan issues and those that will add to my continuing education goals. Meeting topics depend on your area of responsibility within your department.

In addition to meetings outside the building, I also have regular departmental meetings with my supervisor and a part-time reference assistant. During these meetings, we update each other on projects we've been working on, any problematic questions or situations we've encountered, and library issues that affect our department. These regular meetings help minimize problems that might catch us off guard. My library also has scheduled bimonthly in-service sessions where available staff meet to discuss what each department is doing as well as present special programs addressing strategies to deal with library-wide problems. A recent meeting focused on what to do when a patron exhibits symptoms of severe mental problems, an issue well beyond staff expertise.

Every day in this job provides something that reminds me how interesting and rewarding it is to be in this profession.

PROS AND CONS

Working with the public is a two-sided coin. The best and worst parts of the job are your patrons. Oxymoron, you say? Not really. Because the public is made up of many individuals, you're going to interact with someone different in each encounter. I have had patrons ranging from those who come in with relatively simple questions who are incredibly thankful when you find the answer for them, to some who have mental issues that interfere with their ability to interact positively with the general public. Dealing with the latter is often more emotionally draining, and having a colleague take over the desk for you while you go off to a staff area to decompress is invaluable.

I enjoy working with the public. I love helping people find the information they're looking for. Digging up that obscure little fact that completes the mental puzzle for them is enriching and rewarding. Patrons learn from what I am able to find for them, but I also learn from patrons. They often will share little bits of themselves that add to my body of knowledge. With every question that I answer, my own knowledge base becomes broader.

One of the advantages of working in a smaller library is that I can more easily learn how all of the little cogs involved in running the library interact and affect each other. I think having an understanding of technical services, children's services, circulation, and other functions makes me a better reference librarian. If you work in a larger library where the departments are more segregated, I highly recommend taking the initiative to periodically shadow staff members in other departments.

Confession time: I adore books. Yes, I entered the profession partially because I love talking about books with people. Reader's advisory is probably my favorite part of the job. There are so many different aspects to an adult services librarian position that you can easily find at least one (if not more) that excites you.

An advantage that some people may not think of—which won't apply to everyone—is that you work with adults (that is, as opposed to children). I love children. I happily cover our children's desk when needed. I also know myself well enough to know that I would not be the best person I could be if I had to work with kids all day. Some people just need to have some adult interaction on a daily basis.

Cons: Well, there are always cons to any job. One disadvantage (which can also be a con for your employer) is working the reference desk for an extended period of time, such as for six or more hours a day. This can happen because of staffing issues, whether they are intentional or not. *Intentional* means that the person in your position is expected to staff the desk the majority of time he or she is at work. A staffing issue is unintentional when, for whatever reason, an existing position meant to help cover the desk is not filled. When you are on the desk for an extended period of time, you get burned out. Then you are of little use to your patrons, yourself, and your employer. Keep in mind that this applies to you if you work full-time or if you work multiple part-time jobs, and part-time usually means all desk time.

Pros and cons are what you make of them. They're going to differ from library to library, so talk to the adult services librarians in your local public library to get their take on the pros and cons of this type of position.

HOW CAN I GET A JOB LIKE THIS?

There are a number of ways to get your foot in the door. My number one recommendation is to get experience in customer service. In a library or in some other field, customer service is what will separate you from others who have not worked in a service position with the public. Library experience is always preferred, but don't worry if you come from a service background.

If you already work in a library but not in a public services position, take the initiative to shadow a librarian who is in one. See if you can get assigned to desk duty several hours per week alongside an experienced librarian. You may have to work those hours after your normally scheduled hours, but it is worth it!

If you're still in school, get an internship or practicum in the local public library. This not only gives you real work experience, you may also be able to get school credit toward your degree. I repeat the point of getting experience because I cannot emphasize it enough. You will also make the connections you need in local libraries if you want to work in the area after graduate school. These people will be your references and will tip you off to jobs before they are posted.

You've got the experience, so what's next? How do you become aware of vacancies in which you're interested? In addition to scanning the position listings in the major publications and on the major Web sites, try networking. How do you network? There are a number of ways; find out which works best for you. E-mail lists are a great source for interest-specific job postings, and they will also help you become aware of what practicing librarians are concerned with today. Those topics may come up during an interview, and being able to discuss them intelligently will be a point in your favor. Informational interviews are a wonderful way to make personal contact with librarians in your geographic area. They may even encourage you to apply for any open positions the library currently has, may keep you in mind for future openings, or could pass your name along to a colleague who does have an opening.

Conferences are another great place for job hunters. There is a plethora of activities that you can use to your advantage, including programs to increase your knowledge base and constant opportunities to network with those around you. Some library associations offer placement centers at their conferences where you can learn about (and possibly interview for) positions that you may not otherwise have considered.

When you're looking for a job, make sure that you read the posting thoroughly to know how you should apply for the position—by e-mail, mail, online, and so on. Also, distinguish between the *required* qualities of a successful candidate and the *desired* ones; don't be afraid to apply for positions that you think might be a little over your head. What you bring to the table may be close enough to what they are looking for that you could be invited to interview.

When you interview, dress for success, be yourself, and relax. You are interviewing the library just as they are interviewing you. The interviewers are looking for a good fit for their institution, but you are also looking for an institution that will help you achieve what you want in your career.

FURTHER RESOURCES

Print Resources

American Libraries. www.ala.org/alonline (accessed November 25, 2005).
Library Journal. www.libraryjournal.com (accessed November 25, 2005).
Public Libraries. www.ala.org/ala/pla/plapubs/publiclibraries/publiclibraries.htm (accessed November 25, 2005).
Saricks, Joyce G. 2005. *Readers' advisory service in the public library*. Chicago: American Library Association.

Online Resources

Fiction_L (Morton Grove Public Library's mailing list on reader's advisory issues). www.webrary.org/rs/flmenu.html (accessed November 25, 2005).
LibRef-L (a moderated discussion of issues related to reference librarianship). www.library.kent.edu/page/10391 (accessed November 25, 2005).
Public Library Association. www.pla.org (accessed November 25, 2005).

CHAPTER 2

Teen Librarian

SOPHIE BROOKOVER

I'm a senior teen librarian at the largest branch in a six-branch county library system in southern New Jersey. I design and host programs for teens; conduct outreach programming in local junior and senior high schools; staff the children's department reference desk; help children, teens, and their parents with reader's advisory questions; and am in charge of developing the collections for teens. These include fiction and nonfiction books, magazines, CDs, and DVDs.

In addition to my assigned duties, I also participate in professional development activities through the Young Adult Library Services Association (YALSA), a division of the American Library Association, and the New Jersey Library Association (NJLA). YALSA's book discussion e-mail list, YALSA-BK, is an important component of my collection development program, and its daily discussions cover topics from book reviews and read-alike book lists to teen advocacy and handling of censorship issues. I serve on two YALSA process committees: the Publications Committee and the Communications Task Force.

As a member of NJLA, I serve on the executive board of the Young Adult Services Section and am the blog manager for the NJLA blog. I also review books for *Voice of Youth Advocates*, edit and write for Pop Goes the Library (a blog I founded that focuses on improving library services through popular culture), and teach classes on blogging and RSS, popular culture, and the evolving Web for New Jersey's Regional Library Cooperatives.

If it sounds like I am very busy, I am. Fulfilling all of these responsibilities requires discipline, focus, and passion on my part and active encouragement on the part of my library. I am fortunate that both my library director and department head are very supportive of my participation in professional development activities outside the library.

MY DAY AT WORK

A typical workday finds me spending most of my time on the children's department reference desk. Two members of the department staff the desk at all times; between answering patrons' questions, I am able to attend to my other duties.

On the Desk

Checking and responding to e-mail and monitoring and responding to messages on the e-mail lists I belong to. This is ongoing, though if I were more disciplined, I would check e-mail just twice a day: on my arrival at work and after lunch.

Scanning the library blogosphere for interesting posts about popular culture, libraries, and technology. I use the Bloglines aggregator to monitor RSS feeds of about a hundred blogs (I prune and add blogs on an ongoing but highly irregular basis). I check my account three to five times a day, though as with e-mail, I would do better to check less frequently.

Answering reader's advisory questions. This is probably my favorite aspect of on-desk time, and although I didn't know what it was when I applied to library school, it is the reason I wanted to be a librarian in the first place. I love leading kids, teens, and parents to their next "best book ever."

Designing programs for teens, including descriptions for our PR department. We work on a quarterly schedule, so I plan programs for teens about three months in advance. I often find ideas for programs from the YA-YAAC and TAGAD-L e-mail lists. I do my best to honor requests for specific programs, as well.

Working on collection development. My primary print tool for books is *Voice of Youth Advocates* (*VOYA*), though I also use *School Library Journal* and occasionally *Booklist*. When looking for ideas to supplement our magazine collection, I usually hit the magazine stands at local bookstores. For music, I rely heavily on suggestions from teens and to a lesser degree on reviews in magazines like *Spin*, *Vibe*, and *Blender,* plus information gleaned by watching more hours of MTV and MTV2 than is probably good for me.

Posting on my blog. Inspired by something I've read on an e-mail list, a blog, in the newspaper, or seen on TV, I write anywhere from two to eight posts per week at my professional blog, Pop Goes the Library. The discipline of writing on a regular schedule regarding topics I feel passionate about helps me refine my thoughts and my actions. Integrating a personal interest into my professional work has enriched my professional life tremendously, and made me a better librarian. It might not work for everyone, but it has been overwhelmingly positive in my case.

Off the Desk

Two or three times a week, I have a block of off-desk time. I generally use this time to do the following: handle the minutiae of planning programs; draft notes for the classes I teach; read articles in the professional journals routed to me; and clear off my desk, which is often a dumping ground for files, hard copies of e-mails I want to keep, publisher's galleys, and other work-related detritus.

On a somewhat less typical day, I may do outreach by visiting a local school to meet with the school librarian or make presentations to classes. For example, I recently met with the entire sixth grade in three groups, in their school library, and requested their input on their favorite authors, musicians, and comic books. Another time, I spent two days going to all twenty-three sections of ninth-grade English at the local high school to "book talk" some recently published titles and promote teen programming at my branch.

Typically I have two to four professional meetings outside my library each month. The NJLA Young Adult Services Section meets six times annually. The NJLA Blog Committee meets monthly. In addition, I teach classes on blogging, RSS, other Web 2.0 technologies, popular culture, and teen services. On occasion, I also attend professional development activities and courses with colleagues.

Once or twice per month, I make notes for, draft, or polish a book review for *VOYA*.

THE GOOD THINGS

I am in my element working with kids and teens. It's so rare to find a line of work that is a balance of fun and challenging, and that features the added bonus of making the practitioner feel that she's making a difference in people's lives. For me, young adult librarianship is a perfect match.

If I had to select the standout joys of my career, they would be building lasting relationships with teens through personal interactions, outreach, and creating a truly teen-friendly space in the library; developing a comprehensive, high-quality set of current collections for teens, one that accurately reflects their interests and concerns; continuing to develop as a professional through involvement in our state and national organizations, through mentoring relationships (both as mentor and mentee) with experienced and new colleagues, and through teaching workshops of interest to the profession as a whole; and integrating many of my interests— literacy, literature, technology, adolescent development, youth advocacy, and teaching—into every day at work. These things are extremely rewarding.

THE NOT-SO-GOOD THINGS

Not to sound like a Pollyanna, but there are precious few things I don't enjoy about my job. Although the cons are few, they do exist. Here's my list of top three frustrations.

- *Low compensation.* There's no way to gloss over this issue or sugarcoat it. I will never become rich as a teen librarian. A fairly stringent budget will always be a part of my family's life. To me, it's worth it, but it might not be worth it for everyone, so think carefully about how frequently you want to go on a fabulous vacation to New Zealand or about how often you prefer to upgrade the electronics in your home.

- *Budget crises.* These are difficult to predict and can be disheartening to live through. My library recently had its budget cut by over $1 million. Our materials lines were not drastically affected, but our professional development line was. For the foreseeable future, I have to pay my own way to attend conferences, which were formerly subsidized in large part by my library. In addition, the budget crisis has caused a hiring freeze, which means that everyone is overworked and overstressed right now. We'll weather the storm, but it will probably take years for my system to regain its full funding.

- *Lack of recognition by the general public.* When I was in library school, I thought it was funny when I had to explain to people that librarians don't just read books all day, that a master's degree is required for the job, and that we do a lot more than just check books out to the public. I don't think it's so funny anymore. It's not funny that the average person on the street doesn't know what librarians do all day. Thanks to television shows like *Law & Order*, *Boston Legal*, and *ER*, that person probably knows quite a bit about police work, lawyering, and being a doctor. I am now dedicated to raising the public profile of librarians and librarianship.

PREPARING YOURSELF FOR TEEN LIBRARIANSHIP

If you're still in library school, make sure to take all of the youth and teen services courses you can fit into your schedule. If you are applying to library school, look closely at what teen services course offerings are available at your schools of choice. Much of what you'll do as a teen librarian can be learned on the job, but it's very useful to have some background in literature for and services to teens on your transcript.

Take advantage of any and all job-shadowing programs offered by your library school or state library association. (You can do this even if you have graduated from library school and are seeking to change your field of expertise.) Sign up to shadow a teen librarian at his or her job for a day (or better yet, several days), so you can see for yourself what the work is like. It's all well and good to read what I have to say about it, but I'm writing from my experience at my library, where I serve a large, polyglot, predominantly suburban clientele. Conditions will be different at smaller libraries, urban libraries, rural libraries, even at different branches within a county system. See for yourself what the work is like at as many libraries as you can.

Finally, read! Read as much teen literature as you can get your hands on. Read widely and fearlessly—you may surprise yourself. I never thought of myself as a fantasy fan, but since I started working with teens, I've found that it's my favorite genre within YA literature. If you don't know where to start, browse the YA collection bookshelves at your local library, take home whatever appeals to you, and dive in. If you prefer a more structured approach, try looking at the annual lists of Best Books for Young Adults or Quick Picks for Reluctant Young Adult Readers compiled by YALSA.

RELATED RESOURCES

Below are links to professional organizations, e-mail lists, professional journals, and books that I have found invaluable over the years.

Professional Organizations

American Library Association. www.ala.org (accessed February 1, 2006).
Central Jersey Regional Library Cooperative. www.cjrlc.org (accessed February 1, 2006).
Highlands Regional Library Cooperative. www.hrlc.org (accessed February 1, 2006).
INFOLINK: The Eastern New Jersey Regional Library Cooperative. www.infolink.org (accessed February 1, 2006).
New Jersey Library Association. www.njla.org (accessed February 1, 2006).
South Jersey Regional Library Cooperative. www.sjrlc.org (accessed February 1, 2006).
Young Adult Library Services Association (YALSA). www.ala.org/yalsa (accessed February 1, 2006).
YALSA committee, task force, and discussion group descriptions are available at www.ala.org/ala/yalsa/aboutyalsab/yalsacommittee.htm (accessed February 1, 2006).

E-mail Lists

TAGAD-L: Teen Advisory Groups—Advisory Discussion. lists.topica.com/lists/tagad-l (accessed February 1, 2006).
YALSA-BK and YA-YAAC. www.ala.org/ala/yalsa/electronicresourcesb/websitesmailing.htm (accessed February 1, 2006).

Journals

School Library Journal. www.schoollibraryjournal.com (accessed February 1, 2006).
VOYA: Voice of Youth Advocates. www.voya.com (accessed February 1, 2006).

Other Online Resources

Connecting YA. www.connectingya.com (accessed February 1, 2006). This is the Web site affiliated with the book of the same title (and others). It contains a useful preview of the book, now in its third edition, and also provides free downloads of presentations by author Patrick Jones.

Lists of Best Books for Young Adults. www.ala.org/ala/yalsa/booklistsawards/bestbooksya/bestbooksyoung.htm (accessed February 1, 2006).

Lists of Quick Picks for Reluctant Young Adult Readers. www.ala.org/ala/yalsa/booklistsawards/quickpicks/quickpicksreluctant.htm (accessed February 1, 2006).

NJLA Blog. blog.njla.org (accessed February 1, 2006). This is the official blog of the New Jersey Library Association.

Pop Goes the Library. www.popgoesthelibrary.com (accessed March 3, 2007).

yaARC. yaarc.blogspot.com (accessed February 1, 2006). This interactive blog "is the result of conversation on YALSA-BK, the open list for book discussion between YA librarians/friends/advocates. ... Those of us with access to advance reader copies like to share with friends, and this is a handy, mainly self-service way to facilitate all the sharing. Everyone is welcome to lend or borrow ARCs as long as they keep the lines movin'!"

Books

Braun, Linda W. 2003. *Hooking teens with the Net*. New York: Neal-Schuman.

Horning, Kathleen T. 1997. *From cover to cover: Evaluating and reviewing children's books*. New York: HarperCollins.

Jones, Patrick, Michele Gorman, and Tricia Suellentrop. 2004. *Connecting young adults and libraries: A how-to-do-it manual for librarians*, 3rd ed. New York: Neal-Schuman.

LiBretto, Ellen V., and Catherine Barr. 2002. *High/low handbook: Best books and Web sites for reluctant teen readers*, 4th ed. Westport, Conn.: Libraries Unlimited.

Smith, Michael W., and Jeffrey D. Wilhelm. 2002. *Reading don't fix no Chevys: Literacy in the lives of young men*. Portsmouth, N.H.: Heinemann.

CHAPTER 3

Children's Librarian

JENNA INNES

Welcome to my "wubbulous" world as a children's librarian at a public library. A formal description of my job would state that I coordinate collections and services for patrons under age eighteen and their caregivers. This includes providing reference services, craft and story programs, dedicated library spaces, outreach programs, and a variety of services. What it really means is that I do just about anything I can to get kids to use the library and develop a love of reading. It also means that I support families, teachers, and child care providers in their roles. I am an advocate for this segment of our patrons within the library and, I believe, in the larger community. It is as much fun and just as crazy as a barrel of monkeys!

To give you a bit of background, the city of Edmonton, Alberta, has a 2005 population of 712,391. We have a large downtown library, which also serves as a head office with centralized cataloging and selection. There are sixteen branches, four of which are district branches with larger collections and staffed with a branch manager, assistant manager, adult services librarian, and children's services librarian. The four children's librarians in the system work with the downtown children's librarian to coordinate programs that run across all the branches. We also work with many other library staff on project teams, such as the Summer Reading Game and Preschool Programming teams.

In the past, I have also been the children's librarian in areas with only one library, serving much smaller communities. In a small library, you wear many hats—you're the children's librarian, the circulation clerk, the book repair person, the toilet plunger, the computer repair specialist, and so on. At a larger library, I have been able to focus more directly on children's librarianship. Instead of doing every children's program as I would at a smaller library, I share these duties with other library staff and provide a larger variety of services.

PROGRAMMING: FROM STORY TIME TO TEEN GAME NIGHT

Let's start off with what I consider to be the most delightful aspect of my job: programming. By this I mean the various sessions in which young people participate in an activity organized by the library. You may be familiar with story time, where a leader reads picture books aloud to a group of children and does a few songs or fingerplays. This can be expanded to include crafts, games, films, flannelgraphs, guest speakers, and other activities. Programming varies as we move up and down the age continuum. There are baby laptime sessions where moms and babies sit in a circle and learn nursery rhymes, language play, and strategies for sharing books with their little ones. There are sessions for small children with lots of songs, puppets, and simple stories. There are library tours for Girl Guides, kindergarten classes, and day cares to introduce our resources and demonstrate how to care for books. Programs for preschoolers and school-aged children include almost anything from educational homework help to "mad science" demonstrations to booktalking particular titles to reading aloud under a Christmas tree while dressed up as a reindeer. This is an area of immense creative satisfaction with almost endless possibilities!

My programming responsibilities for one day might include planning, promoting, and delivering a program; helping other staff members prepare programs; and working with a team to implement a series of programs that will occur across the city. A flair for the dramatic and a talent for event planning definitely help in this area of the job. For example, many libraries are seeking to develop teen services by starting teen advisory boards and hosting videogame tournaments, book clubs, and karaoke nights. If you are able to join in and sing with both the toddlers and the teens, you will be a big hit. It is enthusiasm, not perfection, that attracts participants to your programs.

COLLECTIONS: WHAT TO BUY, WHAT TO GET RID OF, AND WHERE TO PUT IT

In some libraries, the children's librarian is given a lump sum to spend on materials. In other budgets, the funds are broken down into categories such as paperbacks, hard covers, audio-visual materials, and so on. Our library catalogs and processes these items centrally, then sends them out to the branches. I go through each shipment of new items, checking for a few things: Has this item been assigned the right call number and been labeled correctly? Is it designated for the right location? What else does it connect with—for example, is it a good fit for an upcoming story time or a particular display? These aspects will vary depending on your library, but it is important that someone with a focus on young readers fine-tunes details like these to ensure that an item is in the optimum position to attract its reader.

Although I currently purchase only replacement copies and seek to fill gaps in the collection, at other libraries I was responsible for ordering all of the juvenile material. To do this I read reviews in publications such as *School Library Journal* and *Booklist*. Because our collections now include more diverse formats (such as DVDs, graphic novels, and electronic resources), I have had to work harder to find good resources for evaluating products. Many review sources are not up to date enough to provide information on items that are "new and hot." It can also be difficult to decide how to deal with material that is controversial but in high demand, such as music with profane language or violent subject matter. What do you buy? How should it be cataloged? Where should it be located in the library? How do we process the item so it lasts? How can we prevent theft or damage of the item? Being able to articulate why materials are purchased demonstrates my accountability for our resources and provides a foundation for dealing with challenges regarding my choices.

RECONSIDERATION OF LIBRARY MATERIALS: KEEP IT, SHIFT IT, OR REMOVE IT?

Sometimes changes and challenges will come up after an item is out in the stacks, and it is usually my responsibility to deal with the first stages of any alterations to the collection.

These changes could be as straightforward as reassigning books into a separate collection for reluctant readers or as complex as handling a parent's request that an offensive item be removed from the library. Sometimes patrons just want to have someone hear them out and explain why a particular item is located where it is. They may also have questions about other policies, such as why Internet stations are not equipped with filtering software. Some challenges are formalized in writing and sent to other managers and perhaps to the library board, who make the ultimate decisions regarding library materials. However, most of these issues are dealt with locally.

That being said, a children's librarian is likely to encounter those who want to dictate not only what their child is exposed to but also what is available to all young people in their community. Having a firm commitment to intellectual freedom and being able to effectively communicate that position is one way that you will have a very real impact on children's services in your library. Collection policies, statements of intellectual freedom, procedures for dealing with challenged material, and the support of your library administration are all vital elements to have in place. I must be able to explain why materials and services are provided or excluded from my library and consider the best interests of the youth when setting policy that affects their library access.

READER'S ADVISORY: FINDING THE RIGHT BOOK FOR THE RIGHT READER

Patrons will often find (or fail to find) what they are looking for because of your choices and efforts. I mean this in a very positive way—through reference services and reader's advisory, the librarian seeks to connect patrons with whatever will satisfy their intellectual and recreational needs. The more you know, not only about how information is organized but about particular child-related topics and reading, the better you will be able to address your patrons' needs. In library school, I did not learn much about the stages of reading development. The children's literature courses focused more on the body of writing available for children and its history, themes, and styles.

I recommend getting as much exposure as possible to the process of teaching reading and determining what books fit with each developmental stage. Your expertise will serve you well, for example, when a parent asks for a book about horses for a girl in grade three who is struggling with reading, or when you are approached by a boy in grade six who loves fantasy and wants a challenge.

Here are a few other areas of expertise to include in your repertoire: the many different types of material available; an awareness of different styles of writing, formats, authors, and reading levels; and a familiarity with the various factors influencing a family, such as the economy, popular culture, the media, education, child care, parenting, and teen culture. Also valuable is an understanding of the needs of particular groups, such as children with special needs, low-income families, at-risk youth, and ethnic/cultural groups. This seems like a long list to master! You can't know everything at the beginning, but be open to learning about your patrons' individual needs. You can learn a lot from reading articles, listening to people, and consulting with your peers. An interest in your constituency and a willingness to learn will take you where you want to go.

PARTNERSHIPS AND COMMUNITY BUILDING

The relationships you build with your patrons and your community will not only help get books into the hands that need them but also raise support for the library. A partnership should be mutually beneficial. For example, partnering with schools allows both parties to educate kids and encourage a love of reading. Partnering with a local mothers' group promotes library services while helping parents find good parenting information. Creative partnerships can lead to great successes for the library and community. What about lending books to the YMCA? Allowing language tutoring in your program room? Offering a story time for children with special needs? As we seek to maximize our resources by developing these connections, we also integrate the library deeper into the fabric of our community.

REFERENCE SERVICES: IT'S DUE TOMORROW AND WE CLOSE IN FIVE MINUTES

Although the Internet has changed the way students access information, you are still going to see desperate kids at the library the night before an assignment is due. Developing a pathfinder (a list of relevant resources) for common questions is a great way to help students find what they need quickly. Being familiar with curricula and projects at local schools will help you prepare for the onslaught of kids all seeking information on the same topic. You will likely use more electronic resources to answer your patrons' questions. They will need your help to use these resources effectively; even those who might classify themselves as expert online searchers might find you have a few tips to offer them.

In spite of all the other behind-the-scenes tasks you perform, your daily reference transactions will always be one of your main duties. Empowering patrons by teaching them how to navigate the ever-shifting waters of information can be very rewarding. I have also found it to be very frustrating at times, trying to balance the patron's need for independence with my own desire that they "get it right." For example, I may want to grab the keyboard from the eight-year-old who can't spell and type the terms in myself. I might want to steer a patron away from an endless series of trite novels into a meatier piece of fiction. But I am there to serve *their* needs. So when I offer parents a plethora of great articles about learning disabilities and they turn them down in favor of "Alfie's ADD Web-o-Rama," I must simply state why I believe the articles will provide better information and leave them to decide which sources they will use. Of course, most people are keen to get the best information and are grateful for your efforts to connect them with it. Knowing that my participation in someone's research made a difference in their lives makes me feel useful and blessed.

MANAGEMENT AND FINANCE: PEOPLE, MONEY, AND OTHER RESOURCES

I've found myself in leadership roles more often than I expected. In a variety of situations, I was able to serve as an instrument of change or a champion of intellectual freedom and literacy. There were also times when I let interpersonal conflicts and frustrations get the best of me. My day is full of interactions where I need to get someone else to contribute to projects we are working on. Whether I am serving a customer or meeting with coworkers, being able to get along and get the best out of others is central to my job.

Being able to represent the interests of young patrons and convince others to take action is a skill I will be practicing throughout my career. Unfortunately, it can sometimes be a struggle to convince others that the children's library is a priority. The art of persuasion is an important one to master. A good grasp of management and finance principles can help you explain exactly how you plan to use your resources, what the benefits will be, and how you will account for the results. Being able to speak the language of statistics, outcomes, and bottom lines is just as relevant to children's librarianship as it is to Wall Street. Paying attention to politics and economics has become a regular part of my job, letting me know when to move forward with a particular initiative and whom to approach for support. Any time you are seeking help from others, from the media to the janitorial staff, having a positive relationship in place will often determine your success.

WRAPPING UP

This chapter, like the work itself, is rather unstructured, demonstrating the reality of the position—being pulled in many different directions. But it is the opportunity to experience these diverse elements of children's librarianship that makes the job so interesting. There is a certain magic in connecting children to the inspiring world of books. This magic, and the difference it can make, are what keep me motivated.

CHAPTER 4

Client Services Librarian

Not many people have heard of the role in libraries called client services. I only found it through reading the job advertisement in the paper. There are other titles given to this role with which you might be more familiar, such as circulation services, operations, or customer services. Although this role is often specific to public libraries, I believe it could also exist in academic or large special libraries. In brief, my role as client services librarian at the City of Tea Tree Gully Library in Adelaide, Australia, is to develop and implement an enriching and customer-focused library service for the community.

YES, BUT WHAT DOES THAT INVOLVE EXACTLY?

Before I lose you to another role and another chapter, let me say that my job is very rewarding as it is central to the customer experience. I ensure that all functions that affect day-to-day running of the library service occur and that the written policies and procedures are there to guide and support staff when providing customer service. This includes the creation and maintenance of a roster that includes all staff members across all customer service points within the library. Tied to this are selection, performance management, and training of staff, which helps ensure that service received by our customers is consistent.

Within the library structure, my position is also involved in the overall management of the library service. This involves examining the services we are currently providing and developing services to meet the future needs of the community.

Size Really Does Matter

The tasks I have described sound simple. Indeed, in a smaller library, this role would be easier to manage. However, my job operates within a public library service that has fifty-two library staff in one location, serving more than sixty-two thousand members and a population of more than one hundred thousand. Thankfully, they do not all use the library service at the same time! We are open 52 hours a week. There are nine library staff members scheduled at four service points. Mathematically, this means that 72 hours in a working day are rostered; now spread that over 7 days and a few evenings, and you end up with approximately 525 hours each week being rostered. On a daily basis the library also turns over between six thousand and eight thousand items. It is my responsibility to ensure that those hours and tasks—not to mention the shelving—are managed effectively for the organization.

PLEASE LET ME GET TO MY DESK

My responsibilities revolve around the staff; so does my workload. I find that this position is one of extremes. Sometimes everything happens within the first ten minutes, and this affects the rest of the day; my written list of things to do is put to one side on these occasions. But then there are other days where everything seems to flow well with not too many problems, which enables me to think about the long-term needs of the service.

Getting to work early can allow me to achieve tasks; however, over time I have learned this can have side effects. Let me describe a typically hectic day. As I walk through the door I am told that two staff are sick (one of whom is the person who adjusts the roster), the phones don't appear to be working, and as I'm listening, I also remember that I have a customer service team meeting in twenty minutes. My lunch hasn't even made it to the fridge.

I walk to the call center (where all of the external phones for the whole council are answered), as it is only five desks away, to see if they, too, are experiencing a problem. They are, and they have notified the IT department that there is a problem and they have been told it should be fixed soon.

Back at my desk, I turn on the computer and load up the roster that is put together on a spreadsheet. I grab the folder that contains the list of casual employees who fill in when staff are sick, but I notice that there are no casual staff available. This results in all staff present being given additional desk shifts today. Mental note to self for the to do list: examine the casual staff availability. Do we need more casual staff, or just more casual staff who are available? If we need more casual staff, do we have a number of suitable applicants on file, or will we need to go through a recruitment process?

With rosters changed and staff notified, I go check that the phones are working. This involves going downstairs to get the person who is scheduled to answer the phones to check that he has followed correct procedure when logging the phone in to the system and asking him to test it to see if it is working. I'm relieved to find everything is working again. I run back up the stairs, grab the agenda for the meeting, head back down the stairs.

Due to the number of staff and the fact that they do not all work on the same day, it is impossible to have an all-staff meeting about customer service desk issues in one sitting. To resolve the problem we have four mini-meetings during a week with the same agenda. The agenda is comprised of different issues identified by the other librarians over the previous five weeks. Topics vary from friendly reminders (such as "please keep the desk area tidy; it is looking cluttered with books and water bottles," "if you check in a CD with no CD inside, follow the procedure instead of leaving it for someone else," or "if you find something, either stick it in lost property or bin it"), to updates about new procedures or basic training. After the meeting I go back upstairs—however, not before someone informs me that a shelf has collapsed and something should be done.

By midmorning (and yes, the shelf was fixed), there are ten voicemail messages from people requesting further information about a position advertised in the paper, and one from a student shelver who is unable to come to work. An hour later, after returning calls, e-mailing job descriptions, and contacting another student shelver who was willing to work additional hours, I realize it is lunchtime, and my tuna salad lunch was never placed in the fridge. I'm glad there is a café in the library!

Walking through the library from lunch (while checking the amount of shelving to be done) I am stopped by a patron who tells me he is unable to log on to the Internet. I guide him through the process of logging on. Then he proceeds to complain about children using the computers for games and food being consumed in the library. I listen and try to respond to his complaints calmly by explaining that public libraries are provided for everyone within the community, regardless of age or purpose. It is often difficult for many people to understand the changes that are occurring in public libraries today.

Back upstairs, I stop at the human resources department to collect the applications for another position that closed at the end of the previous week (only fifty-five to read). Finally I sit down and check e-mail. I type up the agenda for the next day's management team meeting and send it, along with a paper on library user statistics, to other attendees.

The telephone ringing interrupts my silent contemplation over library usage figures; a casual staff member is unable to work for the next week due to the flu. I update her availability sheet, which we use when putting the roster together, and begin work on updating recent changes to temporary membership procedures that were being discussed at the mini-meetings this week. During this time, a student shelver drops by to ask questions for a school assignment on the workforce. A short time later, another staff member drops by to complain about the state of the external book chute check-in area, as employees are piling items up high instead of checking them in as they are returned. I understand how she feels and suggest that she speak with the person who was on duty before her. My computer reminds me I am rostered on the customer service desk. Thank you, electronic calendar reminders!

Working at the customer service desk enables me to observe how staff members perform their customer service duties. It is the only way I can truly learn how each staff member works, and it also offers insight into how they work together. However, on this occasion I am specifically concerned over the performance of a new casual staff member. The time passes fast between checking in items, issuing items, and registering new members. Afterward, I speak to the new staff member to ask how he feels things are going, provide him with some positive feedback about his interactions with patrons, and suggest a few areas he needs to work on.

Back at my desk for the last hour of the day, I finalize some occupational health and safety training that all staff will be attending in a few months, and then I begin to read through those fifty-five applications handed to me earlier.

IT IS GOOD ... BUT THEN AGAIN ...

Managing staff to ensure that the library service provides a high level of customer service is the priority of my role. This must be done effectively; otherwise it will be noticed by staff and patrons. Managing the physical presence of staff is like doing jigsaw puzzles, and I believe that rosters, whatever size, are just like a puzzle. To create an effective roster, I see staff members as individual jigsaw pieces that all fit together to make the whole picture. All staff are required to work together (even if X doesn't like Y) in a professional capacity. However, some staff do take assignments and schedule changes personally. Questions often revolve around the number of desk shifts that X has in a day compared to Y (I have yet to find a library where this does not occur), or why Y has been asked to do something that X has not. Be prepared for questions and have all the knowledge and justification ready; otherwise you will be caught on the back foot.

Gathering statistics and reviewing usage of the library during hours of operation are tasks that are standard with this role. Mathematical skills and software skills are useful (mine are improving daily). These are especially useful when justifying a modification to the library's hours of operation or an increase or decrease in staffing numbers. However, one of the most important skills this role requires is the ability to speak to and listen to staff. There are times when things don't turn out the way you expect or you receive an unexpected reaction from your staff (the larger the staff, the higher this probability). You must be prepared for these situations. Do not underestimate the importance that communication plays in this role. The time you spend talking to staff is an important investment for your future success in this role.

In with the New

Having experienced sitting on both sides of the interview table, I have come to realize that interviews are not easy for either party. Yes, it can be an interesting experience, meeting people and hearing about why they want to work for you and what they can do. But you have to make the right selection for the position based on the selection criteria. The decision you make has the ability to affect your library service—for better or for worse—for a long time!

Before a position is advertised, it should be reviewed. Is this job necessary? Are the hours what they should be? How could it be changed to meet our vision for the service? All these questions are investigated. This can be a difficult process, especially if your views differ from others who have input. Recommendations are written and changes to the job description are made. Negotiation with the human resources department is also required. The employment process is never simple.

Before I conducted my first interview, I read articles and books and discussed with others how they performed interviews. Getting an idea of the process and my role in it made me feel more at ease. The most important lesson I learned is how to write effective questions. This enables the candidate to refer to practical experiences and not just recite the standard textbook answer. Internal job interviews are often the most difficult. Often internal interviewees assume that you know them, and therefore they are not always as forthcoming with information.

Informing people that they have not been selected is never easy. I try to focus on what they did well but also let them know how they did not meet the selection criteria. No matter how many of these I experience, giving bad news is always difficult.

Out with the Problem

The number one tip for any person who has to manage staff, regardless of the position: make file notes. I have learned the hard way that you must document your interactions and conversations with staff. Yes, it does take a lot of time, but if you need to use them, these notes will be well worth having. I don't mean you should write down absolutely everything, but definitely when you have counseled people on poor performance or observed substandard work or a negative attitude. There may be a pattern of poor performance that is not apparent until you read your notes back to yourself. There will be systems in place wherever you work that will outline the process for managing poor performance. Know these processes and don't be afraid to use them.

YOU ARE STILL READING ... AND YOU WANT A JOB LIKE MINE?

Fantastic! Libraries, whatever size their roster and staff, need someone like you! Rostering and staff management are not covered in any library course I know, but on reflection they should be, given how crucial they can be to the success of the service. An essential quality for someone in this job is a strong personality that will withstand conflict, stress, and change.

CHAPTER 5

Multimedia Librarian

MARCI COHEN

I am a librarian in the multimedia department of a suburban Illinois public library. Our department includes music, movies, CD-ROMs, and audiobooks. We also conduct music and movie adult programs. I select the rock and pop CDs and create our displays. Beyond the scope of my departmental duties, I edit our staff newsletter.

A TYPICAL WORKDAY

I spend most of each day on a public service desk answering questions. Many of them are variations of "Where can I find the thing whose name I don't quite know?" I explain how our items are shelved, particularly because we use ANSCR, a classification scheme specific to sound recordings. It is therefore unlike the Dewey or Library of Congress systems and unfamiliar to novice patrons. Sometimes, noting that all music is in alphabetical order by call number is adequate. Other times, it requires more clarification; for example, explaining that the beginning of a call number refers broadly to the type of music, such as jazz or classical chamber music, or that classical music is generally alphabetized by composer while popular music is by performer.

Finding classical pieces provides a particular challenge because library catalogs are designed primarily for books rather than music, and consortium records may not be sufficiently thorough for our needs. The same piece can be known by a multitude of names: its English title, its title in the composer's native language, the type of piece (such as a concerto or mazurka), its opus number, another classification number assigned by publishers, or just the ordinal number for the composer's works of that type, as in Fifth Symphony or Symphony No. 5, for example. Adding to the confusion, a recording may include only certain movements rather than the work in its entirety. Coping with such inconsistencies and variations requires a combination of strategies. Familiarity with the collection and its shelving scheme is essential because it is sometimes faster to find something on the shelf than to search the catalog. I also use reference sources, such as *Schwann Opus* or allmusic.com. I devote a lot of time to searching the online catalog, squinting at the content notes, and hoping the patron is patient. My only consolation is that my colleagues with more formal music education or more experience have equal difficulty.

Popular music is my forte and inherently more fun. I take pride in how wide-ranging our collection is because it means that we usually even have obscure songs patrons are seeking. I help patrons figure out who performed a particular song or learn how to search for it on compilations. I determine what will suffice, such as the song "Moon River" rather than the whole *Breakfast at Tiffany's* soundtrack. I deal with confounding spellings, such as "Do Wah Diddy Diddy" by Manfred Mann. Sometimes patrons can only hum a few bars or know only a snippet of lyrics, so discovering what they had in mind is quite satisfying for both of us. I rely on our catalog, allmusic.com, broader Internet searches, and my own memory honed by years of experience as a librarian and previously a record store clerk, music journalist, and fan.

The shelving scheme for our videos and DVDs has a shorter learning curve than our music scheme. However, many patrons are surprised that our movie holdings are in our online catalog and that we do not maintain a paper list for the constantly changing collection of more than thirteen thousand videos and DVDs. Some patrons are looking for any video on a particular topic, but most are looking for a specific movie. They do not always know the complete title, or they may remember details incorrectly. Searching our catalog for stars, directors, and plots usually helps. The Internet Movie Database is great for correcting incomplete or inaccurate titles or for confirming whether a movie has been released on video or DVD; occasionally searching the plot descriptions helps me locate a film about which the patron knows no stars or title. *VideoHound's Golden Movie Retriever* has capsule summaries, lists of actors' and directors' filmographies, and a fun subject index, ranging from the practical (movies taking place in Las Vegas) to the amusing (movies featuring renegade body parts, with a "see also" listing for killer brains).

Helping patrons find audiobooks and CD-ROMs is more straightforward because they are shelved by Dewey number or by author for fiction, schemes with which patrons are already familiar. Besides checking whether a particular item is in, I am also regularly asked for materials for tax and test preparation and typing and foreign language instruction. Familiarity with the latest best-sellers helps answer questions such as "What's that book about the Chicago World's Fair and the serial killer?"

Some interactions are mundane, such as explaining circulation rules or checking carts with hundreds of recently returned CDs to find one for a patron because the catalog claims that it is on the shelf. On a typical day, I spend about half an hour cleaning and inspecting CDs, DVDs, and CD-ROMs that were just returned to ensure that everything is complete, in good condition, and secured for reshelving. Although our department's support staff does most of the cleaning, I suspend other duties to focus on this when we get behind.

I review publications such as *Billboard, Rolling Stone,* and *Spin* and browse new release schedules on allmusic.com to determine what CDs to buy for the library, seeking out both popular titles and anything generating media attention. I study the list of Grammy nominees and critics' year-end "best of" lists, and I skim concert reviews and listings to find out who is selling out shows, all to predict what music our patrons will be seeking. When reading *Entertainment Weekly* on my own time, I make notes of any movie sequels or remakes in the works, check whether we own the originals on DVD, then alert our DVD selector before the demand picks up.

I also troubleshoot, mostly tracking down missing items. I have developed a knack for guessing how items might be misshelved or where they might be tucked away in the staff areas. Although I am not enough of a perfectionist to be a cataloger, I am so good at spotting typos in the catalog that our catalogers joke about my eagle eye. I bring corrections to them in a collaborative spirit to ensure that the patrons can find what they want, so we maintain a good rapport.

Several times a month, I usher our movies. Because we have an aging clientele and poor floor lighting in our auditorium, it is crucial for me to escort people with flashlight in hand. I've seen many terrific movies, from classics to new releases that have left theaters but not made it to video yet, projected from real film onto a big screen. The downside is that I usually miss the first ten minutes of every movie seating the late arrivals. I miss later chunks taking patrons to the bathroom or to the exit when they are offended by controversial movies.

I create and maintain brochures for our department listing materials that are related but not shelved together, in anticipation of patron demand, sometimes in conjunction with displays. Several requests after the September 11, 2001, terrorist attacks prompted me to compile a list and display with patriotic music. Some displays require checking our holdings against existing lists, such as our annual display of Best Picture Academy Award winners. Others require ingenuity in selecting a theme or finding appropriate materials, such as seasonal displays of election-themed movies or romantic music for Valentine's Day. I prepare our monthly print and Web lists of new materials, taxing my computer skills to turn an unwieldy spreadsheet into something useful and attractive for patrons.

Once a week, I edit, print, and distribute our library's staff newsletter, which requires me to keep abreast of what is going on throughout the library. I flex my creative writing skills, both to ensure that staff are enticed to read important announcements and to find library-related filler for slow news weeks.

Outside my own department, I assist with our basic computer classes. Having previously worked in the computer usability field, I do this to remind myself about the common confusion, frustrations, and misunderstandings of novice users. I've learned new things from the classes, and I have become better at coaching our patrons through their initial forays with our online catalog, recalling that not everyone knows how to use scroll bars or hyperlinks.

PROS AND CONS

I focused my library career on working with music because I am passionate about it. Throughout my career, my goal has been to connect great music with an appreciative audience, which I do very directly in this job. I spend taxpayers' money on CDs, which the taxpayers then enjoy hearing. Although I ensure that we are up to date on the latest hits, I always get a thrill whenever I see that a CD by a fringe artist that I love is circulating. When a new album I bought to fill a less-than-obvious hole in our collection has a reserve right away, I feel validated because it shows that patrons value my building a diverse collection. I cherish seeing teenagers who are excited because we already have the CD by a hot up-and-coming band or because we're willing to purchase it just because they asked. Especially as radio becomes more tightly formatted, I'm thrilled that our patrons can explore our entire musical heritage, from Rachmaninoff to the Ramones, for free.

My interest in librarianship grew from admiration for librarians. I had several wonderful encounters at the Free Library of Philadelphia, where I asked different librarians obscure questions. If they did not know the precise answers already, they knew exactly where to look and had immediate answers for me. I entered the field aspiring to do the same—to have magical librarian moments. It is always fun to know an exact item from our collection that fulfills a patron's vague request or to rely on my photographic memory to instantaneously spot a CD in stacks and stacks of unsorted ones waiting to be reshelved. It is also fun to find an answer that isn't so obvious, to know how to exploit our online catalog and reference tools to track down something I did not know previously. My favorite example was determining what song was used in recent Lincoln Navigator commercials; I constructed just the right Google query because I had seen the ads and recognized that it was based on the work of Moondog, an avant-garde musician whose CDs I own. (The song was "Get a Move On" by Mr. Scruff.)

Beyond that, the best and worst part of my job is dealing directly with the public. Some people are wonderful and grateful. They come in with challenging questions and are demonstratively happy when I help them find things. One patron hugged me for locating the score for a particular song. I love when high school orchestra members ask for recordings of the music they're performing, because I was never that motivated as a band member. I've seen patrons both young and old take pride in mastering how to search for materials in our online catalog, a system better designed for finding books than music or movies. They are awed when I zip to the shelf and spot something immediately.

Unfortunately, not all people are so pleasant or appreciative. Some are inherently demanding, cranky, or unreasonable, and others may just be having a bad day. They are annoyed when items they want are unavailable, that we don't own every movie ever made, or that we ask them to respect other library users. I sometimes have a hard time shaking off negative interactions, venting later to coworkers or going over in my mind how I could have prevented the patron's wrath. I usually go out of my way to be kind and friendly with the next patrons I encounter.

HOW WOULD I GET A JOB LIKE YOURS?

Get a library degree and develop subject expertise. I have built my career around working with music, something I have done in most of my jobs. I was intimidated by the thought that music librarians must have a formal education in music. Although many academic music librarians have bachelor's or master's degrees in music, my background in popular music is equally valuable in a public library. I struggle with the spelling of Tchaikovsky but have no problem with Ludacris. Beyond the required education and subject knowledge, some character traits also lead to success in such a position: ease in dealing with the public, attention to detail, a facility with computers, a commitment to doing quality work, and a high level of curiosity.

RELATED RESOURCES

Allmusic. allmusic.com (accessed September 13, 2006).
The Internet Movie Database. www.imdb.com (accessed September 13, 2006).
Music Library Association. musiclibraryassoc.org (accessed February 23, 2006).

CHAPTER 6

Electronic Services Librarian

SARAH HOUGHTON-JAN

I am the e-services librarian for the Marin County Free Library in northern California, a system of eleven physical branches located in both rural and urban communities. I think of my job as being the manager of an additional Internet branch. Ever evolving, my position currently has four main areas of responsibility: I design, code, and maintain the library's Web site of over two thousand discrete pages; direct electronic resources development (including selection and support of databases, Web services, and e-books); coordinate the staffing and training for our three virtual reference services (e-mail, Web-based chat, and instant messaging); and train library staff on a variety of subjects, from basic computer skills to online reference sources.

A TYPICAL WORKDAY

On any given day, I could be out training for three hours, then doing some JavaScript coding, then in a two-hour committee meeting. I might spend the whole day catching up on e-mail and writing policy. I could be creating training materials and then following up with vendors on technical problems with our databases. The only aspect of my job that is constant is that there are 101 things that need to be done in a day, and only time for 10 of them to be accomplished. Following is an outline of the responsibilities and tasks assigned to my position. During the workday I can choose any number of these to focus on, depending on available resources and urgency. They all need to be done all the time.

Web Site Design, Coding, and Maintenance

I make multiple daily updates to the library's Web site, using HTML, CSS, CFM, and JavaScript. I do all of my coding by hand in Notepad; I don't use WYSIWYG programs like Dreamweaver, as I find they actually slow me down. I also do a good deal of graphics work for the Web site, primarily working with Paint Shop Pro and Fireworks. In addition to the regular parts of our library's Web site (pages with graphic and text elements, hyperlinked booklists, online forms), I am also Webmistress for the California Room Digital Archive, an online repository/exhibit of local history materials. Work for this site includes creating online photo albums, oral histories (audio and text), ephemera, and more. I also started a What's New @ the Library blog for the library, using a Blogger template and tweaking the code. I post to this blog regularly as well. I create special Web pages for special library events, such as Banned Books Week. I also edit and post streaming audio files from the library's radio show. A constant source of concern is to ensure that our Web site is ADA-accessible and compliant with national accessibility laws. I also redesign our Web site periodically (every two years), which involves gathering staff comments, many content and navigational changes, graphics and coding work, and usability testing.

Electronic Resources Development

Our library subscribes to a number of databases and e-books collections. I am responsible for purchasing e-resources for the library (including price and contract terms negotiations), and for balancing the e-resources budget. I act as the central contact for technical problems with the databases and e-books collections, and then I work with the vendors to resolve issues. I set up bimonthly trials for new databases (by subject area, to compare databases to one another), solicit feedback from staff, and work with the Database Committee to make purchasing and implementation decisions based on staff and patron input. I conduct periodic reviews of e-resource use and make cost-benefit analyses to determine future renewals or cancellations. In launching new databases for the library, I am responsible for all publicity, training for staff, and integration of information about the new resource into existing Web pages and publications. I conduct periodic needs assessments of staff and the public about e-resources. I also participate in collection development for our statewide e-books collection (through Califa, California's statewide consortium). In creating a balanced collection of e-resources, I am mindful to meet the needs of our at-home patrons, many of whom rarely (if ever) set foot in the physical library.

Training

I am responsible for coordinating the training of the library's ninety or so staff members. Primarily, this involves creating the training materials and teaching classes, although some training is also offered by our integrated library system office, the county Human Resources Department and Information Services and Technology Department, and our statewide training agency. With the help of a staff task force, I created and have since revised a set of technology core competencies for library staff. These competencies, delineated by position, are included in the library's policy and procedure manual, and each competency is linked to a "how-to" page for the task described. Staff members are asked to identify tasks/competencies in which they require training. Based on those self-evaluations, I develop a training sequence with classes geared toward those skill sets people still need to attain. Classes can be one-on-one tutorials or a demonstration class with up to twenty students. Some of the core competency classes I teach are Using Files and Folders, Using E-mail, Introduction to the Library's Web Site, Basic Computer Skills, and a PowerPoint Crash Course. I also teach classes covering the e-resources and e-services that the library offers, including Online Reader's Advisory, A Whirlwind Tour of the Library's Databases, Helping Users Use Our Databases from Home, and Small Business Resources Online. I am also responsible for training staff before new systems launches (e.g., print management system, public-use computer time management system). Through a weekly electronic staff newsletter I also advertise other training offerings available through the agencies listed. If time permits, I also create training materials for the public on our e-resources and e-services.

Virtual Reference

In my years at the library, I have initiated three separate virtual reference services for our patrons: e-mail, Web-based chat, and instant messaging.

E-mail Reference

Users can ask questions of the library using an online form. I supervise the work of the four reference librarians who, as part of their many responsibilities, answer reference questions through this e-mail project. I train these librarians on procedure, review their answers to ensure that we're giving good service, and notify them of any questions that languish in the inbox for longer than twenty-four hours.

Web-Based Chat Reference

The state of California offers a statewide coordinated Web-based chat project, AskNow, which uses QuestionPoint's 24/7 Reference software. Our librarians contribute four hours of staffing per week, and in return we're permitted to advertise the service to our patrons, which is available at any time. I am the coordinator for our library for this service, supervising the work of the three reference librarians who provide staffing. I also staff the service myself one hour per week. I review not only the chat transcripts from our librarians to ensure that they are giving quality service but also the transcripts from sessions our patrons engaged in to ensure that they are receiving quality service from the cooperative's other librarians and to follow up if good service has not been received. I train librarians to participate in this service (a time-intensive endeavor) and coordinate scheduling. I serve as the system follow-up contact for any of our library's patrons' questions that could not be answered through Web-based chat and that require more detailed research.

Instant Messaging Reference

I coordinate the library's instant messaging reference service, supervising the work of our seven librarians staffing this service. I train the librarians on procedure and policy, coordinate scheduling, and keep up on instant messaging trends and news to expand our service to the broadest audience possible. I also staff the service one scheduled hour per week and also any other time I'm at my desk.

Other Duties

Quite a bit of my time is spent going to committee and task force meetings and doing work for these groups. Currently, I am a member of an almost overwhelming nineteen committees, task forces, and teams (one national, three state, six regional/local, and nine internal to our library). I currently chair two of the committees: the library's Database Committee and our consortium's Public Services Committee.

I compile a number of monthly statistical reports for library administration: Web site statistics using WebTrends, database and e-books usage statistics for both our library and our consortium, usage of the library's public use computers (sessions and software usage), and virtual reference statistics from all three services.

I communicate regularly with members of the public regarding comments or complaints about our e-resources, e-services, or Web site.

I staff the physical reference desk in our central branch for up to three hours per week.

I am responsible for all publicity for our e-resources and e-services, so the creation of public service announcements, bookmarks, press releases, flyers, Web graphics, e-mail list entries, posting on Craigslist and other online forums like wikis and blogs, and interviews with the press on these areas of library services falls to me.

I frequently write new policies and procedures, mostly as they pertain to e-resources and e-services.

Occasionally I give presentations to community and library support groups about the library's e-resources and e-services.

I serve as the library's digital copyright expert, ensuring (to the best of our ability) that the library and its users comply with copyright and intellectual property laws.

I compile a monthly list of important library news stories and useful resources for our librarians.

Also, even though we have a separate technical support department, I act as an ad hoc technical support person, supporting staff use of computer hardware and software, Web applications, and other technologies. Because I give the training on almost all technology topics, people tend to then turn to me for support of anything on which I've trained.

I also speak Spanish, so other librarians frequently ask me to speak with patrons and the library administration occasionally asks me to translate documents from English.

PROS AND CONS

The staff in my library system are very good at what they do and they are, as a whole, enthusiastic about trying out new things, including technology. Interacting with them and serving their needs becomes easier because of their generally positive attitudes in the workplace. In positions like mine, one often gets to experiment with new technologies and try new things. This kind of flexibility is great for those of us with geekiness built in from birth.

There are always things waiting to be done; the physical and virtual piles of work never get any smaller. This is good in that I am always kept busy and can choose from a variety of tasks at any given time. However, in truth, my position is severely overloaded. The position was new when I took it several years ago and has at least tripled in responsibilities and duties since then. The position should be broken out among two or three full-time positions to allow adequate time to be spent on each task, avoid delay on most projects and requests (because I am only one person), and avoid staff burnout.

As technologies change and online resources and services become more integral to what the library is about, libraries everywhere will have to refocus staffing on the creation and support of those services and resources. Until now, I think most libraries have considered technology of all kinds to be an add-on to their existing services. Now that technology is integrated into everything we do, staffing needs to be adjusted to account for that.

Because my position is so overloaded, I cannot take any work time to engage in professional development or training. All my efforts to stay current in the profession and in technology training happen during off-work hours. There simply isn't the time at work to do it, so I do it on my own time. In my opinion, not to do so would be professionally irresponsible and limit my ability to do my job effectively. I do hope that some day I will actually have time at work to keep my skills current.

Finally, because I am responsible for so many different areas, the position is extremely high pressure and high stress. This needs to be done, that needs to be done, this project is waiting for you, this service isn't working, on and on and on—the demands from other staff are often overwhelming.

HOW WOULD I GET A JOB LIKE YOURS?

To be an effective e-services librarian, one must have an accredited master's degree in library science or library and information science. Experience as a trainer or teacher is essential. Likewise, Webmaster experience, knowledge of several coding languages and design principles, experience coordinating or staffing virtual reference services, and e-resources (database and e-book) collection development would also be key. The best way to start would be to focus on the technology and training topics while earning your MLS or MLIS and to gain some real-world experience by working in a university or public library.

RELATED RESOURCES

Calishain, Tara. *ResearchBuzz!* www.researchbuzz.org/wp (accessed August 14, 2006).
Crawford, Walt. *Cites & Insights: Crawford at Large.* citesandinsights.info (accessed August 14, 2006).
Houghton-Jan, Sarah. *Librarian in Black.* www.librarianinblack.net (accessed November 13, 2005).
Levine, Jenny. *The Shifted Librarian.* www.theshiftedlibrarian.com (accessed November 13, 2005).
Price, Gary. *ResourceShelf.* www.resourceshelf.com (accessed November 13, 2005).
Schmidt, Aaron. *Walking Paper.* walkingpaper.org (accessed November 13, 2005).
Stephens, Michael. *Tame the Web: Libraries and Technology.* www.tametheweb.com/ttwblog (accessed November 13, 2005).
Tennant, Roy. 2004. *Managing the digital library.* New York: Reed Press.
West, Jessamyn. *Librarian.net.* librarian.net (accessed November 13, 2005).

CHAPTER 7

Technical Services Manager

NANETTE WARGO DONOHUE

I oversee all aspects of acquisition, cataloging, physical preparation, and inventory control of library materials in all formats at Champaign Public Library. Working with staff throughout the library, I determine departmental priorities and deadlines and ensure that all cataloging and processing provides the necessary access to library materials. I run a number of statistical reports on a regular basis, and I supervise and train new staff. I also work closely with our regional library system to cooperatively develop and determine cataloging policies and practices. I also serve on library and consortium committees, and I attend biweekly meetings of the management team.

A TYPICAL WORKDAY

When I give tours of the Technical Services Department, I like to joke that we're the most important department in the library because nobody would be able to find anything without us! Though I'd gladly concede that all departments are equally important pieces of the library puzzle, this little joke is at the heart of everything I do during my workday. As the person who manages the acquisition, cataloging, processing, and item maintenance functions of the library, I've got a lot of people to answer to, both internally and externally. If we don't do our job well here in technical services, no one will be able to find what they're looking for.

One term that's frequently mentioned in technical services is *workflow*. It seems like we're always discussing where materials are in the workflow, where there are bottlenecks in the workflow, and what's going smoothly in the workflow. In my mind, the workflow in technical services starts when the items are received from the vendor, and it ends when they are routed to other departments to be put on the shelves for the public. The standard we have set in our department is four business days or less, with a twenty-four-hour turnaround for high-demand items that have five or more patron holds.

I generally start my day by taking a look around the workroom to get an idea of the workflow. Some things I might notice are backups in a particular area or items flagged for expedited processing. I might find an item or two in my mailbox that requires my attention because of a cataloging question or a database inconsistency. I usually evaluate these items right away so I can get them back to the shelves quickly. I also spend some time in the morning checking and responding to any e-mail that I might have received since the previous workday. Because the library is open until 9 p.m. on weekdays, I sometimes receive e-mail from library staff after I've left for the day. Usually, some of the e-mail is informational, and some may involve requests for statistical reports. Having a general idea of what will need my immediate attention helps me decide how I should best budget my time. Just as with any other library job, organization is key.

I regularly compile several statistical reports, including monthly reports on number of items checked out, number of items borrowed and lent through our consortium's interlibrary loan service, and the number of items ordered from various vendors. These reports are made available to all staff and our library board. I also routinely prepare low-circulation reports for weeding purposes. These reports, which generally consist of titles in a particular collection that have not circulated for a specified amount of time, allow public services staff to remove outdated items from our collections. Fortunately, our integrated library system software is able to automatically generate most of these statistics, and other statistics are easy to compile using basic spreadsheet software.

Part of my day is usually occupied by a special project of some kind. Champaign Public Library has a detailed five-year plan (available on our library's Web site, www.champaign.org) consisting of four key service roles for the library, and each department sets its own goals based on these roles. Any special projects handled by my department are designed to meet one or more of these goals, and they often involve collaboration with other departments. During the past two years, my department has worked through a migration to a new integrated library system, handled several large-scale reprocessing projects intended to improve access to library collections, and started a large-scale collection inventory to improve database quality. Because most of these projects are major undertakings, they require a good deal of advance planning to ensure that everything goes smoothly.

I tend to spend a little bit of time each day handling personnel issues. Usually, this simply means approving requests for time off, though it can also mean writing notes about staff accomplishments or filing comment cards from other staff in my personnel files. This is not the most exciting part of my day, but these notes are very helpful when I write the annual performance evaluations for my department.

Like most managers, I often attend meetings, both in-house and at the library system office. Part of my job description includes serving on library- and system-wide committees. Generally, my committee service relates to either management or to technical services (cataloging in particular), though I also chair the library's Staff Awards Committee. As a manager, I like to be involved in groups or committees that allow me to interact with staff from other departments, especially staff at different levels within the organization. I also handle a weekly shift on the library's instant messenger reference service, and I am trained to substitute in circulation if needed.

At the end of the day, I return to the workflow yet again. Before I leave, I always take a look around and see where things stand. It gives me some perspective on how the day went for the department as a whole and helps me think about what's going well.

PROS AND CONS

I consider myself extremely lucky—I was hired for my dream job right out of library school. I love cataloging, I'm fascinated with acquisitions, and my first library job (way back in high vvschool!) was in database and item maintenance. However, what I really wanted to do was manage. In my job, I have the best of both worlds—I get to manage a department *and* I get to do some of the things I love to do.

Because this field is constantly changing, there's always some project that you can take on to improve access to library collections. There's plenty of room to innovate here, and I've found that changes I've made that seem minor to me have impacted the library and made it a more welcoming place. The pace of change can sometimes seem overwhelming, and it requires a lot of flexibility and willingness to listen carefully and compromise when necessary. This is not a good job for someone who likes to do the same thing every day!

One minor annoyance of working in technical services is that we tend to be misunderstood. Staff who work in public service departments often think it would be relaxing to work in our department. Though we do not have to cope with the unpredictability of library patrons, our workflow is relentless and there is never a moment with nothing to do. Also, this isn't always the best job for a person who longs to be in the spotlight. Staff who present programs and answer questions will always receive compliments from the public, but the cataloger who ensures that the reference librarian can find the right item for a customer won't get any recognition. On a bad day, this can feel like a thankless job, but as the cliché goes, a job well done is its own reward, and the isolated instances where you're singled out for a contribution seem even more special and important.

HOW WOULD I GET A JOB LIKE YOURS?

One piece of advice that I always give practicum students who are interested in technical services work: learn everything you can about technical services, but be a good generalist as well. It is important for technical services staff to understand what goes on in other library departments, because it can help you understand how your work fits into the bigger picture of overall library service. When you're in library school, take as many cataloging classes as you can, but also take general and specialized reference courses and a course in at least one aspect of public service work (children's or teen service, reader's advisory, adult public service and programming, etc.). A solid understanding of the way other departments function will help you make better decisions.

If you have the opportunity, get some practical experience working in technical services. Most libraries have their own way of handling acquisitions, cataloging, and processing, but experience translates well across institutions. Much of what you will learn in library school is theoretical, and though theory is certainly important, much of what you will do in the workplace— particularly in a public library—is practical. An internship, practicum, or other job in technical services will teach you the practical side of technical services work.

It's also important to understand that just because you work behind the scenes doesn't mean that you can get by with poor communication skills. If I were hiring for my job, I'd look for someone who is able to communicate well to staff at numerous levels of understanding without using unnecessary jargon or talking down to them. It's true that not everyone in the library will fully understand what we do in technical services, but I feel it's my duty to serve as a good ambassador for my department and, on a larger level, my field. Because my department works so closely with other departments, good communication skills are vital.

RELATED RESOURCES

ALA's Association for Library Collections and Technical Services (ALCTS) is the dominant professional organization in U.S. technical services. There are divisions of ALCTS for acquisitions, cataloging, collection development, serials, and preservation. The ALCTS Web site (www.ala.org/ alcts) contains information about current trends in the technical services field, information about continuing education, and a bimonthly newsletter with informative articles, committee reports, and news. ALCTS publishes a print journal, *Library Resources & Technical Services*, which publishes research articles in the area of technical services.

There are numerous state and regional groups for technical services librarians and support staff. I am personally involved with the Illinois Library Association's Resources and Technical Services Forum, and many other state library associations have similar groups. A listing of state and regional technical services–related groups can be found on the ALCTS Council of Regional Groups Web site (www.ala.org/ala/alctscontent/crgcontent/affiliaterelatio/directory/directory. htm).

There are also specialized groups that meet specific needs within technical services. Online Audiovisual Catalogers, founded in 1980, addresses the needs of audiovisual catalogers through continuing education and ongoing discussion on their electronic discussion list. Their Web site, located at ublib.buffalo.edu/libraries/units/cts/olac, contains a good deal of information about the organization and about audiovisual cataloging in general. ACQWEB (www.acqweb.org) and its sister publication ACQNET provide a wide variety of information relating to acquisitions in a variety of types of libraries.

I would also recommend looking at the OCLC Web site (www.oclc.org) to familiarize yourself with current and upcoming trends in the world of cataloging. Most public libraries use shared cataloging records from OCLC.

CHAPTER 8

Rural Library Director

JOY HUEBERT

"Can you tell me about the word *eudaemonism*?" asks the puzzled library member who has stopped to talk to me, the director. Of course I can! As I sit at my desk in the middle of our small library, I also work on the board's annual budget, plan a renovation to our children's area, contemplate a union situation regarding a staff job description, arrange for the purchase of two new computers, and think about my upcoming presentation to the Lions Club. The board's first job description for my position was six pages long before they shortened it to read, in a nutshell, "Provide good library services to the people of the Trail area." My community includes twenty thousand people spread over seven municipal areas in British Columbia, the city of Trail being the largest. It is my task to ensure that the collections, programs, staff, facility, and services offered by the public library are the best that they can be for the people who live in this area. It is a job with diversity, challenges, and change. It is a good job for people who like people and who can work with individuals and groups that include boards, city councils, staffs, unions, service clubs, other community organizations, businesses, and librarians in associations. In short, my job is "being everything to everybody."

A TYPICAL WORKDAY

For many years I worked shifts that included days, evenings, and weekends. In Trail I have the privilege of a Monday-to-Friday, eight-to-four work week unless I have an evening program or a meeting with the board, a community group, a library association, or an evening staff member, in which case I work the hours required.

My day starts with e-mail. In the past ten years the world went virtual and now we rarely talk on the telephone or write letters. E-mail comes in all flavors, from reference questions, to vendor sales pitches, to letters from other directors regarding projects we are working on together, to piles of junk that somehow escape our filters.

After the e-mail, I review the events of the day. Usually I have some kind of meeting. On the first Friday of the month I see the Friends of the Library from noon until 1 p.m. and we discuss their projects, which include book sales, membership drives, and other activities. Once a month I attend a board meeting; to prepare for this I write a report, create a financial statement, write up policy changes and issues, and speak to the committees to organize their input. I put together an agenda and a package and make sure it is available the week before the meeting. I also interact on a regular basis with a variety of community organizations like Success by Six, the Adult and Family Literacy Associations, the senior citizens, or the local library association.

My life as a manager and administrator is organized to balance two tasks: the first is to take care of practical daily business; the second is long-range development. Community development takes many forms, one of which is to assist the board with strategic planning. The board and I have spent several years developing a strategic plan, and it is my job to fulfill this plan, which includes many different initiatives. The board's main functions are politics and policies. Managing the politics of the library means that we must be aware of what our seven municipalities are up to and that we must communicate our value to them effectively. To this end, we hosted a reception to thank our donors and stakeholders last year. We invited the local cable company to film the event, and we handed out certificates to those people and organizations that contributed to our organization financially or in other ways.

I work on a lot of future-oriented projects for long-range planning and community development. For example, a speech therapist who had attended a workshop on health literacy came to see me. She was interested in discussing how we could develop a health literacy program in our area. I spoke with her at length, and then we met with the literacy coordinator in our area. We made a plan to begin the project with a workshop that could be presented to health care providers. The speech therapist was a little overwhelmed by the idea of changing the world to become health literate. I reassured her that it was possible to change the world, but that it had to be done in small, manageable, organized steps.

Another example of the long view is the constant need to ensure adequate funds to meet operating expenses and the need to find additional funds for special projects. In a small public library it helps to be aware of money and how to get more of it. Fundraising is a big part of any public library director's job these days. The Friends of the Library raise money in various ways, and so do I, through writing grant proposals, making presentations to service clubs, or in any other ways I can think of. Of course, to persuade municipal, provincial, and federal governments to maintain and increase their funding to public libraries remains the most crucial funding challenge because government funding provides the core of our operating budgets.

Staff members are a big part of my job, and I speak with them every day. I plan training sessions, deal with problems, help them resolve disputes, and answer their questions. Every three years the staff members, through their union representative, negotiate with the management, which consists of the board and me. Then we as individuals turn into *management* and *workers* and figure out what sorts of protocols we will plan to allow us to create a working environment that meets the needs of the organization but is also good for staff.

It's lunchtime! I belong to a noon Toastmasters Club where I make speeches to improve my public speaking and communication skills. Toastmasters is fun; we meet in an Italian restaurant for an hour and get feedback on how we come across to others. Toastmasters has certainly helped me to be a better off-the-cuff speaker, handling difficult situations that require quick thinking or tact.

Daily administrative details come up that I have to deal with. Say the photocopier breaks, or the security system falls apart, or there are forms to fill out for Revenue Canada, or decisions to make about which magazine subscriptions to order. Sometimes these can be planned ahead; sometimes they come up suddenly. The staff feel nauseated, their eyes are burning—has the air quality deteriorated? This must be addressed by phoning the building maintenance crew.

"What's the letter *c* in Greek?" In the middle of writing this chapter, my technology staff member came to me to ask what we should call the third public Internet terminal. We've just expanded and the first two are named alpha and beta. We looked up the Greek alphabet and the answer was obvious: gamma! One big plus for me is the constant learning, and I even get paid for it.

On and on we go. Other duties include ordering books, CDs, videos, DVDs, and other materials; discarding old stuff; planning programs; writing newspaper articles; arranging displays—there are many things to do.

Because of our space limitations, I sit in the middle of the library to do my work. There, people can talk to me whenever they want, and I enjoy the public interaction. Sometimes it's difficult or tiring to engage in conversations with some of our lonely patrons, but generally I like the opportunity that being publicly available gives me to help people find information or fiction or just to chat.

At 4 p.m. it's time to go home. I have put in a useful day and look forward to tomorrow.

PROS AND CONS

My job is interesting and fun. It is a good job for those who like a lot of variety, who are self-motivated, who don't mind interruptions, who can handle the stresses of human interactions that often include conflicts, and who don't mind the need to constantly change and develop services. It is good for someone who, while tracking expenses on a spreadsheet, discovers that in September—oops!—there will be a deficit, and then doesn't mind doing quick fundraising projects to alleviate the sudden lack of funds. It is a good job choice for a person who can stay calm when a carefully arranged plan is completely disrupted.

I personally have two big annoyances. The first is the constant necessity to prove the library's value to its main donors, which are municipalities. I could go on and on about how libraries are often not considered to bring significant value to the community, but I'm sure you know what I mean. It takes constant work to communicate effectively with municipal, provincial, and federal governments. We have made progress, but you can never take it for granted.

The second annoyance is the tendency for libraries to be stuck in rulebooks. I often want to throw all the procedures and rules out and let people have whatever they need to make them happy.

HOW WOULD YOU GET A JOB LIKE MINE?

Library boards usually want to hire a director who is a librarian with a master's degree from an ALA-accredited university. To succeed at the job, it helps to have experience working in a public library, as it involves a lot of detail and complexity. It is also important to understand the many demands of public libraries and to be able to accept interruptions, money shortages, conflicts, and constant change. A potential director should be comfortable with the need to provide leadership in diverse situations. I have known librarians hired to run small public libraries who discovered that they hated the work and much preferred the academic life or a more specialized position in a larger library. Public library work is very flexible. It can accommodate technical services people, children's librarians, reference librarians, detail people, conceptual types, introverts, and extroverts. To run a public library, it is essential to have good communication skills and an ability to see the big picture.

Running a small library in a rural area makes many demands on a person. The librarian has a high profile in the community and may be the only librarian for miles around. She or he may be called on to participate in other organizations and provide leadership for the whole community.

Although there will be other staff, the librarian must be able to do a variety of tasks that can include budgeting, programming, human resources, technical services, public relations, and building repair. A person called on to be all things to all people sometimes has to step back and say, "Hey! I am not qualified to be an accountant, an electrician, a union negotiator, or any one of a number of jobs that it takes a qualified, trained person to do." For example, just the other day I decided to get an actual accountant to design a new spreadsheet for our finances. I was used to doing everything myself but decided it was not feasible to perform this particular task.

If you feel excited or intrigued by my description of working as a rural public library director, I encourage you to pursue this career option. It will lead to an interesting life and many opportunities to make a difference to people's lives and the whole community.

CHAPTER 9

Urban Branch Manager

JIM PEARSON

Before I entered the profession, I served in the army as a paramedic and then as a manager at a large children's hospital. Though I have saved lives using my medical knowledge, I receive no greater job satisfaction than in being a librarian.

After earning my master's in information science in 2003, I was hired by the Harris County (Texas) Public Library System to manage one of their urban branches. The position had been open for at least nine months prior to my starting date. At my first meeting with the staff, they laughed at my remark that I was hired because I was a former army sergeant and trained paramedic. The Aldine branch is in the middle of a tough Houston neighborhood and has experienced gang activity. I had found my home away from home, and the challenge of managing in this environment was exactly how I wanted to spend my time as a librarian.

In December 2004 my supervisor promoted me to branch librarian of a second branch. The High Meadows branch library is located twelve minutes from my first branch and shares some of the same challenges. Both branches are located near middle and high school campuses with large after-school populations. I accepted the challenge of managing two branch libraries, and I find my days filled with the anticipation of not knowing what will happen at either location.

The road leading to success has not been straight; however, each day brings me closer to it. It has been difficult convincing staff to believe that what we accomplish each day for our community goes beyond checking out books. The libraries serve as shining stars in the neighborhood and are a magnet for children and teenagers that live nearby. Finding ways to remain vital to them is what drives my thought processes and focuses each day.

OPENING THE DOORS

I usually begin my day with what for me has become a ceremony that I like to think of as the "opening of the doors." For me, our greatest accomplishment is providing access to the world of information we house within our buildings. My favorite activity is unlocking the doors to this information and greeting each customer as he or she enters the library. Welcoming old acquaintances and meeting new ones as I stand by the open doors sets the tone for their visit.

It also reminds me each day that we are a free society and reinforces the importance of remaining committed to public access to all types of information.

I make a point of pulling my share of reference duty, so I move from door opening to the information desk on most mornings. Both of the branches I manage have transitioned to a service-delivery model where we provide service at one centrally located desk instead of having separate circulation and reference desks. All service is provided at one desk so that customers are not shuttled between desks when they need assistance.

When not providing reference service, I spend time planning library services for both of my branch library communities. High Meadows is served by a state-designated improvement district. Leaders from area businesses and residents meet once a month to plan community initiatives that increase value to the community. The library plays a role, and under my leadership we have partnered with schools and local organizations to raise our profile within the communities we serve.

My passion for service to teenagers led me to develop an afternoon program called TeenTime. It provides a forum for teens to study, play games, or just hang out. The meeting room is opened for their use, and a staff member supervises the three-hour session. I enjoy spending time with the teenagers when I serve as host at least every couple of months. I specialized in young adult services while earning my degree, and service to teenagers remains my passion. I have enjoyed serving as a youth advocate and making the library a destination for teenagers in each community.

A portion of my time each day is spent with staff, either formally or informally, modeling the service behavior that I adhere to in my personal journey as a librarian. I have found that I often provide guidance for others to follow during my interactions with customers. It is my goal as a manager to develop an environment propagated on understanding the daily challenges of our customers. I find that my time in the medical field prepared me for the homeless, frenzied mothers, senior citizens, and teenagers we serve by giving me a foundation of patience. I try each day to pass this attitude on to the staff. For example, I can explain to them that I waived the fines of the single mother returning books late because she is encouraging her children to read by checking out over twenty different items for them.

PROS AND CONS

I enjoy the challenges offered by managing two very distinct staffs and locations. The constant stimulation of not knowing what is going to occur at either location keeps me motivated. I also have the satisfaction of knowing that I am influencing lives in the communities I serve. I have found that it is more difficult to maintain relationships with customers and staff members since my time is split between two locations. I am sometimes frustrated by what I perceive as a lack of progress toward provision of services that I would like to offer, because my attention is easily captured by the pressing issues of each day.

I also sometimes feel guilty about leaving my first branch to visit my second branch because they have had trouble keeping a branch manager in my position for long periods of time. Both branches have experienced a high turnover rate, and it can be difficult for staff to adjust to changing leadership. In the end, the knowledge that I have been able to make a difference at either location offers me peace at the end of my day.

HOW WOULD I GET A JOB LIKE YOURS?

I think that it is important for you, as a new librarian, to realize that just because you have a degree to hang on the wall, this does not mean that your learning is over. You may have worked in a library setting prior to earning your degree, but you still have new things to learn. The fact that you are now a professional means that you have a different responsibility to the people you work with and serve. You should also not be afraid to take a position that does not fit into what you think your career path should be. Librarians are found in all types of environments, and yours may be different from what you anticipated.

CLOSING THE DOORS

I look forward at the end of the day to the closing of the library. This is the time that I spend with customers, reminding them that we will open tomorrow to begin the process over again. As I lock the doors for the evening I begin thinking about what the next day's opening will bring.

CHAPTER 10

Administrator

OSEI AKOTO BAFFOUR

As branch administrator, neighborhood services, I provide direct administrative oversight to branch and regional libraries by coordinating, planning, and evaluating branch library services within the city of Fort Worth, Texas. Under the direct supervision of the library director, I work with the library managers to maintain their facilities, develop collections, and organize programming. I also coordinate services with other divisions within the library system, city departments, and outside agencies. Furthermore, I serve on the Fort Worth Public Library's management team, which is charged with the preparation of policy and procedures, strategic planning, financial accountability, and staff development.

A TYPICAL WORKDAY

In the Morning

I typically start my day firing up my computer and running to the staff lounge for my share of freshly brewed coffee. With a little caffeine surge, I am ready for administration action. First I answer all high-priority e-mails, save low-priority e-mails, and delete the rest. My messages fall into the following categories: messages I hesitate to answer or wish I did not have to read, messages I place on hold, and the messages to be forwarded (my personal favorite). What happens to messages that do not fall into these categories? You guessed it—they are deleted!

Meetings

Beep, beep, beep! The sound of my trustworthy PDA notifies me of important meetings and appointments. I cannot miss those! Naturally, I consult my PDA or digital calendar regarding my schedule. Usually, my day starts with a morning meeting with the division's administrative assistant. We have weekly catch-up meetings during which we exchange information about projects and receive updates. Our discussions center on staffing, incident reports, approvals, and any other issues that she may have handled during the previous week. She always reminds me of city projects that should be on my radar.

MTeam (Management Team Meeting)

The *M* in MTeam stands for management. One of the many hats I wear as a branch administrator is to act as advocate and liaison for branch libraries at the management level. Our meetings are held each Wednesday. This is where I throw on my thick skin. I understand criticism will be pushed my way, so I listen well and prepare to justify all positions. I prepare by making phone calls to my staff for feedback and responses to projects I may have assigned them. I also talk to friends or peers in some benchmark cities about their approaches to policy development and other relevant issues before attending this important meeting. Some of these peers are very sincere and honestly inform me on what will or will not fly. Now I am ready to respond to queries from the rest of the management team and the library director.

Included in the agenda are opportunities for me to answer questions and respond to assignments at the roundtable. I generate important tidbits that help me brag about successes and challenges when it is my turn to talk about my division. Unlike other meetings, the team develops hypotheses that help me in my decision-making processes. The director asks probing and thought-provoking questions that make me think on my feet and come up with solutions that address important concerns. I am always ready to support my positions because she challenges me and the rest of the team to consider all sides of an issue before drawing conclusions. She expects full accountability for decisions I make and conclusions I draw. I always make sure I have all my facts straight before the MTeam. All of this prepares me to go Nutz afterward!

Nutz (Nuts and Bolts Meeting)

After the MTeam meeting on Wednesdays, the management team convenes without our director for the Nutz meeting on Thursdays. The Nutz meeting is like therapy for a library administrator. Our main charge is to address detailed operational issues before presenting them at the MTeam meetings. I submit my agenda items and philosophical questions about library service to the team for discussion. Occasionally, I discuss personnel issues without mentioning specific names to hear my colleagues' points of view. The team becomes my support group. I share my frustrations with them to get their suggestions. They provide me with alternatives for me to choose from. I reevaluate the situation, and choose or ask myself the question, "Should or should I not go with option A, B, or C, as the case may be?"

Unlike the MTeam, I take my own notes at Nutz. The atmosphere is more relaxed and informal. I speak more freely and frankly there than at MTeam because the meeting is less official and controlled. Just like my colleagues do, I use this meeting to hash out policies, plans, and any other initiatives. I work through the nuts and bolts of all items on the agenda. Budgets, staffing, facilities, marketing, and all other operational issues are handled item by item.

After returning to my desk I am all ears, or shall I say, all eyes. Dozens of e-mails await my attention. Frankly, there are times I only click on the ones from the managers and staff in my group. I ask myself: What is going on at these locations? Do they need help covering the branches? Did every manager report to work, and are there any emergencies I need to address?

Other Meetings

By default and virtue of my position, I am a member of all committees that make decisions affecting branches or the whole library system. Beep, beep! My PDA reminds me of my next assignment, a technology planning committee meeting. Members of this group include tech-savvy library staff, other management team members, representatives of Friends of the Library, the library foundation, and City of Fort Worth Information Technology Department representatives. Our charge is to evaluate existing technologies and identify what to support, eliminate, or phase out. The decisions are invariably predicated on the best way to make our services customer friendly. For a library system that recently upgraded all its computers and introduced a new integrated library system, this is a bold transition to the second phase of an overall technology improvement plan as identified in the Long Range Services Plan. This meeting lasts an hour.

The Rest of the Day and Other Routines

If I do not have any emergencies, I plan for my next meeting or grab my scrapbook to review minutes from previous meetings in an effort to follow up on assignments. The real work is often done prior to and after a meeting. Through e-mail exchanges and conversations we formulate opinions before major decisions. The director or other management team members use meetings to distribute or share tasks for participants of the meetings to accomplish.

Conversely, there are those who believe we meet a lot and, for that matter, that some meetings may not be necessary. However, the demands and expectations of the management team make it necessary to meet as often as possible. That is one way of accomplishing tasks and avoiding trouble in the ranks. With this approach and preparation, I am able to respond to queries and assist in accomplishing important objectives for the whole library system.

Branch Visits

I visit branches periodically to observe, audit, have discussions, and answer questions. On selected occasions I meet with staff members individually to chat. I find these meetings helpful because I am able to discover the personalities and potentials of all staff. They get their questions answered, and I share major policy decisions in the pipeline.

Relations with Other City Departments

To achieve results one needs to understand how the whole city operates. I participate in meetings and serve on committees that benefit the library and contribute to the overall success of the City of Fort Worth.

Library department liaisons in selected departments assist and support our operations. I contact the legal department liaison for a review of new or revised policies, decisions about how to handle certain incidents, and other legal issues. The purchasing department and I discuss matters such as changes made to the purchasing software or other changes to the way we acquire materials through the city. As you may already know, dealings with the human resources department revolve around hiring, discipline, training, and firing of employees. The transportation and public works department is instrumental in maintaining library facilities. As a result, I have a special relationship with their management. I visit library buildings with them to seek their advice during the budget process and during new renovation or building projects.

Patron Complaints

The Golden Rule: the customer is always right! Customer satisfaction is very important to the City of Fort Worth and the governing bodies of the library. When a patron calls or writes a complimentary letter or an objection to any library service, I give the praise or grievance fair consideration. To ensure good service, I respond in writing and follow up with a phone call.

Not all communications between me and the public are responses to concerns and problems. There are customers who provide me with positive feedback. I contact them to thank them. One thing I have learned on the job is not to panic or approach situations with a knee-jerk reaction. It helps to investigate the whole case before creating a solution. In certain situations, I am helpless. Sometimes the situation may resolve itself. By asking the right questions and investigating I am able to resolve some of these issues.

Once I received a complaint from a neighborhood association about replacing an outdoor sign at the branch in one particular community. Initially, I thought of fixing the problem right away. Nevertheless, I held back, and after a couple of weeks of e-mail exchanges and phone calls, the organization offered to pay for the sign.

To initiate the project, I discussed it with a divisional head of the transportation and public works department. The library was ready to finance it. However, I believed that it was a better idea to give the community the opportunity to contribute to the upkeep of their branch library. The plan worked! We have a new sign and the neighborhood association is recognized for its good deed.

Personnel Issues: Mentoring, Coaching, Counseling, Disciplining

In an effort to improve communication between library administration and the rank and file, I visit branches monthly to talk with all staff. They chat with me for thirty minutes or less and share ideas with me that I often draw on when making decisions. I also meet with them as a group whenever necessary. I discover who needs more training and receive information that helps me in developing my divisional plan and ultimately performance planning, evaluation, and review for the branches.

I encourage managers to pursue opportunities that will assist their employees' professional development. Managers know that I promote good service and recognize professional acumen among staff. They also know that I do not reward bad behavior and I adhere to the dictates of the personnel rules of the City of Fort Worth with discretion. I believe that staff who violate policies and do not see the need to correct their behavior should be handled according to prescribed disciplinary processes.

Committees

I act as management liaison for select committees to meet goals on the library's business plan. I set up committees, choose conveners, and provide them with instructions and other points of reference. From me they get their answers to questions that only someone in management would know. According to Alec Issigonis, "A camel is a horse designed by committee." When the plans and findings of these committees are completed, I review, revise, and make sure it's a horse and not a camel before sharing with the MTeam. My next steps include approving funds, presenting findings, and making recommendations at Nutz and MTeam. My final acts are to supervise the implementation of the projects, develop policies and procedures related to them, and conduct training if necessary.

At the end of the day, I shut down my computer and I'm off.

WHAT DO I LIKE OR HATE ABOUT MY JOB?

To be completely honest, I became an administrator for the schedule. I work eight to five with no nights and weekends except during special circumstances. What else can I ask for? I have paid my dues as a librarian and library manager. However, in situations such as special systemwide programs or emergencies, I must be available to provide support at any time. I like my job because my duties are more challenging. I get to participate in major decision-making processes and implement them. Besides, I get to plan and develop projects that I support. I also enjoy the unpredictable and challenging nature of my routines. Personally, I get to train, give impromptu speeches, and address major issues ad lib. The rewards are numerous, and I don't mean only the monetary aspect. There are intangible compensations that come with being a branch administrator.

The only challenges I face are those moments when I wish I could have more time to complete projects. Occasionally, I also have to discipline employees due to personnel problems that could have been corrected if they had followed rules. It is fun to recruit and hire new people, but letting workers go is the least enjoyable part of what I do.

TO BECOME A BRANCH ADMINISTRATOR

Managers or librarians with previous branch experience may do well in a position like mine. The main requirements for getting a job like mine are experience in running branch libraries, understanding people, and time management. You will need these skills to handle personnel and customer service problems. Additionally, you must understand how municipal governments work so you can represent the library well on citywide committees and events. You will create interdepartmental relationships and nurture them to achieve results for the library.

Conferences and other continuing education opportunities will improve your professional acumen. Ask for a mentor in library administration who can provide you with insight into what happens in library management. As part of your preparation to secure an administrator's position, read advertisements in library publications such as ALA's JobLIST, *Library Journal, American Libraries,* and library job Web sites to familiarize yourself with job descriptions for skills and expectations needed for a branch administrator position.

RELATED RESOURCES

Nelson, Sandra S. 2000. *Managing for results: Effective resource allocation for public libraries.* Chicago: American Library Association.

CHAPTER 11

Territorial Librarian

ALISON HOPKINS

The Northwest Territories is located in the Canadian Arctic and covers 1.17 million square kilometers. It is populated by slightly over forty thousand people, approximately half of whom are aboriginal. There are eleven official languages: Chipewyan, Cree, Dogrib, English, French, Gwich'in, Inuinnaqtun, Inuktitut, Inuvialuktun, North Slavey, and South Slavey. Yellowknife is the capital city and the largest community (population 18,028). There are thirty-two other communities, all of which are considerably smaller. At the time of this writing, nine communities have public libraries, with six more planned.

In the position of territorial librarian, I manage Public Library Services, a part of the Government of the Northwest Territories. Public Library Services funds community libraries through contribution agreements with community governments and supports community libraries through the provision of rotating collections, interlibrary loan services, training, library visits, and the management of an integrated library system for the territory. We also provide materials by mail to people in communities without library branches. In my position, I also represent the territory in national forums on library services.

A lot of my time is spent traveling. My supervisor, the library system servers, and many of the people I work with are located in Yellowknife, which is a forty-five-minute commute by air. I average one trip a month to Yellowknife.

Many of our public libraries are staffed by one part-time worker with little or no formal library training. To support their work, it is important to visit each library at least once a year in addition to holding an annual meeting.

A TYPICAL WORKDAY

I am going to tell you about a typical workday at the Public Library Services Office. Our office is located in Hay River, which is one of the few communities in the NT accessible by road year-round. The winters are fairly serious, running from October to May, with the mean temperature in January ranging from $-6°F$ to $-22°F$. Our building is owned by the government and contains our offices plus the local public library.

I begin my day by turning on my computer. I check my e-mail, my online calendar and task list, and then turn to my low-tech paper to do list. I use my calendar for appointments, my task list for specific deadlines and reminders, and my to dos for ongoing projects. Between the three, I have a good sense of what needs to be done today, next week, and next month.

I am happiest and most productive when my list runs to about fifteen items, a mix of short- and long-term activities. This week, tasks revolve around three major projects: the addition of six new public libraries, our annual meeting of public libraries, and the need to upgrade our library software system.

Six New Public Libraries

We are starting six new public libraries this year. The libraries will be located in school libraries, with communities receiving funds to hire staff to keep the library open in the evenings and weekends. This week I need to confirm the final contribution agreement, check in on the other communities, communicate with the adult literacy coordinator (my partner on this project), and verify the work that the rest of Public Library Services is doing to order and process materials. I also plan to have a staff meeting to sort out how we are going to go about helping and training the new library staff.

Public Libraries Annual Meeting

This month we are holding a meeting in Yellowknife for representatives of all of our public libraries. It is a two-day event, including a reception with our minister in attendance at the Yellowknife Public Library. This week I need to finalize our meeting agenda, confirm speakers, make reservations somewhere for a group lunch, make sure we have the supplies we need, and confirm that the paperwork for the travel arrangements is in order. Then I will need to get the agenda out to the attendees and answer any questions.

Library Software Upgrade

Public Library Services handles systems administration for a system that is used by public, college, research, and legislative libraries. We are working toward upgrading our software. I need to communicate with our vendor as well as the information systems staff in Yellowknife who assist us with this kind of project. I want to go through the system enhancement list with an eye to training and communication implications. Our system consortium is also talking about having a meeting in November, which I need to start planning. For this project, my timeline is looser. I keep it in mind for times when I need a change from the other projects I am working on.

How I Work

I like to start my day with a few easy tasks, like making some calls or responding to an e-mail; that way I get to warm up a bit and cross something off my list, which makes me feel productive. As the day progresses, I switch to more complex and time-intensive activities.

There are always other things that come up that are not on my list. Weekly, I go through human resources and financial paperwork that needs to be verified and signed. I receive requests and questions by e-mail and telephone that need to be answered.

Toward the middle of the list is an item called "Library Manual." There exists a manual used by current libraries, which I am planning to revise significantly for our new libraries. It is a thorough and complete manual, which I think might scare off the new hires. I want to complete this project in the next two weeks. I have gone through the manual, discussed it with my staff, and have an idea of what I am looking for in the final result. I know that when I start it, I will need at least an afternoon, and it will be difficult to focus on anything else until it is done. I am waiting to start it until it is more fully sorted in my mind, the more urgent work is completed, and I have time to work on it.

I find that in this position, the day wanders in all sorts of directions. A phone call, an e-mail, and suddenly I am finding information for someone, writing a report, or sending a flurry of faxes or e-mails. I work best in this kind of environment, where there are interruptions and interesting things happening.

There are two things that I do every day, fitting them in around everything else that goes on. One, keep current; and two, check in with my staff.

Keeping Current

I subscribe to just over fifty RSS feeds, mostly library related, along with some news and pop culture stuff. I start by checking how many new items there are each morning, and browse through a few. As the day goes on, I return to my feeds when I am on hold, or when I have a few minutes between tasks. Some of the library technology feeds are a bit over my head, but I enjoy reading the headlines and knowing a bit about what is going on.

I also subscribe to a number of e-mail lists that relate to the library software we use. I usually glance at the subject headings each day, but I rarely read through the e-mails. It gives me an idea of what issues others are experiencing, which I find useful and interesting, but they are rarely similar to our problems. At this point, most of our libraries are not using online circulation and instead use a card system. The libraries are small, often located within a school library, and this works well for them. In our larger communities, libraries use online circulation and contend with very different issues. It makes for some challenging and interesting situations.

Our office subscribes to a number of magazines and journals, mainly as sources of book reviews. They arrive at my desk first and I aim to get through them within a week.

Checking In

I manage an office with five staff members. It is important to me to talk to them at least once each day. There are a number of reasons for this. Part of it is my own personality. Working with libraries is exciting and fun, and I want to share that with my staff. Many jobs in the office are fairly routine, but in the larger context they have so much meaning. I want to make sure that everyone has an opportunity to share in the big stuff.

It is important to me that I am visible and present in the workplace. I check in daily, sometimes just a "Hi, how are you?" and sometimes a longer conversation.

My staff have worked at this office much longer than I have and have lived and worked in the Northwest Territories a lot longer than I have. I need their input in our activities so that I have better odds of ensuring that our work is meaningful and useful to our users. I need and value their experience.

The Day's End

At the end of the day, I generally take a few minutes to relax and regroup. The office empties out, the e-mails stop coming, and I go through the papers on my desk and see what is left to do tomorrow. I double-check that today's deadlines have been met and verify if there are any tomorrow. I may highlight sections of my to do list, and rearrange my desk so that I can see exactly what I need to start working on when I come in the next day.

At the end of the week, I rewrite my list so it is fresh and legible for Monday. I go through my e-mails and file whatever I can, so that my inbox is around ten to fifteen items. My paper inbox is sorted and paper files created. Less frequently, I go through electronic and paper files and throw away what is completed.

PROS AND CONS

I really enjoy this position. There is a lot of variety and activity. I get to travel across the Northwest Territories, visiting very interesting places and people. I get to structure my own days and my own office, I can choose the projects that we work on, and I feel like my work has meaning in society. It is hard work and very challenging. I work with staff who care very much about their work and the impact libraries have.

The cons are almost the same as the pros. I don't tend to see them that way, but another person might. Traveling in a harsh climate can be difficult. Responsibility and accountability are serious business and can be scary. Sometimes you have to really work hard and smart over several years to achieve a goal. In this kind of position, you need to be able to self-motivate and reward yourself for your successes. You need to be able to appreciate people and your work and be willing to do the hard stuff.

I tend to be positive and enjoy my job. Some days are harder than others, but that is true with any position.

For someone not familiar with the environment of the Northwest Territories, it can be quite intimidating. The winters are harsh and cold; the communities are small and isolated. But the people are warm and welcoming, and the environment pristine and beautiful. I have found it a different world, but one that I have been welcomed into and am enjoying exploring.

HOW WOULD I GET A JOB LIKE YOURS?

This kind of position does not come up that often. In Canada, each of the thirteen jurisdictions (provincial and territorial) have a position similar to mine, although the organizational structure and scope of responsibilities vary widely. To be considered when applying for this kind of position, it is important to have experience in public library management and familiarity with library technology and systems. Communication skills and experience working with people in different capacities are also key. I have found that experience working within a bureaucratic structure was invaluable, as is experience with library advocacy.

RELATED RESOURCES

Government of the Northwest Territories. www.gov.nt.ca (accessed January 28, 2006).
Northwest Territories Public Library Services. www.nwtpls.gov.nt.ca (accessed January 28, 2006).

CHAPTER 12

Consultant, State Library

MYLEE JOSEPH

Public Library Services at the State Library of New South Wales (NSW), Australia, provides leadership, advice, and support for NSW public libraries, including monitoring local government compliance with the NSW Library Act of 1939, administering state government funding for public libraries, advising councils and libraries on library service management, and managing projects and services that assist public libraries. Public Library Services has ten equivalent full-time positions comprising the managers, consultants, grants and subsidies clerk, and a clerical officer. The service reports to the assistant state librarian, Public Library Services.

Consultants identify needs and participate in the development of statewide strategies to improve the quality of and access to public library services. We liaise with public libraries, local, state, and federal authorities, staff of the state library, and other agencies. Each of the consultants in the team works closely with country and city libraries within New South Wales and also focuses on key service areas (in my case, children's and youth services and services to older people).

A TYPICAL WORKDAY

There are 97 public library services with 363 libraries in New South Wales. My typical day includes communicating with library colleagues across the state via phone or e-mail to discuss all kinds of issues that may arise at their libraries. I have a map beside my phone so I can visualize where the caller is while we are talking. Some of the libraries I work with are in very remote areas. While the outback offers a great lifestyle, it can also be quite isolating professionally, so the Public Library Services team helps provide a link to other library professionals and keep library staff in touch with best practice in the industry.

I also work closely with metropolitan libraries on projects that are relevant to their libraries—for example, services for youth from emerging communities, services for older people, and cooperative projects. We have a regular publication, *Public Library News*, as well as e-lists that we use quite extensively to keep people informed of activities and programs throughout the network.

We are not stuck in the office all the time—a lot of our work involves visiting the various libraries and attending public library conferences and meetings. Along with my colleagues in the

Public Library Services team, I may be participating in on-site consultancies to help develop library services, helping library teams with strategic planning, reviewing a library service, or providing advice on the Library Act for a library committee meeting. I am also involved in hosting continuing education programs at the state library. We have recently held programs on youth services, reference and information services, library building guidelines, library development grant guidelines, marketing, grant writing, and a variety of other topics.

One fairly unique aspect of Public Library Services is the Building Advisory Service. This specialized service provides advice to organizations developing library buildings and regularly updates and publishes *People Places: A Guide for Public Library Buildings in New South Wales,* which is also very popular in other states and overseas as a guide for planning library buildings.

One of the more popular programs we offer is the allocation and payment of subsidies and library development grants to public libraries. In 2005 the program allocated $24.9 million to projects. Libraries compete for these grants; all of the consultants read and comment on the applications, which are then considered by the Grants Committee of the Library Council of New South Wales.

I also attend a lot of meetings to work with public library staff, including the NSW Home Library Service Network, children's and youth services groups, Country Public Libraries Association, Metropolitan Public Libraries Association, and regional library managers' meetings, to name a few. I am also often invited to book launches and other meetings to talk with local, state, and federal authorities and other agencies working with public libraries.

As a part of the larger State Library of NSW team, we also participate in the many programs and activities under way at the state library. Our library provides the largest Australiana collection in the country through the Mitchell Library in Sydney. We also provide multicultural services, document delivery services, and the State Reference Library for the people of New South Wales.

Members of our team are also actively encouraged to submit articles to library industry journals, write issues papers, and present at conferences. As our focus is wider than a single library service, we often draw together the trends we see developing in our industry at a local or perhaps even an international level.

PROS AND CONS

Every job has its pros and cons, but in this job the positive opportunities far outweigh the negative aspects. I have the chance to work with colleagues across the entire state in both city and country libraries. I also have the chance to visit libraries in very far-flung parts of New South Wales. For example, I am looking forward to the opportunity to see the Outback Letterbox Library in the far western part of the state.

There are also times when we are required to read and comment on thousands of pages of library development grant applications, which may seem overwhelming. However, seeing the innovative ideas that people have developed to improve their library services is quite inspiring. The adoption of the "@ your library" campaign in NSW is a good example of a library development grant benefiting the whole state. Other grant projects may include new library buildings, new mobile libraries, and the development of library collections.

On the more challenging side of the job, there are lots of early morning flights and occasional delays due to electrical storms or technical problems, which can sometimes make a day trip turn into a much larger undertaking. There are nights you may wish you were at home when you're on the road. There are times when you wish you could offer more help to a library that is struggling with limited resources.

HOW WOULD I GET A JOB LIKE YOURS?

Qualifications

The essential qualifications are a library degree recognized by the Australian Library and Information Association and relevant experience. In Australia, librarian courses are available at both the undergraduate (bachelor's) and postgraduate (graduate diploma and master's) levels. As a team, we have diverse backgrounds, which give us a variety of perspectives and strengths that support the NSW public library network. The members of our team are all very self-motivated and are excellent communicators, both essential qualities to succeed in these roles.

My job involves a fair amount of travel, so it wouldn't suit someone who didn't like to fly in small planes! We try to do most of our trips in one day, but sometimes that's not possible, so being willing to travel is also a prerequisite of the job. Having good people skills is vital because it is also important to be able to quickly establish rapport with a variety of library staff, council officers, councilors, and other contacts.

Experience

I worked in NSW public libraries for nineteen years before joining the State Library of New South Wales team. I have found that my background working in the field gives me a good understanding of the issues my colleagues face. My specialist areas are children's and youth services and services to older people; however, as I have also worked as a reference librarian, team leader, and library manager, I am able to bring a wide range of experience to the role. I have also been very active in our professional associations, the Australian Library and Information Association and the Metropolitan Public Libraries Association, which helps me develop a wider perspective on issues in the industry.

For anyone who aspires to work in a role like mine, there are a number of things I would recommend, aside from living in New South Wales! Similar roles do exist in other states and other countries, and you would be wise to research the requirements of the positions in your area. It would be to your advantage to become involved in cooperative library projects, working with colleagues from other libraries, establishing your profile in the industry, and expanding your understanding of libraries outside the one in which you work. I also recommend that you develop a good understanding of the broader issues involved in managing a library and take an interest in the wider profession through your professional association. It would also be of great benefit to write papers for journals and make presentations at seminars and conferences.

RELATED RESOURCES

@ your library NSW campaign. www.atyourlibrary.nsw.gov.au (accessed February 2, 2006).

AtMitchell.com. www.atmitchell.com (accessed February 2, 2006).

Australian Library and Information Association. www.alia.org.au (accessed February 2, 2006).

Country Public Libraries Association of New South Wales. www.cpla.asn.au (accessed February 2, 2006).

Metropolitan Public Libraries Association NSW. www.mplansw.asn.au (accessed February 2, 2006).

Outback Letterbox Library Service. www.bhlibrary.org.au/outback.html (accessed February 2, 2006).

People places: A guide for public library buildings in New South Wales, 2nd ed. 2005. Sydney: Library Council of New South Wales. www.sl.nsw.gov.au/pls/publications/pdf/peopleplaces_2ndedition.pdf (accessed February 2, 2006).

State Library of New South Wales. Public Library Services. www.sl.nsw.gov.au/pls (accessed February 2, 2006).

PART II

Academic Libraries

CHAPTER 13

Reference Librarian

AMANDA ETCHES-JOHNSON

To describe my job as a reference librarian in a humanities and social sciences library at a midsized Canadian university in the simplest possible way, I'd say that the tasks I do on a daily basis fall under five distinct categories: reference, library instruction, collections, professional development, and the always vague, ever-essential catchall for everything else that defies categorization, "other projects." Allow me, if you will, to flesh out these categories.

A TYPICAL WORKDAY

Let me start with reference. During a typical work week, I spend about twelve hours on the research help desk, which averages out to just over two hours a day. I assist students with research, help them find resources for their essays, and demystify citation formats, to name just a few of the questions we are frequently asked. In addition to in-person reference, on a typical day I also do some virtual reference. At my institution, we provide instant messaging (IM) reference four hours a day, five days a week, performing this service from our offices in two-hour shifts.

As with most other academic reference positions, library instruction is another key component of my job as a reference librarian. I teach a combination of drop-in sessions (which are organized and developed by our library instruction coordinator) and course-specific classes that are requested by professors and tutorial assistants. Preparation for a course-specific session involves communication with the faculty member, research, and preparation of course materials (presentation slides, handouts, and sometimes a library assignment) and takes anywhere from one to four hours, depending on whether the course is new. Usually, if I've taught a library session for the course in the past, prep time is considerably shorter. The policy at my library is that each librarian teaches a maximum of three library sessions a week, but librarians at other institutions might routinely teach multiple sessions per day.

A third aspect of my job as a reference librarian is collections. As the subject specialist for languages, literature, critical theory, and cultural studies, I am responsible for selecting materials for our reference collection in these disciplines. On an average day, I spend approximately one hour doing collections work, which includes reviewing publishers' catalogs and print/electronic slips, poring through review journals, reviewing tables of contents alerts, and relying on a number of other discovery tools. If you're anything like me, the process of finding and selecting new reference books is one of the most enjoyable parts of the job. You've probably heard the analogy before—it's like shopping for books with someone else's money!

In addition to reference, instruction, and collections, much of the time I spend at my desk (which, depending on the day, is limited) is devoted to working on the varied tasks that are generally grouped together under the "other projects" rubric you see on most academic reference job descriptions. When I applied for my current position, I had two years of experience working at a reference desk at a university, so I felt that I had a pretty decent handle on most of what was involved in an academic reference job. However, the "other projects" reference on job descriptions always mystified me. What could a reference librarian possibly do in the back office when he or she isn't at the reference desk or teaching?

As I quickly learned, a lot! Much of my back office time is spent on committee and project work. When I first joined the institution, I got my feet wet by joining the Library Newsletter Committee, and once I felt that I had enough of a handle on my basic job requirements (which takes six months to a year, I would say), I branched out in search of other committees. I became a librarian member of our faculty association and joined the Web Team (which I now chair). Currently most of my nonreference, nonteaching time is spent doing various Web-related tasks, which I very much enjoy (I'm one of those oddball librarians who can sit in front of a computer and code for hours). I consider myself fortunate to work in a library where librarians are encouraged to work to their strengths, a rare atmosphere indeed.

In addition to committee work, the "other tasks" also include project work. Some of the projects I have led at my library include implementing a new authentication system, setting up a blog on the library Web site, and establishing our IM reference service. The most rewarding part of project work is the opportunity to see a project go from conception through to implementation and completion.

And what of professional development, you might ask? In the little time that remains in an average workday, I try to engage in some professional development, which is encouraged (if not required) at most academic institutions. For me, professional development includes committee work through various library associations, research, conference attendance and presentations, and publication. Though professional development activities are encouraged at most academic institutions, realistically the other aspects of my job take precedence and I usually find myself engaging in professional development activities during the evenings and weekends. On any given day, I consider it an accomplishment if I merely clear out my aggregator of all the professional reading that lines itself up via a multitude of RSS subscriptions!

PROS AND CONS

Pros

For me, one of the biggest pros of my job is working with a group of professional librarians on daily basis. One of the complaints I often hear from librarians at other institutions is that they have to depend on their professional activities to forge connections and foster professional networks. Although I do appreciate the networking opportunities provided by professional involvement, I feel fortunate that I found myself in the position of having an instant network of professionals at my own institution as soon as I started work here. This has been invaluable.

Another overwhelming advantage of being a reference librarian in a midsized academic library is the opportunity for specialization, whether it is focused around a subject area, format, or technology. When you're one librarian in an organization of many, you don't have to be a jack-of-all-trades, and although some might consider this a disadvantage, I personally appreciate having the ability to focus my attention on my areas of interest and am grateful that I work in an institution that is large enough to encourage this.

As I've mentioned previously, most positions in academic institutions come with an expectation of professional involvement. Again, this can either be considered a pro or a con, depending on your own perspective and professional goals. As I have probably made clear, I personally gain a great deal from professional development activities such as attending conferences, researching, delivering papers, and publishing, and I can safely say that I would be very unhappy at an organization that did not encourage, foster, and provide support for these activities.

Cons

Although I would vociferously argue that being an academic reference librarian is an excellent career choice, it might not be the best *first* job for everyone. In a large institution, you might find yourself a victim of the "small fish in a big pond" syndrome. At smaller institutions, fewer librarians are usually responsible for a large majority of tasks, allowing a newly minted professional to gain experience in a wide variety of departments. If you're certain that a career in academic reference is for you (as I was), this shouldn't be an issue, but if you would prefer to gain experience in a number of different areas within a library, you would be well advised to start out at a smaller institution—a community college, for example, is a great place to gain varied experience (Arnold 2005).

Another con to consider is bureaucracy. I don't think I'm giving away any institutional secrets when I say that many (if not most) mid- to large-sized academic libraries suffer from the pitfalls of bureaucracy. Bureaucracy in any organization is often the result of processes that have been put into place that are in all likelihood necessary for decisions to get made. However, these processes often result in the decision-making process becoming mired down, which further results in your library not being as nimble as it could be. The inability of a library (indeed, any organization) to react quickly to change can be frustrating for any employee.

HOW DO I GET A JOB LIKE YOURS?

Education

Having an MLS/MLIS from an ALA-accredited school is the baseline requirement for most professional library positions in North America. In addition, many (but not all) academic libraries require a second master's degree, especially when there are collections or instruction responsibilities involved. The rationale behind this is that to teach library instruction classes or build collections, the candidate should have a certain level of subject expertise. This requirement is fast becoming standard on academic job listings.

Experience

Entry-level positions do not usually require professional experience, but a candidate with paraprofessional experience would probably be favored over a candidate with no experience at all. As a library school student, I worked part-time at reference desks at three academic libraries, and I firmly believe that this experience went a long way toward helping me get my first professional position. If you are not in a position to gain academic reference experience while you're in library school, consider volunteering at an academic library while you're on the job hunt. Also, never underestimate the value of all types of public/customer service experience. If your first round of job applications does not include academic reference experience but does include customer service experience in another type of organization (retail, for example), play that up. Most search committees will value any experience you've had working with the general public.

Coursework

This can be a tricky consideration. For most, the issue of coursework boils down to the tension between depth versus breadth. Do you plan your coursework around a subject field or type of job (depth) in the hope of landing that job once you graduate? Or do you take a wide range of courses that prepare you for a number of different professional positions on graduation (breadth) while risking the possibility that your first job applications will be viewed as lacking specialization? I'm sure you see the conundrum, so I won't belabor the point, but I will offer some friendly advice: if you have a pretty good idea of the type of job you'd like to get after you graduate, don't be afraid to take courses that will prepare you for that job. If you have a faculty advisor, use him or her to help you plan your coursework to best suit your goals while keeping in mind the fine balance between depth and breadth. It's also a good idea to seek out subject-specific reference courses (like government publications, for example) if you know that you'd like to specialize in a specific subject within academic librarianship. Most important, keep in mind that few reasonable search committees will expect you to display highly specialized knowledge or expertise for an entry-level position. They will be much more interested in the skills and abilities you display in your application and interview.

Skills and Abilities

Most academic reference positions require verbal and written communication, interpersonal, and public service skills. I consider these to be basic essentials, so I won't dwell on them here. Instead, I'd like to devote the final paragraphs of this chapter to a couple of the other important skills that usually *aren't* on job descriptions, the ones that will actually help you succeed in an academic reference position.

Public Speaking/Presenting

Good communication skills in an academic library are not just about being able to express yourself in a meeting and writing a clear e-mail (although these are certainly good skills to possess). Good communication skills in this particular setting also mean that you need to be able to get up in front of a class of undergraduates and explain what a Boolean operator is with enough clarity to make them get it and enough charisma to make them enjoy it. If that notion brings on waves of anxiety, take heart! Although it certainly helps if you're a natural-born orator, keep in mind that public speaking can also be a learned skill. There are all manner of excellent books and Web sites devoted to ways in which you can improve your public speaking and presentation skills, so if you're looking for a career in academic librarianship, you'd be well advised to take advantage of such resources.

Project Management

At this point, you might be saying to yourself, "But I want to be a reference librarian, not a project manager! How is this relevant?" Whether or not the job description mentions it, practically every professional position in an academic library involves project work on some level (see the discussion of "other projects"). Given this inevitability, what skills do you need to be a good project manager? The honest answer is that the skill set will vary depending on the project you are leading, but it's safe to say that successful project management involves a combination of good multitasking, time management, organizational and facilitative skills, timely and efficient communication, and the ability to delegate responsibility. If you already have experience leading projects in the past, you probably already have these skills well honed. If not, don't distress! As Marcy Strong (2005) mentions, you probably already have project management experience and don't even realize it: "Have you ever been a student officer? Organized an event? Taken an active role in community service? Coached a sport? Taught a class? You may have more project management experience than you realize."

CONCLUSION

I conducted an informal poll at my workplace, where I walked around the library during my lunch hour and asked my colleagues to complete the following sentence: "Being an academic reference librarian is ..." Here is the compilation of responses I received: Being an academic reference librarian is ... challenging, rewarding, stressful, frustrating, fun, interesting, valuable, demanding, a great career, an awesome profession. On any given day, I could use any of those terms to describe my job, reminding me that one of the best parts of being an academic reference librarian is the constant variety. When I put the same question to myself, my immediate and most honest response was, "Being an academic reference librarian is the best career decision I've made."

REFERENCES

Arnold, Jennifer. 2005. The other academic library: Librarianship at the community college. *LIScareer. com* (May). www.liscareer.com/arnold_commcoll.htm (accessed January 15, 2006).
Strong, Marcy. 2005. New librarians as project managers: A project cataloger tells all. *LIScareer.com* (October). www.liscareer.com/strong_project.htm (accessed January 10, 2006).

RELATED RESOURCES

There are a number of journals devoted to academic librarianship that are worth keeping an eye on, such as *The Journal of Academic Librarianship*, *New Review of Academic Librarianship*, *portal*, and *College and Research Libraries*. If you would like to become professionally involved, the Association of College and Research Libraries (ACRL) is an active division of the American Library Association that works to facilitate discussion about academic librarianship. ACRLog, the official ACRL blog (www.acrlblog.org), is a great resource for discussion about issues of interest to academic librarians. In addition, your state library association might have a division for academic libraries/librarianship to which you could contribute. If you're interested in reference and public service in particular, the Reference and User Services Association (RUSA) is another division of ALA that is worth getting involved with (www.ala.org/rusa).

CHAPTER 14

Reference Librarian at an Overseas American University

NANCY FAWLEY

I am the reference librarian for Virginia Commonwealth University School of the Arts in Qatar (VCUQ). I provide reference services and bibliographic instruction for students, staff, and faculty at a small American design school in the Middle East. I also develop outreach vehicles, such as handouts and Web pages, to promote the library and my services to the university. The library's staff consists of a director, a visual resources librarian, three library specialists, two student workers, and me. The library specialist in public services reports to me.

THE UNIVERSITY

I cannot begin to describe a typical day of work at VCUQ without giving some background information about the school's unique mission and location. VCUQ is a branch campus of the Richmond, Virginia, school and offers bachelor of fine arts degrees in communication arts and design, interior design, and fashion design and merchandising. VCUQ was established in 1998 by VCU and the Qatar Foundation for Education, Science and Community Development. Its mission is to provide a high level of design education for the women of Qatar.

The school is small—180 students as of the fall semester 2005—and all women. Sixty-six percent of the student body is Qatari. Twenty-four nationalities are represented at the school, but the students come primarily from the surrounding Middle Eastern countries. Instruction is in English; most of the students speak English as a second or third language.

Doha is the capital of Qatar, a small country about the size of Connecticut surrounded by Saudi Arabia and the Arabian (Persian) Gulf. There are over eight hundred thousand persons living in Qatar, primarily in Doha. Only about a third of the population is native Qatari; the rest of the population is made up of expatriate workers. Low-wage workers from the Indian subcontinent make up the majority of ex-pats. Oil and natural gas have created great wealth and made Qatar one of the fastest growing countries in the world.

THE STUDENTS

Students who have studied in Arab schools have traditionally learned by rote and memorization. Critical thinking and problem solving are not required or expected. Library usage is minimal; the textbook may be the only book used in class. Women in particular do not have the pressure or expectations to succeed. The students at VCUQ are generally less mature for their age compared with their peers in the States. They can be timid and afraid to approach someone for help unless they know the person.

A TOEFL (Test of English as a Foreign Language) score of at least 500 is a requirement for admittance; our students' scores range from around 500 to over 600. As a result, we have students with a wide range of reading comprehension and writing skills, which also affect their ability to do library research. Most of our students speak Arabic as their native language. Not only are the call numbers in a foreign alphabet, but the books are arranged on the shelves from left to right, not right to left.

A TYPICAL DAY

Before I was hired, there was no reference librarian, and library services were rarely promoted. There was no bibliographic instruction, and many of the faculty and students were unaware of the resources and services our library could provide. As a result, the library was not used as much as it should have been. After one year of promoting myself and the library, my reference services are much more visible and in demand.

Students, faculty, and staff flow in and out of the library and my office all day. We are informal here; patrons walk into my office whenever they need assistance. Students normally come to the library for course-specific material. Design students and faculty are generally visual learners, and this influences the manner in which they search for information. Many prefer to browse the shelves looking for books rather than use the online catalog. In many instances they are looking for images; thumbing through a book or periodical is one of their search methods.

One of my most important duties comes at the start of each semester when I give bibliographic instruction to the first-year students as part of their Introduction to the University course. I initially prepared a lesson similar to one I did in the United States, but I quickly discovered this was too advanced for the majority of our students. Many do not know what a call number is or the difference between a book and a journal article; introducing searching techniques like truncation and Boolean operators is simply overwhelming. I do not want to make the library and research seem so complicated that the students never return. Instead, I developed a more basic lesson on how to use our online catalog, how to find a book on the shelf, and how to do a simple keyword search on our journal databases.

I work with the students one-on-one or in pairs. I initially worked with larger groups but found students needed more individualized attention to complete the required short assignment. It is extremely time-consuming, but it is necessary, and because we are a small school, it is manageable. This is the foundation that their information-seeking skills will be built on.

The other courses that I work with on a regular basis are the English classes. The English curriculum in Qatar adheres strictly to the one established at VCU's Richmond campus. Students are required to submit a portfolio in the introductory class and a research paper in the advanced class to successfully complete the courses. Last year, approximately 30 percent of the students failed their portfolio review and were required to repeat the introductory English course. Poor reading comprehension and research skills and an overdependency on Google and the Internet are the suspected reasons. I initiated a program of increased library involvement in these courses with the aim of improving student performance.

My involvement begins the first week of class when I make an appearance, introduce myself, and hand out a brief questionnaire to gauge the students' knowledge of library resources. An identical questionnaire is distributed at the end of the semester as a means of comparison to evaluate the effectiveness of my services. I stay involved in the course throughout the semester, giving bibliographic instruction and teaching a class on evaluating Web resources. Students are encouraged to seek my assistance in the library as well. The immediate goal is to help them pass their English classes, but I also want them to become self-confident researchers, a skill that will help them in university and beyond.

I have found that handouts are particularly helpful for our students, especially those whose reading skills are better than their conversational skills. I have created handouts on writing citations and evaluating Web resources. I have also developed a research worksheet where a student writes her topic, chooses keywords to search for, and lists the databases she plans to use. This is particularly helpful for the English coursework.

Committee participation is expected at VCUQ and is factored into our annual evaluations. As of this writing I am involved in the committees for our annual international design conference, Tasmeem Doha, and the student fashion show. I have prior work experience in the fashion industry; this gives me the opportunity to use old talents and at the same time interact with students and faculty who may not use the library. It also gives me the chance to promote the library; the more visible I am, the more visible the library and its public services are.

PROS AND CONS

The most rewarding part of my job is working with the students. The small size of our school and the Arab sense of family contribute to a closeness I have not experienced elsewhere. Our students' library skills are less advanced than those of their counterparts in the United States, but I find most are excited about having the opportunity to study in an American college and are eager to learn more about the library and research.

As they are learning, I am learning as well. Not only am I discovering better methods to teach English as a foreign language students about the library, I am learning about our students' culture and their experiences as young women in college in the Middle East. I have only worked here a year, but I have already noticed how the students change from year to year. Last year's first-years returned this fall with increased confidence and a new sense of purpose. I felt like a proud parent, especially of those students who spend a lot of time in the library.

Working in a small school with a small library staff has other advantages, too. We are not segmented the way many larger universities are, so I have an opportunity to be involved in aspects of the library beyond public services. I assist with collection development and technical services when needed. Also, because my position was new, I had a lot of latitude in developing user services.

There is a negative side to having only six full-time employees working in the library. There is no depth to our staff. If more than one person is sick or on holiday it can put a tremendous strain on the library, particularly in public services. There are some library duties that only one staff member knows how to do. When that individual is out, that job does not get done. Additionally, there are very few opportunities to interact with other librarians aside from the two with whom I work.

There are also frustrations that are unique to our location. Inconsistent mail delivery affects the timely and reliable delivery of our periodicals. We are fortunate that we have had no problems in recent years with the censorship of our materials, although some items, especially audiovisual ones, seem to get held up in customs. Library-specific supplies are generally not available. We have to improvise or order items from the United States. This means a long wait to receive them, plus costly shipping charges.

We are an American university library, and I try to stress the importance of policies, such as privacy and intellectual freedom, which are intrinsic to libraries in the United States but unfamiliar in Qatar. It is hard to explain the idea that no one has the right to know what books another has checked out when we are in a traditionally oral society where, according to a staff member, "everyone knows everything about everyone." On a positive note, these cultural differences have led to fascinating discussions and a better understanding of our different cultures.

A more general advantage of my position, and the reason I chose to work overseas, is the experience of living and working in a foreign country. Traveling is one way to see the world, but you will never get to know the people, culture, and customs of a place the same way you would if you lived there.

There are frustrations, of course. Simply adjusting to a country where nothing seems familiar takes time, patience, and an open mind. I am a guest in this country, and I am expected to respect and abide by the laws and customs of Qatar. It is even stated in my contract. I wear conservative clothes that cover my knees, elbows, and collarbone. I would not hold hands in public with a male, even if he were my husband. During the holy month of Ramadan, when Muslims fast between sunup and sundown, I refrain from eating or drinking in public during those hours. These are really just minor adjustments that do not inconvenience me in any way. The opportunity to be a part of the state of Qatar and VCUQ is far more important to me than wearing a short-sleeved shirt in the middle of summer.

A more serious concern, especially in the Middle East, is the threat of terrorism. Qatar is one of the safer countries in the region, but in March 2005 a suicide bomber drove an explosive-laden SUV into a theater in Doha in the middle of a performance, killing himself and one other person. The country and the community condemned the attack, but the possibility of another attack is now a reality we have to live with. I was in the theater when it was bombed, and it was truly a terrifying experience. It did, however, make me even more determined to stay here and work for and support the country that is now my home. My daily activities have not changed since then, but I have learned to be more aware of my surroundings and to think twice before I go to a "Western" hotel or event. VCUQ has an evacuation plan in place and is currently making plans to increase the security in and around our building. I and most of the staff live in walled compounds with security.

HOW DO I GET A JOB LIKE THIS?

Overseas academic librarian positions can be found through many of the same channels you use to job hunt in your home country. HigherEdJobs.com and the International Federation of Library Associations and Institutions (IFLA) e-mail list LIBJOBS are two places that commonly list overseas librarian positions. My job was also advertised in *American Libraries*, the magazine of the American Library Association.

If there is a particular part of the globe you would like to work in, research the universities in the area. There are an increasing number of American institutions opening in the Arabian Gulf countries. Occasionally checking the employment sections of these schools' Web sites can alert you to an open library position. There are no special skills that you necessarily need for an overseas position. Familiarity with the local language is helpful but not necessary if the curriculum is in English. Far more important attributes are an open mind and a sense of adventure.

RELATED SOURCES

Cassidy, Thomas J. Jr. 2003. Education in the Arab states: Preparing to compete in the global economy. In *The Arab world competitiveness report*. Edited by Klaus Schwab and Peter Cornelius. Geneva: World Economic Forum. www.yemenembassy.org/economic/Reports/WEF/Page_222_238_Education.pdf (accessed September 5, 2005).

HigherEdJobs.com. www.higheredjobs.com (accessed September 5, 2005).

LIBJOBS library and information science jobs mailing list. infoserv.inist.fr/wwsympa.fcgi/info/libjobs (accessed September 5, 2005).

Zoepf, Katherine. 2005. In Qatar's "education city," U.S. colleges build atop a gusher. *Chronicle of Higher Education* (April 22).

CHAPTER 15

Reference Librarian and School of Nursing Liaison

Lucky doesn't even begin to describe how I feel about my job and my career. I arrived at the University of Alabama at Birmingham's Lister Hill Library of the Health Sciences in February 2005 after leaving a medium-sized liberal arts academic library in Georgia. The Lister Hill Library (LHL) is one of two libraries on UAB's dynamic urban campus. LHL supports the six health sciences schools on campus: medicine, dentistry, nursing, public health, optometry, and health-related professions, and the Mervyn Sterne Library serves all the other academic programs. There is also a hospital library, Lister Hill Library at University Hospital. So in addition to supporting students and teaching faculty, we also support the hospital. LHL is one of the leading biomedical libraries in the South and is the largest in Alabama. My position in this ever-changing environment is that of a reference librarian. In my role I not only provide reference service but also participate in user education, outreach and marketing activities, Web design, liaison to the School of Nursing, and numerous other projects throughout the library. Furthermore, librarians here have faculty status, so we all serve on library and university committees and are expected to be productive members of the profession as a whole by being active in professional organizations, presenting, conducting research, and publishing.

A TYPICAL DAY

Normal days usually involve a good bit of reference. We all share desk time and provide backup for the telephone, e-mail, and chat service. The department divides up the weekend schedule, and I also cover one evening per week. Some of the reference questions we get are like those in any academic library. Students working on research papers usually need help formulating a search and using the various electronic databases. We are also likely to get really in-depth questions from physicians working in the hospital or any number of on- or off-campus researchers. Sometimes working with a physician or researcher can turn into a long-term research project. So reference questions can take anywhere from five minutes to five months!

LHL is also open to the general public. As a result, we get a good number of consumer health questions. These can be difficult, and these questions were a change from my liberal arts background. You never know when the person standing in front of you might say, "I've been diagnosed with terminal cancer. Can you help me find some information on alternative treatments?" Not all of the questions are this serious, but many of them are. Though these are very hard, they can also be the most rewarding. When I can help someone who is sick or whose loved one is in the UAB hospital, I really feel like I've made a difference, no matter how small. I have also been surprised by the number of attorneys that use LHL. They are often looking for information on specific procedures or state malpractice information. One thing is for sure: you definitely never know what you are going to get when you ask, "Can I help you?"

Serving as liaison to the School of Nursing can also take up a good bit of my typical day. In this position, I am the main contact person for the entire school, which offers undergraduate, nurse practitioner, master's, and PhD programs. The library offers both class and individual instruction for anyone who wants it. I'm called on to do basic library orientations as well as in-depth research classes. At the beginning of each semester, I also speak at the school's orientation session. One of my most challenging projects with the School of Nursing is investigating and learning to use and teach nurse practitioner students to use PDAs. Liaison work also spills over into the most fun part of my job: library marketing and outreach.

LHL has a very active programs and promotions committee, and we do a lot of fun things to increase awareness of the library and its services. In October, we celebrate National Medical Librarians Month with an entire month of activities. One of my favorites is the contest to win an office party. If a school or department adds a link to the library to their Web page or schedules a class, we enter them to win a cake and ice cream party. This is an opportunity to meet people around campus and change people's perceptions about libraries and librarians. Planning these events can really take over our day. One of the most popular events is Snacks on the Plaza outside the library. We gather donations from local businesses and give away free food. The students love it.

If I don't have at least one meeting it is definitely an atypical day! I'm on a number of library committees and groups. One of the most interesting is the Horizon Management Group. This committee is responsible for providing oversight for the integrated library system and all its different departmental modules like circulation, cataloging, and acquisitions, so it includes people from all over the library. Another of my favorites is the Library Operations Committee. Anything can come up in this committee, from furniture to security to signage. Of all the committees I'm on, the Library Operations Committee most embodies what they don't teach you in library school!

PROS AND CONS

There are many more pros than cons to my job at LHL. I love working with the School of Nursing. I also really enjoy all the marketing and outreach we do. There's nothing like hearing a student say, "I never knew librarians were so nice. I won't be afraid to come ask for help anymore." One of the things I like best about most academic libraries, especially here at LHL, is the flexibility of being a faculty member and the encouragement given to pursue your interests. For instance, I have a strong technology background and I like exploring new technologies, and I'm encouraged to pursue those interests within the library even though my research may take me into a different department. Recently I have taken on Web development responsibilities with the systems librarian. We are also encouraged to participate in professional organizations and pursue scholarly work. I enjoy researching and writing about librarianship, so it is nice to be at a place that encourages and values those kinds of activities. An atmosphere that encourages its people to stretch and try things they aren't sure they can do is really hard to find. But the best part of this particular job is the people. The folks I work with are fantastic, and I wouldn't trade them for the world!

The things that annoy me are generally things that occur in all libraries. For instance, I get irritated with people who treat the library like their living room. I don't fall into the crowd that believes libraries shouldn't be dynamic and fun, but I did grow up respecting others people's materials and space. I guess I just like people to remember that others are working in the building, too. I get really annoyed when users complain that a journal is not available online in full text. I think I hide my irritation well when I get this complaint, but I remember that when I was a student, I had to use paper indices, hunt down the correct volume, and then pull out my dimes and make copies! Having all this online access to materials is amazing. I just remind myself that my parents had to walk to school barefoot in the snow uphill both ways! Despite these minor irritations, I can't imagine doing any other job.

A JOB LIKE MINE

I really didn't have any special training for a job in a health sciences library. After earning a master's in history and a master's in information sciences, I fully intended to become a systems librarian, and in fact I still love systems. In my previous library position at Georgia College and State University, however, I discovered I also loved science, so I volunteered to be the library's liaison to the School of Health Science there. As a result, I became familiar with how different the health sciences are from other fields and how to use and teach CINAHL and MEDLINE. I also used my history degree to do some research and publishing on medical history. I'd always heard that old adage "follow what you like and good stuff happens." When I saw the job ad for my current position, I had no idea what the competition would be like, but I had to give it a try. It has worked out really well. For those of you interested in health sciences librarianship, I'd encourage you to volunteer and seek out every opportunity to work with any of the sciences. And don't be afraid to apply for medical librarian positions even if you don't have much science experience. If you have the opportunity to take a related class or do an internship, do it.

RELATED RESOURCES

There are lots of resources for those with an interest in health sciences librarianship. The Medical Library Association (MLA) Web site contains a wealth of information (www.mlanet. org). There are also fourteen regional chapters of the MLA, and all the chapters have Web sites (www.mlanet.org/chapters/chapters.html). Alabama belongs to the Southern Chapter, which is a fantastic organization (www.scmla.org). State organizations, like the Alabama Health Libraries Association (southmed.usouthal.edu/library/alhela), are also an excellent way to learn about health sciences librarianship and become active in the field. The best resources are medical and health science librarians themselves.

CHAPTER 16

Reference/Government Documents Librarian

KAREN DAVIDSON

My position at Mississippi State University is one of a nine-member team responsible for the reference department and also part of a four-member team responsible for the government documents and microforms area. I spend 50 percent of my time in reference reporting to the coordinator of reference and the other 50 percent in government documents and microforms reporting to that coordinator. My responsibility in the reference department is to provide reference assistance to patrons at the ready reference desk and by e-mail, phone, and virtual chat. I assist patrons with their research needs by providing individual consultations by appointment, conducting bibliographic instruction sessions as requested, and assisting in the selection and collection maintenance of digital and print reference resources. My responsibilities in government documents and microforms consist of processing and cataloging U.S. government materials in all formats as well as United Nations materials. In addition, I assist patrons with their research needs, create research guides, and conduct bibliographic instruction sessions as needed.

A TYPICAL WORKDAY

The variety and challenges of each day are what makes this job exciting, ever changing, never boring, and frustrating all at the same time. I work in the reference department on Monday, Wednesday, and Friday mornings and in government documents and microforms in the afternoon. On Tuesday and Thursday it's the reverse.

My day begins at 7:30 a.m. when I open the reference department and get it ready for patrons to arrive. At 8 a.m. I go to my office either in reference or government documents, depending on the day. When I am in the reference department, I might have a bibliographic instruction session to teach or meet with a student to discuss a research strategy and identify appropriate resources. I then spend an hour assisting patrons with their information needs at the reference desk, showing them how to search the databases or locate books, and answering questions. After the reference desk, I may find that I have time to work on an article I am writing for publication, or I might have a committee meeting.

After lunch I go to my office in government documents. My job there consists of processing Marcive batches. Marcive is a company that provides libraries with customized MARC (machine-readable cataloging) records, book labels, smart barcode labels, and authority records for materials received from the Government Printing Office's Federal Depository Library Program. I spend most of my time in government documents double-checking the Marcive cataloging records, adding additional fields to the records, consolidating records, or adding holdings and Internet addresses, making it easier for patrons to locate government documents through our online catalog. I also catalog UN documents, since our institution is also a depository for them. Although a typical day in government documents consists mostly of cataloging materials in all formats, I also assist patrons when needed and work on other projects as assigned.

My position is unique in that I work in two different departments with different responsibilities and separate supervisors, but at the same time I also have responsibilities as a full-time librarian and a tenure-track faculty member. These responsibilities impact both departments and are not specific to my split position. These include research and publishing commitments; promotion and tenure requirements; professional development; state, national, and library committee service; working with academic units on their collections; and providing outreach activities for these departments.

ADVANTAGES AND DISADVANTAGES

Advantages

Knowledge and Skills

The most important advantage to holding two separate positions in two separate areas is the skills and knowledge gained. Even though the two areas are considered public services, my government documents work is much more technical in nature than my reference position. My knowledge of how government documents are cataloged and classified gives me invaluable information with which to help patrons at the reference desk, and my experience at the reference desk has helped me in government documents. The skills I have developed by working in these two positions have given me a broader perspective, which offers me a distinct advantage over someone working in only one area.

Flexibility

I enjoy the flexibility that a split position allows. Libraries are constantly changing to meet the needs of their patrons and the duties of both of my positions have had to change accordingly. For example, once when there were four librarian positions vacant, the reference department needed extra help to cover the reference desk. My hours were adjusted, and I was assigned more hours in reference. It's important to be flexible and able to shuffle duties to accommodate changing needs.

Variety

The variety of my daily responsibilities makes my job interesting and prevents boredom. Switching from a busy public services position to a quiet office where most of my duties consist of cataloging and processing documents provides a change of tasks and keeps my job from becoming routine.

Structure

The cataloging aspects of my government documents position require me to follow rules and regulations that are already set, whereas my reference tasks and patrons' questions are never the same. Even though flexibility and variety are strong advantages to my dual position, having half of my workday more structured and focused helps relieve the stress and unpredictability of the other half.

Improved Communication between Departments

I get a clear idea of what the patron is seeking through my work at the reference desk, and I see through a cataloger's eyes while working with government documents. I work closely with technical services to make sure procedures are correctly followed. I also act as a liaison between departments, relating needed information and resolving problems.

Working with a Variety of People

I feel very lucky to be able to work with a variety of individuals in each department that have knowledge and skills from which I can learn. I also develop professional contacts with librarians in areas of both reference and government documents through local, state, regional, and national committees and conferences.

Job Satisfaction

I enjoy variety in my work, and I look forward to my time in each department. I have enjoyed learning new skills and meeting the day-to-day challenges in each department.

Teamwork

The library functions as a whole, and each department must work together to make the library run smoothly to serve the needs of the patrons. Working with different departments allows for better teamwork.

Disadvantages

Time Management

Managing one's time is difficult enough in one job, but managing time between two jobs can be especially challenging and overwhelming at times. I find it difficult to stop processing and cataloging documents after four hours to go over to my position in the reference department. It is equally difficult to stop working on a research guide or preparing for a bibliographic instruction session when my time is up in the reference department. Often I have to stop in the middle of a project and pick up where I left off the next day. This makes it hard to focus, and it takes time to find the point where you left off, disrupting the workflow. It also is difficult to complete a project in a timely manner when you only have four hours a day in a department.

Feeling Detached

I am only part-time in both locations; therefore when I am in one location, I feel separated from what is going on in the other location and vice versa. There are times when I can't be as involved in an area as I would like because of my part-time status.

Different Management Styles

Each supervisor has individual management styles and ways of doing things. I have to be able to switch back and forth, adapting to each supervisor's management style.

Procedures

The split position has its own set of procedures created from the beginning to eliminate confusion. For example, which supervisor approves time off? Do you call both supervisors if you're sick? What is the annual evaluation procedure when you have two different jobs? How are you to be evaluated by two different supervisors? It has worked well in my position to have both managers sign when a supervisor's signature is needed. It was decided that one annual evaluation document would work best, separating the duties in each department, with each supervisor making comments and the numerical ratings averaged out. It is very important to have open communication with everyone involved, making sure that problems or concerns are addressed as soon as possible.

Training

Training for both departments has taken longer because of limited time spent in each department. Supervisors and employees must be prepared for the longer training time and not get frustrated and discouraged.

Two Offices

Having two different offices can be confusing at times. Each department needs to know my schedule to prevent lost calls and missed messages. Often when I am in one department, I need files from my office in the other department.

Scheduling

It is hard enough keeping track of one schedule, let alone two. Working in two different departments makes it tricky for supervisors to schedule meetings, reference desk, and chat hours to accommodate my schedule along with everyone else's. On occasion I have to shift schedules to accommodate obligations to one department while working in the other. I also try to make sure my research time is split, dividing it equally between the two departments. I try hard to be as fair as I can to each department, giving my work in each department the necessary attention for me to do my best.

Stress

Being able to juggle two completely different jobs, committee responsibilities, research expectations for promotion and tenure, as well as being involved in professional development activities can become very stressful. Supervisors can overload the librarian with work assignments, forgetting that the librarian is only part-time.

MAKING A SPLIT POSITION SUCCESSFUL

A split position may not be for everyone. I truly believe that it takes a special kind of person to be able to handle all the responsibilities, time management issues, and constant interruptions. It takes a mature individual with experience working with different supervisors and different management styles to handle this position. You have to have excellent written and oral communication skills and be well organized, energetic, and self-directed. You must be able to take off one hat and put on another, treating each position as a separate job. It is important to be able to see the big picture and understand how each department can benefit from the knowledge and skills learned in the other. It is essential to work closely with both supervisors, keeping everyone informed and letting them know when the workload becomes too much or when problems arise. You must be able to deal well with multitasking and be able to stop in the middle of a project, continuing the next day without getting confused or upset. As you go into a split position or dual appointment, be aware of the potential problems and be willing to make the position a success for everyone involved. Providing access to information is the common goal and bringing separate departments together to work as a team will benefit everyone. The most important qualification is to love your work.

HOW TO OBTAIN A SPLIT POSITION

Not all academic libraries have split positions like mine. Many rotate librarians so that technical services librarians are scheduled on the reference desk, or librarians may be loaned to a different department as needed. Sharing job duties between departments is becoming more common because of staffing and budget restraints, expanded responsibilities, and the blending of services to accommodate the changing academic library environment. The split position or dual job assignment is usually advertised as a combination of two departments such as cataloging/reference librarian, government documents/reference librarian, cataloging/collection development librarian, or reference/collection development librarian. The best way to find a dual assignment is to review job advertisements in the library literature and visit library and university Web sites for employment opportunities.

CONCLUSION

I have been in my split position at Mississippi State University for a few years now. It has been a rewarding and enjoyable experience for me as well as a benefit to both departments. There have been challenges and concerns, but with good communication and a willingness to make this position a success, it has worked out well. Working in government documents and microforms has opened up a whole new area of librarianship for me. Responsibilities in two departments have given me a better understanding of the work performed in each department as well as the importance of teamwork. I have enjoyed the daily challenges of this dual position and the variety in my work. This is not to say that I don't get frustrated and overwhelmed at times, but the advantages outweigh the disadvantages and I look forward to spending half my day in each department.

RELATED RESOURCES

DeDonato, Ree. 1991. How did we get here: Thoughts on the convergence of reference and technical services. *Reference Librarian* 34: 27–35.

Hardin, Steve. 1993. The servant of two masters: An account of one librarian's adventures in holistic librarianship. *Technicalities* 13 (7): 11–12.

Linsley, Laurie S. 1987. The dual job assignment in law school libraries. *Legal Reference Services Quarterly* 7 (1): 83–88.

Moeckel, Lisa E. 1993. Managing staff with dual assignments: Challenge for the 1990s. *Library Administration and Management* 7 (3): 181–84.

Paster, Amy. 1991. Dual function librarianship: What makes it work? *Reference Librarian* 34: 3–13.

Raynes, Ilene. 2002. Working in public services and technical services: The best of both worlds. *Colorado Libraries* 28 (2): 22–24.

Tice, Beth. 1998. Two hats, one heart: Confessions of a split position librarian. *Technicalities* 18 (7): 4–6.

CHAPTER 17

Social Sciences and Outreach Librarian

SAMANTHA SCHMEHL HINES

The following is taken directly from my job description, which I keep taped to my desk in my office.

Plan, evaluate and maintain total library services and instruction for distance students. Apply new technologies to further develop reference and instructional services for distance education students, and enhance and maintain the distance education library services Web page. Work proactively to further integrate information literacy instruction as an integral part of the distance education experience, and prepare user guides and bibliographies. Participate as a reference team member, providing user-centered general and specialized reference assistance with both traditional and electronic information resources. Participate in collection development and liaison activities with assigned departments: Economics, Journalism, Political Science, Sociology, and Social Work.

A TYPICAL WORKDAY

Does a "typical" workday really exist for any librarian? There are several elements to my job, however, that I work with on a daily basis.

One piece of the puzzle is reference desk time. All librarians in public services at the University of Montana's Mansfield Library are expected to put in some time each week at the Information Center, our reference/circulation/technical support one-stop shop. I average about six hours a week, including one evening shift. On top of the face-to-face reference desk time, I provide three hours of virtual reference desk time each week in our statewide consortium via QuestionPoint, an online chat and e-mail program.

Another element is instruction. Part of my job description is to integrate information literacy with distance education. I accomplish this in part by offering a one-credit online class called Research Strategies via our Blackboard course management system. When the class is in session, I try to check in once a day on the discussion boards, and I also grade assignments. When the class is not in session, I work on improving it by adding new information, thinking of different ways to deliver the material, or searching for outdated links or facts.

As a liaison librarian to five departments on campus, I teach about one library session a week in our face-to-face classroom. These sessions vary from basic introduction to the library workshops (where I demonstrate the catalog, an online database or two, and give a short assignment) to in-depth explorations of particular resources and search strategies. For each session, I create a handout for the students to take away that is unique to the course being taught. I gather evaluations from the students during nearly every session, and I use the results to reflect on my teaching and determine what I could build on.

My other liaison responsibilities include collection development, library budget management, and library outreach for the five academic departments I work with. We are encouraged to promote library use and awareness among students, staff, and faculty in these departments by any means available. Sometimes I attend faculty lectures or presentations on evenings and weekends. I try to attend at least one faculty meeting or gathering a year for each department. At the faculty meetings, I offer them unstructured time to ask questions about library services and discuss how I can help make their lives easier.

I also consider myself to be a liaison to the Department of Continuing Education as part of my outreach coordinator responsibilities. I keep in frequent contact with their office to let them know of available services and keep them up to date on use statistics. In return, they let me know if they have any opportunities for me to communicate with distant faculty or students (on-campus training sessions, a mailing that I can piggyback onto, and so on). Because I have been appointed as one of the library's copyright gurus, questions about fair use and copyright in the distant classroom are routed to me from their office on occasion.

On top of all this, my position is a tenure-track one. I'm expected to conduct research and write for publication, as well as participate in library, university, state, and national associations and committees.

The following is an amalgam of events created to construct a "typical" day:

7:30 a.m. Arrive in my office (I'm an early riser).

7:30–8:30 a.m. Read e-mail; make and return phone calls; peruse RSS feeds or tables of contents e-mail alerts for relevant current literature and innovative ideas from others in the field.

9–10 a.m. Face-to-face instruction for an economics course—demonstrate databases, guide students in search construction and techniques, and allow students to connect a human face with library resources.

10–11 a.m. Collection Development Group meeting—all librarians involved with collection development meet twice a month to learn and share information. Other meetings I may attend within the library are reference department meetings, faculty meetings (consisting of all tenure-track librarians), and ad hoc library committees addressing specific functions or concerns.

11–11:30 a.m. Meet with a student for one-on-one research consultation. When we're on the reference desk, we may refer students directly to subject librarians if we feel the student's question is more in-depth than our time or expertise allows, or a student might contact me after a face-to-face instruction session to ask for further help.

11:30–12 p.m. Lunch! I try to use this as an excuse to get away from the computer for half an hour each day when possible.

12–1 p.m. Reference desk duty—at the same time, I bring out a stack of articles from professional literature that I should read and skim through them.

1–3 p.m. Virtual reference desk duty—at the same time, I check in on my online course, grade assignments, update lessons, and so on.

3–4:30 p.m. Work on committee assignments, research, publications, skimming tables of contents and blogs for articles I should read, or prepare for upcoming classes.

I try to stay in the library no longer than nine hours a day. I strongly believe in balancing work with my outside life. I enjoy my job, but I work to live rather than live to work. Sometimes I take assignments home to work on after having dinner with my family, or I come in for a few hours on the weekend when it can't be avoided. People will tell you that you can't work in academic libraries without putting in sixty- to eighty-hour weeks. Don't believe them. It's up to you to manage your time well, but it can be done!

PROS AND CONS

I can say without reservations that I love my job. The best thing about it is helping out students who might slip through the cracks at other institutions because they aren't physically on campus. I get to research and try out innovative ways to connect with them. I have a lot of leeway with what I can do, and we have a healthy library budget, so I don't usually have to worry about money. The continuing education department is very open and inclusive of the library, and the library in turn is highly considerate of users who are off-campus and at a distance. The people that I work with make it easy for me to get the job done.

The library is very supportive of continuing education opportunities as well, and I am strongly encouraged to go to any conference I feel is relevant. The support also extends to the fiscal arena—it's great not to have to fund every one of these opportunities out of my own pocket anymore!

One of the drawbacks, however, is that outreach to distance education can be a lonely post. You don't normally see your clients. In general, I don't hear from students or faculty unless something has gone wrong. They're often frustrated and aren't able to just stop by and work things out directly. There's a lot of exchanging of phone calls and e-mails.

Another con, and this is pretty general to working in academia, is the pressure to spend as much time at work as possible and take on everything you can manage, and maybe even some things you can't. This is especially true when you are a new faculty member. You may have already gotten the sense that I'm struggling with this! It is important to establish boundaries early on and not get bogged down with too many responsibilities, if possible. Learning to say no is hard but necessary.

HOW WOULD I GET A JOB LIKE YOURS?

I sometimes say that I got my job through blind luck. I was working two part-time library jobs in the Midwest for about a year after I got my degree. While preparing for the 2004 ALA Annual Conference, I signed up for the online job placement center and decided to browse the jobs listed there. I noticed the listing for this particular job, near where I grew up and very close to a town I used to live in. If I hadn't chosen to look at the Hot Jobs Online site, I would have never seen the listing.

In addition, I was well qualified. At the University of Illinois at Urbana-Champaign, I took basic reference and Web design courses. This gave me the background needed to perform reference desk duties and also create and manage Web sites, guides, handouts, tutorials, and other online material that is incredibly useful when dealing with a distant population.

I also took a semester's worth of courses via the LEEP program, UIUC's online library school. This gave me a good insight into what students at a distance have to go through. One of the classes I took at a distance was on library instruction. The tasks of designing instruction for a distant class taught me what professors experience as well.

Also, I involved myself as much as possible in the American Library Association and in school and state library organizations. This activity helped demonstrate to my current place of employment that I was committed to the profession and that I worked well with other librarians. I highly recommend joining ALA to those interested in a job like mine. I also recommend joining ALA's New Members Round Table (NMRT). It's an additional $10 a year, but it provides so many ways to get involved. Try to get a committee appointment either via NMRT or your library school's student associations, and if you can afford to go to ALA or state conferences or some other library organization's meetings, do so. I have heard many people complain about the time and expense of participating in organizations such as these, but it's a great way to meet people, make connections, and show your willingness to be part of the library community.

RELATED RESOURCES

ACRL Distance Learning Section provides information on and about distance librarians and librarianship. caspian.switchinc.org/~distlearn (accessed December 10, 2005).

ALA JobLIST is the Web site on which I found the posting for my job. joblist.ala.org (accessed December 10, 2005).

ALA New Members Round Table gives those new to ALA or the profession many ways to get involved. www.ala.org/nmrt (accessed December 10, 2005).

Weblogs

Here are a few of the blogs that I read to keep updated.

Farkas, Meredith. *Information Wants to Be Free.* meredith.wolfwater.com/wordpress (accessed December 10, 2005).

Pival, Paul. *The Distant Librarian.* distlib.blogs.com/distlib (accessed December 10, 2005).

Vokey, Sherri. *::schwagbag::* blog.uwinnipeg.ca/schwagbag (accessed December 10, 2005).

CHAPTER 18

Distance Education Librarian

MARIE F. JONES

I'm the extended campus services librarian at East Tennessee State University. In that role, I make sure that the library provides services to all of our off-campus students. ETSU teaches courses via a variety of delivery media (online, interactive television, and on-site, for example) and in eight to ten different locations. One of these locations has a full-fledged branch library, and I supervise the two staff members who work there, select materials for its collection, and administer its operation. In addition, Tennessee offers a cooperative online program involving nineteen institutions, and I support students in that program (whether they are taking a course from an ETSU instructor or are registered as ETSU students). As a member of the library faculty, I also serve on committees within the library and in the university as a whole, participate in service activities across campus (for example, I work with our campus diversity education initiative), and I fulfill research/publication requirements. But much of my day-to-day life is taken up with providing library instruction and reference services for the off-campus students.

CIRCUIT-RIDING LIBRARIAN

Others will tell you about the joys and sorrows of administration, collection development, or reference and instruction, but I'm going to focus on the aspect of my job that is very different from the usual academic library position. I call it my "circuit-riding librarian" routine. Imagine this day.

6 a.m. The alarm goes off. I grumble and roll over, because I don't have to be at the office at 8 today. Because I'm conducting library instruction for two night classes, I won't start my day for another couple of hours. Sleeping in isn't a daily event for me, though. At the beginning of the semester, I travel twice a week or so; later in the semester, that slows down and I spend more time on administrative and faculty functions. But today is a traveling day.

9 a.m. Before I hit the road, I log in to my e-mail, answer a couple of reference questions that came in overnight, delete junk mail, add appointments to my calendar, and flag those items that I need to deal with when I'm back in the office tomorrow.

10 a.m. I get in the car, armed with directions to the sites, cell phone, laptop, PDA, LCD projector, and handouts for the classes, not to mention a large cup of coffee!

11 a.m. As I drive down Interstate 81, my cell phone rings. It's my dean, needing a decision about allocating some of my branch library's funds toward the purchase of a set of NetLibrary books. I agree that it seems to be an appropriate use of funds that will help both the students at my branch location and elsewhere, so I allow the allocation. While I have the phone out, I check in with Jackie and Ida, the staff at the branch library, to make sure that everything is all right there and that they know I'm on the road and available by cell phone. They tell me that the new book drop has arrived, but it's a different size than the old one and it needs new bolts installed into the sidewalk. Jackie's already put in a work order with physical plant. It's likely to be a month or more before the physical plant fulfills the work order, so we need to move the drop out of the way and into storage until then.

11:30 a.m. I stop at a Wendy's and have lunch. Five years and twenty pounds later, I've finally figured out that I need to order a salad, not a cheeseburger, on this stop.

12:30 p.m. I arrive at the Starbucks in Sevierville, where I've agreed to meet a group of education doctoral students to help them with their literature reviews for their dissertations. I've met the students earlier in their program, so they recognize me and greet me as I enter. I talk to each of them briefly about their research topics. Then I boot up my laptop, connect to the wireless network, and start by handing my computer to the first student and talking her through an ERIC database search. As she works, I help her identify keywords that will turn up different aspects of her topic. She e-mails a group of articles back to her student mail account. I work through the same process with each of the students. By the time they leave, they have a good sense of the search terms and process to use to get the articles they need. I also troubleshoot for one student who has been having a hard time logging in to databases from her home computer, giving her a handout that may help her set security settings to allow access our proxy server.

Before I leave, I go through the routine with my e-mail again: answer reference questions, delete junk mail, add appointments to my calendar, and flag those items that I need to deal with when I'm back in the office tomorrow. Then I log in to my Blackboard site and check the fifteen classes for which I monitor online discussion boards. There are two questions there.

"I can log in fine from home, but I can't get into the library databases from work. Why?" My answer: "Your work location probably has a firewall or site restrictions. You simply can't access the databases from many worksites."

"I found an article in CINAHL that I want, but when I go to 'Get it @ ETSU' and click the EBSCO link, it doesn't come up." My answer: "Give me the citation of the article you need and I'll see what the problem is with that particular journal."

When you work the reference desk, you answer a lot of "Where's the bathroom?" questions. When you work in a completely virtual environment, those are replaced by troubleshooting and "What do I click on?" questions.

3:30 p.m. I'm due at Northview Elementary School to meet with a counseling class at 4. I check my MapQuest directions (the instructor never did send me the driving directions I requested) and head off. After taking a few wrong turns, I finally arrive at the school. When I go in the front door, I am stopped by someone who looks like an administrator and I identify myself. She directs me to the library. The room is set up for elementary students: pint-sized chairs and small tables. The librarian graciously allows me to use her computer and big-screen TV setup, so I don't have to set up my computer and LCD. The TV is blurry, but the class is small, so I think it will be all right.

Class begins, with these adult graduate students seated in the children's chairs or their own bright orange folding chairs. I tease them about their University of Tennessee colors as I introduce myself and the services the library offers: reference, electronic collections, document delivery. As I tell them how to log in from home, I start to demonstrate the process, but we get page error messages when we should get log-in screens. Something (either firewall issues or security settings) won't allow the proxy server to work. I am prepared for this little glitch; I have a mockup of the appropriate database screens in PowerPoint to show them. When I leave the class, I give them all of the contact information they need to get help, including the toll-free number for the library reference desk, my phone numbers (cell and office), and my e-mail address. I also remind them that they can ask me questions in the online Blackboard discussion board for this class.

5:30 p.m. I head on to Sevierville High School to talk to a technology class. Their research topic is dams, a topic about which my degrees in English and education have taught me little, if anything. But as a generalist librarian, I've learned not only a huge amount about all kinds of topics but also how to draw out keywords from patrons in subject areas I've never heard of before. I had done that background research with the instructor in advance, so I am prepared for this instruction session. Again, in the high school where this class is held, the firewall prevents me from logging in to library databases directly. I pull out yet another PowerPoint mockup to show them the databases. As always, I remind them that librarians enjoy helping people find the information they need, and I give them the library's toll-free number and my e-mail address.

After my presentation and the students' questions, the projector cools down and the students take a break, and I take the opportunity to check my calendar for the next day. It will be a quiet one: faculty meeting from 8:30 to 11:30, lunch with a colleague at noon, two hours on the main library's reference desk, and a committee meeting for the online degree program.

My "to do" list looks like this:

- Update CSA tutorial to reflect interface change.
- Institutional Review Board (that refers to forms that need to be filled out for permissions regarding some research I'm planning).
- Compile monthly statistics.

I add to the list:

- Check on student in Blackboard with the EBSCO access problem.
- Add handouts and PowerPoint slides to course Blackboard sites for today's sessions. (Every "live" class at ETSU has a Blackboard site where course materials can be posted by the instructor. I try to get permission from every instructor I work with to put materials in his or her site, and I often participate in discussion boards where students can ask questions after an instruction session. In other courses, the discussion board is my only contact with the students.)
- Deal with flagged e-mails.

Looking at the size of the list and the schedule of my day, I decide that I'll check my Blackboard classes, see if I can resolve the EBSCO question, post the handouts, deal with some of the flagged e-mails, and, if there's time, I'll work on the statistics. Most of the other things can wait until next week.

7 p.m. I leave the classroom, load the LCD projector and laptop into the car, and get back on the road. Before I leave town, I stop for a bite to eat and then get back in the car for the two-hour drive home.

THE PROS AND CONS

I love this job, but every point that I think of as a positive might be a drawback to someone else.

I enjoy the flexibility of working different hours in different locations, but someone else might find the lack of routine stressful. Generally, I travel two days a week early in the semester and one day a week later in the semester. Because of the locations of our classes, I'm never gone overnight. However, off-campus classes are generally offered on evenings and weekends, and because I can't always flex my schedule fully, some of my days are very long. Still, I feel stifled when I have to work exactly the same schedule every day, and I get sick of looking at the four walls of my office (even though it is in a gorgeous building with a lovely view).

I love watching the seasons change as I drive through the mountains, but my odometer has racked up the miles over the years. Many of the distance education (DE) librarians I know are based at off-campus sites, but I prefer having my office in the main library because it lets me stay in touch with my fantastic coworkers and main library activities. I think that I would feel very isolated if I were based at my branch library.

Because my job includes much more than library instruction and reference, every day is a little bit different. I get the fun of doing library instruction without the burnout factor of having to do twenty first-year English classes in one week. (That was my last job!)

Because I basically run my own department, I have a lot of autonomy. The travel allows me the alone time that an introvert needs, and the instruction expresses my frustrated actress side.

SKILLS

Technological skills are necessary for this job. Much of the reference and instruction I do is through e-mail and online course sites. I spend a lot of time troubleshooting problems with access, which means that it helps to know what might be happening on computer systems that are different from my own. Creating tutorials and building Web pages are mainstays of my work. Excellent writing skills are important for writing clear instructions, especially in e-mail reference. As with any library position, the ability to learn new technologies quickly and the flexibility to adapt to change will help you retain your sanity over time. The ability to see how a new technology might apply to your work is also helpful. For in-person instruction and reference, oral communication skills are important. If you aren't comfortable speaking in front of groups, this is a better job for you than the average reference/instruction job, but the amount of public speaking necessary will depend on your institution. I personally think it's important for off-campus students to see me and make a connection with me so that they feel more willing to call or e-mail in the future, but that is not practical for all institutional settings. Of course traditional reference skills are also important. You need to know how to conduct a reference interview by e-mail or phone as well as in person, how to identify appropriate sources from those available, and how to tell people clearly and concisely how to access and use them.

Communication and networking skills are generally very important. DE librarians have to be proactive because you don't really have a physical library for people to come to; you have to reach out to them. In DE, you often work with departments outside the library. When I first came to ETSU, I made it a priority to meet with people involved in distance education and continuing studies as well as members of the departments that teach a lot of courses off campus. Making cold calls to these people was very difficult for me, but I think it gave me a better sense of what the needs of the campus were right off the bat.

ADVICE FROM THE FIELD

One of the important factors to know about DE librarianship is that it varies quite widely among institutions. Not all jobs that support off-campus students are as integrated into the main library's programs as mine is. Some are branch manager positions; some are tacked on as a portion of another job, usually in reference; some manage large independent departments that provide all reference, document delivery, and other services for off-campus students; some work exclusively with online students. Read job descriptions carefully, find out the location and type of programs offered by the institution, and ask a lot of questions when you interview.

RECOMMENDED RESOURCES

Association of College and Research Libraries and American Library Association. Distance Learning Section. caspian.switchinc.org/~distlearn (accessed November 8, 2005).

Goodson, Carol. 2001. *Providing library services for distance education students: A how-to-do-it manual.* New York: Neal-Schuman.

Miller, William, and Rita M. Pellen, eds. 2004. *Internet reference support for distance learners.* Binghamton, N.Y.: Haworth.

OFFCAMP (Off-campus library services list). listserv.utk.edu/archives/offcamp.html (accessed May 29, 2006).

Off-Campus Library Services Conference proceedings. 1986–2004. Mt. Pleasant: Central Michigan University. Ordering information available at ocls.cmich.edu/conference/proceedings.htm (accessed May 29, 2006).

Slade, Alexander L. Library services for distance learning: The fourth bibliography. uviclib.uvic.ca/dls/bibliography4.html (accessed November 8, 2005).

CHAPTER 19

Collection Development Librarian

ALEXIS LINOSKI

As the collection development librarian at the University of Central Arkansas, my main responsibility is to oversee the development of the library's book and media collections as well as manage electronic resources. This involves developing and updating the collection development plan, handling the allocation of the library materials budget among the colleges and departments, reviewing and monitoring expenditures and purchases for the library's general fund, evaluating electronic resources (databases) and coordinating trials, and tracking database usage statistics. I also coordinate the library liaison program between the departments and the library and act as a liaison to several departments, coordinate the deselection (weeding) of materials, provide information on library resources for department and accreditation reviews and new courses, oversee donations, ensure timely payment of electronic resources invoices, and supervise a department of three. Perhaps atypically, I am also the Webmaster for the library, managing the content and ensuring that it is up to date. Finally, as with many positions in academic libraries, I also work several hours a week at the reference desk.

A TYPICAL WORKDAY

My typical workday is quite varied and involves a bit of multitasking. On any given day, I may carry out some or all of the following activities.

Materials

Collection development positions vary from institution to institution. At my university, I don't actually order the materials. I have a very proficient acquisitions supervisor who does this. However, occasionally a decision or two has to be made regarding the type of material that a department is trying to order and whether it meets the criteria set in the collection development policy. For example, in the past few weeks, several departments submitted orders for software. These requests came to me because we closely monitor software requests due to licensing issues in a university environment. Another part of our current collection development policy states that we only purchase one copy of a title. If a department wishes to purchase more than one copy or a second copy of a title we already own, the request comes to me. Generally, I ask for justification, especially if it is an older publication or if the circulation of the current copy has been less than spectacular. Basically, any request that falls outside of the collection development policy and any nonstandard requests are referred to me.

Database Subscription Renewals

One of my top priorities is to monitor contract dates for electronic resource subscriptions coming up for renewal. If renewal is imminent, a purchase order is initiated to ensure availability of funds when the invoice is received. We are working to get all our database subscriptions synchronized on a fiscal- or calendar-year cycle, so when possible, I negotiate with vendors to reset the renewal date.

Budget

I take the lead on answering any questions from the departments about their budget allocations or dollars spent, ensure the allocation formula is documented, and gather up-to-date criteria needed to allocate the funds at the start of each fiscal year. Monthly reports are run showing the amount each department has spent of their allocated materials budget. I monitor these figures and, as we get closer to midpoint of the fiscal year and then to the end of the fiscal year, I send reminders to departments who have money remaining. Surprisingly, even after being reminded, some departments don't spend all of their money, so we make their selections for them.

Information for Department/Accreditation Reviews or New Courses

As departments perform their own internal reviews or come up for accreditation renewal, I provide the information they need on library resources (including books, electronic resources, serials, and media) that support their programs. Although this is not on a daily basis, generally by the time they realize they need this information, the turnaround time is short. I've developed a standard format, but it still takes a full day to gather all the information and put it into a usable format for the department. I also provide this service for faculty who are developing new courses and need to know what library resources are available to support the course.

Vendors

As the point of contact for database vendors, I speak with vendors on a regular basis. Some are vendors whose databases we already subscribe to who are offering new modules or products, and others are vendors whose databases we don't currently have. Based on my discussions with the vendors and the programs the university offers, I determine which new products or modules we'd like to test and possibly consider for purchase.

Deselection/Weeding

Light deselection/weeding is done fairly regularly. I work with our cataloging department to ensure that as new editions of existing titles are ordered, we pull the older editions. In conjunction with the preservation technician, we have developed guidelines for determining whether we should repair and keep damaged items or simply pull them from the collection.

Web Site Updates

On a regular basis, I update the library's Web site to reflect current information on any trials that we are running, new resources or databases we have added, or updates to subject guides. I also ensure that announcements of special events such as book signings or research clinics are publicized. Although I can plan for some of these updates, purchase cycles for new databases and other larger resources or additions of special events at short notice can provide unexpected changes to my daily workflow. When this happens, I must make time in the day to post these changes.

Meetings, Committees, Professional Activities

Like most librarians, I serve on university committees and on professional association committees (in my case, ALA and the Arkansas Library Association). I am also my library's representative to ARKLink, Arkansas's state library consortium. Some work can be done virtually, and other work requires in-person participation. Either way, they each require time and must be worked into the day. When I am fortunate enough to write articles or present at conferences, they also require time in the day to write or prepare.

PROS AND CONS

Pros

I gain personal satisfaction from the collection development side of this position—working with the budget and determining what direction to take the collection. I am challenged to think beyond traditional resources like printed books and typical databases of indexes, abstracts, and journal articles. There are now e-books as well as other products that are, in my opinion, a cross between databases and e-books. Then there are the products that are e-books but function like a journal database, giving users the flexibility to search across multiple e-books and access them from anywhere at any time. So the joy for me is that I get to grow the collection in a variety of ways to support the needs of the individual departments.

An offshoot of this is the deselection process. Though it sounds kind of scary, and possibly a bit blasphemous, weeding is necessary for any good collection. There are now a variety of software tools available to aid in this process. Thus I can use technology in conjunction with input from our faculty to trim from our collection what no longer supports our programs and at the same time determine which areas we need to build.

I enjoy working with electronic resources and vendors. In working with the vendors, I'm constantly updating my technical knowledge by learning about new modules and new products. Then I take this new information and determine how or if it can support our university's programs; for example, does it duplicate an existing resource, does it enhance an existing resource, or will it support an area or program in which we are currently weak?

Cons

The biggest annoyance for me is the budget. It's never enough (which I'm sure can be said at almost every library). Because our budget remains somewhat static, it's difficult to subscribe to new databases or increase the materials budget for the departments. This in turn makes it difficult to continue providing top-notch services and materials as enrollment rises and an increasing number of distance education classes are offered. However, it's also a chance to market the library's services and educate the university population that the library is more than just books.

Another frustration is the sheer volume of information I receive on a daily basis from publishers. I'm not frustrated by the receipt of the information itself but by the quantity received. Many send large catalogs that cover many areas. Because our faculty determines over 80 percent of what is ordered, these large catalogs make it difficult to get this information to the individual departments. Then there are all the little flyers and letters that seem to be never-ending. I go through as many as I can and set aside those that fit our "general" category for possible purchase through our general fund and forward to the appropriate department when necessary. But there are still days when it feels and looks like a paper bomb has gone off on my desk.

HOW WOULD I GET A JOB LIKE YOURS?

My main recommendation is to make sure you take a collection development class. A good course will cover the basics of a collection development plan, the selection process, publishers and how publishing works, electronic materials, audiovisual materials, acquisitions, jobbers and wholesalers and their roles, fiscal management, budget allocation, deselection, and evaluation. It's also not a bad idea to take a class on preservation and conservation of materials.

Not every institution has a collection development librarian. Those institutions that don't generally include collection development duties for specific areas of the collection, such as business or history, as part of their reference or public services librarian positions. Even if your title isn't collection development librarian, odds are strong that you will be doing some form of collection development and possibly budget management as well. Use these positions to gain experience and move to a collection development position.

Finally, smaller libraries, such as those found in many career colleges, are often overlooked as good places to gain work experience. They offer opportunities to perform a wide range of duties. Professionals at these libraries often work as solo librarians, performing all duties, including budget management, collection development, and acquisitions.

RELATED RESOURCES

Books

Evan, G. Edward. 2000. *Developing library and information center collections*. Greenwood Village, Colo.: Libraries Unlimited. This book was the textbook for my Collection Development class. I still use it as a reference tool.

Web Resources

Charleston Advisor. www.charlestonco.com (accessed June 12, 2006). This Web site provides reviews of Web-based electronic resources. Just a few are free; the rest require a subscription, but it gives one a good feel for what is involved in evaluating electronic resources.

Conferences

The Charleston Conference. www.katina.info/conference (accessed June 12, 2006). Held every year in November, this is the largest conference focusing on acquisitions and collection development. Attendance includes a subscription to *Against the Grain,* which, even with tiny print, is a great journal. I try to attend annually; between the presentations and the vendor fair, there is a lot of good information at this conference.

The Acquisitions Institute at Timberline Lodge. libweb.uoregon.edu/events/ec/aitl (accessed June 12, 2006). Held every year around April or May in Oregon, this is a small conference (currently limited to eighty-five attendees) that provides an opportunity for librarians, vendors, and publishers to discuss current issues and trends.

CHAPTER 20

Curriculum Specialist

ANN BROWNSON

Curriculum specialists, curriculum materials center coordinators, or teaching materials center managers provide assistance to students planning to enter the teaching or school library profession and to college or university faculty. They do this through the collection of textbooks, juvenile trade books, and other materials and through instruction in the use of those materials. People in this position may also provide materials and services to local schoolteachers and library media specialists as well as to the general public. Sometimes they have other responsibilities in the academic library, and sometimes they are not even associated with the institution's library but with the school or college of education.

TYPICAL ACTIVITIES

Rather than focusing on a typical day at work, let me describe the variety of activities that are part of the daily life of a curriculum specialist.

Because my curriculum materials center has an extensive collection of children's books (and that is where my primary interest lies), I spend a significant amount of time developing that collection. I read reviews, search best books lists, write grant applications, and talk to faculty members teaching children's literature courses, all in the name of developing the best collection possible. Students come with requests for juvenile trade books about specific subjects for specific grade levels, so developing the collection based on those curricular needs is also important.

In addition to the juvenile trade book collection, I collect a wide variety of textbooks and other items for the teaching materials collection. Besides pre-K through twelfth-grade textbooks, I select curriculum guides, activity books, and many nonbook materials. Our collection includes puppets, educational games, math manipulatives, books on tape/CD, models, and even a percussion band! Because most of these items are unique, I work on a daily basis with a cataloger to discuss the best way to provide both bibliographic and physical access to the collection.

Developing the teaching materials collection is not simply a matter of looking at reviews and selecting materials. Most teaching materials are not reviewed, and a significant amount of time is spent tracking down materials. Catalogs are not usually sent automatically, so there is a certain amount of detective work that goes into finding what is even available. Part of my search for textbooks has little to do with catalogs and vendors and more to do with talking to education faculty and area teachers, finding out what they are using in their classrooms, what textbook adoptions they are doing in a particular year, and then contacting sales representatives directly. When you think about it, salespeople have little incentive for talking with me. At the most, I will probably purchase one teacher's edition, one set of supporting materials, and one student edition for each grade level, as opposed to a school district that might be buying textbooks for thousands of students. But I keep trying!

There is a somewhat different story for institutions in textbook adoption states. In some cases, curriculum centers are the location of examination collections for a state or part of a state. Those curriculum centers receive examination copies more or less automatically from the textbook publishers.

A big part of my job is direct public service. I work with users both in a reference and in a reader's advisory capacity, helping them find appropriate materials as they work to develop lesson plans and teaching activities for classes and as they work in area schools. Because my library is part of a public institution, we are also open and provide services to local citizens not affiliated with the university. This means that I also work with parents who are homeschooling their children, local teachers looking for specialized materials for their classes, and anyone who calls or contacts me for assistance. I consider myself first and foremost a teacher, providing instruction to individuals or groups in the use of online and print sources. I also work to develop local finding aids, bibliographies, and book lists useful to the center's patrons, and I maintain the curriculum center's Web site. Because I am the education librarian in addition to being the curriculum specialist at my institution, I assist students as they research all kinds of educational issues and topics.

Throughout the semester, many faculty members ask to bring their classes to the curriculum center for instruction in the use of the center and the resources it contains. I am fortunate to have access to an electronic classroom in the building for instruction and to a seminar room where I can demonstrate both online and print resources.

Depending on the size of the curriculum center, the job may involve supervision of support staff and student workers. Because our collection is large, members of the support staff and I must devote a significant amount of time to the maintenance of the collection through constant shelf reading, repairing of damaged items, and processing of new items. Curriculum centers may also have a public service desk to provide circulation and reference services, staffed by both support and professional staff.

Promotion of the curriculum materials center takes place in many ways. For example, I recently wrote a grant that brought 125 fifth graders in from an area school to learn to do research on nonfiction topics. This resulted in the creation of 125 books that the students took home and the addition of several thousand dollars of nonfiction trade titles to the juvenile collection. Promotion of the curriculum center's collection and services also involves networking—making cold calls to busy administrators in local school districts, asking them to encourage teachers' use of the collection and, incidentally, to help me expand the collection. I meet occasionally with local school library media specialists and public children's librarians to discover how we can assist each other. I also provide a weekly story time to local children and their parents and occasional special story times and tours for area day care centers. Within the center, we develop displays highlighting topics of curricular interest as well as new books in the collection.

Because the curriculum center is a part of the larger library at my institution, I have job duties in other parts of the library as well. For example, most of the professional librarians are scheduled at the reference desk for several hours each week and also work an occasional weekend. I participate in a variety of library-wide activities and projects.

In some academic libraries, librarians are tenured or tenure-track faculty, and in others they are considered professional support staff. At my institution, librarians are faculty and participate in the life of the university the same way teaching faculty do. So how does this affect my job? It means we are evaluated based not only on our primary duties as librarians but also for our research and service to the library, campus, and profession. I am a member of several library and campus committees that may also take up part of my day. For example, I am on the library's Web Resources Committee, which determines the look and usability of the library Web site, and I am also a faculty senator involved in the governance of the university. I participate in my profession by serving on statewide and national committees of organizations including ALA, ACRL, and AASL.

My day does not necessarily end when I leave work, either. Because reader's advisory work is a part of my position, I read several children's and young adult books each week, and I do this mostly at home.

PROS AND CONS OF THE POSITION

The best thing about my job is that I work in an academic library, but I have the opportunity to interact with a variety of people—not just college students and faculty but local teachers, parents, and children as well. It's really the best of several worlds. Sometimes I feel like a children's librarian in a public library, sometimes a school library media specialist, and other times like an academic librarian. There is something to learn every day: using new technology, assisting a faculty member with her research project, or determining what new research guide would help students find the information and resources they need.

Within the constraints of the budget and the academic schedule, I have freedom to develop this position into what I think it should be. My time is somewhat flexible in that I am not always expected to be in the curriculum center or even in the library at all. What that sometimes means, however, is that the position becomes much more than an eight-to-five job. If a faculty member wants to bring an evening class in for instruction, I change my schedule to accommodate him. If a grant application is due, I may work additional hours to complete it. Research is often done on my own time, outside the normal workday, though it is expected for tenure and promotion.

I love to order books. When reviews of new books that will be an asset to the collection appear or when new textbook series are published in a subject area that gets lots of use, I can't wait to make them available. Even better is hearing from users that the collection contains "just what I need."

Of course, the downside to ordering books and other material for the curriculum center is that they all cost money. Though I would like to order everything for the collection, this is not realistic, and decisions must be made about the best use of the budget. Do we really need a life-size skeleton of the human body? (It turns out that we did.) How many copies of the latest Harry Potter book should I purchase? (At least three.)

Because many of the items purchased for the curriculum center are nonprint, they require special cataloging and processing. Sometimes this can be quite a trial. Many of the items in the curriculum center require original cataloging, and I must work well with the cataloger who does this for those items. We must determine whether a multipart item should be cataloged separately or as one item; we also must decide how those items should be processed to provide physical access. Should the material be housed on the bookshelves, in bags, in boxes, or some other way? The aforementioned skeleton is housed in a rolling garbage can!

HOW WOULD YOU GET A JOB LIKE MINE?

How do you get the best library job in the world? Because many academic institutions require librarians to hold a second master's degree in a subject specialty, it is a good idea to get a second master's degree, preferably in education. Ideally, you would also have an education degree at the undergraduate level. As part of your library degree, take as many children's and young adult literature and library media specialist–related courses as possible in addition to courses related to work in academic libraries. If you do not have a background in education, you may also want to take courses in the school of education, particularly dealing with reading instruction and educational methods.

If you are interested in becoming a curriculum specialist, one of the best things you can do is to join the Education and Behavioral Sciences Section (EBSS) of the Association of College and Research Libraries (ACRL). You could participate in the Curriculum Materials Committee of that section, and through that involvement you may hear of available positions. The section has an electronic list, EBSS-L, which you can join to hear about issues and opportunities related to education and the behavioral sciences, including curriculum materials centers.

Because some curriculum materials centers are associated with schools of education rather than academic libraries, you may also want to join education associations such as the Association for Supervision and Curriculum Development or the International Reading Association.

The *Directory of Curriculum Materials Centers* published by ACRL is a resource you can use to find many of the academic institutions that have curriculum centers; you could then contact those institutions regarding possible positions.

Of course, there are a variety of online lists of library positions you should monitor, and be sure to fully use the resources offered by your library school and your institution's career center. The *Chronicle of Higher Education* continues to be an important source for library job listings as well.

RELATED RESOURCES

Carr, Jo Ann, ed. 2001. *A guide to the management of curriculum materials centers for the 21st century.* Chicago: Association of College and Research Libraries.

Guidelines for Curriculum Materials Centers. 2003. *College and Research Libraries News* 64 (7): 469–74. Also available online at www.ala.org/ala/acrl/acrlstandards/guidelinescurriculum.htm (accessed August 21, 2006).

Lare, Gary. 2004. *Acquiring and organizing curriculum materials: A guide and directory of resources,* 2nd ed. Lanham, Md.: Scarecrow Press.

Olive, Fred, ed. 2001. *Directory of curriculum materials centers,* 5th ed. Chicago: Association of College and Research Libraries. Available online at acrl.telusys.net/cmc/index.html (user name and password required) (accessed January 28, 2006).

CHAPTER 21

Conservator

WHITNEY BAKER

Conservators are privileged to examine, handle, and repair some of the most unique, rare, and fascinating materials in library collections. The work of conservation involves examining items from libraries and archives and determining what needs to be done to preserve and stabilize them so they are accessible to patrons. As the supervising conservator for the University of Kansas Libraries, I manage the workflow and oversee duties of the Conservation Unit, a hybrid laboratory for both circulating and special collections. This lab is part of the Preservation Department, which also includes commercial binding, reformatting, disaster preparedness and response operations, and environmental monitoring activities. My job description includes more than performing repairs on rare books and archival collections, although this is the part of the position I most enjoy. My other duties include supervising permanent staff, student employees, and interns in the conservation laboratory and serving as a preservation resource for library staff and the public. In addition, I compile the laboratory repair statistics, procure and maintain laboratory equipment, and maintain the laboratory supply inventory. Librarians at the University of Kansas are members of the faculty, so I have research and service requirements as a tenure-track employee, such as serving on library and university committees (including the Preservation Management Team and Disaster Committee) and publishing relevant research in the field.

A TYPICAL WORKDAY

Library conservation falls into two categories: general (or circulating) collections conservation and special collections conservation. The former tends to be characterized by a mass-production approach, such as batching items to be treated and precutting supplies so that the greatest number of items can be addressed. Special collections conservation typically involves more attention to individual items, which are generally housed in closed stacks and are normally of higher value (monetary, sentimental, historical, etc.). No matter the type of library conservation, conservators adhere to the American Institute for Conservation's (AIC) Code of Ethics and Guidelines for Practice that dictates ethical behavior for conservators, such as using high-quality, nondamaging repair materials and doing only what can be reversed easily. (For example, repairing a book with Scotch or book tape is damaging and can be reversed only with the use of toxic solvents, so this practice does not meet the requirements of the Code of Ethics.) I treat items from the special collections library, and the assistant conservator supervises students and staff who repair the circulating collections materials.

When a new special collections item comes into the laboratory for treatment, I first closely examine the object in its current state and note ways in which it is unstable or unsuitable for use. I compile a written report outlining an examination of the materials that compose the object (a book, for example, might be made up of paper, ink, sewing thread, linen cord, wooden boards covered by leather, and metal clasps) and detailed information about the current condition of the item, such as torn pages, a loose spine piece, or water damage. This report is augmented by "before treatment" photo documentation, usually in the form of prints or slides. I compose a treatment proposal to address the condition concerns and share this information with the curator, who retains custody of the item and must give final approval before I undertake a treatment. Once the curator and I agree, I perform the treatment, taking care to record every step performed and the time it takes to carry out the work. Once the repairs are completed, I prepare a final report and take "after treatment" photographs. This final report typically is provided to the curator and an archival copy is kept in the laboratory. The documentation is crucial, as conservators are required to report the work they do so that future generations of conservators will have access to the information should the item require further treatment.

As already stated, an individual book from the general collections does not receive the same level of attention as a rare book. Although we do not take the time to write treatment reports for each item or take photographs of the items before and after treatment, we have a laboratory manual that clearly delineates the steps for each type of repair we perform in the laboratory. If a future conservator should require information about how a particular item was repaired, he or she could reference this manual for a thorough understanding of the repair technique employed. Because we have an established menu of repairs, the books received from circulation and our branch libraries are batched together based on the set instructions. Technicians typically work on three to seven books at once, completing each repair step in a line from the first book to the last to save time as adhesives dry and books are pressed. In this manner, we are able to treat roughly seven to nine thousand items a year with a small staff of 1.5 full-time equivalent (FTE) staff and approximately 1.5 FTE student workers.

A typical workday involves balancing the repair activities in the laboratory with the other duties listed in the job description. As a manager, I usually attend several meetings per day, often with my supervisor, who heads the Preservation Department, on projects that affect the preservation of the collections as a whole. To balance lab time and managerial work, I set aside half a day for administrative duties, such as attending staff and committee meetings, working with interns and students, and engaging in research, and I reserve the other half of the day for time in the laboratory, to the extent that this arrangement is feasible.

PROS AND CONS

Pros

My greatest joy as a conservator is having the chance to closely examine books and paper items, often learning much about how they were made in the process of repairing them. I might treat a medieval manuscript one day and a nineteenth-century newspaper the next. Each item is unique, and I enjoy using my problem-solving skills to tailor a perfect solution to the individual needs of each object. I take great comfort in surrounding myself with the physical and tangible in an increasingly virtual world.

Conservation is a wonderful mix of disciplines and skills, a field that is ideal for someone who is not highly right- or left-brained. It is a perfect combination of chemistry and art, theory and practice, and past and future. Many librarians spend almost all their time in front of a computer; I appreciate spending much of my day working with my hands away from the office setting.

In addition, the conservation field is small and close-knit. As a result, most colleagues are extremely willing to share information and ideas with one another. Likewise, the field has many opportunities for service, and it is generally fairly easy to become involved at a national level. I have gained so much from working with highly placed conservators early in my career. Library and archives conservation is a field still in its adolescence, so there are many research contributions yet to be made.

Cons

Almost universally, most conservators state that the greatest downside to working as a conservator in an institutional setting is that there is never enough time spent at the bench repairing collections. Managerial duties often cannot wait, and these tasks can cut into the time available for repair work. Many of the conservation treatments require uninterrupted blocks of time to carry out the steps. This dilemma necessitates a balancing act.

In addition, a disadvantage of being a library conservator, even one with a master's in LIS, is that we perform work that is quite different from that of the more typical librarian. As such, we have to invest time in education to inform others about what we do. A cataloger and conservator might not speak the same language and might have to work to find common ground.

Depending on where in the country you live, a conservator will most likely hold a fairly unique position at the institution. The highest concentration of library conservators is on the East Coast. Conservators in the Midwest and West might not have any professional colleagues in the same town—or even in the same state—to turn to for advice and guidance. I find it crucial to keep in contact with colleagues by e-mail and through participation in regional and national conferences.

HOW WOULD I GET A JOB LIKE YOURS?

Becoming a conservator requires a good deal of effort. Until the 1980s the most common manner of acquiring conservator credentials was to apprentice with a master conservator for a period of years. Many of the well-respected senior conservators in the field followed this career path. However, as the field evolved, a graduate program at Columbia University was developed that meshed conservation bench skills with a library science degree. In this way, the conservator would gain insight into how a research library operated and earn the degree that would provide a common language between the conservator and the rest of the library staff. When the Columbia library school closed, the program moved to the University of Texas at Austin, where it remains today. Currently, it is the only graduate conservation program focused on library and archives materials. Although there are superb graduate programs in fine art conservation, the Texas graduate program is the only one that awards an MLIS degree.

Conservation training programs are highly selective, as typically only five to ten students are admitted each year. Most programs require extensive preprogram volunteer or paid experience in conservation settings. This work allows the selection committees to gauge interest and dedication to the field and allows potential applicants to meet and shadow working conservators. A typical part of the application process includes a presentation of a portfolio showing examples of one's hand skills, including any previous conservation projects. All conservation degree programs require extensive chemistry coursework prior to application to graduate school, including at least the introductory and organic chemistry courses and accompanying laboratories.

The coursework during school is a combination of traditional library and information science courses; specialized library science courses in areas such as history of printing, history of the book, and archives management; and conservation-focused classes. The latter include preservation management, paper and book conservation laboratories, conservation chemistry, materials science, and courses in other library media, from audiovisual to digital. All conservation programs include an eight-month to one-year internship at the end of the training time, whereby students leave their schools and gain on-the-job training at a research institution elsewhere. This internship time often has a research component, depending on the hosting institution. It is not uncommon for conservators in training to undertake multiple internships or postgraduate fellowships before securing a permanent position.

Fine art conservators often take assistant-level conservator positions right out of school, whereas many library conservators find themselves managing a conservation laboratory straight away, most typically with a staff of one to two FTE and many student workers. Over the past decade or so positions have tended to outnumber trained applicants, but the supply and demand in the field remain steady. Although the path to becoming a conservator is challenging, the rewards are great for those who are successful.

RELATED RESOURCES

The American Institute for Conservation of Historic and Artistic Works. 1994. *AIC code of ethics and guidelines for practice*, rev. ed. aic.stanford.edu/about/coredocs/coe/index.html (accessed November 8, 2005).

———. 2001. *Conservation training in the United States.* aic.stanford.edu/education/becoming/contrain. pdf (accessed November 8, 2005).

———. 2003. *Defining the conservator: Essential competencies.* aic.stanford.edu/about/coredocs/defining-con.pdf (accessed November 8, 2005).

The Kilgarin Center for Preservation of the Cultural Record. www.ischool.utexas.edu/kilgarlin/index.php (accessed November 8, 2005).

Paris, Jan. 1990. *Choosing and working with a conservator.* Atlanta, Ga.: SOLINET Preservation Program.

CHAPTER 22

Cataloging/Training Librarian

ELLEN SYMONS AND ANNE BRÛLÉ

We are the cataloging/training librarians in Central Technical Services at Queen's University in Kingston, Ontario. The Queen's University Library system consists of five libraries: Stauffer Library, the humanities and social sciences library; the Science and Engineering Library; the Education Library; the Lederman Law Library; and the Bracken Health Sciences Library.

JOB DESCRIPTION

As cataloging/training librarians, we are responsible for original cataloging and classification of materials in all formats and subject areas for the libraries, except for the health sciences library. We also act as resource librarians to Central Technical Services staff, providing guidance and support in all areas of cataloging. In addition to day-to-day coaching and mentoring, we are involved in the overall planning, development, and implementation of policies and procedures related to the operation of the department. The other component of our job involves training of library technicians within our department and across the system. Normally, the ratio of cataloging to training is 9:10, but this varies dramatically at times depending on requirements. At the same time that we perform our everyday duties, we are required to participate beyond the department. Following the faculty model by being involved in scholarly activities within the university and within the greater library community is expected.

Although cataloging is our primary duty, it is surprising how little cataloging we actually perform. Central Technical Services is undergoing a substantial reorganization whereby three separate units—Serials Acquisitions, Monograph Acquisitions, and Cataloging—are merging into two multifunctional units, Serials and Monographs. As part of the reorganization, the cataloging and acquisitions staff are being cross-trained in the hope that everyone can perform almost every task within the department. Currently, the balance of cataloging to training has shifted substantially, so that 90 percent of our time is devoted to planning, designing, and delivering training to support the reorganization. We describe a typical day in our lives during a period of intense training.

OUR DAY UNFOLDS

On the day we are highlighting, we're going to be delivering a training session, but of course we still have to attend to our other responsibilities. This is one of the most challenging aspects of this position: juggling the current focus on training with ongoing cataloging and administrative duties. For example, one of the issues facing us is that these sessions, as well as meetings and committee work, often take us away from our desks for blocks of time. This absence has a significant impact on the workflow of the department. Careful planning is required to ensure that regardless of where our focus is for a particular day, we still fulfill the other demands placed on us. This balancing act starts as soon as we arrive at the office.

Early Morning

We arrive at about 8, but due to the varying work schedules of the technicians, training sessions are usually planned for 10:30. This gives us about ninety minutes of work time prior to leaving at 9:30 for the room where the training will be conducted. During this time we have to respond to e-mails that could include questions from librarians or staff outside the department, inquiries regarding committee responsibilities, or messages from the unit head regarding departmental activities. While we are trying to accomplish these tasks in a relatively short time, we must also be available to answer questions posed by the technicians. These can vary from queries regarding cataloging or training to personnel issues in the absence of the supervisory librarians. There is often last-minute preparation for the day's training, such as editing and printing documentation for the upcoming session. It is important that we deal with these tasks and other urgent matters before we leave the department to ensure minimum interruption to the workflow.

Midmorning

The room we use for training is also used by other staff for meetings and is not really intended for training, so not only do we have to retrieve the equipment we need, we also have to set up the room each time we hold a session. We like to allow enough time to have a final rehearsal of the material before the participants arrive. This gives us an opportunity to perfect the content and delivery and guarantee that there are no last-minute technical glitches. There has been some resistance to the reorganization, so we're often faced with negative attitudes toward the training. This adds additional stress to the delivery of the session, so if time permits, we like to have a few minutes before starting for a quick coffee break and a chance to relax.

Training sessions usually last an hour and a half. The topic today is MARC coding, which is the second part of a six-part course. Most of the technicians in the current sessions work in acquisitions or with government documents, and we are teaching them to do copy cataloging of monographs. They recognize basic MARC coding from their work, but they don't have enough knowledge to do derived cataloging. We have created a session comprised of a PowerPoint presentation that introduces them to MARC fields, tags, and subfields, and builds on the previous session that gave them an overview of AACR2. Following the lecture, we conduct exercises to help reinforce the concepts just learned. As part of the lesson, there are usually several handouts or "cheat sheets" that the participants can take away with them to use when they start cataloging.

This training session is part of a broad plan that was initiated as a result of the reorganization. In consultation with the two supervisory librarians and the department head, we devised a comprehensive cross-training plan that will be delivered over the course of the next year. The desired outcome is to have a more flexible staff who are better able to support the service goals of the unit. In addition, there were other gaps in the technicians' skills that needed to be addressed. For example, Queen's Library has recently started to collect media materials. Technicians need to be trained to catalog these materials, and this training has been incorporated into the overall plan.

Noon

After the session, we return to our desks and usually find a pile of rush cataloging. This must be done while we eat our lunches. Rush cataloging is initiated by staff or students who request an item that appears in the library OPAC but is not yet cataloged. The technicians routinely handle these requests unless they are video recordings or items requiring original cataloging or subject analysis and/or classification. On a typical day we can expect to have two to five rush items cross our desks. Of course, there are also e-mails and phone calls that need attention. Since we've been away from our desks, we're often consulted by technicians to answer questions and solve problems.

Early Afternoon

We normally return to the training room in the afternoon to continue planning and organizing future training sessions. However, one or both of us usually has a meeting to attend. These meetings could be anything from committees on which we sit to departmental meetings. For example, Anne is on the Access Services Functional Team, whose mandate is to discuss issues relating to Access Services, such as food and drink policies. Ellen is on the Human Resources and Development Support Team, which is the committee that arranges learning sessions and social events for all library staff. Teams usually meet at least biweekly. Participation in committee work is expected as part of our tenure requirements.

The hour or so we have in the afternoon will be spent creating a completely new training program. Some of the catalogers are being trained to do media cataloging, so we have to prepare the sessions for this course. We begin by brainstorming to come up with ideas, including length of course, style of delivery, handouts, possible examples, and exercises. If time permits, we'll begin preparing slides or a handout. We also have to arrange a meeting with the participants to present the proposed sessions and to give them the opportunity to provide feedback on content and scheduling.

The scheduling of sessions has proved to be problematic. We have to make sure that each person isn't scheduled to be in more than one session at a time, and sessions must be scheduled around other commitments. Sessions often have to be rescheduled at the last minute to accommodate a participant who may not be able to attend for various reasons, so we have to be mindful of possible conflicts. We use a master calendar to keep track of training sessions that will take place during the next six months. Changes must be made on this calendar and communicated to everyone involved. The schedule seems to have taken on a life of its own, and changes have been made almost daily since training began. This takes up more of our time than we ever anticipated.

Midafternoon

The planning of the media cataloging workshops is interrupted today because we have to attend a Technical Services Working Group meeting. This group consists of technical services and systems librarians from across the system who discuss issues such as electronic resource management. Although we return to the training room after lunch with the intention of spending the afternoon working on training, we only get an hour of work done because we must go to the meeting. The meeting usually lasts for an hour, so we have to decide if we want to return to the planning or return to our desks.

Late Afternoon

We decide to return to our desks following the meeting. Our intention is to finish the rush cataloging; however, the department head has just received a brochure for the Ontario Library Association Super Conference, one of the key library conferences in Canada. He would like to know if we are planning to attend and reminds us that the registration deadline is quickly approaching. Participation in conferences is an important aspect of tenure requirements. We make plans to consult the brochure and decide which sessions to attend.

In the time remaining, we discover that there are several rush catalog items that require subject analysis and classification. They are all books on Canadian history, and some of the records have been downloaded from Library and Archives Canada and have Canadian subject headings and classification. Other records have been downloaded from the Library of Congress and of course have LC classification. At Queen's we use the FC schedule for classifying items on Canadian history, but we use LC subject headings, so these records need editing. Canadian literature and French Canadian literature require similar handling. We conclude our day by working on the rush cataloging and discussing briefly what we will do when we return to the training room tomorrow.

THE PROS OF THIS POSITION

This is definitely not the type of cataloging job where you come into work and catalog all day. Our job offers a variety of tasks that make it interesting and challenging. For the most part, we have the autonomy to plan our own time. This allows us to have a more flexible schedule than the librarians in public services who are required to be available for reference desk duty and bibliographic instruction. The academic environment offers many perks; for example, we have access to classes and release time to attend them, and we have access to other services such as the gym. Professional development is encouraged and supported. At Queen's University, librarians have faculty status, which gives us a voice in a large bargaining unit and allows us to reap the benefits awarded to this powerful group.

THE CONS OF THIS POSITION

Although there are many advantages to being grouped with the faculty, there are also some drawbacks. We have the added pressure of trying to meet tenure requirements, which takes time that would normally be devoted to the real purpose of our job. Another downside of this job is the lack of contact with faculty and students. At times we feel isolated from other librarians and the greater university community. The contact we do have is with the library technicians in Central Technical Services. This can be a disadvantage at times because the staff has been here for many years; they are often resistant to change and not always cooperative. This creates a barrier to open communication and flexibility and often stymies attempts to move forward with departmental improvements, including the reorganization. Although the two components of our job, training and cataloging, have the advantage of offering us considerable variety, at times it can feel like two full-time jobs.

HOW WOULD I GET A JOB LIKE THIS?

It is difficult to get into academic librarianship as a cataloger in Canada because there aren't many positions available. This is due to the fact that many university libraries have reduced the number of professional positions in their technical services departments and outsourced much of the cataloging work When positions become available, an MLS is required, a second master's can be useful, and language skills are essential. Cataloging experience is very important, and supervisory experience is desirable. It would be useful to have experience or coursework in the cataloging of serials, media, and electronic resources. For the training component of this position, it would be beneficial to have some formal training in adult education or at the very least some experience in teaching adults. Keeping current with trends, especially electronic resources and their management, is crucial in the new world of technical services.

CHAPTER 23

Special Materials Cataloger

DOUGLAS KING

As special materials cataloger at the University of South Carolina's Thomas Cooper Library, I am responsible for cataloging a wide variety of nonbook, nonprint, and electronic formats. Basically, if the item is not a printed book or a serial (either print or electronic, both of which are handled by our serials cataloger), I catalog it.

I use both MARC (Machine Readable Cataloging) and Dublin Core standards to catalog these materials. Formats that I catalog using MARC include maps, electronic books, audiobooks, microfiche, microfilm, CD-ROMs, sound recordings, video recordings, online databases, and other Web sites. I catalog these nonbook materials not only for the Columbia campus of USC but also for the university system libraries throughout the state. Each campus has unique policies for how its materials should be cataloged or physically processed, but fortunately there is a campus cataloging coordinator who helps.

In addition to MARC, I use the Dublin Core descriptive metadata scheme to establish guidelines for creating descriptive records for digital resources such as electronically scanned manuscripts, photographs, and maps. These records are maintained in a separate searchable database, which is accessible from the library's digital collections Web site. As if cataloging nonbook, electronic, and digital materials were not enough, I also perform original and complex copy cataloging of printed books on an as-needed basis. However, my primary focus is undoubtedly cataloging special materials.

Besides cataloging, I also supervise a faculty-level map cataloger and a staff-level special materials copy cataloger. I also supervise a part-time student assistant and, with the help of other librarians, a fellowship student from the university's library school. In addition, I currently serve as library liaison to the university's philosophy department. This collection development duty requires me to review new material requests and communicate with members of the philosophy department, sharing library news and responding to their library-related concerns or questions. My many in-house committee duties include serving on the Digital Collections Advisory Committee and the Electronic Resources Task Force.

A TYPICAL WORKDAY

As you can probably guess from my job description, my days are filled with a dizzying array of tasks. Fortunately for me, a majority of my time is spent actually cataloging and troubleshooting cataloging-related problems. The special materials copy cataloger is knowledgeable and experienced enough to successfully handle the bulk of the video cataloging, but I help when a large backlog of incoming materials builds up. I answer any questions she might have concerning particularly complicated cataloging or physical processing situations. Also, I perform the majority of the original cataloging for DVDs and videotapes for the library. Otherwise, the copy cataloger takes care of video cataloging.

We have a similar arrangement for map cataloging. The map cataloger handles the bulk of the library's cartographic materials, while I troubleshoot problems, answer questions, and pitch in as needed. This frees me up to concentrate on popular (for us, anyway) and potentially difficult formats such as CD-ROMs, sound recordings, and microforms. There is usually a constant stream of these incoming materials; however, e-book cataloging occurs in spurts. I may go several months without cataloging a single e-book, but then the library will make a large purchase, requiring me to devote much (if not all) of my time to this task until it is completed. E-books and other online resources require occasional URL maintenance, so there is follow-up work to be done for these materials. Also, when a new online database is purchased or when Collection Development chooses to add a Web site to the local catalog, either the serials cataloger or I step in and catalog the resource.

In addition to creating, editing, and maintaining bibliographic records for incoming materials, I also spend time creating and modifying authority records for personal and corporate authors, subject headings, and series titles. This can be tricky when working with nonbook materials, especially videos. Authority control is one of the most challenging and time-consuming aspects of my job, but I thoroughly enjoy it. When I am not working on new materials' bibliographic or authority records, I perform database maintenance on the local catalog, fixing errors as I spot them in my day-to-day work or running reports to discover errors and then systematically correcting them.

When I am not working on MARC bibliographic and authority records for all sorts of incoming materials, I am working on digitization projects, which are spearheaded by the digital collections librarian. I serve as the library's unofficial metadata coordinator for new digital projects. In this capacity, I consult with the digital collections librarian and others involved with the digitized collections on how the Dublin Core metadata records will look. Basically, I help determine what fields will be used, and what level of detail and terminology will be used when inputting data. USC uses a locally customized version of the Dublin Core standard, which we call qualified Dublin Core. This requires me to have a thorough understanding of Dublin Core and how it can best be used to describe and provide access to digital collections. I do very little actual Dublin Core cataloging myself; rather, I serve as coordinator, consultant, and troubleshooter.

Let's not forget my administrative and "other" duties. As a supervisor, I train employees, evaluate everyday work, sign timesheets, approve leave and work schedules, write annual evaluations, discuss workflow and procedures, and so on. These tasks can be very time-consuming and exhausting. Also, nearly every week includes at least one meeting. Department meetings are relatively rare (no more than once a month), but I am involved in a large number of library-wide committees, and we meet on regular or semi-regular bases. Committee work, of course, not only requires me to spend precious time in meetings but also frequently involves research and preparation. In addition, unofficial or impromptu meetings with colleagues or my department head are very common.

It would undoubtedly be a fruitless exercise to try to determine accurate percentages of time spent on my various job duties. However, I think I can estimate that a little over half of my time is spent cataloging incoming materials using MARC, about a quarter of my time is spent working on digital projects using Dublin Core, and the rest is spent doing all those other things that make being a professional cataloger such a challenging but rarely boring job. This position requires a tremendous amount of juggling of duties. I rarely spend more than a few hours on any one task, and I have to be flexible enough to shift quickly and happily from one task to another. It is important that I stay aware of the department's priorities and understand that my professional interests are secondary to the library's needs.

PROS AND CONS

The obvious advantage of working as a special materials cataloger is the inherent and inevitable variety built into my job. I work with many types of formats, both print and electronic, and nearly all of these materials are fun to handle, skim, listen to, or view. I am a strong admirer of maps and other cartographic materials, so I always enjoy handling and analyzing maps that I have the opportunity to catalog. I am also a fan of movies and music, so it is interesting to see what the various USC libraries are purchasing or receiving as gifts. Furthermore, I work with two cataloging standards—MARC and Dublin Core. This keeps me on my toes and prevents me from getting into a mental rut. My job is rarely boring and usually interesting and challenging, and I have a great deal of responsibility, all of which I enjoy.

Another feature of my job that I relish is working with colleagues. I work closely with nearly everyone in my department, but I also talk regularly with noncatalogers, such as the acquisitions librarian, digital collections librarian, government documents librarian, special collections librarian, and various reference librarians. And that doesn't include all the colleagues I work with on committees. Fortunately, I enjoy talking shop with coworkers.

What about the cons of my job? The downside to working on such a wide variety of materials is that I cannot devote enough time to any one particular format to become an expert. I must admit that specializing in one or two nonbook formats sounds very appealing to me, but this is impossible in my current position. This problem is exacerbated by cataloging digital items using Dublin Core while cataloging all other materials in MARC. I am unfortunately unable to specialize in formats that particularly interest me, and sometimes it seems as though I am merely dabbling in the various formats and not cataloging items as well as I think I should or could. It will take me many years to become an experienced music cataloger, for instance, because frankly I do not catalog enough CDs, audio cassettes, or vinyl albums to become proficient in this area. Therefore, I am forced to frequently consult handbooks and other cataloging departments' Web sites, which are often packed with useful, practical information. I also rely heavily on the expertise, experience, and helpfulness of catalogers at other libraries. Thank goodness for e-mail lists and professional organizations!

HOW WOULD I GET A JOB LIKE YOURS?

Cataloging nonbook, electronic, and other "special" materials can be a very rewarding job, if you have the required dedication, flexibility, versatility, interest in technology, and intellectual curiosity. Finding a job as a special materials cataloger, especially if you are fresh out of library school, can be a daunting task. Despite the aging of the profession and the well-documented decrease in numbers of professional librarians, there seems to be a paucity of professional-level cataloging jobs available. However, due to the increased popularity of outsourcing of cataloging for printed books, many of the cataloging jobs that are available and will become available in the near future involve nonbook and electronic materials. Outsourcing MARC bibliographic records for audiovisual materials, electronic resources, and other nonbook formats is relatively uncommon, due to the complicated nature of acquiring, cataloging, and physically processing them. These materials require a great deal of intelligent human involvement to provide optimum access for library users. That's where we catalogers enter the picture. The materials I work with are an important component in many library collections, and they deserve and demand proper care in their handling, preservation, and cataloging.

If you are considering a career in special materials cataloging, I highly recommend that you take as many cataloging and technology classes as are available at your library school. Cataloging classes may be disguised by fancy or vague titles such as Organization of Information, Knowledge Management, and so on. Often these courses take a theoretical approach to library cataloging, focusing on the hows and whys of organizing, classifying, and accessing information, which are important considerations for all catalogers. It is immensely beneficial for future professional catalogers to understand the history of cataloging and gain exposure to current trends and developments in the field. I can almost guarantee that on interviews for your first professional cataloging position you will be asked about the courses you chose to take in library school.

Unfortunately, however, some classes teach students little (if anything) about the practical aspects of cataloging, which are as important to a cataloger's education and development as a firm understanding of the theoretical side of the job. Therefore, it is crucial that future catalogers somehow acquire practical experience cataloging materials, especially nonbook materials that require specialized, complicated, and highly detailed bibliographic records. There are a variety of ways outside the classroom to acquire practical experience as a cataloger. These include internships, volunteer opportunities, and paraprofessional positions. Sometimes you can earn class credit and/or money for internships, which makes them even more beneficial. Working in a library in any sort of cataloging capacity, even if it is merely performing mundane and repetitive database cleanup tasks, will be a tremendous boon to your development as a cataloger and could help you land your first professional position.

As you work side by side with an experienced cataloger, ask lots of questions and absorb as much as you can. Try not to get frustrated, and be patient with yourself and your mentor as you learn all the intricate rules, standards, and procedures involved in cataloging. Allow yourself to make mistakes as you learn the minute and seemingly nonsensical details, and try to focus on the whys and hows (not just the whats) of cataloging.

Also, do not forget to study both MARC standards and other metadata standards, including Dublin Core, Metadata Encoding and Transmission Standard, Metadata Object Description Schema, and others. Research these standards and think about how to best apply them to library materials of all shapes and sizes.

Finally, when you attend conferences and workshops, network with professionals and library science students. You never know who will be on a search committee for that cataloging job you simply must have, and librarianship is a very small world. Forget about six degrees of separation; in this profession, it is more like three degrees of separation at most.

RELATED RESOURCES

Here are a number of helpful resources, both print and electronic, that offer a variety of information that might assist you in gaining an understanding of what my job as special materials cataloger is all about.

AUTOCAT. listserv.syr.edu/archives/autocat.html (accessed January 12, 2006).

Caplan, Priscilla. 2003. *Metadata fundamentals for all librarians*. Chicago: American Library Association.

Cataloging & Classification Quarterly. Available online at catalogingandclassificationquarterly.com (accessed January 12, 2006).

D-Lib Magazine. www.dlib.org (accessed January 12, 2006).

Dublin Core Metadata Initiative. www.dublincore.org (accessed January 12, 2006).

OCLC. www.oclc.org (accessed January 12, 2006).

OCLC Systems & Services. Westport, Conn.: MCB University Press. Also available online at www.emeraldinsight.com/Insight/viewContainer.do?containerType = Journal&containerId = 11150 (accessed January 12, 2006).

OLAC Online Audiovisual Catalogers. www.olacinc.org (accessed January 12, 2006).

Technical Services Quarterly. Available online at http://www.haworthpressinc.com/web/TSQ (accessed January 12, 2006).

University of South Carolina Libraries. Digital collections at the University of South Carolina. www.sc.edu/library/digital (accessed January 12, 2006).

Weber, Mary Beth. 2002. *Cataloging nonprint and Internet resources: A how-to-do-it manual for librarians*. New York: Neal-Schuman.

CHAPTER 24

Serials/Electronic Resources Librarian

As serials/electronic resources librarian at Texas A&M University–Corpus Christi, I am responsible for the acquisition, processing, and maintenance of the print, microform, and electronic serials collections. I facilitate public access to serials in all formats by acquiring, configuring, and maintaining databases of electronic resources. I am head of the Periodicals/Electronic Resources Department, which means that I supervise three full-time staff members and five to ten student assistants. I serve two to four hours per week at the reference desk and have responsibilities as a liaison to the music and sociology departments for collection development and bibliographic instruction.

As an academic librarian, my job also includes service to the library, the university, and the profession. I have served as the library's representative to the Faculty Senate and on a variety of committees within the library from search committees to the Library Student Assistant Advisory Council. There is the expectation at the university that I will attend commencement and other faculty functions and that I will engage in scholarly or creative activity. I also serve on or chair professional committees including committees within the American Library Association and the North American Serials Interest Group.

A TYPICAL WORKDAY

Answers to questions such as "What do you do all day?" are often broad, occasionally vague, and almost always unsatisfying. A job description is not detailed or vivid enough for one who wants to know how someone really spends his or her time and why. I have worked to provide a more satisfying and enlightening glimpse of my typical workday here. It seems natural in describing what I do all day to categorize those functions by the roles that they define. People talk about wearing many hats. It's like a game that is sometimes played in self-development workshops where you find that the way you define yourself is often by the role you play in the lives of others (e.g. a mother, a wife, a librarian, a teacher, a student, etc.). The tasks I perform or the roles I play define the position of serials/electronic resources librarian at Texas A&M University–Corpus Christi.

As serials/electronic resources librarian, some of the tasks I perform are reviewing license agreements, cataloging serial resources, creating title lists, researching and responding to queries about the collection and the department, and reviewing new resources for possible purchase. Reviewing license agreements entails reading contracts for newly acquired resources as well as those updated contracts that often require a signature at the time a resource is renewed. My review includes looking for restrictions that limit our patrons' use of content more strictly than does copyright law, as well as looking for unrealistic requirements (like holding the library strictly liable for the behavior of all patrons rather than requiring us to make reasonable efforts to inform patrons of the rules of use). Because I am not a lawyer, my review does not include an assessment of the legal ramifications of a contract. For similar reasons, I am not authorized to sign licenses on behalf of the library. Instead, from my hands, license agreements and other contracts go to the university's Purchasing Department for review and signature by experts in purchasing and, occasionally, by the institutional legal team. In other words, I review a contract with the interests of the library and its patrons in mind.

Another of my responsibilities is cataloging serials in all formats, which, for a library with a frozen serials budget, takes up a surprisingly large amount of my time. Maintaining local records in the face of title changes, titles that merge, cessations, delayed publications, and all of the other convolutions that serials go through requires a great deal of my attention. Then there are the changes in local practice that often need to be reflected in the catalog. For example, there is the question of whether to link from catalog records to the electronic version of a journal or from our alphabetic journal list, which in my library (although possibly not in others) is maintained completely separately from the catalog. Because I work in a relatively small academic library, I also lend a hand cataloging music and K–12 curriculum materials. For me, cataloging also extends to implementation and maintenance of metadata in the knowledge base (again, separate from the catalog) that underlies our link resolver and federated search engine.

As keeper of all serial-related information at my library, I am the librarian to whom faculty turn when they need a list of the library's journals in their discipline. Faculty need lists of the journals to which the library subscribes for many reasons, the most common of which is accreditation. Title lists are also useful when the library is called on to respond to surveys or provide data that describe the collection to funding agencies. I often use title lists when I review new resources for possible purchase. Both our library online catalog and our alphabetical list of journals are equipped to output lists of journals. Usually, I import those lists into a spreadsheet and then manipulate them based on the particular need, usually by subject.

Occasionally, I get a more unusual request for information about the library's serial collection. For instance, I recently researched the life of an ISSN when a question about its applicability arose. I have also had the opportunity to work with a faculty member who needed a specialized microform reader printer lens for a project he was doing that involved translating a nineteenth-century handwritten journal that had been preserved (rather poorly, unfortunately) on microfiche.

As part of the team of professional librarians, I provide bibliographic instruction in the subject areas for which I serve as subject liaison, music and sociology. Neither department is tremendously demanding of my time in this capacity, so I am also occasionally called on to teach the more heavily requested topics, like biology. My subject liaison duties extend beyond bibliographic instruction to materials selection and some cataloging.

In my role as head of the Periodicals/Electronic Resources Department team, I supervise and participate in the daily operation of the department. Recently, for example, we prioritized print journals for retrospective binding. Another example of my part in the department's daily operation is working with the library systems department to automate requests for assistance from our department by other library departments. Such requests would include notification that a particular electronic resource isn't working properly or that a particular print title did not appear in our electronic list of journal holdings. Of course, it is my responsibility to conduct annual performance evaluations and set goals for productivity.

Then there are committees. Remember all of the group work you did in library school or as an undergraduate? Remember negotiating over the nature of a project: who would be responsible for which part of the project, and when were all of the members of the group free to meet to discuss it? Well, that doesn't end with graduation! All of that continues on the job, but instead of "group work," they call it committee work. Some of the committees I serve on meet in person, and some of them meet virtually by e-mail. The work I do for them is just as important as the rest of my work in the library.

I serve on library committees including the Library Web Committee, the Library Publications Committee, and occasionally a search committee to fill an empty professional position. The Web Committee oversees the content and architecture of the library's Web site. The Publications Committee reviews current and proposed library publications to ensure that they meet university requirements for standardization. They also put on an annual display of recent faculty publications and hold a reception in honor of those faculty members. Search committees are formed as the need arises and meet more sporadically than standing committees. Search committees are always a learning experience and are often time intensive.

The Faculty Senate at Texas A&M University–Corpus Christi "is an advising and recommending body that serves to represent faculty [and librarians] in the governance of the University." Two librarians are elected in alternating years to represent the library. During my term, some of the issues that the senate considered were salary equity among faculty, faculty workload, the possibility of creating a child care facility on campus, the possibility of making the entire campus a nonsmoking environment, and promotion and tenure. I also often serve on and sometimes chair professional committees. Because one of my interests is mentoring new and potential members of the profession, I've served on ALA's New Members Round Table (NMRT) Mentoring Committee as well as the Awards and Recognition Committee of the North American Serials Interest Group (NASIG). The Mentoring Committee matches new members of the profession with mentors both at conferences and on the job. The Awards and Recognition Committee gives grants each year to students and members of the serials profession for conference attendance and to further their research and education.

Training doesn't end at library school graduation either. The speed of the development of new technologies used to deliver library services, especially serials, continues to increase. Continuing to learn is an integral part of my job. In the past year I've attended training sessions on reading and interpreting licenses for electronic resources, electronic collection development, and implementing a link resolver and a metasearch engine in our library. I also regularly attend workshops on topics such as leadership, communication, and supervisory skills.

HOW WOULD I GET A JOB LIKE YOURS?

There's a certain amount of being in the right place at the right time involved in becoming a serials or electronic resources librarian. My interest in serials librarianship developed on the job rather than in library school. Like many library school students, I worked in a library while earning my master's degree. I worked as a paraprofessional in the acquisitions department, where I was responsible for ordering monographic materials and for processing both monographs and some serials as they arrived. When the serials librarian position opened up at the library where I was already working as a paraprofessional, I applied for and was offered the job.

Because there are relatively few library school classes in serials (and the few that exist hardly scratch the surface of their complexities), it's rather more difficult to develop an early interest in serials work than it is to develop an interest in, say, reference or children's librarianship. Serialists are more often born of proximity (and sometimes necessity) than are other librarian specialists. Some, like me to a certain extent, are in the right place at the right time with enough knowledge of serials to lead them to apply (but without enough to know exactly what they are getting into!), whereas others move from more specifically serials-related paraprofessional work into serials librarianship. There are opportunities to increase one's knowledge of serials librarianship if one knows where to find them. NASIG, for example, offers scholarships to library school students to attend their annual conference to engender interest in serials work. Many state library associations have serials interest groups or round tables.

JOYS AND ANNOYANCES

Many of the annoyances that rank high on my list are not unique to serials librarianship or even to librarianship. Those are junk mail, being interrupted, salespeople, long meetings, prioritizing projects, fragmented days, and (this one *is* serials-related!) publications that change their titles. My list of joys is similarly unrelated to serials librarianship: teaching, completing a task, the people I work with, learning something new every day, and solving problems.

Writing reports is among my least favorite duties. We submit monthly reports, as well as an annual report, on our departmental activities to the library director. The monthly report includes a detailed description of my department members' activities (including meetings, training, and other events attended) and progress toward goals (often in the form of statistics). Another annual report I submit on behalf of my department addresses our travel requests for the year. The library director compiles these requests from each department and tells us which will receive funding. I am fortunate to work at a library where both librarians and paraprofessionals are encouraged (and often funded) to contribute to professional associations through committee work and presentations. In my position, writing reports is a necessary evil. It is a form of communication that facilitates understanding among other departments in the library and in the university about what it is we do every day ... but I don't have to like it!

One of the best things about my job is that it has provided me the opportunity to mentor and coach library school students and new librarians. We have a tradition at our library of encouraging paraprofessionals to continue their education by working toward a master's of library science degree. One such paraprofessional in my department recently completed her MLS. I had the privilege of reviewing the résumé and cover letter she planned to submit as a candidate for a serials librarian job. Although I am sad that she will be leaving, I confess I enjoy feeling as if I have contributed to her "growing up" as a librarian. I find encouraging protégés to explore careers in serials librarianship all the more rewarding because serials work is often one of the more mysterious library specialties. Mentoring need not be restricted to one's library. There are a wide variety of opportunities for more experienced librarians (not just serials librarians) to mentor less experienced librarians in professional groups like ALA (particularly NMRT) and NASIG.

Another of my favorite activities is learning new things. The constant change that characterizes the world of serials (title changes, new technologies, etc.) requires me to continue learning about the materials that I work with every day. I also have the opportunity to continue learning in a broader sense; for example, I recently worked with a group of faculty members and librarians to deliver an introduction to open-access publishing under the auspices of the university's Faculty Renaissance Center (FRC). The FRC provides for ongoing faculty development throughout the university. The original workshop took place in January 2006 and will continue to grow and evolve via a wiki site we created to encourage ongoing discussion of open access among librarians and faculty. My participation in this project afforded me an opportunity to learn to use an emerging communication technology (wiki) as well as increase my knowledge and understanding of open-access publishing and the issues that it raises for both librarians and faculty.

My favorite aspect of my job is the diversity of both tasks and people with whom I work. Serials librarianship at a medium-sized academic library affords me the opportunity to wear many hats and to serve many people and purposes ... just the way I like it!

RELATED RESOURCES

NASIG, the North American Serials Interest Group (www.nasig.org), is a professional organization made up of individuals from all parts of the information chain, including librarians, publishers, and aggregators.

ALA's Association for Library Collections and Technical Services (ALCTS) has a Serials Section: www.ala.org/ALCTS and click on Serials.

The Texas Library Association's Electronic Resources and Serials Management Round Table, E-SMART (www.txla.org/groups/e_smart), is an excellent example of a regional association of serials and electronic resources librarians whose purpose is "to promote and improve serials development and librarianship and to foster relations with other branches of library service, publishers, vendors, and other library organizations."

CHAPTER 25

Ordering Librarian

The Stanford University Libraries (SUL) consist of a centralized network of fourteen libraries. The Acquisitions Department serves all of SUL and employs about fifty people. The department consists of three units: Ordering, Receiving and Access, and Fiscal and Data Services. Each unit is headed by a librarian, and all three units are overseen by the head of acquisitions.

The Ordering Unit consists of ten ordering specialists with regional and language specialties. Their work includes all firm, or single, orders in any format from anywhere in the world, but does not encompass approval plans where books are shipped according to a prearranged profile. As head of the Ordering Unit, my job encompasses two main components. The first part involves management of the unit: oversight of the production work in the unit, balancing the workload among ordering specialists, and dealing with personnel issues. This aspect of my work puts me in a role where I perform a range of supervisory functions from tracking leave requests and writing evaluations to answering technical questions about the acquisitions module of our integrated library system (ILS).

The second aspect of my position involves working outside the unit I supervise: interacting directly with other acquisitions managers and SUL bibliographers to implement policy and harmonize the work and priorities of the Order Unit with those of other library units. Most of this work is accomplished through committees. One important Acquisitions Department committee to which I belong is the E-Team, a group recently established to solve problems posed by the increasing number and complexity of electronic resources. Though online resources have been a part of academic library collections for years, recently online versions, supplements, and components have become so numerous that traditional technical services workflows are no longer adequate to incorporate this kind of material systematically. Though online resources were managed by just one person in the Receiving and Access Unit just a couple of years ago, the E-Team is now comprised of six staff members from across the department. The Order Unit plays an important role in e-acquisitions: besides orders, licenses are initiated and tracked by the ordering staff.

I also serve as the liaison from Acquisitions to the Social Science Resource Group, which is composed of the bibliographers doing collection development in that subject area. This group, which serves as a resource to students and faculty in addition to selecting materials for the collection, meets regularly to discuss issues relating to social science research on campus and how SUL can better meet the needs of the campus community. Because members of the group are in regular contact with the public, my role as liaison is to help identify how Acquisitions can support their goals and, in turn, help my department understand our patrons' needs in the social sciences.

A TYPICAL DAY

Acquisitions work is straightforward in principle. The bibliographers (also known as selectors) send their order selections to their respective subject or language specialists in the Order Unit; the specialists initiate the acquisition process by placing an order with the appropriate vendor. This is typically done via the ILS, and orders are either printed and sent manually by mail and fax or transmitted automatically by system-generated e-mail.

As manager of the unit, I play several roles in the ordering process. First, I am responsible for the implementing procedures by which orders are created in the ILS. This means testing new releases of the acquisitions module for the system, checking the accuracy of individual staff members, and writing procedures to guarantee uniformity in output. Procedures are important to ensure that the order is input in a way that will provide an accurate record of the acquisition and payment to the library staff and also so that the output is consistent and complete for the hundreds of vendors who receive our orders. Second, I am the contact point for bibliographers when systematic problems arise in the ordering process, when major acquisitions need to be coordinated, or when someone has questions about the acquisition process. Because all acquisitions start with an order, I am a natural contact point for the collection development librarians when they need information about obtaining materials for the library. Finally, as head of the unit, my responsibilities also encompass some administrative functions, such as granting leave requests and drafting meeting agendas.

In addition to direct supervision of the Ordering Unit, I work with other department managers (librarians, operations managers) to accomplish department- and library-wide goals. This work includes a range of activities from drafting department policies to implementing software modules, such as an electronic resource management system (ERMS). As part of the departmental management team, I am responsible for coordinating ILS upgrades, training staff, and adapting policies to changes in the publishing marketplace. These goals can be accomplished by an entire group, usually in a formal meeting session, but often in an ad hoc manner as problems arise and relevant department managers work out situational strategies.

PROS AND CONS

SUL is a large organization with substantial resources and high expectations; at all times it provides a mix of both complicated problems and rewarding experience. The most interesting aspect of my work is supervising a diverse staff with a depth of experience. The staff is not unlike a network of spies who use their linguistic, geographic, and personal knowledge to obtain rare or hard-to-find information from around the world. Frequently materials can be purchased through regular commercial library vendors, but they might also come from obscure sources like independent filmmakers working out of their vans. I enjoy being at an institution where I am able to participate in a range of acquisitions activities, including monographic and serials purchasing in print and electronic formats.

For me, conference attendance is an exciting element of the job, and several professional conferences apply to my work. Two are especially relevant: the Charleston Conference on Issues in Book and Serials Acquisitions and the Timberline Acquisitions Institute, known respectively as "Charleston" and "Timberline." The former is held in Charleston, South Carolina, and is attended every November by hundreds of librarians, vendors, and publishers. It is a large conference with a varied program, a vendor showcase, and fast pace. Timberline is very different. Held at the historic Timberline Lodge on Mt. Hood every May, attendance is limited to fewer than a hundred participants who all attend the same sessions and take their meals together. In many ways it feels like a casual gathering of colleagues, and the mountain lodge is certainly quieter than bustling Charleston. Both conferences, despite a remarkable difference in scale and setting, provide an excellent opportunity to engage in a dialog with all the stakeholders in library acquisitions: librarians, vendors, publishers, and information technology suppliers.

Like any job, some parts are less enticing than others. The amount of time I spend being a manager cuts into the time I would prefer to spend doing "librarian" projects. Operational necessities such as running meetings or verifying leave time allocations constitute a large portion of my days when I would rather be meeting with vendors or solving a complicated serials problem. Also, the size of the organization creates some inevitable inefficiencies that slow down the whole process. Handing tasks off across units or even between people can bog down even simple tasks, and meetings are required to enact change when new workflows will impact any other unit in the department.

Recently, the number of available electronic resources has exploded, and their acquisition is increasingly dominated by complicated bundling and publisher-direct licensing. On the patron side, growing acceptance and familiarity of e-resources is driving demand. This new publishing paradigm is exciting: pricing and distribution models are taking shape, the traditional nature of collection building is facing scrutiny as old ideas about information are challenged, and the role of librarians is being affirmed. Yet at the beginning of the process, the standard methods of planning and executing basic orders are no longer adequate. Generating licenses, confirming content, and arranging preliminary access absorb a disproportionate amount of staff time, especially considering that many e-resources duplicate print holdings. The biggest puzzle my acquisitions colleagues and I face is how to deal with the emerging regime of complicated e-resources while making do without additional money or staff to tackle the problem.

Overall, though, my work as ordering librarian is interesting and rewarding. It is difficult and even frustrating at times to take on the role of manager and deal with time-consuming personnel and organizational issues. However, now is an exciting time to be an information professional and to be involved in the acquisitions side of librarianship. The business choices made by librarians are shaping the way information is produced, distributed, and eventually used.

HOW WOULD YOU GET A JOB LIKE THIS?

Anecdotally, most acquisitions librarians find their work by accident. Librarians outside acquisitions tend to not understand what this aspect of librarianship entails, and some library schools do not even offer a basic acquisitions class. Therefore, this option is almost invisible to future librarians. To be fair, looking at job postings on any given day will turn up a number of results for reference, access service, or catalog librarians, but rarely does a position identifiably acquisitions-specific appear in the postings.

The management of acquisitions work, however, is still performed by an acquisitions professional at most libraries, so a master's degree in library science is still a good place to start. Like many other technically based areas of expertise, some kind of hands-on experience in an acquisitions department will always be a plus. Unlike other parts of the library, acquisitions work is business in the traditional sense, so experience in management, sales, or other financial sectors can be also be relevant. Likewise, many acquisitions librarians end up working as sales representatives for library vendors because there is a great deal of overlap in the work.

RELATED RESOURCES

Journals

Acquisitions Librarian. See www.haworthpress.com.
Against the Grain. See www.against-the-grain.com.
Journal of Digital & Electronic Acquisitions. See www.haworthpress.com.
Journal of Foreign Acquisitions [forthcoming]. See www.haworthpress.com.
Library Collections, Acquisitions, & Technical Services. See www.elsevier.com.
Serials Librarian. See www.haworthpress.com.

Books

Schmidt, Karen A., ed. 1999. *Understanding the business of library acquisitions.* 2nd ed. Chicago: American Library Association.
Wilkinson, Frances C., and Linda K. Lewis. 2003. *The complete guide to acquisitions management.* Westport, Conn.: Libraries Unlimited.

Web Site

AcqWeb. www.acqweb.org (accessed August 13, 2006).

CHAPTER 26

Access Services Librarian

CHRISTINE CIAMBELLA

Access Services operations at George Mason University include circulation, reserves, and collection maintenance. I am also responsible for coordinating the opening and closing of the law library and monitoring the circulation desk schedule to ensure complete coverage. To do this, I work closely with the two circulation managers (one for day and one for evening) who report directly to me. They in turn supervise the desk attendants. I also coordinate with other law library, law school, and university staff on building issues, including patron safety and security and library care and maintenance. Much of my job is administrative and preemptive. I try to address problems before they arise and try to implement policies and procedures that will ensure that the library runs as smoothly as possible.

A TYPICAL WORKDAY

One of the great pleasures of my job is the variety. I have three areas of responsibility: access services and circulation, reference, and training. For the purposes of this chapter, I shall focus on access services and circulation.

Access services is often the forgotten stepchild of the library world. Take a look at library literature and you'll find that most of it is devoted to reference, technology, and technical services. Access services encompasses the circulation system and the circulation desk staff. It also includes maintaining the collection and physical library building, developing policies on access and usage, and overseeing safety and security. Access services librarians make decisions about when their facility will be open and to whom, what materials will be loaned, and for how long they may be checked out.

A circulation staff member is often the first person a library patron sees or speaks with, so excellent customer service is our primary goal. We are also the troubleshooters for the library and our patrons. Questions and problems are usually submitted to us first. We refer patrons to the appropriate department: reference, technical services, computer services, or administration. We also get lots of questions not directly related to the library. Consequently, the circulation staff must keep abreast of events on the campus and stay informed of the areas of responsibility of the rest of the law school's departments to refer people correctly. We function as the information desk for the entire law school.

The circulation department maintains all reserve materials, both permanent and course reserves. Permanent reserves are popular items that circulate for a short period of time, typically only a few hours. Course reserves are items that a professor wishes to have readily available to students for his or her class. Reserve materials must comply with copyright guidelines, so our staff is very conscientious about keeping current with copyright rules and university policies. Many schools also use electronic reserves. There are many software options available for electronic reserves, and schools will often use their own mix of software. These systems allow a professor to post materials that the students can access from anywhere via computer. Course materials can include the syllabus, calendar, and assignments as well as supplemental reading. The access services staff will often assist a professor with setting up an electronic reserves system.

At George Mason, we are fortunate to have systems librarians who maintain the circulation databases and software. However, at many institutions, the circulation staff handles that responsibility as well.

The circulation staff regularly monitors our collection for problems needing attention and ensures that the books and materials are available and accessible to all of our patrons. We pay attention to patron activities and try to regulate behavior as appropriate. For example, our library is open to the public, but only for the purposes of legal research. We try to redirect people who wish to do other kinds of research, and we try to maintain a quiet, scholarly atmosphere to ensure the students have a comfortable place to study.

We also make sure that the physical plant is in good working order, and we work with other departments at the law school to resolve any issues concerning lighting, heat and air conditioning, cleanliness, and noise. We have to account for weather emergencies and ensure that the library is properly staffed during working hours.

For much of the day, the circulation desk is staffed by student workers. These are usually law students, although we occasionally hire from other graduate departments as well. Supervising these students requires some special considerations. By definition, the law students are temporary employees, and their first priority is their studies. We ask for a firm commitment from them regarding their schedules and are flexible when they need to miss shifts to accommodate assignments or other school-related activities. It's a balancing act, and it usually works pretty well. Most students are responsible and hardworking, even though library work is not their career goal.

We take advantage of the summer break, when there are fewer students and the library is quiet, to handle larger and less pressing projects. These include weeding and shifting the collection, updating maps and signs, working on long-term projects (for example, revising procedure manuals), and dealing with administrative issues. Each spring, the library director takes a survey of the law students and solicits their input on ways the library can improve. Many of our new projects are suggested by the students.

The circulation staff must be flexible and anticipate issues before they become problems. We are constantly evaluating our policies and procedures in light of experience and in response to suggestions from our patrons and the library staff. The old adage about an ounce of prevention certainly pertains to library work. We do allow for flexibility rather than rigid adherence to the rules. Every situation is different and we strive to resolve problems in a way that is most favorable to the patron and to the goal of the library. Our ultimate concern is providing a superior-quality library that meets both the research and studying needs of our students and faculty.

Access services can also be a catchall department for functions that do not clearly belong to reference or technical services. Some examples include interlibrary loan, disaster preparedness, photocopier and computer maintenance, and media services (videotaping lectures and special events for the university).

PROS AND CONS

The variety of work is the biggest plus. I never know what each day will bring. Of course, sometimes that is a curse and not a blessing, but on balance I would not change a thing. I am never bored. Academic settings also lend themselves more easily to self-enrichment. Obviously, education is highly valued, and management is supportive of career development. There are many opportunities to take on special projects that are not necessarily within my job description; thus, I am able to make my job my own.

I love working with students—both as a librarian and as an employer. Most of the time, our circulation desk is staffed by law student workers. Many of them are simply looking for a convenient job on campus, but others genuinely enjoy library work. Regardless, they have a fresh perspective that helps me look at my job with new ideas. Once they are trained, the students do a fabulous job; we could not run the library without them.

I also like helping the students, particularly the new ones. The circulation desk is an ideal place to ask all sorts of questions about the law school, not just the library, and it's rewarding to help first-year students get acclimated to this scary new experience called law school.

No job is perfect, and there are some things about mine that I would change if I could. By necessity, a good portion of my job is reactive rather than proactive. I come in to work with a general idea of what I'd like to accomplish, but that is sometimes derailed by the crisis of the day. I have learned to anticipate that possibility and to shift gears accordingly.

Additionally, I am constrained by the physical design of my work space. The GMU Law Library has a lovely open design, and staff offices are located on the perimeter. It is a beautiful space but not as functional as I would like. For example, I cannot see the circulation desk from my office. This requires me to manage by walking around to overcome the limitations of the space. I do not feel that I am as approachable sitting in my office. The reference suite (where I am located) looks like an office suite, and patrons and staff are constantly apologizing for "bothering" me.

HOW WOULD I GET A JOB LIKE YOURS?

Use every professional development opportunity that comes your way. My first library job required that I assist in teaching training classes, and I was terrified. Over time, I came to enjoy teaching, and my skills improved. That experience was a real asset, as instruction is a central element of working in an academic library.

Remember, too, that although you may not have the exact skill set for a particular job, some skills do translate into others and you may still be the most qualified candidate for the advertised position. For example, I had never worked with an automated circulation system before joining GMU. Most of my career was spent in the private sector, and many law firms do not use automated circulation systems. However, my reference, management, and training skills counterbalanced this lack of experience. I was able to quickly come up to speed on the circulation system.

I encourage everyone to join and participate in local and national professional organizations. They are an excellent way to meet your colleagues, enhance your skills and education, and give back to your profession. You will have a richer experience if you volunteer to work on a committee or project, rather than merely attend a program or meeting. You will also make contacts that not only enhance the richness of your professional life but also provide you with a wealth of resources in doing your work.

RELATED RESOURCES

Ciambella, Christine. 2005. Making the transition from law firm to law school. *Law Library Lights* 48 (Summer): 1–4.

CIRCPLUS. listserv.boisestate.edu/archives/circplus.html (accessed February 1, 2006).

Electronic Reserves Clearinghouse. www.mville.edu/administration/Staff/Jeff_Rosedale (accessed February 1, 2006).

Journal of Access Services. See www.haworthpress.com (accessed February 1, 2006).

U.S. Copyright Office. www.copyright.gov (accessed February 1, 2006).

Web Junction. webjunction.org/do/Home (accessed February 1, 2006).

CHAPTER 27

GIS/Data Librarian

My role as a GIS/data librarian focuses on geographic information systems (GIS) and is central to collecting, managing, disseminating, and teaching about geospatial data. Before discussing a typical day in my position, it is important to talk about GIS: what it is, who uses it, and how it is tied to librarianship.

WHAT IS GIS?

Although once only thought of in terms of the discipline of geography, GIS has become mainstream for viewing, analyzing, and mapping geospatial data. A GIS takes geospatial data (data about something on the Earth) and links it with nongraphic attributes (textual or statistical information). The result is a mapping technology with a database behind it. Almost all data can be mapped. In fact, it is said that 80 percent of all data has a geospatial component. Map creation is important because it allows us to view, understand, and analyze how things operate in the physical world.

Let's dispel a mistaken idea about GIS. A GIS is a *system*, not software. It is comprised of five components: hardware, software, data, people, and methods. See Table 27.1.

Who Uses GIS?

GIS can be used for a wide range of pursuits, both by the general public and by those in academia. In fact, it is used by the public every day. Vehicle navigation software such as Map-Quest or Yahoo! Maps is a GIS. Many automobiles are now equipped with a global positioning system (GPS) unit that is attached to a GIS to show road and route locations. The emergence and popularity of Google Earth points to the public's desire to view and manipulate geospatial data. In academic disciplines such as business, urban studies and planning, and conservation biology, faculty and students use GIS to analyze issues like new site locations for a business, where and how to construct a new community center, and depletion of a species of fish off the coast of Maine.

Components of a Geographic Information System (GIS)

Component	Details
Hardware	Computers, any computer networks, and peripheral devices such as printer or plotter.
Software	GIS software, as well as operating system software, database software, and any other software dealing with mapping or computer functions.
Data	One of the most crucial components of a GIS. Without data, it is impossible to map anything. Remember, even textual data can be geospatial. Data or statistics that relate to a specific country, county, ZIP code, or town can be mapped.
People	As with most computer-related programs, people are necessary to operate and explore the possibilities of the system.
Methods	Information professionals recognize the importance of guidelines, specifications, standards, and procedures. Spatial metadata standards, such as those created by the Federal Geographic Data Committee, ensure that data used in a GIS overlay properly and can be used together.

GIS Librarianship

The area of GIS librarianship is growing. Because GIS is the natural extension of print maps, many GIS librarians have the dual role of GIS and map librarian. Libraries that are fortunate enough to have both a GIS librarian and a map librarian, like the University of Maryland, are able to offer more services related to geospatial data. Data librarians, who report to the GIS librarian, are also becoming more common.

WHAT I DO

I am part of the Government Documents and Maps team at McKeldin Library. The University of Maryland has been a federal depository library since 1925 and the regional federal depository for Maryland, Delaware, and the District of Columbia since 1965. What does this mean and how do I fit in? The Government Documents and Maps Department receives government publications distributed through the U.S. Federal Depository Library Program (FDLP) (Title 44, USC). Many government publications distributed through the FDLP are geospatial, and a few, such as the National Gap Analysis Program publications of the U.S. Geological Survey (USGS), are in a format that either contain a GIS viewer or are only accessible by using outside third-party GIS software. That's where I come in. I make sure that members of the University of Maryland community (students, faculty, and staff) as well as the general public are able to access and use these data. GIS instruction in the form of workshops and individual appointments is available for free.

GIS Reference Service

I provide GIS reference service both by appointment and at the Government Documents and Maps reference desk. Although the number of appointments varies by semester, it is a growing demand on my time. Questions range from specific GIS data needs to assistance with functions, such as plotting locations (geocoding) or spatial analysis. As the GIS/data librarian, my role is to assist and teach patrons, not complete projects for them.

Teaching GIS Workshops

Although not every library with GIS services offers instruction, it is one of McKeldin Library's strongest features. In fact, one of the best parts of my job is teaching. We are a federal depository library and are charged with providing free access to information to everyone. The Government Documents and Maps Department chooses to meet this charge and extend access to include the GIS workshops as well. A series of free workshops are offered every semester that introduce the ArcGIS Desktop software. ArcGIS is a popular software program produced by ESRI. The workshops are by no means comprehensive, but they offer a foundation for those who are interested in GIS. Held in the computer instruction labs, these workshops are hands-on and include color workbooks for class participants.

In addition to the series of library workshops, I create individual GIS classes tailored to specific university courses, such as Introduction to Transportation Logistics (business), Urban Forestry (agriculture and natural resources), and Conservation Biology (biology).

Government Documents and Maps Team

Because I work in a federal depository library, the remainder of my responsibilities is tied to the Government Documents and Maps team. These activities, which include government documents reference, collection development, and maintenance of the GIS workstations in the library, still allow me to focus on GIS but also set aside time for me to grow both as a government documents librarian and an academic librarian.

Non-GIS reference includes desk hours at the service desk and digital reference for the state of Maryland. These reference duties help me keep my other reference skills sharp. I also assist the map librarian with print map resources as needed. Although the Government Documents and Maps Department has a small budget, I contribute to the collection development initiatives of the department for print cartographic information, GIS-related texts, and data purchases. I also make recommendations for software purchases, which come out of the library's budget. Last, I coordinate with the library's Information Technology Division to maintain the department's GIS workstations. This includes troubleshooting, installing software, and coordinating technical support from GIS software companies and the campus Office of Information Technology.

A TYPICAL DAY

A large part of a typical day is spent in front of the computer. I answer patron questions via phone and e-mail. In addition, I spend a great deal of time preparing for appointments (finding data and testing out tools and functions to see how best to analyze and display that data). The only way to become proficient with GIS is to use it as often as possible. Notice that I did not mention mastering GIS. Very few GIS librarians or professionals would—or should—claim mastery. After the period of preparation (which varies from minutes to days), my time is spent instructing patrons how to complete GIS projects.

In addition to the time I spend working with individual patrons, a large portion of my time is spent focusing on group instruction. In 2005 a significant GIS software upgrade on all of the computers was completed. Because the new software contained a completely different interface and additional applications, this upgrade warranted an almost total revision of instruction materials. Library GIS instruction, in combination with specific workshops given to university classes, generally accounts for one to two days of my week.

Future plans involving geospatial data take up a portion of my day as well. The 2005 ESRI International User Conference discussed a vision for the future of GIS in which geospatial data from all over the world would be easily accessible via the Web through portals. Although this is far from the reality, in 2005 the U.S. government made great strides toward this goal by creating the Geospatial One Stop. I'm working to create a similar portal in Maryland with agreements between the University of Maryland and each county to obtain the most requested data, such as building footprints, land parcels, and zoning. The ultimate goal is to provide a service where students, faculty, and staff can review metadata about GIS files and then directly access the files that meet their needs from data stored on a library server or from the counties themselves.

The remainder of my time is devoted to such things as providing and attending staff training, reference at the government documents desk, digital reference, committee/staff meetings, and maintaining GIS-related Web pages. Because librarians at the University of Maryland have faculty status, I also spend time working on projects for promotion and permanent status. This involves development of the areas of librarianship, service, and scholarship.

PROS AND CONS

In truth, my job is full of pros and cons. Depending on the day, there are certain facets of each that can seem positive or negative. In the end, however, the pros significantly outweigh the cons.

Pros

GIS is constantly changing! The most positive aspect of this job is that I learn something every day. GIS and its software are changing so quickly that very little feels routine. For instance, new versions of software with moderate changes come out about every six months. Substantial changes in software have emerged every year or two.

The realm of GIS in the library rests with my position. Because GIS requires very specific knowledge, most libraries only have one GIS specialist. I take pride in shaping the GIS program.

I interact with many different people. This interaction helps me stay connected with the many exciting things people in other disciplines are doing. In addition, because I work at a federal depository library, I also assist members of the general public. For example, last spring I had the opportunity to assist a dentist with the mapping of dental offices that accept certain types of insurance.

A large university has a lot of opportunities. Working at the University of Maryland has a certain amount of prestige and offers wonderful personal and work-related benefits. It is exciting to be a part of such a wonderful institution.

Cons

GIS is constantly changing! Because technology is progressing so quickly, it is challenging to stay attuned to all of the changes and new developments in GIS.

The realm of GIS in the library rests with my position. Because GIS librarianship is both relatively new and very specialized, there are times when I feel isolated. Most librarians do not know GIS, and most GIS specialists do not know the library. I'm very fortunate to have made excellent connections with fellow GIS librarians across the country. This network of colleagues has made all the difference.

I interact with many different people. I found that as demand for GIS instruction increases, so do expectations. Programs on campus want more classes, classes that address more difficult functions, and classes that are geared specifically to their discipline.

A large university has some degree of bureaucracy. I've found that things are not accomplished very quickly. It's frustrating that in a field as fast moving as GIS, plans for services and data often take a long time to implement.

HOW WOULD I GET A JOB LIKE YOURS?

It is incorrect to assume that to get a position using GIS one has to have an advanced degree in geography or GIS. Although a strong knowledge of and experience with GIS is preferred, it is not the only skill required. In fact, my undergraduate degree is in English. I was fortunate to learn GIS through a graduate assistantship while I was in library school studying for an MLS. Through this assistantship I gained valuable experience with GIS, but of equal importance was the experience I gained with teaching, data, maps, government documents, and reference. I highly suggest that you volunteer or work at a library that has a map collection. These libraries often also offer GIS services. Make sure your computer skills are up to date. Read and research GIS, practice using GIS software, and make contacts with librarians who are familiar with GIS. Most important, be willing and excited to continue learning.

RELATED RESOURCES

Adler, Prudence S. 1995. Special issue of geographic information systems (GIS) and academic libraries: An introduction. *Journal of Academic Librarianship* 21, no. 4: 233–35.

Boisse, Joseph A., and Mary Larsgaard. 1995. GIS in academic libraries: A managerial perspective. *Journal of Academic Librarianship* 21, no. 4: 288–91.

Shawa, Tsering Wangyal. 2002. What should a GIS librarian do? Paper presented at the ALA Map and Geography Round Table, June 17. magert.whoi.edu/conf/2002/whatgis.pdf (accessed August 20, 2006).

CHAPTER 28

Metadata Specialist

I run a cost recovery unit from within the cataloging department of the Massachusetts Institute of Technology Libraries. The libraries sought me as an innovative and energetic professional with experience in nontraditional cataloging (i.e., non-MARC metadata) to supervise the Metadata Services Unit, which provides metadata solutions for collections outside the libraries. I don't catalog a single object, digital or otherwise, that is part of the libraries' mandate to provide information resources to the institute.

Instead I provide metadata consulting and production support for MIT departments, administrative units, labs, and grant-funded projects. These organizations have an interest in sharing their own data and digital objects with the world, either by publishing a Web site, creating a podcast, or building a data repository. They need to strategically employ metadata to accomplish their goals. I provide answers to their metadata questions, and I charge them for my work.

It is extremely uncommon to find a service point in a library that is focused on its communities' attempts to build their own libraries. It is even rarer for that service point to attempt to recover its costs. However, we fit right in at MIT.

The unit is part of MIT's entrepreneurial spirit. The MIT Libraries have no significant digital library program of their own. We have recognized that the MIT community isn't waiting for us to deliver digital teaching and research objects; it's actively engaged in the process of creating these objects every day. If there is an information service that is needed, someone will go ahead and build it without consulting the library. They may even repurpose our content along the way. The MIT Libraries do not fear this tendency by our patrons to think that they can do a better job of organizing digital information resources. We want to share our many years' worth of collective wisdom. Lecture videos, data sets, and technical reports are all "born digital" at MIT. They all need metadata to be preserved and disseminated as widely as possible in the spirit of academic openness. Open access is another idea that has captured the minds of the MIT community, and the libraries have been active participants in realizing this goal.

My primary work is developing metadata structures for my clients. Most people, librarians included, think of metadata as similar to the library catalog. I've found that this sort of descriptive metadata is just the beginning of my clients' needs. I also help organize and package complex objects like whole courses that include lecture videos, assignments, reading lists, and applications. Developing structural metadata models, I help clients like DSpace at MIT share educational resources with the world.

A significant portion of the services I provide is teaching and training. Often I don't actually do any of the metadata creation. Instead I provide metadata recommendations, best practices, and user guides, and I meet with the staff that will be creating metadata to walk them through the tricky parts.

I've spent a lot of time recently assisting clients with the preparation of RSS feeds and podcasts. Podcast fever has reached MIT. The administration is strongly committed to making these new technologies easy for the uninitiated and I get to be a part of that. MIT has begun discussion with Apple about joining their new iTunes U initiative, and I have been asked to join this discussion to help participants prepare metadata that enriches the user experience.

One of the best aspects of my position is the opportunity to collaborate with other organizations within MIT. I've found myself part of a suite of services the institute offers for the complete digital publishing process. Again our mission is to make things easier for anyone who wants to share the results of his or her teaching and research. I work with units that provide Web development and audio/video creation services to guide projects from start to finish. I've achieved brand recognition as the metadata expert.

This recognition hasn't come easy. I spend a great deal of time on business development, aggressively marketing my services. Whenever I can, I help my clients write their grant applications to ensure that metadata concerns are adequately addressed.

My position is not permanent. I started with a two-year agreement, and each year the finances of the unit are reviewed to determine whether the libraries can commit to supporting my work for another year. Ideally, I am 100 percent cost recovery, though the libraries do commit to cover any shortfall each year. Fortunately, we have been able to generate a surplus our first two years and have been able to create a reserve to cover the lean times.

A TYPICAL WORKDAY

The best way to provide a clear picture of the work I do is to walk through an average workday. My best days are full of meetings. On my worst I seem to answer e-mail all day.

A Good Day

On a very typical day this past year, I met with the Client Services Group of MIT's Information Services and Technology department. IS&T had received a directive (but not yet a plan) to aggregate podcasts. We discussed what it might mean to let the world know that the institute is podcasting and what service we need to provide to our community to support their podcasts. At this meeting, the other consultants who form the institute's suite of digital publishing services and I shared our enthusiasm and vision for academic podcasting. Two weeks later, I received an invitation to submit a proposal to prepare the user guide for podcast metadata. The user guide was to take the form of a Web tutorial that explains RSS and makes it easy to create a podcast.

Later that day I met with my main client, MIT OpenCourseWare (OCW), to review and assign priorities for the current list of consulting projects. OCW had been the original impetus for the creation of my position when they came to the library for help preparing metadata for their Web publication of educational material. Our early consulting and production work for OCW was very traditional. We defined a metadata structure for them to use in creating descriptive records of their objects, found the right encoding scheme (IEEE Learning Object

Metadata), prepared some rules for formatting metadata values, and defined some controlled vocabularies. At this point in our working relationship, they want to shift efforts on their behalf from this metadata production to consulting projects that will find new avenues for metadata dissemination that increases the discovery and use of their materials.

OCW is in the enviable position of having a great body of content (around 1,500 full courses) that needs as many and as varied channels of distribution as possible. Their ideas include preparing compact discs to send to Africa, where Internet access is unreliable, depositing their content in a preservation archive like the libraries' own DSpace, where it will still be available one hundred years from now, and sending metadata to federated repositories like MERLOT and the National Science Digital Library, and they are especially interested in getting it distributed via Google and iTunes.

This has led them to refocus the preparation of metadata for use by external search engines. Cataloging for systems you don't control is very different from traditional library cataloging. Wherever possible, you refrain from localizing standards. Along with your metadata, you must prepare and publish meta-metadata that provides all the necessary information to interpret your records. You also have to accept the fact that your metadata will be reformatted and edited and your objects will be represented in new ways. You have to relinquish control over your metadata, which is often difficult for libraries.

For the OCW meeting on this day, I prepared a plan for assessment of our metadata in light of the new channels at iTunes and Google. OCW is actively pursuing the deposition of their content in iTunes via podcast and other means. For this they want to create RSS feeds and write their metadata directly onto audio and video files via ID3 tags. So I recommend ways to programmatically restructure and republish their existing metadata in new formats.

The people at OCW are also interested in having their content prominently represented in the new Google Search Appliance (GSA) that was implemented at MIT to search its Web sites. Interestingly, my simple early assessment showed that the GSA was no better at providing access to OCW content than OCW's existing search engine. It has its own different limitations. The crucial difference is that the GSA breaks down where users who are familiar with Google expect their search engine to break down. This is another important lesson for libraries: understand your users' perception of information technology and design your solutions for their expected behavior. Libraries have a tendency to prepare metadata for the 1 percent of its users who will use all the advanced features. The Metadata Services Unit makes metadata recommendations that solve the problems of the 80 percent of users who have simple needs. Our clients are willing to spend the 20 percent of their potential effort that will reach these users and no more.

On a later day, when Google released a new version of the GSA that was more active in its use of metadata, IS&T Client Services approached me to review Google's documentation and devise an MIT-wide solution for implementing the GSA in such a way that metadata created in any format at MIT would be properly indexed.

Back at the metadata projects review, we discussed checklists for the current metadata projects, which involve preparing metadata for export to the library's digital archives, where old content would be shipped via IMS content packages.

After discussing podcasts and meeting with OCW, I then happily spent the rest of the day researching the technical specifics of RSS. This is the true joy of my work. I can never stop learning new technologies. My clients always want to know about the latest and greatest. Often this means that I have to be willing to purport to have expertise on a subject that I then have to go and figure out, but I am comfortable staying just one step ahead of my clients. This is a recognized part of my service—that I will figure out what's coming next and be ready to fit it into their existing process.

A Bad Day

The greatest difficulty of this position is scheduling an even workload. Juggling numerous projects leads me to large spikes in the amount of work I must do under a tight deadline.

There are no bad days, but the most difficult generally involve the intrusion of administrative responsibilities on my efforts to finish all of my work. I sometimes find it challenging to meet my clients' needs while also corresponding with potential clients, responding to existing clients' emergency demands, preparing marketing materials and programs on time, and keeping up with necessary documentation. Although I know my projects and responsibilities would be of interest to my colleagues in the field, I find that I rarely have time to write for publication.

BEING A METADATA SPECIALIST

When I first took this position in the MIT Libraries several years ago, I conducted a quick survey of the field. I found only a handful of other metadata librarians at academic institutions around the country, and only Cornell University was running a cost-recovery metadata unit. I attended the Digital Library Forum, where I met a couple dozen brand-new metadata librarians. We've even started our own e-mail list.

I'm encouraged to see all the new positions and to see many of them, like mine, involved in collaboration with organizations outside the library to make information accessible. The increased need for information professionals with experience beyond the library catalog is reaching nearly every library, big, small, academic, public, or special.

This need is reflected in the increased availability of degree programs in digital libraries. I encourage any interested parties to study the basics of cataloging and indexing, but also information architecture, social software, XML, and most important, project management. The most pressing need of digital libraries is good, pragmatic project managers.

PROS AND CONS

There are three things that make metadata work worthwhile. One is working with colleagues outside your own library on groundbreaking resource-sharing projects. You need to be willing to be an ambassador for the library, to bring your experience organizing information to a broader audience. You also have to be willing to admit that you don't have all the answers and rely on your metadata colleagues for good advice and feedback. Don't be afraid to be wrong. All of this metadata work is still relatively new, and everyone is figuring it out as they go along. You should also want to be an ambassador for users to your library colleagues, sharing the experience of helping library patrons struggle to organize their own information. Metadata specialists have an opportunity to influence the way the library does its work to take advantage of new technologies and make sure our work meets user expectations.

The second great thing about metadata work is constantly learning new things and getting paid to do it. Make sure that your employer expects this of you and gives you the opportunity to stay abreast of the ever-changing technological landscape.

Finally, the best part of metadata work is being part of the solution. I find it really satisfying to see millions using what I helped build. If this is your goal, you're on the right track.

RELATED RESOURCES

The user guide for podcast tagging I wrote is at web.mit.edu/ist/podcasts/podcasting_user_guide.pdf (accessed March 14, 2006).

DSpace at MIT. dspace.mit.edu (accessed March 14, 2006).
DSpace Federation. dspace.org (accessed March 14, 2006).
MIT Libraries, Metadata Services Unit. libraries.mit.edu/metadata (accessed March 14, 2006).
MIT OpenCourseWare. ocw.mit.edu (accessed March 14, 2006).
Podcasts at MIT. web.mit.edu/ist/podcasts (accessed March 14, 2006).

CHAPTER 29

Systems Librarian

DORIS J. VAN KAMPEN

A BIT OF MUSING

Librarianship is a rich and rewarding profession that has come to rely heavily on information technology as the conduit to information. This has been both a bane and a blessing; after all, we now have so many more powerful tools available to us. Yet many prognosticators are calling for the demise of librarianship; libraries (and by association, librarians) are depicted in the popular culture of America as critical, unfriendly, frumpy, outdated, and easily replaced by the Internet.

On the other hand, computers are, to many people, more than a tool; they invite the user into new worlds and relationships with a click of a mouse. One may escape into an online world where information is available for the asking, without any of the negative feelings that may be engendered when using tools and resources with which one is unfamiliar or encountering less-than-friendly information professionals.

Yet people need libraries and librarians. We just need to work on our image, leading the way to a future filled with books, e-books, and all kinds of print and nonprint materials—a friendly, inviting, mentally invigorating space, MP3s and all.

JOB DESCRIPTION

Defining a systems librarian's job as "systems" is a bit like saying that reference librarians "answer questions," especially at smaller academic institutions where everyone tends to wear more than one hat. The formal job description of a systems librarian can only go so far in reflecting reality, leaving unavailable a concise yet useful definition for anyone who asks, "So what do you do at the library?" I could say that I maintain the library Web site, administer the information systems, run the proxy server, contact vendors for technical support as needed, provide training to staff, and so on. Although that might cover the nuts and bolts of the job, it does not accurately describe it.

One useful yet vague description I have developed is "A systems librarian works to make access to information more seamless and user-friendly by creating or implementing resources and services that allow users to complete their tasks more quickly and efficiently." It is the art and science of melding technical expertise with the principles of fair use, and the professional training of a librarian with the capabilities of the systems and the wishes of the user. My job is making optimum use of today's technology without forgetting to include the personal touch. It requires the ability to think on one's feet, work peacefully with many different kinds of people, and to know when to call for outside assistance. It also means being the bridge for several diverse populations, advertising technology changes and the reasons behind them in a manner that does not gloss over potential problems while still communicating the need for the change or upgrade. Setting the right tone for effective and peaceful relations can sometimes be difficult, as everyone may feel the need for greater control over the continued "rising tide of technology."[1]

A systems librarian position at a small academic library is a blend of public services and technical services. On the public services side, I work with circulation, media services, and reference to make the OPAC and library Web site more user-oriented and staff-friendly. There are four broad public service questions I work to address within the framework of my position: Can my patrons find the information they are looking for in a timely and reasonable way? How can we help them when they are not physically here in the building? What technology, resources, or services would make the information search easier? What technologies that are currently being used outside the library have potential within the library? On the technical services side, I work with several departments, bulk-importing MARC records, running reports, generating and posting new titles lists, creating online forms, troubleshooting equipment, and occasionally conducting training. The questions addressed when working with this user group are necessarily different: What equipment or staff person needs my attention now or in the near future? What projects am I currently working on or should I be working on? Are there any reports, queries, or meetings on the task list? Which projects or other commitments that I have made need the most attention?

There are always several items waiting for my attention, usually a couple of short-term projects, a few more long-term projects, and one or two upcoming systems- or network-related events. Migrating to a new server, downloading MARC records and completing a bulk import, determining what kinds of information are needed from usage statistics, setting up e-reserves each semester, updating the proxy server settings, tweaking the OPAC, updating the online forms, discussing with the Office of Information Technology cooperative projects (such as the portal or the integration of the library orientation into student records for tracking purposes), or improving the usability of the Web site, for example, are all part of my job.

A TYPICAL WORKDAY

When I walk into the library in the morning, if there is something urgent, usually someone is waiting in what I jokingly call "ambush mode." If nothing has occurred that needs my immediate attention, I go downstairs to my office and check voicemail and e-mail. Then I go back upstairs for a cruise by the reference desk and a possible stop in the workroom to check my mailbox before wandering into Technical Services. This wandering has a purpose because sometimes I hear things and can assist with potential problems before they become bigger simply by being available.

Next stop is back downstairs to read e-mail, including several critical e-mail lists, and to check the calendar for appointments, reference hours, and meetings. Usually by this time there have been several small issues to deal with, such as the network being slow (call OIT and ask the network people if they are aware of the problem and when it might be resolved) or a database not performing as it should (verify problem, call or e-mail vendor's support desk).

If I have reference desk duty, I am back upstairs for at least two hours, answering the reference desk e-mail and the phone, as well as assisting walk-in patrons. If I am in my office and not on the desk, I might receive a few forwarded calls from patrons who "can't get in," or I might be asked to address a copyright question or deal with issues related to the university portal, a new and interesting thread in the day's fabric. If I am in my office, I try to review my to do list and then, depending on the time of month, I will also work on vendor reports, send out e-mails to OIT concerning any issues we have noticed in the library (we are one of the university's most highly trafficked sites and heaviest users of technology), deal with nagging problems that can't be solved in a few minutes, work on short-term or long-term projects, fulfill requests from library staff for assistance, and try to catch up on other issues that may be awaiting attention.

A TYPICAL WORKWEEK

Just as a typical day has a pattern, a typical workweek has ebbs and flows. Mondays and Tuesdays are the busiest, as I work most of my reference hours on those days, and if I have a course overload, I teach as well. Wednesdays and Thursdays tend to have more meetings than other days of the week, and Fridays are the days with the fewest meetings and a lighter reference schedule. If it is a Friday, I prioritize my to do list for the following week and touch base with Media Services and OIT to see if there are any potential issues or scheduled downtimes for any of the university servers for the weekend. If there is nothing pressing, I try to catch up on the professional literature, reading and (if I see something of interest) e-mailing snippets of articles or citations to other librarians and interested parties so that I can get one or more journals passed on to the next person.

In a typical month, I spend an average of fifteen hours in meetings; thirty to forty hours reading e-mail lists and responding to e-mail; twenty-five to thirty-five hours on the reference desk; thirty-five to fifty hours on projects, tasks, reports, troubleshooting, or other technology-related issues; and three to five hours on professional reading. I also try to block out some time for research or writing (most of my research and writing is done during academic holidays or on my vacation).

PROS AND CONS

This is a small- to medium-sized academic library; the librarians here wear many hats and serve several diverse populations, including militarily deployed students, traditional students, and nontraditional students. The job is rarely boring because there's always a project in the works. Equipment breaks, people change their computer settings and can't get programs to work, connections get lost, databases stop allowing logins, and Web pages disappear. You get to work with books and people who love books. You also get to play with computers and investigate new solutions and new programs, though not usually as much as you really should to stay current.

I enjoy my job very much. I enjoy computers (though I do not consider myself a true computer geek), and I like helping people. The day is fairly varied—something always comes up that needs to be resolved. I have a good working relationship with OIT and the database providers; I know I can count on support when it is needed.

However, I am the only techie librarian in my small academic library. That has positive and negative aspects. When something is not working, I may need to drop everything and try to fix it. There is no other techie with a library perspective I can share ideas and consult with concerning technology, systems, resources, and services. I depend heavily on the e-mail lists for that kind of mentoring and technical support. Other cons include time and assigned duties. Time is a real issue. The staff roster is fairly small, there is very little flexibility in scheduling, and we are open long hours. There is also little opportunity for promotion, and turnover has been somewhat high, resulting in little institutional history and limited documentation from previous efforts or initiatives.

EDUCATION AND TRAINING

An MLS or MIS from an accredited school is required at most institutions. Additional ongoing training is strongly recommended, as your skill set will need to keep up with changes in technology and society. The ability to assimilate new knowledge quickly and good communication skills are highly valuable assets for a systems librarian. An interest in computers as educational and information-finding tools is crucial to reduce the likelihood of burnout.

If you have an undergraduate degree in computer science or have taken graduate-level classes in instructional technology or computer information systems, you will be better prepared. You can also take classes in systems, computer information science, and instructional design as part of your MIS or MLS. If you are already working as a librarian in another position, you can attend professional development workshops and take additional classes to increase your technical knowledge. Previous work as a technical services librarian, technology specialist, or within an IT department can also be an asset. "What is important to remember is that technical skills can be acquired . . . what matters most is your openness to learning, your capacity to both embrace and facilitate change, and your foundation in the principles of librarianship."[2] Showing an interest and taking some initiative to participate in various technology-related projects will indicate to your supervisor and others that you are willing to learn and grow in this area.

Don't get discouraged if you are not offered a position the first time it becomes available; do show your interest if an opportunity presents itself. Sometimes it's a matter of being in the right place at the right time and selling yourself as a viable candidate.

HOW TO GET THIS GREAT JOB

There are numerous avenues to pursue when seeking a systems librarian position. If you have an MLS or MIS with a computer background, it is much easier to find a position; however, even if you don't, there are other ways of breaking in to this area of librarianship. If the systems librarian leaves the institution where you're working and you are interested in the job, speak up—opportunity is knocking! Just make sure you are prepared. Attend relevant workshops and, if possible, look to systems librarians for advice and mentoring; offer to be their backup if needed, and do some networking with other technology professionals.

I was very fortunate when this opportunity knocked on my door; I was working on my dissertation, and I needed to work fewer hours. I quit my job as a media specialist at a local high school and started asking around. I had worked as the unofficial network administrator and technology coordinator for several years and had also taken courses in instructional technology at a local university. I had a smattering of Unix knowledge and could competently troubleshoot Macs and PCs for most computer-related issues, thanks to a few friends and lots of hands-on experience. A friend knew the university had just lost its systems librarian. It was a terrific opportunity, one that I am glad I pursued. If you are interested in computers, Web page design, making the library more accessible online, and working with people and computers, then I encourage you to explore your opportunities.

NOTES

1. Edward Proctor. 2004. Mind the gap. *American Libraries* 35, no. 5: 46–48.
2. Rachel Singer Gordon. 2003. *The accidental systems librarian*. Medford, N.J.: Information Today.

RELATED RESOURCES

Print Resources

Hardesty, Larry, ed. 2000. *Books, bytes, and bridges: Libraries and computer centers in academic institutions*. Chicago: American Library Association.

Ingersoll, Patricia, and John Culshaw. 2004. *Managing information technology: A handbook for systems librarians*. Westport, Conn.: Libraries Unlimited.

Morgan, Eric Lease. 2004. Systems administration requires people skills. *Computers in Libraries* 19, no. 3: 36–37. Also available online at www.infomotions.com/musings/systems-administration (accessed June 26, 2006).

Rossman, Doralyn. 2003. Twenty tips for becoming more computer savvy: Or, how to think like a systems librarian. *PNLA Quarterly* 68, no. 1: 21–22.

Internet Resources

Digital Librarian. digitallibrarian.org (accessed June 26, 2006).

Houghton-Jan, Sarah. *Librarian in Black*. www.librarianinblack.net (accessed June 26, 2006).

Information Today. infotoday.com (accessed June 26, 2006).

Library and Information Technology Association. www.lita.org (accessed June 26, 2006).

LISNews. www.lisnews.com (accessed June 26, 2006).

Search Engine Watch. searchenginewatch.com (accessed June 26, 2006).

CHAPTER 30

Technology Librarian in a Developing Country

The ICT (Information and Communications Technology) Unit at Nigeria's Federal University of Technology Owerri was the result of the adoption of ICT in library operations. As the head of the unit, I report to the university librarian and am responsible for the management of staff and resources in the unit.

Staff management involves a number of responsibilities. I must ensure that the right caliber of staff is employed or deployed in the unit. These staff members must not only be knowledgeable in academic library operations but also must be computer literate or have the capacity to learn the rudiments of computer operation. I also schedule jobs for the staff based on the operational needs of the unit and am responsible for evaluating and disciplining them according to the university's standard for the appraisal of academic and nonacademic staff.

Management of ICT resources includes acquiring, processing, storing, and ensuring effective utilization of ICT facilities. The facilities presently available in the ICT Unit include computers and their accessories, databases, CD-ROMs, networked computers for the eGranary digital library, public address systems, overhead projectors, and televisions and related accessories.

As head of the unit, I am a member of the university library management, and I advise the management on automation of the university library. I also represent the university librarian in the ICT Directorate of the university and the School of Agriculture and Agricultural Technology's Board of Studies.

A TYPICAL WORKDAY

In the morning of every workday, I usually start with general university library housekeeping, such as shelving and shelving supervision. On a particularly eventful day, I was scheduled to supervise shelving of print materials. I drove to the university library premises at 7:30 a.m., entered my office for meditation, and then moved to the stack areas to ensure proper shelving by the scheduled staff. Individual unit operation in the library starts at 8:30 after these housekeeping activities are completed.

When I got to my office, I confirmed with the ICT staff that all the computer systems were booted. Settling down, I instructed the ICT officer for CD lending, writing, and searching of databases to start attending to users even though it was not yet our scheduled opening time. The staff in charge of CD processing was busy with the newly acquired CDs, and the clerical staff responsible for processing the unit's correspondence was typing a memo to the university librarian (UL) requesting a new scanner. Then the attendant in the UL's office came to inform me that the UL needed to see me.

When I arrived at his office, the UL requested information on the status of Internet access donation by the Open Society Initiative for West Africa (OSIWA). He also wanted my opinion on the Alice for Windows library software, which the university library plans to acquire, and he also asked how users are responding to a newly acquired database and the eGranary digital library. Finally, he also sought my opinion on the need for the university library to design and host its own Web site. I responded that OSIWA, an international nongovernmental organization (NGO), may not disappoint the university, but in the event it was unable to donate the Internet access we need, the university should make every effort to provide Internet facilities in the library by soliciting help from other NGOs or donor agencies. Internet access in the library will help us derive benefits including free online databases, virtual library access, and others (Benson 2001). My advice on library software acquisition was based on the knowledge I have acquired from seminars, workshops, and conferences, and readings like those of Rowley (1993) and Burton and Petrie (1991). I also informed him that the university library is overdue for a Web site. Though we need to contract that work out to an expert, I can advise and coordinate the articulation of the Web site's content using the knowledge I have gained by reading appropriate materials.

Back in my office, the officer in charge of public services told me about a staff member in the engineering school who needed to perform an Internet search on triangular distribution. I had to assign one of the library staff the responsibility of conducting the search in one of the cybercafés outside the university because the Internet is not accessible within.

Suddenly a staff member reported that one of the systems was hanging while the printer could not respond to a command. I instructed him to cancel all commands, exit all programs, reboot, and possibly check the printer toner.

The technical services librarian came in to ask for advice on some of the basic requirements of his staff for effective participation in the automation project that will begin soon. I replied that they should have basic computer application literacy and should also endeavor to read computer books written by Parker (2003) and O'Leary and O'Leary (1994). We are going to make training part of the software and hardware package during acquisition. We are also planning to organize training for library users on the use of the workstations.

It was 11 a.m., and I had to attend a School of Agriculture and Agricultural Technology Board of Studies meeting. In the meeting I introduced two new resources to which the university library had recently subscribed: the online portal AGORA (Access to Global Online Research in Agriculture), set up by the Food and Agriculture Organization of the United Nations and major publishers, and eGranary, a WiderNet project that provides digital educational resources to libraries without Internet access. I took time to explain the content of each product so the board members would have a full understanding of their importance to teaching and research. I also asked them to communicate the information to their students.

Back to my office; it was 3:30. What a hectic day, but I needed to gather literature for the proposed article on the university local content. I also needed to read more on the software selection to better advise library management and read more literature on Internet browsing because the university community has come to rely heavily on us for that service. "Oh, I will do those readings at night," I said to myself. "I need to get home and rest."

JOYS AND CHALLENGES

The position of ICT librarian is highly dignified yet filled with challenges. The enviable and dignified nature of my position stems from a number of sources. It gives me a lot of joy to identify and interact with computer engineers and scientists. I have this opportunity when I represent the university librarian in the ICT Directorate of our technological university. I am also exposed to issues and concepts outside the traditional library and information science domain. By so doing I not only learn but am challenged to read and make recommendations on areas that may be alien to me.

The image of the university library is always boosted when I help faculty members find information outside of traditional print sources or give them advice on software and hardware. Thus faculty has come to appreciate libraries and librarians as an integral part of the ever-developing global information society and the university's teaching and research efforts.

Serving as a clearinghouse for all the operations and services in the university library enhances my knowledge of what constitutes university library management. I can only advise on the application of ICT or effectively apply it in the library's operations when I am well grounded in those operations. I expose myself to effective reading and also participate actively in traditional library operations as the need arises.

Despite the institutional and personal gains of this job, the position of the ICT librarian is not easy. Just as the university library is the pivot point around which a university's academic activities revolve, the library's provision of state-of-the-art information using technology revolves around the ICT librarian and the services provided by the unit. I am held responsible for any failure in that aspect. Such high expectations are often not met due to some encumbrances faced by the library. Inadequacy and inefficiency in the areas of software, hardware, and infrastructure tend to impede or, in many cases, bring to a halt all the operations in the unit or the entire library. Poor understanding of the operations in the unit by the university management engenders inadequate support in the areas of finance and training. Underdevelopment of society hampers the availability of infrastructure the unit needs to function effectively, such as electricity and telephone facilities.

Low computer literacy of library users imposes extra tasks for those working with database services. Staff have to make an extra effort to help users who cannot perform effective searches by themselves. In most cases, reference interactions do not elicit the needed information from the users due to poor computer literacy. Furthermore, my limited knowledge and skill in systems maintenance, troubleshooting, and networking often slows down activities in the unit when I am not able to rectify a technical breakdown.

JOB REQUIREMENTS

Though I was previously a cataloger in the technical services unit of the university library, I was called on (as a result of my interest in computers and their accessories) to expand the learning resource center in the library by integrating the new information infrastructure: computers and related equipment and telecommunication facilities.

Before this initiative began, I had acquired training on computer literacy outside the university's sponsorship and was able to write a proposal on the need to have a unit that could provide information resources to the university community using emerging information technology. I started reading books and journal articles on library automation, information technology in libraries, computer science, applications software, and so on. Fully armed with such knowledge, I was able to convince the university library's management of the need to acquire computers. The learning resource center (audiovisual unit) of the library was then converted to the IT unit, now called the ICT unit. I was then asked to staff and develop it.

Though this process is how the ICT unit in my library evolved, I believe such units' development in other developing countries may vary. However, some basic skills are required of an ICT/automation/systems librarian in a developing country like Nigeria. Based on my membership in the IT Section of the Nigerian Library Association, I have identified a number of skills such a librarian needs.

An ICT/systems librarian must be able to advise the library on software, hardware, and staffing needed for the automation of the library, and in most cases will be the one to plan and execute such an automation project. He or she must be able to integrate the Internet and all its paraphernalia into the operations of the library, including the design and maintenance of the library's Web site. The ICT librarian must be in a position to troubleshoot in the event of a breakdown or ensure the availability of a technician who can achieve such troubleshooting. He or she must be knowledgeable in digitization of information resources. Above all, the individual should be well grounded in traditional library operations.

Hence being an ICT, automation, or systems librarian in this part of the world requires basic knowledge of computer hardware, software, and networking and how to apply them to library operations; creating and searching databases; programming; digitization procedures; and management of library resources in print or electronic form. Such a person should also be in a position to keep abreast of developments in academic library management through reading and attending workshops on ICT application to library and information science.

RELATED RESOURCES

Benson, Allen C. 2001. *Neal-Schuman complete Internet companion for libraries*, 2nd ed. New York: Neal-Schuman.

Burton, Paul F., and J. Howard Petrie. 1991. *Information management technology: A librarian's guide*. London: Chapman and Hall.

Kalbag, A. *Build your own Web site*. India: Navneet Publications (I) Limited. www.navneet.com (accessed December, 18, 2005).

O'Leary, Timothy J., and Linda I. O'Leary. 1994. *McGraw-Hill computing essentials*. New York: McGraw-Hill.

Parker, Charles S., and Deborah Morley. 2003. *Understanding computers: Today and tomorrow*. Fort Worth, Tex.: Dryden Press.

Rowley, J.E. 1993. *Computers for libraries*, 3rd ed. London: Library Association Publishing.

Umeano, E. 2000. *TMT teach yourself Excel 2000*. Enugu, Nigeria: TMT Press.

Webster, Kathleen, and Kathryn Paul. *Beyond surfing: Tools and techniques for searching the Web*. www.bstc.az/html/it96jan.htm (accessed December 18, 2005).

CHAPTER 31

Human Resources Librarian

JENIFER ABRAMSON

As an academic human resources librarian, I help administer my library's human resources programs, including recruitment, retention, diversity, equal employment opportunity, employment and staffing, classification and compensation, employee and labor relations, and organizational learning and development. I design a curriculum to cultivate a continuous learning environment across the library. I identify and assess learning opportunities to help employees build skills they need today and prepare them for future work. In this way, I help the library attract and keep the most qualified people and build my organization's capacity to anticipate and thrive on change.

A TYPICAL WORKDAY

My job is made up of two basic parts: human resources and learning and development. The two halves often overlap and may even blur during the course of a day.

Employee and Labor Relations

On the human resources side, I serve as one of my library's employee and labor relations specialists. I need to be familiar with my university's personnel policies and some federal and state laws. My department is large enough that my coworkers and I can be more or less knowledgeable about certain human resources issues, such as those covered by the Fair Labor Standards Act or the Family Medical Leave Act, because we know that we can rely on one another as resources. An HR librarian in a smaller department would need to be very knowledgeable about a broad range of laws and policies.

On any given day, I consult with, advise, and coach library managers and supervisors on HR matters, including staffing questions, strategies for managing employee performance, creating and updating job descriptions, handling conflict effectively, and other similar issues. In each conversation, I deal with confidential information. I need to show that I can be trusted with the information that employees share with me. When I meet with a person at any level, whether a line employee, supervisor, or manager, my goal is to empower the person to identify and handle the problem on his or her own, rather than to fix it myself. Active listening is really important in this process ("I'm hearing you say ... Is this what you meant?"). I sometimes role-play with supervisors and employees to help them find a style that fits them. I find this a rewarding and complex part of my job, because I have to draw on a wide variety of experience and knowledge. I have worked in a number of library departments and performed a variety of types of library work, which gives me more credibility.

As is true of many large universities, my library operates in a union environment. Four different contracts, or collective bargaining agreements, cover library employees on the campus. I need to be familiar with these agreements when I advise any library employee. It is essential that I be knowledgeable about the contract that covers librarians, as academic employees are my main area of specialization.

Peer Review

I assist my director of HR in overseeing personnel actions for librarians across the campus, which includes the library's annual peer review process. I am also responsible for coordinating librarian peer reviews. In this role, I work with the Committee on Appointments, Promotions and Advancements (CAPA) and the university librarian (UL). I forward librarian dossiers to and from the CAPA for their review, to the UL for his review and final decision, and back to my department for final processing.

Recruitment

This part of my job is growing, and I expect to spend more of my time on recruitment in the next several years. Stanley Wilder (1995, 1999) and others who have studied the demographics of academic librarians foresee that more than half of the librarians currently working in libraries will retire in the next ten to fifteen years. On every librarian search committee, the HR director or I serve as the human resources manager. My role on the search committee is to ensure that we follow equal employment opportunity and affirmative action requirements. At the same time, I am a working member of the committee. Each of us on the search committee reads and ranks résumés and cover letters, suggests questions to ask during telephone reference checks, and develops interview questions. We help design the interview schedule (e.g., who will meet with the candidates and when), participate in the interview itself, and contribute to the search committee's final report.

Learning and Development

Recruitment is closely related to retention—finding ways to grow and keep employees who contribute actively to the library's mission. Recruitment and retention make up a key area in which the two parts of my job come together. In the learning and development part of my job, I coordinate the design and development of a curriculum and build a program that fosters learning throughout the library system. In preparing myself for these responsibilities, I have found it valuable to read the works of Peter Senge, Peter Vaill, and others who have written on the learning organization and learning in the midst of change (Senge 1990; Vaill 1996).

I am helping my library define competencies for managers and other "follower-leaders" in the library. I identify, design, and implement activities to orient, train, and develop employees at all levels, whether academic, technical professional, paraprofessional, or student. I continually keep an eye out for training that is available on my campus, at the systemwide level of my university, and in my geographic region to cultivate these competencies. I keep track of consultants who provide training that I want to bring into the library. I also note the types of training that we may need to create and present in-house for managers, supervisors, and other library employees. I think it is essential to ask the library's employees what types of learning they need and want. My organization development colleagues are excellent sources of information on strategies and best practices for surveying library staff to identify training and development needs, and assessing whether and how we are successful.

I also serve as an internal organization development consultant for my library. Organization development (OD) aims to improve the effectiveness of an organization by planning specific activities to improve its culture. In a library these interventions (to use an OD term) could include analyzing and redesigning processes, workflows, individual jobs, even entire departments. If it is to be successful, OD work needs to be planned with and supported by the highest level of the library's administration.

Facilitation

Facilitation is one of the core competencies already identified for library employees. More and more, library employees need to be able to work successfully in groups. This requires more than simply sending out an agenda in advance, although that is important. Group members and leaders need to make sure everyone has a voice at the table. They need to solve problems and make decisions together, address and manage conflict, and know which types of tools will help them do this. I work with a consultant to offer an eight-hour workshop on facilitation skills to library employees, especially managers, librarians, and other supervisors, three to four times a year. I monitor how many and which employees in each library department have completed the workshop and prompt managers for the names of other employees who may attend upcoming sessions.

I also chair a facilitation interest group to ensure that we practice using different types of tools; by doing so, we are working these skills more deeply into the library organization. I set up an electronic discussion list to allow us to share experiences with and ask questions of each other. I chair a monthly in-person meeting where anyone who has completed the workshop can come to discuss and ask questions about facilitation. I plan a quarterly update session with the consultant in which she presents new content or where we use a specific tool. The consultant and I are developing ways to assess the facilitation program and to prove whether the training has prepared library employees to work together more effectively.

Infrastructure and Administration

In my learning and development role, I draft policies for discussion by the council of department managers and approval by the library administration. When approved, they are added to the administrative policy manual. I work with the library's other administrative departments, such as the business services unit, to implement new policies. This infrastructure development usually requires that I also draft forms and develop procedures. When I first bring the policy to the administration, I also recommend a review cycle. This ensures that the policy, forms, and procedures come back to the administration and other relevant groups for review, discussion, and revision.

I also supervise a half-time assistant and a student employee who help me compile statistics and reports on the organizational learning and development program and other related activities.

PROS AND CONS

I enjoy the juggling and multitasking that my job requires. I see much of my daily work as managing multiple projects at once, keeping them all on track and on deadline. Some people might find this frustrating. On some days, it is difficult to focus on one project for long. While I am writing a report or transcribing notes from a meeting that I facilitated, revising a job description, or reading résumés, a manager may call with an urgent question that requires me to make several phone calls to find an answer.

HOW TO GET A JOB LIKE MINE

The skills that I find most valuable in my work include flexibility, active listening skills, a good sense of humor, diplomacy, project management skills, the ability to multitask, and intellectual curiosity. These are critical in both parts of my job. Many of the skills that I use in my day-to-day work I developed as a librarian, doing reference, advising readers, cataloging, and the like. For example, I perceive consulting with supervisors and line employees as another way to use my reference interviewing skills.

I also must be ready and able to ask questions and be willing to wait for answers. Being able to shift between the big picture and a detailed perspective is also important. I need to be able to "zoom out" to grasp where a process or problem may fit into a larger system, and "zoom in" on specifics. These are essential traits for activities such as work redesign and workflow analysis. Problem-solving abilities, good writing skills, and physical stamina are also essential.

To find open positions like mine, search the job listings on the American Library Association's JobLIST or the Web site of the Society for Human Resource Management.

My background of working in many functional areas of libraries, such as cataloging, reference, information literacy, government documents, interlibrary loan, and collection development, has prepared me well for my current job. I have also worked in law libraries and in a laboratory school library (K–6) on my campus. I have been an assistant or interim department head, so I can understand the issues that managers and employees face and give them advice that makes sense to them. If you do not have this kind of experience, I strongly suggest seeking internships or volunteering to work in more than one section of a library. I also think it helps to work in more than one kind of library to broaden your view of people, services, and ways of working together.

RELATED RESOURCES

Works Cited

Senge, Peter M. 1990. *The fifth discipline: The art and practice of the learning organization.* New York: Doubleday.

Vaill, Peter B. 1996. *Learning as a way of being: Strategies for survival in a world of permanent white water.* San Francisco: Jossey-Bass.

Wilder, Stanley J. 1995. *The age demographics of academic librarians: A profession apart.* Washington, D.C.: Association of Research Libraries.

———. 1999. *Demographic change in academic librarianship.* Washington, D.C.: Association of Research Libraries.

Associations

American Library Association, JobLIST. joblist.ala.org (accessed September 22, 2006).

American Society for Training and Development. www.astd.org (accessed February 21, 2006).

Organization Development Network. www.odnetwork.org (accessed February 21, 2006).

Society for Human Resource Management. www.shrm.org (accessed February 21, 2006).

Web Site

University of Maryland Libraries, The Learning Organization. www.lib.umd.edu/groups/learning/ learningorg.html (accessed February 21, 2006).

Additional Readings

Association of College and Research Libraries. Ad Hoc Task Force on Recruitment and Retention Issues. 2002. *Recruitment, retention and restructuring: Human resources in academic libraries.* Chicago: ACRL. Includes extensive annotated bibliographies.

Bradford, David L., and W. Warner Burke, eds. 2005. *Reinventing organization development: New approaches to change in organizations.* San Francisco: Pfeiffer.

Lancaster, Lynne C., and David Stillman. 2002. *When generations collide: Who they are, why they clash, how to solve the generational puzzle at work.* New York: HarperCollins.

Russell, Keith, and Denise Stephens, eds. 2004. Organizational development and leadership. *Library Trends* 53, no. 1 (Summer).

Senge, Peter, Art Kleiner, Charlotte Roberts, Richard Ross, and Bryan Smith, eds. 1994. *Fifth discipline fieldbook: Strategies and tools for building a learning organization.* New York: Doubleday.

Torraco, Richard J., ed. 2005. *Organization development and change in universities.* Thousand Oaks, Calif.: Sage Publications.

CHAPTER 32

Information Literacy Coordinator

MICHELLE S. MILLET

Information literacy coordinator, or library instruction coordinator, is becoming a fairly common job title in a variety of library settings. I equate information literacy and library instruction because the two topics are closely aligned in the profession. This chapter will give you some insight into this kind of job in a small private college.

JOB DESCRIPTION

Trinity University is a selective liberal arts college with approximately 2,400 students. My position was newly created when I began working here in 2003. As information literacy coordinator, my major job responsibility is developing an innovative and integrated information literacy program on campus. This includes motivating the other teaching librarians to develop their instructional techniques, marketing library instruction and information literacy to faculty, developing instruction tools and tutorials that promote information literacy, as well as performing basic department liaison and reference duties. In a job like mine, you can expect to teach fifteen to twenty classes per semester and work on collection development every week, depending on your department liaison assignments.

A TYPICAL WORKDAY

At smaller colleges, librarians usually consider themselves generalists. We often perform duties beyond those of our major job responsibilities in both technical and public services. That means that in addition to being the information literacy advocate on my campus, I also cover the reference desk approximately eight to ten hours a week, devote time to collection development, work on my own scholarly endeavors, and participate in campus committees and activities.

Keeping up with educational trends and issues is an important part of my job because my primary goal is to weave information literacy throughout the curriculum. Assessment is important in information literacy (as it is in higher education), so I continuously work to assess our program and create tools for librarians to assess their individual instruction. Outreach is essential to this position, as is the ability to promote the integration of technology in instruction. I serve as the point person for new strategies toward information literacy and new literature or program ideas. I am the one who finds out what's going on in the field of information literacy and higher education that relates to our environment and puts it forward in our agenda.

My position is also a tenure-track faculty librarian position. Faculty status is not a given in academic libraries. When considering a job like mine, it is important to decide whether faculty status is important to you and whether you wish to pursue a job that has faculty status. When making such a decision, you may want to consult the library's departmental guidelines for promotion and tenure and be sure to ask questions about the process and support.

A typical workday includes a variety of the duties already described and often begins with what I call library triage. When I arrive at work, I need to take care of emergencies right away. That means responding to panic-stricken student e-mails from the night before or ordering course-related materials that need to be rushed for a professor's class next week. Then I devote time to catching up on correspondence (usually e-mail) and preparing for any meetings or instruction for that day. I usually have a two-hour block on the reference desk most days as well.

My afternoon activities involve planning for classes I am going to be teaching or working on information literacy program development. I try to balance my own teaching preparation with programmatic planning as much as possible. I keep up on relevant Weblogs during the day and usually take time out to read appropriate literature or peruse table of contents alerts once a week. In the midst of these projects, I squeeze in student research appointments and committee meetings. I am constantly on the go, both physically and mentally.

Working on instructional development means that a lot of different projects are in process simultaneously. At the beginning of the semester, I may be working on information literacy goals for the year, and at the end of the semester I might be compiling instruction statistics. During the semester, I work on ways to maximize our information literacy Web presence for students or planning a workshop to engage faculty in conversations about information literacy. What makes my job so challenging and fun is that my projects and priorities change continuously. Some days I'll be collaborating with a faculty member on a research assignment, and other days I'm looking at ways to evaluate the effectiveness of research appointments.

Small colleges often do not offer many classes during the summer, so a typical summer day is quite different. The atmosphere is a bit more relaxed and the building is much quieter. Summer days still involve working on the reference desk. My projects are usually a bit more involved and intensive. During the summer I like to work on more demanding projects, like creating Web-based tutorials or adding a lot of online content.

PROS AND CONS OF MY JOB

I enjoy my job, and I am passionate about my career. I like working in an academic environment very much. I have been pleased to find a career in which I can work in higher education and teach with encouraging colleagues. The most positive aspect of my position is the time I spend with students—teaching them in classes and working with them individually. I also like the challenge of developing an information literacy program from the ground up and encouraging library instruction.

The concept of information literacy is more entrenched in some other higher education environments than in the liberal arts, in my opinion. Although it exists in accreditation documentation and has become a major initiative of the Association of American Colleges and Universities, teaching faculty in liberal arts colleges often resist new ideas and initiatives because of the strong academic records of their students and the adherence to a traditional curriculum.

Adaptation is possible—but it happens slowly. A liberal arts school can be an intellectually challenging and stimulating environment, but you have to have patience when bringing new curriculum-related ideas to the table.

I am a strong extrovert, and when I think of ideas, I prefer to put them in action immediately. It is sometimes a challenge for me to reel in my enthusiasm to present new ideas and programs in the most politically correct way on campus. I have to rein myself in to approach things on a small scale and watch ideas take hold and grow slowly. This can be frustrating for someone who is energetic and has new ideas that he or she would like to promote.

Overall, I have had a positive experience working in the liberal arts environment. At Trinity, every librarian teaches, and that commonality brings us together. We all discuss our problems and successes working with students, and we collaborate on goals and objectives for the information literacy program.

Before coming to the private school environment, I worked in larger public institutions. Having experienced both environments, I admit that I miss working with graduate students. When you love to teach and enjoy watching students learn, working with graduate students can be a real pleasure. Missing that pool of hungry students—and teachers—has been one of the only drawbacks of this job.

HOW WOULD I GET A JOB LIKE YOURS?

A job like mine is a gem if you like working with people and teaching. Teaching experience is a must. It would be an excellent addition to your résumé if you attend the Association of College and Research Libraries (ACRL) Institute for Information Literacy Immersion Program. Good inter-personal skills are also helpful, and experience marketing and packaging services is an asset. In a liberal arts college it is an asset if your undergraduate degree is in a liberal arts discipline. I think familiarity with instructional design and instruction software is very advantageous as information technology, instructional design, and information literacy begin to merge. Familiarity with the national information literacy standards from ACRL is important. It would also be helpful to become involved with ACRL's Instruction Section to network with other instruction librarians.

To become an information literacy coordinator, it is often necessary to work in an entry-level instruction librarian position or in a position where library instruction is the main component of your job. Sometimes you can stay at your institution and take on these responsibilities or be promoted to the position. More often, though, it is necessary to relocate when you find an open position. An information literacy coordinator position is not usually someone's first job out of a master's program.

Most information literacy jobs are fairly widely advertised. If you are interested in library instruction, join the Information Literacy Instruction e-mail list (ILI-L), offered through the American Library Association. The e-mail list is very active and includes job advertisements. It will give you a good sample of the important issues in information literacy and help you keep up with the subject.

If you have the opportunity to take a course in information literacy or library instruction in graduate school, take it. Even more helpful would be an opportunity to work in an academic library, collaborating on instruction with an instruction librarian or coordinator. If you do not have a chance to take a course in information literacy in school and cannot get a job in an academic library, try to volunteer with the library instruction coordinator on campus. If you have been a teacher previously, I still encourage you to experience teaching in a library instruction environment. Your experience in teaching is different than the usual fifty-minute, one-shot instruction sessions, so having both will provide you with a good background for a position like mine.

Project management skills are also very valuable. As I have mentioned, a lot of tasks and projects related to information literacy are going on at once in my job. Learning to manage a project from start to finish is great experience. Do your homework on related issues like educational theory, pedagogy, learning styles, and teaching methods as well. Overall, an information literacy coordinator position usually requires two or three years of postgraduate experience, so if you are a new graduate you will have plenty of time to work on beefing up your résumé and acquiring experience.

RELATED RESOURCES

Association of American Colleges and Universities (AACU). www.aacu.org (accessed November 30, 2005).

Association of College and Research Libraries, Information Literacy. www.acrl.org/ala/acrl/acrlissues/acrlinfolit/informationliteracy.htm (accessed November 29, 2005).

———, Instruction Section. www.ala.org/ala/acrl/aboutacrl/acrlsections/instruction/homepage.htm (accessed November 29, 2005).

National Institute for Technology and Liberal Education (NITLE). www.nitle.org (accessed November 30, 2005).

CHAPTER 33

Head of Interlibrary Loan/Document Delivery Services

MICHELLE BATCHELOR

Interlibrary loan (ILL) is an essential part of serving the information needs of an academic institution because no single library can own everything their researchers will find useful. The service we provide is often seen as a mysterious process by which materials are teleported from one institution to another. Some patrons even believe that a book can instantaneously cross the country on placement of an ILL request! Although interlibrary loan does have a certain magical quality, here at the University of Nevada, Las Vegas (UNLV) the daily routines of borrowing materials from other libraries for our patrons and lending materials to other libraries for their patrons are fairly mundane.

Requests to borrow books and articles come in from our patrons via the Web. ILL staff make sure our library doesn't own the item, telling the patron where to find it if we do. We then use a database supplied by OCLC to search for other libraries that own the item. Our request is sent to a series of no more than five potential lending libraries, each of whom are queried by OCLC's automated system in turn. If one of those libraries owns the item, they will either mail it (for books) or send it electronically (for photocopies). Once we receive it, we update our ILL management system, deliver it electronically to the patron if it is a photocopy, or notify the patron via e-mail if it is a book to pick up.

Interlibrary lending is the mirror image of borrowing. Most requests from other libraries come via OCLC WorldCat Resource Sharing into our ILL management system. Requests can also come by fax, e-mail, or paper mail. We check to see if we own the item in question, retrieve it, send it electronically if it is an article and by mail if it is a book, and update the request to reflect that the item was sent. If we cannot supply the item, we forward the request on to the next library and provide a brief reason for why we were unable to fill it.

A TYPICAL WORKDAY

As the head of Document Delivery Services at UNLV, I manage the technology and the people who make this whole process happen. My daily work life tends to be spent partly doing routine tasks and partly engaged in administrative tasks that only need to be done weekly, monthly, annually, or even once every few years.

A portion of my day is always spent responding to questions from our patrons or from staff at other libraries; these questions may come in person, by telephone, by e-mail, or through referral by ILL staff. A few examples include patrons reporting technical difficulties with electronically delivered PDF files, other libraries asking for special rush processing or reporting problems with delivery, and questions about ILL policies or availability of specific materials via ILL. I also try to resolve our most difficult problem requests on a regular basis. For instance, sometimes materials cannot be found in OCLC's resource sharing system because no libraries own it, the patron has cited it wrong, it is only available online, or for some other reason. The reference librarian within me will rise to the challenge and hunt the item down, or at least exhaust every possibility I can think of.

On a less frequent schedule, I keep track of how well our operation is performing by looking at the data collected by our ILL management system. For both borrowing and lending we should have a low average turnaround time (the time it takes for us to receive a request and fill it) and a high fill rate (the number of requests we are able to fill compared to the number of unfilled requests). I also monitor how many items we obtain from libraries that charge us and determine whether we might be eligible for a free reciprocal lending agreement with those libraries. Evaluating and updating our custom holdings is a related task. These prioritized lists in OCLC facilitate automated selection of the closest and least expensive lending libraries. I also have managerial duties, such as training and supervising three classified staff members (though I must note that the staff in my department work very independently), serving on library and university committees, and attending meetings with our interlibrary sharing partners.

As the head of our department, I also have a responsibility to provide leadership and vision to ensure that we are offering the best services we possibly can. The systems that support ILL are constantly evolving, so it is important that I know about the newest, hottest technologies and what the future might bring. Attending presentations and discussion groups at regional ILL conferences as well as large national conferences such as ALA are a great way to stay informed about current developments in ILL.

On a related note, much of my time is currently taken up with implementation of ILLiad, our new ILL management system. ILLiad will streamline the lending and borrowing processes by allowing us to do most of our departmental tasks within one integrated interface instead of switching back and forth between several separate systems. My preparations have included learning as much about ILLiad as possible from the copious amounts of documentation about it, communicating with and visiting staff at other libraries to see how they use the system, meeting with my own staff to prepare them for the change and teach them what I've learned, editing the Web pages that will allow our patrons to use the system, and customizing the system itself to make it work the way we want it to.

PROS AND CONS

There are very few drawbacks to working in ILL. Like any public service, we receive criticism when we are unable to fulfill a patron's expectations. Sometimes items do not arrive as quickly as the patron hoped (especially books that travel long distances to get to us), and sometimes we are unable to obtain items that are noncirculating or simply not owned by other libraries. Because most interlibrary loan people have a strong service ethic, we empathize with our patrons and feel regret when we are unable to obtain something for them.

Problems can also arise from the fact that the technology that supports our service is always evolving, so we are constantly working out the bugs. Transitional times caused by software updates, hardware upgrades, or implementation of new systems can be very stressful. When the systems we use stop working properly, our routine is interrupted and our service slows down or even stops. This brings us to another cause of anxiety. Because our patrons and our library partners judge us by how quickly we process requests, we feel a constant pressure to provide fast and efficient service.

Despite these stressors, working in interlibrary loan can be extremely gratifying. Patrons really do respond to our service with a kind of mystified awe and tend to think we're going above and beyond the call of duty even when we're just doing our everyday jobs. We often get positive verbal feedback—and sometimes chocolate—from the people we serve.

Another wonderful thing about being an ILL librarian is that interlibrary loan touches so many other parts of the library system. I have relationships with subject librarians because they refer patrons to me and I ask them for help with problem requests within their discipline. My job connects with collection development when items cannot be obtained from other libraries but are available for purchase, or when high ILL usage shows that our patrons need something that collection development didn't know they needed to buy. I hope to start having our books picked up at the circulation desk, which will build a new relationship with that department. Reference librarians teach patrons how to search for and find the citations that they will use to order items via ILL. I rely heavily on our systems department for help with technological problems. I even have ties to cataloging, because the information our catalogers enter into the OCLC database and our library catalog affects our lending efficiency. My position also puts me in contact with a whole community of people at other institutions whom I work with and learn from to figure out problems and find ways to improve our services.

HOW TO GET MY JOB

There are many paths to a career as an interlibrary loan head librarian. I gained ILL and supervisory experience as a staff member, obtained my MLIS, and then was hired as an ILL librarian. My mentor began as a science librarian before being promoted to head of ILL. Another librarian I spoke with spent over twenty years as a general reference librarian and later was similarly promoted.

If you are interested in ILL jobs, subscribe to at least one ILL e-mail list. Currently, one of the most active lists is called ILL-L. Reading the discussions there will give you an understanding of the challenges ILL librarians face, and job postings sometimes show up on that list before they appear in other lists for job-seeking librarians. Also know that ILL head librarian positions are rare. There are seldom more than a few positions available at a time nationwide. Therefore, if you have your heart set on ILL, be ready to move to where the job is.

Managing an ILL department requires a unique combination of technological and interpersonal skills. You must be comfortable with computers. ILLers are constantly updating or upgrading software and troubleshooting problems with the programs we use. Understanding databases is extremely useful, because most of our applications are database driven. Web publishing skills come in handy if you want to customize your Web pages to meet your users' unique needs. Good communication skills are also essential because you must maintain excellent relationships with other ILL departments as well as patrons, librarians, support staff, and administrators at your library. If you get excited about technological advances, love problem solving, enjoy networking with other librarians, and have a strong customer service ethic, you'll make a good ILL librarian.

RELATED RESOURCES

Boucher, Virginia. 1997. *Interlibrary loan practices handbook*. Chicago: American Library Association.

Hilyer, Lee Andrew. 2002. *Interlibrary loan and document delivery in the larger academic library: A guide for university, research, and larger public libraries*. Binghamton, N.Y.: Haworth.

Morris, Leslie R. 2002. *Interlibrary loan policies directory,* 7th ed. New York: Neal-Schuman.
OCLC Online Computer Library Center. www.oclc.org (accessed February 2, 2006).
U.S. Interlibrary Loan Code. www.ala.org/ala/rusa/rusaprotools/referenceguide/interlibraryloancode.htm
    (accessed February 2, 2006).

CHAPTER 34

Electronic Periodicals Manager

SUSAN DAVIS

What is it like to work with electronic journals all day? That's right—no print issues to check in, claim, or bind. Truthfully, it has been quite liberating because keeping electronic access on track is definitely a full-time job; many days feel like lifetime employment is assured.

Here is a brief synopsis of my position description: to serve, jointly with another manager, as head of the Electronic Periodicals Management Department at the University at Buffalo, State University of New York; to oversee the day-to-day acquisition, licensing, bibliographic and access control, and monitoring of holdings for electronic periodicals; to establish operational and staff training procedures aimed at making appropriate use of professional staff in the department; to serve effectively on university libraries functional or administrative groups relevant to the activities of the Electronic Periodicals Management Department; to participate in short- and long-term planning in Central Technical Services.

I am also a member of the faculty and am expected to meet the criteria established in the *Criteria for Library Faculty Personnel Actions*. I received tenure some years ago, so this is relevant should I seek promotion to the rank of full librarian and because I supervise another faculty librarian.

TYPICAL ROUTINES

Over the course of my twenty-five-year career in serials, I have heard or used these phrases to describe the work I do: "nail jelly to the wall," "juggle lots of balls at once," and, from a magazine clipping, "thrive on chaos." Because that phrase struck such a chord with me, I photocopied it and pinned it on my bulletin board.

A few caveats about the libraries at the University at Buffalo (UB). There were three technical services units across the libraries that traditionally served distinct clientele. Central Technical Services served the Arts and Sciences Libraries (ASL), Music, and Poetry collections. Health Sciences and Law served those schools. The Electronic Periodicals Management Department (EPMD) was created in 2005. It was formed by merging most of the staff from the Periodicals Section of the Acquisitions Department in Central Technical Services with the head of the Collection Management Services Department in the Health Sciences Library. Collection development and print check-in, claiming, and binding remained in the Health Science Library, and other staff in the Acquisitions Department plus one staff member from Periodicals were given responsibility for print check-in, claiming, and binding. The EPMD was created to centralize overlapping responsibilities for electronic journal acquisitions, licensing, bibliographic control, and maintenance. We manage subscriptions to over six thousand e-journals, either individually or as part of large packages, with expenditures exceeding $3.5 million and access to over two thousand freely available e-journals. We also create separate catalog records for each electronic version, except for journals available in full-text indexing and abstracting products. We use Serials Solutions to help manage coverage data and have implemented the stand-alone Innovative Interfaces Electronic Resource Management system. At the time of this writing, the library is using classic NOTIS for its ILS, but expects to convert to Ex Libris over the summer of 2006.

Most days begin by reviewing incoming e-mail. The EPMD established an electronic journal problem report form for public services and patrons to submit questions and problems. There is also an online journal request/order form. These forms are sent to an administrative e-mail account that is checked several times a day. Once the spam has been cleared, I can focus on the mail specifically addressed to me. I do most of my communicating by e-mail, particularly because we subscribe to journals from all over the world. E-mailing also documents the actions taken on a particular problem or question. I find myself frustrated when I receive a response to a question I posed days earlier without the back-and-forth history to help me remember what was going on!

Most of what I do relates to acquisitions and access problems. Here are some examples of the problems and questions I typically deal with.

I receive an e-mail from our science librarian letting me know that publisher ABC has now digitized backfiles of *Journal XYZ* and is offering them free to current subscribers. Please update our records. This might be simple and straightforward if not for the fact that *Journal XYZ* changed its title and was originally called *Journal BCD* and there is no online record available in OCLC. The other librarians in the department handle original cataloging and derived cataloging based on print records, so I can pass along this particular case for one of them to work on.

A patron reports that a PDF is corrupted in an article from issue A of the *European Journal of STU*. I write an e-mail report to the online provider who later responds that the publisher is being asked for a replacement copy of the article to be reloaded.

A librarian doing bibliographic instruction calls to report problems with ISSNs for various manifestations of *Focus* in Serials Solutions. Researching this problem entangles me in several problem threads regarding holdings for a different *Focus* and results in several e-mails to Serials Solutions to investigate the bibliographic data they are using. I was surprised and heartened to learn that someone outside of technical services does make use of the ISSN!

A staff member discovers that Project MUSE has more issues of a title mounted than the journal Web page indicates. Another e-mail goes out to alert Project MUSE and Serials Solutions because their holdings data matches the incorrect home page indication. JSTOR has a similar problem; they announced that another year of holdings have been added according to the negotiated moving wall, but the journal information pages haven't all been updated to reflect that.

I respond to a question from our subscription agent account representative about a change in the pricing model for *GFE Journal* that offers print plus online or online only. Later in the day she calls to let me know that our renewal instructions were received and the invoice will arrive in about two weeks.

The staff in the Fund Management Section of the Acquisitions Department ask me several questions about potential problems with items on the renewal invoice from our vendor in the

United Kingdom. I send off several e-mails and hope to receive replies the following day because the workday there has already ended.

I take a little time in the late afternoon to create some templates in the Electronic Resource Management (ERM) system so we can begin to add records for individual journal subscriptions that we changed to electronic-only for 2006. Using templates reduces the time required to input records and reduces errors. EPMD began creating records for databases and large e-journal packages in 2005 and completed the work for ASL, Music, and the systemwide purchases. We want to focus now on the e-only journals so that reports on interlibrary loan, e-reserves, and course packs can be distributed to the relevant public services areas. The libraries will no longer have access to print issues, and it will be important to understand what rights we have under the terms of the various publisher licenses. All licenses are not created equal even with the efforts to develop model license language. Until the ERM is populated with license terms, we have had to depend on a paper file of copies of licenses. Plans are under way to scan and mount the licenses on the libraries' Web site (in a staff-only section).

I also consult with the collection development librarians about pricing model changes, serials review procedures, cancellation deadlines, or other questions they may have about online journal subscriptions.

Regular management tasks involve signing the staff's monthly time sheets, preparing annual appraisals, trying to document policies and procedures, and tracking everyone's schedules. I also serve on a library-wide Collections Committee (superseding an Electronic Resources Council) that meets once a month.

I am also active in the profession, holding committee assignments in both the North American Serials Interest Group and ALA's Association for Library Collections and Technical Services. I am a column editor for *Serials Review* and need to recruit reports and edit submissions on a quarterly basis.

PROS AND CONS

My work is incredibly challenging. I love to read mysteries, and I find that similar analytical and observational skills are appropriate to what I do. Almost every publisher is unique in the way they approach mounting and pricing their electronic content, and it's not always easy to find out exactly what they are doing or why. Good detective skills are very helpful. And once you have it figured out, it changes! I really like the variety each day offers and find that multitasking is a necessary skill. Life with periodicals is never boring and has held my interest for twenty-five years. I can't imagine doing anything else (unless I won the lottery!).

The downside is that there is so much to do! We spend a lot of energy trying to make our way through the complex routines needed to establish and maintain access. Some of this is attributable to the newness of electronic information; another factor is the constant change. At first electronic access was included in the price for print, then it was an extra charge, then you could order only electronic access, then you could pay an additional price for backfile access. Publishers have changed online platforms so URLs have had to be changed. Access policies changed so that a subscription entitles you to the latest five years online or from 1997 to date instead of everything available. And there is still a lot of paper around. We keep copies of e-mails, licenses, and examples to document what was, is, or is yet to be.

Some days you feel as though you'll never be able to finish anything. It can be very exhausting trying just to keep up with all the work, let alone actually making any headway. Nonetheless, there is no matching the sense of satisfaction when you are successful in working through a complicated registration process and see access up a moment after you click the send button.

You almost feel like a master serials magician who can snap your fingers and accomplish anything.

WHAT IT TAKES TO MANAGE E-JOURNALS

So how did I arrive at this rather envious (or perhaps overwhelming) position as head of Electronic Periodicals Management, and what do I think are the important attributes for anyone else seeking a similar position?

An ALA-accredited master's degree is a general prerequisite for all professional library positions. I had some experience checking in print journals while in library school and am probably one of a very small minority who actually took a serials course. These experiences helped me obtain a paraprofessional position in serials right out of library school, and I was on my way! Subsequent positions in serials gave me invaluable experience, and I was able to learn on the job as well as through mentors I met at professional meetings. A good foundation in the principles of serials control helped immensely. Also, I cannot overemphasize the importance of establishing an excellent network of serials experts in libraries, publishing, and the vendor community. So a combination of experience and aptitude for the detail-intensive, complex, and seemingly spiraling-out-of-control aura that surrounds electronic journals has made this a successful transition for me.

Anyone who is interested in serials work needs to be detail-oriented, comfortable with ambiguity, and able to juggle many balls at once. The ability to prioritize and manage projects is also helpful, as is an understanding of the scholarly communication process, publishing industry, license terms, and spreadsheets. Excellent communication skills almost go without saying. I have also found that humor and the ability to laugh at some of the more bizarre twists that come with the territory help keep everything in perspective. Serials work really can be fun.

RELATED RESOURCES

Professional involvement is crucial in the fast-paced work of electronic journals, particularly because of the need to be up to speed with the current developments in the area. Contacts with others in the field, especially with vendors and publishers, are invaluable. I recommend participation in the Association for Library Collections and Technical Services (ALCTS) division of the American Library Association (ALA) and the North American Serials Interest Group (NASIG). The Serials Section of ALCTS focuses on all aspects of serials, and there are several discussion and interest groups in ALCTS that are relevant. NASIG holds an annual conference devoted exclusively to serials issues and publishes the proceedings. The NASIG conferences are very informal and offer excellent opportunities to network. Depending on your interest and tolerance for e-mail traffic, these electronic mail discussion lists may be useful: SERIALST, AUTOCAT, ERIL-L, Liblicense-L, and ACQNET. The e-mail lists for ALCTS, its Serials Section, and NASIG tend to focus more on administrative topics. A new conference, Electronic Resources and Libraries, began in March 2006. Reading professional journals is also important, if you can find the time. But most of all, experience is the best teacher. Sometimes just jumping in and plugging away is the best way to learn.

Web Sites

Association for Library Collections and Technical Services. www.ala.org/alcts (accessed March 11, 2006).
E-Resource Access and Management Services (EBSCO Information Services). The e-resource life cycle. www.ebsco.com/home/ejournals/ejournallc.pdf (accessed March 3, 2006).

Electronic Resources and Libraries. www.electroniclibrarian.org (accessed March 11, 2006).
Electronic Resources in Libraries. www.joanconger.net/ERIL (accessed March 11, 2006).
North American Serials Interest Group. www.nasig.org (accessed March 11, 2006).

Journals to Scan

Library Collections, Acquisitions, and Technical Services.
Library Resources and Technical Services.
Serials Librarian.
Serials Review.

Books

Curtis, Donnelyn, with Virginia M. Schenesy. 2005. *E-journals: A how-to-do-it manual for building, managing, and supporting electronic journal collections.* New York: Neal-Schuman.

Grahame, Vicki, and Tim McAdam. 2004. *Managing electronic resources.* Washington, D.C.: Association of Research Libraries.

Tuttle, Marcia. 1996. *Managing serials.* Greenwich, Conn.: JAI Press.

United Kingdom Serials Group. *The e-resources management handbook.* www.uksg.org/serials/handbook. asp (accessed March 11, 2006).

Articles

Case, Mary M. 2004. A snapshot in time: ARL libraries and electronic journal resources. *ARL* no. 235 (August): 1–10.

Cole, Louise. 2005. A journey into e-resource administration hell. *Serials Librarian* 49, no. 1/2: 141–54.

Duranceau, Ellen Finnie, and Cindy Hepfer. 2002. Staffing for electronic resource management: The results of a survey. *Serials Review* 28: 316–20.

Jasper, Richard P., and Laura Sheble. 2005. Evolutionary approach to managing e-resources. *Serials Librarian* 47, no. 4: 55–70.

Srivastava, Sandhya, and Paolina Taglienti. 2004. E-journal management: An online survey evaluation. *Serials Review* 31: 28–38.

CHAPTER 35

Head of Information Services

LAURA TOWNSEND KANE

When I was in the third grade I stuck homemade book pockets and book cards inside the back covers of my Bobbsey Twins books; wrote out a list of titles in my wide-rule, spiral-bound notebook labeled "Books Checked Out"; and proceeded to coerce my family members into checking books out from my "library." I even charged overdue fines. Was I a geeky kid, or what? I found the notebook the other day and chuckled at the short list of entries. My sister checked out *The Bobbsey Twins and the Mystery at Snow Lodge* and never returned it. Typical. My mother, it seems, checked out *The Bobbsey Twins at the Seashore* twice. The entries stopped abruptly after Mother was charged the thirty-five-cent overdue fine noted carefully on line four.

Though my home-based library was short-lived, I never lost my interest in books and library procedures. With such innate (and admittedly frightening) tendencies, you'd think I would have spent my childhood and adolescent years yearning to be a librarian when I grew up. Wrong. It wasn't until after I graduated from college and discovered that I wasn't cut out for teaching that I considered going to library school. A friend of mine had done it, so I thought, "What the heck—why not give it a shot?" And I did. It was the best spur-of-the-moment decision I ever made.

JOB DESCRIPTION

My title is assistant director for information services. It's a long title for a simple concept. Basically, I am in charge of three public services departments within our library: reference, circulation, and interlibrary loan. Lest you become unnecessarily impressed, I should tell you that ours is a small library in comparison with others. Our library, a facility of the University of South Carolina, primarily serves about 320 students and 250 faculty of the School of Medicine. It is my job to see that the medical information needs of students and faculty are met with the help of trained reference professionals, library patrons are able to access the library and borrow the print tools available there, and those who need additional materials not available within the library are able to obtain them from other sources.

A TYPICAL WORKDAY

7:35 a.m.

I'm late! So what else is new? Having spent the first twelve years of my professional life as a cataloger, I have no shortage of nitpicky organizational skills. In fact, I pride myself on being meticulous and disciplined, two highly prized characteristics of a cataloger. Yet I'm forever running late in the mornings. This is an epidemic among working moms. My two boys are the lights of my life, but they make me late. An extra kiss here, an extra hug there, and I'm finally off to work!

8:10 a.m.

Though a tiny bit late, I am in fact the first librarian here this morning. We are lucky to have flex hours, and most of the other librarians (there are seven of us) choose to work from 9 a.m. to 5:30 p.m. I like to get home in the evenings in time to make dinner, so I prefer to start the day earlier.

First things first: coffee! I head for the break room to make my daily cappuccino. Then, armed with my drinkable ammunition, I settle at my desk to read e-mail. I couldn't function without e-mail. This is a strange thing for me to say, since I recall that when I first began working here thirteen years ago, there *was* no e-mail! There was no Internet, either, at least not in the format that we know of today. Funny thing—we functioned just fine without those things. But because all librarians must keep up with technology to remain in business, I went with the flow, and now e-mail and Google are my best friends.

It is a Monday, and therefore I have over ninety messages to sift through. I subscribe to a number of e-mail lists related to medical librarianship, reference work, and public services issues. I have learned through the years that maintaining contact with colleagues around the country is one of the easiest ways to network and to get your name out there. If I have work-related dilemmas, I can get help via a single query to my e-mail list buddies. "No man is an island" has new meaning in the electronic world.

There are a few messages from the graduate assistants who staff the library on nights and weekends. My position includes the oversight of the circulation department and all its activities. Luckily, though, I supervise the head of circulation, whose primary duty is to tackle all the details involved with keeping the library staffed and open when it is supposed to be open. In other words, I help in making departmental decisions and setting policies, but then I can step back and let others do their work. Two e-mail messages involve security within the library. I arrange a meeting with the School of Medicine's security department to discuss the issues. We want our library to be safe.

9 a.m.

It's time for my reference shift! All of the librarians here spend some time at the reference desk. This wasn't always the case. Until about three years ago, only the public services librarians staffed the reference desk. We now involve all of our librarians in reference work, even—God forbid!—the technical services librarians. I'm allowed to say this because I was one of those techie librarians until a short time ago. For twelve years I was head of cataloging and acquisitions, where I spent my days managing all aspects of book acquisition, processing, and cataloging, as well as maintaining our online catalog. My promotion to assistant director for information services was a huge change for me. Now I have gone to the dark side, according to my cataloging colleagues. Conversely, I have seen the light, according to my reference colleagues. Whatever the case, I feel like I am becoming a more well-rounded librarian, with experience in both the technical services and public services arenas.

There are no messages in our AskLib account (an electronic reference question system), so I pick up a file I've been working on for a while. I'm a member of the School of Medicine's Committee on Women, and I promised the group that I would investigate online survey software to conduct our next faculty survey. I play around with the software for a bit and then draft a report to send out to the committee. I'm in the middle of composing the report when the reference desk phone rings. I glance at our circulation specialist, and he makes a funny face at me. The call is a transfer from him, and his expression tells me that this one won't be fun. He is right. One of the school's faculty members is writing an article and needs to know how to find a list of the 500+ enzymes associated with magnesium, ASAP, of course. After conducting a Proper Reference Interview, I tell him, "Let me have your number and I'll get back to you." This is my favorite line these days.

I spend the next hour looking through print and electronic resources for a good source on enzymes. In the middle of this research, I receive another call from an elderly woman who wants to know if cascara sagrada is a laxative and if maybe taking this herbal remedy for two months is the cause of her chronic diarrhea. I jot down the necessary information and then use my favorite line again.

11 a.m.

It is the end of my Monday reference shift, and I am satisfied that I managed to answer the two reference questions to the best of my ability. I pointed the faculty member to a number of enzyme databases to help him with his quest, and I informed the elderly lady that cascara sagrada is indeed a natural laxative and that MedlinePlus (an authoritative consumer health Web site) recommends never taking a laxative for more than one week. You learn a lot doing medical reference work, I've found. I now know more about laxatives and diarrhea than I ever wanted to know! I made sure to suggest that the lady consult with her physician, and she replied, "I already did, but I didn't believe him."

Reference work can be a challenge, but it is definitely rewarding. I like the treasure-hunt feel to it. There isn't always a clearly defined map showing "X marks the spot," though. Some reference quests can lead you down the wrong pathways, and you have to hope you'll find your way back. Just leave a trail of breadcrumbs!

I have just settled myself in my office when I am called back to the front desk, where a patron is complaining about interlibrary loan charges. I put on my Super Librarian cape and fly to the rescue! Actually, all I have to do is show the patron our interlibrary loan policy, which clearly outlines the charges for article requests. I like written policies, because I can whip them out and point to them as if the paper is to blame, when in all probability I wrote the policy myself. I manage to placate the patron using my best de-escalation of conflict techniques.

Back at my desk, I'm finally able to finish the report for the committee that I had begun earlier. Another task completed! I keep eyeing the folder titled "Priscilla Shontz Chapter—due December 1." Should I start that now? Nah, I'll wait. Instead, I walk down the hall to chat with the librarian who took over my cataloging and acquisitions duties. Like me, she is still in training, and I show her how to perform various tasks as time allows. Today we cover her responsibilities for maintaining electronic textbook links in our online catalog. What fun! After thirty minutes I leave her office, skipping a little because it finally hit me—I will never again have to edit 856 fields!

Noon

Lunchtime! Sorry, I can't talk now. I'm not allowed to talk with my mouth full.

1 p.m.

Having satisfied my hunger, it is now time to tackle yet another task I have shoved aside for too long: the library's newsletter. I am the chair of the Newsletter Committee, and it is our responsibility to publish four of those things per year. It is an exercise in coordination from beginning to end. I heave a big sigh, check my calendar, and e-mail the Newsletter Committee with a date for our next meeting.

2 p.m.

I am in a meeting on the main campus of the University of South Carolina. This is the Faculty Senate Steering Committee meeting. Sounds like fun, huh? I am the secretary of the USC Faculty Senate, and as such I am a member of the senate's steering committee. I guess this means we steer things along as best we can (sometimes it's like the blind leading the blind). We meet once a month, an hour before the actual Faculty Senate meeting. We discuss such things as committee reports, vacancies on faculty committees, guest speakers, and so on. Today the meeting flows along smoothly.

3 p.m.

The Faculty Senate meeting begins. I manage to make it through my Report of the Secretary without incident. There have been times, believe me, when I wished I had the ability to disapparate like a wizard from a *Harry Potter* book. There is something about being onstage, in a spotlight, in front of hundreds of faculty senators that makes me put my foot in my mouth more often than not. I recall vividly the time I made a proposal to switch from printed minutes to online minutes. The uproar that ensued was quite memorable. That, incidentally, was my first day as secretary of the senate. It's a miracle I ever went back.

4:14 p.m.

The meeting is over and I'm heading home. Another day, another dollar! Now, what to make for dinner?

PROS AND CONS

I already covered the myriad joys of my position: the satisfaction of helping people hunt for informational treasures, the wide variety of fun and challenging tasks in which I am involved from day to day, interaction with interesting and amusing people. The list goes on.

There are only two drawbacks associated with my position: Supervision and Tenure. Note the capitalization! I am not a natural supervisor; I find it difficult to discipline people and dread any kind of personnel-management-type confrontation. I'm getting better at it, though. I've learned (the hard way) that if you are a supervisor, you need to maintain a bit of distance and not become buddies with everyone. There is a fine line between being a supervisor and being a friend, and you need to be careful to keep the scales tipped more toward the supervisor end of things. It *is* possible, I've discovered, to do this and still be friendly and fun!

Tenure. Ah, the dreaded word! At our institution, librarians are considered faculty. In terms of status, this is a good thing because we are on equal levels with the university's teaching faculty. However, this also means that we must go through the tenure process. In itself, it's not so bad. The problem comes when administrative types try to compare what librarians do with what the teaching faculty do. Librarians, by nature, place emphasis on service. However, to be awarded tenure, you must document that you have been proficient in three areas: service, teaching, and research/scholarly activity. Fulfilling tenure requirements in all three areas is difficult, and requires the pursuit of activities above and beyond your normal job duties. It often seems as though there aren't enough hours in the day for all of this! I have earned tenure, so I can say it's definitely achievable, but it is by no means an easy road. And then there is post-tenure review to worry about. I tell myself to think of it as yet another interesting challenge in my fulfilling job.

HOW TO GET A JOB LIKE MINE

Sorry, my job is not up for grabs. I only just got it, after all! However, there are many academic medical libraries around the country, and many varied positions within each one. The opportunities are there; you just need to be armed with the training and preparation required to make you indispensable! In library school, take any medical librarianship courses available. Work in a medical library as a graduate assistant. Do an internship in a health sciences library. Volunteer to work in the consumer health department of a public library. Join the Medical Library Association and one of its regional chapters. Go online and play around with PubMed, MedlinePlus, and other health Web sites. Any of these experiences will place you one step ahead of competing job applicants. Go for it—and good luck!

RELATED RESOURCES

For more information about medical librarianship, visit the Medical Library Association Web site at www.mlanet.org. Also, take a look at my LIScareer.com article titled "Medical Librarianship: A Niche for Every Interest" at www.liscareer.com/kane_medlibrarian.htm (accessed August 14, 2006).

CHAPTER 36

Head of Technical Services

KAREN DOUGLAS

As head of technical services at Duke University Law Library (DULL—we have lots of fun with that acronym!), I supervise eight people, including two librarians and six paraprofessionals. Together we work at keeping library resources current, organized, and usable by ordering, cataloging, processing, and binding them. We work in an environment that is constantly changing, so I am kept busy training staff, developing new procedures, and creating workflows. I also fill in doing day-to-day work in various sections as needed. As head of technical services, I play many roles. When I try to convince the tech services staff to embrace a new way of doing a job, I am a cheerleader. When I try to convince the administration that a staff member should be promoted or that staff need larger computer monitors to perform their jobs, I am an advocate. When I try to explain to the public services staff why a seemingly ridiculous (to them) technical services function needs to be performed, I am an ambassador. The job requires empathy, diplomacy, tact, and nerves of steel.

A TYPICAL WORKDAY

At the Duke University Law Library, the only thing dull about a typical workday is our acronym. On any given day I could be attending meetings at the main library to discuss procedures concerning our new online integrated library system or attending meetings with the department heads of collection services and reference to design programs to reward staff and boost morale. We might also have a major discussion about which books should be moved to our remote storage facility or why the systems department at the main library has yet to find a way to make our new books list work with the new online system. I also spend time doing necessary projects that no one else has time to do. Right now I am entering a note into the records of each of the two thousand journals that we bind. Fortunately one of our staff members, who is a whiz at creating macros, has made a macro that will allow me to enter this note into the record with two keystrokes. Once this is done, we will create a report from our online system that will tell the staff which volumes of our journals are ready to be bound at any given time. The notes include special binding instructions. Staff will be able to go to the shelves and pull only the issues that need to be bound.

I conduct regular staff meetings, mediate disagreements, and prepare staff performance evaluations. In my spare time, I read and answer e-mail and try to keep up with new developments in technical services by reading professional journals. I also attend continuing education courses conducted by the university to update my technology and management skills.

Several times a year I get to go to "exotic locations" ranging from Lexington, Kentucky, to San Juan, Puerto Rico, to attend meetings of the professional organizations for librarians. This is my chance to network with colleagues, learn about new library procedures and information, go to great parties, shop, and sightsee. (The last two activities vary depending on the location of the meeting.) If you are actively participating in the work of the organization, as I am, your leisure time is vastly reduced. However, your stock rises tremendously in the eyes of your superiors when you are involved with professional organizations. It also makes getting promoted or achieving tenure or continuing appointment much easier. Tenure or continuing appointment is highly desirable for academic librarians. It gives you as much job security as is possible in these uncertain times.

Initially, I became active in professional organizations because I was seeking a promotion. Now I do it because I enjoy it. In technical services, when you are not implementing new technology, your daily work can become rather routine. Service in professional organizations can enhance the work experience. But now, things are changing so quickly that daily work doesn't frequently become routine. I am now chair of the Technical Services Special Interest Section (TS-SIS) of the American Association of Law Libraries (AALL). This is the counterpart of the Association for Library Collections and Technical Services (ALCTS) in ALA. We migrated to a new online system at our library last year, and I thought that our library routines would have settled down by the time I took office in AALL this year. I figured that I would have the time to get as heavily involved in AALL as one needs to be to chair a special interest section. Boy, was I wrong! Since I became chair, I have still been working out major changes in our workflows warranted by the new system. We also had a system crash, which resulted in a loss of six weeks' worth of cataloging, ordering, serials check-in, and budget data.

Somewhere in the midst all of this I have managed to conduct organizational business for TS-SIS, greatly assisted by e-mail, conference calls, and fax machines. Hooray for modern technology! I have conducted a survey of our 625 members, planned programs for next year's meeting, written articles for our newsletter, and appointed committee members while sitting at my desk. It's all in a day's work.

JOYS AND PAINS OF THE JOB

Most days I love the work I do. Even though it can be frustrating, I enjoy planning new workflows and figuring out the quirks of our constantly changing technology. Little things excite us, such as creating a journal prediction pattern that actually works! The serials staff danced and cheered after that victory. Another great success was getting book spine labels to print properly and being able to edit the call numbers on them if needed. I supervise a group of dedicated, hard-working people who are just as excited as I am by the victories that we achieve, however small or large. It's a great feeling when you get the public services staff to acknowledge your existence and realize how important the technical services department is to the operation of the library.

I enjoy going to professional conferences and meeting other technical services librarians and sharing war stories. These conferences are where I get some of the best tips on how to make our section of the library function smoothly.

The work hours are great, too. In most cases, there are no night and weekend hours, which can be the bane of existence for public services staff.

Most of all I enjoy learning about, ordering, and receiving new books and serials. There's nothing like the smell of a new book!

On the other hand, as a department head I have to deal with a lot of administrative details and personnel issues. Writing performance evaluations, especially for staff who might not be working up to par, can be painful and emotionally wrenching. The duty I least like to perform is the difficult conversation. It sometimes affects me physically with headaches or a jumpy stomach. I am somewhat emotional, and conveying information that is likely to result in conflict or a confrontation is very difficult for me. It's also tough for me when people don't work the way I think they should. It's so much easier just to be responsible for yourself. I would love to make my salary and just be responsible for ordering material or managing serials, which is what I really enjoy. However, if you advance in technical services, you usually end up in some sort of supervisory position.

Though I enjoy learning about new developments in technical services, I am suffering from information overload. So much information is coming at me from so many different directions and in so many formats that it's almost impossible to process it all. I try desperately to keep up with all of my e-mail, but it takes hours. There aren't enough hours in the day to read professional journals, perform administrative tasks and special projects, take professional development courses, and do committee work for professional organizations. I need a clone!

WOULD YOU LIKE A JOB LIKE THIS?

A good tech services librarian should be attentive to details, extremely accurate, and maybe even slightly anal retentive. The joke in my library is that the tech services staff always have reports and evaluations ready ahead of the deadline and are always the first ones to arrive at the staff meetings. A person who likes solving puzzles and tracking down elusive details would also be a good fit. Comfort with computers and various Windows applications is a must. Virtually all technical services functions are now done using a computer. If you have the ability to quickly learn to use new computer software and enjoy using it to its maximum capacity, this is the job for you.

To get a job as head of a technical services department, you will need to have worked as a librarian in one or more of the subspecialties of technical services: acquisitions, serials management, cataloging, binding, and preservation. In some cases, collection management and development are also included in technical services. Working as a paraprofessional in one or more of these areas is helpful, too. To plan workflow and projects for a technical services department, you need to know about the functions and how they interact. I spent several years as an acquisitions/serials librarian who also did some work in binding and collection development. The only area in which I didn't have actual working experience was cataloging. To fill in that gap, I took several courses in cataloging. Also, when working in serials and acquisitions, you become familiar with a great number of cataloging functions. I surprised myself by knowing more cataloging than I thought I did.

Much of what I know about technical services I learned on the job and through continuing education. Very few courses beyond a cataloging course or two are taught in library schools these days. If you want to work as a technical services librarian, take as many technical services courses as possible in library school. Join the ALCTS section of ALA as a student. They offer many courses that are useful for gaining technical services knowledge. One of my favorites is the Fundamentals of Acquisitions course offered on the Web. Attendance at the annual meetings of ALA, and AALL if you want to be a law librarian, is very important. If you attend as a student, you can get reduced registration rates. Both organizations offer grants to students to pay for expenses connected with conference attendance. ALA and AALL both have extensive placement services available during the conference. Preliminary on-site job interviews are often conducted at conferences. You will also get a chance to attend meetings and participate in discussion groups where you can learn firsthand about technical services issues, concerns, and new developments in the field. This is often the best way to get a feel for the job. Networking opportunities abound at these conferences. Both ALA and AALL have mentoring programs and special activities for new members in the field. I got one of my first library jobs at an ALA conference and have also hired a librarian that had been interviewed at a conference.

This is an ideal time to consider becoming a technical services librarian. Those jobs are among the hardest library jobs to fill because there aren't enough candidates applying. Many technical services librarians are nearing retirement age, and there will be many openings in upcoming years.

RELATED RESOURCES

The following Web sites will give more information about technical services librarianship in law libraries and other types of libraries.

American Association of Law Libraries, Computing Services Special Interest Section. www.aallnet.org/sis/cssis (accessed August 20, 2006). This Web site contains job descriptions for technical services law librarian positions. Several descriptions for heads of technical services in law libraries are included.

————. Education for a Career in Law Librarianship. www.aallnet.org/committee/tfedu/education.html (accessed January 7, 2006). This Web page gives information about careers in law librarianship in general.

American Library Association, Education and Careers. www.ala.org/ala/education/educationcareers.htm (accessed January 7, 2006). This section of the ALA Web site gives all the information needed to prepare for a library career and find a position as a librarian.

Association for Library Collections and Technical Services. www.ala.org/alcts (accessed January 7, 2006). This is the Web site for the division of ALA that deals with technical services.

CHAPTER 37

Library Services Coordinator

ERIN BARTA

Being library services coordinator (LSC) at a small institution is tantamount to being an information god. Imagine having an intimate familiarity with all the books on your shelves, all of your policies, best practices, and emerging ideas in the field. One minute you're hunting an elusive citation, the next you're a copyright expert. This is the potential that being library services coordinator at a small academic institution has to offer. This is definitely a "big fish, small pond" scenario, for better or for worse. Although the demands of being an "everything librarian" can be a tad frightening, it affords the unique opportunity to have a clear understanding of libraries as entire systems and to be actively involved in each element that comprises the entire structure. So how does it work? How does one juggle all of these responsibilities without losing the love of the job?

WHAT IS IT THAT YOU DO, EXACTLY?

The library services coordinator assists the library director in all aspects of library operations, including staff management, budget allocations, and recommendations for major acquisitions (such as databases or equipment). The coordinator also works in interlibrary loan, cataloging, circulation, Web services, reference, and acquisitions as needed. The library services coordinator is responsible for developing and implementing policies to support operations and may be asked to draft institutional guides as well. Invoicing and billing are executed, and integration of software, hardware, or other services is tested and evaluated by the services coordinator for library or institutional use. Furthermore, the coordinator seeks to streamline workflow, identifies alternative sources of income or ways to offset costs, and develops projects to advance the library as well as the institution.

A services coordinator must be proficient in e-mail, customer service, computer troubleshooting (on a basic level), and have excellent written and oral communication skills. He or she must have knowledge of best practices in library administration, excellent people and supervisory skills, and some foundational knowledge of Web design. Finally, the coordinator should be able to remain informed as to new trends in library and Web services.

A Note on Reality

In practice, at a small school, the library director may have other major responsibilities (like the IT department or campus infrastructure) or an official capacity in institutional advancement, and may subsequently delegate much (if not most) library supervision to the library services coordinator. In such cases, the library director attends to his or her area of primary concern while relying on your direction and recommendations to present them at a much higher level. This means that you'll also need to work well collaboratively with superiors; in this situation, you can't afford to have a strained relationship with your boss.

A BRIEF OVERVIEW

Daily

Daily tasks for an LSC at a small library vary greatly. For the first few hours after opening, circulation may need attention; you may need to check items in and out, fill e-mail and phone requests, or assist patrons in person.

Depending on immediate needs, you may answer incoming reference questions. Reference questions can be unpredictable; they can take minutes or hours, depending on the obscurity of the citation or the difficulty of the question. You will be routinely interrupted with circulation needs, but if you have high-quality staff members, this usually isn't a problem.

Your final hours may be spent toggling between filling interlibrary loan requests, managing your interlibrary loan system, and doing copy or original cataloging. Physical processing of the books is usually delegated to a library assistant. Often you may need to dedicate more of your time to ILL and cataloging, so your days usually vary in focus. The balance of these tasks is specific to each institution, and there are no hard-and-fast rules; whichever is most pressing is done first.

Investigating or keeping current on new trends or technologies will take up your last few minutes or be the work you take home. However, the duties are of such a broad scope that your priorities will shift, being focused entirely on grant writing one day and troubleshooting your automation software the next.

Weekly

Woven into your daily routines are more involved library projects of your own initiation, such as grant seeking, grant writing, investigating new technologies, locating professional development opportunities, implementing improvements to systems, or working on employee morale. Acquisitions, Web services, and other areas may require periodic attention. You'll also be conferring with your superior(s) and meeting with staff regularly to oversee scheduling, help them solve problems, discuss project ideas, and assess their needs as well as their emotional and psychological well-being with regard to their work.

Additional monthly and annual responsibilities exist but are often institution-specific. Monthly statistical reports may be required at one library, whereas another simply may not track such data; some libraries perform routine inventory checks while others do not.

PROS AND CONS

For those who have attended library school or worked in a library setting, these points are fairly unsurprising, so I will focus on the hidden pros and cons of small institution librarianship.

After all, discovering some of the secrets to being successful is more important than learning how to do what you already know how to do, right?

Cons

Small communities, both professional and social, are peculiar because personal and professional oddities become remarkably magnified. In the workplace, to be rather blunt, the goings-on in a small institution can make the streets of *Desperate Housewives* look like the town of Mayberry from *The Andy Griffith Show*. A sea of drama, conflict, and turmoil often fluctuates chaotically just underneath the restful surface. The personality quirks, level of interpersonal communication skills, and attitude that each person brings to the workplace will influence everyone. Whether through direct interaction, indirect consequence, or just old-fashioned office gossip, you will be affected by persons in entirely different departments. This may sound exaggerated, but these days, libraries at small institutions are sometimes considered a bonus, especially as the availability of online databases sometimes causes libraries to go entirely virtual. As a librarian, you may be scrutinized with a keener eye or feel that you are continually asked to validate your departmental existence to administrators. Often, during financially trying times, the library budget is the first to feel the spending executioner's ax, and you'd rather it be out of necessity than due to ugly interoffice politics.

So, with some of these things in mind, remember that in a small institution you should be prepared to do the following.

Make the occasional Faustian alliance. Due to the complex nature of organizational hierarchies, you'll need to be aware of who has authority over you, your department, and most important, your budget allocations ... and then spend some time figuring out who has authority over *those* people. By "authority," I do not simply refer to chain of command; many individuals unaffiliated with departmental directives have enormous institutional influence. By no means should you devolve into a smarmy sycophant or be a traitor to your own character; just be careful whose feathers you ruffle. Upset the wrong person, even on a personal level, and you could find your serials budget unceremoniously slashed in half. In larger organizations, such decisions would be the responsibility of a body of individuals, some completely removed and impartial, but in smaller settings these outcomes in all likelihood will be decided by persons with whom you interact on a daily or weekly basis. Additionally, you may have to collaborate and find agreement with a powerful person whom you dislike, distrust, or feel is manipulative or dishonest—someone who, under other circumstances, you might only meet in a cemetery armed with a cross and garlic. Seek to establish positive working relationships, even if you must invest more time and effort to do so. It can only benefit your library.

Beware of personal scrutiny. You'd be surprised at the number of individuals who are aware of how you present yourself. In a microcorporate environment, it may be said that "news travels fast," which is a euphemism for "gossip runs rampant." Believe it or not, people notice how you dress ("Did you see how short her skirt was?!"), as well as whether you're warm and welcoming. On the member services level, this means that you'll run into your problem patrons with great regularity; you'll identify them and they'll identify you. Part of librarianship involves investing in good marketing. Part of library marketing involves marketing yourself as a respectable representative of the institution. You'd be surprised how disarming a genuine smile can be. A library should represent a community's common ground, and you should display an interest in creating a positive community environment within your institution.

Learn creative ways to say no. Librarians at smaller libraries are often handed the most outrageous requests (often by faculty). Faculty tend to have tremendous influence at smaller academic schools, which means it's a good idea to keep them well fed and happy. However, you can't acquiesce to every request, especially if it crunches your budget, so you must find ways to keep faculty in good spirits while informing them that you can't comply. Offering a list of alternative solutions is a good idea; giving them something useful they can walk away with can preserve the library-faculty relationship.

Learn creative ways to say yes. For example, you may (will) be forced to make a purchase or perform a service for which you truly do not wish to be accountable. If it impacts your budget, sometimes you can find ways to have the funds withdrawn from a more appropriate department (one other than your own) to help ease the financial burden. In such cases, the patron is appeased and your budget is uncompromised. Because you are a small organization, staffing will be sparse. Seeking alternative sources of funding and manpower in the form of grants or internships can allow you to maintain normal operations while carrying a workload that boasts extraordinary projects.

Wear a lot of hats. You will fulfill many roles that would be delegated to various library departments in larger institutional settings. This means that you might be performing a combination of circulation, reference, interlibrary loan, cataloging, acquisitions, and Web services. You might spend days working alone at the circulation desk, which backs up your reference queue, or your cataloging workload might tower behind you as you wrap up your ILL requests.

In my opinion, this is simultaneously a good thing and a total disaster. It's a disaster because you may be overwhelmed and often forced to set aside projects you'd like to tackle to attend to more pressing needs (like the patrons in front of you). It's very good because you will have the rare opportunity to discover how each of your library services interconnect (for example, how cataloging and reference complement one another) and will be able to strengthen each service. Such familiarity with each facet of librarianship makes you a better librarian. I will, however, caution you that holding such a position at a small institution will force you to work overtime hours, many of them unpaid.

Accept the fact that you can't please everyone. Try as you might, you just can't. A policy might delight one person and infuriate the next. This is important to remember when handling complaints about your library, your staff, or even yourself.

Most of these points are common to institutions of all sizes and are not unique. However, do keep in mind that in a diminutive environment these things are magnified to a greater-than-expected intensity.

Pros

Of course, there are many positives that make working for a small library very fulfilling. While there are negatives in any employment situation, there should ideally be a greater number of pros that make your job enjoyable and rewarding. For a manager or coordinator at a small institution, some of the benefits that should make you smile at the end of the day include the following.

Knowing your patrons. As noted, a small institution has the good fortune of behaving like a community, which means you'll have the opportunity to get to know your patrons very well. You'll be able to establish rapport with many of them and follow their academic and professional careers. This alone makes working in a small institution extremely meaningful. You will become intimately familiar with your patrons' areas of interest, making it easier to tailor materials and resources to meet their specific needs. You will have the advantage of providing in house and online services to individuals that you personally know and enjoy. Sometimes you are given the ultimate compliment of an acknowledgment in a publication or student work such as a dissertation or thesis. Either way, good or bad, your patrons will remember you.

Having autonomy. With some exceptions, you will have a great deal of self-determination. How your library looks, feels, and operates (within budget constraints) will be largely up to you. Selection of materials will not likely involve large boards of approval or committees, so you will have a great deal of latitude in the acquisitions process, which will make your job exponentially easier. Furthermore, the tedium of reporting daily to supervisors or the chances of being driven to the brink of madness by micromanagers are more minimal than in other environments. You will decide how your time is spent, which is why I recommend a time management seminar such as those offered by FranklinCovey. You'll have your workplace freedom, but your responsibilities and projects still have to be completed in a timely manner.

Investigating new things. Working at a small library often allows you to investigate new technologies without all of that sticky red tape. Often you have greater freedom to test new software, hardware, or Web-based tools. Professional development budgets tend to be more flexible, or at least negotiable. Additionally, smaller institutions may want to have their own repositories, so you'll have the opportunity to try your hand at archives management as well.

Creating teamwork. This is just plain fun. It's work, but it can give you a pleasant sense of enthusiasm for your workplace. As a library manager, you have the singular ability to provide your staff members with opportunities for teambuilding. Meetings, retreats, discussions of ideas, and collaborative projects are great ways to keep staff participating with interest. Creating a positive work environment ensures colleague cohesion, quickens the workplace, and simply makes work enjoyable.

Giving, giving, giving. In addition to creating teamwork, you'll also be able to plan, design, and implement outreach strategies to reach your population, which may include staff members in other departments, faculty, students, or community patrons. Offering outreach services designed for your fellow colleagues in other departments is a great way to foster a sense of community and increase the feeling of connection and value these individuals have for your library.

The freedoms provided by these advantages allow you to create a distinctive environment for yourself, your colleagues, and your patrons.

GETTING THERE IS HALF THE FUN (YEAH, RIGHT!)

For those interested in working in a small library within a corporate or institutional setting, I recommend a great variety of coursework during an MLS/MLIS program. You'll want to concentrate on courses in academic librarianship, reference and user services, technology tools (fundamentals of Web design, basic and advanced), database design (optional, but handy), cataloging, document delivery, library administration, collection development, archives and rare books, and records management. Also, you'll want some experience; spend extra time volunteering at places, and apply for jobs that will provide basic skills for this position (such as interlibrary loan assistant, cataloging assistant, circulation assistant, or reference assistant). Find ways to obtain progressive experience with increasing responsibilities, perhaps with some supervisory capacity.

IN CLOSING

If you do not thrive in a changing environment or are appalled at the prospect of being involved in every aspect of your library, a position such as library services coordinator will probably not make a satisfying career. Many individuals prefer a more formulaic environment, where methods and outcomes are outlined and predetermined. However, the scale and nature of the opportunities afforded by an LSC position at a smaller institution can make your career as a librarian immensely gratifying.

CHAPTER 38

Learning Resource Center Director

LONNIE BEENE

As director of a community college learning resource center (LRC), I'm responsible for strategic planning, policy formulation and implementation, management of operations and personnel, budget formulation and management, and program development for the library and media services units of the college.

Can you tell I adapted that from my formal job description?

In simpler language, I plan the overall direction for the LRC and make sure we have the resources to take us there. These resources are people, money, and equipment. I make sure we have enough of all of those to get us where we need to be.

Like all academic libraries today, mine has a mix of print, nonprint, and electronic resources. Keeping the right balance is an ongoing challenge, and not just a financial one. Without TexShare (a cooperative program of the Texas State Library and Archives Commission) to provide affordable access to online databases for academic and public libraries across the state, electronic resources would use up a much higher percentage of our materials budget. Microfilm and microfiche have never been popular media in my library, so we have all but jettisoned them, keeping only a bare minimum of titles. Electronic resources have, of course, become increasingly popular in recent years, and now they are the first point of departure for many students seeking to do research. Nevertheless, print materials continue to be in demand.

At my college, the LRC is responsible for media services in addition to library services. Media services means different things at different institutions. Our provision of media services is limited to acquiring and maintaining a collection of audiovisual materials and equipment. Television monitors, VCRs and DVD players, and overhead projectors still constitute over 90 percent of media equipment usage. In our case, we do not have a media production facility, so we do not produce videos and other instructional materials, except for occasionally videotaping college functions. (We also have a graphic arts department that functions primarily as a print shop for the college's printing needs; it is not administratively linked to the LRC, although we share building space.)

A TYPICAL WORKDAY

Although no two days are identical, there are routines that don't change much from day to day. Tasks that have to be performed every day include booting up the public computers and upgrading software as needed; delivering audiovisual equipment to classrooms before classes start; running various statistical and transaction reports using the library automation system; and checking in materials that have been returned through the book drops. However, even simple tasks can become time-consuming and complex depending on the circumstances.

Staffing can affect everything about the day. We're a small library at a small college, so we have a small staff. Every staff member counts. Everyone performs duties that would be performed by three or four people at a larger institution. I'm the director, but I do a lot more than that. Because I spent twelve years in cataloging and technical services before becoming a director, I'm responsible for unraveling cataloging problems, including doing original cataloging. I'm the system administrator for our automation system and the Webmaster for the library's Web site. Those are my basic duties. But if we're shorthanded in any area, I may have to step in. I can work the circulation desk, answer reference questions, conduct tours and instructional sessions, track down orders, deliver and troubleshoot audiovisual equipment, and basically do anything else that arises when no one else is available. We've never been so shorthanded that I've had to close the library, but we've come perilously close sometimes, and most days I feel I'm walking a tightrope in terms of staffing with only the slightest nudge needed to send me into freefall.

Although the LRC has a written policy manual, almost every day some situation arises that doesn't neatly fit into any existing policy. Although my staff would love to have a clearly written policy that covers every situation, that's not realistic. Sometimes I bend the policies a little. However, if a unique situation recurs enough times that it can no longer be considered unique, I may have to amend an existing policy or write a new one. I always use staff input to determine policies, but the ultimate decision—as well as the responsibility if it doesn't work out—is mine.

The most challenging thing about my job is describing what it is we do to people who don't have a library background so they'll give us money. The most frustrating thing about my job is that I have to work as hard as I do at that. It's been a struggle for me to overcome the idea that the value of the library is as self-evident to everyone else as it is to me. I've been using libraries since I could read. Some people, even highly educated people who have gone as far as one can go through the American educational system, still do not understand or appreciate the value of libraries. Even among those who do appreciate libraries, many misperceptions still persist. Asking these people for the money to support ongoing library services, let alone expand them, is a challenge that often takes all my skills at reasoning and persuasion.

There's always something that needs my signature. God help us if I ever break my right hand! Signing invoices for new expenditures and renewals is an almost daily occurrence. Classified staff and student time sheets also have to be signed twice a month.

Because our purchase order system went paperless a few years ago, I no longer have to sign purchase orders. But they require my electronic signature, which basically consists of my logging in to the system and approving or rejecting requests for purchase orders. I'm the one who initiates these expenditures (usually but not always based on what I budgeted for the year), so I rarely reject one unless it contains an error. Once I've approved the purchase order, it is passed along to my vice president for his approval. It will continue along to the business office, which eventually will generate a paper purchase order. So our paperless system isn't entirely paperless after all. Little wonder, as vendors need something in writing.

Interruptions are a fact of life for a director. I've often thought that if I came in to work every morning with no more on my agenda than to sit at my desk and wait for someone to bring me a problem or question, I would never run out of things to do. Between telephone calls, requests for my signature, reports to write, reference inquiries, staff questions, user complaints, committee meetings, and miscellaneous demands on my time, at least I never have time to feel unwanted!

Ah, yes ... committee meetings. How could I forget those? I'm a member of several standing committees, as well as the occasional ad hoc committee. I'm a member of the Instruction and Student Development Council, a committee of department heads who report to the same vice president for instruction and student development. I'm on the Curriculum Committee, which approves new courses and programs, evaluates existing ones, and devises the class schedule every semester. I'm on the Technology Committee, which looks at campus-wide technology issues and makes recommendations. I was recently added to two ad hoc committees. One of them is looking at academic honesty and the college's policies toward cheating. The other is reviewing the college's involvement in the Virtual College of Texas (VCT), a program by which community colleges create distance learning classes and provide them to one another. For my hard work, my college rewarded me by nominating me to participate in the Texas Library Association's TALL Texans Leadership Development Institute in 1999. It was a phenomenal experience and one that I continue to think of as a high point of what continues to be a very satisfying career.

PROS AND CONS

The biggest drawback of my job is never having enough resources to do everything we would like or sometimes need to do. That's hardly a unique situation for community college libraries.

The biggest advantage of being a director is the sense of being in control, not for the sake of controlling—control freaks don't make good directors, or good anything else, in my opinion—but for the sense of shaping the future of your library, your institution, and most important, the people who seek your assistance. There's no greater feeling of accomplishment than the compliments you receive from past and present students, faculty, administrators, and community users who tell you, "You helped me when I needed it. Thanks."

HOW WOULD I GET A JOB LIKE YOURS?

Apply for it. That's not as facetious as it sounds. A lot of people would make excellent directors, but they never seek out and apply for positions. No one is likely to hand you a director's job without your asking for it. If you want it, go out and look for it.

It helps tremendously if you're willing and able to move.

Getting a job like mine is in some ways the easy part. The hard part is making your administration realize you're worth keeping. But that's not really so hard, either. All you have to do is follow some simple guidelines.

First, work hard. It's easy to succumb to thinking that the only reward for hard work is more work. I do this myself sometimes. But more work means you're being trusted to do the work and do it well. If the workload is unfairly onerous, perhaps you're in the wrong place. It happens. Only you know the answer to that. But wherever you go, you must be seen as willing to put in the extra effort.

Second, know what you're doing. Practice your craft. Exercise good judgment. If you don't know what that is, find out. Study best practices. Read everything you can get your hands on that will make you better at what you do.

Third, make sure your administration knows what you're doing. Although it's not necessary to take every little problem to your bosses, that's no excuse for never taking problems to them or for not meeting with them. There are certain categories of problems or issues I always take to my immediate supervisor. Examples include anything that involves spending money beyond what's in my budget; any dispute between the LRC and a person or department that we're not able to mediate successfully among ourselves (fortunately, these are extremely rare); and any proposed change in policy or service that has a potential impact on some other group. (These are, incidentally, the same kinds of problems and issues I expect my staff to bring to me.)

Fourth, don't cry wolf. If you go running to your bosses expecting them to solve every little problem you really should solve yourself, eventually they won't believe you about the genuinely major problems. You have to build some credibility for yourself; you want to be seen as a problem-solver.

Fifth, don't waste time. This goes hand in hand with not crying wolf, but it also goes beyond it. A particular pet peeve of mine is unnecessary meetings. Do not confuse quantity with quality regarding meetings. By the time I left an earlier job, I was spending thirty hours a week in meetings—and my boss couldn't understand why I wasn't getting any work done! Regularly scheduled meetings are fine if they work for you and others. But it's better to have meetings when they're necessary (for example, if one of the situations just outlined has come up) than to schedule meetings regularly for their own sake. Meeting when no one has much to talk about is not a good use of anyone's time.

RELATED RESOURCES

I would have a very hard time doing my job without e-mail lists. I've always found them invaluable, and never more so since moving to a small town and a small college, with very few librarians around locally to bounce ideas off of. To give just one example, I subscribe to CJC-L (www.ala.org/ala/acrl/aboutacrl/acrlsections/commjr/listserv/listserv.htm), an e-mail list for community and junior college librarians.

CHAPTER 39

University Library Director

E. LORENE FLANDERS

I am the director of the library at a state university in Georgia serving just over ten thousand students. The student population has grown fairly rapidly in the past decade, and a few select doctoral programs were recently added. The library has sixteen tenure-track faculty librarians supported by seventeen staff members and a number of student assistants. The library's associate director, who reports to me, supervises four librarians who are division and department heads. The vice president for academic affairs is my supervisor. I am responsible for overseeing library personnel and budget management and for developing collections and services to meet the university's mission.

Three essential elements for serving as a library director are vision, leadership, and ethics, all of which are critical to the operational aspect of libraries. In developing a vision for a library and in planning for its ongoing development, directors must focus on assessing collections, facilities, services, and programs. This forms the basis for goal setting and strategic planning. It is essential that the library's leadership provide an environment in which library faculty and staff are afforded opportunities for collaboration, synthesizing ideas, and participation in decision making. The director must provide a climate in which brainstorming, open discussion, and critique are accomplished with appreciation for the unique talents and differing backgrounds, preparation, and perspective each person brings. Academic library directors must also be very open to seeking input from the campus to plan for the ongoing and long-term development of the library. Ethics plays a critical role in communication, and in a director's approach to personnel issues, budgeting, and allocating resources.

A TYPICAL WORKDAY

Much of my day is spent communicating with library and university personnel by attending meetings and sending and receiving e-mail. There is a large volume of campus e-mail each day, some of which requires response or provides opportunities to involve the library in campus events, programs, and initiatives. Building-related issues must be addressed most days. I also compile information and write reports and other materials. I once heard a candidate for university president describe that job as "explaining things and thanking people." Those are also important aspects of a library director's job, as are initiating, supporting, guiding, and being a team player willing to work side by side with library and university faculty and staff.

Formal and informal meetings allow an organization to run effectively and provide a form of communication for developing ideas. I begin each week by attending a meeting of deans and others who report to the vice president for academic affairs. We discuss issues facing the institution, including program development, budgetary realities, enrollment management, and campus climate. Each month, I meet with the library's division and department heads, the library faculty, and the vice president. I am blessed with faculty and staff who take initiative and who are savvy, forward thinking, and well regarded in the profession. Because I am relatively new to the campus and to the position, I am meeting with individuals and departments to learn more about what they do and the challenges they face, often brainstorming to shape vision and direction for the future of the library.

I also interact with university personnel to assist in furthering their work or learn more about their vision for the library. Faculty often drop by to share ideas, raise questions, or request library input and support for proposals. For example, I am currently meeting with a faculty member interested in seeking a major national grant, brainstorming ideas to shape the focus of the grant application and to identify schools and other agencies to partner with in this endeavor.

Working with library and campus constituencies on vision and strategic planning is an important part of my job. We must explore issues the campus faces, determine how they will impact the library, and make budget requests to meet these challenges. For example, our campus is adding some doctoral programs and may change its Carnegie Classification category. This could raise subscription costs for online information resources, prices for which are predicated on institutional enrollment and classification. My job is to work with the library faculty and staff to identify these issues and communicate to the university administration the costs involved in maintaining and extending the current level of library resources and services. Library budgets are complex, and their ongoing management requires assistance and input from many people.

Library directors from the thirty-five institutions that comprise our state university system have traditionally worked very closely on collaborative initiatives that have put our state at the forefront of providing information resources and services to our citizens. We recently celebrated the tenth anniversary of GALILEO, an online library of databases available to all of the citizens of Georgia. As part of this project, academic librarians developed plans for a universal catalog and other cooperative initiatives to allow students and faculty to request materials from any library in the system. Statewide collaboration requires extensive interaction. I subscribe to an e-mail list of directors and attend two annual meetings that provide opportunities to interact and propose strategies to meet challenges libraries face. For example, the rapid shift to electronic provision of government information is impacting the Federal Depository Library Program, and we are discussing development of a collaborative effort for providing statewide access to this information. My government documents personnel, who are well regarded by their colleagues in the state, will likely provide leadership in shaping this idea. Our library is a member of a metropolitan Atlanta area consortium, another point of contact that requires meetings and other communication.

Whether a library building is old or new, managing a facility is a major aspect of a library director's job. Our library was built in the late 1960s and last expanded in the early 1980s, so the space is dated, somewhat crowded, and not particularly inviting. Some areas face extreme space constraints that compromise our ability to provide services and programs. The campus master plan has identified the need to double the current library space. This project will probably require a decade or more for planning, funding, and construction, as a couple of other projects have precedence. We must find ways to make our current facility work, identify interim solutions to our space problems, and address issues with the building in ways that will make it more secure and inviting. The campus is considering converting an adjacent building to house special collections, and has funded a minor facility project to expand this area in our current building. We are working with an architect and campus facility personnel to finalize plans. Because the expansion will displace some shelving for our regular collections, we must communicate with those responsible for stacks maintenance as well as consider how the construction phase will impact service in special collections.

Hiring, training, and evaluating faculty and staff are ongoing processes. In a university setting, evaluation is the underpinning of the promotion and tenure system. Librarians are rated on their job performance as well as on their service and professional development activities. University personnel often instigate or contribute to community improvement projects. A group of faculty and staff from our university is currently meeting with community educators to discuss ways we can be proactive in furthering information literacy. This initiative, set in motion by my faculty and staff in their various roles as librarians, library staff, parents, and citizens, provides an application of our professional expertise to an issue that needs to be addressed in the community.

Other faculty duties include institutional service such as serving on university committees. As a liaison to academic departments, I meet with the faculty to talk about the library, offer assistance and support for teaching and curricular development, and assist with collection development questions. I order materials to support my departments, review online resources we hope to purchase, and seek departmental input regarding items for the collection. I plan classes on faculty request. The library teaches a for-credit library research unit, and most librarians teach one or more sections of this course each semester. I also work at the reference desk each week, as well as on weekends.

As a new library director, I seek opportunities for training and professional development, another area on which faculty are evaluated. My professional development plan includes identifying courses that address specific library issues, such as space planning or assessment of services, attending conferences offering sessions on topics concerning areas for which I am responsible, and reading about management and about the institution.

THE JOYS AND ANNOYANCES

The greatest joy of my position as director is working with library and university colleagues to visualize and strategize for ongoing development of the library. As a newcomer to the campus, I feel blessed to have landed in a good place. The library has an excellent reputation on campus, in the community, and throughout the state. To support the campus and its mission, the library staff needs opportunities to interact with various constituencies as a basis for understanding how collections and services should be developed. I enjoy bringing people together in the workplace as well as in social settings that extend the teaching, learning, and collaboration that is part of everyday life on campus. This includes hosting library gatherings, introducing new colleagues to my staff or to people in the community, or inviting guest researchers or campus speakers to my home. Better working relationships develop when people meet informally. Ideas and projects are often initiated from casual conversations.

I suppose the greatest personal annoyance is feeling that I have failed to address everything I would like to or that I should address, or that I have failed to communicate with affected constituencies. Sometimes there is too little time, or we assume people know things by osmosis. Learning about campus practices is a challenge, as is prioritizing time, initiatives, and ideas. Whether you are a new director or one who has served in this capacity for some time, you will likely find it challenging to manage being a practicing librarian due to the amount of time and energy that administrative matters consume. For many of us in the library profession, the greatest professional annoyance must certainly be the abysmal salary structure in librarianship. This presents difficulties recruiting faculty and staff. As the ranks thin in the profession due to the large wave of expected retirements in the next decade, this will continue to be a challenge.

HOW WOULD I GET A JOB LIKE YOURS?

Directors of academic libraries combine business savvy with scholarship. Personnel and facilities management, budgeting, and technology implementation will be part of your daily work. You must also understand and participate in the world of academia. A master's degree or a doctorate in a subject field in addition to the requisite ALA-accredited master's degree provides an understanding of the world of teaching and scholarship. Developing experience with institutional funding sources and processes, tenure and promotion issues, and faculty governance is essential.

To direct a library, you need experience in the ranks. Develop diverse expertise, as you may not always have staff who specialize in the many facets of libraries. It helps to be comfortable and knowledgeable with reference services, instruction in the academic setting, and technical issues, because technology is the critical underpinning of library service today. For ongoing professional development, be active in professional organizations, look for opportunities to present and publish, and take advantage of training and development opportunities.

Library directors must be open communicators who are comfortable interacting with many constituencies. University library directors have numerous opportunities to speak to campus administration, committees, faculty, staff, students, parents, alumni, foundation members, and community groups. Learn the art of speaking in group settings and in public. It will stand you in good stead in many roles—as a meeting participant or leader, as a public speaker, and as one charged with communicating the value of libraries to ensure that they maintain appropriate support to serve their clientele.

RELATED RESOURCES

American Library Association. www.ala.org (accessed February 2, 2006). The ALA Web site provides links to two important divisions involved with university libraries and with administrative and management issues: the Association of College and Research Libraries (ACRL) and the Library Administration and Management Association (LAMA).

Cunningham, Nancy. 2001. In search of an emotionally healthy library. *LIScareer.com* (December). www.liscareer.com/cunningham_eiq.htm (accessed February 2, 2006).

U.S. Department of Labor Bureau of Labor Statistics. 2006. Librarians. *Occupational outlook handbook* (August 4). www.bls.gov/oco/ocos068.htm (accessed August 20, 2006).

PART III

School Libraries

CHAPTER 40

Private School Librarian

BARBARA KARP

As the one and only librarian in an elite girls' school of approximately seven hundred students in grades preschool through twelve, I have quite a varied job. My day is divided between two libraries, which means I get a fair amount of exercise traveling between them. Because this is a one-woman show, my duties run the gamut from acquisitions to research assistance.

GOOD MORNING

On most days, my day begins in the elementary library. As soon as I arrive, I make sure my computer is ready to go and clear my desk before the recess rush begins. We are not automated, but we possess an inexpensive circulation program in which all titles are entered as they are acquired. Each morning, there is often circulation information from the previous day waiting to be entered. My first task is to update the records and replace cards in returned books.

This job is barely completed when I hear the bell announcing the imminent arrival of a large contingent of eager readers. At the beginning of a school year, things are especially hectic—girls are issued new library cards, faculty meetings are attended, and policies and services are publicized. In addition, there is the unpleasant task of informing some students that, because they did not return books the previous school year, they will not receive a library card until all obligations are met. I perform a juggling act—I am often simultaneously called on to recommend a book by a certain author, for example, while assisting a student doing online research, providing a book on a specific subject for a preschool teacher to read to her class, and checking materials in and out.

When the bell signals the end of recess, it does not always mean I can catch my breath. First and second graders visit as a class every two weeks, and some sessions occur either immediately before or after the break. Occasionally I read a story, but the visit is normally for borrowing books. It's a pleasure to see the eagerness of these little readers, and sometimes a short discussion with a young book lover ensues. After each class visit, there are computer records to update reflecting returned and borrowed books and varying degrees of straightening up to be done.

TIME TO MOVE

Before I know it, it's time to put on my high school librarian hat. If my schedule permits, I join the teachers in the faculty room at lunchtime for perhaps the only sustained adult company I enjoy the entire day. On occasion, I am still there when a high school student wanders in looking for me. It's amazing that they know where the librarian is hiding.

The high school library routine is very different from that of the elementary library. There is not usually the daily onslaught of readers, with one notable exception: Term Paper Time. I ask teachers to inform me before giving any assignment involving library use, and many comply. However, often my first indication that a research report has been assigned is the bombardment of girls asking for historical fiction, materials on any number of contemporary issues, information about a disease, a biography of a female scientist, literary criticism, a good poem to read aloud, ad infinitum. Thankfully, I am able to fulfill most requests. (It is painful when I must tell a student I don't have what she needs.)

Outside of students requesting help with a class assignment, there is the smattering of pupils looking for a specific bit of information or something good to read. Because the students' days are very full, frequently the only time they can work in the library is when school is dismissed. To accommodate them, the high school library is open late.

BEHIND THE SCENES

All these requests would be extremely difficult to fulfill if I didn't do my homework. Most of the funding I receive becomes available in the early winter and must be spent by early spring. I'm constantly on the lookout for materials that will support the curriculum, meet reference and research needs, be useful for book reports, and/or be interesting to read. I canvass teachers, make notes on what students request, and consult professional literature, vendor catalogs, and other librarians to learn what's out there. Even though some people look askance when I ask for reading or research assignments for the following school year ("It's only October! *This* school year has just started!"), it takes several months to compile the best possible order with the funds available.

New acquisitions are not all that keep me busy when I'm not working with the public. There are books that need to be repaired before they can circulate again. Overdue notices are distributed, and, to avoid error, I search the collection to make sure books really aren't on the shelf before I send the student a "black letter." I regularly check out (sometimes literally) our holdings to determine quality, usefulness, user appeal, and relevance. In addition, there are electronic resources to try so that I am familiar with them when information requests come in. And, lest someone think office items appear by magic, I take inventory of supplies and order more as necessary. (Once I neglected to make sure we had enough library cards at the beginning of the school term. Furthermore, how could I *think* young visitors would be happy to be told there are no bookmarks?)

PUBLICITY

A great library deserves to have the public know about it and the materials it contains. Toward this end, I maintain bulletin boards at both libraries. Outside the elementary library, readers can check out the "Happy Birthday, Authors" feature to learn which writers were born in any given month and become acquainted with some of their books. High school students will note signs throughout the collection providing similar information. Display shelves show readers a variety of new and noteworthy titles. I am a strong proponent of humor, so "Library Laughs" are featured on the wall near the high school library door. And we must not forget special occasions like Elephant Day (September 22), Children's Book Week, Teen Read Week, and whatever holiday or commemoration is coming up. There are so many opportunities to introduce readers to good books!

Speaking of special occasions, the elementary library hosts the school's annual book festival. Inspired by the National Book Festival sponsored by First Lady Laura Bush some years ago, the event provides children with the opportunity to exercise their literary and artistic talents by participating in activities such as completing unfinished stories, writing book reviews, and designing posters. All participants receive a prize, and their work is displayed throughout the elementary library.

To keep young readers (and their teachers and parents) informed about quality titles, I compile and distribute recommended reading lists as well as suggestions of topical and seasonal materials. In addition, I provide annotated, subject-indexed lists of the videos and most valuable reference books in the collection. Occasionally, I am asked for this information, but I try to anticipate users' needs and prepare bibliographies on a regular basis.

SUMMER VACATION? WHAT'S THAT?

When new books and videos arrive, usually in spring and summer, I enthusiastically open the boxes to see what came. (We don't receive every title ordered, as not everything is in stock or in print; therefore, I overorder by approximately 50 percent.) I read or browse many of the new arrivals to familiarize myself with them, determine suitability for the intended age group, and decide if they are appropriate for our girls. Of course, I also read for pleasure.

Once materials have passed inspection, I enter an acquisitions record and assign a book number. The vendor I use for most of my orders sends the books and videos shelf-ready (cataloged and processed). I prepare all other materials for use.

An aside: Occasionally, when teachers hear I'll be working over the summer, they ask, "You are open in the summer? People really come in to borrow books?" Sometimes I think I spend the first half of the summer adding the new acquisitions to the libraries, sending out final overdue notices, checking in materials, and shelving returned items, and I spend the second half rearranging each collection, weeding, and preparing for the school year. By the time the other faculty members begin drifting back, *I'm* ready for a vacation. Even dedicated librarians need to recharge our batteries so we can effectively and cheerfully provide quality service to our patrons.

JOYS AND CHALLENGES

For those of you who think a school librarian position sounds like your cup of tea, I can attest to the merits of such a job. First and foremost is the interaction with eager young readers and researchers and the impromptu book (or audiovisual) discussion that often results. There is nothing quite like the feeling of satisfaction that comes when I successfully help students and teachers with their requests.

I personally find the intellectual stimulation and periods of nonstop activity gratifying. I am aware, however, that school librarians do not have a monopoly on this experience. At a recent convention session devoted to library programming and services, there was a general consensus that a "librarian mentality" exists, manifesting itself in personality traits such as helpfulness and putting others' needs and wishes before our own (including issues of finances and respect).

Another plus of my job is the enjoyable experience of selecting, receiving, and reading new and valuable books. I often compare my reaction to opening a box of recent arrivals to that of a child with a new toy.

There are definitely areas that I refer to as challenges. Because my library staff (like that of many schools) is small (a majority of one, in my case), there is a real pressure to meet the needs of the faculty, staff, and students in the course of a day. Add to that the behind-the-scenes activities of maintaining circulation records, shelving, repairing books, selecting materials, and so on, and it becomes obvious that a school librarian's job is far from sedentary.

Another negative aspect, and possibly the most frustrating, is the fact that some teachers and administrators do not accept the librarian as an educational professional. I say "some," because there are faculty members who, to their credit, consider me a colleague and not a clerical employee.

In addition, a school librarian must always be on guard against children's (and teenagers') natural tendencies to take advantage of the friendly atmosphere of the libraries. Constant vigilance is a necessity to maintain a food-free, orderly environment in which materials are readily accessible and easily located. (A sure sign that a particular author or series is a hit is the condition of the shelf containing the books after eager readers have visited the area. Perhaps this is not a drawback: it's one way I learn of a book's or writer's popularity.)

Related to the occasionally unpleasant interactions with students are the dealings with parents, especially regarding overdue materials. Though most communications are cordial, there is invariably the devoted parent who is certain his or her daughter cannot *possibly* have an unreturned library book, and the librarian or school must be irresponsible to make such a claim.

Finally, budget constraints are a concern. Many desirable resources are not added to the collection because there is inadequate funding for them. Yet this is a blessing in disguise: I must be diligent when selecting materials to ensure (to the best of my ability) that every title is of value.

WHAT IT TAKES TO BE A SCHOOL LIBRARIAN

School librarians need to have a solid background in reference and reader's advisory. This knowledge is essential, as there is seldom leisure time to think about the best possible source of information or most suitable title when forty students need your assistance in thirty minutes. The ability to make quick determinations under pressure and focus on each individual request while not excluding the needs of other patrons is vital. A calm, cheerful personality is definitely an asset, as is flexibility. (If you are preparing an Internet book order and a student needs to do online research on the same computer before she must return to class in fifteen minutes, her requirements definitely take precedence.) A school librarian must always be willing to learn and adapt and to see in any encounter an opportunity to improve library service and programming. (That adorable photograph of a kitten behind a tree can turn into a reading promotion poster with an appropriate caption, like "Maybe my brother won't find me here, and I can read my library book.") And last but definitely not least, you must *love* working with children and teenagers, and be friendly but firm.

WHERE TO FIND A SCHOOL LIBRARIAN POSITION

If you're still a library student, the best place to learn of openings is your university's library. Especially if your library school has its own library, you have access to journals and other valuable sources. In addition, it's important to make your name known. Send letters and résumés (or better yet, pay a visit) to city education departments and private schools. Become a member of ALA's American Association of School Librarians, the Association for Library Service to Children, or the Young Adult Library Services Association. Many states also have their own educational library associations. Librarians seeking positions in religious schools will find organizations devoted to parochial librarianship. Attend conventions and conferences and keep in touch with the professionals you meet there. The Internet is obviously a valuable resource to learn about library associations and to keep abreast of news and developments in our profession. eduScapes (eduscapes.com) is a valuable Web site listing organizations and providing information and resources on a variety of topics of interest to school librarians.

Happy hunting!

CHAPTER 41

International School Librarian

PAULA PFOEFFER

As an international school librarian in Bolivia, I am responsible for the management of the school's K–12 library. The responsibilities include collection development (selecting and weeding materials, managing a resource budget), cataloging, customer service, and implementing programs for each of the year groups. I am also responsible for managing staff and student volunteers and for developing long-term strategies for the school library.

A TYPICAL WORKDAY

I arrive at the school at 7:30 a.m. and open the library. I take fifteen minutes to check my e-mail and see if there is anything urgent to respond to. Students and parents begin to arrive at 7:45 a.m. when the school officially opens. Because classes begin at 8 a.m., many students come in to get last-minute assignment help, print materials, and take out books. Parents come in to borrow books (primarily picture books) for their children. Generally parents need help in choosing books at the appropriate reading level for their children, so I spend some time guiding them in their selections. Many of the parents do not speak English, which gives my Spanish skills a workout. The kindergarteners and first graders are not only learning to read for the first time, they are also learning to read in a second language. This is a huge challenge for their parents.

At my school, every elementary class from preschool to sixth grade has one class in the library per week. These classes are my responsibility. I either tell stories or implement a motivational library or research-skills program.

At 9 a.m. my first elementary class arrives. The first graders come in for a story, after which they choose books to keep in their classroom for a week. The story often fits one of the themes they are studying in class, or I choose an age-appropriate book from the collection. Sometimes the story is followed up by interactive activities, such as a readers' theater, a storyboard, or puppets.

Next, the fourth grade comes in for a library and research skills lesson. I have developed an innovative program of teaching library skills by using visual aids. Our library does not have an OPAC, so I have to teach the Dewey Decimal System (DDC) and explain how to find material in the library manually. To do this I use games such as Research Safari and the Memory Game.

It is a huge challenge to teach search skills to English-as-a-second-language (ESL) learners and to students who don't have access to the kind of library that we are used to. I have found the students react well to visual aids, and it makes teaching DDC much more fun and interesting for me as well.

Research Safari, one of the board games I have adapted (Lee and Edwards 1997), introduces the students to the different types of reference books in the library and how to use them. I have the names of each of these books written on a card underneath another card showing a jungle animal. I read a question and ask the students to decide which reference book they would use to find the answer to the question. Then they have to come up and look under that animal card to find out if they chose the correct book. It's similar to a memory game; however, the students need to think about what type of book they need. I have had huge success with these games with ESL learners.

Now it is time for a break before the high school comes in. The high school classes come into the library primarily to research topics they are studying—for example, history or science projects. There are six computers in the library that have a number of databases and CD-ROMs to assist in research, such as Encarta and World Book. The library also subscribes to SIRS, an online database and an excellent source of information for students. The high school students often need a lot of assistance in finding and evaluating information.

At the beginning of each semester I review Internet and general research skills with each high school class, to refresh their skills and remind them about good search strategies and the different search engines available. These classes take place in the computer lab.

After the lunch break I have two periods left. During period six, the third graders come in for story time and choose early chapter readers. For seventh period (the last period of the day), the sixth graders come in for a book talk. This is a crucial reading age. I have found that many students lose interest in reading once they reach sixth and seventh grade, so I spend a lot of time with the sixth graders talking about interesting, funny, good books to read. I also try to get them talking about books that they have read that they might recommend to their friends.

At the end of the day there is another influx of students and parents into the library to borrow books and to finish assignments before the library closes at 3:30 p.m.

This has been a day with lots of students and teaching on my part. Other days are just as busy with administrative tasks. Apart from the programs I implement with the classes, I am responsible for maintaining a book collection of around ten thousand volumes and a periodical collection. This involves cataloging new items, weeding the collection to keep it up to date, managing the budget, selecting new items for the library, cleaning and tidying the library, and maintaining records of loans. There are a number of staff who work in the library, creating displays, assisting in library programs, and cataloging. Consequently, I also have to manage and direct their work.

School libraries tend to have large display spaces. Each month we design a display to put up. The displays tie into activities designed to promote an author, a theme, or reading in general. Planning these activities takes a lot of time. I take some time out each week to sit down with the library staff and plan. I like to have at least five "themed" months a year. For example, we have had special weeks celebrating Dr. Seuss's one hundredth birthday and Tomie de Paola, author of the *Strega Nona* books.

Of course, my day is not complete without a request from the administration to find some up-to-date research on teaching methods or curriculum development. I spend a lot of time on the Internet or looking through print sources to fulfill the requests of the teaching staff and the administration.

I usually end my day by writing a list of tasks for the following day. Then I shut down all the computers in the library, turn off the lights, and head out the door at around 3:30 p.m. to go to my Spanish class or to my volunteer job at a public library in Cochabamba.

PROS

My life as an international school librarian is busy, creative, and never dull. Working in an international school is both rewarding and challenging. You are able to call on all your creativity and skills to create a dynamic and innovative workplace. You have to be flexible and relaxed about working in an environment that does not have access to all of the resources you are used to. This is extremely challenging, but I feel it has changed the way I work in a positive way.

International schools generally have a small student population, so it is easy to get to know the students and their reading habits. As a result, you are able to recommend books and spend individual time with students, talking with them about what they have been reading and studying.

Living in a foreign country gives you the opportunity to work with students and staff from all over the world. The experience will allow you to broaden your life experience and understanding of the world, not to mention offering you the opportunity to work with innovative teachers who use current methodologies. You also will have the opportunity to learn a second language and travel.

CONS

Certainly in Bolivia, where technology is at a minimum and the country is fairly isolated from the rest of the world, there are obvious challenges. To work in such a country you have to throw out all of your preconceptions and training and get back to basics. This can be frustrating and at times downright impossible. For example, book orders sometimes take up to a year to arrive in this country! This is a huge frustration when you are responsible for keeping a collection updated and having material to support the school's curriculum.

Working in a pre-K–12 school makes for a very busy schedule, and at times you have so much going on it can be hard to keep track of everything and prioritize your projects. I have found that the trick is to stay on top of things and enjoy what you are doing.

In Bolivia, if you don't speak Spanish it is difficult to communicate with some parents and some of the younger students. This can be frustrating, but it's also a great incentive to learn the language. You should be bilingual to carry out your job; you will use English to work with the students and you'll use the home language to communicate with the parents.

HOW TO GET A JOB LIKE THIS

Most international schools recruit through job fairs or the Internet. You usually have to have at least two years of experience in a school library and should be willing to travel and work abroad. Most of the high-profile schools only interview and recruit at the job fairs; however, job seekers should check the Internet and subscribe to the newsletters to keep an eye out for jobs.

RELATED RESOURCES

Council of International Schools. www.cois.org (accessed July 17, 2006).
Lee, Carol K., and Fay Edwards. 1997. *57 games to play in the library or classroom*. Fort Atkinson, Wisc.: Upstart Books.
Search Associates. www.searchassociates.com (accessed July 17, 2006).
TIE Online. www.tieonline.com (accessed July 17, 2006).

PART IV

_____

Special Libraries

CHAPTER 42

Librarian, History of Medicine Library

ALYSON DALBY

The History of Medicine Library is Australia's only actively collecting medical history library and is part of the Royal Australasian College of Physicians. It follows in the tradition set by medical colleges in England and was established with the college in 1938 in the part of town with historically the largest collection of medical establishments (Macquarie Street, for those familiar with Sydney).

The collection comprises some forty thousand items covering all aspects of medical history, with a focus on Australian material and the humanities interpretation of medical history. Our users are fellows of the college (i.e., physicians), staff of the college, historians, graduate students, professional researchers, other librarians, and occasionally members of the public. Despite being privately funded, we are open to the public.

The collection is housed in a heritage-listed Georgian terrace, in dark wood floor-to-ceiling shelving, and in antique cabinets. There are reproduction Art Deco lights, and vellum-bound books galore. It's very pretty, although our basement stacks collection, housed in the usual compact shelving, lacks a bit of ambience. Our oldest item was printed in 1475, and our most valuable item is a first edition of Charles Darwin's *On the Origin of Species*. We hold an original of Australia's first "medical" book, *Journal of a Voyage to New South Wales*, by John White, surgeon to the First Fleet.

Over the past few years the library has undergone something of a transformation. As of mid-2002, the college had spent some years attempting to find alternative housing for the collection—a university, for example. It was felt that the library was a drain on funds, an underused, dated elephant taking up too much floor space. My appointment as librarian coincided with the submission of a plan to rejuvenate the library, which I would describe as halfway complete at the time of this writing. The plan was approved by the College Council, and the History of Medicine Library was saved. It's been an exciting couple of years since then.

JOB DESCRIPTION

My job is to manage the History of Medicine Library. I'm the only full-time staff member, so like most special librarians, my job involves the usual "high-level" management-style tasks such as strategic planning, budgeting, and reporting, as well as shelving, filing, photocopying, and doing the mail—and all the stuff in between. The parameters of *how* I manage the library are pretty fluid. As long as we don't go over budget, and we can display evidence of some kind of semi-regular success (in activity, promotion, whatever), the process is left up to me.

A TYPICAL WORKDAY

The History of Medicine Library is underused. Given the size of the collection, we don't have that many people coming into the library, and we do encourage visitors to make appointments. So the day's schedule for the part-time library technician and me is pretty self-directed, interruptions pending. There aren't "morning" or "afternoon" tasks (at least none of interest—do you really need me to tell you that I check my e-mail in the morning?), but rather just tasks.

There will be reference work, usually on a daily basis. This is pretty standard—any one of our users contacting us to find biographical information on a medical person, finding early evidence of medical opinion (we've had a few law firms looking for early articles on the dangers of cigarettes), compiling a list of citations from our collection on a particular subject of interest to a researcher. I tend to avoid doing in-depth research into a subject, mainly because I lack the medical background necessary at times, but our users are happy to do that research themselves. I see my role as the librarian, not a medico—I focus on ensuring access.

Management tasks occur on a daily basis. Since the library's second chance was granted, I've focused a lot of energy on communication, primarily with internal stakeholders. This means reporting to the council of the college on a regular basis and making connections with senior staff and fellows. The involvement of college staff in the library was minimal at best in the past, and I'm attempting to turn that around. I review the systems and processes in the library, collect and collate usage data, monitor budgets, plan professional development, and supervise staff. I've also established a newsletter, which goes out to our own mailing list. I spend a lot of time writing about what we're doing.

This ties in nicely with the task that takes up perhaps the biggest proportion of my time—marketing. I spend about half of my time on activities related to marketing. This involves, among other duties, running a lecture series; lectures are held every two months, and I manage the administration of the series, from creating a flyer advertising the next speaker to putting together a complementary book display and arranging catering. The series is run jointly with the Unit for the History and Philosophy of Science at the University of Sydney.

Other marketing activities include arranging customized tours and book displays for groups visiting the library or for groups using the college as a venue for a book launch or other function. I write articles about library activities to go in other publications. I promote the library's publications and other merchandise within the college, highlighting it as material suitable for inclusions in information packs and conference materials. I ensure that the library has a presence at the college's annual congress; for example, we recently held a debate on the topic that "the history of medicine is irrelevant to today's practicing physician." I assist documentary filmmakers that contact us wanting to use the library's collection or rooms—this involved, on one occasion, four hours spent just watching a filming to ensure that a particularly delicate book was handled correctly.

Strategic partnerships are vital to us. Apart from our relationship with the University of Sydney, we've been establishing relationships with Australian history of medicine societies, as well as a number of institutions overseas. I've spent time in London in some of these institutions, looking at outreach programs, displays, and activities. These partnerships serve as a support network, and I seek advice on various topics from these people.

The final large component of my days is a huge review of the collection. New collection development and weeding policies were established in 2004, and I spend varying amounts of time each day working through a progressive weed and inventory of the entire collection, something which I can find no evidence of ever having been done before. We have problems with the quality of data in our catalog, and there is no easy, quick way to fix this—we have to check every item, one by one. While doing so, we find books that have never been cataloged, books that need minor repair work, some that need major repair work, and others that have a spelling mistake in the title of the catalog record, ensuring that they will never be found. This is one of those "Will it ever end?" tasks: daunting, but satisfying.

PROS AND CONS

I know every library is different, and every job in every library is different, but this really is a remarkable place to work. Rather than outline pros and cons, I'd rather discuss some of the elements that make the job what it is. These can be considered both pros and cons, depending on your own personal style in the workplace.

History

Something that sets my job apart from most others in the information industry is the role that history plays in my work. By this I don't mean history as a subject—even though the collection I work with is based on history—more important is the history of the job, the library, and the institution.

Before starting at the Royal Australasian College of Physicians, I had never worked for an organization that was, well, older than I was. I'd certainly not thought about it—it just wasn't something I was aware of. But the simple act of staying in touch with the two previous librarians from the History of Medicine Library means that the three of us together represent thirty-six years in the history of this library. In a library this small and specialized, one can't really divorce the concept of the librarian from the library—the collection will, of necessity, be driven by personality. So the history of my library is present, and I'm constantly reminded that, strangely, I'm a part of that story. It adds a sense of proud responsibility to what I do.

The Patrons

My library patrons charm me. I feel that one of the most enjoyable features of working in a small special library is the depth and quality of your relationships with the patrons. We have a very small but incredibly dedicated user group, primarily comprised of retired (or nearly retired) fellows of the college. *Retired* is an inaccurate word to use for them; in their mid-seventies, these people have chosen to stop working and are returning to university, writing theses and completing doctorates. I admire them enormously. They feel a sense of ownership and protectiveness of this library, built in part by the recent fight to keep it open.

Our patrons tend to use our collection in depth. A quick reference query isn't rare, but it's often coupled with hours or days of research, trawling through manuscript material donated by widows. We don't have private study rooms like in a large university library, but patrons' spaces are their own for as long as they need them. That homey, welcoming touch is appreciated.

The Collection

Most visitors to the library who are aware of our recent history are horrified at the concept of breaking up the collection. They are stunned by the treasures we hold, as am I on a regular basis.

Very rarely, I have the luxury to spend some time just exploring, and I have unearthed the most amazing and obscure items, such as items taken by Dr. Robert Scot Skirving on his expeditions to the South Pole with Mawson or an ECG record of John Glenn, the first American to orbit the Earth, as he flew over Woomera, Australia, in 1962. It amazes me that, fresh out of library school, I was appointed as the custodian to such treasures. This job has allowed me direct access to truly valuable material.

The Characteristics of a Special Library

I imagine all special librarians have said the same thing: in a special library, you get to do everything. The opportunities for professional development in a job like this are limited only by my imagination, and the rejuvenation project has allowed me to experiment with a wide range of marketing and redevelopment activities that may not have been considered in a more stable collection. I am given a lot of freedom, but at the same time I have little professional support. If I don't know how to do something, it is my responsibility to find a way to learn—there is no training officer responsible for my skill level. I believe that staying professionally active is a vital element to working in any small library, and this has driven my involvement with both health library networks in Australia and the next-generation librarian movement. These are the people I turn to for professional advice, and they have been invaluable when creating policies and generating new ideas for the future of this collection.

HOW DO I GET A JOB LIKE YOURS?

Honestly, luck. And a whole bunch of hard work.

Unless you have a passionate interest and years of study experience in the subject matter, jobs like this are hard to find. They are often advertised through personal networks, and it's rare for an agency to be involved. It's very common for a nonlibrarian subject expert to be appointed to these positions, so the first hurdle is trying to convince the decision makers of the value of LIS qualifications.

I would not have gotten this job without a series of lucky events. I was fortunate that they used a general administrative temp agency to advertise the job, rather than a specialist recruitment firm, because in the interview stage I was the only one with any LIS studies behind me. I was lucky that the college had difficulty finding a new home for the collection, and that a new CEO happened to come on at that time. I was lucky that he and I shared the same vision for the library.

But beyond that, my own efforts formed the position that I currently hold. It was an early adoption of responsibility beyond the confines of my job description, and a consistently high level of self-motivation and vision eventually put me in the librarian position.

If you want a job like this, you'll probably have to make it happen yourself. Get the closest thing you can find and then adapt it. My job and day-to-day duties are primarily of my own making, and most of my deadlines are set by me, for me. I could have a much easier job of it if I wanted to, but it would be dull and limiting. This is the kind of job you create for yourself.

RELATED RESOURCES

The Australian and New Zealand Society of the History of Medicine. www.anzshm.org.au/index.html (accessed February 4, 2007).
Royal Australasian College of Physicians. www.racp.edu.au (accessed February 26, 2006).
The Wellcome Library (a much larger medical history collection). library.wellcome.ac.uk (accessed February 26, 2006).

CHAPTER 43

Medical Librarian, Pediatric Hospital Library

ELISABETH ROWAN

Hospital librarianship is a specialized area of the profession with a lot of opportunities. Hospitals come in all sizes, from a very small specialty hospital to a community hospital to a large academic medical center. A hospital's mission and size will often—but not always—determine whether it has a library and a degreed librarian as well as what services are required. Sometimes it may simply be that an administrator, board member, or influential physician has taken an interest in having the resources of a library available. In my case, I work in a library for a small, fifty-bed pediatric orthopedic facility. The library developed from a collection overseen by medical secretaries as part of their additional duties to a library managed by a part-time degreed librarian. Early on, the collection included books for the children. These were eventually separated from the medical collection and now are part of recreational therapy. The primary focus of the medical library is to support staff in their clinical care and research.

JOB DESCRIPTION

Unless they are employees of a university or another large medical center, many hospital librarians find themselves flying solo. That's the case in my position, and because it was also my first professional placement, I found it challenging because every aspect of the library—from administrative to routine tasks—fell to me to get done. Sometimes if you're lucky you can find a volunteer to help, or perhaps you can try partnering with a library school for an intern. Regardless, it certainly helps to have a good grounding in several different areas of library science going into such a position, because in the end you will be responsible for every aspect of the library.

Within hospital librarianship, the core services tend to be doing literature searches and obtaining articles for patrons. However, there is also a collection to maintain, which makes cataloging, serials and monograph processing, and the provision of access just as important. Although most patrons of health sciences libraries are doctors, nurses, and allied health professionals, it is also common to have patients, families, and visitors stop in with questions. Therefore it is important to offer both materials that are highly specialized and those better suited for consumers.

One of the areas I oversee as part of my position is a family resource center, which has books on parenting, living with disorders, education rights, grief—a variety of topics of interest to families. A computer gives families e-mail access and allows them to research information of interest. Because we strive to provide family-centered care, these resources are important in supporting the hospital mission. Originally located in the library, the family resource center is now on the inpatient unit, so this gives me the opportunity to get out into the actual workings of the hospital.

Because we are a pediatric facility, there is one other area I oversee—an early literacy project called Reach Out and Read (ROR). ROR was developed for use in private pediatric practices but was adapted at our hospital for our outpatient clinic. Age-appropriate books for children aged six months to five years are kept in the clinic and given to the children during their appointments. Care coordinators discuss books and the benefits of reading with the parents and even make literacy referrals if the parent needs help with reading. Volunteers read to the children in the lobby, modeling the behavior for parents. The idea is that each child will start kindergarten with a small library of books that otherwise might not be available in the home. Books are available in different languages and in Braille. I order the books from publishers, oversee provider training, secure funding, and make sure that the books are available in the clinic for the children. I'm not sure if other hospital librarians are involved in ROR or similar programs, but it's been an excellent opportunity for me to be involved more directly in patient care. We also take donations of books for older children so that siblings are not left out. It's another way to address the needs of the whole family.

A TYPICAL WORKDAY

Because I'm part-time, a typical workday for me begins at 10 a.m. and ends at 2:30 p.m. Most of the medical librarians I know work standard hours, usually from 8 or 9 in the morning to 5 p.m. My day is spent doing literature searches, obtaining articles through the National Library of Medicine's interlibrary loan system (DOCLINE), and assisting patrons with their own searches. We often have residents or nursing students in the library searching for a particular book or article. We also have computers for hospital staff use, and I walk people through the use of software on the computer. Another common use of the library is recreational reading: people stopping by on break to read the newspapers.

The main copier for the hospital is located in the library, so I am often called to help with copying issues. Having a good technical sense can really help with this sort of thing, and although my job is so much more than babysitting the copier, it's one of the main forms of customer service that wins me recognition from my peers.

I keep current in the field by subscribing to various electronic lists, including those for medical librarians, solo librarians, and pediatric librarians. I also belong to the Medical Library Association and receive their journal and newsletters. I network with other librarians in our hospital system and with librarians in my geographical area through consortia. This is especially important when you're a solo librarian.

Over time I have built a reputation for being creative (by, of all things, helping with bulletin boards) and as a result was asked to serve on several committees or teams ranging from patient education to employee appreciation. Several of these have made decisions for the whole hospital, and it's been very satisfying to have a voice in planning.

Otherwise my time is taken up with maintaining the collection, shelving, tracking statistics, budgeting, ordering supplies, paying invoices—basically, anything that needs to be done to keep the library running smoothly. If only those people who are convinced that librarians sit around and read all the time could see all we do!

PROS AND CONS

One of the most rewarding aspects of hospital librarianship is that you often get instant feedback that your efforts have gone to a good cause. The classic case is a call from the operating room where information or a resource is needed to help with the case. Patrons come into the library looking for answers to questions that matter a great deal, and they should always be respected as such. Health is such a basic part of our lives; when it is threatened it can cause a great deal of stress. Having information that impacts one's own health or that of a loved one is empowering because it helps us begin to put the situation into perspective. The librarian, of course, cannot interpret the information, but just having information on an illness, procedure, or medication can mean a great deal. It also allows the patron to discuss health choices more intelligently with a health professional.

Pediatric settings, for whatever reason, seem to be more laid-back than other hospital settings. Scrubs and even doctors' ties tend to have cartoon characters on them, and everyone goes out of their way to put patients and families at ease and make their stay as "unhospital-like" as possible. Hallways may have colorful murals. Hospital management may have philosophies geared to having fun while still doing a wonderful job. The object is to strike a balance between professionalism and approachability, and the library should take its cue from the general organization's lead.

One of the drawbacks to working in a hospital is that they go through fads of management that sometimes lead to reorganization or drastic changes in budgeting. The library is always at risk because it's not generating revenue directly. It's important to be able to justify your existence. Some librarians research the cost it would take to outsource their services. Others belong to consortia with important provisions for membership, such as a minimum number of journals or minimum number of staff hours to receive free interlibrary loans. Sometimes cutbacks are unavoidable, and at that point the emphasis must be on core services. I used to work thirty-five-hour weeks and was cut down to twenty during an economic downturn. My challenge became maintaining excellent service in a limited number of hours per day.

Another problem is that hospital libraries usually require twenty-four-hour access, with patrons either using a key or being let in by security at all times of night and day. Of course, the library staff, especially a solo librarian, can only supervise for a limited time. This makes controlling the inventory of the collection difficult. Most hospital librarians count themselves lucky if the patron remembered to fill out a book card and leave it on the desk before absconding. Self-checkout systems are prohibitively expensive for many libraries, and although informal circulation is not ideal from the point of view of the library, it works best to see that patrons can access materials whenever they are needed. Some hospitals simply do not allow materials to leave the room, but again, this is difficult to police.

Many hospital libraries allow food or drink near the materials. Don't panic if this is the case with yours. It actually tends to work out all right. In eight years the worst we've seen is spilled coffee, and that didn't get near a book. The books themselves may come back worse for wear (I swear sometimes I think they've played hockey with them in the clinic), so you might want to get some basics of book repair down. Medical books are quite costly (and serials are even pricier), often go out of print quickly, and can be difficult to replace.

Of course, another problem is that new editions come out very quickly. Keeping a collection up to date can be very difficult, especially on a limited budget. Many books come out with new editions every year, and having an out-of-date collection can translate into incorrect procedures or inadequate patient care, so the consequences are graver than in most libraries.

HOW WOULD I GET A JOB LIKE YOURS?

I saw the ad for my position in the local paper. You might also want to check a state job line or call your library school for more information; many keep an eye out for positions for alumni. Regardless of how you find out about the job, be sure to stress any experience you have that might relate to working with children's services or apply in a medical setting. I didn't have a health sciences background, but I do have a classics degree, and my knowledge of Latin and Greek help immensely with medical terminology. It also piqued the interest of the chief of staff emeritus, who was largely responsible for creating the library during his tenure. If you talk with other health science librarians, you'll find they came from all sorts of backgrounds.

The candidate must be flexible, as he or she will jump into what amounts to a culture all its own. Be willing to work as part of a team approach. Teams do everything in hospitals; one may even interview you. Willingness to learn is also important. Although I had not had a class on health sciences libraries, I took one at the first opportunity. I also took classes on storytelling and children's literature, which helped with the ROR program. Also, snap up any chance to serve on a team or otherwise become visible outside the library; one of the best ways is by eating lunch with different groups. You have to market your services and train your users to think of you and your library as a solution to their needs. It not only builds job security; it truly integrates the library into the patient care team.

RELATED RESOURCES

One of the best things you can do to learn about health sciences libraries and get connected into a network is to participate in a consortium, which is normally made up of institutions but may also accept personal or student members. State and national associations are also great. Here are some resources you may find helpful.

Darling, Louise, ed. 1982. *Handbook of medical library practice*, 4th ed. Chicago: Medical Library Association. A three-volume classic, meaning technologically out-of-date, but the principles remain.

Journal of the Medical Library Association. www.mlanet.org/publications/jmla (accessed September 29, 2005).

Medical Library Association. www.mlanet.org (accessed September 29, 2005).

MEDLIB-L (Medical libraries discussion list). www.mlanet.org/discussion/medlibl.html (accessed August 20, 2006).

Pedhosplib (Pediatric hospital libraries discussion list). listserv.tamucc.edu/mailman/listinfo/pedhosplib (accessed August 20, 2006).

Reach Out and Read. www.reachoutandread.org (accessed September 29, 2005).

SLA-DSOL (Solo librarians discussion list; formerly SOLOLIB-L). units.sla.org/division/dsol/discussion.html (accessed August 20, 2006).

CHAPTER 44

Library and Information Officer, Nonprofit Health Organization

NATASHA DAVIES

Cancerbackup is the only independent United Kingdom charity that specializes in providing high-quality information on all types of cancer. Its services are provided free and confidentially to anyone affected by cancer. Information, support, and practical advice are delivered via a free telephone helpline staffed by specialist cancer nurses, an interactive Web site, and a network of local drop-in centers across the country. The charity also supplies an extensive range of free booklets and fact sheets and supplies health professionals with up-to-date information on controversial and difficult cancer topics.

Cancerbackup's Library and Information Service (LIS) is part of the Cancer Support Service (CSS), one of four organizational departments. Other departments are Fundraising, Information and Marketing, Partnerships and Finance, and Administration. Cancerbackup has offices in London and Glasgow, each with its own phone room.

The LIS aims to support the work of all of Cancerbackup's nurses (wherever they are based) and provide assistance to other staff where possible. The LIS is a multisite operation, with the main print collection in the London office and a smaller collection in Glasgow. The LIS is staffed by two full-time information professionals: I am the library and information officer, and I work with the LIS manager at the London office. There are two part-time library and information assistants, one in London and one in Glasgow.

The LIS hard copy collections comprise one thousand book titles (key texts are held in London and Glasgow) and about ten thousand other items, including journal articles, reports, guidelines, and patient information resources. There are print and electronic subscriptions to ten journal titles; print copies are held in London. All collections are reference only. Access to the collections is through STATUS, a legacy database package.

JOB DESCRIPTION

The main purpose of my job is to support the LIS manager in providing high-quality service; there is a lot of overlap between the two posts, and I am expected to take charge of the service in her absence. I contribute to the development of LIS policy and procedures and stock selection. The only things I don't get involved in are finance and staff management.

About one-third of my time is spent dealing with inquiries from nurses and other members of the staff. Inquiries range from the directional ("Where is the purple book?") to the very in-depth ("Can you get me some recent articles about optimum scheduling of adjuvant chemotherapy for breast cancer?"). Helpline nurses often make inquiries while they have callers on hold, so speed is of the essence. When answering an in-depth inquiry, I normally start by checking STATUS, as it is something that nurses often forget to do.

Depending on the nature of the inquiry, I might then try searching the Internet. If I'm looking for scholarly articles and don't have a lot of time, I'll try searching Medline, one of the National Library of Medicine's bibliographic databases, via PubMed. If I have more time I'll log on to Dialog Datastar to take advantage of its increased search functionality to search Medline and EMBASE, another bibliographic database with a pharmacological and European emphasis. As a medical charity, Cancerbackup is fortunate to benefit from free access to these databases and other electronic resources via the National Health Service's (NHS) electronic libraries.

Another one-third of my time is spent on cataloging, classification, indexing, and abstracting new resources. The classification scheme we use is a bastardized version of National Library of Medicine (NLM) Classification. It uses a lot of free-floating subdivisions to account for commonly occurring specialist cancer concepts; for example, the subdivision .710 represents chemotherapy treatment. The NLM classmark (or call number) for breast neoplasms (cancer) is WP 870. The subdivision for chemotherapy is then added to the NLM classmark to make WP 870.710, Cancerbackup's classmark for "chemotherapy for breast cancer." Indexing terms are taken from the Cancerbackup thesaurus.

My other activities include maintaining the listing of clinical guidelines on the health professionals section of Cancerbackup's Web site and chairing Resource Update Meetings (RUM). RUM is a form of journal club, where helpline nurses get together to discuss new scholarly and patient information resources. I represent the LIS at the Black and Minority Ethnic group projects reference group meeting, the only regular cross-departmental meeting apart from that of the senior management team. I also contribute to the development of an information skills training program for the helpline nurses.

MY TYPICAL WORKDAY

I always listen to Radio 4, the BBC's "intelligent speech" radio station, while getting ready for work, and I usually scan a free newspaper during my commute. Media coverage of cancer-related stories can generate a lot of calls to the helpline. I'm not responsible for picking up on such stories, but it is good to have advance warning of what might be in store when I arrive at the office. Cancer news is prone to exaggeration by the media; reports of miracle cures are often based on in vitro research or trials of new drugs on very small numbers of patients. The helpline nurses have to be forewarned and briefed on the facts; LIS staff often get involved in tracking down the original medical research that gave rise to the media interest.

If there is no breaking news, I can press on with more routine tasks, such as cataloging and classification. LIS tends to send a lot of e-mails, so I try to make time during the day to telephone my colleague in Glasgow to maintain personal contact. On a busy day I could answer ten or more directional inquiries and two or three in-depth inquiries. LIS does not keep any performance statistics, so I'm not able to quantify this work. Our library assistant is responsible for maintaining an archive of cancer-related press stories from the previous two months. Because she does not work full-time, I cover this duty on Mondays and Fridays.

Most weeks I'll have a booklet update to work on. Cancerbackup produces sixty-five booklets on different types of cancer, which are updated on a rolling basis at least once every two years. LIS is responsible for checking the "other useful organizations and resources" section at the back of the booklets. I check that the organizational contact details are correct, and then I'll check STATUS for any relevant patient information resources that have been added to stock since the last update. I also look on Amazon.com for potential new purchases for patients or health professionals; anything interesting is forwarded to the LIS manager to assist with stock selection.

PROS AND CONS

Cancerbackup's nurses provide an important, useful service, and it can be very satisfying to help them give a timely, accurate answer to a tricky question from an anxious caller. Our newly appointed library assistant is studying for her postgraduate LIS qualification, so I'm often able to act as a source of information and ideas for essays and dissertation proposals. It is nice to be involved in what UK librarians sometimes refer to as "growing people" for the profession.

Like most library and information services, Cancerbackup's LIS is afflicted by the perennial problems of lack of money and space. LIS impact and efficiency is particularly restricted by the limitations of STATUS, our legacy database software. Its shortcomings include having to use a DOS-based program to enter new records in their entirety (you can't import skeleton records from Bookdata or other providers, or even cut and paste); inability to include hyperlinks (you can include URLs as text but have to cut and paste them from the STATUS record into your Web browser); limited search functionality; lack of flexibility with respect to entering different information formats; and lack of a designated field for publication dates. I estimate that a new system could cut in half the time that I spend entering new records and formatting outputs to make them presentable for users. The possibility of a replacement system has been mooted for several years, but core funding has not been available. Cancerbackup is just over twenty years old, and the organization is running a major fundraising appeal; it is hoped that this will fund a replacement system.

In my previous post I was responsible for developing and delivering information skills training to health professionals in the North Essex area. In my current post I don't have a lot of personal or professional responsibility or autonomy, and I miss the job satisfaction that goes with that. In addition, Cancerbackup is an independent organization, so I don't have the same opportunities to attend training and networking events as I did when I worked in the NHS. This can lead to a feeling of isolation when I'm puzzling over a particularly difficult inquiry or classification conundrum.

HOW WOULD I GET A JOB LIKE YOURS?

Many UK library and information jobs are advertised in the *Library and Information Gazette*, a fortnightly magazine produced by CILIP, the Chartered Institute of Library and Information Professionals; these vacancies are listed online at the Lisjobnet Web site. CILIP also operates LIBEX (library and information job exchange), a clearinghouse for CILIP members and library and information staff in other countries who are interested in arranging temporary job exchanges. Jobs are sometimes advertised via the LIS-MEDICAL mailing list.

Knowledge organization and information retrieval skills are essential for this kind of job. Attention to detail is important when working with the complex classification scheme and specialist terminology. Useful transferable skills include teamwork and communication; I often pick up half-finished or poorly defined tasks, so it is important to know what is expected and exactly where to start. Nurses might interrupt my work routine at any time, so I do a lot of multitasking. Cancer is an emotional subject, so it is helpful to be able to maintain a level of detachment when processing particular types of information resources.

RELATED RESOURCES

BBC Radio 4. www.bbc.co.uk/radio4 (accessed February 5, 2006).

Cancerbackup. www.cancerbackup.org.uk (accessed February 5, 2006).

Chartered Institute of Library and Information Professionals (CILIP). www.cilip.org.uk (accessed February 5, 2006).

LIBEX. www.cilip.org.uk/jobscareers/libex (accessed February 5, 2006).

Lisjobnet. www.lisjobnet.com/Lisjobnet (accessed February 5, 2006).

LIS-MEDICAL. www.jiscmail.ac.uk/lists/LIS-MEDICAL.html (accessed February 5, 2006).

National Cancer Institute. www.cancer.gov (accessed February 5, 2006).

National Library for Health. www.library.nhs.uk (accessed February 5, 2006).

NHS Scotland e-Library. www.elib.scot.nhs.uk/portal/elib/pages/index.aspx (accessed February 5, 2006).

NLM Classification 2006. wwwcf.nlm.nih.gov/class (accessed August 22, 2006).

CHAPTER 45

Librarian/Vice President, Financial Company

DAN CHERUBIN

I work in the New York office of Rabobank International, a global financial company that is headquartered in Utrecht, The Netherlands. I report to the Food and Agribusiness Research (FAR) Division, a group of about eighty analysts worldwide, although I serve the entire bank community as the corporate librarian for the Americas. In my region, Rabobank has offices throughout the United States, as well as Canada, Mexico, Argentina, Brazil, and Chile. I handle requests related to the bank's major work in agribusiness (which covers all sectors of farming, livestock and crop production, food processing, distribution, and retail), and I am also responsible for general financial research. In addition, I serve as the go-to resource for general information on North and South America for our offices in other regions.

A TYPICAL WORKDAY

My day starts around 8:30 a.m., though sometimes I begin earlier (and end much later) so as to be available to clients in other regions. I check my e-mail and phone messages for any new research requests and place them all in a spreadsheet. This serves as my request triage and helps me see if similar requests have been previously posted. It's also useful when it comes to producing end-of-the-year statistics. I then check my calendar to see if there are any internal meetings or appointments with vendors on my schedule. I often get to sit in on other departments' meetings to get a better idea of their information needs and offer my assistance for different projects. I may also give brief presentations on new resources in the corporate library. I work at the level of vice president, so there are also a variety of corporate meetings and events I need to attend throughout the year.

I then go through my morning industry e-mails. These come from a variety of trade associations, commodity groups, and government Web sites. I also look into credit alerts from Moody's and Standard & Poor's and, if it's the beginning of a financial quarter, I check to see if equity analysts have released any reports on some of our clients. I also check our online and print periodicals in and route pertinent issues or articles to various parties. A lot of this work is for my standing order research requests, where various people in the bank receive regular information packets (monthly, weekly, or FYI) on any industry, company, or event for which they need updates. Along with some of the FAR analysts, I regularly update time series for commodity prices, sales volume, export data, and so on.

I receive more e-mail and phone reference requests throughout the day, and people can also come to my desk to ask questions. I spend a certain amount of time talking with many of my clients, as reference questions often need to be discussed. Many of my regular users know that I need to chart a specific path for research and not just have someone ask me, "I need everything there is on dairy in Canada!" But I get new clients every week (through my presentations around the company and through word of mouth), so bibliographic instruction always comes into play.

Because my client base is international in scope, there are also language issues to take into consideration. I often need to order material for the library in Spanish and Portuguese, and on occasion Chinese and Dutch. Many of my required reference sources have no English-language equivalent. These resources have helped bring attention to the global span of the library's coverage.

I also spend time updating the FAR intranet Web site, which is used by offices all over the region. I add and update industry links, reports written by FAR analysts, and other information pertinent to the agribusiness sectors addressed in the Americas. I also work with my colleagues in other parts of the world to have our intranet sources complement each other and work on a more global scale. Often this involves sharing contracts and licensing for certain resources, and I get to represent the group for any products coming out of the Americas.

If possible, I try to eat lunch with different people from the bank so we can discuss different issues. The rest of the day may be spent on research requests, which take anywhere from a few minutes to several days. I keep track of all material used, so if similar requests come up later, I'll have the resources ready. Some of the results of my research are posted on shared drives on the company server or on the intranet. However, due to compliance and security issues, much of my work has to be kept private on my personal drive. I usually leave the office around 6 p.m. unless I need to stay later to talk with someone in Asia or Australia. I tend to keep a to do list on my computer for any top-priority research that I need to continue first thing in the morning.

There is also travel involved in the job. I make trips to various offices in my region, usually to do basic bibliographic instruction but also to sit in on larger meetings of various groups. The FAR Division has an annual weeklong Team Days event in the Netherlands, which includes one day set aside for an information officers meeting. I also get to travel for professional development and conferences, although I am usually limited to two such events a year.

PROS AND CONS

The top of both my pro and con list is the same: I am a solo librarian. On the positive side, I get to create policy for material acquisition, negotiate vendor contracts, and establish policies and practices, all without too much bureaucracy and red tape. I am seen as *the* reference source for material and information, and I'm included in discussions all over the bank. My feedback is considered important, and I get to have a large say in how information resources are used throughout two continents. On the negative side, I don't often get a chance to bounce ideas and questions off people in similar situations. There are a handful of other librarians in the company, but I am the only one in this geographical region, so in-depth conversations have to be planned via several days of e-mails. Although there are many financial and agricultural experts around me, it would be nice to have someone else who understands the unique roles of librarians.

Other pros of the job include the international aspects of working at Rabobank. I am surrounded by people from a variety of countries, and my daily tasks are different each day. I get to travel around the world and share knowledge and information on a variety of subjects.

Each day brings a new type of request: news of the Uruguay eucalyptus pulp industry, frozen food retail in China, the U.S. beef trade, Canadian biofuels ... you name it. With each new topic, I learn about more resources and different cultures.

I also enjoy the very different sort of corporate culture that comes from working in a non-U.S. company. The Dutch understand the need for a personal life. Even though everyone works hard, the friendly, open atmosphere and generous vacation policies make work easier. And how can one hate regular wine and cheese gatherings in the afternoons? It's much better than some enforced weekend company picnic!

However, the international aspects of the job can also be a disadvantage. Each region has its own compliance and security issues. Sharing information is not always easy. It can be frustrating to only communicate via e-mail. Cultural differences can make electronic discussion more difficult than it should be.

Other negative aspects would be what one might find working in any large financial institution. No matter how well you do your job as a librarian, when corporate culture is faced with downsizing, you may not be immune. It's a sad fact of life. There's also the general corporate culture of a bank, even a Dutch one. It may be a bit staid for some, and there can be long hours. However, there are so many positive aspects to his job that these downsides are fairly easy to deal with.

Finally, one of the best pros is the salary! The library world is filled with tales of underpaid labor. During my time in public and not-for-profit libraries, I went into crushing debt (which I'm still climbing out of) and I had to hold down several additional part-time jobs. In the corporate world, working hard often leads to a bonus and a raise. Banks tend to pay better than public libraries. For all the comments I hear about selling out, I know my company supports causes I believe in, and I now make enough at one job so I can use my spare time on causes and activities that matter to me rather than looking for extra work just so I can pay my rent and eat. I couldn't make that statement in previous jobs.

HOW WOULD I GET A JOB LIKE YOURS?

My first response to this question is, "Be a good librarian and stay flexible in your knowledge!" My next response would be, "Have no fear and believe that you are worth every penny."

My path was rather roundabout. I began my professional career as a music librarian. After ten years, I left the library world to become director of marketing at a software company. I returned to the profession as a solo librarian in an insurance company before landing my current position. Although I had done some food retail research at previous jobs, my knowledge of agriculture and agribusiness was somewhat limited—I am a lifelong resident of New York City. However, my belief (which I always mention in job interviews) is that if I know how to use 100 different databases, who says I can't learn 101? Being a good librarian means knowing how to find and disseminate information and learning about new resources. My experience in marketing helped me learn to market myself and my services. I knew I could do a good job at this company and keep increasing my user base. My employers knew I had that ability. When I took this job, the Americas region had never had a library or central information resource. I'm now an invaluable part of the organization. I've had librarians ask me how I could have possibly made the jump from public music librarian to corporate agriculture librarian. I call it being good at what you do.

I will add that having some command of foreign languages is also helpful. Even though the official language of Rabobank International is English, much of my research (and that of my clients) delves into other languages, particularly Spanish and Portuguese. My fluency in French has helped find key elements of information in other Romance languages. My knowledge of Russian, which I didn't think would be too helpful in this job, has proved valuable for many different offices looking for information on Russian companies. I am also in the process of studying Dutch, which isn't mandatory for the job, but I find many of my colleagues are quite happy about this. It helps in day-to-day communications.

RELATED RESOURCES

For my particular subject (the finance of agriculture), I have found there aren't too many other librarians like me in America. Most financial librarians rarely (if ever) deal with agriculture, and most agricultural librarians focus on the scientific side of the sector. But the ability to talk with other librarians is priceless. Here are a few librarian groups that have been invaluable resources.

International Association of Agriculture Information Specialists (IAALD). www.iaald.org (accessed February 1, 2006).
———. The IAALD blog. iaald.blogspot.com (accessed February 1, 2006).
Special Libraries Association, Business and Finance Division. www.slabf.org (accessed February 1, 2006).
———, Food, Agriculture and Nutrition Division. units.sla.org/division/dfan (accessed February 1, 2006).
U.S. Agricultural Information Network (USAIN). www.usain.org (accessed February 1, 2006).

CHAPTER 46

Technical Librarian/Document Controller, Oil and Gas Company

JENNIFER MORRISON

I work in the international branch headquarters of an independent oil and gas exploration and production company. I am based in Aberdeen, Scotland. My job covers two roles that are quite distinct, although both are related to information management. First, I am the sole librarian for the company. As a solo librarian my role is very varied, but it can best be described as being responsible for providing library services, in the widest sense of the term, to the whole international division. I manage all the company's subscriptions (electronic and print). I also manage a small technical library that contains books, conference proceedings, technical papers, standards, and so on. I am also responsible for the management of the company's collection of technical standards (BSI, ISO, API, etc.). I conduct research projects for the business, as well as compiling bibliographies and annotated literature searches. I also compile a daily press review.

I am heavily involved in controlling the company's engineering documents. As part of a team of three, I manage the company's engineering records. Again, this role is varied. Because some of our oil- and gas-producing assets are now thirty years old, we have accumulated a great deal of documentation regarding them. Our role is to manage this documentation, which is in a mixture of hard copy and electronic formats. We set up procedures and build relationships with suppliers to ensure that the delivery of new or updated information is efficiently controlled and delivered in a format compatible with the company's information systems. We also plan and execute data quality exercises so that we efficiently manage our existing documentation in line with company policies and industry standards.

With both of these roles I am part of a multidiscipline information center. We are primarily responsible for providing information services to the people who work in our head office, international field offices, and offshore installations. However, we often need to make information accessible to partners and third parties.

A TYPICAL WORKDAY

A typical workday for me starts around 8 a.m. I arrive in the office and check my e-mail. We are a very reactive service and are heavily used by the business, so every day is very busy. I need to have every task written down so that I don't overlook any requests. We also keep a team log of requests for the information center, which helps the team leader demonstrate work levels to management, so it is very important to keep track of everything that we do.

Press Review

Every morning, my first major task is to compile a press review for distribution within the company. This is probably the only task that I conduct without fail every day. I use an online news indexing and abstracting service. I have set up standard searches that run constantly, matching my required keywords with the keywords indexed in the article. The press review aims to cover major developments in the oil and gas industry worldwide as well as within our operating areas. I also look for articles covering sociopolitical events that may affect our activities in the countries where we operate. I also look for articles mentioning our company, its activities, and its market performance.

I review the results of the searches and try to narrow the list down to about twenty articles. I then reformat these articles, along with key company performance figures at the close of the previous day, into a press review document. The review is then distributed to key individuals within the company. My review goes to the highest levels of the company, including the chairman of the board and the entire management committee of our parent company.

I am responsible for managing our subscription to the online news service and making sure that we abide by copyright and distribution licenses. I am also constantly monitoring that the services to which we subscribe are the best on offer in terms of content and value.

Typical Library Service Requests

Compiling the press review normally takes about an hour and a half, depending on the levels of activity in the industry. Once I have finished the press review, I move on to addressing some of my requests.

For the most part, my work involves responding to direct requests and dealing with the issues that arise from them. However, I feel it is essential to remain always vigilant and ask lots of questions of requestors, because I often find that simple requests lead to greater issues, such as users not getting the best use out of products because they are unfamiliar with them or problems with the delivery of our resources. I find that by asking questions to discover bigger problems and then addressing these problems, we build stronger relationships with our users and provide a better service.

Typically library service requests tend to fall into three categories: requests for or issues with access to existing resources, access to resources we do not currently offer, and research inquiries.

Due to space constraints I recently had to pack up my technical library and send it to the archives. We get archive deliveries twice each working day, so it is not a problem to recall items. I kept the most heavily used reference manuals and technical standards on-site, so this doesn't really inconvenience users.

I currently manage over ninety separate subscriptions, ranging from low-cost hard copy journals with limited appeal to extremely high-cost electronic information products that are widely used within the company. For all subscriptions I am responsible for ensuring the value and usefulness of the services. I am also responsible for ensuring that the company makes the best and most efficient use of these products. This may involve giving demonstrations of products, explaining the content of the subscriptions to new users, or arranging training for new and existing products.

I often get requests for access to new resources, ranging from state-of-the-art products on the market and updated revisions of books or standards to requests for very old and often out-of-print copies of legislation or standards that specify the standards to which aging equipment was built. I deal with all aspects of purchasing. I contact vendors directly and always compare to be sure I am getting the best deal. I get new materials delivered directly to me so that I can catalog them before loaning them out. We use a customized content management system as our catalog, so although I follow the general principles of cataloging standards, I have created my own standard in response to the kind of information I manage.

I also conduct research inquiries. These range from our finance team requiring business information reports or company accounts to corporate and business development teams wanting industry comparisons. I will often be asked to create annotated bibliographies or to run literature searches for individuals. Some recent examples of topics are

- Search for literature on a specific field or technology.
- Produce a table showing major milestones in worldwide deepwater developments (for example, project sanction, contract awards, FPSO sailaway, first oil).
- Produce a table of offshore deepwater fields (producing and in development) showing discovery date versus first oil date (actual and expected).
- Compile a list of applicable standards to be used in the design of stairs on a floating production vessel.

I also realize my limitations as an information provider and sometimes outsource certain types of work to specialists, such as specialized patent searchers.

Typical Engineering Document Control Requests

My day involves a mixture of library and document control requests. Because I work as a solo librarian, I have to make decisions and develop work practices myself. As a document controller, I work as part of a team. It is vital that we all work according to common practices and standards and that we are in constant contact with each other to know what the others are working on. To do this, we have weekly team meetings where we discuss what we are working on and raise any issues we have encountered. We strive to be aware of all current projects as much as possible so that if someone is out of the office or overwhelmed with requests, we can provide instant backup.

Again, requests are extremely varied due to the type of information we manage. Because our assets are mostly mature, we are rapidly approaching a million records in our document management system, the majority of which are historical information. Many of these were bulk-loaded to the document management system when it was created and, due to the volume of records involved, data quality problems appeared. We often find poorly cataloged information. Titles of engineering documents can be misleading and are frequently not detailed enough to allow the user to find the record again. We find that drawing numbers were altered on the records from the way they actually appear on the document to make them easier to file. Due to the acquisitive nature of our company, there are large portions of our records that were imported from other content management systems with different cataloging requirements and quality standards. This also causes problems.

However, we can improve the quality of inherited information by slowly yet constantly making small improvements. I have recently worked with my team leader and our purchasing department to create a set of new purchasing procedures that should greatly increase our capture of documentation. We also run intensive document control on every new project. This involves liaising with contractors and creating document control procedures that standardize the delivery of documentation and the internal company access to that information. Once projects are up and running, we receive, catalog, and issue documentation to provide information and gather comments. We manage the interface between our company and its suppliers in terms of documentation delivery and comments on documents. We make sure that our engineers can access the most current information as they need it.

We also actively seek, plan, and execute data quality exercises. This could include recataloging a data set to improve the records or giving a supplier access to our document management system so that they can access the information they need quickly.

Although we strive to conduct our projects electronically as much as possible, we are also responsible for managing a hard copy set of key safety critical drawings and documents that the company requires in an emergency response situation. We therefore need to exercise the strictest control over these sets, regularly auditing them to make sure that they are current and in good physical condition.

Typical document control requests range from being asked to provide information to issuing new documents for internal or external review. Some recent examples include

- "We are upgrading a system on platform X. I need a list of everything we hold on that system, and I need a copy to be sent to the contractor doing the work."
- "I can't find this drawing/document in the system, but I know it exists."
- Issuing basis of design documents for review by other disciplines before work proceeds.
- Providing orientation to new users in finding information in our organization.

PROS AND CONS

Getting such wide and varied experience in information management is one of the best things about my job. In a company like mine, you deal with a variety of disciplines, including finance, human resources, engineering, geology, and geophysics. I even provide medical information to our offshore medics. It is fantastic experience. You also get a great deal of responsibility in a position like mine. For library work, especially, you often have to work solo, which gives you the freedom to run your services as you see fit. Of course, it also has the potential disadvantages of leaving you isolated from your peers and lacking professional support.

For these reasons I feel it is especially important to become involved in professional activities. National professional associations work through networks of local branches. I am on the committee of my local branch, which has allowed me to build a network of other professionals whom I can call on for advice if needed. There are also other local networks that are great to be involved in, as you can keep up to date with what is happening in other sectors of information management and can also meet fellow professionals.

HOW WOULD I GET A JOB LIKE YOURS?

Most positions require a library or information qualification, often at the university level. Relevant work experience is also often required, although graduate positions are occasionally available. If you are unable to secure a graduate position, it is still possible to get relevant work experience. Most public and academic libraries have science and engineering sections; those in areas with a higher oil and gas industry population often have a business and technical section. Experience gained this way can be very valuable.

Document control entry requirements (for jobs above basic issuing and cataloging positions) would normally be either a suitable qualification and relevant work experience or a good deal of basic document control experience. Many people working in document control were school leavers who started working as office juniors or clerks and moved up through promotions.

Most important, given the nature of the industry, certain personality traits are attractive to prospective employers. Applicants need to be very confident, yet open to the ideas of others. They must have a great deal of common sense and be very methodical and persistent. They should have good negotiating skills and not just accept existing practices. They must embrace change and keep up to date with new technologies. Above all else, they must have a genuine belief that what they are doing creates value for the business and must be able to communicate this, with enthusiasm, to all levels.

RELATED RESOURCES

ARMA International, Standards/Best Practices. www.arma.org/standards/index.cfm (accessed June 22, 2006).

Chartered Institute of Library and Information Professionals (CILIP). www.cilip.org.uk (accessed June 22, 2006).

EngLib: For the Scitech Librarian. englib.info (accessed June 22, 2006).

Grampian Information. www.grampianinfo.co.uk (accessed June 22, 2006).

Internet Resources Newsletter. www.hw.ac.uk/libwww/irn/irn.html (accessed June 22, 2006).

Issues in Science & Technology Librarianship. www.istl.org (accessed June 22, 2006).

OilOnline. www.oilonline.com (accessed June 22, 2006).

Special Libraries Association. www.sla.org (accessed June 22, 2006).

CHAPTER 47

Librarian, Internet Start-Up Company

STEVEN M. COHEN

It started with a standard e-mail exchange. While quickly checking my e-mail at the business center during a library conference in Monterey, an interesting note appeared. A CEO of a start-up Web company (one that I had been using and writing about since its inception two years earlier) was looking to hire a library scientist to help out in query creation, general Web collection development and classification, and other duties. Having read my blog posts discussing several presentations at the conference, he noted that he had become acquainted with my blog over the past few days and would like to get together to talk about possible referrals. Included in his e-mail was an invitation to an end-of-the-year party that the company was having, where many A-listers (those popular in the blogging community) would be present.

Although I couldn't attend the party (I would get back to New York too late), I responded that I was interested in talking to him and his colleagues about the company and, in what came as a surprise to him, the possibility of sending him my résumé and discussing future employment for me. Because I was very familiar with what the company did as well as the community in which they were entrenched, it seemed logical for me to pursue options for future employment. He agreed to discuss this and we set up a meeting. And so began my work for PubSub Concepts and its cofounders Salim Ismail (CEO) and Bob Wyman (CTO), along with twelve other employees.

After I returned home from the conference, I worked on a prospectus for what I could add conceptually, theoretically, and practically to the company. Because my training was in library science, with a specialty in online research (including fee-based databases, free search engines, emerging technologies, and competitive intelligence strategies), I decided to pursue the search angle in my initial write-up before the formal interview. PubSub is a prospective search company that matches new content in real time to queries created by users. Prospective search is a natural progression from retrospective search, which is what happens when users put queries into any search engine (such as Google, Yahoo!, LexisNexis, etc.) where the past is searched. PubSub will "search the future" for users rather than the past, which is important for ongoing research and discussion on any topic. Mixing my knowledge of the search engines, the formats used at PubSub (XML and RSS), and my training in library science made me an ideal candidate for a job that, after meeting with Bob and Salim, I was eager to have.

A librarian employed at a start-up Web company *in the role of librarian* was not a novel idea (Yahoo! and Amazon.com hired many new graduates of library schools in their hopes to organize the developing Web; in fact, one of the earliest employees of Yahoo! was a librarian, hired to head up their directory, which at the time took up major real estate on their site), but it was an anomaly. When blogs started to hit the mainstream in early to late 2002, there seemed to be a need yet again to organize and prioritize the incoming data. And there was a lot of it. PubSub was in the blog business (most of the content that comes into the matching engine comes from blog posts) and decided that it needed a librarian on staff to help in this process.

A TYPICAL WORKDAY

A typical day starts with me taking a train on a ninety-minute commute to New York City. Some may not see the benefits of such a long trip, but it gives me time to either read for pleasure (which I love to do) or get ready for the day ahead by checking e-mail or writing weekly reports. This gives me a head start on what I have to do for the day, getting my schedule ready and intact for what lay ahead.

Like many librarians, I find it hard to schedule a day when I know there will be many changes ahead. This is true for all aspects of librarianship (especially those in the front lines), but not as much for those of us that don't work directly with clientele. Also, my work at PubSub (being a start-up) involves more than just library work. I am heavily involved in community outreach and public relations and have to schedule my time based on these demands as well. The key is to be as flexible as possible with scheduling a day's work.

The library-related work that I do at PubSub is based on the online research skills I learned in library school and improved over the years while working at a law firm (using LexisNexis and Westlaw) and by continuously keeping up with the trends in the search engine industry. When using any search service, it's necessary to know all aspects of the logic inherent in the system. Librarians are known to be expert researchers. It's my job to be an expert at the PubSub search system, create subscriptions (our term for query creations) based on that knowledge as examples for new users, and educate end users on how to create better subscriptions.

In addition, I also use the query creation knowledge to build "precanned" subscriptions that are used on various themed content pages that we put out to the public. One of the benefits of creating these precanned subscriptions is that the user doesn't have to. For example, in 2005, PubSub released PubSub Government, a place for users to go to find out what is being said about every member of Congress, the Supreme Court, committees, and departments and members of the Cabinet. All of the subscriptions for this project were created and continuously and carefully edited over a month-long period to be as accurate as possible. My job was to make sure that each subscription did not bring back any false results and to edit as needed. The same concepts were put into place for other features that we put out over the course of the year, including PubSub Baseball and PubSub Football. In relation to subscription creation, I also keep the front page of our Web site up to date with sample subscriptions that we use to educate users on the many different uses of PubSub.

Although it wasn't part of the initial job description, I have recently joined the public relations team and now head up the community outreach department. I attend weekly **PR** meetings and work with the **PR** agency in setting up speaking engagements for our executives. The community outreach position builds on my ten years of experience as a public librarian, working with the community and assisting in information retrieval, educational training, and information literacy. Also, due to the business and social network that I formed in the library profession as well as in the Weblog/RSS community (where PubSub is a major player), this outreach role was perfectly suited for me.

In addition, I have been on the library speaking circuit for three years, with over twenty presentations per year on my slate. Any small company is always trying to market its services as much as possible to as many people as possible. By speaking at conferences and local library events, I have had the opportunity to do just that. Also, because of my experience with speaking in front of large audiences, I also speak at nonlibrary events. In 2005, I had the opportunity to attend four technology-related conferences and speak at three of them. Having a third employee with presentation experience has been very helpful to the executives, who are always on the road at meetings and conferences touting our company's core services.

I also proofread much of the copy that will be sent to journalists, placed on the Web site, or released on the press wires. As I mentioned earlier, I work closely with our public relations agency; my experience writing my blog, articles, columns, and book has made my desk one of the stops for press releases as they make their way from draft to final form. In addition, my experience with the written word also helps in communicating feedback to our users' questions.

On a typical day I may perform all of the tasks I've mentioned, from writing queries to sending off feedback e-mails to our vast user base. Sometimes I'm doing this at the office, and other times I'm attending teleconferences in my hotel room while attending a library or technology conference. For me, the unpredictable part of my job is not the work that I am asked to do, but where I will actually do it.

PROS AND CONS

Because I work in the virtual environment, I can accomplish most of my work at home, at the office, or on the road. All of the employees in my company can communicate with each other via e-mail or chat software, so I don't have to be physically present in our offices in New York (although I find it extremely important to be available in the office as much as possible). This has made for a more flexible work time, so that if I need to help out my family at home for a few hours, I can do so without having to worry about traveling back and forth on the commuter train. Having this option available has been one of the better aspects of this job, as I tend to work better independently rather than in an office situation. My position in the company entails many meetings, most of which I can do via teleconference.

Most jobs have negative and positive aspects, but I have found that working at PubSub is a good fit for a certain personality and those negative and positive conditions may be determined by the employee's perspective. First, there is a sense of insecurity when it comes to money. All start-ups have money issues when they first, well, start up, unless the founders are wealthy enough to keep the company afloat (which usually isn't the case). So there is always the uncertainty in the back of many workers' minds that the company could close shop if they run out of money. (Editors' note: PubSub laid off all employees in 2006.) It takes a certain personality type to work in such an environment, but the payoff may be greater, so this may be seen as a positive job aspect.

WOULD YOU LIKE A JOB LIKE MINE?

In this type of position, you must be a self-starter. Although there are managers that can guide you in your work, creativity and the ability to work independently are musts. You should not be afraid to come up with ideas and do everything possible to make sure that the idea is seen through to the end, because most of time, you will be the sole owner of the project. Of course, you will work with others in the company, but the onus falls on the one who initiates the idea.

The job also requires patience. Managers in start-ups can be very busy at times and may not be available at every step in a project. You must be confident in the decisions you make and try to make decisions that would benefit the company as a whole and not waste precious company time and resources.

Also, a librarian at a start-up may not be performing "librarian" duties. Although I have done research as well as create queries using my skills as a researcher, I also found myself reviewing press releases, performing outreach services (which does have some library-related aspects), writing content for the site, and more. On a related note, if a start-up does employ a librarian, it will most likely be only one. Not working side by side with other library colleagues may be a concern for those who are used to being surrounded by other librarians.

Working for a start-up takes creativity, the ability to work independently, the ability to create and follow through with initiatives, and a willingness to perform nonlibrarian duties. It's exciting, challenging, and stressful. Sometimes, it's not for the faint of heart and requires careful interpersonal and internal negotiations. Other times, it's just plain fun.

CHAPTER 48

Director of Library Services, Law Firm

KELLY DEVLIN

Help wanted: Law firm seeks professional librarian with excellent communication skills to manage staff, develop the collection within budget, and maintain the facilities; provide reference services, bibliographic instruction, and online resources training; and make sure the candy dish is filled with the "good stuff" for those late-night research sessions. MLS and sense of humor required/JD optional. Excellent benefits and salary available for qualified candidates.

The ad for my position could have read like that, and it wouldn't have been far off the mark. But truth be told, the candy dish actually gets filled with whatever I or my library colleagues choose to buy, and it gets put in the cupboard for a bit if we get more complaints than kudos for the offerings. As for the other tasks completed in the course of my workday, please read on.

A TYPICAL WORKDAY

Being a director or manager of a law firm library requires the typical management skill set of organizing, planning, budgeting, staffing, and coordinating, but the workdays can be surprisingly atypical compared to those of other professional librarians. Every day is a bit different than the one before and quite likely to be different from the next. The result is a job that one day stimulates and strokes the researcher in you as it challenges your ability to provide the highest level of professional reference service you can muster in a time-sensitive environment, and then the next day tests your managerial skills and ability to make progress on large library projects. Yes, the two "days" are often rolled into one; you can wear many hats in a span of eight to ten hours, including the following.

- Researcher: "Sure, I can find a case that says that in the next twenty minutes."

- Supervisor: "The firm understands that you need that time off. You take care of things there, and we'll take care of things here until you get back."

- Instructor: "Those two legal research tools are supposed to provide the same information, but they don't because they are produced by competing publishers using different analytical and editorial methods."

- IT support technician: "To allow the print dialog box to appear, you need to add this site to your trusted sites list. Here's how."
- Accounts payable clerk: "Check #124346 was sent two months ago to pay that invoice and has cleared our bank. Is it possible the payment was posted to another account?"
- Office assistant: "Three copies of that statute: one to fax, one for the court, and one for the file? Your assistant will have them in ten minutes."

The amount of time I wear each of these hats varies greatly due to my personal management style. Though I don't delegate high-level managerial tasks to other members of our library services team, I do like to work closely with them on major projects, such as implementation of our new library management system, reorganizing and relocating the collection, and working with the law students employed by the firm, commonly referred to as summer associates.

More importantly, I try to encourage a team atmosphere and cross-training when practical. My preference is that we each can fill in to a certain extent when one of the members of our team is away, out sick, on vacation, or just not available. I know it sounds hokey, and honestly it doesn't work well if the players don't play well together. In addition, while I may be the team captain, I also try to be a team player. Consequently, each time I answer the phone, I don't know whether I'll be asked to confirm a book order or find legal authority for an appellate brief. Very similarly, the other members of the team work on administrative and research tasks as required. The difference is in our varying skill levels and the time devoted to the tasks.

I'll admit it—I don't make a lot of copies at this stage of my career. I don't think firms pay directors the salaries they do so there will be an extra pair of hands to copy legal opinions. I believe I'm paid to have vision, plan ahead, and make sure that information services are delivered promptly and accurately each day. To that end, I have to apply my knowledge about computers, networks, information classification systems, research, law, and my firm's collection of resources to make sure that happens. That said, if an attorney needs an opinion copied and the other members of the team aren't available, I do remember how to turn pages and press the little green button. Moreover, I'm glad to do it because it's all part of providing information services with an emphasis on service.

But what I tend to enjoy most are the more challenging research and technology questions I get in the course of a day. For instance, an attorney might need legal authority to support an argument to be made in front of a judge during a hearing or trial. If the attorney can't find that authority, I use my experience and skill to locate it in our books and online resources.

Law school does teach attorneys how to research, but the classes are limited in coverage, and research skills often atrophy if the attorney doesn't research regularly. In addition, online legal resources tend to get improved and revised frequently. A busy attorney may not have time to keep up with these changes, but a primary part of my job is to keep up with those very same changes so I can quickly find information for others and show them how to use legal information systems for those moments when they want to complete their research projects independently. Consequently, a tough research question challenges my abilities both as a researcher and, if time permits and the attorney is interested, as a teacher.

In contrast, I may also get a call from an attorney informing me that one of our online systems isn't working. To respond to calls like these, I might do some technical troubleshooting or call on the firm's technology staff for assistance. I might also realize that there's nothing wrong with the system, and that the attorney needs an introduction to a new database interface. These situations allow me to work as the library liaison and marketer. Here, communication skills are key, and I have to use them along with my technical knowledge to get things up and running. I also often have to multitask in these instances because the attorney's need for the information continues, and I'm expected to locate the information in an alternate resource.

Some might find the pressure of having to multitask like this to be too stressful. For me, it's usually intellectually stimulating. I hate to be bored, and being presented with different challenges each day keeps me interested in my job. Of course, the positive feedback I get when I find information the attorney couldn't find is a powerful motivator. Frankly, it's quite rewarding to be appreciated at work. If you're the same way, enjoy challenges at work, don't crumble under pressure, and like positive feedback for a job well done, then you probably can see why I like what I do on the very varied days I spend as a law library director.

PROS AND CONS

Many firm administrators still view librarians as book-stamping, shushing introverts instead of the highly skilled, computer-savvy, well-educated modern professionals most must be today to succeed in a law firm environment. Unfortunately, the result can often be a false devaluation of the services provided and the professionals who provide them. Practically speaking, that means that although library directors and managers in law firms must bring a great deal of education and experience to their firms and handle a fair amount of managerial tasks, they are often not recognized as professionals on the same level as the firm's other administrative leaders in the accounting, human resources, or information technology services areas.

Similarly, the level of responsibility given to library managers is often quite disparate from the level of authority enjoyed by them in their positions. In addition, salary surveys often show that compensation is comparatively low for library directors compared with that of other professionals required to hold at least a master's degree and have several years of practical experience.

Still with me? Good. Here's the positive side.

If you get professional satisfaction from meeting a quick research deadline, enjoy choosing the tasks of the day yourself (instead of being micromanaged by another), seek fair compensation and good benefits, and want new challenges and a different workday every day, then you will be quite happy as a director in a law firm environment. The research assignments will stimulate your intellectual curiosity, and those who cannot find what you can will be very grateful for your efforts and skill. Furthermore, the managerial projects will give you opportunities to shine. The library may be a small department in the firm, but your annual bonus will probably be a reflection of how well you meet your budget goal, manage your staff, and keep operations running smoothly.

Moreover, you will get to work with legal professionals at various levels: law students, associates, experienced attorneys, former judges who have returned to practice, and retired partners. Though attorneys are often the subject of jokes about greed, thievery, and deceit, many are highly ethical and honorable professionals who use their knowledge to help others in their community in the pro bono publico tradition. As such, I've found that many are sterling individuals.

In addition, lawyers' personalities and backgrounds can be quite diverse, so you are likely to interact with several different, interesting, and personable individuals on a daily basis in any medium- or large-sized firm. For example, in patent practice firms, you'll work with lawyers who are also scientists, but in corporate practice firms, you'll encounter tax attorneys who are also CPAs. Most are very professional and defy the negative stereotypes at every turn.

HOW WOULD I GET A JOB LIKE YOURS?

Law library directors in law firms generally hold two or three advanced degrees: a master's degree in library science, a juris doctor degree, or both. They also must know legal bibliography and be able to teach others how to use legal resources properly. Preparation for a director's position includes taking a legal research course and providing legal reference services as a paraprofessional and professional for several years under the guidance of experienced law librarians. You must be very adept for this level of law librarianship because you will be the go-to research person expected to locate information and documents that no one else can find.

To find an opening in a firm, it's important to scan job listings on professional association, library school, and law firm Web sites regularly. You should network with trusted colleagues as well so you'll hear about openings promptly, often before an ad is placed and the position is announced. In addition, check area newspapers dedicated to the legal profession. These specialized newspapers predate the Web, and in past years were the only place to find ads for law library openings. Of course, it's a good idea to check the newspaper Web sites, too, because ads can be placed there exclusively.

Once you hear about an opening, find out as much as you can about the position before applying. You should not only check to see if you can meet the firm's qualifications, but you should also check out the firm. What kind of reputation does the firm have? In what practice areas do they work? How does the firm treat administrative employees? What are the other library staff members like? How long has this position been open? Has this (or other library positions) been filled and open and refilled several times in recent years? If so, why?

To get this information, you'll have to do some research, but that shouldn't scare you. After all, you're an expert researcher or else you wouldn't be applying for this job! Learn about the firm through its Web site, news searches, client list, and your professional network. If you're lucky, you'll learn which firms are likely to offer both the position and the work environment you seek before you send that cover letter and résumé. Moreover, you'll be able to honestly and candidly write that the library director opening at their firm interests you because you have the qualifications they seek and they offer a work environment you just know you would thrive in.

Above all, be specific! If the firm's attorneys practice corporate law and you've got great business research experience to go with your legal research experience, tell them that. Demonstrate not only that you can fill their needs as stated in the ad but also that you will bring other valuable skills, knowledge, and experience that they will be able to use for marketing, recruiting, and other business purposes. If you're an attorney and they have a large litigation practice, let them know that you understand how to get documents from courts and government agencies. Former medical professionals should stress their knowledge of biological sciences and how it can help with assessing personal injury and workers' compensation cases. It's not a time to be shy. Go against the librarian stereotype and prove you are a valuable professional they absolutely must hire before someone else does because you're talented, knowledgeable, and can be an asset to their business.

RELATED RESOURCES

American Association of Law Libraries. www.aallnet.org (accessed March 11, 2006).
Association of Legal Administrators. www.alanet.org (accessed March 11, 2006).
Special Libraries Association. www.sla.org (accessed March 11, 2006).

CHAPTER 49

Law Librarian, Private Law Firm

KATHERINE COOLIDGE

It's Tuesday morning after a long weekend. This week I am scheduled to attend two practice group meetings and am preparing to conduct the monthly Library Committee meeting and a legal research training session the following day. My part-time assistant is out sick, my incoming mail stack is about a foot high, there is a backlog of materials to be cataloged, and there are fifty messages in my e-mail inbox, several of which are reference requests and two of which relate to problems using the electronic resources (the frustration of the senders is noted). Two of the research tables are covered with books needing to be reshelved, there are two reference projects left on my chair by attorneys who worked over the weekend, a paralegal is waiting by my desk to ask a question, the voicemail message light is glowing red, and the phone is ringing. What do I do first? I smile, because I am in an interesting, challenging career that allows me to work with highly educated and motivated people.

Needless to say, learning to prioritize and remaining calm and pleasant under fire are essential to succeeding as a solo law librarian. I came to law librarianship after practicing law and have found that it has allowed me to keep all of the aspects I loved about law, such as researching, writing, negotiating, managing, counseling, and advising, while leaving behind the aspects I did not enjoy so much, such as litigation. Solo law librarianship offers the opportunity to learn something new every day.

JOB DESCRIPTION

As a solo law librarian in a private law firm, I maintain and control all aspects of the firm's research collection housed in the law libraries and in the attorneys' offices in Springfield and Boston, Massachusetts. I conduct legal and nonlegal reference research for forty-one attorneys and six paralegals; plan for changes in research collections; process new acquisitions, serial circulation, and interlibrary loans; prepare and monitor the library budget and payables; negotiate contracts for print and electronic resources; maintain the firm's intranet page; and contribute to the firm's knowledge management and legal research training initiatives.

I report to the executive director and to the Library Committee, which consists of two partners, one associate, and the executive director. I prepare the agenda and budget reports for the monthly meetings that I conduct. I supervise one part-time employee who is responsible for serial circulation, looseleaf service interfiling, and reshelving of borrowed materials.

A TYPICAL WORKDAY

Legal and nonlegal research and reference services take priority over all other responsibilities and tasks. Consequently, I start my day by checking my e-mail and desk for written reference requests. I also receive requests in person and by telephone. Reference requests may include conducting research on electronic resources such as Westlaw, LexisNexis, RIA Checkpoint, Tax Analysts, Dun and Bradstreet, and federal and state-hosted Web sites as well as searching the firm's and other libraries' catalogs for useful resources. My goal is to provide excellent reference service above and beyond what the original requestor may have asked. Quite often the answer to a question leads to more questions. Providing that additional information and service saves time and effort on the part of attorneys, a valuable asset in the billable hour setting. New and varied reference questions keep my career challenging and fresh.

In between providing reference services, I may be monitoring legal and nonlegal newspapers and slip opinion services that are delivered daily by e-mail, attending a practice group meeting so that I have a better understanding of the issues on which my patrons are working, cataloging new arrivals, or working on our retrospective cataloging project. I also spend time redesigning the intranet page, preparing monthly reports, assisting patrons with access to print and electronic resources, processing invoices, purchasing new titles, negotiating contracts, and scheduling and conducting legal research training. Once a month I conduct the Library Committee meeting. Each day brings opportunities to develop my research and managerial skills.

PROS AND CONS

The most significant positive aspect of solo law librarianship is the intellectual stimulation and the opportunity to work with highly intelligent people in a fast-paced, professional setting. In my particular firm, I am constantly reminded that I am valued and important to the firm as a member of a team that provides high-quality legal services. My opinions matter, and I am consulted in the areas of knowledge management and continuing legal education. Providing legal reference is as much about counseling as it is researching law and facts and communicating the results. The personal human interaction is very rewarding.

The downside of solo law librarianship is that you are it—from fixing paper jams and pasting card pockets in new acquisitions to typing and filing all your own correspondence, reports, and spreadsheets. At times, the cataloging backlog can be overwhelming, and the printer always seems to jam only when you are in a hurry. Receiving a lengthy reference request while you are trying to prepare to conduct a meeting or a training session can test your patience. Having a good sense of humor and an understanding that your position is a career, not just a job, can help immensely to keep everything in perspective.

Both a pro and a con of solo law librarianship is the independent nature of being the only person in the firm who provides the services you do. Although it is a blessing to be able to structure your own time and determine your activities, it can be rather isolating not to have a counterpart with whom to discuss ideas and methods of practice. Additionally, when you are not in the office, there is no one available to cover your workload. Reaching out to other law librarians and creating a network in the legal field as well as in other subject areas is absolutely essential to improving your own skills and providing reference service coverage in your absence.

ENTERING THE FIELD OF LAW LIBRARIANSHIP

I made the decision to transition into law librarianship after practicing law for over seventeen years. My practical experience in researching the law, advising clients, and applying the law to their needs is invaluable to my ability to assist the attorneys in my firm. However, you do not need to have been a practicing attorney to become a law librarian. A master's degree in library and information science along with an interest in learning and understanding legal resources would qualify you to become a law librarian in a private firm. Some firms only require experience in a law library whether or not you have obtained an MLIS.

Though it may sound like a cliché, excellent communication and personal skills are essential to a career as a solo law librarian. You must be able to listen to the question being asked and clarify any questions you may have about the reference request. After conducting the research, you must be able to organize and communicate the answer. Often your patrons will come to you after conducting their own unsuccessful research that has left them frustrated and impatient. It is helpful to remain centered on basic research skills and approach the question with fresh eyes. Sometimes, just the reference interview and a suggestion of a research strategy helps the patron refocus on the heart of the issue. A smile and an empathetic statement go a long way to diffusing the tension and pressure inherent in the practice of law.

Strong skills in the use of electronic resources—especially how to frame an effective search—and a willingness to learn legal terms of art so that your searches are precise will make legal reference easier to manage. Basic accounting skills and practical experience with Office software are necessary to manage the daily processes of the law library and to organize and conduct legal research training, committee meetings, and annual budgeting and reporting. You must be able to work independently with little direction and be able to prioritize your responsibilities and tasks. Finally, you must be flexible enough to accept interruptions with grace and adjust your work schedule as needed while remaining focused on the fact that you are part of a professional team in a service industry. Rigid adherence to a routine or set schedule is not characteristic of solo law librarianship.

To prepare for law librarianship within a law firm, I recommend working as a library assistant or clerical worker in a law firm or as a library assistant in a courthouse library. These jobs allow you to work closely with attorneys, gain experience with legal reference resources, and also understand the pace of a law practice. Taking a legal reference course in library school or obtaining a certificate in paralegal studies would also help you learn legal research skills and terminology. I also highly recommend becoming a member of a professional association so that you may meet other law librarians, attend educational conferences, and read the literature of the profession. Joining a professional association at both the national and regional levels is the best way to network with others in the profession. The American Association of Law Libraries (AALL) and the Special Libraries Association (SLA) both offer student memberships at a reasonable rate. Membership in their regional chapters and practice divisions may be included or added for a nominal fee.

CONCLUSION

Even though I am a solo law librarian, I am not flying solo. That is by design, not by accident. Often I draw on the expertise of colleagues both inside and outside the firm. The development of this chapter is an example of this process.[1] If you remember that collaboration is paramount, you will flourish as a solo law librarian in a law firm. You should try to learn something from everyone in the firm (by "everyone," I mean attorneys, paralegals, and bookkeeping, information technology, administrative, and secretarial staff), and you should aspire to become valued as a team player. Take advantage of every opportunity to network with colleagues in the many subject specialties of the library profession. Striving to listen effectively, think critically, research efficiently, and communicate precisely will keep you in good stead in the profession of solo law librarianship.

NOTE

1. I thank attorney Robert B. Atkinson, partner at Bulkley, Richardson and Gelinas, LLP, and Professors Sheila Intner and Terry Plum of Simmons GSLIS West for their time and consideration in reading this chapter and for their valuable editorial comments. I also thank Priscilla Shontz and Rich Murray for giving me the opportunity to write about my profession.

RELATED RESOURCES

You may obtain more information about AALL at www.aallnet.org/index.asp and about SLA at www.sla.org.

CHAPTER 50

Public Law Librarian

Working in a quasi-public library located in a county courthouse in Texas means my patrons range from the unsophisticated, uneducated, and computer illiterate to the computer-savvy legal professional. My job description, originally written for a clerk,[1] actually ranges from librarian to office clerk and unofficial information technology employee. I am responsible for the library's administrative tasks, all public and technical services, and occasionally public speaking. My office hat includes miscellaneous typing for the district attorney's office, as well as handling anything concerning electronics and maintaining the second-floor courthouse display rack.[2] I also handle a variety of special projects, ranging from locating and compiling county ordinances into one accessible location to coordinating a library move to creating and maintaining an online catalog.

A TYPICAL WORKDAY

It is 7:55 a.m. and already people have requested directions to a criminal courtroom, the child support court, and the central jury room. Unlocking the library's door, I am stopped by a fourth person with a request to skip jury duty. He unhappily returns to his hallway seat when I suggest he talk to the district clerk. Two more people request directions to the restroom and a coffee pot. Before I can complete opening procedures, a Hispanic family enters looking for the juvenile courtroom. I call the district clerk's office, only to be told that all juvenile hearings will be in my building tomorrow. As I share that information in my limited Spanish, the father, speaking rapid-fire Spanish, waves a document at me. It turns out their case involves Child Protective Services, not Juvenile Services, so I call the district clerk's office back with the correct information and obtain courtroom information. Next, I receive a call from an attorney with a request for an oil and gas article. Jotting down the citation, I advise him that it may take several days to obtain a copy and ask if he would be willing to pay a reasonable fee if the owning library charges for interlibrary loans.

By now it is almost 8:30 and I still have to catch up on yesterday's leftover office work. As I pull the office files and typing out of my inbox, I notice I have five files to scan and distribute to the appropriate defense attorneys,[3] sixty documents to type, twenty-five case files to dispose, and fifteen scanned files awaiting quality control audit. While working on the office tasks, I have several requests from the public for divorce, name change, and deed forms, as well as a request for probate information. Although the print collection provides resources for the first three questions, the probate question requires using one of our databases, so I teach this patron to use the public access terminal.

About half of the legal professionals I see request assistance. Today an attorney is upset when I tell him we have only the digital edition of a book he needs. He is uncomfortable with computers, so I accompany him to one of the database terminals and teach him how to access that title.

Halfway through the clerical work, I take a shelving break and check on the two patrons still in the room. The attorney on the Westlaw terminal appears to be doing fine, so I do not disturb him. The second patron, a paralegal student, complains she does not understand why she has to use a digest to access a case reporter. I show her how the digest serves as an index to the print reporters.

While shelving, I notice that the divorce book I use with the majority of the general public is in need of more major surgery, and I put it in the office for repairs. I also notice that the cleaning crew forgot to dust and vacuum the library, so I make a mental note to remind them to clean the room every Wednesday.

At 10:30 a.m. I am almost finished with the quality control audit on the part-time employee's scanning. She scans old department files so we can destroy paper files to save space while still complying with the state's record retention requirements. After five months she is ready for random audit, so I will no longer review every file she touches.

Before I can start on the case disposals, the phone rings again. I have had several calls this morning, but all except for the first call have been requests for library hours and location, a telephone number for legal aid, and a wrong number. This time it is one of the prosecutors requesting a case law search regarding spousal privilege in grand jury hearings. Generally, if an attorney asks me to perform research, it is because he is looking for a second opinion. In this case, the prosecutor has performed several database searches and found nothing directly on point—that is, he has found no legal decision or ruling that is identical or similar enough to be cited as precedent in his case. Jotting down the details, I set it aside, check my e-mail, and post my oil and gas interlibrary loan request to an e-mail list.

By 11:15, I am finished with the case disposals and begin my library work with the case law search on spousal privilege. After finding nothing directly on point using both natural language and Boolean techniques with two different online vendors, I check a secondary source. Deciding there is probably nothing on point, I type a memo for the prosecutor.

I have just enough time before lunch to open the mail, call our CD-ROM vendor about an update mailed three weeks ago but never received, check the budget, and process today's bills. Shortly before noon, I give both patrons a five-minute warning, suggest they take a lunch break, and remind them that they are welcome to return at 1 p.m. As I leave for lunch, a child tells me the display rack at the end of the hall is broken.

On my way back in at 1 p.m., I check the display rack. It looks worse than it really is—the pins holding the bottom two shelves in place have slipped from their holes. After reopening the library, I grab a pair of pliers, a screwdriver, and a wire hanger, and I wire the shelves to the frame and restock the rack.

Returning to the library, I find a voicemail from one of the office's investigators with a request for a two-year-old local weather report that she cannot retrieve from the news media. Five minutes later, I have it (courtesy of a free Web site) and e-mail it to her. The next telephone call is from a public library employee with a request for materials on international adoptions. After making sure the patron is looking for legal information on the adoption process, I suggest the librarian send the patron over.

Checking my e-mail, I see a response from my earlier posting on the oil and gas request; the article should be on my fax machine by morning. I also see a request from a Maryland librarian looking for a Texas jury charge. I respond, asking her if she would like it e-mailed or faxed. She responds with a fax number. I finally have a few minutes to order some materials from the Government Printing Office and the state attorney general's office.

The next patron requiring assistance is a legal professional who has difficulty operating a mouse due to tremors. When she has exhausted the print collection, she will have to use one of the legal databases. Because of her inability to operate a mouse, I spend more time with her than I normally spend with my patrons to help her log into the database and input her search. Once the search has been entered, I can set the computer to respond to keyboard commands.

The phone rings, but before I can return to the office, a poorly dressed, possibly homeless man enters the library. He looks unkempt, mutters to himself, and generally makes my two remaining patrons uneasy. Deciding to keep a closer eye on him, I let voicemail answer the phone call while I do some shelf reading and shifting. When he approaches the paralegal student, I intercept him with an offer of assistance, politely explaining that he can stay as long as he respects everyone else's space, adding that I will call the sheriff's department for assistance if I think it necessary. While he considers my statement, I notice a jailer has arrived with a small stack of inmate requests. Paging through the requests, I note they are all easy this week: a request for divorce and child support forms, anything on blue warrants, a case citation, and information concerning the sentencing options for DUI. Before leaving, the jailer asks if I want him to escort the man out. Because he has settled down with a book, I thank the officer for his offer but indicate the man can stay for the time being.

I finally notice the time and realize the part-time employee has been scanning for over an hour. As I begin processing the books I cataloged yesterday, I tell her she has graduated to random audits. After the potential problem patron leaves, I ask her to watch the room while I deliver the book order requisition to purchasing and the bills to the auditor. I then check with the legal professional to make sure she is not waiting for assistance with the computer before I load a box of files onto the book truck and head across the street to the Justice Center. While over there, I check my box for tomorrow's office work and follow up with a couple of prosecutors who had difficulty accessing the CD-ROMs on the intranet yesterday (I'm hoping the IT staff and I found and fixed the problem this morning).

Returning to the library, I find two messages from private attorneys. One cannot access his electronic discovery account, so I walk him through the process. The second call is actually from a legal secretary in need of the correct citation format for a brief she is typing. I look it up in *The Bluebook* and read it to her over the telephone.

The legal professional is now ready for one of the online databases, so I set her up on the Westlaw terminal and seat myself at the Lexis terminal. Late yesterday, I received requests for the current Library Systems Act, library districting legislation, and contact information for a little-known oil company. I save the state's Library Systems Act and library districting legislation to a floppy disk to work on in the morning. The contact information for the oil company takes more research and a little creativity. Between the free Internet and the subscription databases, I have learned that it is most likely a privately held Canadian company that could be either an oil company or a pipeline company. With that much information, I call a colleague at a library with a good-sized Canadian business collection. She checks one of her directories and provides what information she can while stressing that her directory is several years old.

Shortly before closing for the day, the county judge stops by and reminds me that he plans to institute the first part of the new records retention policy and wants to make sure I have a current copy of the state requirements for each department. Shortly after he leaves, the jailer returns to pick up the materials I have already checked out to his department for inmate use.

PROS AND CONS

Pros

A public law library is a unique environment in which I have daily contact with both the general public and legal professionals. I especially enjoy the challenges created by the wide variety of patrons, bibliographic instruction, computer instruction, mind-bogglingly complex reference questions, and in-depth research. Although this library was established in the 1960s, I am their first professional librarian, and after several years I am finally beginning to receive requests from county officials, employees, legal professionals, and members of the general public. A few of my patrons have recently commented they think I can walk on water due to my ability to locate almost any information, given enough time and clues.

Cons

One downside to my job is the low salary. Whereas some of the large public law libraries on the East and West Coasts pay over $60,000 a year, the average salary range for public law librarians is on the low end of the professional scale—between the mid-$20s and mid-$50s. I often find myself creating policies and procedures from scratch as the situation warrants, while combating the "No one ever said I could(n't) before" syndrome, as policies and procedures did not exist when I took this job. Another downside is the difficulty convincing the general public that I am a librarian, not an attorney, and although I frequently make that statement to a patron during the initial contact and reference interview, not everyone hears it.

Being a one-person show is also a disadvantage. If I need to be out of the room, I have to make arrangements to have someone watch it or close it and modify the hours accordingly. If I ever call in sick, the library is closed the entire day, and I will spend the next two weeks fielding complaints about the unscheduled closing. To attend a conference or take a day off, I have to make arrangements to have someone monitor the room and defer all questions to a future date or suggest the patron contact the next closest public law library. Continuing to split my time between library and nonlibrary responsibilities is another con, but one that will eventually work itself out as the library side of the job continues to expand.

HOW TO FIND A JOB IN A PUBLIC LAW LIBRARY

Generally, an MLS with advanced coursework in or experience with legal resources and government documents is adequate for positions in most public law libraries. A strong reference background is also helpful. Some library science programs offer advanced certificates in law librarianship. It is also possible to brush up on legal resources by taking a paralegal or legal assistant research course at a local community college.

Finding a public law library job can require some creativity. When I applied, the ad was for a clerk or secretary with a little library experience who would monitor the room while performing clerical work for the office. That job description changes as my supervisor discovers new ways to utilize the skills, knowledge, and training of a professional librarian. Already two of the office tasks listed in the original job ad have been reassigned elsewhere.

Positions may be advertised in the local newspaper, in trade journals such as *Law Library Journal*, on an e-mail list such as Law-Lib, by word of mouth, on a library science department job board, and on some Web sites such as the American Association of Law Librarians or Monster.com. You can also try to create a position by showing the key people what a professional librarian can do and how it can benefit them by volunteering your services or by sneaking in a back door like I did.

NOTES

1. At the time of my hiring, the job description merely stated, "Maintaining and balancing cash drawer, updating and reshelving books, pulling books for jail inmates, assisting public with use of law library, preparing responses to discovery requests, disposing of files, assisting with intake and preparing various outgoing correspondence for the County Attorney's Office" (Grayson County, Tex. Human Resources. www.co.grayson.tx.us).

2. My clerical duties for the district attorney's office include typing correspondence and internal documents, managing the district attorney's online database passwords, auditing the office's database invoices, and overseeing all archival and electronic document delivery procedures.

3. This is part of the discovery process. Discovery occurs when opposing attorneys share case information with each other. My involvement in the process is limited to scanning and distributing those case file documents the prosecutor indicates he or she wants shared with the defense attorney.

BIBLIOGRAPHY

Grayson County, Texas. Human Resources. www.co.grayson.tx.us/Human%20Resources/HRMain.htm (accessed September 18, 2006).

Manion, Terrance. American Association of Law Libraries. Task Force to Enhance Law Librarianship Education. Education for a career in law librarianship: How can I learn about law librarianship as a career? www.aallnet.org/committee/tfedu/education.html (accessed November 25, 2005).

ADDITIONAL RESOURCES

Job Search Resources: Web Sites and Professional Organizations

American Association of Law Libraries. Job placement hotline. www.aallnet.org/hotline (accessed June 21, 2006).

American Library Association. Employment opportunities. www.ala.org/ala/education/empopps/employmentopportunities.htm (accessed June 21, 2006).

Gordon, Rachel Singer. *Lisjobs.com.* www.lisjobs.com (accessed June 21, 2006).

Law-Lib e-mail list. lawlibrary.ucdavis.edu/LAWLIB/lawlib.html (accessed August 20, 2006).

Monster.com. 2005. www.monster.com (accessed June 21, 2006).

Personnel services, such as Kelly Services. www.kellyservices.us (accessed August 22, 2006).

Special Library Association. Career center. www.sla.org/careers (accessed August 20, 2006).

Additional Information

Partial lists of public law libraries can be found at:

FindLaw. www.findlaw.com/05libraries/public.html (accessed November 27, 2005).

State Court and County Law Libraries (SCCLL). American Association of Law Libraries, SCCLL libraries. www.aallnet.org/sis/sccll/membership/libraries.htm (accessed November 27, 2005).

Yahoo! Public law libraries in the Yahoo! directory. dir.yahoo.com/Government/law/legal_research/libraries/public_law_libraries (accessed August 20, 2006).

General Resources

Law Library Resource Exchange. *LLRX.com.* www.llrx.com (accessed November 27, 2005).

Noe, Christopher. Law-Lib e-mail list FAQ. home.olemiss.edu/%7Enoe/llfaq.html (accessed August 20, 2006).

CHAPTER 51

Librarian, Art Museum Library

JONATHAN W. EVANS

My job entails overseeing all reader services, including reference and research activities, at the Museum of Fine Arts, Houston. Additional responsibilities include bibliographic instruction, publication exchange, and interlibrary loan service to the museum's professional staff. Related to these functions are the creation of policies and procedures for reader services, as well as the development of strategies for the provision of services. Other key duties involve participating in collection development, assisting in the preparation of the annual budget, and advising in matters related to space planning.

A TYPICAL WORKDAY

Stare into the eyes of a female sitter in a painting by Rembrandt and wonder about her role in prosperous seventeenth-century Dutch society. Reflect on the significance of a hand gesture in a thirteenth-century Hindu bronze statue. Admire the sinuous line and bold coloration of a Matisse portrait while looking for clues about technique. Question the artistic merit of a minimalist sculpture by Donald Judd. Each of these scenarios or ones like them are played out daily in art museums across the country. The simple yet profound act of contemplating a work of art can generate a series of intellectual inquiries. It can also elicit a range of emotional responses that leave one confounded or in a state of euphoria. Whether through intellectual curiosity or emotional necessity, the end result frequently culminates in a desire for more information.

This is where art museum librarians come into the picture, helping patrons locate biographical information about an artist, place a work within its historical context, identify a style, explore technical aspects of creation, assess the theoretical underpinnings of a work, or simply revel in the wonder of creation. In my role as reference librarian at the Hirsch Library at the Museum of Fine Arts, Houston (MFAH), I am fortunate to work directly with staff and patrons who are as passionate and curious about the visual world as I am. This position affords me the opportunity to learn and challenge myself each day, which I feel is a luxury.

Etched in the Indiana limestone facade of the original entrance to the museum are the words "Erected by the People for the Use of the People," underscoring the fundamental democratic principles of the institution. The MFAH is a privately funded entity that provides an essential public service by opening the eyes of its visitors to the value of art in their lives.

Although museums have often been viewed as daunting and even intimidating places, the art museum architecture boom in recent decades has transformed many traditional structures into new temples of populism that have their ideological roots in the museums of the late nineteenth century. The MFAH is at the forefront of exposing its riches to the broadest possible range of citizens, intent on enhancing appreciation for and knowledge of art.

I can't imagine working in a place that didn't aspire to these democratic values. As I daily cross the threshold of the museum, I recognize that I'm privileged to work in an environment where sharing information about our collective cultural heritage is not only appreciated but at the core of our very mission. That's why I find the field of art museum librarianship so alluring.

The MFAH is a large, privately funded urban museum that possesses an encyclopedic collection renowned for its Impressionist and post-Impressionist paintings, African gold objects, photography, and Texas art. It is now the sixth-largest museum in the nation in terms of physical size. It employs over five hundred individuals on a full-time basis.

The Hirsch Library is the research facility for the museum. Our mission is to meet the art information needs of the museum's staff as well as the general public. The library is of medium size by art museum library standards, with a collection that weighs in at just over one hundred thousand volumes and attendance that exceeds five thousand visitors per year. The library employs four full-time professionals, two full-time paraprofessionals, and four part-time paraprofessionals, in addition to a small cadre of dedicated volunteers. What sets us apart from a large contingent of art museum libraries is our accessibility to the general public. The library maintains public hours five days a week for a total of thirty-seven hours. It is accessible solely to staff an additional twelve hours per week. This level of service displays an unusual level of commitment put forth by the institution to educate the public about the visual arts. It also requires a great deal of flexibility on the part of the reference staff as demand and complexity of need can fluctuate significantly from day to day.

This demand comes from three distinct user groups. Our primary users are the research staff of the museum, which constitutes approximately seventy researchers. A secondary group of users are those closely associated with the museum but not under its employ, including docents, interns, committee members, and volunteers who commit their time and effort in support of the museum. A final group constitutes a broad spectrum of users, including college and university students, outside scholars, appraisers, educators, artists, collectors, gallery owners, and those simply curious about the relics that reside in their attics.

Part of my delight in working in this environment comes from this diversity of patrons. For some, this may be seen as a burden. My philosophy about both art and libraries is that they are intended to be appreciated by all, regardless of educational background or prior experience. At the Hirsch Library this means that we regularly serve patrons ranging from those on their first trip to a museum to curatorial staff members with doctorates conducting research for a forthcoming exhibition.

Two recent exchanges exemplify the range of inquiries that we receive at the library. One of the more than 1,500 local college and university students who patronize our library recently embarked on her first visit to a museum, arriving at the library somewhat overwhelmed. Following a brief reference exchange, it became evident that she required documentation about a Ptolemaic-period Egyptian coffin in the museum's permanent collection. For objects such as this that receive frequent attention from students, the library has produced a series of research guides to assist students in grasping basic concepts associated with the object while providing a detailed bibliography of related sources. A reserve shelf near the reference desk allows us to work directly with students in identifying potentially valuable resources. In this way we have become adept at making the best use of staff and student time. This, combined with an in-depth knowledge of the museum's collection and a familiarity with key print and online resources, makes our library a valuable resource for students.

Staff requests tend to be more time consuming to address, because they are typically narrowly focused and less predictable. They can also be some of the most challenging and stimulating, allowing library staff to probe the collection in ways that refine our research skills and increase knowledge of our holdings. For example, a staff member recently asked me to compile material related to the early painting techniques employed by Joan Miró, a twentieth-century Spanish painter. The body of literature on Miró is formidable, and there was no single source of scholarship that dealt with his technical practices that I could identify. I consulted a sampling of encyclopedias, bibliographies, exhibition catalogs, monographs, periodical indexes, and articles. In the process, I learned a great deal about Miró's practices, as well as about some of the strengths and weaknesses of our collection. Additionally, I was reminded of the limitations of library catalogs and periodical indexes as a fair amount of browsing was required to amass the necessary materials in this case. Regardless of who the patron is, we strive to provide high-quality service in an efficient, effective manner.

Responsibility for interlibrary loan services to staff falls to me. Our ILL operation has increased dramatically in recent years with annual borrowing exceeding 650 items, while lending surpasses 225 items. I particularly enjoy this aspect of my job because it keeps me close to the pulse of research activities at the museum. Additionally, it hones my database-searching skills while requiring me to stay familiar with a range of union catalogs, periodical indexes, and auction indexes.

Collection development in many art museum library settings is a complex and very hands-on endeavor. Our library maintains a close eye on its selection practices and as a result has steered away from approval plans. This is due in part to occasional lean and fluctuating budgets. An additional complicating factor is the acquisition of materials through gift or exchange. More significantly, we recognize that the specialized nature of staff interests and the unique quality of our museum's collections make approval plans impractical. As a result, the three or four of us engaged in collection development spend a fair amount of time poring over publisher and dealer catalogs, book review sources, periodical literature, and bibliographies. Equally important in this environment is the cultivation of relationships with museum staff who depend on the library for their research needs. Working closely with these subject specialists is vital to developing strong collections, as their insight about important authors, publications, and sources is invaluable. Ultimately, the challenge for library staff is to ensure that the collection is built in a balanced fashion over time, while reflecting the strengths of the museum's permanent collection.

Unique to museum librarianship is the exchange program. Essentially we trade our publications for those of other museums as a cost-cutting measure and a way to disseminate our scholarly endeavors. Our library has developed an active exchange program over the years that comprises more than a hundred domestic and international partners. Exhibition catalogs in particular have become a staple of this exchange arrangement. These specialized publications are an essential part of any art museum library in that they serve to document exhibitions as well as the objects that accompany them. Not only that, larger catalogs now incorporate multiple essays that provide context and even varying disciplinary approaches to a subject. Many catalogs also feature detailed entries devoted to each work in the exhibition, giving provenance, exhibition history, and associated literature. They have superseded their original function as checklists of events and have become vital tools for scholarship.

Over the past year or so, the library director and I have had the opportunity to exhibit materials from the library's collection in the museum's galleries. These relatively small but content-rich exhibitions typically feature between five and eight works from our collection in conjunction with a similar number of objects from the museum's holdings. A recent show paired works from the library's extensive holdings of postwar Japanese photography books with complementary photographs of the period that emphasized the important role that books played and continue to play for Japanese photographers in disseminating their vision. These exhibits afford us the chance to show another side of the library in a more prominent fashion. Furthermore, they encourage us to look at our collections with fresh eyes, as well as contemplate the medium of the book as an artistic endeavor in its own right, while underscoring the important role that these materials play in supporting scholarship within the museum.

Working in an environment that is relatively small in comparison to colleagues in academic and public libraries allows for a diverse and rewarding experience. I value this because it provides the ability to understand the complex functioning of a library in a microcosm. No less significant, it keeps me directly involved with research activities and collection building while simultaneously requiring my consideration of policy decisions and their implications. Furthermore, it allows me to think and work creatively to implement worthy services for our patrons in an environment that is flexible and open to change.

PROS AND CONS

As I have mentioned, there are plenty of reasons to pursue a career in art museum librarianship. Chief among them is the opportunity to work in a field that is challenging and stimulating, where one can truly make an impact. Working with intelligent and interesting colleagues and patrons is another benefit. One cannot underestimate the privilege of being surrounded by art on a daily basis.

On the downside, the pay scale for museum librarians is often lower than those in academic or public libraries.

HOW WOULD I GET A JOB LIKE YOURS?

An MLS from an ALA-accredited program is essential. Beyond this, one should possess a bachelor's degree in art history at a minimum. A master's degree in art history is advisable and would make one highly marketable. That said, the pay does not always reflect or reward an individual for an advanced degree.

Regardless of your educational background, take as many art history courses as possible. Brush up on your language skills, particularly German, French, Italian, and Spanish, as all are valuable assets in this field. Volunteer or pursue an internship in an art library to gain experience and establish contacts.

Become active in the Art Libraries Society of North America (ARLIS/NA), which is the premier organization for art information professionals. There are seventeen active chapters across North America. Attend an ARLIS/NA conference and participate in the strong mentoring program. Review the current job postings on the ARLIS/NA Web site. Subscribe to the ARLIS-L e-mail list, which regularly posts job opportunities and provides a sense for the issues confronting art information professionals. Consult *Aviso*, the magazine of the American Association of Museums, for further job listings.

CONCLUSION

Interested in working in an environment that offers a diverse range of responsibilities? Want to be intellectually challenged on a daily basis? Care to work for an institution that places a high priority on enlightening its patrons? Would you like to impact change within a specialized library setting that allows for a high degree of autonomy? If this sounds appealing, then perhaps the field of art museum librarianship is right for you. And the visual perks aren't so bad either.

RELATED RESOURCES

Art Libraries Society of North America (ARLIS/NA). www.arlisna.org (accessed March 5, 2006).

Benedetti, Joan M., ed. 2007. *A handbook of art museum librarianship*. ARLIS/NA Occasional Papers. Kanata, Ontario: ARLIS/NA.

Jones, Lois Swan. 1990. *Art information: Research methods and resources*, 3rd ed. With a foreword by Caroline H. Backlund. Dubuque, Iowa: Kendall/Hunt.

Pacey, Philip, ed. 1985. *A reader in art librarianship*. New York: K. G. Saur.

Wilson, Terrie L., ed. 2003. *The twenty-first century art librarian*. Binghamton, N.Y.: Haworth.

CHAPTER 52

Public Access Coordinator, Film Archive

SNOWDEN BECKER

As access coordinator for the Academy Film Archive, a branch of the Academy of Motion Picture Arts and Sciences, I serve as the primary point of contact between the archive's motion picture collection and the world at large. Our holdings include over 110,000 pieces of moving image material—film in many formats, video media, and digital files—dating from the 1890s up to last year's nominees for the Best Picture Oscar. With a collection that broad and that large, you can surely guess that our research audience is similarly varied, and in a typical day I may speak to undergraduate students working on term papers about historic animated shorts, reporters doing fact checking about actors' Oscar acceptance speeches, documentary producers who are looking for stock footage for their latest project, and ordinary folks who are trying to find a copy of an older movie that Blockbuster doesn't have.

As the first person to hold this position at the archive, I also helped set up our new Public Access Center, updated the information on our Web site, started tracking access statistics for the first time, and worked with the rest of the archive's staff to establish new policies and procedures for everything from general reference questions to footage licensing and commercial services. The Academy Film Archive's primary mission is film preservation, but it's axiomatic in the film archive world that "film preservation without access is pointless."[1] So I see myself as an essential partner in the work that our preservationists and curators do, helping the films they preserve continue to reach an appreciative audience.

A TYPICAL DAY IN THE ACCESS CENTER

I begin my workday as most people do, by checking voicemail and e-mail. All but a handful of our many inquiries come in via phone calls or e-mails—and I get between ten and twelve new inquiries every day, though only about 10 percent of these work out to be serious research requests that lead to an on-site viewing appointment. One of my first projects here was to set up a Web-based viewing request form that researchers could use to send collections inquiries when they found us during online searches,[2] and I now get about ten of these e-mails per week. I also get a certain number of e-mails and calls from researchers who are referred to the archive by the academy's research facility, the Margaret Herrick Library. As I like to say, we collect everything that moves, and the Herrick Library has everything that doesn't: a rich collection of still photographs, periodicals, books, posters, and special collections materials that are the perfect starting point for any research project relating to the history of motion pictures. Quite a few of the researchers who visit the Herrick Library in search of documentation and written records about a film are also interested in the outtakes, behind-the-scenes footage, and rare prints of films that we have here. They end up visiting both facilities in the course of their research—so I work hand in hand with the library staff.

For simpler inquiries, I often reply with a quick phone call or a form letter e-mail. The easiest responses are to people who have contacted us to request a video copy of a particular film or a previous Academy Awards show broadcast; our collection is noncirculating, and we don't reproduce or distribute most of the films and videos in our collection (this would be like a librarian photocopying an entire book for a patron!).[3] I may refer the inquirer to online retailers for titles that are readily available on consumer video formats, or let them know that the silent film from 1911 they are asking about has been missing for decades and is presumed lost. Many people are surprised to discover that the vast majority of silent-era films—those produced before 1930 or so—are now lost, and many films released before about 1980 are still not available on VHS or DVD. Communicating some sense of *why* those films have not survived and how we are trying to make sure the remaining titles do live on in accessible formats is a part of my job as well. The film archive community differs substantially from the library world in that we have not traditionally been very forthcoming about our holdings; for instance, there is no such thing as a national or international union catalog for all motion picture collections, although some recent projects are attempting to remedy this. Our own collections database reflects fifteen years' worth of gradually improving internal standards for description,[4] as well as the effects of migration from older database systems to our current collections management software, MAVIS, which is designed especially for moving-image collections. Our MAVIS database is not accessible to the public, so I often serve as a sort of living, breathing OPAC that translates search requests into information about our holdings when calls come in to the access center.

When a researcher has a legitimate research interest in a film or video copy of something in our collection, I'll book an appointment for an on-site viewing session. All appointments are booked at least thirty-six hours in advance, because materials must be paged from our cold storage vaults and climatized for at least twenty-four hours before they can be brought into the room-temperature viewing environment of the access center. Our access center has viewing equipment for 35 mm, 16 mm, 8 mm, and Super-8 film; VHS, DVD, ¾" Umatic, Betacam, and laser disc video players and television monitors; we also have an inspection bench with hand rewinds that we use to prep film materials before viewing or, in a pinch, allow access to elements other than projection prints (such as negatives and shorter film fragments) that cannot be run on mechanical viewing equipment due to preservation concerns. Whenever possible, we offer viewing access to videotape reference copies; however, there are some cases where the researcher's needs make access to a film original necessary, and in those cases I consult with our preservation staff, curators, and archive director to determine whether access to rare or fragile materials should be granted or restricted.

In all cases, my job requires a working knowledge of a wide variety of film and video formats, terminology, and viewing equipment. I often spend time before a researcher arrives physically inspecting and preparing the materials he or she is about to see. The prep time involved in providing access to motion picture materials is another reason we ask for ample advance notice on viewing appointments, and it's a big part of why I try to keep viewing appointments down to one per day—they're a lot of work! More than one researcher in the room at a time means I can't devote the promptest attention to technical problems, or guarantee the quietest viewing environment possible, either. If the researchers are not experienced film handlers themselves,

I also supervise their entire viewing session to eliminate the possibility of the material being inadvertently damaged. At the end of the viewing, I'll see to it that the material is rehoused and sent back to its proper place in the vaults by our traffic department staff.

At that point, I often sit down at my desk with a sigh and catch up on all the e-mails that came in over the course of the day—normally, there will be follow-up messages about a couple of print loans in progress, either from new borrowers who are returning our detailed venue information and loan request forms or from established borrowers who are forwarding rights clearance information from studios or distributors so we can safely release prints to them for screenings. I may also have a few licensing requests to deal with, from producers of new documentaries or biographical productions about famous directors or movie stars. Our collection includes quite a bit of behind-the-scenes footage and home movies of people involved in the motion picture industry, and it seems like we always have one or two licensing requests in the works for materials of this sort that were donated to us with rights. Streamlining and tightening up our rights and licensing procedures, as well as our print loans processes, has been another big part of my job here. It's very satisfying to have made progress in these complex areas, because they have a direct effect on how visible we are to the outside world, and I think they help keep our work and our holdings relevant.

I LOVE THIS JOB ... I HATE THIS JOB

The job of access coordinator in a film archive definitely qualifies as a service industry position. Like any restaurant server, retail salesperson, or reference librarian, I am asked for and paid to deliver a product—in my case, information in the form of motion picture materials, instead of books, food, or a V-neck sweater in size large. I like to be helpful, so this job is a great fit for me; nevertheless, it does have its share of annoyances and even its own equivalent of the bad tipper! The limitations of our noncirculating collection mean that I get a fair number of calls from people I simply can't help—like when we have the last remaining film copy of a silent picture from 1917 here at our archive in Hollywood, and the doctoral student who needs to see it for his or her dissertation research is in Nebraska. These callers are simply out of luck unless they can travel to Hollywood to view the material in person. It's really not helpful at all to say they should be grateful the film even survives, given that 90 percent of silent-era films have been lost or destroyed since they were first produced.

Also, because we're a preservation-oriented facility, we don't place a strong emphasis—or spend a big chunk of our budget—on the staffing and equipment that would support a major footage licensing program. Even so, I often deal with producers and directors who want to license footage we own the rights to and who are on extremely tight production schedules. When I emphasize that we need ample turnaround time to supply the footage they've requested, they'll expect that to mean "later this week" (or even "later today") when I mean "later this month!" Managing expectations and working out solutions that meet the needs of the various audiences we serve is a challenge, but it's one I enjoy. It's also *very* rewarding to work with our donors and depositors, with filmmakers developing interesting new projects, and with people who have finally found the motion picture they've been looking for everywhere. The endless variety of this job is a source of amusement and stimulation, and I often feel I learn as much from my researchers as they learn from me and our collection.

GETTING A JOB LIKE THIS

I have used almost everything I learned in library school at this job. Anyone applying for a position like mine would be well served by previous experience on a reference desk, or in another position that involved frequent work with a (nonspecialist) public constituency. A good knowledge of cataloging practices, especially for motion picture materials, is also very helpful; in my case, I don't do a lot of actual cataloging, but it certainly helps to know where certain data are recorded and why it may be done differently for moving images than for other formats. Experience with MAVIS, our collections management database, was not something I had when I started here, but my previous experience with relational databases and different collections information systems for museums and libraries certainly helped me get up that learning curve faster.[5] Because I'm often the first point of contact for potential donors or depositors, an understanding of our own collection priorities, and collection development practices in general, is very helpful. I work on our commercial services policies and with potential licensees, so a robust working knowledge of copyright and intellectual property law is something I couldn't do without.

Of course, familiarity with lots of film and video formats and the equipment required to view them is essential for any motion picture archive job. There are several new graduate and certificate programs that provide training in motion picture preservation.[6] These programs often include training in archival practice and theory as well as the technical aspects of motion picture collection care. As yet, a degree or certificate from one of these programs is not an absolute requirement—an equivalent combination of skills and experience is acceptable for many posted film archive positions—but the field of motion picture archives is undeniably in the process of professionalizing, and such credentials are advantageous. Those who cannot afford the time or money needed to go back to school again are in luck, though; the resources needed for self-study in motion picture preservation have never been better or more readily available.[7] A motivated person working as a practicing professional in a library or archive could certainly acquire on his or her own or through volunteer work elsewhere the knowledge and skills needed to become a film archive access coordinator.

NOTES

1. See the 1993 statement made by the Committee for Film Preservation and Public Access before the National Film Preservation Board of the Library of Congress, online at www.cinemaweb.com/access/pre_stmt.htm.

2. See www.oscars.org/contact/archivereq.html.

3. For more details about our access policies and procedures, see www.oscars.org/filmarchive/usingthearchive.html.

4. The International Federation of Film Archives (FIAF) has created a Treasures from the Film Archives database that lists silent film holdings for many of its member organizations. This project was voluntary for FIAF member archives, and participating institutions contribute only those records they choose to, but it is still the most comprehensive listing of surviving silent film materials available. The Moving Image Collections online project (abbreviated MIC, pronounced "mike") is also being developed as a clearinghouse of information on motion picture collections worldwide. MIC's key components include an archive directory, where institutions with motion picture materials can create an institutional profile, and a searchable collections area, where users can search across collections for catalog entries related to specific works. MIC is a growing resource and one that certainly has the potential to become that union catalog the motion picture archive world is missing, but it will take considerable time to develop.

5. The MAVIS collections management database is specifically designed for motion picture collections. It was originally developed by the National Film and Sound Archive of Australia and is also used at the Library of Congress in their Motion Picture, Broadcasting, and Recorded Sound Division. MAVIS allows multiple copies of a work in multiple formats to be associated under the same intellectual entity. This is extremely helpful for motion picture collections, where one may have multiple 35 mm prints at seven reels each, a 16 mm print on three reels, and VHS, DVD, and laser disc access copies of the exact same

commercial film release—all from different sources, all stored in different vault locations, and all with varying degrees of accessibility. For more information about the various approaches to motion picture cataloging, see the *AMIA Compendium of Moving Image Cataloging Practice*, available from the SAA Bookstore at www.archivists.org.

6. A list of these programs is available on the National Film Preservation Board Web site at www.loc.gov/film/schools.html.

7. See, for instance, the National Film Preservation Foundation's recently published *Film Preservation Guide*, which is available for free download as a PDF from their Web site, www.filmpreservation.org; the Home Film Preservation Guide, online at www.filmforever.org; and the many publications of the International Federation of Film Archives, www.fiafnet.org.

RELATED RESOURCES

The Association of Moving Image Archivists (AMIA). www.amianet.org (accessed February 2, 2006). AMIA is a nonprofit professional organization, similar to ALA or the Society of American Archivists. AMIA's membership is international and includes many individual archivists as well as institutional and commercial members; the AMIA-L e-mail list is also an important forum for information exchange and discussion among the community of people who care for and work with motion picture materials.

The International Federation of Film Archives (FIAF). www.fiafnet.org (accessed February 2, 2006). Established in 1938, FIAF is an association of the world's leading film archives, dedicated to ensuring the proper preservation and exhibition of motion pictures. Membership is available to institutions only, not individuals, but FIAF's various projects continue to have a major influence on the work of all who are involved in motion picture preservation and access.

Moving Image Collections (MIC). mic.imtc.gatech.edu (accessed February 2, 2006). This site combines a growing union catalog, archive directory, and targeted information portals to offer comprehensive information about moving image collections and motion picture preservation efforts worldwide.

CHAPTER 53

Librarian, Private Social Club

MARY JO P. GODWIN

With one foot in the nineteenth century and the other firmly in step with current issues and events, the librarian for the Metropolitan Club, a private club in Washington, D.C., has to span this gap with aplomb and a constant focus on customer service. From its founding in 1863 at the height of the Civil War by six officials with the U.S. Treasury Department, the club has been an institution for and about its membership. It was organized as an establishment for literary purposes, mutual improvement, and the promotion of social interaction, where members could enjoy conversation and the pleasure of one another's company.

The library at the Treasury Department was the gathering place for club members in the early days until a permanent facility was acquired where members could meet, eat, and relax. This first clubhouse was destroyed by fire in 1904 along with several thousand volumes in the library. The current home at the corner of H and 17th Street NW, a four-story building designed by prominent New York architectural firm Heins and Lafarge and completed in 1908, is listed on the National Register of Historic Places and is also a District of Columbia historic landmark. In addition to the library, the club facility includes an athletic department with exercise and locker rooms, squash courts, and indoor pool; a barber shop; a wine cellar; overnight accommodations in nine comfortably furnished guest rooms; three formal dining rooms, a member's lounge, and bar; and two beautifully decorated rooms used for large functions. Crystal chandeliers and stained glass windows illuminate the public rooms and a marble grand staircase, casting a warm glow on the elaborate moldings, paneled walls, silk draperies, antique porcelains, and plush Oriental carpets. The four working fireplaces are popular gathering spots on chilly days. The walls are hung with portraits of the founders and others who led the club over the years, many of whom distinguished themselves in the military and foreign services.

It takes a staff of nearly a hundred individuals to operate and maintain the facility on a twenty-four-hour schedule. Their dedication and job satisfaction is evidenced by the large number of employees who have more than a decade of service. The club's proximity to the White House and other seats of U.S. power has made it among the world's most fascinating waypoints for local, national, and international leaders, including almost every U.S. president since Abraham Lincoln. The club's unique location and dedication to the traditions of social civility provide its nearly 2,500 members with a convenient haven from the bustle of Washington business while offering the amenities of contemporary urban living.

JOB DESCRIPTION

From the very beginning, the Metropolitan Club members focused on organizing a book collection, mostly with donated volumes and a few subscriptions to the popular newspapers and magazines of the day such as *Harper's Weekly*. The bylaws established a library committee charged with collection development and setting up procedures for lending books. To help generate much-needed revenue, members were charged modest fees for the privilege of borrowing books. The first professional librarian was hired in the 1920s. Today, the club librarian is an integral member of the team of professionals that delivers quality service to members.

I was attracted to the job because of two words in the lead sentence of the job announcement—private club seeking a "diplomatic" and "flexible" individual. This emphasis on people skills rather than library management skills intrigued me, and I immediately wanted to learn more about the institution that placed the ad. During my interviews with the club management, it was made very clear that although they were seeking a candidate with library experience and expertise, their primary concern was for someone who could meet their high standards of customer service and interact positively with the diverse membership.

Flexibility is needed because this is a one-person library and the librarian performs *all* of the functions and tasks associated with its operation. Additionally, the librarian is responsible for organizing, classifying, and maintaining the club archives. The managers knew from past experience that the person they hired would need to have the maturity and confidence to deal effectively with the twenty-member Library Committee. This committee's function is very similar to that of a public library or foundation's policy-making board of trustees. The librarian serves as the secretary to the committee, taking minutes, sending meeting notices, and handling correspondence. He or she works closely with the committee chair and key subcommittees for operations, policies, archives, and activities to plan, execute, analyze, and report on all aspects of the library's operation. Because the club members are primarily professionals, executives, and leaders in their respective professions, they have strong personalities and are not shy about expressing their views. They also can be formidable advocates for the library with the board of governors. The librarian must also work closely with the club managers, reporting directly to the assistant general manager.

A TYPICAL DAY

The librarian's duties are basic and primarily involve the areas of acquisitions and collection development, cataloging, and circulation. Because the members have all-hours access to the club and library, the materials are readily available and displayed for easy browsing and self-service checkout. I arrange my work schedule to staff the library during the hours when the most members use the club. The heaviest traffic times are in the mornings until around 10 a.m., during the lunch period, and from 4 p.m. until the dinner hour. The club furnishes meals to the staff, so I rarely leave the building after arriving for work. The priority task each morning is to display the nine daily newspapers and any new issues of the more than seventy periodicals to which the library subscribes. Members use these materials more than any others in the collection. Back issues are archived in easily accessible storage beneath the new book display table. Although periodicals are not permitted to be removed from the library, a daily accounting usually turns up misplaced issues in guest rooms or the bar.

For many years, circulation transactions were recorded in a ledger. Today members sign their names and club number on book cards, and the librarian records these transactions in the circulation module of the online library management system so that the book rental fees can be computed and charged to the member's club account. Materials can be returned via two book drops (one in the library, the other in the entrance lobby) and cleared from the system by the librarian. Circulation statistics are reported monthly to the Library Committee.

Materials are ordered monthly from library jobbers and tracked with the acquisitions module of the system. Because this is a Web-based catalog, the members can easily see if the title they want is on order and can enter a reserve request online. Catalog records are downloaded from the jobber's site into the OPAC. Members readily make recommendations for purchase and also donate materials, which the librarian must acknowledge, catalog, and process for circulation. Current fiction and best-sellers, biographies, American and military history, politics, current affairs, and sports are the most popular subjects, so knowledge of these subjects is helpful. Audiobooks are also popular items in the collection. There is a card catalog, but no new acquisitions have been added to it since 2002. Many of the older members and those who lack computer expertise consult it or ask the librarian to search the online catalog and retrieve items for them.

Acting as a reader's advisor and retrieving materials for members are important functions the librarian must perform daily. The more than fourteen thousand items in the collection are shelved in handsome English oak bookcases that are recessed in the walls around the library's perimeter. Ranging from the floor to the ceiling for fourteen feet, these shelves must be accessed with the help of a twelve-foot ladder—another reason the librarian must be "flexible" and definitely not afraid of heights! There is a catalog record for almost every item in the collection, but there are three classification systems: Library of Congress, Dewey Decimal, and a subject section shelf arrangement, which was the original system. About two-thirds of the books are classified by the unique section shelf system and the remainder is split between Dewey and LC. All titles acquired in the past two years use LC classification, and a project is under way to reclassify the older titles. When completed, all of the books will be reshelved according to LC. All new titles are shelved temporarily on custom book racks that rest on the tops of the two large tables in the center of the library. The librarian makes decisions about when and whether to shift a title to the permanent shelves, so one is constantly weeding and enriching the collection. The librarian posts monthly lists of new acquisitions on the club Web site as well as on the library bulletin board.

Because most of the members use the library for personal use and recreational reading rather than business and research, the reference section is very small, and there is little demand to answer reference questions. There are lots of requests to locate titles by a particular author and to leave books at the downstairs lobby desk or in the athletic department because the member will be at the club but will not be dressed in the required attire (a coat and tie for men or business clothes for women) to come to the library.

The club librarian is also in charge of organizing and classifying the club archives, which are stored in a climate-controlled special collections room adjacent to the library. Consisting of board minutes, membership records, newsletters, and other club publications, along with selected financial records and papers dealing with the construction and renovation of the building, the archives are also the primary project of the Archives Subcommittee of the Library Committee. The librarian works closely with the committee to develop work plans and oversee volunteers.

PROS AND CONS

This is a very stress-free position in a beautiful work environment with an endless flow of interesting people who are well mannered, polite, and appreciative of the service I provide.

To some, the job may sound more like that of a concierge than a librarian/archivist. It is most certainly one that demands a commitment to customer service. After all, the club is a hospitality business grounded in satisfying the dues-paying members. Librarians seeking a high-tech workplace and considerable research work probably would not find the low-tech environment and slow pace challenging enough. For me, this is the ideal job for a former public library administrator who spent the past twenty years working in library reference publishing. In this twilight period of my career, I find that my librarian skills are not too rusty to perform the critical tasks and that my people skills and years of experience are a definite advantage in dealing with club members. I also draw on my marketing expertise in organizing the monthly literary luncheons and other author events and book promotions. Working in a one-person library requires the librarian to be self-motivated, well organized, and able to prioritize many tasks. I never feel isolated, though, because the club staff is available and willing to help if a problem arises. Additionally, there is an informal network among the other private club librarians in the Washington, D.C., area.

The major disadvantage to the job is that smoking is permitted in an area of the library. Special air handling equipment was installed to remove the smoke, but to someone who is sensitive, this would be a problem. The Library Committee plans to revisit the possibility of a smoking ban.

A healthy respect for protocol, etiquette, and club tradition is an important attribute for anyone seeking employment in this type of library. Change can be initiated, but the process is slow, methodical, and can get bogged down in a committee. Individuals who can successfully build trust and confidence with the members will find it easier to propose new ideas and changes in procedures.

HOW TO GET A JOB LIKE THIS

Most private clubs are located in major metropolitan areas and job openings are advertised in the local paper. Sending query letters with your résumé to club human resource directors is also an effective approach. The club members themselves are sometimes solicited for prospective candidates for openings such as that of librarian. The Metropolitan Club contacted local library school faculty and placed announcements on local library association job lines. As with most jobs, networking is important, and getting to know librarians who work in clubs or other special library settings is another way to get into the job loop. The Independent Librarian's Exchange Section of ALA's Association of Specialized and Cooperative Library Agencies is one such group.

CHAPTER 54

Golf Librarian

The United States Golf Association (USGA) is the governing body for golf in the United States. Founded in 1894, the USGA's mission is to preserve and promote the history and best interests of the game of golf. The USGA accomplishes its mission by conducting national championships, writing and interpreting the rules of golf and amateur status, and serving as the authority in all matters relating to the game of golf.

The museum collection includes antique and vintage equipment, clubs of USGA champions, architectural plans, trophies, and decorative arts. The historical archives include a library of books, manuscripts, and periodicals, as well as collections of historical films, videos, and photographs. Our library is regarded as the most complete collection of golf literature in the world.

The mission of the museum states, "The USGA Museum and Archives is an educational institution dedicated to fostering an appreciation for the game of golf, its participants, and the Association. By collecting, preserving, and interpreting the historical developments of the game in the United States, with an emphasis on the Association and its championships, the Museum promotes a greater understanding of golf's cultural significance for a world-wide audience."

JOB DESCRIPTION

Being the USGA librarian entails a variety of duties. As the title suggests, my primary function is overseeing the library. The USGA library is the most complete golf library in the world. It contains more than twenty-five thousand volumes on all subjects, including biography, history, rules, instruction, humor, reference, and so forth. The library also contains a rare book collection that dates from the turn of the century, as well as more than seven thousand club histories. Often a club, on celebrating an anniversary, will commission a book to be written about its history. Our collection of club histories is the world's largest and proves to be a valuable resource to researchers. In addition to the book collection, the library contains magazines, personal papers, subject files, material about the association, files on all our championships, and an extensive scrapbook and audio collection. The collection touches on most every aspect of golf history.

My primary responsibility is to manage the collection, acquire new material, answer reference requests, and assist researchers who make appointments. In addition, I develop and monitor the library budget; supervise a research assistant, interns, and volunteers; oversee vendor relations regarding preservation projects; and prepare all forms and regulations regarding the governance of the department. Some of these forms include a preservation plan, disaster plan, environmental monitoring plan, collections management plan, and collections development plan. Finally, I coordinate the USGA Herbert Warren Wind Book Award, the top literary prize awarded by the USGA.

The library is part of the museum and, as such, some of my duties include assisting with exhibition development, giving tours to school groups, and collaborating with other museum departments on collections issues. Because the USGA is comprised of member clubs, some of my work can entail consulting with clubs about organizing their own archives. As a result, my job description extends beyond the confines of the library to include assisting the association and being a resource to its constituents.

A TYPICAL WORKDAY

What makes this position interesting and rewarding is the variety of tasks I face from day to day. Given that the focus of the job is the library, some of my daily responsibilities include overseeing it. First and foremost is answering reference requests, whether from the staff of the association or other researchers who call or e-mail with a question. We field more than two thousand reference requests annually from writers, the media, students, and the general public. People research all topics, including biography, rules decisions, fashion, championships, and assorted statistical data. In addition to answering reference requests, I also assist the more than 250 researchers who make an appointment to use our facility and consult our archives each year. Researchers who come to our facility are provided with individual attention.

In addition to answering reference requests, I also acquire new materials. I work with book dealers, book suppliers, and private individuals to acquire the latest golf publications. As the most complete golf library in the world, our mandate is to seek out all publications. We look for books, club histories, magazines, and course and club material. Our focus is not just national but international as the library contains material from many countries, including Japan, Germany, and France. Furthermore, we work with potential donors on acquiring their personal papers. Within the collection, we have the letters of Robert Jones, the Walter Travis papers, and an assortment of scrapbooks beginning in the late 1890s. Our goal is to add to this collection and become the premier golf repository. The eventual goal is to encourage all golf writers to consult our collection in the course of their research.

In addition to acquiring collections, I work to catalog the material and make it available on our Web site. Our goal is to more fully develop our presence on the Web and allow researchers to access our collections from anywhere in the world. We have also begun a digitization project that is focusing on turn-of-the-century books and magazines. We want to reduce access to the originals and create a surrogate copy for researchers to consult. In some instances, we are the only repository with a complete run of certain golf magazines, so preserving the originals is a top priority. One of my responsibilities is to work with an outside vendor in coordinating this project.

Along with my library duties, I serve as the archivist for the collection. I process archival collections, create finding aids, and organize the scrapbook and audio collections. Other than managing the library, my duties can vary each day. Some days, I might be supervising interns on collections-related projects. Other days, I might be developing a preservation plan for the library. And at other times I could be researching for an exhibition or publication. The variety of the work is what makes the position interesting.

PROS AND CONS

Working as a golf librarian at the USGA has many benefits. One is the ability to combine an interest in museums, archives, and libraries with sports. Being a golf librarian allows one to develop a greater appreciation for how the golf industry works. For those who have an avid interest in golf, the USGA provides a unique opportunity to see how the sport is governed on all levels. This includes how championships are conducted, how equipment is tested for conformance standards, and how rules are written and interpreted. In addition, one can see how regional and state golf associations as well as member clubs all rely on and work with the USGA.

Because we are a corporate museum and serve the association, our funding is supplied by the association. As a result, the USGA provides the museum and archives with a budget each year to carry out its mission. We do not need to raise money to support ourselves, nor do we charge admission to the museum. Obviously, this is an advantage, and it allows us to focus more fully on our mission, which is to preserve and make accessible our collection. Our energies are focused on supporting this mission.

The diversity of the collection and the varied nature of the work is an advantage for the staff. Assisting with video projects, exhibitions, or educational programs shows how library and archival material can be used to promote history and educate the public. Attending USGA championships fosters a deeper understanding of and appreciation for the material we collect; it helps us see why we collect and what we should be collecting in the future. There is a direct link between the collection and the mandate and operations of the association.

Overall, serving as the librarian at the USGA is a positive experience. Like any job, there are some downsides. The association has a rich and long history. Unfortunately, much of that history has not been kept or is not centralized in one place for staff to access. A formal records management program would greatly benefit the association by keeping its vital historical documents in one area, which would help with long-term planning as well as legal and financial matters.

The museum is part of the association and functions as a corporate museum. Corporate museums present some unique challenges. Our museum is not a core function of the USGA. The association is concerned with conducting championships, writing rules, and other assorted functions relating to being the governing body for the game. It is important to understand where the department fits into the overall hierarchy of the organization. This is not necessarily a con, but it is important to be cognizant of this fact. Not everyone is working toward the same mission you are, which is preserving golf's history and making it accessible through the museum.

HOW WOULD I GET A JOB LIKE YOURS?

This job was advertised in the North American Sport Library Network (NASLIN) Web site and newsletter. At the time, the USGA was seeking an individual to manage all library operations, including acquisition, reference, organization of the collection, and access. In addition, the association wanted a candidate who had experience with sports museums, sports organizations, or a membership-based museum. Prior to joining the USGA, I served as the librarian and archivist at the Basketball Hall of Fame. In that position, I had worked with a highly specific sports collection, understood the sports industry, and was trained in organizing collections. That combined experience made me an attractive candidate to the USGA. Although I had limited knowledge of golf history, my experience in organizing collections was seen as an asset. By performing my duties as a librarian, I knew I would begin to learn golf history.

Although I have received all my jobs by answering an advertisement in a professional trade journal, I recommend that job seekers develop a more diverse approach to finding a job. In many ways, the dynamics of finding a job is similar to creating an investment portfolio. Diversification and asset allocation are the keys. Reading trade publications is valuable, as are networking, sitting on professional committees, attending conferences, and looking at Web sites. Finding a job is as much about what you know as whom you know. Going to conferences, serving on committees, and networking will broaden your contacts in the field and help identify you as a potential candidate with certain areas of specialty and interest. Many people apply for positions that they see advertised. In fact, organizations are often flooded with applications referring to a specific listing. However, there are an equal number of positions that are never advertised, and knowing the right individuals can help get you in the door.

RELATED RESOURCES

One of the best ways to learn about sports museums and halls of fame is to visit the International Sports Heritage Association (ISHA) Web site (www.sportshalls.com). ISHA has a yearly conference, a newsletter, and an e-mail list that can keep you connected with the industry. All types of sports museums are represented, and the yearly conference provides an easy way to network with colleagues, attend seminars, and find out about job openings. It is a small network of individuals that includes museum professionals and former athletes and administrators.

In addition to ISHA, the North American Sport Library Network (NASLIN) is also a good organization with which to be involved (www.naslin.org). While ISHA is geared toward sports museums, NASLIN is focused on sport libraries in the United States and Canada. NASLIN has a yearly conference and publishes a newsletter. The newsletter is an especially good resource that provides links to other sports organizations, job listings, publications, and other information that may be helpful. Together, ISHA and NASLIN provide more than enough information for anyone interested in seeking a career as a sports librarian or sports museum professional.

Another useful organization is the Special Libraries Association (www.sla.org). I recommend that any future librarian become acquainted with this organization. The strength of SLA is its focus on the nontraditional library and the unique challenges and characteristics of a special library.

CHAPTER 55

Information Resource Director, U.S. Embassy

PETTER NÆSS

I manage the Information Resource Center (IRC) in the Public Affairs section of the American embassy in Oslo, Norway. Public Affairs is a small section numbering eight members altogether: two American foreign service officers (these are U.S. diplomats, who are usually assigned to an embassy for a period of two to four years) and six permanent locally employed staff. Two colleagues and I work in the IRC, which is an integral part of this close-knit environment and is involved in virtually every aspect of the work of the Public Affairs section. That includes many assignments: for example, penning speeches and translations, organizing U.S. speaker programs, and assisting American officers in learning the ways of the country. The great range and variety of tasks are a challenging and rewarding aspect of my work and also provide an interesting example of how traditional library services may be adapted to meet new demands and new environments.

A distinguishing feature of the job is that it applies tools of the library profession toward two separate objectives and audiences. One part of the job is a traditional company library function of supplying American diplomats and in-house members of the embassy staff with the information they need to do their work. The other part targets the Norwegian audience and supports the embassy's overarching goal of promoting the United States and its interests in Norway. By reaching out to Norwegian opinion makers, media, and the general public with information and information services—along with a variety of cultural, educational, and exchange programs—our section works to improve public perceptions of the United States.

TYPICAL RESPONSIBILITIES

The dual roles of company library and library as public relations agent make for an interesting mix of duties. There's hardly any limit to what a U.S. diplomat working in Norway might want to know about the United States or about Norway, and our Norwegian audience will ask about everything from Route 66 to details about the U.S. legislative process. We must be prepared to research just about any topic that might be asked at a public or government library in either country, and we have to be knowledgeable about both American and Norwegian sources of information. Moreover, because we are a small library covering a big field, we have to be well connected within the library communities of both nations. We also need to know how to package and distribute the information. Setting up an intranet, developing hard-copy and electronic in-house alert products, and using technology to inform and communicate with the audience in the most efficient manner possible are essential concerns for a good company library.

The other part of the mix—contributing to the embassy's effort to influence the Norwegian public in a way that will benefit U.S. interests—poses different challenges. This particular aspect of an embassy's diplomatic activity is known as public diplomacy. Although all embassy IRCs are used as in-house information repositories by staff, this outward-directed public diplomacy function is the raison d'être of the approximately 160 American libraries and information centers that the U.S. State Department maintains around the world.

A permanent challenge in my job is to think about how the IRC can best use information services and communication technologies for the purposes of public diplomacy. What kind of services should we be providing and to whom? Do we simply answer questions about anything, the way a public library might, or do we proactively push information we would like the community to have? Do we answer anybody's questions, or do we give priority to audiences that wield power and influence? Do we concentrate our efforts on explaining and defending U.S. foreign policy, or should we try to accentuate other aspects of the United States (for example, arts and culture, higher education, science and technology) that might be less controversial and more attractive to a foreign audience? Is it our duty to strive for balance and credibility and show both sides of the story, or should we, as governments typically do, show only the pleasing side of the story? Are our efforts having any impact, and how can we measure it?

This continual questioning of one's activities, the nonegalitarian practice of discriminating between different kinds of audiences according to their importance to the public diplomacy cause, obsessing over how to remain relevant, and working toward rather lofty, long-term, and intangible goals are some aspects of the job that might prove frustrating to a librarian who simply wants to concentrate on the tools of the trade and see the results of his or her work. Personally, however, I find it is this librarian-cum–public diplomat aspect of my job that makes it particularly rewarding, but it is perhaps not for everyone.

The overarching public diplomacy objective and tight integration with the rest of the Public Affairs section brings with it other interesting tasks. Although these vary somewhat from embassy to embassy depending on the particular aptitudes of the IRC staff, it is not unusual for IRCs to be involved in nominating candidates for U.S. government exchange programs, finding appropriate American speakers for programs and events in the host country, writing speeches for the ambassador and American officers, testing out new technologies and coming up with innovative ways to use them, identifying relevant audiences for embassy programs, providing input to the American officers on public diplomacy strategies, and accompanying American foreign service officers on trips around the country to get a taste of the hinterlands outside the capital cities where embassies are located. One of my more exotic assignments was setting up a "getting to know Norway" visit to the Lofoten Islands for the embassy's administrative officer. Our itinerary included a stop at a whaling station, where we were fed whale-beef steaks and taken for a spin on a whaler. Although whaling is one of the very few divisive issues between Norway and the United States, the hospitality we were shown was nothing less than overwhelming! On another occasion I was tagged to travel to Kirkenes, three hundred miles north of the Arctic Circle in the extreme northeastern corner of Norway, to open an art and jewelry exhibit of pieces by American artists.

Although such assignments are not the stuff of a typical workday, neither are they particularly unusual for an embassy IRC director. In Norway it is sometimes said of a person that he is "like a potato"—meaning that the person is versatile and can be used for many things (this also says something about the drabness of Norwegian cuisine). My impression, after many years of close contact with my colleagues at other embassies, is that IRC directors are often first in line when embassy staffers are recruited for yeoman potato service. I believe it is often the case that the interests, aptitudes, and skills that a librarian naturally brings to the job are particularly well suited for such a wide range of public diplomacy assignments.

PROS AND CONS

I've mentioned some of the more obvious job satisfaction returns of the librarian as public diplomacy agent role—exotic assignments, dealing with interesting people, and having a good deal of latitude in determining where to focus one's efforts. On a more profound level, however, my work provides a continual and healthy reminder of the deeper values that underlie the library profession and that can easily become obscured by its more mundane workaday problems and challenges. The questions that arise when considering how to apply library services toward public diplomacy ends are not unlike the questions public administrators confront when allocating funds for public services such as art museums, concert halls, parks, and public libraries. Most agree that these things are valuable, but some of us would also claim that this value is immeasurable and should be tacitly acknowledged and honored rather than scientifically (or economically) proven.

In an age where the value of every expenditure is carefully calculated and measured, it is particularly eloquent testimony to the value of libraries that for more than sixty years the U.S. government has found it worth its investment to use overseas American libraries in its effort to tell America's story to the world and generate goodwill for the United States. One of the first of these libraries was the Benjamin Franklin Library in Mexico City. Former director of the U.S. Information Agency George Allen quoted Mexico's foreign minister as telling him, "The United States has done many fine things for Mexico. You spent fifty million dollars helping us eradicate hoof and mouth disease; you have constructed sewage systems in each of our towns along the border; and you have helped us build health clinics and other public works throughout the country. But the finest single thing you have ever done for us, in my opinion, was the establishment of the Benjamin Franklin Library" (Kraske 1985, p. 246).

The public diplomacy role of embassy libraries has undergone many changes since the opening of the Ben Franklin library. From being large walk-in public library–like facilities with collections that provided a multifaceted presentation of the United States, the IRCs were reduced in size and scope during the 1970s and 1980s to provide a more targeted kind of service to elite audiences. The IRC aimed to gain greater acceptance for U.S. policies by providing focused policy information to opinion makers, government officials, and movers and shakers. Large collections containing not only policy information but also art, music, and literature were pared down to concise reference collections. The general public's access to these libraries was limited, and a greater emphasis was placed on outreach and advocacy to a segmented market.

In the current international political climate, however, when creating goodwill for the United States is a bigger challenge than ever before, it seems that the value of the broad public library approach is again being acknowledged. For security reasons, the days of large walk-in public libraries like the U.S. Information Service libraries of yore are probably gone forever, but IRCs are now partnering with host country libraries to create "American Corners" that try to convey—both through general collections and through exhibitions, concerts, speakers, and other programming activities—an understanding of the United States that is often broader and more sympathetic than the message conveyed through its official actions and spokespersons.

I hope I've imparted some sense of the varied and interesting nature of the assignments that can make up a day in the life of a U.S. embassy IRC director. There are also frustrations, of course, and one of them is that in a large organization like the State Department, change comes slowly. Resistance to change is inherent in any large organization, but in the State Department there are some additional factors that impede that process whereby a new idea is introduced, acknowledged as useful, and implemented in practice. One of the impediments involves security. The State Department, like the foreign ministry of any government, must protect sensitive information and play its cards carefully. Diplomacy is by nature a cautious and guarded profession; frankness and candor are not the hallmarks of a diplomat. Public diplomacy, on the other hand, seeks to engage the outside audience and thrives on mutual openness and accessibility. In my experience, confidentiality and openness are not reconcilable, and priority— necessarily, I suppose—goes to the former concern. This can be frustrating for a librarian who wants to stay abreast of the latest and greatest technology!

A second frustration concerns the State Department's organizational structure; a central headquarters in Washington, D.C., tries to determine the correct approach for achieving its aims in some two hundred countries around the world. Naturally there will be some disagreement about what those aims should be, but that comes with the turf; personal politics yield to official policies in an embassy. A more valid disagreement concerns how those goals should be achieved. Sometimes people in the field, particularly locally engaged foreign nationals, will feel that headquarters are not sufficiently mindful of the insights we bring to the job. This is surely less of a problem in Western Europe, which has more commonalities than differences with the United States, but in parts of the world where cultural and political differences are significant, field personnel (local as well as American) may feel that their advice is not being heeded, and that Washington-driven public diplomacy campaigns are misguided, ineffectual, or downright alienating.

A more mundane frustration is the hierarchical nature of command in an embassy. Managing the manager is a challenge in any workplace, but in an embassy, as in the military, there is not even the pretense that things should be decided democratically. Your consolation is that you, as a locally engaged staffer, represent the continuity in the embassy, and your supervisors, the foreign service officers, come and go. I should say that during my nearly twenty years at the embassy, my supervisors without exception have been easy to deal with, but this will not always be the case for everyone.

I should also mention that there are some major advantages to working for a large organization like the State Department. Ever since the inception of its overseas library programs, the State Department has maintained a team of information resource officers (IROs; foreign service officers who are also librarians) who supervise the libraries, organize training and conferences, negotiate centralized contracts for database resources for the field, and liaise between the field and Washington. IROs can also step in and mediate if there are problems between IRC staff and American officers at post, and they are often involved in the hiring of new personnel for IRCs. The IROs spend about 60 percent of their time on the road. Some (those who cover Western Europe, for example) are based in Washington, whereas others are posted to an embassy and use it as their headquarters for covering the region. I've always found the IROs to be unfailingly supportive and essential to the success of the library program, which is a program the U.S. government has every reason to be proud of.

Perhaps the single most rewarding feature of my job is the powerful feeling of community and friendship that exists in the family of IRC staffers and IROs around the world. Although we see each other only occasionally and communicate primarily via e-mail, there is a spirit of internationalism, collaboration, mutual fondness, and respect that I think embodies the best of both the library and diplomat professions.

HOW WOULD YOU GET A JOB LIKE MINE?

To get a position like mine, you have to have residency and a work permit in the nation in which the embassy is located. You do not need to be a citizen of that country, but you must be fully fluent in its language and conversant with its culture. In addition, of course, you need an excellent command of English. Having studied aspects of the United States and/or spent some time there is asset, but not a requirement. The director of the public affairs section at the post has some discretion regarding the formal requirements for the position, but an MLS degree is strongly recommended (and normally required if an IRO is involved in the hiring process). Personal qualities that are absolutely essential to the position include flexibility, creativity, intellectual curiosity, and pleasure in working with people. This job is not for someone who wants to catalog in peace, but I personally cannot imagine a more exciting and fulfilling way to use an MLS.

RELATED RESOURCES

For information about the U.S. Foreign Service and pursuing a career or internship within the U.S. State Department, please see careers.state.gov (accessed June 17, 2006).

For information about what goes inside an embassy and the kind of work done by foreign service officers, see the State Department's description of "Diplomacy at Work: A U.S. Embassy" (www.state.gov/r/pa/ei/c6177.htm), the American Foreign Service Association (AFSA) Web site (www.afsa.org), or the book *Inside a U.S. Embassy: How the Foreign Service Works for America*; available for purchase at www.afsa.org/inside/index.cfm (accessed June 17, 2006).

If you are a U.S. citizen and interested in pursuing a career as an IRO, see the article "IROs: Into the Cyber Age," by Ruth Mara and Cynthia Borys (*Foreign Service Journal*, September 2003; available online at www.afsa.org/fsj/sept03/maraborys&melun.pdf; accessed June 17, 2006).

An interesting history of libraries in the service of U.S. public diplomacy is Gary E. Kraske's *Missionaries of the Book: The American Library Profession and the Origins of United States Cultural Diplomacy* (Westport, Conn.: Greenwood Press, 1985).

For a recent account of the history of U.S. embassy libraries, see Cynthia Borys and Martin Manning's article "U.S. Embassy Libraries," in *Encyclopedia of Library and Information Science*, 2nd ed., first update supplement (Boca Raton, Fla.: Taylor and Francis, 2005).

CHAPTER 56

Head, Legislative Relations Office, Congressional Research Service

ROBERT R. NEWLEN

I work for one of the most interesting federal agencies in Washington, D.C.: the Congressional Research Service (CRS), which is part of the Library of Congress. Congress created CRS to serve its needs for nonpartisan and objective research and analysis of legislative policy issues. CRS provides timely, confidential, and authoritative research and analysis to members of Congress, committees, and their staff. It has no public mission. The service provides comprehensive support in foreign policy, economics, law, science, political science, and social policy. CRS also covers the operations and procedures of both chambers, legislative processes for the federal budget and appropriations, and all constitutional issues, including separation of powers, war powers, impeachment, and electoral procedures.

Our staff consists of analysts, attorneys, and librarians who work closely with members of Congress and committees to define policy problems, develop options and legislative proposals, conduct legal analysis of pending legislation, deliver testimony before congressional committees, prepare products on current legislative issues, write confidential memoranda, and provide personal consultations. The service also conducts seminars on public policy and legal issues as well as training in the legislative and budget processes.

As head of the Legislative Relations Office, I have an opportunity to work closely with congressional clients and CRS staff on a daily basis. Amazingly, I have spent my entire career in CRS (a good sign that I like what I do) and have been fortunate to have a wide range of experiences in many different types of jobs. Among other positions, I have worked as an information specialist conducting reference interviews with clients, as a librarian providing public policy information to members of Congress and congressional staff, and as a manager of a research center located in the U.S. Senate.

A TYPICAL WORKDAY

Things move very quickly on Capitol Hill, and the workday is especially busy when Congress is in session. We receive many research requests from Congress, and one aspect of my job is to make sure that each request is assigned to the best analyst, attorney, or librarian. Often these requests involve the expertise of multiple staff, so a good deal of time is spent working with clients to ensure we understand their expectations precisely and that we bring the right mix of staff together to make sure they receive a timely response. This often involves some quick negotiation.

One of my highest priorities is outreach, which is especially important for any service-oriented organization. I help ensure that members of Congress and congressional staff are aware of our full range of services. This is a big challenge because members and staff can turn over very quickly. So I am involved in the development of the content and graphic look of print and Web sources that describe our services, how and when we brief new members and staff, and development of new strategies that quickly convey the key services provided by CRS. I also ensure that CRS research staff are conversant about our full range of services.

Managing technology issues is another important aspect of my job. As in most organizations, the competition for technology resources has become especially intense, so I need to be sure that senior management is continually aware of our needs. This includes making sure our daily operations are fully supported as well as exploring and recommending new technologies that would help streamline operations, improve efficiency, or provide enhanced services to our clients.

I also oversee the logistical aspects of training and public programs that we offer to Congress as well as client feedback and evaluation. As a manager, a good deal of my time is spent on personnel administration, the budget, and space issues.

PROS AND CONS

There are many things I like about my work. No two days are alike—there is always something new and different. Throughout my career in CRS, I have worked with individuals who are highly motivated, smart, and committed to providing high-quality client service. I've also had the good fortune to work for individuals from whom I could learn a great deal. This is probably one of the most important things I've learned in my career: who you work for is as important as what you do. CRS has also placed a high priority on training and professional development, which has helped me grow professionally and kept me fresh in my job. Another thing I value about my workplace is the flexibility to try new things that I believe will provide better service to our clients. I've certainly had my share of successes over the years, but I've also had some ideas that were not as successful. This has been a great learning experience.

The cons of my job are not unlike the management challenges faced by many of my colleagues in other libraries and research organizations, especially those in the governmental and nonprofit sectors. Chief among these challenges are working in a resource-constrained environment, keeping up with and supporting new technologies, and dealing with the need for greater data security.

Human resources are also a big challenge. Basic issues of keeping staff motivated and making sure they have all the tools they need to serve our clients well are especially important. Maintaining continuity of service and institutional memory in my office is also a big challenge. Unlike the baby boomers of my generation who worked continuously for one organization for their entire career as I have, I've observed that younger workers are much more likely to job hop and change careers with greater frequency.

Like many other managers, I face the challenge of making sure that I continually take a big picture approach to managing my operation. It is often easy to get caught up in the day-to-day activities without taking time to step back and think about strategic direction.

I'm also coping with challenges I never could have imagined when I was taking management courses in library school. All client-centered organizations are dealing with the issues presented in the post-9/11 world. Managers devote an increasing amount of time to planning and testing business continuity plans and how services would be restored in emergency or catastrophic situations. Having survived a serious anthrax scare, we spend more time preparing staff for evacuations, chemical threats, and shelter-in-place scenarios.

HOW WOULD I GET A JOB LIKE YOURS?

One of the best ways to learn more about a particular job or area of librarianship is to speak directly to someone already in the position. If you are not acquainted with someone in your target job or library, you can probably make a contact through someone in your professional network. If not, don't hesitate to make a cold contact and request an informational interview. Everyone loves to provide advice. Employers are generally very willing to assist someone new to the field who is trying to choose a career path. This opportunity can provide you with excellent advice and referrals.

Another good way to learn more about library jobs and careers is through professional associations at the local, state, and national levels. Involvement in organizations like the American Library Association, Special Libraries Association, or state library associations can provide a wealth of contacts. It can also give you experience that can enhance your résumé. For example, experience you acquire by volunteering as a committee chair, secretary, or treasurer of a professional organization can translate into important skills in the workplace.

This chapter represents the views of the author and does not represent the views of the Congressional Research Service or the Library of Congress.

CHAPTER 57

Information Specialist, Government Research Organization

CELIA WATERS

Dstl (Defence Science and Technology Laboratory) is a technical consultancy providing advice to the United Kingdom's Ministry of Defence (MOD) and its armed forces. It has approximately three thousand staff members spread over six main sites, four of which have libraries provided by the Knowledge Services Department. I run the library on Dstl's headquarters site at Farnborough, about thirty miles south of London. This site has about seven hundred staff members. The library was opened in 2003 with the goal of providing a small, focused, well-proportioned stock to deal with everyday needs, with a relatively small collection of periodicals, access to the Internet, easy access to a wide range of electronic resources, a quiet place to work, and an intelligent, responsive staff.

In practice this means that I have overall responsibility for a small library—everything from physical equipment, stock, and budgets to health, safety, and security issues to service delivery and development. We provide an inquiry and advice service as well as customer training on electronic resources. I also play a part in a number of wider information management projects and I act as a "super user" for several corporate e-systems. I also have a professional role, liaising with library and information professionals in the MOD Library Services and beyond.

A TYPICAL WORKDAY

The library is left open twenty-hour hours a day during the week, but is only staffed from 8:30 a.m. to 4:30 p.m. While I sort out the newspapers in the morning and unlock the coffee machine, Andrew pops in to collect some spare copies of *Aviation Week & Space Technology* to circulate around his department. He's followed by Natalie returning her overdue British Library book on robust nonparametric statistical methods. She asks us to buy a copy for her department's retention; luckily my colleague has arrived because she looks after the purchasing. That frees me to work on the monthly usage statistics. In the four and a half years we've been in existence, we've been used by three-quarters of the site staff. Daily visits to the library average about 36; we reach between 14 and 34 new customers per month, and we deal with up to 196 inquiries in the same time frame.

Midmorning I'm caught eating a chocolate biscuit, and I try not to laugh when Jonathan comes in to confess that he was up until 1 a.m. tackling the sudoku puzzle in yesterday's *Times*.

He retreats to a seat with a cappuccino and the latest issue of *Mathematics of Computation* and is soon discussing a poster design for the internal symposium with another colleague. The library has become an informal meeting area, which is great. Not only does it allow us to help facilitate internal networking, it also provides us with an instant source of inquiry assistance. When a call comes in requesting contacts for immersion survivability figures, we know just the person to ask. Two weeks ago we spotted that two customers had recently asked us for similarly titled journal articles, so we put them in touch and they discovered that they'd worked on the same floor for six months without knowing of each other's existence. It's what the MOD calls "stovepiping." The library has adopted the responsibility of helping break down these barriers by recommending internal contacts based on our ever-growing knowledge of the site's work and the staff's expertise.

Martin, the chief executive, pops in. "What? No chocolate cake today?" We've gained a reputation for providing home-baked goods on special occasions, and it works, because visits to the library double on those days. Now, however, he needs us to clear the copyright for him to use a photo of Isambard Kingdom Brunel in his Dstl roadshow.

The mention of cake reminds me to speak to Conferencing and Communications about refreshments and posters for our next training event. We've put the library on the map through a series of promotional events which have ranged from coffee mornings to support the Dstl Microsoft Challenge teams to marking national events such as Children in Need Day to inviting in the local college to promote their new academic year prospectus. One of our biggest events is Learning at Work Day, held each May, when we arrange a mixture of activities about work/life balance issues, including training by key e-product suppliers such as Jane's and British Standards Online, lunchtime hobby demonstrations, information stands about clubs and societies, and guided walks in the site conservation area. Last year one of the staff members used that walk as a way of achieving his goal of managing a mile's walk after suffering a mild stroke. The library does really make a difference here.

From midmorning to midafternoon, it's busy. As systems administrator for a number of e-products, I receive a steady stream of phone calls and e-mails from other Dstl sites, but most of our own site inquiries are received in person. We've got an ideal location on the ground floor, just off the main reception area by the door leading to one of the main staff car parks and near the chocolate and soft drink machine. By lunchtime it's standing room only in the library. Although it may be a bolt-hole for users to escape from open-plan offices and desktop screens, the library is far from being a quiet haven. We know practically everyone by name, and no one escapes a cheerful greeting.

We have our regular customers, of course. Nigel dashes in and calls us over to the Internet terminal to show us the Webcam at a fish restaurant in Sydney. He's flying out to Australia tomorrow night and will be meeting a colleague for a meal there on arrival. Meanwhile Major Daniel urgently needs access to a defense contract. While I send him an e-mail with the link attached, the Linguaphone language series on the new arrivals shelf also catches his eye; he told us last week that he's being posted to Germany in August.

Early in the afternoon, two knowledge agents appear for their weekly drop-in session. We're all part of Knowledge Services, and the agents' role is to serve as free agents who use their scientific subject knowledge to get directly involved in customer project work. Our role is that of gateway to these and other specialists within our department. That means they use the library to increase their visibility, but we also pass inquiries and customers between us so that they get to deal with the best person for their task. Today we let them know that the new squadron leader in Air and Weapon Systems will be coming along to discuss access to MOD strategy papers on space.

In return the knowledge agents bring Simon to our attention; he's been in their open-plan office for a few months, but based on his comments he still doesn't seem to be aware that thousands of Dstl's reports are available electronically on the library's Unicorn catalog. We give him a call, and he pops down later for a coffee and ten minutes of training on the system. As we chat with him we discover that he's actually most interested in anything that's been written about waves in random media over the past four years. We show him how to use ISI's Web of Knowledge and then how to place requests for papers from the British Library directly from his desktop. He then starts talking with another of our regular customers who's searching our reference collection for electrical circuit diagrams because he's building a bat detector at home.

PROS AND CONS OF THE JOB

At a day-to-day level I thoroughly enjoy my job, so I can think of far more pros than cons.

There are, of course, annoyances and frustrations when working as part of such a large departmental team and particularly one that is spread out across six main geographical sites. A lot of time is spent traveling between sites for meetings, for example, and it's difficult to keep up with what everyone else in the department is working on. Getting decisions made, changes accepted, and anything done can also sometimes be a painfully slow process because input is required from so many people. Due to the nature of the organization, there are also countless procedures and security issues that can further slow progress down.

There are never enough hours in the day! Because my office is also the library, there's no privacy, and there are constant distractions throughout the day. It can be difficult to concentrate on some projects.

All that said, here's a job in which you really have a chance to make a difference to the people around you, be appreciated for it, and share many chats and laughs en route. I have the opportunity to get to know on-site customers, find out about their varied areas of work, put them in contact with each other, guide them to resources that will make their jobs easier, and help them use their time more effectively to achieve the organizational goals. I get to see the bigger picture of the organization because on a daily basis I'm dealing with everyone from the Year in Industry students to the chief executive. It also makes the job wonderfully varied; with the size of my to do list, there's no chance of getting bored!

Working as part of a large information department means that I have a backup network of colleagues whom I can call on for assistance in specialized areas such as patents, database design, literature search and analysis, and document digitization. This means that we're in a position to supply a very comprehensive package of information solutions for our customers without one person feeling the pressure to become a jack of all trades. It also means that I have colleagues from whom I can seek advice and expand my own knowledge. It's therefore a job in which I'm constantly learning. I can also take advantage of countless personal development opportunities, such as finding ways to enhance my facilitation and presentation skills, taking on event and project management, marketing, and learning how to provide training.

Furthermore there's support for my professional involvement and networking, particularly within the UK defense and government library communities. For example, I'm chair for the Aerospace and Defence Librarians Group , a subgroup of CILIP (Chartered Institute of Library and Information Professionals); my department has supported my committee work, my writing for the professional press, and my presentations at key library/information conferences, such as the biennial Umbrella Conference held in Manchester. It's vital to consider organizational support for these things if you intend to gain your chartership as well as for your own continuing professional development.

Finally, I really enjoy being responsible for a whole unit and having a fairly large degree of autonomy on a day-to-day basis. There's the opportunity to plan service delivery and development, put it into effect, and see firsthand the difference that it makes. Within the bounds of organizational procedures, departmental and personal objectives, and a daily timetable partly set by my customers, I rule the roost in the library. Its success—or otherwise—is very much dependent on me and on my attitude, my actions, and my working relationship with my assistant. That may not suit everyone, and it's certainly not an easy option. It can, however, provide for a very high level of job satisfaction; that satisfaction (and not just the pay packet) makes your working week feel worthwhile.

HOW WOULD I GET A JOB LIKE YOURS?

This is always a difficult question because specific posts can depend on being in the right place at the right time. You can help yourself, though.

Skills. There's nothing wrong with specializing, for example, as an e-librarian or in a specific subject area such as science and technology, but make sure that you also develop more generic and transferable skills, because those are the ones that will ultimately put you in a strong position when applying for any job. Transferable skills may include communication and interpersonal skills, leadership, organizational skills, customer service, decision-making abilities, time management, problem solving, presentation skills, and information and communication technology. I recently facilitated a discussion based on the question "Do we need to be subject specialists or specialists in acquiring subject knowledge?" and the resounding response was the latter. The best thing that you can do is keep notes about your experience and examples of your work. Use those to provide evidence of your transferable skills. Demonstrate that you are also flexible, positive, open to change, can work as part of a team, and that you have a good sense of humor! Very few organizations will then turn you down even if you don't have the subject experience because most employers are looking for employees who will fit in, apply their core skills to pick up the job, and move with the times.

Contacts. Network at every opportunity. Keep in touch with contacts and be prepared to help them out; you never know when they might be in a position to do the same for you.

Current awareness. Read the professional journals, subscribe to key library/information science mailing lists, set up alerts, and keep your ear to the ground. Not only will this keep you up to date with the latest developments in the profession (which are useful to mention at job interviews and may allow you to consider new career opportunities), but these are also good sources of information about jobs with organizations that you may wish to work for in the future. I've always kept a file of job adverts that have appealed to me but that I've not wanted to pursue at the time. This is useful to spot which organizations have been taken over, for example, or have a high turnover of staff, or are expanding. It also helps you learn what skills and experience employers are looking for, which in turn may help you plan your future training and development opportunities. They're also a potential source of contacts if you wanted to apply on spec at a later date or seek more information.

Finally, when applying for jobs, be truthful and realistic. Be confident and believe in yourself.

RELATED RESOURCES

Aerospace and Defence Librarians Group (ADLG). www.adlg.org.uk (accessed January 28, 2006).
Chartered Institute of Library and Information Professionals (CILIP). www.cilip.org.uk (accessed January 28, 2006).
CILIP job vacancies. www.lisjobnet.com (accessed January 28, 2006).
Defence Science and Technology Laboratory (Dstl). www.dstl.gov.uk (accessed January 28, 2006).

CHAPTER 58

Armed Forces Librarian

STEPHANIE DECLUE

Armed forces librarianship is not an active-duty military job; it is a civilian position. An armed forces librarian in a typical base library will be one of only a handful of professional staff (my library has two, including me). As a result, you will have to do it all. The job can involve reference, collection development, programming (both youth and adult), interlibrary loan, budgeting, report writing, and at times, circulation duties such as checking out books and shelving. And of course, there are those dreaded "other duties as needed." Actually, my job is very similar to that of a librarian in a small public library, with a few exceptions.

HOW ARE MILITARY LIBRARIES DIFFERENT?

My typical workday consists of routines and duties that are often similar to those of a reference librarian in a public library. I answer reference questions from customers ranging from seven years old to eighty-seven years old. We have programs for preschoolers, middle schoolers, high schoolers, and adults. Much of military librarianship is the same as public librarianship, but a few things are very different. This chapter focuses on the things that make an Air Force library different from a public library.

Collection Development

Buying books for an armed forces library can be a joy if your previous library was strapped in the budget department, because we are very well funded. However, it can also be a challenge. Air Force libraries have three separate missions: mission support (related to the mission of the base military operations), education support (for everything from grade school to graduate school students), and quality of life (the fun stuff like children's story time and best-sellers). I have to buy materials that will be useful to the Air Force in carrying out its mission, materials that will be useful for students in varying stages of education, and materials that will be useful for people who want to read for pleasure, take up a new hobby, start a business, and so on.

In addition to the wide-ranging subject matter that I order, the Air Force has specific rules about how certain money can be used. There are local base funds and central Air Force funds.

Local funding is sporadic (we have gotten almost none for the past few years) but can be used to buy books for any of the three missions. Central funds are fairly abundant and consistent from year to year, but they can only be used for mission support and education support. Ironically, the most used materials in our library are quality of life materials, but they are the worst funded.

The Air Force also likes to order only at specific times of the year. We get our central funds budget in February, and it has to be spent by mid-April. Contrary to what you might think, it is not that easy to spend $50,000 in two months. So I spend most of my year gathering files of Amazon.com printouts, pages ripped from catalogs, and sticky-note reminders of things I need to buy so that I can be ready to spend, spend, spend when the time comes. Local funds, when they are available, also come and go quickly. In the military, if you don't spend the money you are given quickly, there is always another department that is willing to take the money off your hands. That principle can work for you as well as against you. I have found that if I spend my central funds quickly, sometimes I am rewarded with extra money (presumably from someone who was not as quick to react).

Active-Duty College Students

Many active-duty military personnel are in the process of getting a college education. For most of them, college was a major part of their decision to join the military. However, because of the transient nature of military service, many military students try to take some shortcuts in getting their degree. The College-Level Examination Program (CLEP) is extremely popular on military bases. This program allows students to gain college credit for a course by taking an examination that measures their mastery of the subject matter without ever setting foot in a classroom. We provide textbooks and CLEP study guides for almost every subject the program covers. These materials are in high demand and can become outdated very quickly. As a result, we are always on the lookout for updated versions of CLEP study guides and new editions of textbooks. Without the CLEP program, many airmen and -women would not be able to receive a college education, so the library serves a valuable mission in providing the materials necessary to maintain a well-educated military.

Active-Duty Families

The active-duty family unit differs significantly from the family of a non–active-duty member. The military puts tremendous focus on personal responsibility. Active-duty members and their families are taught that their actions in and out of uniform reflect on their branch of service. They are ambassadors of the armed forces and are expected to act accordingly. As a result, the active-duty member of the family is held responsible for everything that the rest of the family does, whether it is bouncing a check at the grocery store, spray-painting graffiti on a wall, or failing to return an overdue library book. The privacy that most libraries hold near and dear does not exactly exist here. Active-duty family members can ask us at any time what their families have checked out and we have to tell them, because they are responsible for their family's library accounts.

This rule also helps the military library with an issue that plagues many public libraries these days: unsupervised and unruly children. The Air Force has specific rules stating at what age a child can be left unattended and for how long, so we have very few unattended children in our library. The children of active-duty members also understand that their behavior can get their parent in trouble at work, so the children and teens we do have in the library are very well behaved. The failure of any member of the family to abide by the Air Force's rules can result in disciplinary action against the active-duty member. Personal responsibility is a thread that runs through every choice that active-duty family members make.

Here Today, Gone Tomorrow

Active-duty personnel typically only stay at one duty station for an average of three years. That means that every year, roughly one-third of your customer base moves away and new customers move in. Military libraries are constantly promoting their services to new residents. The transient nature of the military base allows the library to constantly reach new customers. It also requires us to constantly assess our collection to ensure that it is meeting the needs of the current population. One year, a large group of science fiction readers might transfer onto base. Three years later, many of them will be shipped to other bases and a new group of customers come in who may be big mystery fans. It is up to the librarian to make sure that the collection the library has is what the current population wants to read. That is a challenge, but thankfully, military libraries do receive sufficient funding to make these periodic changes to the collection.

Safety First

One of the main differences between a public library and a military library is that many of the people on a military base are armed and well trained in how to use the weapons entrusted to them. Every time I drive onto base I am reminded that we are at war and that these men and women are serious about protecting the base from any outside threat. Periodically, the base will go into higher states of alert, either for real threats gathered through intelligence or for an exercise (like a fire drill times twenty) so that we are prepared when a real threat does occur. For the library that can mean many different things based on how high the alert is. At the lowest level, we can be asked to check the military IDs of everyone entering the building; at the highest, we can be told to lock down all entrances and exits, allowing no one to enter or leave the building.

Another threat to safety is the proverbial loose lips syndrome. You hear that your favorite regular customer is going to be deployed overseas (which, by the way, doesn't necessarily mean Iraq). You run into a mutual friend at the grocery store and tell her Captain Smith and his squadron will be going to Iraq next month. You are overheard by a terrorist (they do actually spend time in the towns around military bases for just this purpose), and they have gained valuable intelligence about our troop movements. It seems like such a little thing, but it could be potentially hazardous. If you are a habitual gossiper, military librarianship could be a challenge for you.

WHAT I LIKE, WHAT I DON'T LIKE

There are many pros of military librarianship.

1. It is very rewarding to know that I have a hand in helping these men and women do the job of protecting our country.
2. Military libraries are typically better funded than public libraries.
3. The customer base and the collection are constantly changing, which makes for a challenging work environment.
4. Due to the high degree of personal responsibility, there are very few behavior problems.

And there are also some cons.

1. The military jargon—they like to speak in acronyms. As a civilian worker, I felt like I was in a different country at first!

2. Military families move often, and it is hard to say goodbye to favorite customers.

3. Military funding, though abundant, is mired in red tape and difficult to access at times.

4. There are a lot of airplanes. I mean *a lot*. It's like being situated next door to the runway of a major airport. After a while you tune them out. And of course the patrons are all used to the noise, so they don't even notice.

SO YOU WANT TO WORK IN A MILITARY LIBRARY?

If you want to try for a job in a military library, you should probably be willing to relocate, unless you already live near a military base. Military library jobs come in three different types: general schedule (GS) positions, nonappropriated funds (NAF) positions, and contractor positions. Each base makes the determinations as to whether they will use GS, NAF, or contract librarians.

GS employees work for the Department of Defense (DoD) and receive DoD benefits. The best source for GS library positions is the USA Jobs Web site of the Office of Personnel Management (www.usajobs.com). Each job posting contains detailed instructions for how to apply. Read the instructions carefully—they tend to be complicated! The salaries listed in the job posting include a low range and a high range. Don't assume that you will get hired at the high range because you have library experience. GS jobs have highly structured pay scales; you need to be willing to work for the low range or you might go through all the trouble of applying only to turn down the job offer in the end. GS library positions are rare these days. If you find one, jump on it!

NAF employees are also government employees but are not subject to DoD benefits. The pay for NAF library jobs is typically lower than that for GS positions, but they are more common. Each base advertises separately for its NAF positions. A Google search for "NAF library jobs" returned over seventy thousand hits in almost all fifty states. Each job posting contains instructions for how to apply. One caveat: NAF employees are technically eligible to be deployed to other locations (even sandy ones where people could shoot at you) with or without their consent. There are no reported instances of this happening in libraries, but the possibility needs to be kept in mind.

Librarians in contractor positions are not considered DoD employees. They are employees of a private company that provides library staffing to the base library. All benefits are provided by the contractor. The pay is set by the Department of Labor and is determined by the prevailing wage in the closest major city. These positions are harder to find, because there is no single place for all of the job postings. Regular searching of the library job posting Web sites will turn up contractor positions when they are available. Contractors are sort of in limbo when at work on a military base. They are granted the ability to get on base to go to work but cannot use other base facilities. This can make it difficult for the librarian to really feel like he or she is a part of the community.

Whether the job you are looking for is GS, NAF, or contract, there is no one clearinghouse for military library jobs. Finding these positions takes thorough searching and patience, but the job is so rewarding that the effort is more than worth it.

FOR MORE INFORMATION

Block, Marylaine. 2004. Military life. *Library Journal* (September 15). www.libraryjournal.com/article/CA452291.html (accessed February 1, 2006). A good overview of what military librarianship is like.

Metz, Edward. 2003. Paths to becoming an army librarian. *Info Career Trends* 4, no. 5 (September). www. lisjobs.com/newsletter/archives/sept03emetz.htm (accessed February 1, 2006). Good information on the application process for military library jobs.

Special Libraries Association, Military Librarians Division. www.sla.org/division/dmil (accessed February 1, 2006). The Listserv is a good source for finding open positions.

CHAPTER 59

Police Force Librarian

TOM RINK

I have not always been a librarian. Like many, I've entered the field of special librarianship via a most unlikely route. I'm a police officer who felt the twinge of burnout midway through my law enforcement career, pursued my master's degree to prepare myself for a career change, and ended up using this degree to launch my library career while still at the police department. When I transferred into my current position (originally a policy-writing position), a library/librarian position did not exist. I was tasked with creating a library from scratch "in my spare time." What a great challenge early on in my career! My first priorities included the development of an operational budget, the completion of a space planning analysis, and an inventory of the existing materials and resources. Only then was I told that there were no budget monies available and that I'd have to seek my own independent funding. Well, I did (drug forfeiture monies), and the rest is history.

JOB DESCRIPTION

As a solo librarian for an organization in an industry that rarely has a library or any form of organized collection, let alone a degreed librarian, I am forced to wear many hats and fulfill many functions. Let's start with a description of my job. The resource center serves the management of the police department by providing library, information, and support services that meet the professional, educational, and research needs of the department. This mission includes the development and maintenance of departmental resources (print as well as electronic), which include (but are not limited to) books, magazines, videos, government documents, policy and procedure, tactical and operational guidelines, and the completion of special projects as required. Although I serve the department as a whole, I am specifically assigned to the Training Academy, where I have some rather unique nonlibrarian tasks to accomplish as well.

A TYPICAL WORKDAY

Though I do not actually start each day with a doughnut (as surprising as this may seem), I do find coffee an absolute necessity. Armed with my coffee, I settle in to review and triage my e-mail and voicemail. One of the next things that I try to do each day is review my task list to check for upcoming deadlines and prioritize my tasks for the day. However, throughout the course of the day I often find myself playing the role of a firefighter as I respond to and handle assorted "brush fires" (emergency crises) that tend to crop up in any large, bureaucratic organization. Many of the academy crises will generally occur first thing in the morning; they are usually equipment-related (computer, projector, Internet connection, or PowerPoint problems), and I'm the one called. Department crises could be anytime during the day and usually involve the provision of critical information or documents quickly. Service is the key.

Anyone who takes the time to personally come to the resource center has my undivided attention as we attempt to fulfill his or her immediate information need. I generally use the lunch hour to get away from my desk and often go for a run (and then eat lunch at my desk). The afternoon and end of my day arrive quickly; each day presents its own challenges and opportunities. My daily activities can be broken down into two distinct types: those that are library-related and those that are not.

Library-Related Tasks

The majority of my requests, whether received by phone, e-mail, or in person, are basic reference or document delivery inquiries: "Where can I find … ?" "Could you send me a copy of … ?" "What materials do we have on … ?" Having worked here as long as I have, my general knowledge of the organization certainly helps in providing answers. Providing reference easily fills at least 30 percent of my time. I handle the quick and simple requests and questions immediately, and I add the ones requiring a bit more of a response or research to my prioritized list to deal with as time and conflicting deadlines permit.

I'm also responsible for the acquisition of new materials in a variety of formats. This is easily achieved by reviewing the professional literature, glancing through publishers' catalogs, and considering third-party recommendations. In addition to the normal purchase of books, videos, CDs, and DVDs, I keep track of a multitude of subject-specific periodicals and serial subscriptions and collect government documents produced by the various branches of the Department of Justice. As highly specialized as our collection is, many of the items within the collection are classified as "law enforcement only" and cannot be shared with the general public. But I do receive numerous reference calls from the non–law enforcement community, usually wanting statistics, historical data, demographics, or other sharable facts. Being housed within our training division, I'm a resource for many of our instructors who are always on the lookout for new items to update their teaching materials and lesson plans. I've been asked to produce organization charts and flowcharts and have also provided bibliographies, pathfinders, and other navigational tools.

Once these new materials are acquired, they must be cataloged (classified, described, and organized). I have no staff, so this task falls to me as well. I do not have a specific library automation system but must rely on Microsoft Office software to accomplish all of my tasks. I designed a database in Access to gather all of the bibliographic data of the collection. Except for periodicals and journals, our materials are allowed to circulate, and I continually strive via reminders and overdue notices to retrieve the checked-out items from persons who truly believe that possession is ownership.

My administrative tasks include the requisitioning of appropriate supplies and materials, developing library policies, providing monthly updates for my Web page on our intranet, alerting many of our subject matter experts whenever I see an article of interest, keeping usage statistics, and filing. I always seem to be filing something—vertical file materials, catalogs, training flyers and brochures, policies and procedures, and so on. From time to time, I've even been asked by other police agencies to consult with and assist them in establishing a library for their organizations. Twice a year, during new supervisor training, I provide instruction on the resource center to all of the new supervisors: what it is, where it is, and what it can provide.

Nonlibrary Tasks

In addition to being the go-to guy for audiovisual and other equipment-related issues, I also serve as the on-site computer guru for troubleshooting both hardware and software questions.

At the department-wide level, I provide research assistance whenever required, assist with policy development, proofread documents for accuracy and correctness, serve on the occasional committee, and house all of the current and historical policies and procedures and tactical and operational guidelines (print and electronic). I'm also called on to assist in locating and providing the necessary documentation to comply with national accreditation standards. I complete surveys and benchmarking studies with other police agencies, and I produce ad hoc reports on a regular basis. One of my newest tasks has been to coordinate our Managing Law Enforcement Initiatives Program. In a nutshell, this program is our attempt to use project management techniques to conceptualize, create, introduce, and enhance new police products and services to our community. I coordinate, communicate progress and updates, and assist with all aspects of the proposal life cycle from launch to closure for the more than sixty proposals to date.

At the academy level, I am frequently called on to assist with training new recruit classes. I'm actively involved with their physical training—running, specifically, but I stay involved and assist with their other aerobic and strength training activities as well. I also help coordinate and plan some of the reality-based training exercises that the recruits must undergo in preparation for field training. And of course, there are always those "other duties as required" type of assignments that we all fall victim to.

PROS AND CONS

Let me start with the pros (though it may be hard to separate some of these from cons). First and foremost, I'm the only information professional in my organization. Not everyone may consider this a pro, but there is a wonderful sense of freedom and independence associated with being the sole information provider. And even though I must report to others who are nonlibrarians—which in itself could be considered a pro as well as a con—the sense of being in control of the resource center is very liberating. I have the ability to schedule and prioritize my time and tasks with minimal interference or supervision, though obviously with some limitations, as a police department is very hierarchical. With this independence comes the responsibility to do the best job possible; there's no one else to blame when things go wrong (a con?).

Second, having built the collection from the ground up, and having been employed with the organization for more than twenty years, my knowledge of the collection and the organization is extensive. I know exactly what I have and where to find it, and this is very valuable to my customers. I enjoy being the go-to guy when people are looking for documents or information.

Another pro that relates to my status as a solo librarian is the variety of tasks that I'm asked to perform day in and day out. I must do it all; I can delegate nothing. Due to this variety, I always manage to stay busy and avoid getting bored.

One of the more obvious pros is that I love my job! It is both challenging and rewarding at the same time. The sense of accomplishment is not too shabby either.

The last pro may be specific to my situation: job security. Being a civil servant first and a librarian second certainly provides me with a much more secure employment picture. Even if I were downsized and the library were closed, I'd still have a job (albeit back in patrol, but employed nonetheless).

On the con side, I still do not have a dedicated budget. Monies are available, but there is no line item specifically for the resource center. (This could be considered a pro from the standpoint that I do not have to prepare a budget.)

There is also the feeling of isolation from professional peers. This is easily combated by becoming active in a professional association—I highly recommend the Special Libraries Association, especially if you find yourself working in a highly specialized field—and by networking with other information professionals within your area.

Some other cons include the lack of clerical support to do some of the more routine tasks and the seeming lack of time to get everything done. But with improved time management skills, you can gain control over both of these issues; you may not conquer them completely, but you can come close.

One last con that I would like to address deals with the dilemma that when I'm gone or out of the office, no one picks up the slack or does my job! I always return from a vacation or conference to a swamp load of work, mostly of the routine filing variety.

Regardless, I wouldn't change a thing. Have I mentioned that I love my job?

HOW WOULD I GET A JOB LIKE YOURS?

Municipal police departments are slowly realizing the value of information and are beginning to take the steps required to collect and organize their information by creating libraries. Federal and state agencies are much more likely to have already taken these steps. All governmental agencies have human resources departments or the equivalent that are responsible for all of their hiring decisions. You'll have to apply for posted job announcements and traverse through the voluminous layers of bureaucratic red tape to end up on a ranked list. But the advantages to doing so far outweigh the disadvantages—namely, the benefits and general job security. The Web would be a great place to start searching.

I attribute my success to planning and preparation, patience, persistence (I did not give up easily), productivity, professionalism, and problem solving. Some additional skills that would be helpful to possess include organizational skills, attention to detail, communication skills, flexibility, creativity, a sense of humor, and above all an indomitable spirit. Allow yourself to dream and keep your mind and your eyes open to the existing possibilities. My organization did not have a library before I was offered the opportunity to create one. You never know when an opportunity will present itself, and you must be prepared to jump at the chance.

RELATED RESOURCES

Rink, Tom. 2004. Librarians—on the cutting edge of the information age. www.rose.edu/lrc/careers/rink. htm (accessed February 6, 2006).

———. 2005. A really alternative career in librarianship. *LISjobs.com* (March). www.lisjobs.com/ newsletter/archives/mar05trink.htm (accessed February 6, 2006).

StateJobs.com. statejobs.com (accessed February 6, 2006).

USAJOBS: The Federal Government's Official Job Site. www.fedjobs.gov (accessed February 6, 2006).

CHAPTER 60

Coordinator of Correctional Libraries

GLENNOR SHIRLEY

As the coordinator for correctional libraries, I am responsible for providing leadership and direction for development and maintenance of library and information services to inmates in twenty-three state prisons in Maryland. I also coordinate services that support the various goals and objectives of the Correctional Education Program; manage system services and grant-funded programs; develop service plans for each institution and plan for new facilities; negotiate service agreements with appropriate partners, including public, academic, and special libraries; administer centralized purchasing of library materials and equipment; and recruit, hire, and train library staff.

LIBRARY SERVICES TO PRISONERS

Our prison libraries are under the auspices of the Maryland State Department of Education, but they are located across the state in facilities that are operated by the Division of Corrections (DOC), a separate agency whose primary focus is public safety.

Prisoners have the same leisure reading interests and information needs as individuals in the wider society, although a disproportionate number of them are illiterate or have mental illnesses and poor social skills. Prison libraries may be law libraries, recreational reading libraries, or a combination, many operating on a public library model using guidelines established by *Library Standards for Adult Correctional Institutions* (1992). The *Standards* were designed as a tool to plan and evaluate general library services and stipulated that "library services shall address the basic needs of inmates for information on institution regulations and procedures, information to maintain contact with the outside community, information of vocation skills, educational information, rehabilitative programs, self-directed reading for lifelong learning and personal needs, recreational reading, information on reentry into the community."

A TYPICAL WORKDAY

The only typical feature of my workday is the morning ritual of checking and responding to e-mail, voicemail, and my immediate attention file. After that, my day consists of a swirl of activities that may include attending meetings, responding to the public defender about library services, dealing with personnel issues, initiating contacts with outside agencies, assisting librarians to meet audit standards, signing documents, managing budget issues, and developing procedures for new DOC regulations. I will try, however, to capture components from an actual day in July, the beginning of our fiscal year.

Of my thirty new e-mails, the high importance one from the director requests library statistics for a legislative report. Librarians send monthly statistics of circulation transactions, general reference and legal reference use, collection development activities, and patron visits, so it is fairly easy to compile the required statistical information.

At the forefront of my attention file are a request from a librarian for information on certification, four situations with implications for collection development, book orders from three libraries, a note reminding me to begin to contact magazine vendors in preparation for competitive bid for magazine subscriptions, and data for today's visit to a prison library with a prospective applicant for one of our vacant positions.

My Attention File

Librarians with an MLS degree manage our libraries; their salaries and job status are dependent on an advanced professional certificate that must be renewed every ten years. I check with the Certification Branch in our agency and fax the required information to the librarian.

At least three times per week vendors, writers/self-publishers, and citizens call to sell or donate materials or equipment. This week's pile consists of an ex-prisoner, now an author, who wants to sell copies of his book; a bookseller who wants to donate his overstock of Bill Clinton's memoirs; a citizen offering to donate books from the basement of her dead relative; and a law firm with hundreds of legal books to donate, stipulating that we must go collect them.

Our written material selection policy outlines our philosophy to purchase current, popular interest materials based on the guidelines in the *Standards*. With tact and diplomacy, I question the donors about condition, date, subject, and so on, before deciding to refuse or accept their offers. From the author, I request reviews and a complimentary copy of his book to route to librarians for their input. I arrange a pick-up point for the copies of Clinton's book, and politely decline the offers from the citizen and the lawyer, because the former's offer consists mostly of old textbooks and the latter's requires more shelving space than we have in any of the libraries. I rarely accept donations of law books because our libraries have more up-to-date databases with the same content, access to online legal databases, and an annually updated required reference list.

Each fiscal year, librarians receive a budget based on my assessment of circulation, material use, and population size. I encourage them to spend the allocated amount soon after notification of its availability, because the libraries are often the first group to lose funds in a budget crisis. Before authorizing book orders, I check to ensure selections are balanced, in compliance with our materials selection policy, and congruent with population needs. For example, in minimum-security prisons where the inmates are preparing to return to their communities, there should be some purchases on family relationships, career options, credit repair, continuing education, job hunting, and skills and trades.

Technology and Correction Libraries

The fact that I operate with an open-door policy means I rarely have uninterrupted times. While I am on hold on the telephone, the computer technology manager enters with an expression that indicates she needs my attention *now*. The two computers on the cart beside her and the paper she is waving means that she needs a signature that will allow her to take equipment outside the building. We had previously discussed purchasing new computers for one of the libraries. This library is seventy miles away, and she must leave early in case installation is complicated. The manager reminds me to set the date, location, and content of the next training workshop for the librarians. Having recently signed a three-year contract with a new legal database vendor who offered a significantly lower price for comparative legal products, we must now train the librarians before installing the software in the institutions.

Prison librarians are one-person managers who operate the library and negotiate multiple transactions on any given day, with no other on-the-spot professional help. To provide some assistance to the librarians, I have increasingly relied on the use of technology as a medium of communication and a forum for questions and answers. Each librarian has access to e-mail and the all-librarian group e-mail. They use the group e-mail to perform interlibrary loan transactions, request photocopies to replace missing pages, and inform one another of happenings in their institutions. I use e-mail to forward information on conferences, relevant prison and library stories, and tips; I also use it to ask librarians for suggestions for training.

To provide more support for the librarians, I developed a Web site that has links to information on many of the topics that they need to answer questions, especially those that are unique to the prison environment. As I encounter topics of interest, I e-mail the Web manager to include them on our site.

Staffing

Two librarians retired earlier this year and I worked closely with our human resources department to advertise the positions in various media. One prospective applicant who saw the announcement on our Web page called to request a tour of a prison before making her decision to apply. Visitors to a correctional facility must submit information for a background check and receive a signed authorization to enter the institutions. Having submitted the information two weeks prior, I call the prison to confirm we are expected.

Visit to a Prison

During visits, I encourage the institutional librarian to answer questions frankly and take visitors to the reading areas instead of remaining in the office. The library manager explains that she hires, trains, and supervises the inmate clerks who are stationed at the circulation, reference, and magazine desks and in the processing room.

Because visitors provide a respite to the routine life of inmates, most inmates are willing to answer questions, especially if they think the visitor has authority to improve their situation. For example, when inmates realize that I am in charge of correctional libraries, they offer suggestions, complaints, and praise. I consider this good feedback and an opportunity to observe collection and database usage as well as to address concerns of the librarians.

When visitors bring up the inevitable question of safety, I point out the reality: that the library is so valued in the institution that inmates are unlikely to do anything to jeopardize their chance to have access; that the library is the one place in the institution where an inmate is sure to get unbiased information; that of the many choices they have (recreation, TV, school, group activities, etc.), many choose to visit the library; that there are more crimes in shopping malls, in parking lots, and in homes than in prison. One hour into the visit, a correctional officer announces that the library is closed for lunch. The librarian explains that this is the quiet time that she uses to catch up on paperwork or access the Internet, because institutional rules forbid use of the Internet when inmates are around, although they have access to computers with CD-ROM databases.

If I visit a prison that is 130 miles away, most of the day is consumed in driving. Today's visit is only seventeen miles away, so I am able to return to the office for the afternoon. I responded affirmatively to e-mails from two librarians interested in attending the Correctional Education Association conference, assuring them that I would pay for their registration.

JOYS AND TRIBULATIONS

Joys

I like being in charge. As the coordinator I have the power to initiate and design services for this special group of users. I am able to conceive and implement ideas that have positive effects. One such idea was when I created a CD-ROM tutorial that explains the Internet for inmates who have never used it. I copyrighted the CD-ROM, which has become very popular among the inmates in Maryland as well as in prison and juvenile centers in other states. I like the trust inmates place in our information services. Some use our libraries not only for themselves but to do research for family members outside the prison. Former inmates often associate the library with good experiences during their incarceration. One poignant moment for me was a chance encounter with a former offender who was the guest speaker at a forum I attended. The first person in the United States to be exonerated with DNA evidence, he began his presentation by acknowledging my presence, detailing the ways the library helped him with the books that gave him the idea to seek DNA testing.

I get bored with routine, and this position provides little opportunity for monotony. Instead it tests my ability to find creative solutions for myriad unpredictable situations. Few of these situations stem from prisoners; more are caused by the rigidities of security personnel who are often whimsical in their support of the library and education programs. On those days when I feel mired in paperwork, I often visit a prison and talk with the prisoners and librarians. Invariably I return inspired by the inmates' positive feedback and motivated by the many possibilities to improve services.

Tribulations

As the correctional coordinator, my greatest frustration is having to deal with correctional personnel who see their role as maintaining security with minimal or no concern for inmates' educational well-being, or correctional officers who try to act as censors wanting certain library materials removed for no good reason.

Another frustration is the inability to recruit librarians, especially younger ones, to the profession. Our vacancies take up to a year to fill, and our pool of qualified applicants is usually limited to librarians who, after decades of working in other library systems, are within a few years of retirement.

I have no counterpart to my position in Maryland; therefore my support group consists of library coordinators from other states, prison libraries e-mail lists, and other librarians who are active in the Library Services to Prisoners Forum of the American Library Association's Libraries Serving Special Populations Section.

SO YOU WANT TO BE A PRISON LIBRARY COORDINATOR?

You need a master's degree in library and information sciences and knowledge of current library practice, including telecommunication and electronic technologies. You need the ability to work in an atmosphere of diversity, handle budgets, perform multiple tasks, and work with various agencies. You should have experience in working with institutionalized populations. You also need good people skills as well as a passion for providing information services for disadvantaged persons.

Begin by working in a public library. This will give you a sense of the variety of information needs that you might also encounter in the prison environment. Then apply for a job as a prison librarian. If you prefer to work with young people, look for a position as a librarian/media specialist in a juvenile institution. If you are successful as a one-person manager—dealing assertively with the various issues such as prisoners, security personnel, information needs, supervisory tasks, budgets—there is nothing to deter you from applying for the next vacant coordinator position.

RELATED READINGS

Association of Specialized and Cooperative Library Agencies. 1992. *Library standards for adult correctional institutions, 1992*. Chicago: American Library Association.

Lehmann, Vibeke. 1999. Prison librarians needed: A challenging career for those with the right professional and human skills. Paper presented at the 65th IFLA Council and General Conference, Bangkok, Thailand, August 20–28. Available online at www.ifla.org/IV/ifla65/papers/046-132e.htm (accessed April 3, 2006).

Shirley, Glennor. 2003. Correctional libraries, library standards, and diversity. *Journal of Correctional Education* 54 (June): 70–74.

———. 2004. Prison libraries and cultural diversity. www.ala.org/ala/olos/outreachresource/prisoncol4. htm (accessed August 20, 2006).

Vogel, Brenda. 1995. *Down for the count: A prison library handbook*. Lanham, Md.: Scarecrow Press.

Web Sites of Interest

Association of Specialized and Cooperative Library Agencies. Library Service to Prisoners Forum. www .ala.org/ala/ascla/asclaourassoc/asclasections/lssps/lspf/lspf.htm (accessed April 3, 2006).

Maryland Correctional Education Libraries. ce.msde.state.md.us/library/libraries.htm (accessed August 20, 2006).

———, Collections. ce.msde.state.md.us/library/collections.htm (accessed August 20, 2006).

CHAPTER 61

Librarian for the Blind and Disabled

SARAH PITKIN

My main responsibility is serving as a reader's advisor to the visually impaired or physically disabled at the Utah State Library. I sit at my desk for most of the workday with four other reader's advisors, answering phone calls requesting book orders, asking questions, seeking information, or concerning other library business. Between calls, I work on my other assignments, which include management of our library's Web site, choosing locally published books to be recorded and added to our collection, cataloging and reporting these books electronically to the National Library Service for the Blind and Physically Handicapped for its national database, and creating and implementing the Summer Reading Program.

The Program for the Blind and Disabled is a national program that is an extension of the Library of Congress. There is a system of regional libraries throughout the United States for users who qualify for these services. An application is required that is signed by a medical or other professional who can verify disability. When we receive this application, we add the user's name and information into our database and provide a cassette player for him or her to listen to books and magazines on cassette tape. These books are recorded at a slower speed that allows recording on all four tracks of the cassette tape, resulting in half the number of cassettes per book, and requiring a special player.

Those who read Braille material can also check out Braille books from our collection. Our library contracts with about twenty other states to provide Braille books for their patrons as well. Patrons from these states can call our toll-free number to order Braille materials, which are sent to them postage-free through the U.S. Postal Service.

Our other services include a collection of books in large print, a local radio reading service (broadcast from our building through a sideband of a local radio station), and a descriptive video service. All materials and equipment can be mailed to and from our patrons postage-free through the U.S. Postal Service to accommodate any of our patrons who cannot physically visit the library.

Although we serve a wide range of people of all ages and disabilities, the majority of our clients are older adults who have lost some or all of their vision to eye problems, which prevent them from reading regular print. There are four other people in the Library for the Blind who also serve as reader's advisors; each has a major area of responsibility in the library, such as cataloging and production of catalogs of our local collections, outreach, inventory control, and responsibility for the large-print collection. We each have our own cubicle and work in a small call center of sorts where we take patron calls throughout the day, answer questions, update patron information, and fill requests for library materials.

I have an additional assignment from the state library, which is separate from the Library for the Blind but shares the same building. I currently serve as the state Summer Reading Program coordinator. This assignment involves coordinating and distributing summer reading materials to public libraries throughout the state and then reporting statistics for those programs to the state librarian, who uses this information to promote the value of summer reading programs to our legislature and other funding agencies.

Utah, along with roughly thirty-two other states or library districts, belongs to the Collaborative Summer Library Program (CSLP), an organization that develops, produces, and distributes summer reading materials for its member states. I attend an annual conference where state representatives meet to discuss organizational business and develop program ideas for future summer reading programs. Then I spend the rest of the year coordinating the distribution of summer reading materials, workshops, and promotions for CSLP. I enjoy this assignment because it gives me the opportunity to be in contact with librarians across the country as well as those in my own state. We share ideas and efforts, which lightens the load for all the members.

A TYPICAL DAY IS A WEEK

Monday morning seems to hit like a ton of bricks. There are so many different things to accomplish and the phones seem to ring nonstop. We consistently receive more phone calls on Monday than any other day. If there has been a holiday on Monday, then Tuesday is what we call a "double Monday," meaning it feels like having two Mondays in one day as calls can be even more plentiful than on a regular busy Monday. We also have a few walk-in patrons each day who are directed to one of the reader's advisors for individual service. This visit may involve a lengthy reference/instructional interview, especially if a patron is signing up for the service for the first time. We tell new patrons how our program works, how to order and return books and other materials, and how to use the tape player that we provide for them, and we try to resolve any questions or concerns they may have.

Most of my day is spent on the phone with patrons. Most calls involve taking down a book order or helping a patron choose what to read next. A fair amount of detective work may be involved when patrons either don't know what to request, or they *do* know what they want but don't have enough information about the book for me to figure out what it is. Because most of our patrons are older adults, this is a common occurrence. Amazon.com has become one of my best friends for book information; I use it to find out exactly how to spell a title or author's name, or if a book is even in print. Many patrons who want the latest titles are also frustrated because it can take up to a year before a book in print is recorded on the four-track cassettes and added to our collection. Locally produced books can take up to eight months, based on the availability of volunteers to read and record each book.

Along with the challenges of helping an aging population, the very nature of phone communication can present unique problems, such as not being able to understand the name of the patron or trying to understand the speech of someone with a disability that affects his or her speech. Many of our patrons are also hard of hearing. Yelling into the phone isn't one of my favorite things to do! Because we serve many other states for Braille, I sometimes have a hard time understanding some of our out-of-state patrons who have a thick accent. But even with these specific challenges, most patrons are pleasant and patient with our service and grateful that it provides them a way to read that they wouldn't have otherwise.

As the week progresses, the number of calls usually diminishes each day, so between phone calls I work on my other assignments. I'm usually working on several projects at once, so I am usually tied to the phone and the computer for most of my workday. Our supervisor keeps track of times that any of the staff will be away from their desks for a long period of time (such as lunch, meetings, workshops, or training) and arranges phone coverage accordingly.

Although there are occasionally unexpected snags in the regular routine, days and weeks follow a similar pattern. Each day, glued to my phone and computer, I try to spend time on each of my assignments, prioritizing according to need and deadline, while taking calls and helping walk-ins.

IN A PERFECT WORLD: PROS AND CONS

Many of the challenges I face on the job are both beneficial and frustrating at the same time. I am constantly thinking about and trying to develop better service to visually impaired and physically disabled people of all ages, within the bounds of available resources. It is often difficult for me, as a sighted and enabled person, to know how to develop helpful materials for our patrons. Patron feedback is critical for me to do my job well. For example, we solicit feedback on our Web site's accessibility and effectiveness. Also, I sometimes get requests to adapt materials. A parent of one of our Braille-reading young people requested that summer reading activity sheets be provided in a format that combines large print and Braille. Currently, summer reading activity sheets are mailed to our young readers in a large-print format, and a separate Braille format if requested. These activity sheets are mailed back to the library to earn prizes. I have sought suggestions from several e-mail lists and have worked with our in-house Braille producer; we hope to be able to come up with a feasible format. I share any new products that help our young readers with other librarians who have a similar clientele, as we are all working together to provide the most beneficial service we can to our patrons.

An important benefit of my job is the opportunity to learn different aspects of library service by taking on various assignments. Collaborating with knowledgeable people who specialize in different areas expands my knowledge and experience. A completed project is always a relief, but working with other people who can teach me new things makes the process more satisfying.

Although I rarely deal with rude or overly demanding patrons, it is sometimes difficult to be tied to the phone and computer for so much of the day. Being aware of and handling my restlessness or any other negative mood I might have is part of my daily practice. I suspect most librarians deal with this, because work performance is usually directly related to how one is feeling. Luckily, most of our patrons are pleasant to talk with and grateful for our service to them; most of the maddening calls really have nothing to do with the person who is calling but with my *reaction* to the call. Being interrupted by the phone when I'm trying to concentrate on another project can be frustrating. Our library is an interruption-intensive place to work, and it's my responsibility to be pleasant to patrons all the time, no matter how I may feel, even if I have to fake it!

Sometimes patrons may be genuinely annoying, continually interrupting me as I'm trying to help them or talking to me as if I were stupid (I hate that!). In these cases, I employ my best voice acting skills to interact pleasantly with the patron and hide my frustration. On the other hand, cheerful or favorite patrons can quickly lighten my mood with their fun personalities and gratitude for our service to them. Like anything else, there are ups and downs and in-betweens, but overall, I enjoy my job very much.

GETTING THE JOB

An MLS is required for my position, and applicants must follow the official job application process online through the State of Utah Web site. There are regional libraries like ours throughout the United States that are often affiliated with a state library, so the hiring procedures of the state where the library is located must be followed.

I was surprised to be hired shortly after completing my MLS program because I had no professional library experience, but I came to find out that sometimes those who make hiring decisions prefer inexperienced librarians because it can be easier to train someone to serve our unique clientele than to try to change previous training. I've also learned that a patient, pleasant personality will help in getting hired at a library like ours. I've heard my supervisor say on more than one occasion that she can teach someone the different aspects of being a librarian, but, as she says, "I can't teach you how to be nice."

There are good and bad days, but for me, the satisfaction I feel doing my job outweighs any temporary frustration I may feel along the way.

RELATED RESOURCES

Collaborative Summer Library Program. www.cslpreads.org (accessed February 15, 2006).
National Library Service for the Blind and Physically Handicapped. www.loc.gov/nls (accessed February 15, 2006).
Utah Department of Human Resource Management. Applying for jobs. statejobs.utah.gov/faqApply.jsp (accessed February 15, 2006).
Utah State Library for the Blind and Disabled. blindlibrary.utah.gov (accessed February 15, 2006).

PART V

Consortia

CHAPTER 62

Internet Trainer

MICHAEL SAUERS

The Bibliographical Center for Research (BCR) is a multistate library cooperative that offers Online Computer Library Center (OCLC) services, group purchases of databases, and training for libraries in eleven member states. My job as BCR's Internet trainer is to travel around the region offering workshops on the Internet and other technology topics to librarians and library staff. I also perform technical support for our members and staff on an as-needed basis in addition to working on the BCR Web site.

Outside of my official duties I am a member of the board of trustees of the Aurora Public Library, and I'm a member of the board the Friends of the Aurora Public Library. I am also an author with seven published titles and several magazine and journal articles. I regularly present at state and national conferences.

TYPICAL WORKDAYS

I will describe two types of workday routines because on some days I teach and on other days I don't.

On the Road

BCR currently has eleven member states (Colorado, Kansas, Iowa, Utah, Nevada, Montana, Wyoming, Idaho, Oregon, Washington, and Alaska), and I teach workshops in all of them. This requires a great amount of travel. When workshops are scheduled, I travel to the city on Monday, teach classes Tuesday through Friday, and return home Friday evening (if I'm not close enough to a major airport, I drive to the city with the airport Friday evening and return home on Saturday morning). Most of my trips require air travel, though when I teach in southern Wyoming or western Kansas, I usually drive.

Workshops are offered from 9 a.m. to 4 p.m. with an hour for lunch and morning and afternoon breaks of ten to fifteen minutes each. Teaching days include either one full-day workshop or two half-day workshops. (My Introduction to XML workshop is my only two-day seminar.) I arrive at the workshop location (normally a university or public library computer lab) at 7:30 a.m. on the first day to meet the host, check out the setup, and solve any equipment problems that arise at the last moment. As the week progresses, I arrive at the lab closer to 9 a.m.

With few exceptions, my classes are hands-on and move at a quick pace. Before I know it, it's time for lunch, which means going to a local restaurant with the host and some of the students.

By 4 p.m., class is over and I'm exhausted, so I head back to my hotel to change into more comfortable clothing and go to dinner. Usually I'm on my own for dinner, but some hosts enjoy showing me the best places to eat in town. After dinner I either look for a coffee shop or used bookstore, or go back to my hotel room to work on an article or book and enjoy some relaxing reading. (This usually depends on the size of the town and whether I've been there before.)

I also teach workshops at the BCR offices. The schedule for those days is the same as my workshops on the road, but things are less stressful because the travel is my usual morning commute to the office, and I have complete control over the training environment.

In the Office

When I'm not on the road, I'm in my office recovering from one trip or preparing for another. The first day in the office after a trip is always filled with the trip paperwork: logging receipts, making sure I stayed under budget, and requesting any reimbursements. I also have snail mail to catch up on, along with any e-mail that I couldn't handle from the road. This usually takes up all of the first weekday back.

Because BCR has recently started to offer our workshops online, on days that I'm in the office and at my desk I may also be teaching a workshop online to students in several other states.

Other days in the office are generally a blur of activity to me, but to other people it probably looks as if I'm just playing or not doing much of anything at all. These activities include tasks such as updating training materials to reflect changes in the systems I'm teaching, creating new materials for workshops, investigating hot technology topics for possible new classes, attending meetings for both BCR and OCLC, and writing for publication.

These activities could be boiled down to one descriptive phrase: trying to keep up. As a trainer I need to keep up not only with the technology I teach but also with what's coming down the pipeline. I do this by reading blogs, listening to podcasts, trying out new Web sites and software, reading articles and books, and generally poking around both online and offline to find what might be interesting to the librarians who come to my workshops. When I'm not working on a specific project, my time is spent trying to keep up (if not get ahead) on all these things.

Periodically, I am asked to do presentations at meetings at which BCR has no official relationship, such as the Computers in Libraries and Internet Librarian conferences. I develop and prepare for those events just as I would any of my other workshops.

My official job description includes offering support for BCR's member libraries, but honestly, I don't do this often. I am available to answer questions as they come in, but in most cases, because I'm dealing with the Internet instead of particular databases or OCLC services, the questions I receive are few and far between. (Librarians typically contact their own local tech support person with this type of question.) I do, however, work with BCR staff, assisting them with Internet, Windows, and Web design questions whenever I'm available.

PROS AND CONS

The greatest part of my job is that I get to meet so many different librarians in my travels. I especially feel like I'm doing some good both when those "aha!" moments happen in my classes and when students return for more workshops.

The biggest con to the job is Murphy's Law: if it can go wrong, it probably will. I've been in training rooms that are way too small for the number of attendees, dealt with nonfunctional technology (or worse yet, nonexistent technology), and had uncooperative hosts who are unwilling to let me run the workshop the way I need it to run. After eight years of these problems, very few surprise me anymore, and I look on them as a challenge and a learning experience. However, when I was starting out in this position, these unexpected problems took a heavy psychological toll.

The amount of travel that I do is both a pro and a con. On one hand, I've seen much of the country and been to places that I never would have visited otherwise. On the other, I'm a suburbanite at heart, and I've spent weeks in towns where the local Wal-Mart is the most interesting place to go. The travel has also prevented me from having any pets, and I've only successfully kept one plant alive in the past eight years.

HOW WOULD I GET A JOB LIKE YOURS?

In her book *The Accidental Trainer*, Elaine Weiss says, "Chances are you did not wake up one morning when you were eight years old and say to yourself, 'I don't think I'll be a firefighter after all. I think when I grow up I'll earn my living by teaching people to use computers.' If you are like many computer trainers, you fell into the role accidentally." I have yet to meet a trainer that doesn't agree with this wholeheartedly. None of us *intended* to be a trainer; we just ended up doing it.

In my case it was because I insisted on opening my mouth during my Internet 101 class in library school back in 1994. There was this new technology available on campus called "the Web," and I insisted that the instructor needed to know all about it. I ended up teaching that part of the class for the next three semesters. From there I taught the first Internet classes that the university library offered (I also created the library's first Web site). After graduation, I moved to Las Vegas to run my own Internet consulting firm for two years. Once I finally decided that consulting wasn't my gig, I drove myself off to ALA's annual conference in San Francisco and spent several days at the job fair. I found this position as a result of that conference. So in my case, ending up as a trainer was completely accidental.

However, if you're *planning* to become a trainer, here's a bit of advice. First, train every chance you get. Offer some free workshops at your local public library or bookstore. The more you train, the better you become at it. Second, read everything you can about the topics you're interested in teaching. Third, attend sessions taught by other trainers, especially those who are training on the same topic you're interested in teaching. You may not learn new material, but you may learn new teaching methods. Third, read everything you can on the larger issues that envelop what you want to teach. For example, I once read James Surowiecki's *The Wisdom of Crowds* because it sounded interesting. A year later, when I started putting together a class on wikis, I immediately recognized concepts from that book. The material didn't seem directly relevant at first, but it came in handy in the end.

RELATED RESOURCES

Bibliographical Center for Research (BCR). www.bcr.org (accessed June 11, 2006).
Sauers, Michael. *The Travelin' Librarian*. travelinlibrarian.info (accessed June 11, 2006). My blog.
Surowiecki, James. 2004. *The wisdom of crowds: Why the many are smarter than the few and how collective wisdom shapes business, economies, societies, and nations*. New York: Doubleday.
Weiss, Elaine. 1997. *The accidental trainer: You know computers, so they want you to teach everyone else*. San Francisco: Jossey-Bass.

CHAPTER 63

Member Support Coordinator

CYNTHIA I. WILSON

When I tell people I am a librarian their first response is, "What library do you work in?" It's a common perception that librarians work in a library. However, librarians are information sources who can provide references within or without the physical library building. I work in an office building.

PALINET, which once stood for Philadelphia Area Library Network, is a nonprofit membership organization of libraries, museums, and organizations primarily in the mid-Atlantic states. PALINET joins libraries together to get discounts on electronic resources and to establish cooperative agreements to share information. PALINET also provides varied training opportunities and offers members a place to go for support when they need help with their purchases. As the member support coordinator, I establish procedures for orders, general software support, and communication with members handled by PALINET's support desk. I do this while also providing support to librarians and library staff within the approximately six hundred libraries that comprise our membership.

PALINET is also a regional service provider for Online Computer Library Center (OCLC). Our region includes libraries and cultural institutions in Pennsylvania, New Jersey, Delaware, Maryland, West Virginia, and beyond. A large part of my job is providing technical and ordering support for OCLC products and services. I also answer members' PALINET-related questions, such as those related to e-mail lists, workshops, annual invoices, or cooperative purchasing liaisons.

WHAT COULD POSSIBLY HAPPEN IN A DAY?

Every productive day starts with a good cup of coffee. For many months, I have logged in to my computer and gotten my coffee while waiting for my computer to warm up. Recently my computer has been upgraded, so it runs much faster now, but I still am in the routine of getting some morning caffeine as I start the workday.

Throughout any given day, my workload can include such things as e-mail or telephone support, editing and disseminating news, going to meetings, placing orders, or communicating with members and OCLC.

I frequently check my e-mail for member support needs and look for any important messages that are posted on the OCLC discussion lists. Important items might include system outages that affect workflow, new technology, product discounts, or educational opportunities that will benefit our members.

It is a big part of my job to be aware of industry-related news and OCLC news. I check e-mail lists, blogs, and news sites to help keep me informed about updates within the OCLC software systems that PALINET supports. Biweekly meetings called OCLC Hours help keep me abreast of changes in the OCLC software and within the OCLC organization. I also gain this information through the American Library Association's annual and midwinter conferences and through service meetings that are held at OCLC twice a year. I then disseminate this information to our membership through the PALINET e-mail list, PALINET blogs, and an online newsletter called *OCLC Watch*.

The computer is a large facet of my job, but I also communicate with members on the phone. The majority of support calls that come my way are related to OCLC products. I also receive questions about the PALINET e-mail list or member invoices, but primarily I provide support for cataloging, interlibrary loan, or reference products.

While covering the support desk, it is important to consider the needs of our members and make sure that their voices are heard by our vendors. Our members frequently request enhancements to OCLC products and services, and I forward these requests to OCLC.

Members also place orders for OCLC products through the support desk. I process some orders (for example, OCLC FirstSearch, WorldCat Collection Analysis, and WorldCat Collection Sets), and others go to our trainers, who are the product experts. Quotes are often provided by our experts, so I gather preliminary information for them and send them the specifics so they can assist the member. I am able to provide quotes for a few products that have more standardized pricing.

The trainers are also the providers of more specialized support for the cataloging, interlibrary loan, reference, and digitization products and services. My interaction with the trainers is a key factor in helping our members. They also help with the support desk coverage during meetings, lunches, or vacation time.

Because I maintain the support desk schedule, I schedule time away from the desk for myself so I can look for ways to improve or expand our member support. I have worked with our technical staff to streamline the internal e-mail processes so that multiple e-mail addresses filter into one account and items or orders can be easily transferred to other staff if needed. I am also working on establishing our second blog and moving our static Web page for *OCLC Watch* into a regularly updated RSS feed.

As a continued effort for member outreach, PALINET has agreed to perform service checks on certain OCLC products and services such as CONTENTdm, eAudiobooks, ILLiad, WebDewey, and WorldCat Collection Analysis for libraries in our region. It is primarily my responsibility to contact the members about the newly purchased or renewed OCLC products and services. I maintain a spreadsheet for the orders and service checks and send the members' answers to OCLC.

I spend a large part of my day in meetings where we discuss how to help libraries take advantage of emerging technologies. Currently I serve on two committees at PALINET. I am the chair of the Staff Activities Committee, and I am a part of the Web team, which is managing the redesign of PALINET's Web site.

The Staff Activities Committee plans events such as birthday and holiday parties, staff outings, and community-related activities. As chair, I handle the communication to the staff about these events.

The Web team has a specific goal to redesign the Web site. My responsibilities have included assisting with determining the features we need, organizing information, performing usability testing, and writing survey questions. At PALINET's annual conference, we also hosted discussions about the Web site to incorporate our members' opinions and suggestions.

As the meetings, calls, and e-mails of the day come to a close, I review my notes documenting calls and go through my e-mail to flag what needs to be done for the next day. I finish the last sip of my second cup of coffee, shut down my computer, and run out the door to catch my train home.

REWARDS AND FRUSTRATIONS

There are many rewards to being the member support coordinator. Constantly learning new things is on top of the list. I became a librarian because I enjoy helping people. This position allows me to fulfill this desire and it also makes me feel like an information source with whom people feel comfortable. It's also a good feeling to be able to help those who taught me.

PALINET's location is also a big reward for me. It is right across the street from 30th Street station and only two blocks away from the World Café Live, a music venue that has "Free at Noon" concerts on Fridays hosted by the University of Pennsylvania's radio station WXPN. I often coerce my coworkers to join me for a lunchtime concert. That aside, working with a fantastic group of people is always a bonus for any employee. In this regard, I'm very lucky to have not only great coworkers but also very understanding members.

On the downside, there are times when frustrations occur. Telling people about system problems is one of the toughest tasks. Generally these problems are resolved quickly, but the longer it takes to fix, the harder it becomes to calm people, especially when the ability to fix a problem is outside my control. Another challenge is scheduling a large number of people for the support desk. Schedules are constantly changing, and it's often a challenge to plan ahead.

THE ROAD TO LIBRARY SUPPORT

My previous work with PALINET's Preservation Advisory Group helped me move into my current position. This group provides guidance to PALINET staff related to preservation program development, workshops, communication to members, resource evaluation, references, and member outreach efforts. I joined the advisory group while in library school and working for the law library at Reed Smith LLP, a PALINET member. If you are interested in working with a consortium that promotes cooperative arrangements among libraries, then I suggest that you look for ways to volunteer with the organization. Committee work is also a great way to make contacts that could help you in the future.

Another factor that helped me get this position was my wide range of experience, particularly in interlibrary loan, cataloging, and preservation. My job in the interlibrary loan department at Temple University led me to go for my master's in library science. I was able to move into various positions while in library school. As I mentioned earlier, I worked in a law firm library. I later worked in the library at Moore College of Art and Design. I took on an internship at the Temple University Urban Archives, cataloging photographs even before I could receive school credit for it. I wanted to gain knowledge for my coursework and also help discover what type of job I wanted after graduation. I had a second internship with Washington State University in their Manuscripts, Archives and Special Collections department. I cannot highlight the importance of internships enough. Experience is essential for a job search. I wouldn't recommend a series of short-term jobs to everyone because it's risky, but I was lucky enough to have the opportunity and ability to be flexible with my career.

Flexibility is a key factor in working in any support environment. My position is one that is regularly transforming. The member support coordinator has to be ready to switch gears at any given moment. Another key personality trait that someone in this position would need is the steady desire to learn. As the information is constantly changing, it is important for the member support coordinator to be on the forefront of those changes.

FOR MORE INFORMATION

Dotolo, Lawrence George, and John B. Noftsinger, eds. 2002. *Leveraging resources through partnerships.* San Francisco: Jossey-Bass.

Ensor, Pat, ed. 2000. *The cybrarian's manual 2.* Chicago: American Library Association. OCLC. www.oclc. org (accessed April 4, 2006).

———, OCLC regional service providers. www.oclc.org/contacts/regional/default.htm (accessed April 4, 2006).

———, 1997. *What the OCLC online union catalog means to me: A collection of essays.* Dublin, Ohio: OCLC.

PALINET. www.palinet.org (accessed April 4, 2006).

———, PALINET ILL blog. palinet-ill.blogspot.com (accessed April 4, 2006).

Woodsworth, Anne. 1991. *Library cooperation and networks: A basic reader.* With the assistance of Thomas B. Wall. New York: Neal-Schuman.

CHAPTER 64

Metadata Specialist

OCLC (Online Computer Library Center) is a major library services company that offers myriad services for academic, public, corporate, and special libraries in the United States and around the world. The company is quite large and covers many different specialties. I work in OCLC's Metadata and Contract Services Division. In this division, there are three major work areas that offer customizable services for libraries: Language Sets, Cataloging Partners, and TechPro. I work in TechPro's Contract Cataloging division, which, true to its name, offers custom contract cataloging services for libraries in search of high-quality, efficient cataloging for various kinds of materials. For instance, a library might get items in a language that none of its staff speak or read. Similarly, formats such as DVDs, microfiche, maps, musical scores, and electronic resources have specialized cataloging rules and may require additional expertise that a library's staff may not possess. Sometimes libraries have a large backlog of uncataloged materials or receive gift collections that they might never get around to working on because the established priority is to keep up with new acquisitions. TechPro was created for situations just like these. TechPro's catalogers have a wide variety of skills and expertise. Some have cataloging expertise in many languages, ranging from Russian to Arabic to Urdu. The format expertise is also wide-ranging: for example, there are catalogers who focus exclusively on music recordings, maps, or books. The majority of items received are print materials, but there are also catalogers who work on audiovisual or electronic formats.

A TYPICAL WORKDAY

A typical workday for a metadata specialist consists chiefly of project cataloging and possibly some meetings. Each workday varies greatly, depending on the types of materials included in projects and the cataloger's area of expertise. Depending on how many active projects I have and what kind of materials are included therein, I may, for example, work a few hours cataloging maps, a few hours on local genealogical materials, and a few hours on theses and dissertations. Some people specialize in non-English languages, others focus on serials, and some of us simply work on whatever is in the project.

Problem-solving skills are especially useful in this position. I have often encountered an item or type of material I have never seen before and used problem-solving techniques to determine the best first step in the process. It is important to be able to understand the scope of the project and have a sense of the resources required to complete it.

Contract Cataloging tends to receive more complex materials, and sometimes the more difficult items require consulting cataloging tools and standards to determine whether an item requires special treatment, and deciding how to best represent the information based on the *Anglo-American Cataloging Rules*, 2nd revision (AACR2), the current cataloging standard. Proficiency with AACR2 and other cataloging tools is a major part of the position, one that proves very useful when I need to do research on a specific kind of situation.

Another typical activity is tracking the allocation of time spent on each project. The billing process is not handled by catalogers, but we are required to document the amount of time spent on each project by using specialized time-tracking software and note the number of records created or updated each day. This enables the project managers to accurately bill the library or organization at the end of the month.

PROS AND CONS

One major advantage of my job is the opportunity to learn. There are so many different kinds of materials that come into the department that it would be difficult to go through a day without learning a new rule, using a new resource, or encountering a new type of item. The department is very supportive of employee training and development and works with employees who want to further their language skills, cataloging knowledge of special formats, or other specialties. Often employees are sent to workshops and training sessions (in-house and at other locations) to increase the knowledge they can bring to the team. The environment is also very supportive of asking questions. It is comforting to know that there is always someone who might have already encountered my tricky situation or is at least able to offer suggestions on finding an answer.

OCLC is a great place to work. Beyond departmental training, there are often company educational initiatives with speakers on topics of interest in the library community. There are two cafeterias and a workout facility on site, as well as a good number of other benefits, including discounts for local services and dry cleaning drop-off. The flexible hours are also a tremendous asset.

This position also has its challenges. The work can seem repetitive, with few distractions, although I have found that my attention span has greatly increased since I have had this job. If I am working on a big project with many similar items, I sometimes become tired. Being able to focus is an important skill, and I find it useful to listen to music to help maintain concentration. The environment is also largely sedentary with little physical activity. I usually take walks outside around the campus to get my blood flowing again.

HOW CAN I GET A JOB LIKE THIS?

The most important skills for this job are an interest in cataloging and an attention to detail. I have long been interested in how and why things are organized in certain ways, and I've found that this helps me maintain a high level of interest in my work. The position of metadata specialist requires a master's in library science and some cataloging experience, but there are positions at varying levels within the department that may require more or less experience.

If you think you might be interested in a cataloging position, the first thing you should do is to take the cataloging course offered in library school. Some programs do not require this course, but it is integral in understanding the structure of the catalog. It also helps with search skills and can ultimately help you better serve the users. Once you take the course, you will have a better idea about what exactly is involved in cataloging and whether this kind of work is right for you. To be candid, not everyone enjoys cataloging. If you decide that you do, it is a great skill to have and will help you in whatever career path you ultimately follow.

In addition to taking a cataloging course, it is also very helpful to get some practical experience. You can try to find an entry-level position in the technical services unit at a local library. There you can begin to become familiar with cataloging and other technical services processes. Knowledge of databases, metadata, and other computer skills are also very useful, especially because most cataloging tasks are performed using specialized cataloging software.

Once you have some experience and your degree, you can begin to look for professional positions. One great resource is AUTOCAT, an important cataloging-related mailing list. There are always interesting topics being discussed, and the subscribers collectively represent a wealth of knowledge on cataloging and catalog-related topics. Many cataloging job postings are also listed here.

There are many library job posting services online, and it is also useful to visit the Web sites of libraries and organizations in the geographical region in which you would like to work. Though the job-posting services usually cover most of the vacancies, there are sometimes openings that slip by. Other great resources are conferences and meetings. Meeting people who are in the field can be a valuable way to learn about job openings and get insider information about what it is like to work at a specific place.

RELATED RESOURCES

AUTOCAT. ublib.buffalo.edu/libraries/units/cts/autocat (accessed November 27, 2005).

OCLC, Contract cataloging. www.oclc.org/customcataloging/services/contract/default.htm (accessed November 27, 2005).

———, Custom cataloging. www.oclc.org/customcataloging (accessed November 27, 2005).

CHAPTER 65

Knowledge Manager

As a knowledge manager at the North Suburban Library System (NSLS), I find my days consumed with locating, analyzing, and sharing information with both coworkers and the library system's member libraries. Funded by the Illinois State Library, NSLS is a consortium of 650 member libraries and is one of nine library systems around the state that supports the public, school, academic, and special libraries in its membership through a variety of services.

My responsibilities involve several of the system's major initiatives, particularly overseeing its knowledge management (KM) initiative, coordinating professional development, and assisting with the development of technology projects. My day's activities can range from talking on the phone with a potential speaker to posting on our special libraries online discussion board to providing technical support for one of our services. My work keeps me close to home, serving on various staff teams and assisting with projects assigned by the assistant director for administration, but it also provides opportunities for outside involvement with other library organizations. A library system serves many libraries, each with different needs, so my work spans many different areas of the library system. By providing access to information and resources to its member libraries, the library system serves its own unique community of libraries. I see myself as a librarian helping other librarians.

KNOWLEDGE MANAGEMENT 101

My role as a knowledge manager began when I oversaw the development of the system's KM initiative, with its vision to "capture, share and transfer our organizational knowledge to connect our members and employees to each other, to meaningful content, and to NSLS." I use my KM skills to identify knowledge gaps and then create processes to fill those gaps, so that necessary information gets to the correct people when they need it. My work with KM over the initiative's five-year span has affected the way the system, its staff, and its member libraries use their knowledge in several ways. Identifying member needs that lead us to create new services, enhancing a current service so it better meets member expectations, connecting members who have similar needs—these are just a few of the outcomes of my work with KM.

Anticipating Members' Professional Development Needs

My work as a knowledge manager is embedded into my daily work on several major initiatives at the library system, one of which is overseeing the system's professional development classes. Providing adequate professional development for hundreds of member libraries can be a time-consuming process on some days. The library system's face-to-face and online classes are the second most requested service, and planning classes that meet the needs of our members involves more than just identifying potential topics and speakers. It's a responsibility that requires daily attention. My contribution to the development of over two hundred classes each year involves calling potential speakers, booking dates, developing class descriptions and learning objectives, assisting on the day of the class, and processing any follow-up.

Our classes change as our members' needs change and as training itself evolves. I manage this continuous process of learning by monitoring current trends in training, observing what other organizations are doing, and then sharing this information with staff. Over time this information adds up to knowledge, which can be applied back to meeting the professional development needs of NSLS's member libraries. One way I keep tuned to our members' needs is by closely monitoring what they are saying about our classes in their evaluations, from which I create monthly, quarterly, and yearly reports to track our professional development's overall progress. These reports include information such as the most popular class topics, speaker ratings, particular libraries or library types in attendance, and how a member learned about the class. I share the findings at staff meetings, through e-mail, and in a formal yearly report. This constant management, organization, and communication of knowledge enables system staff to reduce the time and work spent on class development and better identify future trends and anticipate needs of our members.

Serving Members, One Visit at a Time

Another way I combine my work duties with my KM skills is through my role as the liaison to our Special Librarians and New Librarians networking groups. Networking enables me to connect members who have a particular need with another member with that expertise. The more I visit special member libraries and meet librarians at their meetings, the better sense I have of their needs and how the system can support them. Being a staff liaison to a particular member networking group involves assisting them with questions, promoting their accomplishments in our weekly e-newsletter or Web site, and planning quarterly networking meetings. For the New Librarians networking group, I pick a theme for each meeting, arrange a guest speaker or provide resources around that theme, and then facilitate the discussion. Both member groups have online discussion boards called CoPs (communities of practice) that enable members (and me) to keep in touch between meetings. Several times a week I try to post something I feel might be of interest to the group.

Inventing Innovation

Library system work involves staying current on new technology, because often the staff at our member libraries are more focused on day-to-day operations and therefore rely on system staff to alert them to future trends. By serving on the system's technology team, I play a part in monitoring new technology by reading literature, attending conferences, and collaborating with other library organizations and then sharing information with our members. As part of the technology team, I attend monthly team meetings to review current system projects that may have a technology component. Daily I may be assigned technology requests from other staff needing assistance with a printer jam, computer errors, or testing a new Web site feature. As a member of this team I also contribute to the ongoing development and maintenance of many of the system's technology initiatives. I play a role in supporting our online community network, called NorthStarNet (NSN). NSLS serves as administrative and technical support for more than fifty public libraries that work with their local community organizations to establish a Web presence. My responsibilities with NSN are to provide technical support to the library staff by answering e-mail and phone requests. I also contribute to the ongoing development of NSN and attend quarterly member planning meetings.

Knowledge Is Power

I've found that an organization can learn and benefit even more from the knowledge that exists outside its walls. I've had the opportunity to collaborate on projects with other library systems and library organizations. I've also been able to use my storytelling abilities by participating in speaking and writing opportunities to promote the library system's efforts and my own accomplishments. One example was a collaborative opportunity I had with another library system, the Metropolitan Library System, and the Diversity Office of ALA; we created a one-day conference that focused on the issues of recruitment and retention in the profession. Over sixty participants attended to discuss issues such as the value of diversity in libraries, generational differences in the workplace, and the need for mentoring, higher pay, and a more positive image for librarians and libraries. My work on this project involved coordinating presenters, identifying additional resources for distribution at the event, promoting the program, ordering food, and being master of ceremonies on that day. An outcome of the conference was the establishment of NSLS's New Librarian networking group. Through the creation of an opportunity for our member libraries to share their knowledge, a need was identified, and NSLS was able to create a new service to meet that need.

PROS AND CONS

One of the biggest rewards working at a library system provides is being able to participate in a wide variety of opportunities. There are always new things to learn, new technologies to play with, and any number of collaborative projects to get involved in. You can become an expert in a particular library type, such as school or special libraries, or focus on one particular area of librarianship like advocacy or marketing. You'll meet people working at all levels at all types of libraries, including other library systems, the state library, even libraries across the country. The variety of opportunities available at a library system can also be the ultimate double-edged sword, for each opportunity has its own cost of time, effort, and evaluation of what's in the best interest of the member libraries versus the system.

One of the biggest challenges I face in working for a membership organization is the desire to meet all of our members' needs. Because we have so many staff members from varied types of libraries, the system has to provide different types of service that meet each member's need. This can pull system staff in many different directions and create a heavy workload of demands and expectations. Another challenge is balancing members' daily needs with the future goals of the system. For example, although answering member NSN technical questions is one of my daily priorities, it's also essential that I find the time to get member input on their future needs so system staff can plan developments for this service. In the end, the rewards are definitely worth the challenges. If you thrive on change, challenges, and continued learning, then a library system is a place for you.

HOW WOULD I GET A JOB LIKE YOURS?

I suggest first visiting a local library system or consortium, if one exists in your state, to get a better sense of this type of work. Although not a requirement, having a sense of what type of library you prefer can be helpful. If your background is in school libraries and you want to continue in this area, you can potentially do this at a library system, but keep in mind you may find yourself working with all library types. Having particular expertise is good, but having the flexibility to take on new skill sets and be willing to work with other types of libraries is essential at a library system. If KM appeals to you, I'd suggest taking an introductory class or reading some of the beginner's literature, such as *Working Knowledge: How Organizations Manage What They Know* by Thomas Davenport and Laurence Prusak. Elsevier's KM bookstore also has a great selection of KM literature. Consider getting experience with technology support, grant writing, or library advocacy. Become more involved with your state library, other larger organizations, networking groups, or associations within your particular area of interest. I guarantee, whatever road you pick at a library system, it will be an adventure.

RELATED RESOURCES

Davenport, Thomas H. and Laurence Prusak. 1998. *Working knowledge: How organizations manage what they know*. Boston: Harvard Business School Press.

Denning, Stephen. 2001. *The springboard: How storytelling ignites action in knowledge-era organizations*. Boston: Butterworth Heinemann.

Elsevier. Knowledge management bookstore. books.elsevier.com/knowledgemanagement (accessed March 1, 2006).

Illinois Library Systems. www.ilsdo.org (accessed March 1, 2006).

Illinois State Library. www.cyberdriveillinois.com/departments/library/home.html (accessed March 1, 2006).

International Federation of Library Associations and Institutions (IFLA), Knowledge Management Section. www.ifla.org/VII/s47 (accessed August 21, 2006).

KM World. www.kmworld.com (accessed August 21, 2006).

McGuckin, Patrick, ed. 2005. Illinois regional library systems: 40 years, 1965–2005: Past, present, future. Special issue, *Illinois Libraries* 86, no. 1. Available online at www.cyberdriveillinois.com/publications/pdf_publications/lda1042.pdf (accessed August 21, 2006).

NorthStarNet (NSN). www.northstarnet.org (accessed March 1, 2006).

Srikantaiah, Kanti, and Michael E. D. Koenig, eds. 2000. *Knowledge management for the information professional*. Medford, N.J.: Information Today.

Stoll, Christina. 2004. Writing the book on knowledge management: A library system brings knowledge-management tools to the information industry. *Association Management* 56, no. 4 (April): 56–63.

PART VI

LIS Faculty

CHAPTER 66

Assistant Professor

LYNNE C. CHASE

It is the middle of the week, and I am preparing for a teaching trip to one of our off-site teaching venues. I am a new professor at the School of Library and Information Management at Emporia State University. My charge is to teach three courses per semester. Before each semester begins, the faculty get together with the dean to discuss what courses will be taught by whom for the upcoming semester. Of course, we have several core courses that are taught in rotation each semester. My core course teaching responsibility is Theory of Organization of Information. Besides teaching the courses, I am charged with interacting with students throughout each semester, continuing with my research and writing, and serving on various committees within our school, the university, and within state, regional, and national library studies associations.

As a new professor, I work very diligently to become acclimated to this environment and to the mode of course delivery. Our school's program is somewhat different from others in that we travel to various sites to deliver the courses to cohorts of master's students. We also teach at the school and via the Internet. All of our teaching is done during intensive weekend sessions (two sessions per course), except for courses delivered online. That means that I teach on Friday evening, all day Saturday, and Sunday morning. This format requires somewhat different skills for teaching, and I constantly try to improve my strategies as I develop as a teacher. My earlier teaching experience (as a doctoral student) was in a traditional face-to-face setting with classes scheduled for sixteen weeks per semester.

A TYPICAL DAY

Teaching

Teaching responsibilities typically include conducting three courses each semester using learner-centered approaches that engage students in unique, creative, and transformative learning opportunities. It is particularly challenging to craft the course content and format to match the cognitive styles of the students and the individual cohort cultures.

This morning, I have e-mailed the site coordinator to make sure preparations have been made for this teaching weekend. The coordinator confirms that I have transportation between the airport, hotel, and classroom site. She has photocopied some handouts for me and will check all the technology equipment when we arrive at the classroom. As usual, I have a question about the weather. This is the first weekend for this course. I am anxious to meet the students. This is also the first time I will be teaching this course, so I will try to be particularly attentive to what is working in the classroom and what is not.

I make another check of the texts and materials that will accompany me to the site and review the lecture notes and PowerPoint slides I have prepared. Then I turn my attention to individual student needs.

The practice of excellence in teaching is a central component in my life as an assistant professor. Each day begins with questions: "Do I need to communicate with students today?" "Are any assignments due?" "Have I entered grades for the latest assignment in the digital grade book?" "Should I revise that lecture on diffusion of information?"

I have several e-mails from students today. I do not think I could fulfill my teaching responsibilities without access to e-mail, the Internet, and the excellent teaching software that is available to me. Students at a distance, in particular, need to know that I am here and will respond in a timely fashion. Three of the e-mails are from students at the distance site asking for clarification on the first assignment. This course is about transfer of information in private sector enterprise. I have asked the students to find a newspaper or short journal piece on transfer of information in the private sector enterprise to share in class. I respond and then send out a group e-mail to the entire class further clarifying the assignment. I am learning that a group e-mail can assuage the uncertainty of students at a distance. As soon as I receive two or more queries on the same topic, I usually respond to everyone. I know that if a few students are asking, others are probably uncertain but not asking.

Research

When I feel that my teaching responsibilities are under control, I spend some time thinking about my research. Responsibilities include conducting research in an area of expertise, publishing in appropriate venues, and presenting at conferences. I have just received notification of acceptance of a presentation proposal for a national conference on information management. I need to make progress on writing the actual presentation, which is based on my dissertation research. I am fortunate in that I belong to a writing circle of new faculty, chaired by an experienced full professor with an impressive publishing record. Today, we receive a group e-mail from the chair of the writing circle asking about the progress of each circle member.

I respond to his e-mail and assure everyone that I will be sending a few pages from the presentation after my weekend of teaching. I find that I am able to write more and better when I know that others are counting on me to submit writing in a timely fashion and to offer comments on the writings of other members. I work on that piece for about an hour. Then I remember that we have a faculty meeting after lunch. These meetings are extremely important for several reasons: a chance to talk to our faculty colleagues, an opportunity to hear from the dean, and the likelihood of working on important policy issues for our program.

Service

Service responsibilities include participation on school, university, and professional association committees, as well as participation in other activities that further the development of library and information management. It is also important to attend training sessions offered by our school and the university. We are also expected to attend functions such as general assembly, doctoral proposal and dissertation presentations, and colloquia.

During the faculty meeting today we will be discussing the creation of a new low-performance policy that has been mandated for all departments and schools. I am on the committee that has looked at current standards across campus to compare and revise these standards. The other committee members are not able to attend our meeting today, so I will deliver the report. I set to work reviewing our conclusions and thinking about additional information that faculty may need.

I suddenly realize that I am getting hungry. One of my colleagues stops by to invite me to lunch. We proceed across the street to a sandwich shop. Although our main intent is satisfying our hunger and catching up on news, we find ourselves talking about various issues at school. I am discovering that being a professor means becoming immersed in academia. It is not an eight-hours-a-day endeavor.

After lunch I attend the faculty meeting. We review the agenda, take care of old business, report on committee work, and move on to new business. We hear from a professor who has received a grant to extend our teaching venues to a fourth distance site. We talk about demographics of this group of potential students and ask the following questions: What technology will be needed? Where will the teaching take place? What are the information needs for this population?

We then move on to a planning discussion for a series of colloquia to be held over a six-month period. Our first speaker, one of the designers of our current curriculum, will be arriving in a few weeks. Today we work out the details of transportation and lodging. The rest of the meeting is spent on hearing from faculty who have committee responsibilities on the university level. We adjourn on time. That is fortunate because I am scheduled to attend a workshop on a revised electronic teaching software package.

I am making a real effort to take advantage of these workshops. Sometimes, of course, I am off-site teaching or have a conflicting responsibility. Today's workshop is an introduction to the software; the second part will be taught next week. There will be several other faculty members there. This is a good opportunity to meet some non–library school professors. The workshop goes smoothly and I am back at my desk within one and a half hours.

Service duties take up quite a bit of time. I am a member of several committees. My library school committees include scholarship review committee, progress reviews, technology, and vision and mission statement. It is also important to participate in university-wide committee work. I am a member of the vice president of academic affairs' advisory council and the affirmative action committee. These meetings allow me the opportunity to assist in resolving issues university-wide and of networking with others. I am also a member of a national association committee that will meet early next year.

Now it is midafternoon. After making sure that I have confirmed dates for upcoming meetings, deadlines for reports, and any other university-related obligations, I decide to pick up some scholarship applications in the main office for my scholarship committee work. Each semester three of us review the applications and determine the eligibility of each student and the amount to be awarded. Although this process is somewhat tedious, it gives me a good feeling knowing that I am assisting in facilitating the education process for these students.

I look at the applications, rate each one based on scholarship, need, letters of reference, and completeness of the application. Then I enter my ratings into a table. After one hour I decide I had better complete some small tasks before I leave the school.

I read a report that was e-mailed to me yesterday. I look briefly at an article that has drawn my attention (which I will review at length during the plane trip to my distance teaching site), and then I call my graduate assistant. He is updating my Web pages, and I want to tell him about some new material I would like included on the site. It is time to leave. I feel good about the work I completed today. I am, however, already thinking about all the tasks I need to work on tomorrow.

BECOMING A PROFESSOR

I had thought about the possibility of becoming a professor; it was always a goal for "the future." As I worked my way through the MLIS program, I had occasion to interact with doctoral students at our school. My interest in doctoral studies was piqued by these interactions. After receiving my master's degree, I did some independent consulting work with my advisor (a professor at my school) for the U.S. government. This work was challenging and fun. It was then that I decided to pursue the doctoral program in hopes of gaining the expertise I would need to engage in more of these challenging projects. Along the way, I discovered that I love to teach, and then I decided to enter the academic world. In other words, for me, it was a series of steps that built one on the other, not an overriding desire that drove me throughout my entire academic experience.

Becoming a professor starts long before you may realize that is the road you are taking. I think to be a professor one must have a very curious mindset—that is, the ability to question the world around you. Many people who earn a doctorate in library science do not have a master's in library science. We are a very interdisciplinary group with members from various disciplines such as anthropology, communications, history, education, and the sciences.

I think that sometime during the master's degree process one may begin to look more closely at how the information one needs is organized, how it can be accessed, and, in general, the information transfer process as a whole. If that is the case, one may investigate library science or library studies.

If you are interested in becoming a professor, one way to explore this area is to review Web sites of associations for library educators, such as ALISE. If you are fortunate enough to live near a university that offers a doctorate in library science, you would be well served to visit the school and talk to professors and students there. Advisors at library schools would be happy to discuss the requirements for entering the doctoral programs at these schools.

It is always advisable to gain teaching experience before you enter a doctoral program. These programs vary widely; not all will give you teaching opportunities. If you cannot teach an entire course as a master's student, perhaps you can deliver one lecture or present a poster or short paper at a conference. Any experience will help you begin your university teaching career with more confidence. Of course, your colleagues can usually also offer teaching strategy suggestions.

PROS AND CONS

For me, the pros of being a professor far outweigh the cons. Being a university professor has been one of my long-term goals. Although some of my duties are not particularly challenging, most are exactly what I hoped for. Pros include having intellectual exchanges with colleagues and students, fostering the development of students into practicing professionals, networking with others who share similar research interests at conferences and workshops, and conducting research that may shed light on some of the issues we face.

Cons include the never-ending list of tasks, including the ongoing university, regional, and national association meetings and committee work. Sometimes you may have to teach a course that is not in your area of interest. Grading assignments can be a lengthy, tedious process.

RELATED RESOURCES

Association for Library and Information Science Education (ALISE). www.alise.org (accessed August 24, 2006).

CHAPTER 67

Visiting Instructor at an International University

DALLAS LONG

ANOTHER DAY IN HUNGARY

"*Jo reggelt. Sziasztok*. Good morning," I greet my students as I enter the classroom. They push away their chairs and stand. I motion for them to sit, and they bring out their notebooks, waiting to write down my every word. A few of them smile, but most are nervous. This morning's class is Business Information Resources, which is a fourth-year course. The fourth-year students are among the last to move through the system of education that the Hungarians endured under Soviet administration. Consequently, their English isn't good, and many struggle to understand my lecture and to express their questions. My Hungarian isn't good either, so I rely on the advanced students to translate. Sometimes I answer in German, which the students understand better.

This morning I'm feeling more confident about lecturing because my Hungarian has improved tremendously now that I'm nearing the end of my second year. The students understand English better, too. Nonetheless I'm wishing I were teaching my afternoon course, which is with first-year students. The first-year students were the first Hungarians to receive a more Western style of education after the fall of communism here, and their English is vastly better. They are also more relaxed, slouching at their desks and joking with each other and with me. They ask a lot of questions, and our discussions are lively. The fourth-year students tend to repeat what I've said in previous lectures and look confused when I try to engage the class in discussion.

I'm a visiting instructor at Berzsenyi Daniel College in southern Hungary. I teach undergraduates because library science is a baccalaureate degree here. I'm offering courses in business information and digital libraries because the Hungarian professors decided that an American librarian knows considerably more about business and technology. My students can find work in public libraries and institutions of higher learning after they graduate, but Hungarian library schools are trying hard to train their graduates for careers in Eastern Europe's emerging markets as information managers, analysts, and information scientists. The older professors don't have this business or technical training or experience.

I was an information specialist with a pharmaceutical company before I entered library school. I conducted competitive intelligence, researching rival pharmaceutical companies by using electronic databases like Dialog and Factiva. I scoured press releases, sales data, proprietary databases, rumors posted on online message boards, annual reports, and filings with the U.S. Securities and Exchange Commission. Then I presented my company's executives with reports so they could decide how to lead our business or leverage an advantage against a rival.

Today my students are doing the same tasks. They're charged with discovering everything they can about a company of their choice using electronic databases and Web sites, and then presenting it in a format usable by a business professional. They're learning to search Dialog and Factiva, which is challenging. The searching isn't difficult for the students—we've already covered Boolean operators and strategies to expand or narrow a search. However, I'm clarifying a lot of questions caused by the barrier of searching an English language database—explaining the concept of a "product mix," helping a student find an appropriate synonym for a search term, and soothing a girl's frustration when she misspells search terms and doesn't understand why she receives no results.

A FEW DAILY SURPRISES AND CHALLENGES

Bzzzt! The lights flicker briefly, and the computers wink out. All the students' work is lost. The electricity has failed again. The students groan. Silently I groan with them. How can I teach with no electricity to power my electronic databases? Teaching without electricity is a frequent occurrence—the power fails at least once a day. Sometimes we experience brief intervals; sometimes we lose great chunks of class time.

I keep the students focused and immediately use the time to spark a discussion on controlled vocabulary—were they having trouble finding information because the English words or phrases they were taught by their UK-educated English teachers weren't necessarily the words or phrases used as keywords in American databases? Yes, a few of the students note that they had to allow for differences in spelling (i.e., *color* or *colour*). "Isn't it enough to speak Hungarian?" says one young woman, humorously but not without a touch of anxiety.

I'm hoping the electricity will return, and I watch the students review the notes they copied from the articles they retrieved online. They would have printed out what they found, but we don't have paper for the printers. The students copy everything in their notebooks, and I print handouts and syllabi on the backs of old, discarded handouts.

The electricity doesn't come back on until after the class has concluded. The students depart noisily, and I pray that I'll have power in two hours when I teach Digital Libraries.

In the meantime, I leave campus to walk to the train station. I'm going to buy a railway ticket to Budapest for the weekend. I'm offering a continuing education course at the National Szechenyi Library two weekends each month. Practicing librarians across Hungary come together to practice their English with me. They're very interested in learning the English words for library terminology so they can converse with vendors and participate in library conferences. Of course, not only do they have to learn the vocabulary, they have to learn how to communicate with each other in conversations and through written exercises. So not only am I learning how to teach library and information science, I'm finding myself an English teacher as well!

I'm also developing a course called Special English for Librarians and Information Managers, which offers instruction to first- and third-year students in the English vocabulary of library terminology. The students learn all the vocabulary and jargon associated with public services and technical services and the library field. I'm not really an English teacher, so I'm collaborating with an Irish woman who teaches English at a university in neighboring Austria. She's helping me develop the exercises that improve their English ability while I concentrate on the library content. I find this to be a lot of fun, and I wish I could remain in Hungary to see the course established as part of the regular curriculum. Currently a pilot program is being introduced to the first-year students who have had advanced English in their secondary schools.

After I buy the ticket, I return to campus. I head toward the dormitory, where I live in a private room, but right now I'm going to the small library that is housed there. I describe it as a public library for students—a small collection of Hungarian literature, popular reading, newspapers, magazines, and CDs. The college is essentially a teacher training institute, and many of the students are studying to be foreign language teachers. However, the library lacks a significant collection of English-language works and the students have little opportunity to practice their language skills outside the classroom. I'm working ten hours a week with the librarians, identifying magazines and popular literature the students can use to sharpen their command of English. I'm writing to family and friends to ship copies of classic literature so we have numerous copies of the materials they study in the English curriculum. (The college has no bookstore, and students have to travel three hours by train to Budapest to find bookstores that carry English-language novels.) I catalog most of the materials, too.

HOW DID I GET HERE?

I never thought I'd find myself working at a small college in Eastern Europe. My colleagues treat me with respect. My American library degree affords me credibility—I'm skilled at working with technology but also with business sources. I'm experienced at answering reference questions, a skill that is relatively new to Hungarian librarianship. The communists didn't encourage the pursuit of knowledge by the workers, and libraries were little more than depositories for government documents and cultural artifacts. Librarians were trained as catalogers and are only now adopting customer service, reader's advisory, reference, and information literacy into their skill set. But I have a more highly prized skill: I am a native speaker of English. That, more than anything, is what secured my job offer.

When I was finishing my library degree at the University of Illinois, I decided it was a good time to pursue my dream of living in Europe. I asked my professors if they knew of colleagues who could host an American librarian for a year. They wrote letters of introduction on my behalf, and I included my résumé and highlighted the skills I'd developed working at a public library for two years and a corporate library for one year.

I received two responses: Warsaw University, who wanted an American to edit their English-language library science journal, and Berzsenyi Daniel College, who wanted a visiting instructor. I was surprised—me, without a doctorate, a teacher? However, Hungary requires only a baccalaureate degree to qualify as a librarian. With a master's degree, I was fully qualified to be a member of the faculty. Unfortunately, the college couldn't afford to pay my travel and living expenses.

Currently the U.S. State Department, under the auspices of the Fulbright Program, funds my stay in Hungary. I thought their financial support would be a long shot, but I applied and was surprised to receive an award letter six months later. One of the program advisors informed me that they wished more librarians would apply for Fulbright grants. They are trying to award grants to people from disciplines other than the traditional fields of political science, law, medicine, and history. The money isn't very much by American standards, but it is more than enough by Hungarian standards.

AND NOW IT'S TIME TO SAY GOODBYE

I'm eager to return to the United States, however. I've accomplished my dream of working overseas, but now I am starting to think fondly about hot showers, laundry that I won't have to wash by hand, and not choking with cigarette smoke whenever I enter a coffeehouse. I'm the lone American and one of the few foreigners living in Szombathely. Everyone knows me—I can't enter a shop without a clerk nodding to me with a murmur of "That's the American man!" I've learned a lot about Hungarian culture as well as about the Hungarian character. I've made many friends, celebrated their holidays, and shared their sorrows over past atrocities committed by Ottoman Turks, Nazis, and Soviets. I partied when Hungary joined the European Union in May 2004. I've learned to drink their vile, brown, herbal liqueur, and I'm not sure how I survived for so long without powerful shots of espresso and cups of steaming mulled wine in the winter.

I'm not renewing my grant with the U.S. Department of State. I've refused an offer for a six-month assignment at Kabul University in Afghanistan and from a women's college in Polynesia. After many spotty transatlantic phone calls with search committees and an expensive flight for a jet-lagged interview, I am delighted to report that I've accepted a library management position with the University of Illinois at Urbana-Champaign. My new supervisor remarked that my experience in Hungary caught their attention; my willingness to move overseas and immerse myself in another culture proved to them that I'm a risk taker and that I'm very comfortable with unfamiliar situations. I will miss Hungary and the friends I've made here, but I know that new adventures await me back in central Illinois.

PART VII

Library Vendors

CHAPTER 68

Director of Sales for North America

DENA SCHOEN

As director of sales for North America for Harrassowitz, a German company founded in 1872, I head a team of three people who visit all our North American book and subscriptions customers. The territory covers both the United States and Canada, with our primary customers being academic and research libraries. Because 88 percent of the company's business is in North America, this is a hefty assignment, especially as Harrassowitz is now the third largest agent on the continent. I train and supervise my two colleagues in all facets of the job: customer service by e-mail, phone, and site visits; sales presentations; and representation at industry conferences. Extensive travel is involved, and the position requires superlative communication and presentation skills, full knowledge of the book and serial trade (as well as knowledge of music scores), command of library collection development and technical services practices, and the ability to convey North American library culture to the Europe-based management and staff. I also have my own territory to cover, and I work with management on crafting responses to RFPs (requests for proposals). My colleagues and I are dispersed throughout the country, so I have to manage my team and communicate with headquarters from my home office.

MY TYPICAL WORKDAY: HOME ON THE RANGE OR ON THE ROAD AGAIN

I have two types of workdays, and that is one of the many great things about my job. When I'm not visiting libraries and am off the road, I work at home. No commute, no cubicle, and no boss watching over me—I just turn on my laptop and start my day. But it is long, hard, constant work covering numerous time zones, so I can't really be a couch potato, even if I am on my couch. First I'll read reams of e-mail from headquarters in Germany and call the managing director to discuss any crises, pending RFP submissions, or sales strategies.

As the morning wanes, North American customers also begin to contact me. This will be the first wave of customers in my time zone. The ones from California and even Hawaii will come in about the time I'm ready to have a glass of wine before dinner (and believe me, I do, and I think it enhances customer service!). The messages, to be quite honest, range from the ridiculous to the sublime, from petty to profound, from disheartening to totally invigorating. The invigorating ones are the grateful letters thanking me for my "excellent service" and telling me I am "the best rep they've ever seen in the library" (salespeople need ego boosts on a daily basis, and we get paranoid easily when we work at home). My favorite e-mail is when I learn that we have won new business. After all, this is the shameless commerce sector of our industry, and our raison d'être as salespeople is to sell. But the quotidian reality is that many of the e-mails involve submitting claims for missing items, setting up a username and password for one of our databases, forwarding an expense report to headquarters, or reading e-mail lists and sending out about a zillion FYIs to colleagues. Do not consider this job if you do not like being online and have no potential for becoming an e-mail junkie.

A significant portion of my time online is spent setting up itineraries for site visits. This is not easy, because not everybody likes to be visited by vendors and everyone's schedules are amazingly busy. I'll write to a key customer and cross my fingers that she will write back to confirm a date and time. As soon as that's done, I can contact other libraries in that area and lock in a week's worth of visits. I then outsource travel arrangements to an agent and happily pay a service charge for efficiency's sake. (If only my customers were as open to service charges for *my* company's services, but I digress.) Then I surf over to Mapquest, my new best friend, to print out driving directions. University and college Web sites also have driving directions, which I use regularly. One wonders what my vendor ancestors did before the Internet.

I might spend a week or two off the road having days like the one I just described. And then the road trip begins! If you think constant travel is exciting, think again, since it's become pretty onerous in our post-9/11 environment. Schlepping around with a laptop and having to put it through security (along with one's shoes) a zillion times a year is pure drudgery, not to mention a sobering reminder of how our world has changed. But no matter how exhausted or stressed I might be, the adrenaline rush begins when I walk into a library to start my real work: schmoozing. If you like to engage with people, this is a job for you! I meet with a variety of library staff, from directors right on down to clerks.

Every facet of this is interesting, even when it is boring. Why do I say that? Because I have learned so much about libraries by experiencing them in all their uniqueness and monotony. I'll answer the same questions for weeks on end, but it is incredibly fulfilling to realize how much information I have assimilated since I crossed over from librarianship to the so-called dark side. Often I get up in front of a fairly large group of people to do a full-blown sales presentation. This requires a complete mastery of our company, industry norms and trends, the ability to teach, and a knack for nimble thinking. It also requires that you learn how to say "no, we cannot do that" and that you develop a thick skin when criticism is slung your way. It takes some measure of humor, so if you have a comedic streak like I do, this is a great job for you. I also have to balance the laughs with diplomacy. This job has changed me as a person irrevocably, because my career trajectory from librarian to vendor has proved to be the quintessential growth experience.

After caroming from library to library (maybe three a day), I'll go to my hotel and catch up on e-mail. I might even write my travel report right then and not put it off until I'm off the road. This will go on for a week or more until it's time to go home.

PROS AND CONS

I'll never regret having decided to become a vendor, though there are many days when I want to bail out of the industry altogether and become a professional dog walker, talk show host, or teacher. (After all, the grass is always greener …) But as a vendor, you can only strive for excellence, or you'll fail to represent your company successfully, keep your unbelievably demanding customers happy, and win sales. I've never worked so hard in my life, but I've never learned so much either. You have to be somewhat of an autodidact, but it really pays off. Library school didn't prepare me for any of this, I can tell you that. You have to soak up information like a sponge and synthesize quickly. You have to know your own company thoroughly, as well as knowing the wider industry and libraries. I have learned about collection management, library technology, software companies, publishers (oops, "content providers"), contracts, and business-to-business relations. I have also learned more about people and my country than I ever expected during a time when our culture is changing rapidly. I've traveled everywhere and learned to relate to people completely different from me and it's made me a more tolerant person. I've learned about poverty and privilege as I've watched the service class throughout the airports and hotels of the land cater to the needs of us spoiled business travelers. As a former educator, I've learned incredible lessons about higher education as I've visited more colleges and universities than I knew existed.

But every job has its downside. Long stretches of solitude can really get to you. Travel, as I said, can be a total drag. You cannot imagine how tedious it is to listen to other people's cell phone conversations on a plane, especially the ones that should be kept private, please! (No, I don't want to hear the details of your doctor's appointment, thank you very much.) Going to conferences and having booth duty gets old really fast, and every convention center looks alike. Sometimes I feel completely rootless, unable to have a personal life and connect to my community because I leave home so much. If you have young children, forget about this job. I only have two fox terriers, but it's painful to leave them so often. Did I mention having a partner or spouse? Not easy.

Then there is the really big one: vendors versus librarians and vendors versus vendors. Librarians usually do not understand or like the commercial side of the information industry. The level of antipathy is amazing, and as budgets shrink and the competition gets fierce, things can be pretty unpleasant. Very few librarians understand that service comes at a price. They think we make a lot of money, but we don't, especially when compared to certain behemoth scientific, technical, and medical publishers and software companies. Often, nobody wants you to visit them, but it's in your job description to visit them! And if you don't visit, they'll complain that you don't care about them. Sometimes you even get stood up, which is pretty bad when you're far from home, not to mention that they've just cost your company money even as they complain about rising costs. If you don't follow up with customers right away, they will complain and move the business to a competitor, but sometimes they don't answer your e-mail for weeks or never answer at all. You have to hold your head up high and do your job well, and for me this challenge has been valuable. If you are outspoken at conferences (which I am) and if you have novel ideas and convictions, you can get into trouble. You can take blows, but learning to take them, as I have, has been part of the beauty of this job. Beyond this threat of ego insecurity, there is also job insecurity. This is the commercial sector, not academia: no tenure.

WANT A JOB LIKE MINE?

If you want a job like this one, pay your dues. Work in a library and diversify by taking both technical services and collection development positions. Learn about all formats, digital and print, and emerging technologies. Get into the position of interacting with vendors—they might recruit you (one of mine did). Do presentations at conferences and be on panels with vendors. Visit vendor exhibits at conferences and try to meet the sales managers of the companies that interest you. Watch the ads in trade publications.

CHAPTER 69

Sales Coordinator for International and Special Markets

ANN SNOEYENBOS

My job is to represent Project MUSE in the library communities outside North America and in nonacademic library markets in the United States. I exhibit at trade shows and attend library conferences around the world to make contact with specific library markets and identify sales opportunities for the Project MUSE journal collections. I work with librarians, consortium leaders, and subscription agents. In brief, my job is to be "the face of Project MUSE" in my market segments to increase visibility and distribution of our journals.

I attend both library conferences and academic publishing conferences so that I can continue to learn about the publishing industry and stay connected to the library community at the same time. Talking with both library and publishing colleagues helps me analyze the potential for Project MUSE in new markets such as special libraries, high schools, music conservatories, and public libraries, to name just a few. When I'm in the office I work with my colleagues to create materials that will help us reach new markets and retain existing subscribers.

The Johns Hopkins University Press (JHUP) manages Project MUSE, so I am employed by JHUP, and I enjoy the benefits of working at Johns Hopkins University. Project MUSE is a collaboration of more than sixty not-for-profit publishers and the university's Milton S. Eisenhower Library. MUSE offers online journal collections in the humanities and social sciences.

A TYPICAL WORKDAY

I really have two typical workdays because I have one set of activities when I'm in the Project MUSE office in Baltimore, and another very different set of activities when I'm on the road for a conference or trade show.

In the Office

When I'm in the office I spend most of the day reading and responding to e-mail. Project MUSE has a small staff of fewer than 25 people, and JHUP employs about 125 employees in total. I only interact with four to five coworkers on a regular basis, so it is easy to have impromptu chats when needed, and we don't schedule formal meetings very often. I like the agility that comes with being part of a small staff because when something is important we can move from concept to implementation very quickly. This agility reflects the Internet startup mentality that allowed Project MUSE to succeed and thrive during its early years. My boss and I constitute the entire Sales and Marketing Department, so I have been given a lot of autonomy simply out of necessity. I like not having to participate in a lot of meetings, but it can also feel lonely because I see so few people in a typical day at the office. MUSE employees are a distinct subset of JHUP. To generalize a bit, we are younger, mostly single with no kids, and most of us work 10 a.m. to 6 p.m. as opposed to the 8 a.m. to 4 p.m. schedule that is common in the Books Division.

My typical day in the office revolves around e-mail. I divide my e-mail activities into three main categories: customer service, requests for pricing and the management of agent relationships, and product development.

Customer service includes answering questions about the license, usage statistics, trials and subscriptions, and setting up linkages between MUSE and other products. Because I often get messages from people who aren't native speakers of English, I need to be able to read between the lines to understand what the person is really asking. I consider myself an advocate for the customer, but I must always keep in mind that we are a small staff, so special requests can easily become burdensome. Because we serve a clientele that is increasingly from outside North America, I try to come up with ways we can refine our Web site and the printed materials we distribute to meet the needs of our new audiences. Some of the refinements have to do with language and cultural concerns, and some have to do with the way we invoice and receive payments.

Requests for pricing usually come in through a Web form. Either an institution or a subscription agent acting on behalf of an institution submits the request, and I respond to the ones from my market segments. U.S. pricing is made public on our Web site, but the international pricing is not on the site because it is tiered and the pricing model is more complicated. Pricing questions can be quick to answer because I look at the institution's Web site and then check a price list. Sometimes, though, the institution doesn't fit our classification scheme or the Web site is in a language I can't read. Then I do a little basic research to find out about the educational system in that country. For a complex consortium request, I use my reference skills to find out about the political and economic context, trends in library funding, and similar information for that country. It is great to be part of a university because I have access to all the online resources offered by the Johns Hopkins libraries.

Cultivating relationships with subscription agents is something I work on both in the office and at trade shows. Subscription agents play a vital role in my work because of language and cultural issues, and also because of library purchasing regulations; in some countries libraries can't make payments to vendors outside the country. Subscription agents provide me with information on the local market for MUSE and they let me know whether my product meets local needs. I have been surprised by the need for face-to-face meetings with libraries and subscription agents to facilitate sales. The way I understand it is that I sell a high-cost intangible product. In many countries Project MUSE is not a recognized brand, so I need to build the trust of both agents and librarians. I need to trust that the agent will represent us accurately to libraries and that they will pay the invoices on time. The librarians and agents need to trust that if they send me money I will provide the promised journal access. In selling e-journals, the old-fashioned handshake and eye contact are far more important than I imagined they would be. Once we've had the initial face-to-face meeting, then we can work easily for a long time by e-mail and fax without additional meetings.

Product development constitutes the third category of work that I do in the office. In libraries this type of issue is most often discussed in committee meetings, but because we don't all work the same schedule and the MUSE team is split between two floors, we discuss a lot of issues by e-mail. Product development includes discussions about content to be added in the future, functionality upgrades, links with other products, new materials to add to the Web site or to have printed, and so on. For particularly complex issues we have face-to-face meetings that are supplemented by e-mail discussion.

Only a few of my projects are long-term. For those, I do research on my own and check in periodically with my boss. We sometimes bring in outside companies when we need expertise we don't have in-house. Most often we work with an advertising agency, but we have also brought in market research firms, publisher's agents, and the like.

When I want to take a break from the endless flow of e-mails, I always have work trips to prepare for. I spend quite a bit of time checking airfares, researching and booking hotel rooms, and scheduling meetings. I enjoy these activities because it feels like goofing off even though it isn't!

On the Road

When I'm not in the office, I am either in transit (I spend a lot of time in airports) or working from the Project MUSE booth at a trade show. The spring and early summer are when I am busiest traveling to library conferences; in the fall I go to publishing industry trade shows. Last year I exhibited at twelve trade shows and attended two conferences for my own professional development. With that much travel it can be hard to schedule vacation time, but vacation is a necessity because international trips and trade shows require a lot of mental energy and can be very draining.

You can probably imagine what the travel part is like: laundry, packing, airports, hotel rooms, unpacking, setting up and tearing down the booth, repacking, and home again to do more laundry. As soon as I'm back from a trip, I need to catch up on things that happened while I was away, prepare my expense reports, and follow up on the meetings I had while I was away.

Trade shows can take place over several days as part of a library conference, as with the American Library Association's Annual Conference and Midwinter Meeting, or they can be a single-day vendor fair, as with OCLC's regional networks. Some trade shows are stand-alone events, like the Frankfurt Book Fair, where the exhibits are the main draw and the programs and speakers are a minor attraction.

When I work a multiday trade show, I set up my exhibit space the day before the show opens to the public. For a one-day event I set my booth up one to two hours before the attendees are allowed in. During the build-up phase of a multiday trade show it's amazing to watch a big warehouse full of forklifts and wooden crates be transformed into a carpeted and well-lit space that is inviting to visitors.

Setting up the MUSE booth is not complicated because I have learned to use things that I can bring in my luggage. My job description said that I should be able to lift forty pounds because of the booth materials. Boxes of printed handouts are heavy! The most stressful part of booth setup is testing the Internet connection. When the Internet connection is bad, it can make the whole show difficult. I like having portable booth materials, but it does mean that I have to weigh my luggage before I leave home and before my return flight to avoid excess weight charges.

During the exhibit hours I take appointments, most of which I've arranged in advance. I also enjoy talking to anybody who comes to the booth to find out what's new. At some trade shows I talk with subscription agents about how to sell our journal collections in their country and what I might do to help them with that. My personal interests do not really lean toward the financial side of these arrangements, but I like to make a good match between the MUSE journals and the needs of the institution.

PROS AND CONS

In many ways this type of sales work is a lot like working the reference desk. People bring you questions, and you answer what you can right away, then work to find answers to the rest. The most enlightening part of my work so far has been to see just how similar libraries and librarians are all around the world. We all have budget concerns and we all have demanding patrons.

There are a few negative aspects to the travel and trade show circuit. It is fatiguing to be on my feet all day in a ten-foot-by-ten-foot booth. I get dehydrated from the processed air, and it can be hard to find healthy food in exhibit halls. It can be lonely to be on my own in a new city, although I am making friends among the community of international salespeople who exhibit at the same trade shows I do. It is hard to maintain a consistent exercise regimen when I change locales and time zones frequently.

HOW WOULD YOU FIND A JOB LIKE MINE?

If you would like to find a job like mine, you should have a solid background in libraries. I find that my reference, liaison, and collection development experience serves me well, although I really wish I knew more about serials acquisitions or acquisitions work in general.

You should also refresh your foreign language skills. These are extremely useful but not always required. You must have excellent written communication skills; my job is probably 70 percent written (e-mail) and 30 percent face-to-face communication.

You need to be patient and resilient. All kinds of things can go wrong when you travel, and you need to maintain grace under pressure and be able to think on your feet.

You should have some physical strength and a strong constitution. I have logged six or more miles in one day at a trade show, which directly contrasts to sitting for six to twelve hours at a time on an airplane.

Vendor jobs for librarians are often posted on Libjobs.com, on the *Chronicle of Higher Education* Web site, and on other library discussion lists. They are also posted to publishers' Web sites and to publishing association job banks.

RELATED RESOURCES

Association of Learned and Professional Society Publishers (UK). www.alpsp.org (accessed March 1, 2006).
Society for Scholarly Publishing (SSP). www.sspnet.org (accessed March 1, 2006).

CHAPTER 70

Training Resources Manager

JULIE HARWELL

My two roles as training resources manager of EBSCO Industries are to fulfill the duties of a training specialist and serve as the leader of our four-member team. Most of our work within Training Resources is to provide training to customers and colleagues on products and services provided by EBSCO Information Services, which is one of a few dozen companies that comprise EBSCO Industries. EBSCO Information Services sells research databases, an A-to-Z service, an OpenURL-compliant link resolver, an e-journals gateway, and an e-commerce book/journal procurement service; it also provides a subscription management system to customers of our subscription service. Many of these products have an end user or patron site and an administrative site used by librarians to customize or manage the end user site.

Most of the training we provide is via Web conferencing. After reviewing a schedule of classes and registering via our Web site, customers receive an e-mail confirmation that includes several hyperlinks, including one to prepare the computer that will be used for the training and another to join the session up to ten minutes prior to the scheduled start time.

Just as an instruction librarian or bibliographic instruction coordinator within an academic library does not lead classes every day, nor does a training specialist. In addition to training, I want to share some of the tasks that keep me busy between sessions, the pros and cons of my job, and how an interested librarian might go about getting a job like mine.

TASKS

My job as a trainer draws on my experience as a reference librarian—I help our customers understand a specific product or feature and how to use it based on their specific needs. I also help my colleagues that sell or support a product understand it—to make sure they do not over- or undersell a product.

We sometimes train our customers and colleagues via on-site training, but we mostly use a Web conferencing service. As manager of training resources, I coordinated a request for proposal (RFP) to investigate various Web conferencing providers and negotiate our contract. All of the training we provide is complimentary because we consider it a value-added service; in other words, it's an incentive for using us as your subscription agent. The phrase "serials agents" or "subscription agents" refers to the vendors that libraries often use to facilitate the management of magazines, journals, and newspapers.

As a manager, I ensure that the training sessions we offer serve the needs of our customers; this includes the content of the training and the frequency. We offer training sessions at various times to attempt to accommodate customers in different time zones around the world. We also remain flexible when scheduling dates and times to train in-house colleagues who are sales representatives or account services managers because their primary responsibility is serving customers. When major enhancements or new products become available, we routinely offer sessions over the weekend and in the evenings.

Although Web conferencing offers a video streaming component, this feature is problematic because it often delays transmission and prevents a seamless experience for all attendees. Therefore, we rarely see the people we train and instead look forward to putting faces with names when we meet attendees at conferences. Library Basics, a course for EBSCO employees who do not have a library background, is a session we hold regularly that follows a more traditional classroom experience. All of my training specialist colleagues enjoy connecting to an audience in this setting, and we also look forward to this class because it provides an opportunity to highlight the importance of supporting local public libraries and educating people about our state's virtual library.

One task that I enjoy most is product development and testing. This brings all of a training specialist's collaboration skills and experience as a librarian together with our various stakeholders: on-site colleagues, external EBSCO colleagues, and customers. On-site colleagues at our international headquarters in Birmingham, Alabama, include developers or programmers, software quality assurance testers, customer care or help desk associates, technical writers who write online help screens, and creators of marketing materials. External colleagues include sales representatives, account service managers, e-resource specialists, customer service representatives, and training liaisons within our thirty-two offices operating in twenty countries on every continent except, of course, Antarctica. Participation in product development includes involvement in requirements documents, usability reviews, and alpha testing.

When I worked in interlibrary loan, one of the things I loved about it was how it brought so many pieces of the library together. When an item is requested via interlibrary loan, it reflects on the library as a whole, beginning with collection development. And if an item is held locally, what part of cataloging, inventory control, or reference impeded its discovery? One of the things I love about my job is how it brings many people together; a training specialist does not simply specialize in education but collaboration, bringing people together with diverse viewpoints and backgrounds to facilitate better understanding and knowledge of a common interest or need.

I know that no matter how many training sessions my colleagues and I offer each month, someone will still need on-demand training, so we have created how-to demonstrations that are available from online help screens to serve as just-in-time training. Training Resources creates the content of these demonstrations, and our colleagues in marketing create the finished piece in Adobe Flash. To facilitate the recording of the voiceover portion of an audiovisual demonstration, we create scripts that are distributed to training liaisons at our regional offices outside the United States. These scripts and other training materials we send to the training liaisons facilitate the support of our customers in their native languages and local time zones.

As another example of our collaboration as librarians, we are on call to assist User Services Web Support and EAMS Customer Care when they have a question about a complex library-related inquiry. In other words, if a customer references an unknown term or workflow process, we are one of the resources Customer Care and User Services can call on. Finally, a fair amount of our time is taken up with maintaining our skills as librarians—committee work; association and conference commitments; review of professional literature, Web sites, and blogs; as well as the deluge of e-mails from discussion lists.

I encounter some special issues in my job because I am a trainer not just for EBSCO Information Services. Remember I said that I am a trainer for EBSCO Industries, which is comprised of a few dozen diverse companies, including PRADCO, the largest manufacturer of fishing lures in the world; several manufacturing companies; and a real estate division. So do I get to train people on how to use fishing lures or other manufactured products? No, but I am called on to learn some of the workflow tools our various subsidiaries use, such as a point of sale (POS) system. A POS is used to enter a credit card transaction, and I train our subsidiaries on how to use a Web-based POS system so they can accept credit card orders for their products. Training specialists also work with our colleagues within EBSCO Information Services and other divisions, like PRADCO, on the use of Web conferencing to facilitate collaboration with customers.

PROS AND CONS

One atypical benefit of working at EBSCO compared to a traditional library setting is how supportive the company is of our continued professional development. We are actively encouraged to attend and contribute to conferences and given adequate support to meet our professional goals. We don't have to vie with one another to attend conferences, nor do we have to share a room with five people just to be able to attend. We do not have a blank check to attend any conference we want, but on average, each training specialist attends two conferences each year plus other professional development workshops and standard skills training in office applications.

How does working for a vendor differ from working in a traditional library? When Katy Ginanni, a librarian who hired me, began working at EBSCO more than thirteen years ago and met Lynn Fortney, MLS, vice president and Biomedical Division director, Lynn asked about her background. Katy began, "When I was a librarian ..." and Lynn immediately reminded her, "You are still a librarian; you just don't work in a traditional library." I think that's the best advice I can share—no matter what job you take, you will always be a librarian.

So, then, what is the downside of being a librarian working in a nontraditional library setting? For me, there are two things. One is that not all of our librarian colleagues think the way Lynn does. At conferences, on discussion lists, and on committees, when people read my name tag they see my employer first. Some people assume I have an agenda to sell, sell, sell EBSCO. I am proud to be a part of our organization, and I believe in what we do. However, when I offer opinions at a conference or as part of a committee, I do so as a librarian. When I am at an EBSCO function, when I'm working at our booth at conferences, or when I am asked about EBSCO, I provide information on and represent the company. It is a distinction that few people can accept unless they have worked for a vendor or who have close friends who work for a vendor.

The second issue or downside is that I do miss helping patrons discover how a library empowers them. I still have patrons that I enjoy serving, but there is a different feeling to reaching a patron who is discovering a library for the first time or maybe rediscovering what a modern library is. When schedule constraints prevent me from recapturing this feeling by volunteering at my local public library, I am lucky that I can still experience it through the stories my husband shares from his job as a librarian in a local university. In the end, my job is still rewarding because I am helping my patrons or customers discover the tools available to them and providing information to help them make informed decisions or do their job.

HOW TO BECOME A TRAINER

Significant library experience or an MLS/MLIS is required to be a training specialist; at the time of this writing, all of our trainers are librarians who together have more than thirty-six years of library experience. Some other requirements for my team are experience in development and production of training or instructional materials and strong writing and presentation skills. Although we don't have to be techies or able to quote a NISO standard, we do have to converse comfortably about standards—their role within the industry, what in the world does EDI mean, and what EDI services are available with EBSCO, and so on. We have annual personnel reviews like most organizations, and we evaluate our training services via a Web form that is displayed after each session.

If I were to leave this job, I would recommend that in addition to the skills required of a training specialist, my replacement should have at least three years of management experience, extensive project management skills, including coordination of RFPs, and a true dedication to working in a team environment.

"Team building" and "a team environment" are easy catchphrases, and everyone always says that they want to work as part of a team. True teamwork, however, is some of the most challenging, complex work that exists. Teamwork means sacrifice and selflessness. My best preparation for team building came early in my life via concert and marching band, where our band director routinely drilled into us that we were only as strong as our weakest member, a paraphrase of a quote by William James. There is wisdom in this paraphrase and the original quote: "A chain is no stronger than its weakest link, and life is after all a chain." Some might feel this principle isolates someone who is struggling and targets him or her for removal, but that is not my view. In band and in my life, I see it as the responsibility of a group, community, and country to look out for those that need assistance and not simply serve as a figurehead of a leader but actively seek out ways to empower individuals and help them realize their potential. This is an ongoing process for everyone in a group because every person has areas or skills that can be improved. Teamwork is rarely easy, even after years of working with colleagues and knowing how they think and approach projects. But I have found that my proudest and most meaningful accomplishments are actually the result of group effort. As John Donne wrote far more eloquently, "No man is an island entire of itself; every man is a piece of the Continent, a part of the main."

RELATED RESOURCES

EBSCO Training Resources. training.ebsco.com (accessed February 11, 2006).

CHAPTER 71

Cataloger

BRYAN BALDUS

As a cataloger at Quality Books Inc. (QBI), in Oregon, Illinois, I create full-level MARC 21 records to describe and provide access to the books, video recordings (VHS and DVD), sound recordings, and CD-ROMs carried by QBI. I also create prepublication Publisher's Cataloging-in-Publication (P-CIP) blocks and assist in maintaining the company's database of MARC records. In addition, I recently did some MARC-related programming for customization of records and generation of labels for processing.

A TYPICAL WORKDAY

QBI sells books, video recordings, and a few sound recordings and electronic resources, to libraries across the United States and Canada. The company deals mainly with small/independent presses. Currently, we provide full-level MARC 21 records, based on AACR2 and Library of Congress (LC) practice, with Dewey Decimal (both twenty-second full edition and fourteenth abridged edition) and LC classifications, and LC Subject Headings (LCSH) (as well as Sears subject headings if libraries request it) for all of our books. We also provide publishers with P-CIP as a service to those who are unable or unwilling to receive Cataloging-in-Publication data from the LC CIP program.

On a typical day, my first task is to catch up on any e-mail that has come in, including scanning messages from the electronic discussion lists I monitor: AUTOCAT, PUBLIB, OCLC-CAT, OLAC-L, MLA-L, and two lists for publishers and authors.

After I check my e-mail, the majority of the rest of my day is devoted to cataloging. For each set of books or videos on an order for a library, our first task is to search for an existing record in the LC database. If successful, we save the record to a disk. If not, we create an original record, often based on an existing record in QBI's database or in LC's catalog. We occasionally look at records in OCLC or RLIN to aid in creating the original record. Our goal is to generate records as close to LC's quality as possible and to use LC's records (whenever available) as a basis for ours. After searching for records for the order, I move to a second cataloging program in which I edit or create a record for each item, print the finished edit sheet, and place it in the item. During the cataloging process, I do any necessary authority work, which involves searching the authority file for an existing heading and resolving any conflicts that might exist. This occasionally involves contacting publishers or authors via e-mail or phone, attempting to obtain a middle initial, full middle name, or date of birth so that a unique name heading may be established.

After finishing all of the records, I run them through a Perl script to check for common coding errors, and then I turn in the set of items for proofreading. The proofreader marks necessary corrections on the edit sheets, and at the same time adds information such as LC and Dewey classification numbers to QBI's inventory control database. When the proofreading is complete, I make the corrections and add a workmark to a field in the record indicating that it has been proofed. I then upload the records to a database linked to the company's inventory control software, as well as to our cataloging software's database, and return the materials to the proofreader to look over the edit sheets a final time to make sure nothing obvious was missed the first time.

In addition to the cataloging related to our customers' purchases, we also provide P-CIP for authors and publishers. When we initiated this process, we offered a choice of ten-, thirty-, or sixty-day turnaround, depending on their needs. Now this is done on a first-come, first-served basis, with a timeframe based on how busy we are with orders from our library customers. We moved to a Web form P-CIP submission and e-mail delivery process in 2004, hoping to speed up the process. In 2005, we hired an off-site cataloger to assist with P-CIP records and other cataloging tasks that don't require access to the physical item.

Although most of my time is devoted to producing MARC records, I also assist in training. QBI currently has two MLS-degreed catalogers and one paraprofessional copy cataloger. We anticipate hiring an additional degreed cataloger in the future. All of the records we produce are examined by one of the catalogers before being uploaded. This is to ensure that the headings are established in the authority file and that the subject headings and classification are appropriate.

Each week, QBI holds a title selection committee meeting. Membership on the committee currently includes QBI's general manager, two people from the publisher relations department, the head cataloger, and me. During the meeting, we go through each of the books, videos, or other materials publishers have submitted for selection and vote on whether to take them in for distribution. When we reject a title, we have to give a reason, such as poor binding, too many titles on that subject already, personal stories (i.e., autobiographies), fiction (we accept children's fiction but not usually general novels or poetry), among other reasons.

In 2003, QBI changed inventory management systems, from an old DOS-based system to a modern, relational database-based system. This required a change in the way the MARC records were stored to be extracted as needed for customer orders. During the development of the new MARC database, I undertook a database cleanup project, as QBI was looking into a partnership with OCLC to upload our records to WorldCat. As part of the cleanup project, I began teaching myself Perl programming and wrote some programs to look for MARC coding errors. In 2004, QBI's catalogers were asked about the possibility of customizing our records for one of our customers. Using what I'd learned during the cleanup project, I was able to write some programs that facilitated the customization, including producing the necessary data for labels. As a result, I have the additional task of maintaining programs for generating customized label data.

PROS AND CONS

Working as a cataloger for a vendor, I enjoy being able to devote most of my day to cataloging interesting materials rather than having to manage a department or conduct meetings. QBI's focus is selling small and independent press materials on subjects from all areas of knowledge, from books about arts and crafts, sports, and library science to more esoteric topics like witchcraft, how to use bullwhips, and UFOs.

I also enjoy being able to create high-quality, full-level records. Unfortunately, because I work for a business, sometimes the MARC record load and timeframes create pressures to increase productivity by producing MARC records to industry standards rather than QBI's normal high-level standards. Because of the way our record delivery system is set up, though, we currently catalog to full-level standards for those libraries that demand such records. By providing such records to libraries and contributing them to OCLC and other utilities, my hope is that the quality of those record sources will improve, and that the end users of the records— the patrons of our library customers—will have improved success in accessing the materials they need. Libraries should demand the best records *possible* from their vendors rather than the best *available*. Unfortunately, that also requires them to be willing to pay the high cost of creating such records. In today's world of constrained budgets, the opposite is more often the case.

Something that is both a joy and an annoyance is our contact (or lack thereof) with others outside the building. The catalogers don't usually communicate directly with our library customers and try to avoid speaking with publishers whenever possible. For me, part of the reason for that is my personal dislike of the telephone, but the main reason for trying to avoid contact with publishers is to maintain objectivity. Some publishers see the P-CIP block as a sales tool. For the cataloger, it is supposed to be an objective description of the material being cataloged, created to assist libraries in providing access to the item as efficiently as possible. A separate department at QBI, Customer Service, deals with library customers. However, we have recently begun dabbling in custom cataloging for some of our customers. As a result, it has been necessary to speak directly with libraries, or with their consortium's head cataloger or systems administrator, to determine their requirements. In some cases libraries have no one on staff to clarify apparently contradictory specifications in their cataloging profile, making the creation of programming to automate customization more difficult. As a result, both sides have been left a little frustrated—on our end because we want to do what the library wants but cannot if they are not clear; on their end because we have to send constant follow-up messages asking for more detail than they think is necessary or than they have the ability to provide.

In addition to my typical job activities, QBI pays for my membership in the American Library Association (ALA), the Association for Library Collections and Technical Services (ALCTS), the Association of College and Research Libraries (ACRL), the Western European Studies Section (WESS) of ACRL, the Public Library Association (PLA), and OLAC (Online Audiovisual Catalogers). QBI's catalogers usually take turns attending ALA, where we always try to attend two committees, PLA's Cataloging Needs of Public Libraries Committee and ALCTS's Cataloging of Children's Materials Committee, because those deal with QBI's main customers, public and school libraries.

HOW WOULD I GET A JOB LIKE YOURS?

Someone wanting a cataloging job at a vendor like QBI would want to be certain they enjoy cataloging. Taking an introductory cataloging class should be required of all library science students and is essential for a cataloging job like mine. Practical experience in an internship or graduate assistantship program would also be helpful. While in library school, I had an assistantship in a rapid cataloging (copy cataloging) department, where I gained a great deal of experience that gave me a strong start at QBI. Other catalogers at QBI have started with less experience and have learned on the job. Attention to detail and a familiarity with cataloging tools, such as AACR2, LC Rule Interpretations, LCSH, and both DDC and LC classification systems, are useful skills.

To find a job like mine, I recommend checking electronic discussion lists such as AUTOCAT, OCLC-CAT, OLAC-L, and ALA's New Members Round Table (NMRT) list, as well as job sites provided by library schools and regional library systems. If one chooses to work in an entry-level position in a rural setting, particularly in times such as these when library budgets are not what they once were, the job seeker may need to be willing to accept a salary somewhat lower than one would expect in a larger urban setting. Private, for-profit companies may offer lower salaries than libraries. In an ideal world, the pay would be much higher for such a position, but in that world, all librarians would be receiving a top salary; libraries would demand high-quality full- or core-level records from their vendors and in-house catalogers, and be willing to pay for it; library patrons would recognize the value of such records and be willing to support their libraries with sufficient funds to maintain the collection, high salaries, and other needs of the library. Unfortunately, this is not possible in today's world.

That being said, for those interested in working as a full-time cataloger, a job at a small vendor like QBI is a great choice. I have the opportunity to work on a good variety of materials with excellent coworkers. The workload can be a bit overwhelming at times, but it is never boring.

RELATED RESOURCES

QBI's Web site, www.quality-books.com, offers details on the company.

I monitor several electronic discussion lists, including the following.

025.431: The Dewey blog. ddc.typepad.com. A blog devoted to the Dewey Decimal classification system.

AUTOCAT. ublib.buffalo.edu/libraries/units/cts/autocat. A good general cataloging discussion list that anyone interested in cataloging should monitor.

Catalogablog. www.catalogablog.blogspot.com. A blog that offers daily news related to cataloging.

LC Cataloging Newsline. www.loc.gov/catdir/lccn. An irregular publication of the Library of Congress that provides updates on LC's cataloging activities.

OCLC-CAT. listserv.oclc.org/scripts/wa.exe?SUBED1=oclc-cat&A=1. Focuses on OCLC-related cataloging, but some general discussions do take place.

OLAC. www.olacinc.org. An organization devoted to audiovisual cataloging. The organization holds meetings at ALA conferences, as well as a biennial conference typically taking place in the fall of even years. OLAC-L is a discussion list open to all those interested in nonbook cataloging.

MARC list. www.loc.gov/marc/marcforum.html. Devoted to MARC 21-related discussion.

MLA-L (Music Library Association Mailing List). listserv.indiana.edu/archives/mla-l.html. A discussion list for those interested in music librarianship.

Perl4lib, perl4lib.perl.org, and Code4lib, dewey.library.nd.edu/mailing-lists/code4lib. Discussion lists about the use of Perl programming, and computer programming in general, for library-related tasks.

PUBLIB. lists.webjunction.org/publib. A general discussion list for those interested in public libraries.

VideoLib. www.lib.berkeley.edu/MRC/vrtlists.html. A discussion list sponsored by the Video Round Table of ALA and devoted to general video-related topics in libraries.

CHAPTER 72

Senior Product Strategist

CANDY ZEMON

The primary tasks of the senior product strategist are to gather, digest, and contribute information needed to guide overall product development and convey this information to the company leadership. To do this effectively requires broad and deep knowledge of the library industry, awareness of current and developing trends both inside and outside the industry, a technical understanding of software and relevant standards, and excellent communication skills, including the ability to explain technical subjects in readily understood nontechnical terms.

My position at Polaris Library Systems also includes responsibility for the development of two of the subsystems in the Polaris Integrated Library System: cataloging and public access (PAC). Add responsibilities as NISO (National Information Standards Organization) voting representative and participation in various standards bodies and you have the full measure of my job description.

A TYPICAL WORKDAY

What my day looks like depends on which primary role I am filling at the moment: strategist, product analyst, or standards representative. Some days are full of work for standards bodies. Some are exclusively devoted to writing programming specifications. All involve attentive curiosity.

One of the facts affecting my work life is that I work from my home in Saint Louis, Missouri, for a company whose office is in Syracuse, New York. This means that a regular part of my life is travel to the Polaris Library Systems office. On average, I spend one week out of six in Syracuse. Seven hours en route each way each trip means lots of time available to read and think!

Product Strategist Role

When I wear my product strategist hat, my life is full of breadth. Looking thoughtfully into the future requires casting a wide net to catch present developments and trends. I read widely. I cover a regular roster of news sources, professional bodies, technology and programming resources, blogs, newsletters, publications, and personal networks. I think about what I am seeing and hearing, whether it is at the grocery store (self-checkout), the hardware store (microelectronics for the home), the school parking lot (what *are* those gadgets everyone has?), or in any of the various libraries, physical and virtual, that I frequent. I track commercial offerings. I read, contribute to, and review standards and other protocols in the making. I send (and respond to) endless streams of e-mail to various colleagues about the things I am discovering or thinking about.

In my strategist role, I serve as a resource for anyone in the company for questions like "What do you hear about ... ?," "Do you know about ... ?," or "What do you think we should do about ... ?" When the inevitable prioritizing of efforts occurs in product development planning, both a reasonable map of the territory and a fairly detailed guesstimate about the future are helpful. It is my job to provide those.

One way I keep myself open to change is to imagine uses for things I hear about—how could one combine the new with the new or the new with the existing? There are some gadgets made (TV/cell phone combo) whose usefulness is hard for me to understand—or at least hard at this moment in U.S. society. But there are other combinations, once in the realm of science fiction, that have become such a part of our lives that we hardly notice them, like the personal assistant software that lives on our cell phones or the talking GPS navigators in our cars. When trends coalesce or converge to create something completely new and previously unimagined, it changes our assumptions about what is normal, what is possible, and how problems should be addressed.

Product Analyst Role

When I wear my product analyst hat, my life is full of detail and spans at least five years of development. I live partly in the current release, answering questions about how released features work and dealing with any bugs that arise. I also live in the next release, for which I write the detailed programming specifications that underlie new features to be added to the product. And I look beyond that to future releases.

Spec writing is the central reality for a product analyst. We write specs throughout a release cycle, but most heavily at the start—about six to twelve months before the next release. In writing specs, we take input from various sources, including our customers, our sales force, our customer support department, market trends, and industry discussions. We use that input to decide which features need to be added next (and how). Spec writing involves detailed knowledge and description of how the product currently works and of the changes necessary to add the desired features. It also involves conversations with programmers, the quality assurance team, the documentation team, and focus group members (customers). In this role, I also contribute to answers to requests for proposals and other sales-related issues coming out of library visits or demos. Besides actively working on both the current and the coming release, I concurrently plan about two years into the future, prioritizing what will best be done when and sequencing development projects to get us from point A to point B.

Standards Role

When I wear my standards hat, I am steeped in the technical details that make it possible for different applications to interoperate. The standards on which much of our library software relies, from Z39.50 to NCIP (NISO Circulation Interchange Protocol) to XML, are developed and maintained by standards bodies. NISO is the standards body for the library world in the United States. NISO also works with ISO, the International Standards Organization. Institutions are members of NISO, and those with voting membership have an obligation to review and comment on any standards up for either initial or maintenance votes.

Representatives of member institutions and other interested parties form the working groups and committees that produce the standards documents. Much of the work these groups do is accomplished over e-mail and with conference calls on a regular (sometimes weekly) basis. Sometimes face-to-face meetings are also scheduled, often around major industry conferences. Participation in several groups means many hours a week devoted to the actual calls, review of the e-mailed documents, and research to contribute to the group's efforts.

Other non–library-specific standards are increasingly important to the library world, given the Web-enabled nature of many library tools. Blurring boundaries between standards specific to the library industry and those not specific to the library industry opens new possibilities and forces standards bodies to reassess their role.

To be effective in standards work requires several strengths, including a detailed understanding of the problem area to judge whether the standard is useful, some familiarity with how standards are written and generally how they work to judge the soundness of the approach, and some detailed technical understanding of how software works to assess the boundaries within which a standard is likely to be practicable. It also helps to be involved with several standards bodies to see the similarities, differences, and possible synergies or duplications of effort among particular groups. Working well collaboratively is essential to all standards work.

PROS AND CONS

On the whole, I think I have the one of the best jobs in the world for me at this point in my life. But as with any job, some aspects of the work are more fun than others.

The Positive Side

On the plus side, I am rarely bored. There is so much to explore, think about, and contribute to that the biggest problem I have is choosing what to do each day in the discretionary bit of time I try to work into my routine.

I live much of my working day about two to five years in the future, speculating about and working toward the potential and the possible. But the rest of my working day is spent in the immediate past (assessing problems and bugs) and the immediate future (current development projects and the next release beyond that). Jumping around in the development timeline keeps me alert and gives me a broader perspective.

Working from home gives me control of my schedule and the isolation I need to concentrate. Polaris Library Systems works hard to keep me in the loop and include me in meetings and conference calls. They once offered to exempt me from those office e-mails like "cake is in the kitchen" or "someone left car lights on," but I really enjoy receiving those—I get to be part of the office ambience without being physically present.

I experience enormous satisfaction when something new and useful results from my investigations and ideas. I have a lot of fun in being able to wonder "what if" about technological solutions and tools.

An unexpected bonus from my heavy involvement in standards groups is that I get to work closely with people I would never otherwise meet. There is a relatively small group of us who have long been involved in standards work. I value the friendships I make there.

The Negative Side

As any telecommuter will tell you, physical isolation can cause problems. I depend on connectivity for basic productivity. A day when the Internet connection is spotty or there are firewall problems or a storm knocks out power or my laptop feels colicky is a day in which I get little done. Because my problems do not generally affect the home office, I deal with them without the camaraderie of coworkers stuck in the same boat.

I live in a constant time warp—my business day and my laptop are on Eastern time, but my physical life and the desk where the laptop sits are on Central time. My work context dances between the immediate past, the present, the immediate future, and up to five years beyond that. My mind and body can become confused, especially when I am tired or traveling.

Focusing on the right things can be a problem. There is such a broad range of information to cover that it is easy to become lost in a sea of disconnected data. There are few guidelines to help me make the right focus decisions. What if I am following a passing fad rather than a growing trend? What if I miss something fundamental? I try to guard against this by purposely having a set of things I watch regularly and a piece of time where I just surf and browse outside my regular paths. And I have to accept that sometimes I will be wrong.

It takes work on my part to maintain connections and conversations with Syracuse-based staff. It can be lonely working from home. Without the give and take enforced in an office environment, it is too easy to become stuck in a particular mood or idea, misinterpret e-mail messages, or fail to call to discuss something.

But back to the positive side, when frustrations like these arise, I can defuse them by taking the dog for a walk.

HOW WOULD YOU GET A JOB LIKE MINE?

Get that MLS—you will need it. Get some real-world library experience. There is no substitute for that. Be curious. Be active in technical bodies—NISO committees or MARBI (ALA's Machine-Readable Bibliographic Information Committee) are great for this. Understand how standards help (and where they can hurt) the industry. Publish—any experience in this realm is useful, from notes at conference sessions to blogs to articles in peer-reviewed journals. Learn to code or at least understand some programming languages. Play with new products. Speak whenever asked. Develop a group of folks you can bounce ideas off. Be sure some of those folks are not in the library industry. Be willing to share what you know and think. Work in committees and be fearless in volunteering and faithful in following through. Learn about the library vendor world—how it works, who is in it, where the opportunities are. Watch what toys and tools teenagers and young adults are buying and using. Notice changes in common workplace technologies. Listen to older adults in your life and understand their technology world. Get some business experience. Learn about business cycles, return on investment, management, and other corporate truths. Be patient; this is not a job one tends to get straight out of school. One essential requirement is experience.

RELATED RESOURCES

Polaris Library Systems is a major producer of integrated library systems with a focus on serving public libraries or consortia of multitype libraries in the United States. www.polarislibrary.com (accessed June 11, 2006).

NISO is the standards organization in the United States involved in the library industry. www.niso.org (accessed June 11, 2006).

The Library of Congress's Web site is full of useful standards-related resources. www.loc.gov/marc (accessed June 11, 2006).

PART VIII

Publishing

CHAPTER 73

Editor, Publisher, Author, Speaker

JUDITH A. SIESS

The U.S. Bureau of Labor Statistics estimates that the average person in the United States has seven careers in their lifetime. I am currently on careers five, six, and seven—all at the same time. (For the record, numbers one through four were anthropologist, secretary, agricultural economist, and practicing librarian.)

A bit of history first. At the end of 1996, I quit my job as librarian for a large international corporation that valued neither information nor my role in its provision. I wasn't sure what I was going to do, but I knew that a change was necessary. Just as I was recovering from one sprained and one broken ankle (from a fall at a professional conference), I received a call from Guy St. Clair, founder of *The One-Person Library: A Newsletter for Librarians and Management*. He asked if I wanted to buy the newsletter. I immediately said yes. (Note: Never respond immediately—you lose your negotiating position.) After lengthy negotiations, *OPL* was mine. The rest followed naturally.

EDITOR/PUBLISHER

Actually writing the newsletter takes only about thirty hours a month, but deciding what to include adds to my workload. I try to include articles written by others as often as possible and getting permission to quote people takes a lot of time, especially because I might have found the quote several years ago and now have to find where the author is working (thank goodness for Google). After the newsletter is written, it goes to my proofreader, John Welford. John is located in England. This wouldn't have been possible before the Internet—an example of how technology makes my life easier. The work doesn't end there. I have to make address labels and take them and the printed copy to the publisher. I send electronic copy to my Webmaster to post on my Web site for those who have subscribed electronically. After the issue is published, I have to send copies to all those who have been quoted and checks to all those who wrote articles. Keeping the subscription database up to date takes some time, too. By the time I get this done, it's time to work on the next issue. It never really ends. (Actually, I am usually working on at least two issues at a time, often three.)

OPL has been profitable almost from the start. I found a low-cost printer who takes camera-ready copy and prints, folds, and mails the newsletters. Delivering the information electronically is nearly free; there is still a cost for postcards for reminding people to renew their subscriptions, but that isn't much. In fact, if all my subscribers chose the electronic option I would double my profit.

AUTHOR

In addition to the newsletter, I also write books and articles on library management issues. The first book, *The SOLO Librarian's Sourcebook*, was written while I was still a working librarian. I saw a need for a book containing not only management advice but also lists of resources that could make the librarian's life easier. People often ask me how to get a book published. I am the wrong person to ask. For the first one I just approached Tom Hogan, owner of Information Today, whom I knew from fifteen years of going to SLA conferences, and asked him if he wanted to publish it. He said yes. Four years later, John Bryans, his book editor, asked me to update the sourcebook, so *The OPL Sourcebook: A Guide for Small and Solo Libraries* was written. While exhibiting at an SLA conference, the acquisitions editor at Scarecrow Press saw my speaker ribbon and asked what my topic was. When I told her that I gave a workshop on time management, she asked if I would write a book about it. That encounter led to my third book, *Time Management, Planning and Prioritization for Librarians*. An e-mail from the American Library Association's book division led to my next book. They asked me to write a book on marketing and advocacy from the viewpoint of holding onto your job. This was a pet subject of mine, so I agreed, and *The Visible Librarian: Asserting Your Value with Marketing and Advocacy* was published in 2004, making it three books in three years. In 2005, I had two books come out: *The Essential OPL, 1998–2004: The Best of Seven Years of The One-Person Library* and *The New OPL Sourcebook*. Another book is in the works, this time a collection of writings by Stephen Abram.

Fortunately, writing comes easily to me, and I love the research part. When writing a book I read between 30 and 50 books and 100 and 150 articles, taking notes on index cards. After organizing the cards according to my outline, I transfer the notes to the computer and start linking them together into paragraphs. The draft goes to the publisher for editing. (I never start a book without having a signed contract.) A month or so later, I get the edited manuscript, go over it, and send it back for another edit. My final look at the manuscript is the galley proofs, which both my husband and I read over carefully. This process usually takes about eighteen months, although I have done it in less time.

You are unlikely to make a lot of money writing books for librarians. It is a small market, and sales of fewer than two thousand copies are considered very good. Most contracts provide you with 15 percent of gross sales. Do the math: two thousand copies at $30 times 15 percent equals $9,000. But two thousand books is a lot, especially for a first book. You won't always get 15 percent royalties, and you have to subtract your expenses (buying books and articles, copy costs, postage, and maybe paying a proofreader, editor, or indexer).

SPEAKER

A natural outgrowth of both the newsletter and the books is being asked to speak to groups of librarians. This is what I *really* enjoy. My first workshop was "Management Strategies for One-Person Libraries" and was based on my first book. Of the other two, "Time Management, Planning and Prioritization" came after the book, but "The Visible Librarian" was developed before the book was written—in fact, the workshop provided the outline for the book.

Developing a workshop involves a lot of thinking time, but really very little actual writing time, especially if it is based on a book. I once wrote a workshop in a waiting room while my car was being serviced. Every time I give a workshop, I customize it for the audience. This takes a few hours. Each workshop lasts no more than eight hours, but you have to add travel time to that, which is usually one day before and one after—that is, three days per workshop. I do between five and fifteen workshops per year. In addition, I have done a few shorter talks to SLA chapters and student groups for which I do not charge.

The workshops are, by definition, profitable. In addition to my fee, I require payment of all expenses. About fees: I charge relatively little because I feel that my major market—small libraries and library groups—cannot pay a large fee. However, other speakers have told me that I do not charge enough. You'll have to decide this one for yourself.

A TYPICAL DAY

What I do depends on which hat I am wearing, but here is my usual routine when I am at home. I work out of my house, which gives me a lot of flexibility. At 5:30 a.m., my cats (Harry Potter and Hermione Granger) demand that I get up. After breakfast, I make my first check of e-mail. I get a *lot* of e-mail. Because I no longer work in a library, I keep up with what's going on through electronic lists. I subscribe to at least fifteen of them, including SOLOLIB (my mainstay), LIBREF, BUSLIB, NEWLIB, and lists in Australia, New Zealand, Canada, the United Kingdom, South Africa, and India. (About one-third of my subscribers are outside of the United States.) I get some of my best ideas for articles from the lists. I check e-mail at least three times a day.

I usually work until about 9 a.m. and then go back to bed (to make up for all those mornings when I just wanted to roll over and go back to sleep but had to work) for an hour or so. I then work until lunchtime, usually with the TV on and a cat by my side. After lunch the mail brings more work, in the form of claims for missing issues and, I hope, checks for new or renewal subscriptions.

What I do in the afternoon depends on what needs doing or how close my next deadline is. I run errands (both personal and corporate), write, or even catch a nap. I quit working when my husband comes home about 5:30 p.m. and fix and eat dinner. After dinner we usually sit in the living room, watch TV or a video, and both work on our laptops (he is a self-employed accountant). He goes to bed at 10, but I usually work or read until midnight or later. (That's why I need a nap in the afternoon.) This may not sound like a bad schedule, but, remember, this is seven days a week. Weekends and national holidays make no difference to the self-employed; if there is work to do, you work. But my life is not all about work; I figure I average about twenty hours per week.

I also get to travel a lot. In fact, my father said that I didn't buy a business; I bought an excuse to travel. We try to take at least one foreign and one domestic trip each year. So far we've been to Norway, Australia (I've been three times), New Zealand (also three trips), the United Kingdom, Mexico (many times), Canada (several times), Germany, Kenya, Tanzania, and South Africa. I try to combine pleasure and business as much as possible by e-mailing librarians in the country I am going to vacation in and offering to do a workshop or speak to a group. This has led to many enjoyable meetings with non-U.S. librarians, some of whom are now valued friends.

I just *love* my job!

DO YOU WANT TO DO WHAT I DO?

I never intended to become an entrepreneur/author/editor/publisher/speaker. Now that I am, I'm glad I tried it. However, there are pros and cons.

Pros

1. No one to tell you what to do.

2. No fixed schedule.

3. You get to keep all the profits.

4. No boss or bureaucracy to deal with.

5. You make all the decisions and get all the credit.

Cons

1. No one to talk to about problems (though you can talk to people on the Internet or find advisors through groups such as SCORE—Service Corps of Retired Executives).

2. You have to be disciplined about getting work done, especially if you work from home.

3. There may not be any profits for several years, so you will need another source of income for a while (a spouse or partner, a pension, or substantial savings).

4. No parent organization means no benefits. You need to arrange for health insurance. Ideally, you have a spouse or significant other who is a working stiff and has benefits that you can take advantage of. If you don't, although it is likely to be expensive to purchase insurance, you should budget to do so. Look into programs designed for small businesses or entrepreneurs. (My husband—who is also a one-person company—and I get our health insurance through the Cleveland, Ohio, Council of Smaller Enterprises at about one-half of the nongroup rate, but it is still almost US$1,500 per month!)

5. Although you get all the credit for your decisions, you also must take all the blame for your failures.

Here are some additional things to consider. Plan to set aside a part of your home for an office, at least to begin with. You may want to move into a real office later, but wait until you have enough money to warrant it. (I prefer to work out of my home because I don't need to meet with customers. My husband needs a real office to meet with his clients.) You will have to advertise your newsletter or workshops or books. For a newsletter, this presents problems. At least half of my subscriptions come through subscription services such as EBSCO, so it is very difficult to determine if advertising is working. Don't forget the importance and usefulness of having a Web site (an additional cost if you can't do it yourself). There are two good ways to let people know about your availability for workshops or speeches: electronic lists and networking. Talk to people (online or in person) as much as you can, mentioning your services. Be subtle, not pushy. Don't count on your publisher to promote your book; carry one with you wherever you go and tell people about it. For some of my books, I estimate I have sold as many as the publisher.

Finally, make sure that this is what you *really* want to do. It is not easy. You have to be very confident in your abilities and have plenty of patience. But, if this is really your passion, go for it!

CHAPTER 74

Assistant Editor

TRACY SHIELDS

The Medical Letter, a nonprofit organization, does not receive any outside funding or financial support through advertisements, relying solely on subscription fees to publish two independent newsletters. Its publications—the biweekly *Medical Letter on Drugs and Therapeutics* and the monthly *Treatment Guidelines from The Medical Letter*—provide physicians and other health care professionals unbiased critical evaluations of drugs as well as articles on the treatment of common diseases and disorders.

WHAT I DO

As an assistant editor, I am assigned articles written by experts and medical consultants, although I have also researched and written articles on my own. I am responsible for researching, fact checking, evaluating, editing, revising, and reviewing my article to ensure the most recent, accurate information is presented in a clear, concise manner. I also index articles for our Web site's collection search and develop the yearly print index for both publications. It is a challenging job, but intellectually stimulating and varied.

HOW I SPEND MY DAYS

Most of the work I do is in two-week cycles coinciding with the publishing schedule for *The Medical Letter on Drugs and Therapeutics*. I must continually manage my time and various projects to meet specific deadlines. My daily duties are dependent on what stage I am at in the article's life cycle, but several major areas stand out.

Research, Research, and More Research

The importance of comprehensively researching a topic or drug for an article cannot be overstated. Although we have a librarian on site, her duties are mainly collection development and management, interlibrary loans, and other support services for the editors. I conduct my own literature reviews and database searches, things typically done by a science or medical reference librarian. I spend the equivalent of several days during the two-week publishing cycle just on research. Because I am responsible for every aspect of my article, I must become an expert on my article topic in a very short amount of time. I depend a great deal on finding authoritative information and data to ensure the accuracy and balance of the article. Knowing that doctors and other health care professionals may determine a patient's treatment based on my information (or lack thereof) really adds to the pressure.

Every article has references for supporting data or studies related to the drug or topic being discussed. Many of these references are included with the article from the time it is written; other sources result from research in databases, textbooks, and other works uncovered during my research for the article. These sources include published studies from peer-reviewed journals, safety and prescribing information from the Food and Drug Administration (FDA), abstracts and/or posters from conferences or meetings, and any other unpublished data or information that might be relevant to the article. Our editorial process includes soliciting feedback from Medical Letter consultants, drug manufacturers, government agencies such as the FDA, and the primary author(s) of studies and papers cited in the article; I depend on this feedback to provide expert opinion and information for my article.

My major source for research is the National Library of Medicine's PubMed database, which indexes every major published article in a wide range of biotechnology and biomedical peer-reviewed journals. It is the first and most important place I look for the latest research and published studies related to my article. The FDA's Web site is also an invaluable resource for drug information, especially when approval documents contain unpublished data or research for a specific drug. Google is my preferred search engine to augment searches in PubMed. I have used other sources with success, but I find myself using Google and Google Scholar as my standards. I have learned advanced- and expert-level tricks for my preferred reference sources and use them religiously.

Current awareness is another essential element to my research. Knowing what is in the news means I can use the latest available scientific data to help answer some of the questions patients may ask their doctors. I always have a stack of journals to read or skim through to keep up to date and catch anything I might have missed in my other research. I also browse major newspapers (*The Wall Street Journal* and *The New York Times* are two favorites) and online news sources (RSS and other news aggregators are great tools) for important topics in the news that relate to drugs and the pharmaceutical industry.

Cut, Copy, and Paste

Besides content, I am responsible for the article's tone and written presentation. No matter how many experts and grammar gurus look at an article, there is always something that could or should be changed. Although a degree in English would be helpful in this position, it is not essential, especially when the latest edition of *The Chicago Manual of Style* is close at hand. When I have a grammar question or issues about usage, I often consult with the other editors and consider the tone and style of *The Medical Letter* established after forty-something years of publishing articles.

The week before going to press I spend most of each day reading through and editing my article and the other articles from other editors; all editors read and review every article in the current issue, offering suggestions or edits for content, tone, and clarity. Ideally, the nearer the print deadline is, the more polished an article is and the less likely it is that it will undergo major revisions. That said, sometimes major revisions or edits are needed near the end due to layout issues (being over the standard length is the most common), new information that has come to light, or necessary revisions in what is said and how information is presented.

Copyediting, which is preparing the issue for printing by checking layout, spacing, font size, formatting, and overall look, becomes important in the final days before going to print.

Other Projects

My duties also include indexing our articles for our Web-based collection search and the yearly comprehensive index. I did not take a course in indexing during my graduate studies because I did not plan on being an indexer, and now I dearly wish I had. I had the basics and underlying principles of indexing as part of other classes, but I have had to learn a great deal on my own. I have also been involved with redesigning our search program, which has used a great deal of the theoretical and abstract discussions from my graduate coursework that I never thought I would use in the real world. Usability, user needs and wants, search structure, thesaurus building, and related topics have all played a part in my duties.

THE GOOD PARTS OF MY JOB

My job is intellectually challenging and always changing. I learn about new drugs and effective treatment options and keep up to date on important medical issues. Working for a small nonprofit organization definitely has its perks compared to positions in academic research libraries—the work environment is casual, I have a great deal of autonomy, I never work weekends or holidays, and I have a flexible schedule.

THE BAD PARTS OF MY JOB

Time limits and deadlines are probably the biggest pain about my job. It takes a great deal of time, energy, and resources to do the job right and on time. Considering the variety and potential disparity of articles in any given issue, it can be a major challenge to get things finished before the press deadline. There is never quite enough time to do everything and search everywhere I need to get the most accurate and timely information.

HOW I GOT MY JOB

I took quite a convoluted path to my current job and career track. I never planned to be an editor, and never really knew what I wanted to do after realizing that I did not want to go through medical school, my original goal. Unexpectedly, my varied postuniversity jobs and experiences provided the experience and skills for this job. After earning an undergraduate degree in biology, I worked as a medical assistant for a dermatology private practice, contracted as an editorial assistant for a pharmacology textbook project, and conducted pharmacology research in an academic research laboratory. After I realized I still did not know what kind of work I wanted to do, I decided to go back to school; information science appealed to me because of personal interests and an annoying tendency to research things to death.

While in Graduate School

I decided early in my master's program to focus on science and medical reference services. I tailored my coursework to reflect my desire for reference services and tried to incorporate scientific and medical topics in special projects. By the end of my program, I was ready to be a science or medical reference librarian. I searched for jobs in academic research libraries, but also checked out nontraditional positions, which is how I found my current job posted on the Special

Libraries Association (SLA) and Medical Library Association (MLA) Web sites. Although the position was not the reference librarian position I thought I wanted, I applied for it anyway. The job sounded interesting, and I met all the requirements and preferred qualifications. In hindsight, working as an assistant editor for a medical publication is a great fit for me and uses my strengths and interests in exciting and novel ways.

Do You Really Need a Graduate Degree for That?

Having a degree in science and an advanced degree in library and information science may not be essential for this type of job, but it definitely makes it easier. Two other editors have a library background as either the former librarian at The Medical Letter or as a librarian in other libraries. Although my previous experience working on an editorial project helps, my science background (for terminology and concepts) and information science degree (for search skills) are what I depend on most to do my job effectively.

Other Important Factors and General Advice

A willingness to accept new challenges, continually learn new things, and adhere to deadlines is vital in this position; time management and organizational skills are a must. If you cannot work independently and without structure, this job is not for you. It also really helps to be a perfectionist, because the work is all about details and getting things right. Editing in general and copyediting in particular benefit from a strong attention to detail. Having a slight tendency toward obsessive-compulsive behavior is also an asset. I do not think these traits can be learned. It takes a certain personality type to really enjoy and thrive in this kind of work.

Take a chance and consider jobs that may not exactly fit the librarian or information science graduate stereotypes. Be cognizant of jobs that use the skills and knowledge gained in other positions (even if they at first seem like they have no relation) and that may not necessarily require a degree in information science; the SLA Web site is a great resource for finding positions. Finally, be open to new opportunities that make the most of all life experiences. Do not be afraid to try something new. Your dream job may be under another name.

RESOURCES

FDA Center for Drug Evaluation and Research. www.fda.gov/cder (accessed February 6, 2006).
The Medical Letter. www.medicalletter.org (accessed February 6, 2006).
Medical Library Association (MLA). www.mlanet.org (accessed February 6, 2006).
PubMed database. www.pubmed.gov (accessed February 6, 2006).
Special Libraries Association (SLA). www.sla.org (accessed February 6, 2006).

CHAPTER 75

Author of Young Adult Novels

CLARE B. DUNKLE

When I was young, I had such vivid dreams that I believed I lived in two worlds. During the day, I played with my friends in a world that seemed solid but dull. As I fell asleep, details of last night's dream would begin to wander through my head like memories coming back to an amnesiac, and I would doze off into that same dream again, picking up where I had left off. These days, I understand that memory is state dependent, meaning that what we learn in a sleepy state, we remember best when we're sleepy. But back then, I assumed that as I fell asleep "here," my other self was waking up "there" and recalling where it was and what it had to do that day. I was returning to my other world.

By adulthood, I viewed my overactive imagination as an embarrassing waste of time. I wanted a real life and a real job, so I earned an MLS and became a university librarian. For nine pleasant years, I maintained my library's computers, keeping that other world at a distance. I gave no indication to myself or anyone else that I was on the brink of a creative career. But even then, in the comfortable surroundings of the library, the call of my other world would become too insistent, and I would spend my break in the stacks staring at a blank wall.

Novelists are born like this. We can't help ourselves. Our imagination sweeps us away. In the middle of a committee meeting on the public services mission statement, we are commanding the last battle of an epic war, watching magicians cast gruesome spells, declaring a hopeless love, or perhaps undergoing the terror of a public execution. We appear to be in the same room with our colleagues, and we feel guilty for deceiving them, but the only thing we've left behind is a body staring at an agenda. We're off somewhere in that land dreams are made of. Novelists spend every day commuting between two worlds.

JOB DESCRIPTION

I am a published novelist of young adult (YA) novels, making my living by selling the publication rights of my book-length manuscripts to major trade publishing houses. Henry Holt Books for Young Readers bought and published my first four manuscripts, and Atheneum Books for Young Readers (Simon & Schuster) has acquired my latest one. I focus almost exclusively on book-length projects suitable for readers aged twelve and up, and my goal is to complete and sell one new manuscript each year. Writing this year's novel and keeping earlier projects moving smoothly through the publication process are my top priorities. Beyond these critical tasks, I feel that certain other duties belong to the role of a YA novelist. I visit schools, conduct workshops, and give talks at various events. I respond to even the most badly spelled reader mail. I maintain a Web site so that interested readers can learn about my books and career. And, as a way to give back to the craft and develop new ideas for my workshops, I participate in an online writer's forum that gives amateurs advice about breaking into the publishing game.

A TYPICAL WORKDAY

How well does an overactive imagination fit itself into a schedule? It isn't as much of a problem as it might seem. I spent years trying to squeeze it into the leftover moments of my day, so I know how to turn it loose in a second. Other professional writers would probably back me up when I say that there is no such thing as writer's block. Some days, I write a little, and some days I write a lot, but I don't have the luxury of being blocked any more than a reference librarian has the luxury of avoiding patrons.

I spend about four hours a day working on my top priority, fiction writing, although that figure changes depending on how soon the project is due. Another hour a day on average goes toward research, an activity that may consume entire weeks before the commencement of a rough draft or dwindle to practically nothing during later stages of manuscript work. Although I write fantasy and science fiction, I frequently have to check historical details. Some drafts require research trips and consultation with expert sources.

Writing books for publication is a cyclical process. First, I complete a rough draft, which usually represents four months of effort, but the interruptions of other projects break up that time considerably and extend it over the better part of a year. The rough draft goes to my agent while she and my editor negotiate the sale, and the manuscript reappears on my plate two or three months later in the form of revision comments from my editor, detailing which aspects of the storytelling are splendid and which are weak or unbelievable. I drop what I'm working on (usually another rough draft) and devote serious brain power to reimagining the story. Then I make numerous modifications, some as small as changing a few words here or there and others as significant as adding an entire plot thread with newly written scenes. A revision takes one or two months to complete, and each manuscript goes through two or three revisions, with a break of a couple of months in between during which my editor reads the new draft and prepares the next revision letter.

When my editor decides that the revision work is over, she sends me the line-edited manuscript. Up to this point, her comments have mentioned general things: storytelling problems and bad writing habits that I should avoid, such as overusing adverbs. Now we deal with the words themselves. The line edit is a printout of the manuscript, marked up with her suggestions for changes. Again, I drop what I'm doing to work on the line edit, which is usually due very quickly. I spend a week or two poring over word choices, reading sections out loud, and cornering members of my family to ask which sounds better, sentence A or sentence B. By the last page, not even my cats will come near me.

The completion of the line edit means that my editor and I are finished with the creation of this manuscript. The project is about a year from publication, and it's time for the art department, book designers, and marketing director to take over. But during this final year, the manuscript comes back for several more brief visits. When the copy editors read it, I have a couple of days to respond to the problems that they find. When the printer sends back the page proofs about five months before publication, everyone involved with the manuscript gets a copy, and we all read it like fiends to try to find printer typos or overlooked problems.

The project closest to publication takes precedence over newer stuff, so I may set aside a rough draft to work on the revision of an older manuscript and pick up that rough draft two months later only to drop it again in a week to read the page proofs of the book that's about to hit the shelves. Projects leapfrog along, interrupting one another until they finally appear in print. A writer has to be very good at shifting gears.

So far, because I live overseas, my publishers have not involved me in book tours, but my editor has already indicated that my next book's release date will trigger a whole new set of interruptions. Right now, I'm keeping a low profile here in Germany, making professional appearances only when someone learns about me and invites me. It is March as I'm writing this, and my tax diaries assure me that I have made five author visits so far this year. One of them was a weeklong trip to England, where I conducted a fiction-writing workshop at one school and then visited another to share career information about being an author. I love school visits because they frequently center on the library and give me a chance to talk all day long.

My Web site usually occupies me for a couple of days a month, but when a book is close to publication, the Web work can soak up several weeks. At the moment, my Web site is holding steady at about three thousand visits a month. As my own Webmaster, I've enjoyed learning Dreamweaver MX, Paint Shop Pro, and other Web-maintenance applications. The site is my baby because here I can think like a librarian, determining which items visitors want to learn about and how best to organize and present that information. I try to be creative about adding fun elements, like extra short stories, photo galleries, question-and-answer pages, and "deleted scenes" that didn't make it into the books.

The last obligation in my workday is professional correspondence, to which I turn after the fiction writing is finished. Last month, I sent out eighty-three professional e-mails, of which sixteen were to my editors, fifteen were to educators needing information or inviting me to events, and fifty-two were replies to readers. I also posted forty-one times in the writer's forum to which I belong, giving advice to the new writers and encouragement to the professionals who form our online community.

PROS AND CONS

Any job that allows me to work in bunny slippers is pretty close to ideal. Most of the advantages are obvious: I run my own workday, and I can work almost anywhere. I get paid to trek off to that other world and write down the wild things I see. I'm making a living off daydreams. What's not to like?

There's the money situation, for one thing. Authorship is a tricky business, so it's hard to predict income from one year to the next. Although I'm replacing my old librarian's salary right now, I have no clue what I'll be making five years from now. And as a sole proprietor filing a 1040 Schedule C, I have to save receipts and keep meticulous records and diaries so that we'll be prepared when tax season rolls around. This year, I think I'll deduct my bunny slippers.

Another disadvantage of the writer's life is that the work proceeds slowly. I am working, generally speaking, on manuscripts that are scheduled for publication up to three years from now. By the time a book hits the shelves, it's two or three projects back in the past, and I'm not nearly as excited about it as I am about the stuff that no one can read yet. The process of earning advances and building up royalties also takes time. The story I've just invented may wind up on the best-seller list, but that isn't going to help me for about four years. Book publication is all about delayed gratification.

Also, writing is a solitary job. Some people might consider that an advantage, but I miss the friendly bustle of the library. I can't hide behind the anonymity of a committee, either; I have to be willing to take responsibility for what I write. My editor's revision comments are long, critical e-mails, and I can't just ignore them or try to argue my way out of them. Even when my editor decides the book is perfect, I still have to face the gauntlet of public opinion. Ranganathan's rules apply here: some readers will "get" my book, and others won't like it. And my fans, with their strong devotion to one or another of my books, lobby me vigorously to write more books just like their favorites. I can't let all those eyes on my work change what I think I should do. I have to be flexible enough to listen to my editor to improve the manuscripts but confident enough not to try to please everyone.

HOW TO GET A JOB LIKE MINE

Becoming a novelist is either easy or impossible, depending on your gifts and skills. According to a 1995 survey, over 50 percent of the authors who responded had an advanced degree, but no degree or certificate guarantees a manuscript sale (Smith 1995). Ultimately, a would-be novelist has only one career option: sit down and write a novel—and then another and another. If several novels sell, and editors and readers want more, then that person has become a novelist.

How lucky am I to have succeeded at this career? Very lucky indeed. First, a new novelist's book-length manuscript must interest a reputable literary agency because the majority of mainstream publishing houses accept submissions from agents only. Hill and Power note that literary agencies generally agree to represent only one manuscript out of every five hundred. Having charmed an agent, that manuscript then goes to the publishing houses, where editors generally accept one or two manuscripts out of every hundred (Hill and Power 2005). So, for each manuscript published, approximately twenty-five thousand submissions have not found a home. Those are painful odds.

But this business is not a lottery, and at the end of the day, those numbers don't mean very much. Success is largely a matter of skill and experience. My MLS prepared me well for YA publishing. I learned how YA librarians think about books. Various courses introduced me to the important review journals, exposed me to the names of the most prestigious publishing houses, and gave me a wide introduction to that field of literature that would later become my competition. In spite of the odds, my debut manuscript landed with a respectable publishing house on its first trip out into the world, and not a single one of my manuscripts (so far!) has received a rejection letter. So if you want a job like mine, remember that your MLS is your ace in the hole. Just sit down and write that first novel.

RELATED RESOURCES

An amateur wishing to read more about the joys of writing and the perils of publishing might be crushed under the weight of the available how-to books and magazines. Just as helpful is the Internet, in part because published authors often include on their Web sites good advice reflecting their own experience. A well-constructed Google search can pull in fascinating reading and will soon steer you toward the best of the print sources, such as *Writer's Market* (published yearly by Writer's Digest Books), which includes detailed listings of the literary agencies that might want to represent your new masterpiece.

The Internet can substitute for a great deal in print, but the one time I would be absolutely sure to consult the best print sources available is when you are reviewing a contract. I keep the following volumes on hand.

Kirsch, Jonathan. 1999. *Kirsch's guide to the book contract: For authors, publishers, editors and agents.* Los Angeles: Acrobat Books.

Levine, Mark L. 2006. *Negotiating a book contract: A guide for authors, agents, and lawyers,* 2nd ed. Wakefield, R.I.: Moyer Bell.

REFERENCES

Hill, Brian, and Dee Power. 2005. *The making of a bestseller: Success stories from authors and the editors, agents, and booksellers behind them.* Chicago: Dearborn Trade.

Smith, Nancy DuVergne. 1995. *The freelance writers' lot: The NWU American writers survey profiles.* New York: National Writers Union. Also available online at members.aol.com/nancyds/wlot1.html (accessed March 11, 2006).

CHAPTER 76

Indexer

ENID L. ZAFRAN

AN INDEXER'S DAY FROM A TO Z

Arise to another fun day of indexing!

Business seems slow, but then I get the unexpected project. Each day has the potential for a new client to call me with a surprising project. One day business looks slow, and the next day I have been signed up to index an encyclopedia on "daily life through the ages." Eight thousand pages to index in a couple of months. Steady work. Now I need to line up some subcontractors to help me with a project this size. Plus I don't want to lose my regular customers while I work on a huge job for one client who may or may not become a regular, so I need the subcontractors' help on other projects during this time.

I **call** about the pages that I don't have despite many promises on the part of the editor. The editor told me to expect the material by a certain date. The deadline is tight, and I have promised to meet it. But the material has yet to appear, and the deadline is almost here. This requires an urgent call to see if I can renegotiate the timeframe.

I **deposit** checks in the bank. As a self-employed individual, I have to take care of business details. Debt collection is the part of my job I like the least. I have learned the payment schedules of regular customers, so I can tell when an invoice is most likely lost versus when a client is slow to pay.

I **edit** the index. When I am done creating index entries, the index is not yet ready for submission. It has to undergo an edit for structure, consistency, and sense.

Filing the index entries is done automatically by indexing software. This has taken much of the tedium out of my job. It allows me to concentrate on the substantive part of indexing and leave the mechanical part to the computer.

I **go** through e-mail regularly. I never know when a client may need to make a change to the deadline, pagination, or other things. Most customers now communicate via e-mail. I have lost jobs because of not responding within an hour!

The top level of the entry is the main **heading**. These are the ones that best represent the essential topics in the book. They usually are nouns or adjective-noun phrases and have to be strong keywords. Sometimes authors will provide a list of the terms that they expect to see in the index, and sometimes that works very well. But once in a while, they have terms on the list that are nowhere to be found in the book. I spend a lot of time searching for them before I admit defeat and tell the author. It frequently turns out the book has been edited and that material removed, or the author is confusing this article with another one. Very frustrating!

Indent the levels. There are primarily two styles for indexes: indent and run-in. The run-in style limits the indexer to two levels (i.e., a main heading and one sublevel), whereas the indented style allows for more sublevels. The run-in style came about to save space, but I think it is harder to use. So I try to persuade clients to use the indented form.

I **juggle** projects. This is one of my best indexer tricks. I frequently have five or six indexes all in process at one time. Material comes in piecemeal and out of order. Deadlines slide as authors decide to revise or update what they have already submitted. I typically work eight to ten hours a day so I may work on several different projects in one day.

I have to **keep** it short. Many publishers give the indexer a page length for the index. That means the indexer has to balance being selective with being thorough. Usually I hire a typist to pick up all the names of people in the material and then see how much room I have left to make topical entries. I sometimes beg for another page. It is unlikely that I will get it, though—books are published in folios of eight, sixteen, or thirty-two pages, so it is impossible to add just one page without needing many blank pages to fill out the folio.

I **link** up related terms. An index should not have a bad split of information. That defeats its very purpose of bringing material on a topic together in one place. So I build a running list (an authority list) of main headings as I index, and as I read more of the book, I keep adding consistently to it. Memory skills are very important for indexers.

I **market** my business. I explain indexing and what it is on almost a daily basis. Sometimes I find people who want to learn indexing. In general, people need to be educated about indexing and learn about the field. It is a great option for parents staying home to attend to children because they can fit it around school schedules and kids' activities. I have recruited many indexers to work with me this way. When I have the time, I also try to market to prospective clients. I find Web sites and get addresses so I can write to editors, publishers, and institutions.

I **negotiate**. Although I have established rates with longtime clients, I negotiate my rate of pay with new customers. I either ask to be paid by the page, by the hour, or by a flat fee for the job. If the potential customer is acting difficult on the phone, I will raise my rate to compensate me for what I anticipate to be a troublesome job.

I need to be very **organized**. I have usually committed to take projects a month or two in advance. Then those deadlines start sliding and in the meantime I am offered other work. I need to know the jobs to which I have committed, the amount of work they will entail, and what level of indexing competence they will require. Because I use several subcontractors and each one has different strengths, I try to find a mix of work to keep everyone busy doing what they like.

I **proofread**. Yes, I run spell check, but that is not enough. Indexes are full of people's names and strange terms. I have to do a lot of careful proofreading.

I **question** the editor. I need to make sure I understand all aspects of the assignment, deadlines, format, means by which they would like to receive the finished index, and so on.

I **read** the material. One of the questions I am asked most often about indexing is whether I have to read the material. And the answer is yes, I read it all. And most days this is what takes the bulk of my time. I love to read and learn new things, and this makes indexing a great profession for me!

I **stop** for lunch and breaks. Sitting at a PC all day in one position makes my body stiff and unhappy. So I try to remember to take breaks and move around—in fact, I have workouts with a personal trainer and a massage during the week to make sure that I do.

I **train** new indexers. A frequent question I get from those interested in entering the field is how to get started. I advise them to look at the Web site of the American Society of Indexing (www.asindexing.org), which offers lots of good advice. They can also get guidance from a book I edited, *Starting an Indexing Business* (ITI 1998). In terms of learning how to index, they should take one of the basic classes; I recommend the one ASI offers via distance learning. After that, the next step is to work with an established indexer who can mentor the newbie. I usually take this role for one or two fledglings a year.

I need to **understand** what I read. This is critical for indexers, and this is why, for example, I do not index medical or scientific works. I have no background in those areas, and there is no faking it. The index reflects your knowledge and comfort with the subject matter. For me, that means law, government, public policy, art, history, education, language, and psychology. I like this mix because every few days I am reading something in a different area and avoid boredom (if a topic is boring, I know it will be over soon and then it is on to something new).

I **vet** the pages. When a book comes in, I go through the print pages and mark on them the ranges—for example, the chapter ranges, the subchapter ranges, and ranges for any parts that have bold or italic headings setting them off. This saves time later when I key the entries into my indexing software, plus I can check that I have received all the material.

I have a nice **work** area. My office is in my home, and it is comfortable, functional, and conducive to productivity. I listen to my favorite CDs while I work. I am surrounded by paintings I truly love. And I have a view out to the street to see any activity in my sleepy neighborhood.

I make **xrefs**, or cross-references to those not familiar with indexer lingo. I have to check the xrefs before handing in the index to make sure I don't have any blind or circular references. My indexing software has a utility to do this.

I try to keep busy **year**-round. My busy period is from June through November. In October and November, I typically work fourteen-hour days, seven days a week. I turn away work during that time and wish that work would have come during the slower months. To counter this imbalance, I am always looking for clients that need indexing from December through May.

I **zip** up my file to send the finished index to the client. I pat myself on the back; another day in the life of the indexer has ended.

CHAPTER 77

Freelance Book Producer

VERNON R. TOTANES

I get hired to make sure that a book gets published. The job includes most (if not all) of the following: correcting grammatical or factual errors; improving readability and consistency; laying out the text; designing the cover; and coordinating the project with the authors/editors, cover designers, printers, and publishers.

FROM MANUSCRIPT TO BOOK

My work begins when I receive a digital or soft copy of a manuscript that is intended for publication. It ends once the printed book is delivered to the publisher. I have been involved in the production of ten books, ten issues of two journals, six pamphlets, and three newsletters, all published in the Philippines.

What exactly do I do between receipt of the manuscript and delivery of the books? I usually print a hard copy of the manuscript that I can read and mark using my own system. Then I start looking for inconsistencies in facts, punctuation, capitalization, spelling, and so on. At the same time, I try to see whether the text makes sense to me. I may not be an expert on the subject at hand, but I've learned that this can be an asset instead of a liability.

For instance, I once edited the work of one of the best-known historians in the Philippines, and I noticed that some of the years mentioned in the text seemed to be in the wrong century. When I asked the author about the inconsistencies, he realized that he had made a few errors.

At other times, authors use language that makes me wonder if they misspelled some words or are just using very technical terms unique to their fields. Most of the time, it is one or the other. If it's jargon, they often decide that if I can't understand it, then perhaps other readers won't understand it either. But there have been instances where the authors themselves couldn't make heads or tails out of what they wrote. When this happens, I usually leave it up to them to rewrite the enigmatic portions.

After going through the manuscript for the first time, I usually meet with the publisher and author(s) to discuss my questions and concerns regarding style and substance. At that meeting, I explain what I did and ask them to go over the corrections I made—just in case I changed something I shouldn't have—and answer the questions I've written in the margins.

If there are very few corrections or questions (which rarely happens), I leave the meeting with the manuscript in hand. But most of the time, I leave the manuscript with the authors and they return it to me when they've revised it. In some cases, I have worked with authors who were an ocean away. Boy, am I glad that e-mail exists—it makes communication so much easier.

The Internet also helps make life easier, especially when I have doubts about the bibliographic information provided by authors in their footnotes or bibliographies. This is where the online catalogs of the Library of Congress and other libraries become very useful. Instead of asking the authors, who are usually too busy for such trivial questions, I look for the information myself. I only ask authors about bibliographic information when I can't find the book or journal. I've spent a lot of time at libraries verifying quotes and even basic facts.

Sometimes, after my first reading of the manuscript, meeting with the author, and sleuthing in the library or online, I'm reasonably sure I can lay out the pages. More often than not, some more back-and-forth needs to be done. In the meantime, I also start work on the cataloging-in-publication data, which is not as common in the Philippines as in other countries; discuss the cover with the designer; obtain quotations from prospective printers; and even go over copyright and marketing issues with the publisher.

Once everything is ready, and the necessary approvals have been obtained for the text, layout, front and back covers, and so forth, I turn over all the camera-ready pages and other materials to the printer selected by the publisher. And then the waiting begins.

PROS AND CONS

Pros

There is nothing like holding a book that I worked on after it's published. I suppose it's as close to giving birth as I will ever get. (Unless, of course, I ever write my own book.) One other thing that makes it all worthwhile is the gratitude expressed by the authors and publishers. When they thank me publicly at the book launch, I feel almost as if the many months I spent working on the manuscript have evaporated.

Recently I was asked to write the foreword for a book that I personally conceptualized, as opposed to other projects that were brought to me. After spending so much time working on scholarly books that I was afraid very few were buying—much less reading—I realized that I actually knew someone whose work had never been compiled in a book, and I believed there was very likely a large audience for that topic. That was several years ago. The book is ready for distribution, but due to copyright issues—which I can't write about in detail—I don't really know if it will ever be sold in bookstores.

It may not have ended as happily as I had hoped, but as a result of that experience, I gained a better understanding of copyright law. I've also learned many new skills over the years, especially the principles of layout and the use of desktop publishing software. In addition, I've sharpened my reading and writing skills, and I've learned more about the subjects of the books and journals I've worked on.

There's nothing like struggling with fonts and printers to give you an appreciation of the amount of time and effort that must have gone into printing a book when Gutenberg came out with his first Bible. In fact, the computer has made things so easy that I can now do in a few weeks what used to be done by many people over many years.

Finally, the best thing that happened to me because of my work as a freelance book producer was that I found my vocation. I was spending so much time in libraries that I wondered whether there was such a thing as a master's degree for librarians. There was! That's how I came to decide to get my degree in library and information science.

Cons

People have difficulty understanding exactly what I do. They're never quite sure whether I'm an editor, publisher, or editorial assistant. Some even think that I just code changes in manuscripts. It's not very different from the image problem that librarians have. Actually, I didn't really know what to call myself either until I read a book that detailed all the kinds of jobs available in publishing. According to Mogel (1996), book producers "provide all the services necessary for a book's production, from concept to complete physical book, and delivery to a publisher's warehouse." That's when I realized there was actually a name for what I had been doing.

The American Book Producers Association, however, emphasizes the role of book producers in the creation of "complicated" books, defined as "just about any book that involves more than a straightforward, single-author text." They refer, though, to book producers as companies "with experienced publishing professionals and equipped with sophisticated design and production technologies."

The work I do, on the other hand, is limited to relatively uncomplicated projects. Unless you get into the big leagues, the money will not be enough to survive on. Though the work I did helped me pay for my MLIS, it must be noted that tuition fees in the Philippines aren't even one-tenth of the fees for the MBA I initially thought of pursuing.

I've had some rather difficult times with a few authors who, even though they had master's and doctorates (some were even editors themselves), couldn't get their facts right—especially in their notes and bibliographies. There have been a few times when I had to reconcile footnotes and endnotes or abbreviations and references within the same book! It can be very tedious trying to track down the first mention of a certain name, for example, when all I want to do is finish the book and go to sleep.

Aside from the manuscript-related problems, there are the practical ones. The editing process, for instance, can take forever because of the constant interactions with authors and publishers who are also doing other things at the same time. Sometimes, I'm the one who doesn't have time to devote to the manuscript. I've had a few projects that took several years from manuscript to book.

Finally, this job makes it difficult to enjoy reading a manuscript because I'm constantly looking for mistakes. And there's no way to enjoy the book after it's published because I always find things that I could have done better. The worst is that my disease, which I call "editor-itis," spills over into my real life and sometimes makes me wish that I could have edited certain books myself.

HOW WOULD I GET A JOB LIKE YOURS?

I got into the publishing business purely by accident. I've had many different jobs from the time I finished my undergraduate course to the time I started my MLIS. But one common thing among them was my involvement in editing and desktop publishing.

My interest in publishing began when I became features editor for the annual yearbook in sixth grade. By the time I graduated from high school, I was the yearbook's editor-in-chief, responsible for editing student write-ups, finalizing the layout, and dealing with the printer. After I graduated from university, I became involved once again with publishing when I became dissatisfied with the printing of our company's newsletter. I began studying the desktop publishing software and ended up taking over. I went on to edit and design other newsletters and books just because I liked doing it. Eventually, the work I did attracted the attention of academic publishers who hired me to produce books for them.

At first, it was difficult trying to put a price tag on what I did because I had always done things for free. But over the years, I've learned to charge a retainer fee (half of the project fee, in case delays are caused by the author) and adjust my pricing to account for the length of manuscripts and how much work needs to be done.

Most of my projects were referred by friends and satisfied customers. If you'd like to do something similar, I suggest you try to help as many people for free while you're learning what you need to know, and then ask those you've helped for referrals. Don't be embarrassed to tell people what you do. You can also try telling those who express interest that you have too much work so they'll think you're in demand and line up for your services. This is not quite a joke—some people are still waiting for me to say yes!

RELATED RESOURCES

American Book Producers Association. www.abpaonline.org/what.html (accessed March 31, 2006).

Mogel, Leonard. 1996. *Making it in book publishing*. New York: Macmillan.

CHAPTER 78

Rights and Permissions Manager

ALISA ALERING

When an author signs a book contract, he or she usually also assigns a number of subsidiary rights to the publisher while the book is in print. As rights and permissions manager at a university press, I try to find a market for those subrights through negotiations with foreign and domestic publishers, online aggregators, film producers, and other content providers. Because making informed deals means I have to keep up with copyright laws and interpretations, I also serve as a general reference resource for the press's editorial staff about copyright issues of all kinds.

A TYPICAL WORKDAY

In publishing jargon, *permissions* refers to any request to reuse a portion of a book, such as a single illustration, a chapter photocopied for a class, or an excerpt from a monograph used in a compiled textbook. *Rights* are requests to republish an entire book: a cheap paperback reprint of a once expensive monograph, a foreign translation, inclusion in a full-text database or e-book system such as NetLibrary, or film and TV rights.

Most of my hours are taken up with processing permissions, but most of my intellectual capital is spent on rights issues. Permissions are numerous but usually follow a predictable pattern, though a particularly frustrating one can pop up from time to time. Rights requests are less frequent, but each situation is unique and requires greater thought, deeper research, and more cautious communication. A permission is often handled in a day, whereas the negotiation of a rights deal can go on for several months.

In the mornings, I check my e-mail, mail, fax, and phone for new permissions requests, the bulk of which are handled automatically by the Copyright Clearance Center (CCC), a clearinghouse with an automated Web system for instant approval. However, I have to preapprove each title the press publishes before handing it over for administration by the CCC. For those titles referred back to me or that come direct by fax or e-mail, I check the requested material individually and reply directly to the requestor.

Often clearing a permission involves sitting down with a copy of the physical book and turning the pages, looking for clues. I check the title page, verso, other front matter, acknowledgment, preface, captions, footnotes, endnotes, and so on, for copyright information and attributions. Every book has a unique design, and the vital clue to making a determination is hidden somewhere different in each one.

Keeping good records is essential. Books last a long time, and modern copyrights even longer. Uncovering the rights situation for a particular book may rest on finding an e-mail or a fax from fifteen years ago in a moldy file in the basement. What someone said or jotted down on a memo can be very relevant, so there's an archives aspect to my work. Because I'm the only one in the press who deals with the books once they're no longer in print and who can regularly be found rummaging in the moldy basement files, I like to think of myself as the unofficial librarian of the press.

Requests for new and different forms of electronic usage are increasing all the time. This is an exciting part of my job because I'm helping define new areas of use, but it can also be a headache because often the requestors are equally unsure of their intent. Each request that comes in differs from the previous one, and though I may have formulated a rough policy, the next situation may not fit it. There are e-reserves, e-books, subscription databases, highly indexed metadata-based databases, universities who want to compile an online archive of all of their faculty's research, authors with their own Web sites, e-journals, and so on. The old rules don't apply, and nobody's sure what the new rules are.

A current issue is licensing books to NetLibrary. Every book we publish now is considered for submission to NetLibrary. Every last thing in that book must be checked, from all of the text to all of the pictures. We want to provide these books to the library, but because of the restrictive nature of permissions we receive from other publishers, we often are not able to.

Negotiations for movies are rare, but in a commercial publishing house these are obviously very important and potentially lucrative. Often in these cases an author's agent will have a hand in the deal. At the university press level, most authors don't have agents, and it is up to the press to negotiate a fair deal on a film or option. We've only had one feature film (starring Robert Redford!) actually made, but there have been options and smaller independent films and documentaries.

I try to put aside a chunk of time in the afternoon to work on long-term projects: writing computer scripts for my database (notes for which I write down on a pad when a good idea comes to me), entering rights information for newly contracted books into the database, checking full-text electronic rights, improving workflow. Processes can be very important, but you need free time to think about them, which is difficult when fulfilling request after request. I try to make time for creative thinking so that I don't get bogged down in the minutiae and fail to improve the overall situation.

Being comfortable with database design is also important for financial reasons. I'm responsible for the billing and reconciliation of all of my accounts. I respond to thousands of permissions requests a year, and not all requestors are prompt about paying. Recently, a new request prompted me to look into a license that dated back about five years or so. When I wrote for more information to the company who was selling our product, it turned out they had neglected to pay any royalties for the previous three years, and the press was owed several thousand dollars. I have since overhauled the database, adding fields to track expected/anticipated payments and quick-check display screens to keep on top of current payments. I also do quarterly searching for unpaid accounts that may have been missed during regular maintenance.

Many presses, especially academic ones, are struggling financially. Rights are something a publisher already owns, and it has become more important to exploit them, at times trying to make enough money through rights to make the publication of a book worthwhile. For a librarian there is an ethical dilemma between providing information for the public good and the publisher needing to stay afloat.

At my press, editors and their assistants are responsible for requesting permissions from other publishers for use in the books we are publishing, and the rights manager is concerned only with the sale of rights controlled by the press. In a larger, commercial publishing house, a rights manager or director may oversee the entire permissions process from both sides, selling the rights of their house and buying rights for use in their own publications.

I do spend a lot of time explaining things to people: to authors, editors, and requestors. I rely on research and personal knowledge developed over a history of previous questions. There's not much of a reference interview–style process, digging to find out what the customer really wants to know—usually it is, "Will the press get in trouble if I use this article/photograph/musical score in my book?" Sometimes it can take quite a lot of research to find the answer. There is a lot of responsibility in being the one who makes that decision. Being comfortable with decision making may be the most important aspect of the job. I have to decide with authority, even when the facts are fuzzy. If you aren't comfortable making judgment calls multiple times a day, this may not be the job for you.

PROS AND CONS

Authors and academics can be difficult to work with. Authors sometimes forget that they have ceded their rights to the press, and that can cause sticky complications. Most are lovely and understanding, but some seem to feel that their book is the only one being published by a press—or at least the only one that matters. The day their book comes out they will want to know why it hasn't been sold for translation in at least six different countries.

It is gratifying when I finally hold a published copy of a book that has been licensed for a foreign translation. Japanese editions are invariably beautiful, with great design and quality paper and binding. Authors are really pleased with the whole publishing process when you send them three copies of their own work translated into Turkish or Croatian.

For a press working on a tight budget, the extra income from rights sales can be very important. Frequently I find that we are owed money but haven't been paid. With foreign presses, you sometimes have to hound them to get them to pay the advances that are agreed on. They're all the way on another continent, and it's hard to exert real pressure.

There's a lot of unspoken responsibility. Usually a university press will have a legal counsel available for consultation on important matters, but small everyday matters can turn into important ones when your press is sued due to your oversight.

Hours can be flexible because a lot of work can be done by e-mail, fax, and mail. I probably only speak with people on the phone about deals 10 to 15 percent of the time. Particularly with international contacts, e-mail has really been a boon.

The pay for a rights manager isn't outstanding, but is about on par with that of a starting librarian. If you advance in your career to a director of rights at a large publishing house, your salary could increase substantially.

HOW WOULD I GET A JOB LIKE YOURS?

If there's a press at your university, volunteer to intern for them. They may not have an internship specifically in the rights field, but working in marketing or even the editorial department would give you an edge in applying for any publishing job in the future.

Before getting my MLS, I worked in public television. I've found that media companies are almost always sympathetic to employees of other media companies as prospective hires. It doesn't seem to matter if you're going from radio to print to television to whatever; just having worked in any kind of media can make it easier to get anther media job in the future.

Be aware of and have opinions on the overall meaning and purpose of copyright. Read up on current changes in copyright law. Have a vision for the future of books and the Web. Know how you feel about electronic books.

Writing well is important for marketing and promotion. You need to be able to put together a convincing description of a book and three reasons why it is worth publishing. Foreign languages aren't strictly necessary for the job but are always valued in a university press.

Every job description includes "good communication skills," and they are certainly crucial in this field. You need to be able to communicate regularly and politely with people around the world and from different cultures. Authors can get panicky and need to be soothed. You have to get along with the editors. They provide a lot of the information needed for the rights process, but they sometimes don't see rights as an important part of the publishing process. You need diplomacy in approaching them and getting them to see subsidiary rights as an important contribution to the overall health of the company.

There are definitely other librarians kicking around publishing houses, but you may need to compel your interviewer to consider your MLS an asset. Pointing out how many skills librarianship and publishing have in common may help you land an interesting job in the publishing field.

RELATED RESOURCES

Association of American University Presses (AAUP). www.aaupnet.org (accessed February 1, 2006).
Copyright Clearance Center (CCC). www.copyright.com (accessed February 1, 2006).
Current Copyright Readings. copyrightreadings.blogspot.com (accessed February 1, 2006).
U.S. Copyright Office. www.copyright.gov (accessed February 1, 2006).

CHAPTER 79

Electronic Marketing Manager

BETSY VAN DER VEER MARTENS

The electronic marketing manager (EMM) position is fairly new at most university presses, as opportunities to promote scholarly books and journals electronically have exploded over the past decade, often making it advisable to shift some resources from more traditional press positions (publicity manager, direct mail manager, advertising manager) to these new responsibilities. This job requires the same strong basic organization and presentation skills as those positions but is generally more technically oriented, as it involves managing as well as using new information and communication technologies. The electronic marketing manager usually reports to the head of the marketing department, who in turn reports to the head of the press.

TYPICAL JOB DESCRIPTION

The electronic marketing manager uses e-marketing tools to reach both scholarly and general audiences through various electronic alternatives to print media, such as e-mail announcements, e-mail discussion lists, online periodicals, blogs, and Web sites. He or she works with colleagues in editorial and marketing to develop e-marketing plans for each title published by the press both before and after initial publication; adapts and implements all press marketing strategies for the electronic environment; maintains and enhances the press Web site and other related electronic content; communicates with online booksellers to manage content and data exchange; prepares, monitors, and analyzes the electronic marketing budget; and scans the electronic environment for trends and news that may impact the press's electronic presence and then disseminates relevant items to management and colleagues as necessary.

TYPICAL RESPONSIBILITIES

At a recent Web marketing workshop at the American Association of University Presses annual conference, several participants noted that the EMM position is just now emerging as a separate set of activities from the management of more traditional nonelectronic marketing channels. A typical workday, therefore, often involves many non–electronic-related activities, such as direct mail list analysis or classroom textbook adoption sales calls, depending on the

EMM's portfolio of other responsibilities. Focusing only on the electronic marketing portfolio, standard responsibilities for the EMM would include the tasks described next.

Making Sure that the Web Site Is Functioning Correctly

This responsibility includes elements that are both technical (communicating with programmers to identify and solve problems) and informational (responding to inquiries from customers, authors, and others seeking information about in-print, out-of-print, and forthcoming books or other questions). As part of my daily routine, I ensure that content is current and comprehensive, as our Web site includes book descriptions, book reviews, subject headings, book jacket images, tables of contents, links to author sites, editorial contacts, and much other information about our press.

This part of the day could include anything from a phone call from a colleague informing me that the Web site seems to be sluggish, to a request from one of our authors for a hyperlink from her book's page on our Web site to her personal Web site, to an e-mail from an overseas scholar requesting help in locating one of our long-out-of-print titles, to a discussion with the press copy supervisor about why a particular book review quote doesn't represent the book accurately and shouldn't appear on our Web site. However, when the Web site is down, getting it back up again becomes the primary task—downtime costs us sales!

Developing Ways to Improve and Promote the Web Site

This involves researching cost-effective ways to improve the usability and functionality of the Web site, as both the technology and the expectations of our users are evolving rapidly. At many more conservative presses, the value of the Web site and electronic marketing in general isn't necessarily widely accepted, so improvements to the site often have to be sold internally before they can be made available to external users. Another ongoing task is promoting the Web site to the rest of the press through monthly reports on our Web site sales, hit statistics, and hyperlink and blog activity analysis, as well as statistics on sales from other third-party electronic channels such as Amazon.com.

Most university presses are also dealing with tight budgets and the legacy of older computer systems and software, so the emphasis is always on doing more with less. At my press, the Web site is fed from an internal FileMaker database, which in turn is updated from an even more primitive database that contains inventory and pricing information from our warehouse, so there is a good deal of behind-the-scenes manipulation in putting that data into Web-friendly order!

Some of the interesting things that are being done on university press Web sites include the development of special course book sections, in which instructors interested in using a particular book for their courses can download sample chapters; the creation of Web site–related blogs or wikis in which press personnel can post their comments on books of interest; the addition of supplementary material for some books (maps, bibliographies, footnotes, discussion guides, sounds and images, author biographies, and links to additional resources); the creation of electronic catalogs, which may eventually replace the hard-copy versions of our seasonal catalogs; and the creation of "born electronic" books and journals in a variety of fields.

Other Electronic Marketing Activities

Beyond the daily operations of the Web site, there are other ongoing electronic marketing opportunities that the EMM may manage or coordinate. These usually involve developing and implementing the electronic components of the marketing plans for each of our books.

Planning

Planning for the electronic marketing of books that will be published during the next season takes place during launch season, the three months or so following the release of each of our two seasonal catalogs (spring and fall). Planning involves researching relevant electronic marketing channels (blogs, e-mail lists, Web sites, electronic bibliographies, etc.) and discussing their potential effectiveness with other colleagues in the editorial and marketing departments. Another component of our launch process is adding information about these channels to our marketing research database for future use. The other major planning component is development and monitoring the budget for Web site maintenance and electronic marketing.

Promoting Frontlist Titles

Shortly before publication, we begin promoting our current (frontlist) titles through electronic channels. We encourage our authors to self-promote their books through their academic communities and provide them with the necessary electronic materials to do so, and we also use any other electronic marketing channels identified during the book launch discussions. These promotional activities take place throughout the year, clustering around the publication of new books.

Promoting Backlist Titles

Although there is a great deal of emphasis on new books, much of our reputation and revenue comes from older books that we've published, so we also pay considerable attention to promoting our older (backlist) titles through electronic channels by identifying new or existing communities to which they may be of interest. This often happens as a result of research performed for new titles, as university presses tend to publish within a similar group of specialties, such as Russian history or comparative literature. For example, subscribers to an academic e-mail list who are interested in our latest book on Thoreau may also be interested in our book on Emerson from three years ago.

General Electronic Content Coordination

These activities involve coordinating the movement of electronic content on an as-needed basis and include working with the production department to send book images to electronic booksellers, working with the rights department to provide PDFs of book chapters for electronic course use, and working with the editorial department to assure an agitated author that a last-minute change to his book's description *will* appear on Amazon.com shortly. In addition to the purely technological aspect, because of copyright considerations the EMM has to be familiar with appropriate press policies regarding each of these activities and their possible ramifications within a rapidly changing electronic environment.

PROS AND CONS OF THE JOB

This job is terrific for someone with a library background because it involves many of the research and retrieval skills used in a more typical library setting (and often involves interaction with the library community). It offers a wide variety of intellectual challenges (for example, which groups of scholars might be interested in a new book on allegorical interpretation, and can they be reached via electronic means more effectively or efficiently than through more traditional channels such as sending the book to a particular journal for review or renting a disciplinary mailing list from the Modern Language Association?), communication challenges (once you've identified several groups interested in the topic of allegoresis, how do you create an appropriately engaging message to sell the book to each group?), organizational challenges (the allegoresis book is only one of the 150 new books that the press is publishing this year; how do you determine the appropriate amount of attention to devote to it?), and public relations challenges (the Web site is now the most visible embodiment of a scholarly press's mission, and is often the first point of contact for its various constituencies, from a potential author sending a manuscript proposal for consideration, to a foreign customer asking about international shipping options for a particular book, to the university development office inquiring about possible gift books for major donors).

For someone who likes books and the book world, the day is never boring. One of the great perks of the job is the chance to read a lot of fascinating things long before they're officially published. In addition to the interesting individual projects, there is also much collaboration with other press personnel because promotional opportunities for scholarly books often cross interdepartmental lines. For example, an ad for a book in a particular journal often features a special link to the press's Web site for a discount on that book, and the press's Web site will often list and link to the scholarly conferences at which the press will exhibit that year.

The only downside is something common to all university press work: it pays relatively little compared to other high-level marketing jobs outside academia, and the workload is very heavy, as there are any number of potential marketing opportunities for any given book (we hope!). Because university presses are under increasing financial pressure, that pressure is of course passed on to the marketing personnel, including the EMM, to increase overall sales and to pay more attention to the potential for best-selling books on the list.

HOW TO GET A JOB LIKE THIS

There are approximately 125 scholarly presses that belong to the American Association of University Presses, ranging from very large ones such as the MIT Press in Cambridge to very small ones such as Trinity University Press in San Antonio. Some specialize in regional books that primarily interest the local audience around their host university, whereas others have international reputations and global interests. University presses, like all publishers, are going through a continuous process of trying to adapt to the new communication and marketing environment while attempting to accomplish their central mission, which is to advance scholarship through publishing and distributing important books and specialized academic journals.

The best way to advance in scholarly publishing is to get in and either work your way up internally or take that initial experience to another press for the job you really want. There is always too much to do at a university press and not enough people to do it, especially in areas that may seem less glamorous (that is, the tasks that aren't editorial—editorial work always attracts plenty of English majors).

The AAUP Web site at www.aaupnet.org provides a list of its members, and I suggest that you contact the ones at which you might like to work and describe your interest and qualifications (those library skills will come in very handy) and offer to spend a month or so as an unpaid volunteer to see whether there is a good fit. If there is, you may find a fun and rewarding career, and even if there isn't, you'll still have a unique experience in which you can learn a lot about scholarly publishing and its ongoing efforts to contribute to society's knowledge.

CHAPTER 80

Web Marketing Coordinator

MICHELLE MACH

The Web marketing coordinator at Interweave Press maintains the Web sites for six craft magazines and a growing book publishing program. The major job responsibilities include creating and updating Web pages, tracking Web usage, writing and editing Web copy, and responding to technical or content questions from customers. It also entails working closely with the editors, sales and marketing, and circulation staff, who supply most of the initial text and graphics for the site. Required job skills include Web design, organizational ability, and communication skills.

A TYPICAL WORKDAY

My first day on the job in March 2005 was the day the Martha Stewart poncho story broke. What poncho? The handmade one Martha Stewart wore leaving prison, inspiring thousands of knitters and crocheters to create their own gray, scalloped-edged ponchos (Young 2005). Interweave Press offered a free pattern for the "freedom poncho" on its Web site, garnering more than ten thousand downloads an hour. As a TV crew crowded into the lobby, my coworkers repeatedly reminded me how unusual this was. (Of course, the very next day I was asked to post photos of actors Orlando Bloom and Kate Bosworth on the Web site, because the pair had recently attended an Interweave Press–sponsored event in Hollywood. *Was this typical? I wondered.*)

In reality, a normal workday includes a mix of scheduled and unscheduled Web activity, with only occasional "celebrity" interaction with people like the world's fastest crocheter or an editor commissioned to design a sweater for Fred Rogers of children's television.

In the morning, I typically read my e-mail and respond to any customer e-mails or urgent messages from colleagues. Today I respond to a customer who can't figure out how to change her e-mail address for the *Beadwork* e-newsletter. I change it, and also send her directions for future reference. Occasionally, customers call when they cannot find certain links or have other technical problems. These calls sometimes spark ideas for new Web site features.

Next, I tackle magazine content. Generally, every week I post new online content for at least one magazine before subscribers receive their issues in the mail. Today I post the *Handwoven* content, which includes the table of contents, an editorial, a guest column, two free Web-exclusive weaving projects, a calendar, and advertising. I read the short project descriptions in the PDFs and compose two short blurbs for the Web site. The editor resides out of state, so we e-mail back and forth as I prepare the issue for the Web. In addition to the standard content, the results of the recent poncho contest are in. I look over the photos and text and decide that a slide show that pops up in a second window would work best. I crop the photos and arrange the captions. *Handwoven* is also offering an e-book for sale. My boss and I (the entire Web department) test the shopping cart procedure for this new product and write download instructions for customers.

After lunch, I tackle a number of small projects. I begin by removing a recent random drawing giveaway, which offered prizes like a hand-stitched linen tablecloth. I pull the names from the database and send them to the circulation manager. The assistant editor for *Interweave Knits* sends me corrections to the fall 2005 issue, which I add to the Web site. Then an advertising manager asks how often an advertiser-sponsored pattern on the Web site was accessed. I pull the data and send it to her. A frantic e-mail from the publicist arrives, followed by a phone call. A press release needs to be added to the online press room and a book signing added to the *Hip to Stitch* Web site, a standalone microsite for a single book title. When I look at the site, I'm reminded to send an e-mail to the twenty-four-year-old author, asking if she wants to change her online poll question. The current poll, "What are you itchin' to stitch?," was designed to appeal to *Teen* readers who saw her jeans embroidery pattern in the magazine last month. I convert the press release to PDF, adding our standard header and footer. One of the marketing managers comes by to tell me about a new Web promotion—a free pattern to those attending Knit-Out events—and another e-mail arrives. This one is from a sales manager asking me to change a shop address in our online directory.

Before I leave for the day, I check the production schedule and send an e-mail to a magazine designer, asking about a certain necklace project that must be posted in a few days. I also write out a list of remaining tasks so I can stay on track. Other than a weekly departmental meeting, my time is my own.

Other tasks this month include creating an online reader survey, adding reviewers' quotes to our book pages, posting new magazine submission guidelines, posting online holiday subscription forms, designing a new microsite for a special issue publication, and creating a pink button for the *Knitted Babes* Knit-Along (a blog where everyone works on projects from the same book).

In addition to the day-to-day tasks, I've also tackled some larger projects that use my librarian background. I've expanded the new books pages to include more information, such as tables of contents, sample page spreads, author photos, and review quotes. When I worked a traditional reference job, I sometimes found book descriptions to be scarce. It feels good to offer solid, detailed information about our books.

Another large project involved the article archives for two magazines. This required indexing and cataloging skills as I skimmed the articles and grouped them into categories. I've also reorganized the project pages for the various magazines by category like "bracelets" or "quilting," offering customers another navigation option besides date.

PROS AND CONS

When reviewing the pros and cons for this position, it's important to remember that what is positive to one person may be negative to another. For example, this job requires long periods alone at a desk; it also is susceptible to interruptions and switching gears. Some might find these work conditions pleasant or invigorating; others might find them isolating or confusing.

Pros

There are several positive aspects to working in a Web-related position in a small publishing house.

Control over Web site. Traditional libraries tend to operate under an umbrella organization, whether it is a university, government, or corporation. This can make it difficult, even impossible, to reconcile your Web goals with those of the larger organization. A publishing Web site, however, is self-sufficient. You can respond quickly to new ideas or customer needs. Coming from an academic background, I found it quite an adjustment to be told to go ahead with an idea immediately rather than wade through layers of committees over several months.

Flexibility in job duties. A small organization offers the opportunity to undertake tasks outside your job description. One fun aspect for me, for example, is being able to comment on the effectiveness of several possible magazine or book covers.

Creativity. Publishers, especially in the crafts niche, tend to be visually oriented. This means that your work with the Web site involves colors and images, not just words. You may, as I have done, create Web sites with hot pink or turquoise and no one will blink. In addition, because you are surrounded by creative people, you may find yourself open to learning new things or feeling more inspired than usual. Since I've been here, I've learned to string beaded necklaces and even had a quick knitting lesson in the cafeteria.

Helping others. Altruism is not a quality normally associated with business, though it is apt for this particular company. One of my joys in this job has been to post our eBay charity auctions.

Cons

There are three challenges in this type of position.

Lack of other librarians. One possible downside to working in a nontraditional environment is the absence of librarian colleagues. You may be the only librarian in your department or the entire company. Your boss is unlikely to be a librarian and may have different philosophies or goals. You may even have difficulty communicating. (Publishers and librarians are both overly fond of their own acronyms.) On the other hand, you may be asked in meetings, as I have, "What do librarians think about Google Book Search, e-books, Amazon.com?" As a librarian, you have a unique perspective to share.

Communication. People who gravitate toward publishing typically view themselves as good communicators. But because the Web falls outside of normal publishing workflow, it does not always merit the same attention as print publications. One Web editor notes, "Those who supply content to Web teams don't take the content seriously" (McGovern 2003). You might find yourself repeatedly asking for late content or have mysterious (and usually pressing) Web content arrive on your desk without any warning. Or you might only learn about forthcoming Web content by flipping through the latest copy of the magazine and seeing a note to customers telling them to check the Web site. I have encountered all those situations more than once.

Technology. The use of technology in publishing appears to lag somewhat behind other fields. Though many employees are experts in their narrow technological niches, they are less tech-savvy overall than typical academic library staff. With your broad technology training, you may find yourself answering questions about e-mail or spreadsheets. You may also experience some resistance toward tech-heavy solutions like database-driven Web sites. This appears to be changing as younger, more tech-savvy people enter the field.

HOW WOULD I GET A JOB LIKE YOURS?

Although the traditional career ladder for publishing is well defined with numerous steps from editorial assistant to editor-in-chief, the path for IT-related folks is less clear. The Internet is new territory for many publishers, although more of them are seeing the benefits of moving beyond a static, brochure type of Web site.

"Magazines are a natural fit for a web presence, because magazines share many characteristics of web based communications: well defined content that appeals to a relatively narrow audience sector, and timeliness of information" (Bury 2005). An article in *Folio* goes a step further: "The web has placed huge new demands on publishers, creating new departments and job descriptions out of whole cloth" (Klein 2005). This newness can help you shape your ideal career path.

Common college backgrounds for publishing include journalism, English, marketing, and information technology (LearnDirect 2005). For example, my boss has a journalism background. In the craft publishing niche, hobbies can be your most important job qualifications. Another librarian-turned-Webmaster at a publishing house, Michael McCulley, cites "editorial skills, business savvy, technical skills, and Web knowledge" as valuable assets for Internet-related careers (Eberts 2004).

Librarians with a technical bent are uniquely qualified for this type of job. As a library student, you've probably spent hours analyzing how to improve Web site navigation, organize information, or explain technical things to nontechnical people. Who better than a librarian to explain why lumping content under the heading "general" is a bad idea, or why just a sentence of marketing copy and a thumbnail book cover isn't enough to persuade someone to look at— let alone buy—a book?

Several organizations and publications may be helpful in researching this type of job. My particular job was advertised on the Society for Technical Communication Web site. This organization is geared toward technical writers who often work in online environments. The Special Libraries Association and the *Chronicle of Higher Education* may also list relevant positions. The *Chronicle* also features a column titled "Beyond the Ivory Tower," which offers insight to academics, including new graduate students, who choose careers outside the university. Reading trade publications like *Publishers Weekly*, *Folio*, *Electronic Publishing*, and *Library Journal* will help you learn about current publishing trends.

While in library school, consider an internship or practicum to try out the publishing field. Often these experiences turn into full-time opportunities. Like traditional librarianship, publishing is a small field, and you may hear of openings by word of mouth. For traditional entry-level publishing positions like assistant editor or marketing assistant, a summer publishing school like that at the University of Denver often leads to interviews and job offers. As with libraries, the transition from print to online media has made this an especially exciting and challenging time to work in publishing.

RELATED RESOURCES

Works Cited

Bury, Scott. 2005. Cross-media publishing. *Electronic Publishing* 29, no. 6: 18–22.

Eberts, Marjorie. 2004. *Careers for cybersurfers and other online types*. Chicago: VGM Career Books.

Klein, Jeffrey S. 2005. Human resources: The key to the business. *Folio* 33, no. 5: 28.

LearnDirect. Web content editor/manager (job profile). www.learndirectadvice.co.uk (accessed February 5, 2006).

McGovern, Gerry. Content management: Web publishing needs real discipline. *New Thinking*. www.gerrymcgovern.com/nt/2003/nt_2003_11_03_discipline.htm (accessed February 5, 2006).

Young, Tara. 2005. Knitters hooked on prison poncho. *Washington Post*, March 13.

Additional Resources

Chronicle of Higher Education. Chronicle Careers. chronicle.com/jobs (accessed August 22, 2006).

Crafts Report. www.craftsreport.com (accessed February 5, 2006).

Electronic Publishing. www.electronicpublishing.com (accessed February 5, 2006).

Folio Magazine. www.foliomag.com (accessed February 5, 2006).

Henderson, Harry. 2004. *Career opportunities in computers and cyberspace*. New York: Ferguson.

Interweave Press. www.interweave.com (accessed February 5, 2006).

Library Journal. www.libraryjournal.com (accessed February 5, 2006).

Publishers Weekly. www.publishersweekly.com (accessed February 5, 2006).

Society for Technical Communication. www.stc.org (accessed February 5, 2006).

Special Libraries Association. www.sla.org (accessed February 5, 2006).

Yager, Fred, and Jan Yager. 2005. New media departments. In *Career opportunities in the publishing industry*. New York: Checkmark Books.

CHAPTER 81

Database Librarian

Entertainment Weekly (EW) is the magazine for everything about pop culture. We cover movies, music, TV, DVDs, books, and everything in between, from Internet sites and video games to the latest kids' toys. The Web site is an extension of the magazine that contains PopWatch (a blog), TV Watches (day-after snarky recaps of the most popular shows on television), and original feature stories.

I am responsible for all of the data found on *EW*'s Web site. Most of my time is spent managing the category tool. This includes adding and deleting categories and deciding where certain products fall. (Is Gregor Samsa an indie rock band or a character in Franz Kafka's *The Metamorphosis*? This is, of course, a trick question because both answers are correct, but it is something I deal with on a daily basis.) Every article that is in the magazine is found online, so the rest of my time is spent coding those stories with XML. I also manage the intern program for the site and pitch and write stories.

A TYPICAL WORKDAY

I never thought that I'd be the type of person that could work from home and love it. After all, I am one of those people that *has* to be around others; at least, I thought I was. But ever since relocating away from *EW*'s New York office, I don't know how I could go back to a cube farm.

My day lazily begins around 9:30 a.m., when I make my five-second commute down the stairs and turn on the TV to check out what's on the *Today* show, *CNN This Morning*, and *Regis and Kelly*. I know, I know, it's painful, but it's part of my job. I have to be informed about what's going on in pop culture!

Once 10 a.m. hits, I head over to my office area, which is elegantly decked out in band posters, piles of CDs, video games, books, and mountains of press releases. I turn on my laptop, log in to Instant Messenger, and check my e-mail. But has the real work really begun? Not yet; I still have to check a plethora of blogs, news sites, and entertainment portals to see what's being reported that the major networks missed. After this gets done, *then* I can really start my day. And how does that happen? Well, by going to the EW.com site and reading over the newly posted stories, making sure there are categories attached to those stories, and, most important, that they are the right categories. The last thing I want to see is a story about the new Madonna record with a category for the Donnas attached to it. (It could happen!)

With the morning routine out of the way, I head to the physical mailbox to see what has arrived. Will it be the new issue of *Interview*? Maybe it's the *New York Observer* or the always scintillating *IT Architect*! Alas, all I got today were four CDs and two video games.

After returning to my office I start going through my e-mail, dealing with reader comments that come in to the Webmaster account and those that are sent directly to me. (I have the honor of being the person listed on the site to contact if you have technical issues.) Many of the comments that come in actually aren't for me but for the promotions and marketing department of the magazine. Sometimes, though, readers let me know that they are having problems finding a specific article on the site or they let me know that something is not working on the site. (It's usually an incorrectly placed date in a film's category entry that is breaking the site. Lucky for me, it's an easy fix.)

If there is a new e-mail from Exhibitor Relations, a movie-tracking firm, I'll go through it and add new film projects and release dates into the category tool. I'm probably the only person who flipped out on seeing *Return of the Living Dead: Rave to the Grave* on the schedule. (I was later crushed when it was pulled from major theatrical release, but at least it still aired on the SciFi channel, sans curse words.)

If it's a Monday, it's teleconference time. I call down to New York for the weekly staff meeting, where the executive editor goes over what needs to be done that week for the site. On Wednesdays, I call down for the weekly news meeting, where anything goes when it comes to pitching entertainment-related stories. Occasionally there are other meetings I'll need to be in on, sometimes with the manager of the e-content group for Time and other times with the senior database librarian for Time Interactive regarding the new ontology that's being developed.

When not participating in meetings or surfing the site, I focus on cleaning up the data from the magazine's previous issue. All of the text from each issue is online, but it must first be coded and have the correct categories attached to each article. Many times the articles must be created from scratch using our content tool. It can be an intense and laborious process, but it's something I quite enjoy, because I get to see everything that's coming out.

The magazine that is available on newsstands on Friday actually closes on Tuesday night (so it can get to the printer and out to stores in time), and the raw text usually arrives at EW.com sometime on Thursday. My interns and I spend Thursday and Friday cleaning up the text before publishing the electronic version of the issue on the site. Cleaning up the issue consists of not only coding but also writing. We write decks (the secondary headline below the main headline) for all the articles so that online readers will know what the article is about. A headline that says "The Cowboy Way" doesn't let an online reader know that the article is about Clint Eastwood. We write what's called tout-link text for the article that may say "Clint Eastwood talks about a B-movie hero," giving the reader more context.

Another big job is monitoring the message boards. Every single review and TV Watch on the site has a message board attached. This allows readers to respond to what has been written and share their own perspective on the product being talked about. However, people can sometimes get out of control, using expletives or veering off-topic. We have a banned word list that has over six hundred entries; it contains full words, derivations of words, and partial words with wildcards. Even with this in place, our users find creative ways to get around our safeguards. These boards are monitored daily, and during *American Idol* season, they are monitored every hour during the workweek.

I don't always spend my time off-site. When I'm looking for new interns I travel down to the city for interviews. I also go down to the city on interns' first and last days on the job. After all, I do have to train them! I usually spend two to three days training new interns before returning home. While I'm in the city, I also make time to meet with the technical folks at Time Interactive to let them know of concerns I have. Not a moment of my time in the city is wasted.

Other duties that I have that aren't specifically library-related include writing the Download This (music) entries for the site's blog, PopWatch; writing the occasional feature story; managing, hiring, and training the interns; ordering office supplies for the staff; maintaining the vacation calendar; and dealing with most of the reader e-mails that come in to the site. The day is never long enough to get everything done, but I can't complain, because I'm surrounded by entertainment all the time.

PROS AND CONS

One of the best things about working for *Entertainment Weekly* is that it comes with a lot of perks. Where else can you have a job where you have an expense account from day one that allows you to get reimbursed for going to the movies, joining professional organizations, and anything else you can think of that is entertainment-related (within certain limits, of course)? The environment is extremely relaxed. My typical work dress consists of a band T-shirt and jeans; it really doesn't vary except for the sweater or hoodie over the shirt in the winter. I also get to be on top of all the latest entertainment news. Music is my other love; because I write for the site, I get new releases months before they are available to the public.

If there is one bad thing about working the site, it's dealing with outdated technology. The site has recently gone through a redesign that should take away many of the hiccups. The other con about my position is that I can't keep my interns, which means I have to train a new slew of them every six months—sometimes earlier if they leave for a full-time job! It can be frustrating, but it is great when an intern leaves for a job at another magazine (one is currently an associate editor at *Life & Style*).

HOW WOULD I GET A JOB LIKE YOURS?

The first place to start would be by joining the NewsLib e-mail list. Almost every librarian working in magazines and newspapers is a member, so many jobs get posted there and, most important, *only* there! Other places to look for positions include JournalismJobs.com and Ed2010.com. Although those two sites are mostly for journalism students, you never know what you may find. Another good source to read about the state of journalism is Mediabistro.com. I highly recommend reading the site and keeping up to date with the industry. Jobs like mine aren't generally posted in traditional library outlets.

If you ask me how I got my job, my answer is simple: luck. But I was also passionate about the subject. I was lucky enough to intern at *People* magazine's research center in the summer during my two years of graduate work. After I finished my degree, I waited five months for the right job to come along. Then my first job at *EW* opened up (I worked in their library for one and a half years). I sent one simple e-mail to the manager, and I was interviewing a week later. In that interview I let my passion for pop culture shine through. *EW* is not a typical work environment. A cookie-cutter professional cover letter won't get you an interview, at least not with me. Many others who hire at the magazine are the same way. Passion for pop is what gets you in.

PART IX

Associations and Agencies

CHAPTER 82

Director, Library Association

JENIFER GRADY

This young organization, ALA-APA: the Organization for the Advancement of Library Employees, is yours. I am helping build, with lots of assistance and input from colleagues and volunteers in the library community, an organization with two missions: to encourage and manage certification programs for specializations within the field and to support salary improvement initiatives for the nation's library workers (including librarians and support staff). National certification using the course/evaluation model is new for the profession of librarianship, whereas promoting the pay equity movement has a twenty-year history in the American Library Association. ALA-APA has no membership but serves the library community through programs, products, and policies. My activities include implementing promotional/outreach campaigns, advocacy, monitoring career trends, and editing and promoting an electronic newsletter, *Library Worklife: HR E-News for Today's Leaders*, focused on human resources issues. Administratively, I support projects of the four standing committees in ALA-APA, cultivate the board relationship, oversee an annual budget of $250,000, and manage fundraising activities.

A TYPICAL WORKDAY

The First Half

On this particular day, I check e-mail, as I will do countless times during the day. I peek at e-mail list digests for news and career and human resources–related trends in libraries, nonprofits, and corporations. I believe that we should take tips from outside the profession, and I save possible topics and writers for *Library Worklife*. I check my calendar for the previous day and the next day, as well as the current day, to see what I missed, what I need to prepare for, and what I need to do today.

I hit the jackpot on two electronic discussion groups, MONEYTALKS and NEXGENLIB-L. In one was a message about a book called *Why Men Earn More* (by Warren Farrell), and in the other was a response to an article called "Digital Dirt." I e-mail Farrell's publisher, who responds immediately and directs me to the author's Web site. Farrell contacts me right away.

We set up a time to talk about his research and how it applies to a predominantly female profession like librarianship. I e-mail the reprint office of *Newsday* (N.Y.) newspaper and receive a quick approval to reprint the "Digital Dirt" article. When I call the office, the person who gives permission is a librarian! And the son of a librarian! I love the serendipity of this work.

This gets me thinking about the next month's newsletter. Publishing a monthly electronic newsletter is rewarding, but the pressure to fill it each month can be vexing. I look to see what I already have in the hopper, whom I need to nudge to get their submissions in, and which gaps I need to fill before the deadline. With an electronic newsletter, the deadlines aren't as strict, but *every* time I have published it there has been a human or technological glitch, so I have to keep plans in motion. Even so, it always gets out on time, and I thank everyone involved.

For a break, I get my snail mail, and this time it's a donation check. This doesn't happen often, so I'm giddy! For efficiency, I check e-mail for any online donations as well. I get two donations of $25, so I print out thank-you letters and call the donors to ask whether they want a DVD or VHS copy of *Working @ Your Library: For Love or Money*, our advocacy video. I package the videos, finding odd pieces of cardboard to protect the DVDs, and mail them to the donors. I fill out donation forms and submit them to the Development Office with copies of the check and e-mails.

I remember that I need to order more letterhead paper. I used the last of it for the Certified Public Library Administrator (CPLA) Program RFP, for which I sent letters to potential providers like library schools, ALA divisions, ALA chapters, and regional consortia. The supply manager gives me prices and quantities. This order reminds me that I need to send a box of promotional materials for a state chapter conference, so I search for the contact person's address. I call to find out the estimated audience number and package our promotional materials (everything you want to know about ALA-APA, Give $5 in '05 donation, *Library Worklife* information, and Top 10 Ways to Get Involved with ALA-APA brochures).

The phone rings, and it's the director of a participant library asking when the *Survey of Librarian Salaries* is going to be in the online ALA store for purchase. She doesn't want to hear about our struggles to improve the content and aesthetics of the survey, or the myriad reasons why the survey was delayed. The letter says it was to be available in September (it's now November) and she wants her 25 percent discount. I humbly explain that we appreciate her response to the survey and that she will be very happy when she sees that the survey now includes state as well as regional data. Then I tell her that the survey will be in the store next week.

This reminds me that we must settle how to process the discount for survey participants. This is the second year the survey has been available for purchase online and we—meaning a specialist from ALA Editions, the director of the Office for Research and Statistics, and I—have to figure out a way to give the discount without causing undue burden to the distribution office. We also have some software hindrances around pricing that we must work out for the next edition. I send an e-mail to all the relevant parties and leave my desk, reading the latest issue of *American Libraries* as I take the elevator and walk down the halls. I have impromptu meetings with each person to devise a solution. Another crisis averted. I check my e-mail again and get the same question about the discount from another anxious participant, and now I have a concrete answer. I print out the answer and put it in the "to be filed" pile.

Lunch

I put any ideas that come to me during lunch in my PDA with an alarm to remind me to take action when I return to the office, or I leave myself a voicemail. Ideas generated now may be useful later, and I know they'll flee from my mind if I don't capture them. Work/life balance is something we talk about in the newsletter, so I try to practice it myself by getting away from my desk (sometimes) during the day.

The Second Half

I contact the chairs of the certification committees to discuss what we need to accomplish before the ALA Midwinter Meeting. Both committees, the CPLA Certification Review Committee (CRC) and the Certification Program Committee (CPC), will be meeting, but with different goals. The CRC will be reviewing applications from providers for the CPLA program and planning for reviewing applications from certification participants in the spring. The CPC is the overseeing body that will be meeting about developing new certification programs. The chair and I talk about how we will split speaking engagements at ALA division leaders' meetings (executive boards, committees) about why certification is important in their fields and how to begin the process. I update my already full conference schedule with the "what" because we don't yet know the "where."

I receive a phone call from a potential provider who has a question about the RFP. I answer him and send my response to the CRC so they'll be aware of the type of questions we're getting. This reminds me that I need to send a reminder to the institutions that might want to be providers, so I schedule a time to do this next week.

The board of directors will be here in a few weeks, so I edit the minutes from the Annual Conference based on input from the executive director of ALA-APA (and ALA) and resend the file. I review the minutes from several past meetings to make sure that I have attended to all of their recommendations. I place a reminder in my calendar to take a few hours next week to delve deeply into my current actual budget and compare it to the proposed budget. To do this analysis, I need a block of time to set my mind to the task. Though I monitor the budget monthly, I find that I have more "aha!" moments when I give it the time it deserves at the end of each quarter. I also have to compare it to the next year's budget, so I know I'll probably be calling the accountants and even the chief financial officer.

Is ALA-APA Council talking about the certification program? Let me search their discussion group before I leave so I can answer any questions.

At 11:30 p.m. I call and leave myself a message at work to ask the ALA-APA Bylaws Committee Chair about the Midwinter Meeting agenda.

GROWING PAINS

I am one of the few people I know who really loves her work. I have the responsibility for undergirding this small association with a huge mission by providing a strong foundation of early successes and sustainable financing. It is sometimes overwhelming to be the only person completely dedicated to these missions. However, because I know that I am not alone in my efforts to make it happen, I stay encouraged and enthusiastic about the possibilities. When I hear that someone got a higher salary because of the negotiation workshop at the Annual Conference, I know that ALA-APA fulfills needs.

It's so exciting to be a part of what grew out of powerful movements for certification and better salaries. There are people in the field who are proponents of one or the other, and a few who feel the two are complementary. I enjoy the challenge of finding more people to join those three camps and to believe in our future enough to pledge time, money, and effort to ALA-APA.

Speaking and fundraising go hand in hand with my interlinked goals of increasing awareness and strengthening the budget. The first is easy, but corporate fundraising is more difficult.

I am dedicating more time to investigating entities that might have an interest in our mission, structuring a compelling "ask," and having planned responses for questions and rejections. Answering "What's in it for me?" is easier for individuals and libraries than it is for those outside of our arena, but it's a critical question that all of us need to think about as we seek funding, whether it's for our own salaries, purchases for the collection, or a new building.

THE SPIRIT OF A LEADER

Those with an entrepreneurial spirit would do well in a position like this. Even so, there's no place for lone rangers. A well-established nonprofit must still grow, and staff and volunteers are key, so you can't think you can do it alone. We carry forth all of the suggestions of governing bodies and committees. There is some routine from year to year, like publishing deadlines, conferences, and board and committee meetings, and there are special events like National Library Workers Day (the Tuesday of National Library Week), but the organization has to continue to find ways to meet the changing needs of its constituents, even those who do not belong to the organization. Doing more with less is a situation we are used to. You have to be creative by extending yourself and using the talents, experiences, contributions, and advice others are willing to give.

Heading a nonprofit is not for fearful people. You will need help, so be comfortable asking for it. You also have to be confident enough to ask for assistance from anyone—leaders in the field, CEOs, editors, directors, political figures, and so on. Little should deter you from fulfilling your mission. I hope that you find, as I have, that boldness comes from your passion for the work that you will be doing.

It's important to be able to prioritize because member needs, meetings, and requests will shake up your plans. You must be able to shift your focus, even if only temporarily, to attend to urgencies, and then return to your other business.

Finally, you must celebrate *every* success, small and large. Only you know what it takes to reach your personal and organizational goals, what brilliance you've shown, what adversities you've overcome. Tell others!

FIND OUT MORE

ALA-APA: The Organization for the Advancement of Library Employees. www.ala-apa.org (accessed January 7, 2006).

———, Certification News. www.ala-apa.org/certification/certification.html (accessed August 20, 2006).

———, *Library Worklife.* www.ala-apa.org/newsletter/newsletter.html (accessed August 20, 2006).

———, Salaries. www.ala-apa.org/salaries/salaries.html (accessed August 20, 2006).

American Library Association, Office for Human Resource Development and Recruitment. www.ala.org/hrdr (accessed January 7, 2006).

———, Office for Research and Statistics. www.ala.org/ors (accessed January 7, 2006).

American Society of Association Executives. www.asaecenter.org (accessed August 20, 2006).

CHAPTER 83

Director of Information and Communications/ Privacy Officer, Advertising Association

JO-ANN MCQUILLAN

I have one of those long and ambiguous job titles: director of information and communications *and* privacy officer. I prefer Information Goddess, Queen of Information, or on certain days, InfoBitch!

I work at the Institute of Communications and Advertising (ICA), Canada's professional trade association for advertising agencies. My job is multifaceted: I oversee all library operations for our private collection, run an information service that assists over seven thousand members in approximately one hundred ad agencies, manage four Web sites, run informational seminars on many topics, edit and publish our association newsletter, and oversee our association's other publications. On top of that, I manage our association's privacy policy, which can be quite tricky considering that we have a professional development division, charitable fundraising, and other complex initiatives throughout the year.

There are usually at least five current projects on the go—today, for example, we are researching airports, apple juice, gas nozzles, electronics, retention rates, and home renovation trends. All of these projects are considered urgent by the frantic people requesting the information.

I do research for nonmembers such as industry partners, our education faculty, the government, and other librarians. We also work with research partners from several different countries, sharing information and developing new information products.

We have an active publishing division, with a focus on disseminating marketing communications best practices documents. I also work on other book publishing projects, including project management, research, editing, marketing, and sales.

Because intelligence gathering is such a huge part of my job, my assistant is crucial in this area. I find information about new studies, statistics, reports, and other info nuggets. My assistant retrieves the information, I tag each item with a subject designation, and then the information is stored in our research files, of which we have over six hundred and counting. This allows us to analyze industries and products quickly, using the clippings for clues that help us build customized packages of information.

In my new role as privacy officer, I have developed our privacy policy and protocols in response to new legislation in Canada that changes how we handle personal information. Educating staff and implementing new internal policies and procedures is trying, as is any major corporate change. I now handle all privacy issues, access to information requests, and mandatory reporting.

The ICA has a corporate Web site, an ad agency profile Web site, an informative advertising educational site, and our Canadian advertising awards online archive. I am responsible for keeping these sites current, troubleshooting, and developing new formats.

A TYPICAL WORKDAY

I am one of those freaks who loves to get up really early and go to work—in fact, I arrive at the office two hours before everyone else. I use the two quiet hours to serve clients on the Atlantic coast, scan four newspapers, and go through hundreds of e-mails before the doors open.

I get thousands of e-mails daily, and I really enjoy dealing with them. I start my day by looking for information requests that have arrived overnight by e-mail, fax, or telephone.

I scan the *Toronto Star*, *National Post*, *Globe and Mail*, and *USA Today* each day, as well as hundreds of industry and trade publications. We subscribe to over fifty print journals and countless electronic alerts. This constant reading allows me to gather information and clippings for our subject files. This is a huge part of my job—proactively gathering nuggets of information in anticipation of the tricky reference question that will inevitably come to me.

Members of our association are allowed to use my services for free as part of their membership package. Their fees pay for me to be here and for the library collection. I am the person they call when they have quick reference questions or need custom research tools or larger information packages on any topic. Because we work in advertising, there is no limit to what we research. We have researched sex shops, restorative hair tonics, Sanskrit nouns, magnets, dialysis equipment, soup, and a million more wacky subjects. Last year, we completed close to seven hundred such projects of varying degrees of depth and complexity.

You might wonder exactly what kinds of requests we handle for our clients. I believe there are three levels of assistance we provide: quick reference, handholding, and information dumps.

Quick reference. Quick reference questions are those that we can answer easily by referring to a specific resource that is readily available. We are frequently asked to determine which ad agencies are being used by a specific company—in Canada, there is no comprehensive resource that answers this question. We have developed a proprietary process that allows us to find the answer quickly. Often, we will be given a list of companies (sometimes up to one hundred) and we are charged with determining the advertiser-agency alignment. Conversely, we also help determine full client lists for competing agencies—Agency X might want to keep an eye on Agency Z, and one way of doing this is to watch the projects they are working on and new clients that they are acquiring.

Handholding. Handholding works on the assumption that some clients want to be autonomous, to a degree. As all info pros know, sometimes a client can't describe exactly what he is seeking, but he would know it if he saw it in front of him. I develop pathfinders for clients to allow them to do some guided searching of targeted resources. For example, a client might need to get a better understanding of the car rental industry or a specific product category, such as kosher foods. I use my resources, including our subject files, to develop a hyperlinked list of online reports, associations, statistics, primers, and so on. This allows clients to have a snazzy little pathfinder to click away at when it suits them and to build on their initial research findings. These types of tools are also very educational for me; often I am creating pathfinders on topics about which I know nothing.

Information dumps. The final level of assistance is the most complex and involves a level of service that traditional librarians do not provide. Information dumps, literature reviews, and evidence to support specific arguments usually involve at least a day per request and often even longer. An information dump is when we retrieve something very specific; we buy information and supplement it with free information to make an organized package or primer on a specific topic. This could be about new media trends, menu trends, or the use of sound cues in broadcast ads—anything that requires painting a holistic picture. Literature reviews are what I do for my clients because I love them and I know that they are "lazy." I say *lazy* with the utmost respect—these people work dreadfully long hours, have huge obstacles to overcome, and face extreme pressure. Reading fifteen scholarly articles and summarizing them is simply not feasible for my clients. My favorite extreme information request is providing magical statistics—those statistics that prove an assertion, however insane it might be. For example, someone might need a statistic to prove that women eat more lima beans than men do or to prove that people in Toronto are more likely to be victims of an assault. Even if these assertions are wrong, there is usually some evidence to support anything. I like using these opportunities to impart sound methodological wisdom to my clients.

There are some types of work that I do not do. I do not give my clients proprietary information, but I will tell them exactly where to find it. I will rarely go out and do field research, although I have been asked. I will sometimes do off-site research for clients, but only if I think it is going to contribute to my research in the future. I am given access to extremely confidential information when working with clients, and I never share this with other clients, although I have been asked. I have had some questions over the years that are simply un-reasonable: my favorite one was a request for me to get a photo of the front of *every* convenience store in the United States. The client asked for this one with a straight face, believe it or not.

In addition to an abundance of office work, I also travel to member agencies to tutor staff on effective research techniques and tools. I get to spend time with teams of all sizes and help them find the information they always thought was on the Internet but could never find.

I couldn't do all of this by myself—I am blessed to have a great library technician working with me. She is able to take over a number of tasks that bog me down, like serials management, circulation, and filing.

Other tasks that I might undertake on a typical day are editing our newsletter (published four to five times a year); preparing publications for release; collection development; internal research requests; and research projects with members of government, other associations, academics, and miscellaneous experts.

I am also a huge fan of mentoring; each year I try to take on two library technician interns from a local college. These students are crucial in helping with the intense backlog of work we always seem to have, and it allows me to teach new info pros about alternative jobs. At the time of this writing, I have mentored six students, and all have left the ICA with new skills, increased confidence, and a fresh attitude.

I have a soft spot for students who call me requesting research assistance. I have a policy of helping students who are polite and articulate, on the condition that they share their papers or projects with us afterward.

PROS AND CONS

Pros

1. Extremely stimulating and interesting work.
2. Fast pace.
3. Fascinating industry.

4. No limits on types of information explored.

5. Lots of responsibilities.

6. Lots of opportunities to do different types of work.

7. Networking with SLA Advertising and Marketing Division peers.

8. Nontraditional library work.

9. No cataloging!

Cons

1. Clients in five time zones.

2. Research in both official languages (French and English).

3. Periods of extreme stress.

4. Lack of peers in Canadian advertising industry.

5. Highly competitive client base.

6. Clients are demanding and often don't articulate what they really need.

7. The other ad librarians in Canada are becoming obsolete, putting more pressure on me to fill the void.

HOW WOULD I GET A JOB LIKE YOURS?

I found this job because I wanted to. I set a job goal early on: I needed an extremely interesting job that would prevent boredom. I looked at companies whose work interested me and then pursued opportunities with them. I actually found my position by employing a simple online search strategy: using Monster.com, I searched for job ads with the word *information* and chose not to limit the search to any specific industry. That helped me find the ad for my current job.

I specifically chose to work in the not-for-profit sector, and I highly encourage other information misfits to do the same. I have never been comfortable contributing to anyone's bottom line (aside from my own), and I like having lots of responsibility combined with independence. In associations and other not-for-profits, one is more likely to have a much larger swath of influence and to have a lot of responsibilities. I wear a lot of hats, and for me, that is ideal. I know a lot of info pros who would not enjoy my workload, the pressure, and the "other duties as required," but I thrive on these things.

I am also essentially a solo (despite the fact that I have a technician on staff) and as an only child, I think I am well suited to working alone. If you thrive on group work and real-time peer support, being a solo might not be a suitable career path for you.

Everyone has a unique history, and mine made me an ideal fit for this job: it required high energy, a lot of creativity, and a fearless renegade attitude. I didn't have industry-specific experience before I got this job, and sometimes I think this gave me an edge: I came to the job fresh out of school with an open mind and enthusiasm. I had to learn everything very quickly, which is easier if you are still on a grad school learning rush.

RELATED RESOURCES

CASSIES: Canadian Advertising Success Stories. www.cassies.ca (accessed June 10, 2006).

Institute of Communications and Advertising. www.ica-ad.com (accessed June 10, 2006).

———, Agency search. www.agencysearch.ca (accessed June 10, 2006).

My Big Future. www.mybigfuture.ca (accessed June 10, 2006).

Here are a few of the resources I use on daily basis.

Adnews. www.adnews.com (accessed June 10, 2006).

AMPQ. www.ampq.com (accessed June 10, 2006).

Dialog. www.dialog.com (accessed June 10, 2006). Favorite files: Advertiser & Agency Red Books (files 177 and 178) and TableBase (file 93).

Eloda. www.eloda.com (accessed June 10, 2006).

Factiva. www.factiva.com (accessed June 10, 2006).

FoodNavigator. www.foodnavigator.com (accessed June 10, 2006).

Globe and Mail. www.theglobeandmail.com (accessed June 10, 2006).

Google Alerts. www.google.ca/alerts?hl = en (accessed June 10, 2006).

Infopresse. www.infopresse.com (accessed June 10, 2006).

Marketing. www.marketingmag.ca (accessed June 10, 2006).

Media in Canada. www.mediaincanada.com (accessed June 10, 2006).

MERX. www.merx.com (accessed June 10, 2006).

National Post. www.canada.com/nationalpost/index.html (accessed June 10, 2006).

NPD Group. www.npd.com (accessed June 10, 2006).

PubZone. www.pubzone.com (accessed June 10, 2006).

Statistics Canada. www.statcan.ca (accessed June 10, 2006).

Strategy Magazine. www.strategymag.com (accessed June 10, 2006).

Toronto Star. www.thestar.com (accessed June 10, 2006).

USA Today. www.usatoday.com (accessed June 10, 2006).

World Advertising Research Center. www.warc.com (accessed June 10, 2006).

CHAPTER 84

Senior Program Officer, Federal Agency

"So where do you work?" is the usual question at any library conference, workshop, or seminar. When I worked at an academic library, I could just tell someone the name of my university and they would nod and smile. Today when I respond, "I work at the Institute of Museum and Library Services," I'm usually confronted with a quizzical look or a blank stare. On the other hand, if they have heard about the Library Services and Technology Act, I usually get a warm handshake and a wide grin. Usually people are pleasantly surprised that I am a librarian who works at a federal agency. What is harder to understand is that although the agency has "library" and "museum" in its title, the agency is not a museum or a library. The agency does not have access to hundreds of online databases or books you can browse on the shelf. Yet I decided to leave my tenured academic job to become a federal employee.

BACKGROUND INFORMATION

The Institute of Museum and Library Services is an independent federal agency. Its mission is to grow and sustain a nation of learners because lifelong learning is critical to both societal and individual success. Through its grant making, convening, research, and publications, the institute empowers museums and libraries nationwide to provide leadership and services to enhance learning in families and communities, sustain cultural heritage, build twenty-first-century skills, and provide opportunities for civic participation.

We administer a federal law called the Museum and Library Services Act, which contains the Museum Services Act and the Library Services and Technology Act (LSTA). The agency receives an annual appropriation from Congress to carry out the mission of the law. In 2006, Congress appropriated $247,144,000 to the agency: $36,547,000 for museum programs and $210,597,000 for library programs. LSTA is perhaps best known for its formula grants to states. Each year every state and the territories receive money from IMLS to support library services. LSTA also provides grants to tribes and Native Hawaiian organizations for library services and National Leadership Grants and the Laura Bush 21st Century Librarian Program.

I am one of the program officers for the Laura Bush 21st Century Librarian Program. The program has been in existence since 2003 with an initial annual budget of $10 million. In 2006, the budget was approximately $23 million. The program supports programs at the master's, doctoral, and preprofessional levels; these programs build the institutional capacity of graduate schools of library and information services and support continuing education and targeted research. Since Laura Bush announced the president would support a multimillion-dollar initiative to recruit librarians in 2002, the institute has funded 1,537 master's degree students, 119 doctoral students, 660 preprofessional students, and 378 continuing education students in the library sciences. We've also supported important research like the Future of Librarians in the Workforce study.

TYPICAL JOB RESPONSIBILITIES

Most of a program officer's job responsibilities revolve around the grant cycle. For the Laura Bush Program, the current grant cycle runs from December 15 to June 30. But the cycle starts weeks before the December 15 deadline because that is when potential grantees call, e-mail, or sometimes make appointments to stop by and talk about their grant ideas. At the busiest times, usually a few days before the deadline, I receive approximately twenty to thirty urgent phone calls and e-mails per day. I was formerly an academic librarian, and the phone activity feels like working with students a few days before a final paper is due. I love hearing from people all over the country with questions about all types of innovative projects. It puts my reference librarian skills to the test and gives me an opportunity to use my strong public service orientation.

After the December 15 deadline, program officers work with our program specialist and contractors to get the applications entered into the computer and send acknowledgments to the applicants. Afterward, we work in conjunction with the assistant deputy director and the director to determine who will be selected to serve on an expert technical panel that reviews the applications. From there, we determine who will be assigned to review each application, and we prepare materials for each reviewer.

In the midst of this activity, we read all applications in preparation for the technical panels. When the technical panel meets in Washington, D.C., we usually facilitate reviewer discussions as they make recommendations about each grant. After the technical panel, we prepare the grants that received the highest ratings for a second review. If the grant passes the second review, the grants are sent to the director of IMLS for the final approval. Program officers are also responsible for negotiating with the grantees if they need to modify their budget or change the scope of the project before receiving the grant.

We monitor the grants in our area and answer any questions that arise. Finally, we read all the grant reports and on occasion call people if we need additional information or have any questions.

PROS AND CONS

In my opinion, variety is the biggest reward to being a program officer. If you are curious about librarianship as a profession, then this position is for you. As I said before, I come from an academic librarian background, but in my work at IMLS I am involved with people and projects from many types of libraries (academic, public, special, school, and state) as well as with schools of library and information science. In addition, because IMLS really encourages collaboration and innovation, program officers get a close view of the best of libraries working, collaborating, and developing creative projects.

Program officers attend several national conferences every year, and sometimes we showcase our grant recipients' work to disseminate basic information about our grants. This is a very different conference experience from my academic librarian days when I was running frantically from one committee meeting to another, waving to good friends in the hallways. Now that I'm a program officer, I still serve on committees, but I cannot chair a committee because it could pose a conflict of interest. This gives me a lot more time to talk and interact with people.

Another perk that comes with working for a federal granting agency is being a part of the government where we promote library programs to the public, Congress, and the administration, and place a spotlight on the role of libraries in American society. We also interact with other federal agencies like the National Science Foundation and the National Endowment for the Humanities. Before I arrived at the agency, I thought I had a good grasp of the federal government process, but after working here for two years I realize that I was very naive. It's not an easy or a necessarily intuitive process to understand, and I find myself learning something new every day.

The biggest con for me is although I am working for the Office of Library Services at the Institute of Museum and Library Services, I am not a practicing librarian. I am a federal employee. So if you really enjoy direct interaction with the public, accessing electronic databases, or just like being around lots of books and other print resources, this position is not for you. When we are in the middle of the grant cycle, there are a lot of things to do, and we receive a fair number of questions. But there are other times where we are just doing more process-oriented work and the phone doesn't ring for days. In addition, after the grants are awarded, we monitor them and contact the recipients if we have questions, but program officers are not directly involved with the implementation. So it's like watching the profession from a distance instead of having your hands, elbows, and knees involved in the outcome. I enjoy hearing about lots of projects and being part of the early stages of development of innovative projects. Sometimes these ideas are so exciting that I'd like to jump right in and be a part of the implementation team, but in the end it is a great experience to be in the role of a donor and see so many projects grow and develop.

HOW WOULD I GET A JOB LIKE YOURS?

If you would like to work for IMLS, my first recommendation would be to sign up for our free monthly electronic newsletter, *Primary Source*. There is a link on our home page. *Primary Source* not only provides employment information but also keeps you informed of grant deadlines, alerts you to where our staff is presenting during that month, and provides a look at some interesting projects throughout the country with highlights of IMLS grant recipients. Just browsing the newsletter provides helpful background information that could be used to fill out the employment application. An important thing to remember is that IMLS is a federal agency and the application process involves more than sending a résumé and cover letter. Check out a federal government employment book to get a general understanding of the application process. I spent a little extra time addressing all the criteria and providing very specific examples.

A final tip would be to seek out IMLS staff if you're at a meeting we're attending. We are often moderating or presenting at sessions, staffing our exhibit booth, or sitting in the audience when people are talking about IMLS grants. Any one of us would be happy to talk to you about employment or grant opportunities at the Institute of Museum and Library Services.

RELATED RESOURCES

Future of Librarians in the Workforce Study. www.libraryworkforce.org/tiki-index.php (accessed February 15, 2006).
Institute of Museum and Library Services. www.imls.gov (accessed February 15, 2006).

CHAPTER 85

Senior Planning and Development Specialist for Library Services, Federal Agency

NANCY G. FAGET

WHAT DOES A PLANNER DO?

Planning and development specialists in the federal government typically analyze data and information to identify program trends, assess current activities, and determine direction for various agency library programs. At the U.S. Government Printing Office (GPO), librarians work as planners for the Federal Depository Library Program (FDLP) to develop services for the program and the 1,266 library participants. The library program is changing dramatically to align with the agency's strategic vision and take advantage of emerging technologies.

The FDLP was established by Congress to ensure that the American public has access to its government's information. The program employs librarians to locate and acquire government documents, convert documents to other formats when necessary, create systems for managing content in many formats, and disseminate depository materials to a network of federal depository libraries in the fifty states, the District of Columbia, and U.S. territories. As a planner for the GPO, my job is to examine all aspects of the FDLP and recommend policies that could help the program operate more effectively in the twenty-first century. Beatrice L. Warde describes the printing office on a broadside entitled *This Is a Printing Office* (1932): "From this place words may fly abroad not to perish on waves of sound, not to vary with writer's hand, but fixed in time having been verified by proof." The libraries in the depository program are firmly committed to maintaining free and open access to government information, and I am firmly committed to supporting them.

As a planning and development specialist, I view the network of libraries as a system and examine how the system is operating. Do the libraries understand and comply with the rules for depositories? Do those rules make sense, or should they be changed? Are libraries entering or leaving the program, and why? How can I better support the network? Are things working from the library's perspective? I research and analyze ways to improve the system, create a plan for improvements, discuss the plan with stakeholders, sell the proposal to senior level managers, obtain funding if needed, and work cooperatively with thousands of the best librarians in the country to implement those improvements. Planners toss lots of projects into the air and keep them afloat like balloons. The work is fast paced, exciting, and satisfying when you can make a positive contribution to the program.

JUGGLING FOR A LIVING

Our agency hosted the 2005 Fall FDL Conference and Depository Library Council Meeting where training and informational sessions were offered to library staff working in depository libraries. The conference was an excellent opportunity to hold a meeting with regional depository librarians and representatives from the White House Initiative on Tribal Colleges and Universities, the American Indian Higher Education Consortium, and the Smithsonian Institution's National Museum of the American Indian. To set up this meeting, I invited speakers, reserved the room, created an invitation, outlined the agenda, and finalized handouts and materials for distribution. Our shared goal is to recruit Native American libraries as new depository libraries. I work cooperatively throughout the year with regional librarians in states where tribal colleges are located to recruit new libraries to act as depositories for government information resources. The regional depository librarian is principally responsible for ensuring federal government information is made available in a state or territory to satisfy the needs of that region. I write a follow-up report on the meeting on the types of information the tribal libraries might collect and how we might celebrate tribal libraries as new depositories during the next year's conference. In addition, I circulate a follow-up e-mail to the attendees to recap the discussion and detail ways we might collaborate in the future.

The Depository Library Council, an advisory group to our agency, is developing a new vision for the depository library program. I review the discussion paper, blog, and recap of the conference sessions to better understand the proposals for the FDLP. The advisory group is gathering input from the library community to describe the program and services in the future. As the FDLP transitions to a twenty-first-century digital information environment, there are many new functions and services the FDLP might provide. My job is to plan for and implement these new services.

A possible new service is a national virtual reference service for people seeking information about and from their government. At my former job, I helped build a virtual reference service for all users on the Army Knowledge Online Portal (1.2 million users) providing "any time, any place" reference service. This experience will be very helpful if a consortium of depository librarians is formed to provide government information reference service. My colleagues help me brainstorm ideas about possible ways to initiate such a service, which technology might be employed, how much it might cost, and how we might advertise it.

A phone call from a regional librarian to discuss a possible new depository library prompts me to review the list of depository openings. There can be only a certain number of congressionally designated depositories in each congressional district and state, so I update the list of vacancies after the census reapportionment or redistricting in each state. A new depository library in the northern part of the caller's state would certainly provide citizens better access to government information. The process of identifying openings for libraries should be performed in a more systematic way, so I begin to write a proposal for generating a list of openings that might be included in the annual directory of depository libraries. The list of openings might be circulated to members of Congress and their staffs to inform them about the designation process and how a U.S. representative or senator can designate a library in his or her district or state.

I also draft a response to a librarian who works in a depository library. Depository coordinators ask many types of questions, such as how to operate a depository, what to do when renovations limit access to the library, or when new technologies and processes will be activated. My duties also include drafting responses to congressional inquiries and questions from the public about the depository library program. Questions are routed through the customer relationship management application, so mastering this software is important. If the question seems to be a developing hot topic or one that the wider community might be asking, I suggest the question and answer as a frequently asked question in the knowledge base. There may also be a need to post the explanation to a discussion list or Web page, so I write an e-mail message with this same information to be sure it is widely disseminated.

The department I work in recently took on the responsibility for managing special partnerships with depository libraries. I accept a meeting invitation to learn about the projects that will be transferred to our department. Partnerships are agreements between the FDLP and libraries or government information publishers to provide special services to all program participants. A partnership is an exciting opportunity to work closely with the library community to develop cutting-edge information dissemination practices. Here is an example of such a partnership. Have you ever tried to find a publication that was issued by a presidential commission that is no longer active? Thanks to the University of North Texas Libraries, you can find those publications in the Cybercemetery, a partnership that provides permanent online access to publications of federal entities that are no longer in operation.

After Hurricanes Katrina and Rita, our office gathered material and resources to assist the depository libraries in damaged areas. I relay information from FEMA to the regional librarians in Texas and Louisiana so that filing on behalf of the damaged collections can be initiated. I contact publication departments at the National Institute of Child Health and Human Development, the National Institute of Mental Health, and the Center for the Study of Traumatic Stress at the Uniformed Services University of the Health Sciences to obtain special publications to distribute to evacuees. The libraries that are serving evacuees have requested such publications, so I provide that list to the GPO distribution manager who will ship the next batch of twenty thousand fact sheets. It is a pleasure to draft a letter of thanks to the agencies for providing publications on coping with stress and trauma after disasters. The depository librarians will distribute these materials in the libraries and in the shelters.

It's time to review my calendar before leaving for the day. I look at upcoming events, read messages from my favorite electronic discussion groups, and consider travel plans to the ASIST (American Society for Information Science and Technology) conference. Because this is not a work-related event, I tally up the costs to see if I can afford to go. As a volunteer posting content to the Blogs, Wikis, and Podcasting Special Interest Group, I would like to travel to the conference to help blog it and attend the International Conference on Knowledge Management. I gather materials to read during my commute home on the subway. This is an ideal way to save money (my employer pays for my travel to and from work) and find time to read. Keep your thinking cap on when reading! You just might find the next big idea.

TAKING THE GOOD WITH THE BAD

The best part of my day is when I know I've satisfied my customers. Remember, my primary customers are the staff in depository libraries, which means all of my customers are very well-informed consumers of information resources. Librarians understand the service a fellow librarian should provide and can be very tough customers! Librarians are also generous and frequently your greatest asset in planning and developing excellent services. When you've satisfied a patron who happens to be a librarian, you know you've done a good job.

Some librarians see visible progress each day. As a planner, I push plans for projects through long, collaborative processes before seeing any results. It is difficult to have patience knowing that the patrons need the services now. So why take time to collaborate with others? I have seen project plans greatly improved by input from stakeholders who bring a different perspective, fresh ideas, and new information to the meeting. A one-hour meeting with stakeholders might produce a great idea or additional opportunities to improve the plan. By maintaining open lines of communication and involving the community in the decision-making process, you end up with a plan the community participants feel ownership of, understand, and accept.

ARE YOU READY FOR A JOB LIKE THIS?

Librarians that work for the federal government are federal civil service employees. My agency, the GPO, is in the legislative branch of government. All federal jobs that are open to the public are posted at the USAJOBS Web site. Think outside the box when searching this site. Try running a series search, and enter "14, 03, 17" as the job series number. These results provide a larger pool of jobs for which you may qualify. You may find an opportunity to create Web-based tutorials or manage a network of libraries. The GPO posts unique job opportunities for librarians on their employment Web page.

Accepting an internship or student job are smart ways to begin a federal career. My federal career began when I accepted a Department of the Army internship. The internship provided me a year of funding and support to learn about the Army library program, visit possible places of employment, attend conferences and educational events, meet hundreds of librarians, and receive on-the-job training in all areas of the library so I could chart my career path. My mentor, Lee Porter, provided valuable guidance throughout the internship and patiently taught me the unwritten rules. Seek out a mentor either through your job or a professional association. It's a great gift you can give yourself and a wonderful way to learn the politics!

Housed at the Library of Congress, the Federal Library and Information Center Committee fosters excellence in federal library and information services through interagency cooperation. Their publication on job-hunting tips, *Looking for a Federal Information Job?*, and descriptions of federal libraries, FLICC's *Handbook of Federal Librarianship*, are excellent professional resources.

RELATED RESOURCES

Federal Civil Service Jobs at Office of Personnel Management (OPM) and GPO

Studentjobs.gov. www.studentjobs.gov (accessed January 7, 2006). Internships and student jobs (an excellent way to get your foot in the door).

U.S. Government Printing Office, Employment. www.gpo.gov/careers/index.html (accessed January 7, 2006).

U.S. Office of Personnel Management. *Handbook of occupational groups and families.* www.opm.gov/fedclass/text/HdBkToC.htm (accessed January 7, 2006). Learn about jobs in each job series (especially 1410, 1412, 0301).

———. Information on federal pay and leave. www.opm.gov/oca (accessed January 7, 2006).

USAJOBS. www.usajobs.opm.gov (accessed January 7, 2006). Jobs the public may apply for are posted here.

Federal Library and Information Center Committee (FLICC)

FLICC. *Handbook of federal librarianship.* www.loc.gov/flicc/pubs/federalhandbook.pdf (accessed January 7, 2006).

———, Human Resources Working Group. www.loc.gov/flicc/wghr.html (accessed January 7, 2006).

————. *Looking for a federal information job?* www.loc.gov/flicc/wg/looking.pdf (accessed January 7, 2006).

My Favorite Discussion Groups

DocTech-L. list.lib.usu.edu/mailman/listinfo/doctech-l (accessed January 7, 2006). Devoted to technical processing of government documents.

FDLP-L. listserv.access.gpo.gov (accessed January 7, 2006). Announcements from the Federal Depository Library Program.

FEDLIB: Federal Librarians Discussion List. www.loc.gov/flicc/listsrvs.html (accessed January 7, 2006).

GOVDOC-L. govdoc-l.org (accessed January 7, 2006). Discussion forum about government information and the FDLP.

KM-LIST. listserv.gsa.gov/archives/km-list.html (accessed January 7, 2006).

Knowledge Management Working Group (www.km.gov) of the Federal CIO Council which includes taxonomy and semantics groups.

SIG-BWP: American Society for Information Science & Technology Special Interest Group on Blogs, Wikis and Podcasting. mail.asis.org/mailman/listinfo/sig-bwp (accessed January 7, 2006).

CHAPTER 86

Program Coordinator, Health Organization

SHELLEY HOURSTON

I am the program director for the AIDS and Disability Action Program (ADAP), the Wellness and Disability Initiative (WDI), and the Health Literacy Network (HLN) at the British Columbia Coalition of People with Disabilities. My primary responsibility is promoting HIV prevention education for people with all types of disabilities throughout the province. I supervise one or two part-time staff (depending on funding) and several volunteers. I also write and publish two quarterly newsletters and develop plain-language HIV prevention education material in print, audio, and Braille formats. I perform consumer health research for both consumers and service providers (public health nurses, front-line workers in community agencies, and educators working with disability support staff). Finally, I am responsible for educating people with disabilities regarding their right to health information in formats that they can use, and for raising awareness among service providers of the importance of accessible health information for their clients.

A TYPICAL WORKDAY

My job requires the ability to multitask and prioritize multiple demands and a never-ending stream of work. I recognize that this is hardly unusual—especially in the information field—but I do find it challenging to monitor and keep on top of both the micro and the macro perspectives. I should acknowledge that some of my workload has been self-inflicted. I was originally hired as a librarian to manage a resource center for ADAP. When the program director left three months later, I stepped into that position and have been expanding and adding complementary programs and services for eight years.

My typical workday consists primarily of research and writing with a sprinkling of information and referral calls (referring callers to the appropriate organization for information) and current awareness/information dissemination for our executive director, other program directors, and occasionally for consumers who have asked to be informed of developments in specific areas. Depending on the day of the week, I monitor the workflow for one part-time staff person and various volunteers who manage our newsletter subscription database, newsletter distribution, and promotional activities such as creating mailing lists and sending out sample copies of our publications. Like most nonprofit organizations, we depend heavily on volunteers.

Ensuring that large projects are stitched together effectively and seamlessly, however, can be challenging as volunteers have varying skill sets, schedules, and ability to come to work regularly.

One of the newsletters I publish is for consumers and is called *Tips for Living Well*. It covers practical and positive tips for living well with a disability or chronic health condition. Now in its sixth year, this newsletter was developed as a way to convey HIV prevention information in a regular and nonthreatening way. In each issue we include an article on some aspect of HIV prevention within the publication, but never on the front cover, where it could make people feel uncomfortable if someone were to see them reading an article about HIV/AIDS.

The research, interviewing, and writing for *Tips for Living Well* are an absolute delight. Topics I've written about include nutrition, sleep, pain management, laughter yoga, ways to stay positive while living with a disability, and the impact of pets on health. I encourage people with disabilities to submit tips for coping as well as articles and poetry. In each issue I include a "Pets and Wellness" section in which a person with a disability and his or her pet are profiled. In addition to the usual assortment of dogs and cats, I interviewed one person who has two pet ducks living in her apartment and another woman who is quadriplegic and has two pet llamas that she boards at a friend's farm outside the city. The "Pets and Wellness" feature has become very popular and encourages people with disabilities to subscribe to the newsletter. Along with positive information about wellness, subscribers also receive reader-friendly information about HIV prevention in the "HIV/AIDS Reality Check" column.

The second newsletter I publish is also quarterly and is called *HIV/AIDS Prevention Resources for Educators: Reaching Students with Special Learning Needs*. Articles include profiles of unique HIV prevention initiatives around the world, reviews of new sexual health education programs for people with disabilities, and reports on research relating to HIV prevention education for youth with different types of disabilities. I have had articles written by experts in the fields of disability and education and have a health promotion professional who writes a regular column called "Research Notes" covering significant research in the field of sexual health for youth with disabilities. Whether it is research, writing, arranging permission for reprints, or coordinating writers, publishing a sixteen- to twenty-page newsletter requires considerable time.

I also do consumer health research for people with disabilities, family members, and service providers. Topics vary and have included benefits of meditation for people with disabilities; accessibility barriers and their effect on people with disabilities; identification of experts for a workshop panel on ADHD (attention deficit/hyperactivity disorder), Prader-Willi syndrome, and Asperger syndrome; Pilates classes for a woman with multiple sclerosis; chronic pain management for young adults with cerebral palsy; anti-ableism and disability etiquette; location of needle exchanges in British Columbia; and labor law for service providers working with a young man with fetal alcohol syndrome/effects. In some cases, the information is required in alternative formats, such as plain language or audio.

To promote our HIV prevention publications, our volunteers mail samples of our materials to community groups and health centers throughout the province, with an offer of free copies for distribution. To reach professionals working with people with disabilities, we exhibit and present at relevant conferences. When exhibiting at local conferences, my coworker or I set up the exhibit early in the morning and field questions from conference attendees throughout the day. This can be a great opportunity to gather information about information needs from service providers and from consumers when we are at disability-specific conferences.

My programs also take advantage of events such as International Health Literacy Month in October and World AIDS Day on December 1 to create awareness of health information accessibility issues for people with disabilities. We introduced annual Access to Health awards as a way to commemorate International Health Literacy Month. Each year we ask people with disabilities across the province to nominate either a health care professional or a community agency worker whom they feel has provided extraordinary service. We take nominations through October and then select a winner in each of the two categories. The winner then receives a commemorative plaque. Organizing the Access to Health awards begins in June when we update mailing lists and contacts and identify potential new promotional options. Announcements are sent to community groups and professional organizations in mid-August, with reminders sent out in September.

World AIDS Day provides an opportunity to raise awareness of the fact that HIV/AIDS affects everyone—including people with disabilities. Three years ago we introduced a partnership initiative with disability support centers at college and university campuses across BC. The centers create an information display with copies of our HIV prevention publications, a World AIDS Day poster, postcards, and pins.

Two years ago, after publishing a booklet called *Know about Seniors and HIV*, we approached seniors' organizations to participate in World AIDS Day displays. We had an extremely positive response and have partnered with these groups each year.

Planning for World AIDS Day activities begins in midsummer as we update contact lists for invitations, ensure that we have enough copies of our publications printed, and update or develop new posters. Invitations are mailed to campuses and seniors' organizations by September 1 with a reminder faxed or e-mailed by mid-October. All materials are packed and shipped by November 15 to arrive just before World AIDS Day.

My routine also includes attending meetings of advisory and steering committees. For example, I am the chair of the Provincial Literacy and Health Research Advisory Committee and a member of the Rural HIV/AIDS Information Networks Project Advisory Committee, the Self Help Resource Association *Online Self Help Project*. I also serve on a thesis committee for a master's degree student studying nutrition and people with disabilities. I have been a member of the BC Provincial Literacy and Health Workshop Planning Committee, the International Health Literacy Month Advisory Committee, and the Neil Squire Foundation National Literacy and Disability Research Project Advisory Committee. In addition, I am asked to speak to community, professional, and student groups regarding various aspects of health literacy and health information for people with disabilities.

PROS AND CONS

My job requires creative thinking to try to bridge the divide between people with disabilities and HIV prevention information. Stigma, poverty, geographic isolation, low literacy skills, accessibility issues, and poor health literacy skills are a few of the barriers that separate individuals from the information they need. I enjoy the challenge and am grateful to have an executive director who is supportive and recognizes the value of trial and error and innovative approaches. I am very proud of our newsletters, which have received positive reviews from subscribers and provide regular access to our target audience. Each year we introduce at least one new educational booklet, which is then converted to audio and Braille formats. In the coming months we will work on two publications: one about communicating with your doctor and one on finding sexual health information in your community. There is an enormous sense of satisfaction in identifying and focusing a topic, doing the research, and working with our writer and design contractor to eventually produce new materials.

Another positive feature of my job is the respect I have for my coworkers in the other programs. The BC Coalition of People with Disabilities is recognized as a leader in advocacy and bringing about political and social change in the disability arena. It is rewarding to be a part of the organization.

Finally, I have learned a great deal from my coworkers, our executive director, and the people with disabilities who are clients or members of our organization. I have also had the opportunity to attend and present at many conferences on topics such as public health, health literacy, information and referral, patients' rights, special education, and disability.

The downside to working with a nonprofit organization is the lack of funding. It can be difficult to decide where to focus attention and dollars when there is so much to be done. Limited funding also impacts salaries and staffing. Even when I had two half-time staff members a few years ago, there was always far more work than we could manage. It is the nature of work in the social service/education field. For people unable to come to terms with a never-ending and staggering workload, burnout is certain. Learning to focus your energy where you will get the most benefit—however it is measured by you or your organization—and then letting go of what cannot be done is imperative.

Often, jobs in the nonprofit sector are unique. This can be exciting, but it can also mean considerable isolation and lack of understanding and appreciation from coworkers and even from professional colleagues. If you require a lot of external affirmation and appreciation in your work, the nonprofit world may not be an ideal fit.

HOW WOULD I GET A JOB LIKE YOURS?

I have largely created my own job description by proposing innovative ways of reaching program and organizational goals. To find similar job opportunities, you must think creatively about your skills and the results you can achieve. Reframe library-related language and expertise. Consider the goals of the organization you want to work with and devise a plan to achieve them with your skill set. Librarians are extremely resourceful.

Managers hiring in nonprofit organizations prefer applicants who have experience in this sector, even if only in a volunteer capacity. If you want to work in a particular organization or type of organization, volunteer your time. Showcase your passion for the cause and the value of your skills. Writing relevant and practical articles in publications read by nonprofit managers is an excellent way to gain recognition; if you don't have experience in the field, interview those who do and publish the results. Successful job applicants should convey an ability to work independently and creatively and indicate their willingness to work as a team with others in the organization. Job descriptions can sometimes be fluid; when a deadline is imminent, everyone sits down to stuff envelopes. As in many environments, managers working in the nonprofit sector frequently do not understand what a librarian or information professional can offer. Before you are hired, focus on results and benefits you can provide and have provided in the past. After you begin the job, take every opportunity to use your skills to support your executive director and board of directors. Learn what their information needs are and educate by example. Finally, be prepared to learn about nonprofit culture—people, politics, and other community organizations—and how they work (or don't work) together. Nonprofit organizations offer extraordinary opportunities for librarians to apply experience and training and to make a difference.

RELATED RESOURCES

Canada

Charity Village. www.charityvillage.com (accessed January 7, 2006).

United States

Idealist.org: Action without Borders. www.idealist.org (accessed January 7, 2006).

CHAPTER 87

Project Coordinator, Nonprofit Corporation

MELODY D. PARKER

I work for a nonprofit corporation called the Michigan Public Health Institute, a full-service research, development, and educational organization. As a project coordinator, my job is to provide operational oversight for the Michigan Local Public Health Accreditation Program. The institute is contracted by the state health department, which provides administrative oversight for the program in addition to funding to provide project coordination services. The list of these contractual services includes development and coordination of operational processes, development and implementation of tracking processes, project financial management (including budget development and monitoring), facilitation of continuous quality improvement (CQI), staff selection and training, grant writing, and representing the program through local and national presentations (i.e., conference sessions) and article writing.

A TYPICAL WORKDAY

My position title implies that I coordinate the accreditation program in the state of Michigan. What it truly means is that I create, organize, coordinate, and execute the tasks that keep the program running on a daily basis and beyond!

My day usually begins by sifting through e-mail to prioritize how I'll deal with ongoing and new tasks. Because this is a statewide program dealing with forty-five local public health departments, three state agencies, and a local public health association, the sheer amount of e-mail can be daunting at times. Rapid response is key to the success of my job, so I maintain an eagle eye on my e-mail, almost to the point of obsession, so that no matter what else my day might entail, a fair portion of it will be spent processing messages and completing the tasks that arise from their content.

The program accredits the state's local public health departments in a three-year cycle, so at any given moment, the progress of at least six to twelve departments in the accreditation process needs to be monitored. Additionally, I am responsible for writing and assembling the bulk of the tool that the local public health departments use to complete the accreditation process. (They must also meet minimum program requirements that are developed and written by the state agencies themselves.) Any updates to the program's tools, local public health department progress, and other information must be updated on the program's Web site, which I created and maintain.

More often than not, there are myriad meetings to attend. I meet with the representatives from the state funding entity at least weekly. There are interagency meetings, which include managers from the three main stakeholder health agencies; workgroup meetings dealing with standards development, CQI, and other topics that run simultaneously in support of the program; and my own in-house supervisor and staff meetings. My staff and I participate in the program's advisory commission that meets quarterly. Occasionally there are additional funds awarded through grant writing from other funding entities, such as foundations or the federal government, that require additional committee creation and meeting attendance.

With all that said, what does a typical day really look like for me? I can illustrate it by pulling a page from my calendar, presenting an annotated version of one of my days.

9–11 a.m. Meeting with clients to discuss training development for the program's on-site reviewers and local health departments as part of the program's efforts to provide CQI to the accreditation process. Additionally, we discuss any other relevant issues that have arisen since our last meeting. These meetings take place monthly.

11 a.m.–1 p.m. Work on action items from the morning's meeting, which includes parceling out applicable pieces to staff. Deal with tasks generated by e-mail and voicemail that have arrived since last checked, such as researching topics for a financial meeting, continued work on an article I am coauthoring, and posting an updated form to the program's Web site. Somewhere in there, I'll get lunch, usually at my desk. I can't forget that I must prepare for the next day's meetings!

1–2 p.m. Attend unit staff meeting.

2–2:15 p.m. Meet with a member of the unit's tech team to clarify a few points regarding the new Web reporting module that's being created for the program's on-site reviewers.

2:15–3:30 p.m. Continue deskbound tasks as already described. May include taking phone calls on issues such as walking users through the Web site, discussing the next steps in the process with a local health department, and coordinating responses to program participant issues with clients. Impromptu meetings with my own supervisor can also occur as staffing allocation issues arise.

3:30–4:30 p.m. Final meeting of the day. It could be a meeting with the team I supervise to follow up on tasks we're working on or to distribute further work. I work on another project that goes hand in hand with this one, and it could be a regularly scheduled meeting with that project's director to provide her with updates. It could also be a unit supervisors' meeting, which is also regularly scheduled.

4:30–5 p.m. End-of-day clean up. I use this time to ensure that all the tasks that could be completed within the day have been, and those that couldn't be finished are placed in the proper queue and the relevant individuals are updated on progress. I'll also use this time to finish preparation for the next day's run of meetings. It is not out of the ordinary for this to extend beyond 5 p.m.

PROS AND CONS

There are several aspects of my job in which I delight. One is the feeling of autonomy that I have. I am free to pursue development of grant opportunities in which I am interested, such as those dealing directly with library and information science or delivery of information services within the organization. For example, I am developing a survey of the employees of my organization to assess their reference tool needs. Additionally, the salary and benefits are above par for information professionals, falling well above the median starting salary for academic librarians.

Because accreditation of public health is a national topic, support for attendance at national conferences and the ensuing networking is a bonus as well.

The most obvious frustration with this position is that it is fraught with politics, and the possibilities for mistakes are endless. Every e-mail that I send must be carefully constructed for the individual recipient to ensure that the subject matter is appropriately and successfully handled. With the implementation of our CQI process, I do not have messages from anxious local health department representatives in my inbox or on my phone as often I did in the past, but it still happens from time to time; these situations must be handled delicately and cheerfully to achieve positive outcomes. I also walk a fine line because the program is handled administratively by the state's current administration. I've survived one change in the governor's office since I've been with the project, and the personality of the project has changed significantly in that time. Adaptability is a must.

The most disconcerting thing about my job is that I work for a nonprofit entity. Because the program is funded with state dollars, there is always the possibility that the continual budget shortfalls each year may cause funding to be reduced or even cut completely.

HOW WOULD I GET A JOB LIKE YOURS?

This type of job would most likely appeal to information professionals with a background in or desire to work in health sciences. Having a master's degree in public health wouldn't hurt, either. Postings for jobs like these on both the state and national levels can be difficult to find if you don't know where to look, as they are often posted solely on Web sites of organizations or schools of public health, or in trade publications such as the journal of the American Public Health Association.

The field of public health accreditation, which falls within public health systems research, is relatively small (but growing exponentially), so networking is of utmost importance.

What is most important about looking for work in this field, however, is that it must be a good fit for you personally. Skills you must possess are effective project coordination, experience in coordinating collaborative efforts with diverse participants, strong written and oral presentation skills, excellent customer service skills, the ability to deliver high-quality work with discretion while facing political pressure, and above all, a very diplomatic and unflappable demeanor.

RELATED RESOURCES

The following Web sites are indispensable in understanding where I am and what I do.

Centers for Disease Control and Prevention, National Public Health Performance Standards Program. www.cdc.gov/od/ocphp/nphpsp (accessed May 28, 2006).

Exploring Accreditation (national accreditation development project). www.exploringaccreditation.org (accessed May 28, 2006).

Michigan Local Public Health Accreditation Program. accreditation.localhealth.net (accessed May 28, 2006).

Michigan Public Health Institute (my employer). www.mphi.org (accessed May 28, 2006).

National Association of County and City Health Officials. www.naccho.org/topics/infrastructure/exploringaccreditation.cfm (accessed May 28, 2006).

PART X

Nontraditional

CHAPTER 88

Personal Librarian

A "KEPT" LIBRARIAN

I work as the personal research librarian to writer and cultural visionary Kevin Kelly. Kevin is best known as the founding editor of *Wired* magazine. My work is disproportionately divided among five areas. Research and reference related to Kevin's writing and project-founding activities are often the focus, but I also provide support for his self-publishing interests, assist with Web site management, perform some administrative tasks, and most recently, have begun organizing his four-thousand-volume book collection.

A TYPICAL DAY

First, let me paint the backdrop. I work out of Kevin's home. He lives in the picturesque coastal town of Pacifica, south of San Francisco. His home is at the dead end of a quiet street that meanders along a stream and ends at a densely wooded ridge. Our office is a bright, airy, two-story workspace in an open loft design. I usually work nine to five from our office although occasionally I work from home or a library. Although I am free to choose my hours and work location, I find it productive to have a set schedule and location. It took Kevin a good while to get used to this. His work experience had put him around writers, hackers, creatives, and others for whom it was typical to come in at noon and work for twelve hours or stay up all night on the job for three nights and then disappear for a week. My work hours were too predictable and this, for Kevin, was suspect. Now, unfortunately, he gets it all too well and has come to rely on my constancy.

Although I usually don't work in all five areas of my job on a given day, it might be constructive to give an account of typical projects or tasks for each area. I'll start with research and reference. I provide research for Kevin's current book writing project. There are thirty or so broad questions he is contemplating that translate into research questions. For instance, he is interested in an exhaustive list of all the times in history that a culture rejected a technology. He wants to know how intelligence is measured in animals. He wants to determine how and to what extent the kill power of weapons has increased over time. Then there is the endless barrage of questions we call his "how manys." "How many miles of roads are there?" "How many books has Google scanned?" "What is the total information storage in the human genome?" And my personal favorite: "How many things are there?" Most of these questions remain open; thus, his deliberations guide my research. In addition to the book, there is research for shorter pieces (he is writing a cover story for the *New York Times Magazine* on the concept of the universal library) and other projects he is interested in both professionally and personally, although at times, in this type of arrangement, those lines blur. For example, after returning from a family vacation in Mexico, he asked me to find current academic papers on traveler's diarrhea to help resolve a dispute he was having with his wife. This was a seemingly personal request; however, once he probed further, he decided to publish a little booklet about traveler's diarrhea for his Cool Tools Web site. That's a good segue to another of my capacities, which is support for the print and Web projects he publishes.

Kevin has authored and self-published a number of his own books. He designed a coffee-table book of photographs from his travels throughout Asia, called *Asia Grace*, printing the first prototype on his large-format printer and subsequently selling the publishing rights to Taschen. Next he published two sketchbooks: *Bicycle Haiku*, which consists of sketches with accompanying haikus from his bike ride across the United States; and *Bad Dreams*, sketches made after he took a photography class from a renowned photographer, where he was asked to draw what he saw in his own photographs. His last two books are catalogs, *Cool Tools* and *True Films*. *Cool Tools* is a book of reviews for "the best of" outdoor gear, how-to books, hand tools, gadgets, software, educational films, catalogs, and machinery, all of which he loosely calls "tools." From early on, Kevin liked recommending to friends the cool stuff that he had discovered. Being publisher at Whole Earth during the 1980s gave him the means to cultivate his practice of discovering and sharing really good tools. One of the inspirations for the book is to give to his three children, when they leave home, a selection of the best tools and manuals for living. *True Films* is a book of one hundred great documentaries that are easily available for a reasonable price. We are currently working on updated print editions of both books. Both have companion Web sites with their entire contents, plus frequent additions, freely available.

In his publishing undertakings, my role has been supportive. Kevin typically does the design and content layout and I do the formatting, proofing, access information for the catalog entries, scanning and input of photos, and conversion to print-ready format. I handle the requests for proposals from small-run printers. On one occasion, we were given access to an organization that prints its own books. I was permitted to go in after hours for several days to print, trim, and bind one of our titles.

Another of my stations is his Web site. I'm not a Webmaster, but I've learned enough on the job to be able to make minor changes and additions to the site when needed. Mostly, however, this part of my job involves the daily updates to *Cool Tools*. Kevin gets hundreds of recommendations for tools to include each month. He carefully screens each review, often obtaining the item to test prior to reviewing it. He includes only those items that either he or someone he trusts has used.

I also bear an administrative responsibility. This involves financial bookkeeping, payroll (mine), and managing Kevin's interviews, speaking engagements, and travel.

To wrap up the typical day, just recently, Kevin deemed that his massive book collection needs organizing. Thus a great deal of my time of late has involved scanning ISBN numbers, organizing, and cataloging this collection.

PROS AND CONS

My job is exceptional and, to some, enviable. It is inherently engaging, empowering, progressive, and imparts an uncommon opportunity for making connections. Kevin has a diverse range of interests and relationships with fascinating people, which yield absorbing projects. I prize the empowering circumstances of my job, which allow me unprecedented freedoms. I have a great deal of independence. Most days, the only contact I have with Kevin is if one of us has a question for the other or he has a special request. Otherwise, I control my workflow. I can work from the office, home, or anywhere, really. Probably the most freeing aspect of my job is the absence of a dress code. I'm not really into dress codes and have a history of subverting them. But no matter how grungy I arrive at work, Kevin always looks more casual than I do. He is a creative, visionary thinker and encourages that in me. My job has exposed me to a realm of new ideas and ways of thinking. Having only one patron, I am intimately connected with his information needs. I feel very lucky to have landed such an opportunity.

As desirable as my job is, it has a couple of downsides. I'm lonely. I miss having coworkers. Without them, I miss out on the unique gifts that work friends can bring to my life. I have only the boss to turn to for advice, gossip, griping, or just to waste a little time. Undoubtedly, I can manage all of this virtually, but I covet the real thing. The other piece I find lacking is that as interesting as I find the projects and as excited and intellectually stimulated as Kevin is about them, they are *his* projects. If I were in the business of being Kevin Kelly, different things would move me to think, write, and create. Simply put, Kevin is passionate about the culture surrounding technology. My passions lie in issues of social justice, corporate accountability, and environmentalism.

HOW TO GET A JOB LIKE MINE

When I tell people, especially other librarians, what I do for a living, I usually get three questions: "How did you get your job?" "What do you do all day?" and "How can I get a job like that?" The first two are easy. The third is not. I'll be downright honest with you: I'm not aware of many jobs like mine, but I suspect opportunities exist.

Let me start by telling you how I got here, but I must warn you that my tactics were unconventional and certainly aren't meant as counsel in your own search for such a position. I include this part of my story because its first-draft omission begged the question. I graduated from the University of Tennessee School of Information Science in December of 2000. At the time I was working two part-time library jobs. I also had a very part-time information brokering business. I wasn't actively job seeking because I had offers from both libraries to continue working. One day I saw a posting on a library discussion list for this unbelievably cool-sounding job to assist this unknown (to me) writer with his personal writing and project-founding activities. I thought, *What the heck, I'll never get it*, so I applied.

Applying comprised a simple response via e-mail. Kevin wasn't interested in a résumé or credentials; in fact, his posting read, "I am completely unimpressed with credentials." His casual nature must have inspired the madness that followed because I did something no sensible job seeker would do. I wrote him a personal letter sharing intimate, deeply private, and even dreary details of my life. I broke every rule of the job-seeking process. If there are any recruiters reading this, you may want to put the book down. In the course of telling Kevin why I wanted the job, I told him about losing both my parents—my mom to cancer and my dad to heart disease—within the previous two years, euthanizing my thirteen-year-old dog, and ending a ten-year relationship with a man to start my first relationship with a woman (yes, I came out to him on my job application). I somehow managed to make all of this relevant to the job. I would have done anything to be able to reach through that machine and jerk that e-mail back. *He is going to think I am completely unsound*, I thought. Kevin called me three days later on New Year's Day.

Thus began a hiring process that lasted several months. First, he hired me to do a couple of research jobs. Then he flew me out to San Francisco to interview. I had no idea what to wear.

A suit didn't seem suitable, but I wasn't sure. So I wrote to Kevin and asked that since he wasn't impressed with credentials, did that mean he was equally unimpressed with formal interview attire? His immediate response was, "Don't you dare come in anything formal. This is San Francisco and I'm an old hippie. Wear what you'd like to work in." So worn-out jeans it was. The interview lasted four hours, most of which we spent hiking on the coastal hills around his home. Three days after the interview, he called me at home in Tennessee and offered me the job.

Just recently, at my request, Kevin sat down with me to talk about how a librarian might presently "sell" a position to him. (It's tough to condense his expansive thinking into a couple of paragraphs.) The first couple of points that he made about the Web are self-evident to librarians. I summarize them here. There is a whole body of work outside of the Web that information professionals have the knowledge and means to get at. The ascendancy of Google has increased the value of other types of research that take more ingenuity of search skills and resources, such as market research, library research, telephone research (contacting experts to see what they know), and primary research. There is a competitive advantage to being able to do research outside of the open Web. I add to this, even for the omnipresent Web search, the laziness of relying on its first page of results advances the sublimity of an information professional's deeper, more intelligent and industrious manner of Web searching. His third point is about what the Web, online search, and information retrieval in general have failed to do, which is to *ask good questions*. Kevin believes that good questions are more valuable than answers. Advances in search will make good answers ubiquitous, but good questions will always be at a premium. Kevin relies on his friends, peers, and me to ask these questions. Finally, having me in his workflow provides a reflection of how he is spending his time. Our interactions become signposts for where he has been and where he is heading with various projects. Otherwise, the temptation to drift lies unchecked. His productivity rises as a result. Kevin suggests that these are the cogent points to stress when selling your position.

Kevin knows many serial entrepreneurs (inventors, writers, artists, musicians) who would like to have someone like me in their employ but don't know where to look because they are not necessarily looking for librarians, researchers, or information professionals. He believes this misconnect is a failure of title. Although I do research for Kevin because he is constantly doing new things as a writer and thinker that require new knowledge, I do many other things that help him manage the results of his success. The more productive he is, the more work he generates, and the more help he needs managing the fallout. Many creatives don't think they need a full-time researcher (although they know they need research) or a full-time assistant (although they need other kinds of miscellaneous help). Presenting yourself as strictly a researcher or librarian may cast your value in insufficiently narrow terms. Instead, underscore the roles you could fill outside of research.

Here's one tactic you might try. If you have a person for whom you would like to work, give him or her a high-value sample of your work and offer to do a project for a low fee to prove your usefulness. Let the person know you hope to establish a working relationship in the future. Even if he or she isn't looking to hire someone right now, that can change at any time. For example, if I were trying to get a job with Kevin doing research, I would take one of the articles he has already published and provide a value add (additional statistics, analysis, citations, experts, etc.). Then I would give this to him, in lieu of my business card or résumé, and offer to provide research for his next writing project.

CHAPTER 89

Independent Information Professional

Life as an independent information professional (IIP) can be exciting and challenging. I began this career path directly out of library school. I had flexibility in my first career as a laboratory technologist doing genetic and agricultural research, so when I completed my MLS, I decided to try my hand as a consultant. When I started earning my degree, I thought that I would become an academic or special librarian, but I realized quickly while working as a library student employee that I didn't want to work in a large organization or have my hours dictated by an employer.

JOB DESCRIPTION

Since 1991 I have been working as an independent information professional under the business name Apex Information. I specialize in health-related research and library services. My primary focus is on research and writing, but I occasionally take on projects such as setting up small specialized libraries, helping libraries merge collections or catalogs or move from a paper-based to a computerized system, or developing "how to" manuals. I have also worked with a telehealth start-up company, conceptualizing and developing their librarian business unit and helping develop a workflow model of the company's user interface. I work with a variety of health-related clients (including academic institutions, government agencies, private consulting firms, and nonprofit organizations) primarily based in North America but also around the world. My areas of concentration are health policy, health technology assessment, health economics, and other similar health delivery and administration topics. I conduct most of my work electronically or by phone, even with my local clients.

MY TYPICAL WORKDAY

I start most days by looking over my daily file and then moving to e-mail and phone calls. I update and respond to current clients and answer questions from potential ones. I quickly review and respond to professional and subject-related e-mail lists unless I am facing a dead-line. I then proceed with the work of the day, whether that is project work for a client or administrative work for my business. I end most days by reviewing my daily file for the next day to set priorities; for example, if I need to phone overseas, I can plan what time I have to make calls to reach contacts during their regular working hours.

Depending on the project, I might conduct comprehensive literature searches for systematic reviews of the literature, or I might conduct an environmental scan, which involves doing a literature search, selecting and analyzing documents to review, and writing a report on the current and historical state of a specific topic. Some projects have me spending time on the phone tracking down experts and interviewing them. The pace varies greatly from fairly leisurely, with a timeline of one to several years, to fast-paced, with a tight turnaround time of a few days. I rarely have clients who need information within a few hours. I am sometimes involved in the document supply end of a project, although this is work I often contract out to an associate.

Communication with clients is extremely important. At the start of a new project, especially with new clients, I find it helpful to communicate often. Initially, we have either a fairly long phone conversation or a detailed e-mail exchange about the specifics of a project. Once work starts on a project, I contact clients periodically to report on initial findings and review the parameters of the project based on these initial results.

JOYS AND FRUSTRATIONS

Many of the pros and cons of working as an IIP are interchangeable: the lack of routine provides relief from boredom, but it can also add to the stress of working independently; isolation can be difficult, but working in quiet and solitude, without the distractions of a busy office, is often most efficient. Working as an IIP demands that you be self-motivated, disciplined, and able to structure your time.

I consider the biggest benefit to be the variety of work I find landing on my desk. I rarely get bored, because I never know what will be coming my way. Other pros include the ability to choose projects and clients (a luxury that comes with being fairly well established), allowing me to work on things I think are important and have an impact on the world. I enjoy my independence and control over my schedule. The freedom to take my dogs for walks during the day, attend art classes during the workday, or do shopping and errands during quieter times is invaluable to me. Another benefit of life as an IIP is the opportunity to work with some very impressive research teams and a variety of movers and shakers in both the health and information fields. I'm always learning new things and am able to attend conferences or continuing education courses that I consider important or interesting.

The most obvious drawback to any type of self-employment is the lack of traditional job-related benefits, including pension plans, vacation pay, and insurance coverage. For me, the greatest disadvantage is the lack of security that comes with being an IIP. The lack of security is the flipside of the flexibility afforded by absence of routine. It's important, however, to note that today few jobs are truly secure. This lack of security ensures that I don't become complacent and forces me to keep my professional skills and knowledge current.

The second greatest con is that I must market and promote my services—a challenge for many information professionals. Many of us are introverts who find selling our expertise difficult. Although I have known many of my clients for years and know that they value my services, asking them for referrals can be difficult.

Another downside is the need to do everything myself. There is a lot of administrative work, and it often doesn't get done until the workday is over or on the weekend. When I am working on large or multiple projects, I often work twelve hours a day, seven days a week. Not always having access to well-qualified help can mean longer hours for me. I've purposely kept my business at a level where I don't have to hire permanent staff. I don't want to become an employer and manager; if necessary, I prefer to contract someone to do clerical work and subcontract professional work to other independents.

Working as an IIP can lead to a feeling of isolation. I combat this by belonging to and volunteering in professional associations, meeting both formally and casually with other members, and getting together for the occasional coffee or meal with some of my local clients. I also maintain friendships with colleagues, both local and distant, with whom I share personal interests; we e-mail, talk on the phone, and visit from time to time.

Managing the relationship with clients and their expectations can be tricky. If I can't find information that the client wants, it's easy to feel as though I've failed—even if that information doesn't exist. This might be good news to a client (indicating an open area for research), but it's important to be able to control that nagging feeling that there just might be something out there that the search didn't reveal. Success has to be judged project by project; a client might be happy to stop the hunt before I am, and I have to let it go at that point. It's also important to be able to say no—to set boundaries with clients in a way that doesn't jeopardize the relationship. I find that I do a great deal of client education about the information world and how it operates. Issues such as "free versus fee" and copyright come up repeatedly, and conversations with clients often revolve around these issues.

Finally, it is important to know when to put the work down and take time off. It can be difficult to leave work behind when deadlines are looming and your work time isn't structured by an office atmosphere. I seldom take full days off on weekends and rarely take more than a week off at a time for vacations. This is common in the world of consulting. Sometimes, though, I just have to shut down my computer, put my work out of sight, and take some downtime so I can come back to my work refreshed with new ideas and approaches.

Despite the number of drawbacks I have outlined, the pros far outweigh the cons for me, and I plan to continue consulting until I retire.

BECOMING AN INDEPENDENT INFORMATION PROFESSIONAL

Many of the IIPs I know have gotten into the field after working in a traditional library setting. Although I set myself up in business right out of library school, I had worked as a student employee in the medical and science libraries at a university and in the science division of a public library. This experience and the connections I made gave me a leg up in the search for my first clients. I also visited libraries of the type I wanted to target with my services and spoke with many librarians working in the field.

My first two contracts involved setting up specialized libraries (both collection development and services to users) in two very different health-related organizations with very different needs. One was a health policy research unit at a large university (where I worked with researchers, academics, visiting scientists, and students), and the other was a community mental health nonprofit providing services to people with severe and chronic mental disorders in a large urban setting (where my clientele included frontline workers, administrators, and consumers). I continued working with these organizations for many years on a contract basis, providing ongoing library support for staff and researchers. Both of these organizations were excellent learning environments and provided me with experience, breadth of subject expertise, and crucial contacts to help with my marketing efforts as I was building my business.

I recommend finding a good mentor, if possible—someone who is providing a similar service to what you would like to provide. If you don't know someone suitable, consider a professional mentor. Amelia Kassel of MarketingBase is a professional librarian who offers an excellent mentoring program for both beginning and established IIPs.

Recognize the importance of communication and hone your skills. Relationships with clients are critical and play a large part in the future of your business. It's imperative to understand what your client needs and expects. Never underestimate the value of high-quality work— especially when it's time to look for more work. The success of my business has been largely due to satisfied clients, word-of-mouth marketing, and referrals.

RELATED RESOURCES

One of the best resources for anyone contemplating becoming an IIP is the Association of Independent Information Professionals (AIIP). I can't overemphasize the value of a membership in this organization. Not only is it a welcoming international community, membership also comes with excellent benefits from a number of key vendors (e.g., discounts on subscriptions, free training sessions and materials). Discussion on the AIIP members-only e-mail list is worth the price of membership alone. Members discuss all aspects of the business, from administrative functions to specific resources to answer research questions on subjects as disparate as chemical structures for a pharmaceutical company, patent searches for an inventor, and regulations for importing raw materials for a manufacturer.

There are also a number of books that provide guidance. Information Today's list includes books on various types of information services you can provide, specific subject areas, research techniques and resources, and administrative tasks such as marketing. Mary Ellen Bates's book on running a research business provides excellent advice on almost all aspects of the business. Contents include setting yourself up initially, finding a niche market and clients, negotiating contracts and fees, networking, marketing, and research approaches.

Finally, I suggest you check out small business associations and information centers where you live. They are often a wealth of information for the details and regulations of running a business in your own jurisdiction.

RELATED RESOURCES

Allen, David. 2001. *Getting things done: The art of stress-free productivity*. New York: Viking.

Association of Independent Information Professionals. www.aiip.org (accessed July 18, 2006).

Bates, Mary Ellen. 2003. *Building & running a successful research business: A guide for the independent information professional*. Ed. Reva Basch. Medford, N.J.: Information Today.

Kassel, Amelia. Frequently asked questions about information brokering. www.marketingbase.com/faqs.html (accessed July 18, 2006).

———. Information broker mentor program. www.marketingbase.com/mentor.html (accessed July 18, 2006).

Rugge, Sue, and Alfred Glossbrenner. 1997. *The information broker's handbook*, 3rd ed. New York: McGraw-Hill.

United States Small Business Administration. www.sba.gov/smallbusinessplanner/index.html (accessed July 18, 2006).

CHAPTER 90

Consultant, Entrepreneur, Marketing Manager

CAROL A. BERGER

My latest title is manager, marketing/communications for C. Berger Group (CBG). This position is ultimately responsible for keeping CBG's name visible and generating new and reoccurring business for our library staffing and information management consulting organization. My duties include developing and implementing promotional, sales, and public relations programs and identifying and assessing new venture opportunities. I evaluate advertising and sponsorship opportunities, conduct new service and competitive intelligence research, and develop content for CBG's Web site. I'm responsible for preparing collaterals, coordinating exhibit events, and participating in educational and professional activities, all duties that utilize my writing, speaking, and creative skills. In addition, I am a library consultant for CBG, delivering recommendations that are instrumental in creating knowledge centers and solving information problems for clients nationwide. I also provide library executive search management consulting services to clients, and I serve on various national and local professional boards and committees.

A TYPICAL WORKDAY

What is now CBG started as a one-person operation headquartered in the corner of my basement in 1982. During my twenty-one years as president, I performed every task necessary to establish, publicize, fund, populate, nurture, and reshape the business, teaching and delegating those responsibilities to hundreds of CBG's office employees who were hired during that time. In 2003, I relinquished daily oversight for the less time-consuming but more challenging position of marketing manager, although I retained my title as chairperson of the board. Our new president now sets marketing standards and direction for me.

Being CBG's corporate memory (and longest-serving employee), I have a great deal of flexibility in my job. I often start and leave later than other staff members: my day begins at 10 a.m. and extends to 6 p.m. most of the time. Because I spend time at home each evening outlining my goals and activities for the next day, I follow a predetermined schedule. Mornings are devoted to returning calls or responding to e-mailed inquiries and requests. Afternoons are spent on the computer, either trying to locate information (for example, verifying contact data or monitoring competitors); drafting copy for press releases, interviews, or letters; sending cold e-mails; or planning for events and updating budgets and timetables.

Meetings break up my routine. I may meet on-site with staff at weekly management meetings and strategy sessions or at vendor presentations, or I go off-site for prospect or client visits and professional lunch and dinner events. Travel makes up less than 15 percent of my work time, especially now that conference calls are so common. I spend at least an hour each day reading library science, trade, and business periodicals, and I spend at least that much time lurking on discussion lists. I'm the one who routes worthy ideas, news items, or statistics gleaned from articles on to other staff members, and I also maintain my own files for future use in speeches and writing projects. I review potential government contract opportunities, recommend specific ones to pursue, and write proposals to get them. I keep a daily accounting of my work, which is reported weekly, summarized monthly, and used to flesh out an annual report for marketing, planning, and budgeting.

PROS AND CONS

The primary joy of owning your own business is being your own boss (as I was at the beginning). That exhilarating feeling began when C. Berger Group received its first contract and ended when I relinquished the title of president after more than twenty years. I was the one who set company hours, established corporate policies and standards, and figured out how to solve problems. As the company grew, I began to rely more on internal and external advisors, although most major decisions were mine, ranging from setting the direction for the company to rewarding employees with surprise bonuses and gifts.

In my current position, I consider being asked to be interviewed a benefit. I'm a spokesperson both for the library and information science profession and for the temporary staffing industry as a niche service supplier. Being recognized by my peers for support we've provided is also gratifying. I love to see something I wrote picked up by the press or quoted in the literature. Now that I am back in the marketing saddle, I enjoy seeing how a marketing project such as a call, letter, e-mail, or proposal can help land a new client or job.

In CBG's early days, the cons revolved around two issues: offering benefits and growing the client list. Trying to develop a benefits package for employees that included add-ons like health insurance, paid leave, and other perks, which are taken for granted in a large organization, created huge financial challenges for our small business. Expanding the client base was a labor-intensive effort because no one else offered our services locally. I became a missionary, explaining at every opportunity that potential buyers had to add a budget line for temporaries and consultants to use our services in the future.

Now my challenges are caused by piles of filing (the byproduct of the creative process) and the need to track marketing activities. Just making room for new materials in drawers or erasing files from the computer can use time that could be focused on bringing in more new business. It is also distressing to recognize that even the best marketing or sales efforts may have little impact, as we have no control over general economic conditions or competitors.

GETTING A JOB LIKE MINE

There are three distinct components of my career and each builds on the other. To be successful, one needs the following.

Skills, training, and experience of a consultant. Start by getting academic credentials such as an MLS or MBA. It's difficult to have credibility as a consultant without those initials after your name. Next, take as many positions as you can with different employers in your selected specialty. I had experience working in public, school, and academic libraries; I handled reference, cataloging, and management responsibilities before starting my business. One should also volunteer for assignments to acquire the broadest range of knowledge. Learn as much as possible from each assignment—that's how to train to be a consultant. I worked on committees that planned events, recommended candidates, and produced publications. I accepted nominations to run for office myself. That's how consultants get to know a lot of information about particular topics and develop many reliable sources and connections to call on for support. They also tend to be great communicators who are highly visible at professional venues where other consultants and potential customers congregate. Professional conferences are great places to be seen and heard. Although being published may enhance one's image, in the long run a consultant's main job is living up to his or her reputation—advice that holds true in any field.

Skills, training, and experience of an entrepreneur. Unfortunately, entrepreneurship is a state of mind. The best start-up business developers are people with a vision who are willing to assume the risks of delivering a new entity and who, because they are self-driven and relentless, will devote endless hours to birthing it. They are naturally inquisitive and great researchers. Although the mechanics of starting a business can be taught, the spark that enlivens it cannot. I advise potential business owners to work in the industry or type of business they want to start so they can acquire hands-on knowledge of management and pricing basics; after that, they should take training and utilize resources provided by government and academic experts. This will help them confirm that their ideas are worthy, test their abilities, attract funding, and ultimately translate their vision into a viable organism.

Skills, training, and experience of a marketing manager. Persistence, attention to detail, creativity, strong communication skills, and a thick skin are the minimal requirements for becoming a successful marketing or sales professional. On-the-job assignments and formal courses are the main tools for learning the trades. Many colleges offer degree programs, and there are also continuing education and organization-sponsored activities to choose from. Some of the marketing activities I used as a special library manager were good practice for my early years of developing CBG. Two techniques I brought with me were branding the library and sending out frequent personal communications and newsletters. The marketing courses I took in graduate business school were also relevant to growing CBG.

No business can thrive without some marketing efforts; even a one-person operation can't succeed if prospective buyers don't know it exists. Besides networking, which is a one-on-one tool, the second most important resource in marketing today is a Web site. It showcases a business, service, or idea without requiring a large physical presence and is not dependent on the size of the business to be effective or reach buyers.

RELATED RESOURCES

Learning about C. Berger Group

Please visit www.cberger.com for an overview of C. Berger Group and the services we provide. The Web site has background on its history and staff as well as notes on presentations, sponsorships, and marketing activities. Additional information about CBG can be found in directories of providers compiled by such groups as the American Library Association (ALA), the Special Libraries Association (SLA), and the American Association of Law Libraries (AALL), and in Thomson Gale and Kennedy Information publications.

Career Options

Professional and trade organizations are good starting points for careers with the following specialties.

Entrepreneurship. The U.S. Small Business Administration (www.sba.gov), Service Corps of Retired Executives (www.score.org), and Women's Business Development Centers (see the Chicago center at www.wbdc.org) have basic information. Many colleges and universities can test you to help determine if you fit the profile. Once you have a business established, join the local chamber of commerce for visibility and leads and consider approaching a Procurement Technical Assistance Center (www.dla.mil/db/procurem.htm) for help in getting government contracts.

Consulting. To learn about activities of library consultants and to find a mentor, see the Web sites of ALA (www.ala.org), Independent Librarian's Exchange section of ASCLA (www.ala.org/ala/ascla/asclaourassoc/asclasections/ilex/ilex.htm), the Consulting Section of the Leadership and Management Division of the Special Libraries Association (units.sla.org/division/dlmd/aboutconsulting.html), and the Association of Independent Information Professionals (www.aiip.org).

Marketing. Library-related marketing advice is available online and through courses offered by ALA, SLA, and AALL. Go to the American Marketing Association (www.marketingpower.com) for information on marketing as a career.

CHAPTER 91

Senior Program Manager

SAMANTHA STARMER

I am responsible for managing strategy and implementation for the Microsoft Market Research internal Web portal. This site is the central place for Microsoft employees to find all of the valuable market research that is done by the centralized group of researchers in my department. My duties encompass a very wide range of activities, and although much of what I do requires project and business management skills, I would not be able to be as successful in this position without the specialized knowledge I gained from earning my MLIS degree. As the main business owner for this Web site, I plan new features and manage projects that encompass everything from front-end visual design and information architecture to back-end database functionality and IT innovation. I also oversee the tools and processes related to the Web site, such as how it gathers, organizes, and displays information. This includes areas like content management, editorial workflow, Web publishing, and taxonomy governance.

A TYPICAL WORKDAY

Because I'm a morning person and I like to have some quiet time before the rush of a day at a high-tech company begins, I try to get to work by 7 a.m. This generally gives me a couple of hours to check and respond to any e-mail sent the previous night and try to make a bit of progress on one of my high-priority projects before the onslaught of meetings begins. The Market Research Web site that I manage is used internationally, so at times I have a 7 or 8 a.m. conference call with someone in a different time zone. Our IT and software development is currently handled offshore, so in the morning I often have e-mails and issues to review that have come in overnight due to the time difference. If I don't have any early morning meetings or "fire drills," such as a site problem or a short-notice deadline or presentation that day, I will usually pick up one of my in-progress projects and get some planning or tasks accomplished during this time This may involve creating wireframes to diagram a new feature or Web page, deciding to schedule a card-sorting activity to assist with taxonomy improvements, or reviewing the effectiveness of our search engine and content and metadata tagging processes.

I am then often in meetings from 9 or 10 a.m. through much of the day. As a program manager, I tend to be the one planning and running the meetings I attend. This requires advance preparation to make sure that the meeting runs as smoothly as possible and no one's time is wasted. Each meeting request needs to be thought out carefully, and I work to ensure that a meeting is not scheduled unless it is truly the best way to make progress on the issue. People skills and the ability to learn individual styles and communication preferences are extremely important to being successful in running meetings. I believe that meetings are really just another way to share and manage information, so I find that thinking about this part of my job from an information science perspective can be very helpful. I consider my "users" and try to match the style of the meeting and the decision making to their needs. This means that some meetings may include a lot of discussion time to enhance collaboration, whereas others may be short and direct to reach the goal most efficiently.

When I return to my desk after the usual series of meetings, there is always more e-mail to read and answer. The culture at Microsoft is very e-mail focused, and much of my communication is done this way. As the main point of contact for the Market Research site, I often get e-mails from users either within the group of research managers who contribute content to the site or from the broader base of Microsoft employees who look for information on the site. I also get e-mails that require thinking on more strategic issues. For example, my manager may send me an e-mail to make me aware of a new departmental initiative that I need to reflect on to determine how it might impact the Web site. I need to be able to quickly prioritize my incoming e-mails and respond promptly and concisely to those that are most important. Other e-mails can be filed away for a later or more researched response. A good e-mail classification scheme is critical when you get over one hundred e-mails a day!

Any time I have remaining after e-mails, meetings, or other forms of communication with my coworkers and vendors is usually spent continuing to work on one or more of my ongoing projects. These generally fall into one of two categories: strategic initiatives or tactical operations. With the tactical operations tasks I am often working to ensure that the Web site and its processes are running smoothly. I have other researchers who assist in this work, but each week I still spend some time answering user support questions, investigating bugs and reporting them to IT, and working on areas like content management workflow or analyzing metadata use. Because the running of a content-heavy Web site can be very complicated, it is easy to get caught up in these tactical endeavors. However, I also make sure that a large portion of my project focus is spent on strategic initiatives. These are most often driven by the needs of the people who provide or access the information available on the Web site. Right now I'm working on a few big projects, including a navigation and information architecture redesign, a taxonomy and metadata redesign, and a project to research our users and their information needs. I am also working on the long-term vision and measures of success for our site to continue to plan for both increased user satisfaction and technical innovation.

Because I am responsible for the end-to-end workings of this Market Research intranet, I am always managing a number of active projects relating to the site in addition to determining upcoming initiatives, ideas, or improvements that I would like to move forward on. Although some of the site-related projects are driven by external forces such as changes in the organization or requests from management, I focus most of my priorities around creating the best possible experience for our users. Because the site is reasonably complex and contains a large amount of rich content, many of the daily tasks and longer term projects that I work on directly relate to getting people to the information they need in the easiest, most efficient manner. In this area, all of the studies I did during my MLIS are directly applicable. I have found myself talking about information-seeking behavior in meetings and have recently realized that many of the user questions that I answer about how to use the site are best answered when I do a mini-reference interview. My job may not seem like an obvious career path from an MLIS degree, but every day I have a task or a project that deals directly with a subject covered in library school.

PROS AND CONS

I could work one hundred hours every week and I would still have more ideas than I could get accomplished in the allocated time. That is probably the biggest challenge of my role and might be hard for someone who likes to end the day or the week at work with a nicely completed checklist. I continually balance my priorities to make sure that the things at the top of my list are not only important for my specific role but are also aligned with departmental and company priorities. To meet business needs, a shift in management priorities or a departmental reorganization may occur with fairly short notice, and these changes often directly impact my own set of goals and plans for the year. As with most high-tech jobs, it can be easy to feel overwhelmed by the heavy amount of work, high-energy communication style, and very short timelines.

In many ways, though, the challenges of this job also contribute to its wonderful benefits. The fast-moving, constantly changing environment is one of the most exciting and pleasurable aspects of a position like this. Although it can feel hectic to know that I have more ideas than time, it is great that every day will require new knowledge and skills to be learned. I might be fully immersed in taxonomy issues one week, only to find that the next week I need to look into all of the ways to dynamically push information to users, set up a usability testing plan, or determine which part of the necessary information architecture work should be outsourced. I am very fortunate to be able to have a significant role in defining the goals and vision of the site and all related strategy as well as to work on more tactical areas, such as which new features should be added and how various processes and operations should work.

HOW WOULD I GET A JOB LIKE YOURS?

Because I had experience with high-tech program management and business analysis before obtaining my MLIS, I may have a somewhat different combination of experience than other MLIS graduates. I have known of recent graduates who have been successful at moving into project management–type jobs without much official experience by emphasizing how library or other work they have done in the past was very much about managing tasks to completion and getting the right work done at the right time. Program management positions are generally filled based on experience and skill set, but this doesn't always mean that you must have had a previous PM title to get this kind of job. Think about all of your past experiences, regardless of the environment. Chances are that you have actually managed many projects and can highlight why you were successful and can illustrate some of the tactics you used.

Because many people in program management or analyst jobs have often come to these jobs rather accidentally, there isn't necessarily a direct path for getting into these positions. This knowledge can be very helpful for anyone with an MLIS who is thinking of working in a corporate environment in this kind of position, because you can often parlay your previous background and skills into something relevant for project management. Many people drawn to an MLIS would be great at project management and analysis work, as many of the organizational, communication, and people skills that are so important to a librarian are also critical in these roles. Even if you don't think you want to be a project manager forever, the skills are greatly beneficial and transferable to just about any kind of job. If you want the opportunity to both dream up cool information management ideas and use all of your creative facilities to determine how they can be executed, project management can be a great way to get there.

RELATED RESOURCES

I rely heavily on the benefits of professional organizations for learning about the latest in various fields relevant to my work. These organizations are a great place to meet people who are involved in similar activities, find answers to tough challenges I might be having with a particular project, or brush up on a particular skill such as creating site wireframes for layout and design or doing a card sort exercise to learn about users' categorization for specific terms. Here are some of the organizations I use the most.

American Society for Information Science and Technology (ASIS&T). asis.org (accessed March 9, 2006).
Content Management Professionals. www.cmprofessionals.org (accessed March 9, 2006).
Information Architecture Institute (IAI). iainstitute.org (accessed March 9, 2006).
Special Libraries Association (SLA). www.sla.org (accessed March 9, 2006).

CHAPTER 92

Information Architect

LYNN BOYDEN

An information architect is the person who decides what happens next when you click on a link on a Web site. This explanation is a very simple but useful way of describing what I do daily. The title of information architect (or IA) is relatively new, coined by Richard Saul Wurman in the 1970s and first appearing in print in his 1996 book *Information Architects*. The profession remained marginal until the early twenty-first century, with a surge in practitioners entering the field during the dot-com explosion. Just as a building architect interprets the client's needs and wishes for a home in a series of documents from which a contractor builds, an information architect interprets needs and wishes for a Web site and documents them for the programmers who write the HTML code and develop programs for the backend systems. IA encompasses activities such as interaction design, usability testing, taxonomy and nomenclature development, and questions of wayfinding and information design (navigation), information storage and retrieval (search), indexing (metadata), information-seeking behavior (usability), and marketing, statistics, and security. The job can be performed as an employee for the employer's sites, or in an agency environment, working on different projects for the agency's clients. Often these positions are hired out to independent contractors.

I am an information architect for a large software firm that specializes in information security and availability. I am a member of the larger customer experience (CX) team, which encompasses my smaller group, the user experience (UX) team. CX owns about 80 percent of the corporate Web site. We are responsible for maintaining and updating the content, visual design, and structure of the entire site as well as supporting internal Web tools and sites. The public site consists of seven main sections: three market segments, three business offerings (support, security updates, and mandated corporate information), and an intranet for our sales partners. Each of these sections has subsections, functionality, links to a wide variety of content types, and satisfies different, often conflicting, business rules. The site is also limited by backend systems (content management systems, search engines, content repositories, and Web-serving systems). Our company recently acquired another, larger company, and we are incrementally merging the two Web sites. This lengthy, multiphase, and multiteam effort requires extensive documentation to interpret the merged goals of the business as a consistent and robust user experience. My role on the team is to support the UX managers for the different sections. I am also responsible for the user experience of searching on our site.

A TYPICAL WORKDAY

On this day I had two important meetings, both involving incremental work on projects that were in progress.

The first and potentially most troublesome meeting was with the representatives of the Education Services marketing team to review our proposed site map for the revision of their section of the site. They have been very involved clients, but they are not information architects, and their solutions for the site are often not consistent with our site conventions, nor do they make for a strongly usable site. The team entertains our suggestions but requires convincing to agree to implement them. It is a process of education, but they are eager pupils.

We have proposed a number of changes, mostly to bring the style and functionality of the training site into conformity with our site conventions. We recommended a four-column approach to each page, with the subsection navigation confined to the left-hand side, page content in the two center columns, and the right-hand side dedicated to promotions and widgets (an area of the Web page with controls dedicated to a specific function).

The training team approved the elimination of three frequently asked questions (FAQ) files on the site in favor of distributing the contents of the files to the appropriate area of the site. We have recommended removing the login link from the left-hand navigation, as our philosophy of information architecture calls for a clear distinction between navigation elements and site functionality. The login link gives access to the six different backend training systems used by the two companies. These will be merged and reduced to a more manageable number in a later phase of the site merger plan, but for now they must all be accommodated. The link has been moved to a widget in the right-hand column. We have reorganized the site content areas to incorporate the training-related content from both companies and have recommended several nomenclature changes.

Most important, the team agreed to delay the delivery of the site documentation for a week to perform user testing of our recommendations. Because usability is one of our guiding principles, and because the training organization generates a healthy percentage of revenue in this market segment, we proposed some microtesting of the site to ascertain that we are on the right track with our recommendations. This involves recruiting user testers, observing their use of the site, recording and interpreting the observations, and then incorporating the findings into our site. Microtesting means that we will not be doing a full usability analysis of the entire section of the site; rather, we will ask five to eight members of our primary user group to answer key questions designed to elicit their needs in a couple of key areas. Microtesting provides a quick, low-cost opportunity to learn more about our site's users.

I spent the rest of the morning revising the site map to record the outcomes and action items from the meeting. A site map diagrams the pages and sections of a Web site, and often contains information about site functionality, navigation, or site conventions. Ours are maintained in Visio and printed to PDF files for distribution to client groups.

On this day I had lunch with a colleague (also trained as a librarian) from the support documentation division of our company. During lunch we had a lively discussion of the value of metadata to the knowledge base, and how our users search for documents—with one- or two-word queries. It was a quick lunch, as we both had 1 p.m. meetings.

My second meeting of the day was with the search manager for our CX team. I needed her approval to launch a quick metatagging initiative and I wanted her assistance in getting the Symantec divisions to talk to each other and act quickly.

At the end of October a news story broke about copyright protection software released on music CDs from a major record label. The software required the user to install a program known as a rootkit on their computer in order to play the music. A rootkit executes certain computer files, and although it is usually installed for a legitimate purpose, it can be exploited by malicious software (malware) to install and execute harmful code.

As the story continued to grow, I monitored our daily query logs and found a half dozen terms related to the story. Before the meeting, I also searched for these relevant terms on our site, and determined that none of the top search results produced by these queries was relevant to the malware issue. I had also identified the rate of increase associated with each of the query terms over the last two weeks. These searches totaled nearly a thousand per day.

My plan was to attach some of these query terms as metatags to relevant documents in our security write-up document repository. These write-ups are owned and maintained by a separate division of the company.

The search manager is located in Oregon, so our meeting took place over the phone. Most of my team is located in Silicon Valley, with a few outposts in southern California, Utah, Massachusetts, and Alaska. I explained the situation to the manager. She was not aware of the story, so I used an instant messenger program to send a link to a newspaper article on it. We use instant messaging extensively, as it is very useful for quick exchanges, such as answers to closed-end questions or links to Web information.

She agreed that the metatags were an easy opportunity to quickly improve our users' experience on our Web site. She sent an e-mail to the manager of the malware information portion of our Web site. The malware information manager responded with two alternate write-ups. These addressed the specific rootkit used by the record label, describing its behavior and giving step-by-step instructions on how to remove it from a computer. We gave him a list of five specific queries that users had searched over the past two weeks, and he relayed them to another colleague who managed the content of the security write-ups, asking him to tag the appropriate documents. The colleague responded quickly that the documents had been tagged and would be reindexed within twelve hours.

I then turned to recruiting the users and developing the materials to be used for the microtesting effort of the training section. We wanted the users to perform a card-sort exercise to ascertain whether the information on our site was sorted into the appropriate sections. I used an Excel spreadsheet, Word's mail merge utility, and perforated business card printer sheets to make five sets of ninety cards for the users to sort into groups. I planned to ask each user to sort the cards into whatever groupings made sense and name those groups. I hoped to learn how users describe our content. We planned to ask them to name the sections on a site map that had been stripped of section names. I spent half an hour preparing the stripped maps. Finally I worked with another IA on my team to develop a questionnaire to record each user tester's background and familiarity with our products, our site, and our content.

The last part of the day was spent responding to the e-mail solicitations I had sent to potential user testers. Because I would be traveling to their offices rather than asking them to come to us, I had recruited high-level functional information technology managers and administrators only from UCLA. The response rate was high, and I confirmed appointments for the following week with five users in five different areas of the campus. I also wrote a plan for the microtesting and submitted it to my manager for approvals. I wanted to keep within any company policies regarding user testing, and I wanted to submit a reimbursement request for a gift certificate for each user tester. My manager gave his approval and asked me to present my efforts and the outcomes, with emphasis on metrics and budget, at our next biweekly team meeting.

Before shutting down for the day, I searched our site for the rootkit malware query terms. They had been reindexed already, and the appropriate documents were ranked first and second for most of the queries.

It was a very productive day.

THE JOYS AND TERRORS OF INFORMATION ARCHITECTURE

The joys of being an information architect are many. I love seeing my work on the Web and hearing from other people that my work has made their experience of our Web site better. Believe it or not, I love hearing from other people that my Web designs don't work for them, because I get to look at my design with new eyes. I can then make recommendations for improving the design of a user's experience. With two hours' work identifying queries and tagging some key documents in a content repository, I improved the user experience of a thousand users a day for two weeks. That is very satisfying.

Entry-level information architects holding a degree in library science earn nearly twice what entry-level librarians earn. The corporate environment offers the opportunity to develop my abilities and to be rewarded for taking initiative and performing well. When I worked at an agency, I worked on a wide variety of sites and business models. As an in-house information architect, I have the pleasure of watching a site improve over time, and I am less subject to the vagaries of unreasonable clients and the incredible time pressure that often exists in the agency world. My colleagues have incredibly diverse backgrounds. IAs are not only trained as librarians; they come from anthropology, graphic design, business, marketing, behavioral psychology, and programming, to name just a few. This diversity keeps the practice and theory of IA in evolution. There is always something new to learn.

The terrors of IA work are big ones. Because good information architecture is almost invisible (by reducing the barriers between a user and his or her goals in using a Web site), it is often a challenge to demonstrate the value that our work brings to a Web property. The field is developing methods for measuring an improved user experience through the use of such statistics as click-through rates, shopping cart abandonment, changes in revenue, user feedback forms, usability testing, query logging, and other techniques. Another barrier to our success has been the feeling that information architecture is easy and that anyone can do it, or that it isn't necessary. On the whole, however, these drawbacks are fairly easily overcome by demonstrating the quantifiable value of the information architecture practice. I often find that informing clients of my library degree does a great deal to diminish their resistance to my recommendations.

HOW CAN YOU BECOME AN INFORMATION ARCHITECT?

A library science background is a very strong preparation for information architecture, and many leaders of the field have come out of the area of information studies. Most library science degree programs offer some sort of coursework in information architecture, although it may have other names. Others provide courses in information design, usability, systems design, and information-seeking behavior. All of these courses are relevant to a career in IA. Strong presentation and project management skills will help you throughout life as well as in information architecture. Writing well is an important component of IA for deliverables and site content. If you can obtain direct hands-on experience with Web site development and ongoing maintenance, you will have a broad understanding of the underlying issues related to the practice. If your program offers internships or work-study employment, find one that will use your abilities in this area. Take advantage of your mentoring program. If your school doesn't have one, set one up with help from the alumni association or the faculty. Find mentors at meetings of professional associations and alumni gatherings. Job postings are found online at job boards such as Craigslist, Monster, Yahoo!, and CareerBuilder, as well as at corporate and agency sites. Often posting a résumé on a networking site can also be productive, especially as a job market becomes more growth oriented. Most facets of a library science or information studies education can facilitate a career in information architecture.

RELATED RESOURCES

Books

Garrett, Jesse James. 2002. *The elements of user experience*. Berkeley, Calif.: New Riders.

Reiss, Eric L. 2000. *Practical information architecture*. Reading, Mass.: Addison-Wesley.

Rosenfeld, Louis, and Peter Morville. 2002. *Information architecture for the World Wide Web*, 2nd ed. Sebastopol, Calif.: O'Reilly.

Wurman, Richard Saul, ed. 1996. *Information architects*. Zurich: Graphis.

Online

Boxes and Arrows. www.boxesandarrows.com (accessed February 1, 2006).

Garrett, Jesse James. *Information architecture resources*. www.jjg.net/ia/resources.html (accessed February 1, 2006).

Reiss, Eric L. *Community*. www.e-reiss.com/Community.aspx (accessed February 1, 2006).

Associations

American Society for Information Science and Technology, Information Architecture Special Interest Group. www.asist.org/SIG/ia.html (accessed February 1, 2006).

Association of Computing Machinery, Computer-Human Interaction Special Interest Group. www.sigchi.org (accessed February 1, 2006).

Information Architecture Institute. iainstitute.org (accessed February 1, 2006).

Usability Professionals' Association. www.upassoc.org (accessed February 1, 2006).

CHAPTER 93

Competitive Intelligence Analyst

MICHAEL RUSSELL

Competitive intelligence (CI) is simply learning about the competitive forces that envelop your organization, then using these insights to make informed, timely, strategic, and tactical decisions. CI is not espionage—that's what the CIA does. CI has ethical standards that are taken very seriously. Librarians have told me that their research skills and value-added insights, ability to classify and disseminate information, or ability to build intranet portals is CI. They are correct in that their efforts are part of the CI chain. But CI is the end product of transformed information, and many hands are involved in its delivery.

As a CI analyst working in the health insurance industry, I gather relevant information and use my industry expertise to develop it into knowledge that I can share with the decision makers. This targeted gathering and analysis is part of the CI process because it ultimately leads to knowledge about the environment. Transforming information into actionable intelligence is the core of competitive intelligence. It is the domain of those with the talent to take what is known and unknown and synthesize it into something more. CI analysts are a professionally diverse group that includes a fair share of librarians.

A TYPICAL WORKDAY

I work directly for senior management and my daily routine revolves around the needs of the business. Handling multiple projects with short turnaround times is normal. I adapt to role changes by being a team player with a strong streak of independence and self-motivation. Although I am assigned to a corporate research center, I do not work in a traditional library setting. The collection is very narrow but exhaustive in its depth and is almost completely digital.

Information Gatherer

Business information is a broad subject area. As a librarian working in competitive intelligence, I compile legislative histories, find government reports, talk to the experts who wrote those reports, and engage them to tell me more. I have to stay well read in my industry to be able to ask questions and understand the implications of the answers.

The job is not so much about finding information as it is about finding out if credible information exists at all. I read and evaluate the alerts from the commercial database vendors, blogs, wikis, the Internet, print sources, and all the hidden corners for my competitors and industry. As an industry expert searching for information, I have developed a keen sense of what is happening in the field. I give value-added insight that initiates the transformation of information into intelligence. I read everything I find, understand most of it, and must be able to communicate its significance to management. Telling the story of information's impact on my organization, our competitors, and the relation to other market forces is a big part of my job. I republish the gathered information via an intranet portal and news bulletins to targeted areas of my company.

Filtering content based on my knowledge of the end user's needs and organization's current position is critical. Think of it this way. It's like turning a fire hose into a garden hose. Just as drinking from a fire hose is practically impossible, being flooded with a huge volume of information will drown the users. People do not have the time to sort through a hundred or more news stories every day. They need the dozen that are going to make a difference. So on-time delivery of relevant information to targeted end users begins the CI analysis chain. This is my value to the organization—getting them the information gems. Think you are going to spend a lot of time talking to people and selling your abilities? You're right!

Web Specialist

As an intranet portal editor I help in the publishing process. Relevant information is targeted to the correct audience and pushed out in newsletters or e-mail alerts, but increasingly it is being disseminated through intranet portals powered by very sophisticated databases, Flash, XML, RSS, and ASP.NET. I have formal training in Web design and development, but I am not the nuts-and-bolts Web person. My role is to follow emerging technologies to anticipate future needs and applications.

Analyst

As an analyst I look at the available data (research, interviews, and analysis), make an opinion as to what the company should do in light of the competitive forces, and communicate it to the decision makers. But my analysis is only as good as the quality of the information I am able to find.

As the CI analyst, I am involved in evaluating the content of the information in relation to what I know and would like to know. The range of information can be staggering and will include everything from personal conversations to financial statements. There are ways of approaching this analysis that draw on my creativity and sense of intuition. Analysts track the workings of competitors, suppliers, and buyers within the industry by bringing all relevant information that can be legally and ethically obtained. I listen to investor conference calls and try to anticipate the investor analyst's questions. I also read financial statements, compare them within the industry, and decipher where they are glazing over problems. It's important to understand the competitor's marketing, sales, research and development, distribution network, and IT capabilities in comparison to those at my own organization and other competitors. It is my job to know about anything that can give a competitor an edge over my organization in the marketplace. But more important, I need to evaluate what will give us the competitive edge over them.

PROS AND CONS

If it feeds CI, responds to CI, and supports CI, does that make it CI? Ask the librarians in the CI crowd and you'll hear a resounding "yes." Ask the nonlibrarian CI analysts and they will tell you they could not do corporate research without the librarians, but the librarian's role is not really CI. To me, that is like the supermarket telling the farmer that food is not food until it is in a plastic package. Information is turned into competitive intelligence, and a lot of hands are involved along the way. CI is a process as much as it is an end product.

This is a lesson I learned in the military and heard repeated at conferences. Within some organizations, if you get labeled as the information gatherer, your fate is sealed. It is not that an analyst deplores getting his hands dirty gathering information but that he does not have the time to sort through all the information. Instead, the analyst relies on trained gatherers who can sort through the vast amounts of information and send on the gems.

The people requesting analysis do not fully understand or appreciate the ethical and legal considerations involved in competitive intelligence gathering. You need to be familiar with what constitutes copyright, trademark, or trade secret infringement. This will include maintaining a close working relationship with a company's legal department.

The MLS and its variants are professional degrees just like the MBA, but the MLS lacks the financial respect. My employer cares that I have the skills and experience to get the job done, not that I am a librarian. Stereotypes die hard deaths, and unfortunately, being labeled as a librarian often means lower pay and fewer opportunities in the business world. Information knows no bounds, and we must evolve to meet the shifting paradigms. Focus on being a professional and getting the job done to create a place for the future professionals.

HOW WOULD I GET A JOB LIKE YOURS?

Library school did not prepare me to read financial statements, SEC filings, annual reports, or to read between the lines during investor conference calls. It did not prepare me to develop a truly professional network of contacts, or to communicate in a corporate environment. Library school *did* prepare me to critically think about and evaluate information as well as people's need for it. This is one of many core competencies for being a CI analyst.

Having some type of business degree or an MBA helps, but it is not mandatory. There are several places to get CI training. The best is the world is the Fuld-Gilad-Herring Academy of Competitive Intelligence; it is expensive, but worth every penny. In addition, excellent workshops and seminars are offered at the annual conference of the Society of Competitive Intelligence Professionals (SCIP); CI-101 and CI-102 are the best beginning courses. The Special Libraries Association (SLA) has a Competitive Intelligence Division that offers training and seminars at the SLA annual conference. It is worth investing time to participate in an SLA division that covers your organization's industry. There are also professional societies outside of librarianship that offer training and credentialing.

If you do not have a business degree, then I suggest college-level courses in accounting, economics, marketing, financial management, psychology, sociology, anthropology, communications, strategy, business writing, business statistics, and business law.

I found the following library school courses valuable: government documents, business reference, industry subject reference, advanced database searching, statistics, taxonomies, and cataloging.

Additionally you should have expert proficiency with Microsoft Office, as well as the ability to use Web editing software, graphics programs, and Adobe Professional products.

A better-than-average understanding of database design and integration will come in handy. Also, an intermediate understanding of computer operating systems will be valuable.

RELATED RESOURCES

Additional Readings

Bates, Mary Ellen. Read everything she writes.

Baumohl, Bernard. 2004. *The secrets of economic indicators: Hidden clues to future economic trends and investment opportunities*. Upper Saddle River, N.J.: Wharton School Publishing.

Fleischer, Craig S. 2002. *Strategic and competitive analysis: Methods and techniques for analyzing business competition*. Upper Saddle River, N.J.: Prentice Hall.

Gilad, Benjamin. 1994. *Business blindspots: Replacing your company's entrenched and outdated myths, beliefs and assumptions with the realities of today's markets*. Chicago: Probus. Read everything Ben has written and seek out his presentations.

————. 2003. *Early warning: Using competitive intelligence to anticipate market shifts, control risk, and create powerful strategies*. New York: AMACOM.

Hasanali, Farida, Paige Leavitt, Darcy Lemons, and John E. Prescott. 2004. *Competitive intelligence: A guide for your journey to best-practice processes*. Houston: APQC Publications.

Porter, Michael E. 1980. *Competitive strategy: Techniques for analyzing industries and competitors*. New York: Free Press.

Journals

Competitive Intelligence Magazine.
Cyberskeptic's Guide to Internet Research.
Information Outlook: The Monthly Magazine of the Special Libraries Association.
Information Today.
Intranets: Enterprise Strategies and Solutions.
Searcher: The Magazine for Database Professionals.

Additionally, read local and national newspapers (including the *New York Times* and *Wall Street Journal*) and your industry's trade and professional journals.

Organizations

Fuld-Gilad-Herring Academy of Competitive Intelligence. www.academyci.com (accessed August 20, 2006).

Society of Competitive Intelligence Professionals (SCIP). www.scip.org (accessed August 20, 2006).

Special Libraries Association (SLA), Competitive Intelligence Division. units.sla.org/division/dci/cihome. htm (accessed August 20, 2006).

CHAPTER 94

Knowledge Management Specialist

LANA KROLIKOWSKI

My job is to manage an internal database (intranet) of information for a series of call centers for Comcast, a large cable company. This includes reviewing current information for correctness and completeness, seeking out new information, networking with those agents in my call center to make sure they are using the database, networking with the other call centers to make sure the information is being understood and used there, as well as making sure that the most current information and policies are flowing from the corporate, division, and regional levels to the call centers and, more important, to the agents who work there.

A TYPICAL WORKDAY

The first thing I do when I arrive is start up the computer. This may seem mundane, but quick communication is very important in a rapidly changing business. I begin every day by checking for new e-mails and voicemails. Because so much of the communication I send out is time-sensitive, it is important that I check to see what new information has been sent to me over the night before. Communications come from many different levels, and because we are a nationwide company and many of our facilities are open twenty-four hours, e-mails come in day and night. We have many employees who are not co-located, so it is important to be considerate in responding to e-mail in a timely fashion so that people do not think you have forgotten what they have asked you to do. E-mail also works as a great tool for me to remind people about deliverables they said they would give me to be posted to our intranet. Because people are working on many projects at once, I also make sure to mark e-mails so that I remember to follow up to get responses. Also, I set up reminders in my online calendar so that I make sure to get weekly and monthly reports out by their due dates. I find having an organized e-mail box and calendar is rather important because it keeps me on task and makes sure I do not miss important calls or meetings. Keeping an up-to-date calendar is a way of letting others know if you are busy, something that is very important if you don't want to be scheduled for 2 a.m. meetings.

Another mode of communication that is becoming more popular is Communicator, a Microsoft product that allows coworkers to chat within a company. This has been adapted by a number of my closest contacts, which is wonderful because it allows communication without exchanging multiple voicemails and, better still, without filling up our e-mail boxes, which have a strict size limit. Given the amount of communication that occurs by e-mail, any chance to communicate without using that precious space is something that I love. Plus, as many readers will understand, chatting allows for multitasking, which is useful when you are working on multiple projects or are on the phone. Conversations can be extended in time so that they can continue after lunch breaks or meetings and act as reminders of what you were working on when you had to leave your desk or shift your attention. In addition, chat can be a nonobtrusive way to see if your fellow workers are available. It allows you to interrupt without being as disruptive as a phone call would be, and allows them to get back to you in their own time, but carries more urgency than an e-mail would.

After responding and following up with e-mails, my next duty is to respond to feedback that has been left in the past few days. Our intranet allows users to enter feedback into an automated form. Each day a report is pulled from that feedback that shows us what the users are having problems with, what problems the developers need to be aware of, and what information gaps need to be filled. The rest of my day is filled with meetings of various committees, updating and redesigning documents, and walking the floor, reminding the agents of any new information that has been recently posted and answering any questions they might have.

JOYS AND ANNOYANCES

To be a successful knowledge manager in a large, distributed company, you have to be an outgoing person who is willing to work in a number of different circles to get the information your users need. The aphorism "information is power" holds very true in a large corporation. Being new to the company, the most challenging aspect has been to figure out who the gatekeepers are for all the information my agents need. And when I say "my agents," that is really how I feel about them. It is my responsibility to make sure that they get the best, most timely information available. Although you can imagine that a company would like its employees to have the most updated information, sometimes people forget to pass on information, send it on too late, or just don't have it yet themselves. No matter how proactive I want to be, I am often in a reactive position when posting and distributing information. This means that I have to be able to multitask, not on just a few projects but on several dozen projects, from small updates to design revisions. After a year of experience, I recommend this type of position to someone who is able to move from project to project at a moment's notice, who does not mind being interrupted for emergencies on a daily basis and who is able to stay organized so projects do not fall through the cracks.

Another one of my huge daily challenges is user acceptance. For many years, the system I am currently working with was not maintained, and the agents have a negative attitude about it. Because the system was not maintained in the past, many of the agents do not check it now, even though it is now maintained on a more-than-daily basis and has undergone a complete interface change. In addition, in the past the database was used for the cable side of the business, so it did not contain much information about Internet and telephone services that are covered by my home call center. The tenured employees are not used to checking this database, so it does not even occur to them to use it when they have a question. An interesting observation is that the new hires who have been taught to go to this intranet recognize its usefulness and have fewer problems finding the information they need. We completed a revision of the interface and organization of the system, and to my great pleasure, it is being used more often by all agents. The information is often still questioned, but the agents, through use, are becoming more accepting of the information and are using the system on a more consistent basis.

Some of the joy I get out of my job is being able to work with a wide variety of people at a wide variety of levels within the company. I work with divisional people to redesign and evaluate our intranet, with regional people to set goals and expectations of use, and with call center managers to confirm that we have all the information that the agents need and to inform the agents of new information pertinent to their jobs. Additionally, working with the agents can be a blast. Those agents who want to do a good job and want to earn extra incentives find the database I work on a great resource to make them more knowledgeable about what we are offering to our customers. When I send out information, I am glad to get questions back from the agents because then I get a better idea about who doesn't understand what; that lets me know what areas I need to address in training sessions.

This is not a job I would recommend to someone who is not outgoing and willing to ruffle a few feathers to make sure that users are being served. You must know when to fight the battles for information and when to involve your supervisors for help. As with all jobs, networking has been key, and getting to know people has been a challenge at times. One thing that helps me is that I have two counterparts who have been with the company for several years. We all bring different skills to the position and complement each other well. Having a team that works well together makes any job better.

Another joy of my job is that I get to do so much outside of my job description. That category "other duties as assigned" can be deadly at times, but it can be really fun at others. I have gotten to design meeting invitations, do benchmarking and usability studies of different aspects of my intranet, be in charge of our call center's efforts to raise money for the United Way and other charitable organizations, and do a promotion launch—all within the first nine months of working here.

HOW DID I GET MY JOB?

I think in part my getting this particular job was a bit of kismet and a bit of finding a job that fit my interests. I had been applying for academic library jobs when I heard about this position. A friend of mine from library school worked for the company and had been trying to find someone from our school to apply because she knew that the company could use someone with our education and skill set. Although I had started in the library and information science track, I had switched to the human-computer interaction specialization offered at the University of Michigan because it appealed to my scientific side. Because of my customer service experience from working at a reference desk and my technical skills from my undergraduate and graduate education, I seemed uniquely suited to work with a group of people who were in a similar situation. Having experience talking to the technically and nontechnically inclined has turned out to be one of my greatest assets so far because communication with people of different education levels and technical ability is so important in my job.

CHAPTER 95

Community Evangelist

JENNY SPADAFORA

I'M SORRY, DID YOU SAY EVANGELIST?

In the business world, "evangelist" is still an unusual (but not unheard of) job title. Guy Kawasaki is credited with introducing the term to the high-tech world in the 1990s as a way to describe "the process of convincing people to believe in your product or idea as much as you do" (Kawasaki 1992).

I work in Intuit's Innovation Lab as part of a small team focused on customer-driven new product development. I'm responsible for leading and critically evaluating community-centered offerings exploration and building relationships with business units and functional groups inside Intuit to encourage the flow of ideas and collaborative projects. In other words, I'm a Web geek with a passionate focus on users and the online community. I want people to believe in the possibilities of tapping the wisdom of the digital crowd.

THE DAILY DOSE

I can get very little work done without my laptop and a Wi-Fi connection, so my day starts with logging on and logging in. I connect to the corporate network, and then I fire up my e-mail, feed reader, and browser. Most of the information I sift through comes from the public Web, but not all of it, and I need to feed it back behind the firewall in any case. (I'm probably not in the office. This community evangelist frequently telecommutes.)

After I read my e-mail and follow up with any issues, I start reading feeds.[1] I subscribe to approximately 150 feeds, mostly blogs, which cover a range of topics I want to pay attention to; right now, those topics include social software, Web 2.0, findability, user experience, marketing, and the subject of attention itself. I read blogs by technologists, academics, venture capitalists, and other Web geeks.

I'm looking to see what is new, who is talking about what, and what the buzz is on these different topics. I'm looking for sparks—the provocative, thoughtful ideas I'll want to come back to later. I tag and bookmark those sparks, and the brighter ones I write up and post on the Innovation Lab's blog, so I can kick around the idea with my coworkers.

Next, I might discuss the pros and cons of using a blog for disseminating project-related information with someone in another department in the company. I might consult on information architecture issues involved in building and maintaining a wiki. Maybe I'll participate in a brainstorming meeting where the team generates ideas for new projects to work on, decides on directions to take with existing projects, or figures out who we need to talk to so we can learn more than we know now. One of the things Intuit prides itself on is listening to the customer, so part of figuring out who we need to learn from often means thinking about what types of customers we need to talk with. (Then we go visit them, spending two hours asking questions, listening to answers, and probing for reasons why things are working or not working for them today.)

I'll also devote time to moving forward whatever projects I'm working on directly (rather than consulting on). This might mean creating a simple graphic to illustrate features I want to add to a wiki, editing blog templates, proposing a timeline, or providing feedback on a document generated by someone else on the team.

The home page I've set in my browser is the main page of the wiki I installed on my laptop, and the header says "Thinking only gets you so far ... go do something." Underneath that is an image from Hugh MacLeod's "My 10 Best Ideas" (2004) about how quality isn't job one; being totally amazing is job one. This keeps me from staring into space for too long, and helps me remember that failing is all right (Kirkpatrick 2006) as long as I get out there and do something and learn from it. Every day.

THE GOOD AND THE LESS GOOD

The best thing about my job is getting to work with really smart people who push my thinking. Everything after this is gravy. Here's what the gravy consists of.

- There is constant change and variety in my work. There is always something new in the pipeline, so I am never bored.
- Being a thought leader at a big company (with approximately seven thousand employees, Intuit is roughly the size of the town where I grew up) means my ideas can potentially have wide impact.
- My work is passion driven, largely unstructured, and not micromanaged.
- My work environment is literally my living room or my favorite coffee shop or occasionally an actual office.

Good jobs—even great jobs—have a downside, but I don't think of this next list as being in the "con" column by comparison to the gravy. They are more caveat than con: things to carefully consider your tolerance for if you consider this kind of work.

- Web-centered work moves at a fast pace, and it isn't strictly nine-to-five. I'm happy with my work/life balance, and that's largely because I'm passionate about what I do. This is a job that you do for love, not just money. (Yes, as you probably want to know, the money is good—on the more lucrative side of things as library science options go.)
- Being an evangelist for something presupposes that everyone doesn't already agree with you. Pushing the envelope means occasionally you have to deal with pushback. It can be challenging to deal with smart folks who nevertheless don't understand your position.

- Being a thought leader means eventually people are going to ask you to stand up and think in public. Giving presentations isn't everyone's cup of tea, and in a role like this you need to be able to squelch the "umms" and crank up some enthusiasm in front of an audience.
- Working for a geographically dispersed organization means travel, not always with a lot of notice. I don't really like to fly, but I'm getting used to it.

THE PATH TO COMMUNITY EVANGELISM

Given that community evangelist isn't a traditional library science job (and that evangelism isn't yet what I'd call a traditional corporate gig), can I accurately plot a path that will lead you to it? The answer is no, if you are looking for a guaranteed direct line. But if you can tolerate a bit of uncertainty and are willing to enjoy the journey as well as the destination, then yes.

Things You Need to Be Able to Do

When it comes to skills, I can come close to giving you a tick list. I live on the Web, a task made much easier by the fact that I know something about how it works. I wouldn't be comfortable taking on the role of system administrator, but I do know at least one blogging tool inside and out, I can hand-code when needed, CSS (Cascading Style Sheets) doesn't scare me, I can configure server-based software, and I have a dozen or so extensions installed with my browser. The exact tools I use aren't as important as my confidence level when it comes to using them and choosing the right tool for the job at hand. This confidence comes from being willing to try new things, and from lots of practice.

The "squishy" skills are easy enough to identify, but harder to learn. What exactly are these softer skills? Curiosity and critical thinking. Paying attention to good experiences online and offline. Most important, the ability to recognize good ideas when they aren't your own and to think about the possible implications and implementations of those ideas.

Creating the Right Place at the Right Time

This job found me—I was recruited by someone I previously worked with, because she saw my skill set as something she needed as part of her team. She knew I had the "things you need to know" stuff covered, as well as solid experience in knowledge management, information architecture, and Web content management. These are all things I first learned about in library school and then learned how to practice on the job.

How did I put myself in the right place at the right time? The frustratingly uncertain part of my answer is that I focused on doing good work that I cared about, kept up an online presence that reflected the way I thought and most of what I thought about, and didn't worry about what my next career move was supposed to be. Because you are probably looking for a more proactive approach, I'll tell you a bit about *how* I knew this job was the right move for me.

I knew this job was right because I wanted to be at a forward-thinking company or organization where people saw the Web as an opportunity, not a threat. I wanted to use the most interesting (to me) things I learned in library school and on my own. I wanted to be someplace where others thought my blogging was a plus, not a weird hobby. Finally, cultural fit is extremely important to me. Intuit's goal—to provide tools that give people a way of doing things that is so much better that they won't go back to the old way—made sense to me. So did their nondiscrimination policy, and yes, even their lack of a dress code. The lesson here is: articulate what is important to you well enough that you can explain it to someone else. Then go look for it, unless it finds you first.

Advice I Wish I'd Been Given

The most important thing I learned in library school was something I didn't realize was that important at the time. I took cataloging because it was required, and between the syllabus set by that particular instructor and my disinclination to investigate on my own, I didn't actually learn very much about cataloging. What I did learn is this: *there is no such thing as a natural, inherent organizational system.* Different systems might feel right to us, but that is our perspective, not fact. Now this theory is great if you are approaching Web site information architecture (and perhaps not so good if you work in a university library technical services department).

Don't get too hung up on the details of every little subject offered in library school. Instead, put that energy into trying to figure out which details you need to know. Sometimes the theory or pattern that emerges is more important. For instance, the database management software I learned in class is outdated now, but understanding how databases work isn't. I wish someone had told me explicitly that there was value in being something of a generalist techie. By that, I mean being comfortable with technology but keeping the focus on the people—the *why* half of tech. The other thing I would have liked to hear (but in fairness would not have believed) is that following your passion will pay off, and the trick is learning to live with uncertainty until it does.

NOTE

1. A feed is a method for a Web site to syndicate content. The point of feed readers is one-stop shopping for new content, because the reader polls your resources for you. You no longer have to click on link after link just to see if there is something new, and the time it saves means you can track exponentially more sources of information. See K. G. Schneider, "Getting Started with RSS: The Fifteen-Minute Tutorial," *Free Range Librarian*, November 18, 2003. freerangelibrarian.com/archives/111803/getting_started_with. php (accessed February 6, 2006).

GOING DEEPER

If you are interested in learning more about evangelism in a business context, curious and critical thinking, or Intuit, these are the resources I recommend.

Online

Church of the Customer. customerevangelists.typepad.com (accessed June 21, 2006). Maintained by Ben McConnell and Jackie Huba, this blog's focus is marketing and evangelism, and reading it is a great way to get what evangelism is in a business context.

Corante Web Hub. web.corante.com (accessed June 21, 2006). This site aggregates posts from a variety of contributors who are known as leading thinkers on issues of Web-based communication, collaboration, social networks, and tool development. This aggregated blog is a great way to follow the conversation.

Kirkpatrick, David. 2005. Lessons in leadership: Throw it at the wall and see if it sticks. *Fortune*, December 12. money.cnn.com/magazines/fortune/fortune_archive/2005/12/12/8363128/index.htm (accessed June 21, 2006). This article is about the culture of innovation at Intuit, and how "failure is very much an option as long as you learn from it."

MacLeod, Hugh. 2004. My 10 best ideas. *Gapingvoid*. (September 18). www.gapingvoid.com/Moveable_Type/archives/000988.html (accessed June 21, 2006).

Offline

Kawasaki, Guy. 1992. *Selling the dream: how to promote your product, company, or ideas, and make a difference using everyday evangelism*. New York: HarperBusiness.

Kawasaki, Guy, with Michele Moreno. 1999. *Rules for revolutionaries: The capitalist manifesto for creating and marketing new products and services.* New York: HarperBusiness. Accessible (dare I say fun?) introduction to competitive business culture. If you have never read a *Business Week* best-seller because you thought it would be too boring, this book will change your mind. If it excites you, this kind of work might be for you—if not, then it isn't.

Pink, Daniel H. 2005. *A whole new mind: Moving from the information age to the conceptual age.* New York: Riverhead Books. Pink makes the case for knowledge workers developing "high touch" and "high concept" aptitudes for keeping the creativity and connection alive at work or seeing their jobs move overseas. He presents a different perspective on career planning by positing "meaning is the new money."

Surowiecki, James. 2004. *The wisdom of crowds: Why the many are smarter than the few and how collective wisdom shapes business, economies, societies, and nations.* New York: Doubleday. It may seem counterintuitive at first, but diverse groups are smarter than individual experts most of the time. Thinking about this opens up whole new possibilities in a networked world full of user-generated content.

Taylor, Suzanne E., and Katherine K. Schroeder. 2003. *Inside Intuit: How the makers of Quicken beat Microsoft and revolutionized an entire industry.* Boston: Harvard Business School Press. A company biography, if you want to learn more about the only software company to compete head-to-head with Microsoft and win. You probably don't need to know this much about Intuit, but in case you do, have at it.

Epilogue: A Day in the Life of Priscilla and Rich's Editor

SUE EASUN

July 10, 2005
Sue—I had a new idea for an edited collection. See below a message a friend sent me for LIScareer. "I had an idea for LIScareer. It'd be a series of articles called *A Day in the Life* ... and you'd have people do a summary of what a 'normal' workday is like." Last night it occurred to me that this might make an interesting book. If you think it's interesting, I can work up a proposal.—Priscilla

July 10, 2005
Priscilla—Oh, I really like it! (Wish I'd thought of it.)—Sue

July 20, 2005
Hi, Priscilla! I am pleased to announce that we would very much like to publish *A Day in the Life*!—Sue

August 12, 2005
Hi Sue, I'm looking for MLS grads who work in publishing. If you'd like to write a chapter for this book, you're quite welcome.—Priscilla

August 12, 2005
Priscilla—I think it would be fun if I wrote an epilogue. I've been a librarian (academic and public), faculty member, editor, and wholesale book buyer, so I could really cover the gamut. I could also make it funny, informative, and supportive of your efforts.—Sue

November 15, 2005
Sue, I have never had someone write an epilogue. Would you like to see a rough draft of the entire manuscript before you write it?—Priscilla

November 15, 2005
Hi, Priscilla! I think the easiest thing to do is send me, by e-mail, your final draft. I will read it, write my epilogue, submit it to you for review, revise as requested, then return it for you to add to the whole. Does that seem doable? In the meantime, I can think about what I'm going to say, so that I don't hold up the works.—Sue

March 1, 2006
Sue, are you still willing to write an epilogue? If so, I would probably need your piece by August 1 at the latest, since my deadline is September 1.—Priscilla

March 10, 2006
Priscilla—Yes, I'm still willing to write an epilogue. I will make a note to have my part to you by August 1, if not before.—Sue

April 13, 2006
Sue, I need to ask you to make some changes to the *A Day in the Life* book contract. Rich Murray has agreed to join me as coeditor.—Priscilla and Rich

April 13, 2006
Welcome aboard, Rich!—Sue

July 13, 2006
Sue—There *is* a possibility that we may need an extra one or two months.—Priscilla and Rich

July 13, 2006
Priscilla and Rich—Hey, if you're asking me, I'd be happy for you to submit a month late. That would certainly ease a little pressure in terms of my epilogue!—Sue

July 14, 2006
Sue, as for your epilogue, please be honest with us, did you offer to write the epilogue just to be nice? I mean, would you sigh with relief if we let you off the hook? We don't want to stress you out! But on the other hand, if this is something you would really, really like to do, then we would love for you to do it.—Priscilla and Rich

July 14, 2006
Priscilla and Rich, don't worry about the deadline; as far as I'm concerned, you have until September 30. I rarely know what I'm going to write until I start, but I'm thinking of "a day in the life of Priscilla and Rich's editor," thus giving a sense of what I do while poking a little fun at me and the process.—Sue

July 30, 2006
Sue—We're making good progress on the book, but we do think we'll probably need at least a couple extra weeks, so we'd like to make October 1 our official deadline. So we can give you more time to write the epilogue. Would a new deadline of August 31 work for you?—Priscilla and Rich

July 30, 2006
Priscilla and Rich, I definitely need an extension … and it works beautifully into what I'm writing. So you shall have my deathless prose by August 31 (if not before), and you now have until October 1 to submit the whole thing.—Sue

September 2, 2006
Sue—How are you? We don't mean to bug you, but we did want to check in to see how the epilogue is coming.—Priscilla and Rich

September 3, 2006: I commit the first words of this epilogue to print.

LIFE AS AN ACQUISITIONS EDITOR

The e-mail exchanges give a pretty accurate snapshot of life as an acquisitions editor (except for a little role reversal toward the end. It's the editor who's supposed to do the prodding!).

Note, too, the ease with which I send assurances, then promptly move on to other matters: it puts me in good company with about 90 percent of the author universe. (The remaining 10 percent are paragons of virtue and beyond the scope of this comparison.)

Making sure that 90 percent produce their manuscripts by deadlines that often resemble moving targets is a big part of my job. At our company, none of our authors work for hire where, in exchange for a fee, they give us exactly what we ask for when we ask for it. Our agreements, just as legally binding, are far less one-sided. Although I'm sure many of you feel that the publisher holds all the cards, a savvy acquisitions editor endeavors to stack the deck so that both parties come out winners, each convinced the victory is theirs! It is as detrimental to my employment future for the company to thrive at the author's expense as it would be to privilege an author without regard for the bottom line.

Some authors have agents to help them break into the business and ensure a fair shake. None of my authors do. I suspect it would change the dynamics of what I've described, although I have read enough acknowledgments to know authors can and do develop strong bonds with editors as well as agents.

SO WHAT EXACTLY DO I DO?

A typical day finds me involved in at least one of three asterisms, composed of prospective authors, contracted authors, and coworkers, respectively. In short, I am either looking for new blood, ministering to the converted, or feeding the various members of my publishing family whatever information will help them produce, market, and sell our titles. Although I work in a corporate environment, where output (preferably profitable output) rules, the true measure of success lies in my ability to transcend quotas and bean counting and, for want of a better phrase, go with the flow. There is no right answer to whether time is better spent presenting a proposal, negotiating a contract, or reading a manuscript, nor whether it is better spent filling in forms or sending follow-up e-mail after a conference. The only right answer is the one that ensures continual movement. Stuff in, stuff out. Too much of either and the rhythm breaks down.

Is it Monday at 3 p.m.? If so, and I have book proposals in hand, that's the deadline to put them on the agenda for tomorrow's weekly meeting. I don't circulate the actual proposals; instead, I present them to my colleagues and my boss. My ability to do so successfully is contingent on my knowledge of the market, the strength of my conviction in the author, and the believability of my sales projections.

Is it Tuesday at 3 p.m.? If so, I will soon know whether I have good news for my authors and we can begin to discuss the terms of the contract. Sometimes this part goes quickly, other times it seems interminable. Questions range from "What does 'indemnity' mean?" to "Only five free copies? That won't begin to cover my Christmas gift list!" I find I'm always a little on edge about a project until the contract has been signed and countersigned. After that, the ball's back in my court.

Other than a monthly staff meeting and fall/spring title launches to our marketing and sales teams, that's it for my scheduled time, and not just because I work from home. What I said about flow, about keeping things moving—this is where it begins.

It is no coincidence that this epilogue is the first real writing I've done since I became an editor eight years ago. Truly, this eleventh-hour effort has as much to do with guilt as procrastination. If I am writing, I am not editing, and any one of my authors could rightfully say, "She has time to write an epilogue? I'm still waiting to hear back!"

Some authors are content to sign their contracts and work away in relative oblivion until they have completed a draft. Many more have questions, or simply a need to hear from the only other person they know to care as much about what they have to say as they do. But at some point, all are ready to share, and I must read the fruits of their labors with kindness, discernment, and tact. I also determine whether to send it out for review and, in so doing, accept that I have acquired yet another person to prod and another set of revisions to incorporate.

At the same time, I am tending my contact database—people I've met at conferences, via journals and discussion lists, from referrals and past employment—nearly all of whom need to be approached at least twice before I can begin to traverse the six degrees of separation between me and the culmination of an idea. Such contacts are my stock in trade. No acquisitions editor can afford to rely on authors coming to us first.

In between, there are forms and queries and checkpoints and reports, all generated by or for the in-house team. As is the case with much of early twenty-first-century life, they eat up an inordinate amount of my time.

So which of these activities did I perform today? Which will I perform tomorrow? Let's just say I have created a number of mechanisms that allow me to monitor activity or lack thereof (from preproposal to postproduction) that are, of course, only as effective as the data I put into them. To say more would be imprudent; it might tip off a competitor, wondering how the heck I found the time to write an epilogue.

Which now has me wondering the same thing.

September 5, 2006: I commit the final words of this epilogue to print.

Index

About the Contributors

For updated biographies, see www.liscareer.com/dil.htm.

Jenifer Abramson is assistant director of library human resources at UCLA. Her professional experience includes work in cataloging, information literacy, reference, government information, reader advisory, and collection development, as well as work in multiple settings, including law, academic, and elementary school libraries. She is an active member of ALA and several of its divisions and round tables. She received her MLS from UCLA in 1977.

Alisa Alering received her MLS from Indiana University in 2004. She has been rights and permissions manager at Indiana University Press since 2003. Sometimes she has a hard time making her inner librarian think like a publisher.

Chinwe Anunobi is a graduate of biological science at the University of Nigeria Nsukka and also holds an MLS from Imo State University. She is presently the ICT librarian at the Federal University of Technology Owerri. She is a member of the International Reading Association, Nigerian Library Association, Reading Association of Nigeria, and the Editorial Board, Nigeria Library Association Imo State chapter.

Osei Akoto Baffour is a Ghanaian-trained sculptor who joined the library profession after conducting African art workshops for The New York Public Library. He completed his MLIS at Pratt Institute in Brooklyn, New York. During the seven years that followed, he became a senior young adult librarian and assistant branch librarian. In 1998, Osei left the New York system and joined Dallas Public Library, where he managed two branch libraries and set up three teen centers. He is currently a branch administrator at Fort Worth Public Library and continues to create and exhibit art.

Whitney Baker is the conservator for the University of Kansas Libraries and previously held conservator positions at the University of Kentucky and the Library of Congress. She holds an MLIS and advanced certificate in library and archives conservation from the University of Texas at Austin.

Bryan Baldus is a cataloger at Quality Books in Oregon, Illinois. He obtained his MSLIS from the University of Illinois at Urbana-Champaign in 2000. In his spare time, he enjoys working with Macintosh computers, programming in Perl, watching TV, and playing video games.

Erin Barta is a self-proclaimed "everything librarian" and has been working in libraries for the past eight years. She is library services coordinator for a small academic institution in California. In her spare time, she volunteers with animal rescue organizations, cares for five rescued special-needs parrots, and studies kung fu and Filipino kali.

Michelle Batchelor began her library career as a student employee in interlibrary loan at the University of Oregon. After graduating with a BA in English, she worked as classified staff in ILL until she was promoted to student supervisor and assistant to the unit manager of the circulation/reserves and videos department. She obtained her MLIS at the University of Washington in 2005 and was hired into her current position as head of document delivery services at the University of Nevada, Las Vegas.

In addition to her work as public access coordinator for the Academy Film Archive, **Snowden Becker** is an active member of the moving-image archives community. She was the founding chair of the AMIA Small Gauge and Amateur Film interest group and is a cofounder of International Home Movie Day and the nonprofit Center for Home Movies. Her research and writing on amateur film has examined the use of home movies in the scientific community to study autism and schizophrenia, early independent film productions, and the increasing use of historic footage in new documentary productions.

Lonnie Beene is director of the Northeast Texas Community College Learning Resource Center in Mount Pleasant, Texas. Since 1983 he has worked in a variety of academic libraries including a small private liberal arts college, a law school, and both public and private four-year universities before moving into his current position in 1995.

Carol A. Berger is manager, marketing communications, and chairman of the board of C. Berger Group, a woman-owned library personnel and information management services firm in Illinois. She founded CBG in 1982 after working fifteen years in association and corporate libraries in Chicago and Washington, D.C., and was president from 1982 to 2003. She participates as a committee member and elected official of local/national sections of SLA, ALA, and AALL and in the Illinois Library Association, Association of Independent Information Professionals, and National Association of Women Business Owners. She is quoted in *Library Journal*, the *Chicago Tribune*, and CareerJournal.com as a speaker on library and entrepreneurial topics. Carol received an MSLS and a BA in English literature from the Catholic University of America and holds an MBA from the University of Illinois at Chicago. She served as an advisory member of GSLIS, LTA, and association boards.

Lynn Boyden is an information architect teaching in the graduate information studies program at UCLA. Prior to that, she was with the user experience team at Symantec. She has worked at a variety of other positions, ranging from photo editor at *Hustler* magazine to public information officer at the Italian consulate, each of which has in some way informed her approach to information architecture, usability, and site design. She earned an MLIS from UCLA in 1997 and is one of the four original instigators of the Information Architecture Slam. Outside a brief stint as a page, Lynn has never worked in a library. She lives in Los Angeles with her husband, two children, a fish with no name, and two Husqvarna sewing machines.

Sophie Brookover is a senior teen librarian at the M. Allan Vogelson Regional Branch of the Camden County (New Jersey) Library. When not waxing rhapsodic about the joys of serving teens, she can usually be found knitting; reading; trawling used record shops, used bookshops, and used clothing shops for hidden treasures; or just hanging out with her daughter and husband.

Ann Brownson is a reference librarian, education bibliographer, and coordinator of the Ballenger Teachers Center at Booth Library, Eastern Illinois University, in Charleston, Illinois.

Anne Brûlé is a cataloging/training librarian at Queen's University. She has an MLIS from the University of Western Ontario and an undergraduate degree in art history/architecture from Carleton University in Ottawa. Before coming to Queen's University in 2003, she worked at Okanagan University College in British Columbia.

Lynne C. Chase is an assistant professor at the University of Emporia School of Library and Information Management in Emporia, Kansas. Her research interests include information transfer and interactions in the state and federal government setting using a social informatics approach.

Dan Cherubin has worked as the vice president, corporate librarian at Rabobank International for two years. He has a BA in music from Bard College, an MSLS from Columbia University's School of Library Service, and a master's in media studies from New School University. His prior library positions include the New York Public Library for the Performing Arts, the American Music Center, MONY Life Insurance, and work as a freelance cataloger. He has also worked as director of marketing for G2X. He is a regular contributor to "Commodity of the Quarter" in the *Journal of Agricultural & Food Information* and has been recently published in *Counterpoise* and *Revolting Librarians Redux*. Online, he is known as the Ska Librarian and has a not-so-regularly updated Web site at www.geocities.com/ska_librarian. He lives in New York City.

Christine Ciambella received her MSLS degree from the Catholic University of America in 1995. Prior to that, she had been a practicing attorney for five years, having also earned her JD from Catholic University. She spent most of her career working in private law libraries before joining George Mason University as circulation/access services librarian in 2005. Special areas of interest include legislative history, tax, and government contracts research. She is active in several professional organizations, including the Law Librarians' Society of Washington, D.C., and the Southeastern Chapter of the American Association of Law Libraries.

Marci Cohen is a multimedia librarian at Northbrook (Illinois) Public Library. She has worked with music throughout her career, mainly as a popular music critic, and also as a usability specialist at RollingStone.com. She earned a BS from the Wharton School of Business, University of Pennsylvania and an MSLIS from the Graduate School of Library and Information Science, University of Illinois, Urbana-Champaign.

Steven M. Cohen worked at PubSub Concepts from 2005 to 2006. He is now senior librarian at Law Library Management, providing law library services to law firms or corporate legal departments. He is the creator of the Library Stuff Weblog (librarystuff.net) and a columnist for Information Today. He has spoken at numerous conferences on such topics as Weblogs, RSS, keeping current, search engines, social networking, and reader's advisory. He was one of *Library Journal*'s Movers and Shakers in 2004 and is the author of *Keeping Current: Advanced Internet Strategies to Meet Librarian and Patron Needs*. He holds an undergraduate degree from SUNY Stonybrook, an MA in mental health counseling from Long Island University, and an MLS from Queens College. He and his family live in New York.

Katherine Coolidge is the law librarian for Bulkley, Richardson and Gelinas, with offices in Springfield and Boston, Massachusetts, where she has been employed since 2002. She is a graduate of Western New England College School of Law and of Simmons College Graduate School of Library and Information Science. She is a licensed attorney in the Commonwealth of Massachusetts and a member of the Massachusetts Bar Association. She is a member of the American Association of Law Libraries and its New England chapter, the Law Librarians of New England, as well as its practice division, the Private Law Librarians. She is also a member of the Special Libraries Association and its Connecticut Valley chapter, where she holds the office of archivist, and its Legal Division, where she holds the office of treasurer.

Alyson Dalby graduated from library school in 2003 and has been working at the History of Medicine Library, part of the Royal Australasian College of Physicians, since 2002. She is involved in the Australian Library and Information Association New Graduates Group, and served as convenor of the 2006 New Librarians' Symposium in Sydney. Alyson was the Special Libraries Association Australia-New Zealand chapter's Information Professional of the Year for 2006.

Karen Davidson is a serials cataloger and assistant professor in the Mitchell Memorial Library at Mississippi State University. She holds a master of education degree from the University of Georgia and an MLIS from San José State University. At the time she wrote her chapter, she was a reference/government documents librarian at Mississippi State University and had been in this split position for two years.

Natasha Davies was awarded a BSc (Hons) from King's College London in 2000 and took up a graduate trainee information assistant post at the Science Museum Library, London. She received a grant from the Arts and Humanities Research Board to study for an MA in information studies and graduated from the University of Brighton in 2002. Natasha was elected to the register of chartered members of CILIP in 2004, while working as assistant librarian at North Essex Hospitals' Library and Information Service, Essex Rivers NHS Trust. After working as librarian and information officer at Cancerbackup, she took up the post of intelligence analyst–life sciences at IPEEX in 2006.

Susan Davis has been a serials librarian since 1980 and is currently head of electronic periodicals management at the University at Buffalo, State University of New York. She was previously head of the periodicals section at UB and head of serials at the Illinois Institute of Technology. She is active in both NASIG and the Association for Library Collections and Technical Services of ALA and was a column editor for *Serials Review*.

Stephanie DeClue was the public services librarian at Whiteman Air Force Base from 2002 to 2005. She is currently the director of library services at State Fair Community College in Sedalia, Missouri.

Kelly Devlin is a recovering attorney working for a regional law firm. A native Rhode Islander educated in Indiana and Massachusetts, she now lives in Massachusetts and on most days commutes to the firm's Providence office, which is just five blocks from where she grew up, proving that you can go home again.

Nanette Wargo Donohue is a 2003 graduate of the University of Illinois Graduate School of Library and Information Science. She joined the Champaign Public Library as technical services manager in 2003. Nanette currently serves as president-elect of the ALA New Members Round Table, assistant editor of the *ALCTS Newsletter Online*, and chair of the Illinois Library Association Resources and Technical Services Forum. She is a member of the 2005 class of Synergy: The Illinois Library Leadership Initiative.

Karen Douglas grew up in the borough of Queens in New York City. She has a BA in history from Boston University and an MS in library service from Columbia University. Karen has been a librarian for over thirty years, working in public, school, special, and academic libraries. Her career began as a reference librarian at the Queens Public Library. After thirteen years as a reference librarian, she made the transition to technical services as an acquisitions/serials librarian at Newark Public Library in New Jersey. Karen began technical services work in law libraries at the U.S. Department of Justice Library in Washington, D.C. She has also worked as acquisitions/serials librarian at George Washington University Law Library and Georgia State University Law Library, where she was promoted to head of technical services. Karen assumed her current position as head of technical services at Duke University Law Library in 2004.

Clare B. Dunkle received her MLS from Indiana University and earned tenure as the monographs cataloger at Trinity University in San Antonio, Texas, before moving overseas and starting a writing career. She published four novels with Holt and is currently working on two manuscripts for the Ginee Seo Books imprint of Atheneum Press. Her debut novel, *The Hollow Kingdom*, won the Mythopoeic Award as well as a spot on ALA's "Best Books for Young Adults" list, and her books have garnered various honors and starred reviews. She lives with her husband and daughters in Obermohr, Germany.

After graduating from the University of Illinois at Urbana-Champaign's Graduate School of Library and Information Science in 2003, **Katie Dunneback** started the Young Librarian Web site and Weblog (www.younglibrarian.net). Currently, she is a reference librarian with the Westchester Public Library in Westchester, Illinois.

Sue Easun is acquisitions editor for textbooks and scholarly/professional monographs in academic libraries, information science and systems, and instructional technology at Libraries Unlimited. She has been a paraprofessional at the Chatham (Ontario) Public Library, a reference librarian at the Ontario Institute for Studies in Education and the University of Victoria (British Columbia), and an adult services librarian at the Toronto Public Library. She also worked for three years as children's book buyer for the National Book Centre (now National Library Service). A 1992 graduate of the University of California, Berkeley's doctoral program, Sue held a faculty position at the Faculty of Information Studies, University of Toronto for seven years, followed by five years as an acquisitions editor at Scarecrow Press. While at Toronto, she served as founding publisher of *The Looking Glass* (www.the-looking-glass.net), the first children's literature e-journal, created an online community known as InfoMOO, and served as founding executive director of the Toronto Centre for the Study of Children's Literature.

Lisa A. Ennis is a reference librarian and liaison to the School of Nursing at the University of Alabama at Birmingham's Lister Hill Library of the Health Sciences. She holds an MA in history from Georgia College (1994) and an MS in information sciences from the University of Tennessee (1997). Only really happy when she has too much to do, Lisa is the author of numerous encyclopedia entries, articles, and book chapters on a variety of topics. She especially enjoys writing about weird medical history and library marketing and leadership. Her free time is spent working on her house and playing with her dog, Gracie.

Amanda Etches-Johnson has an MA and MISt from the University of Toronto and is a reference librarian at McMaster University and a lecturer at the Faculty of Information and Media Studies at the University of Western Ontario. She authors the Weblog blogwithoutalibrary.net, and frequently publishes and presents on topics such as emerging technologies and social software in libraries. She considers herself extremely fortunate to have found her dream job right out of library school.

Jonathan W. Evans is reference librarian at the Museum of Fine Arts, Houston, where he has been employed for the past fifteen years. His professional experience includes work in reference, bibliographic instruction, interlibrary loan, collection development, and cataloging. He is an active member of the Art Libraries Society of North America, where he is presently working with a group to provide better access to artist files. He received his MLS from the University of North Texas in 2000.

Nancy G. Faget holds a BS in marketing (1981) and MLIS (1998) from Louisiana State University, where she was inducted into Beta Phi Mu in 1999. She began her career as a librarian in a community college library, completed a one-year internship for the Department of the Army library program, and worked four years as an electronic services librarian at the Army Corps of Engineers Headquarters Library. She is now a senior planning and development specialist in Library Services and Content Management at the U.S. Government Printing Office. For the past several years, Nancy held a leadership role in the Knowledge Management Working Group of the Federal Chief Information Officers Council, where she helped start taxonomy and semantics communities of practice. She advises librarians to learn all they can (especially about knowledge management, metadata, content management, taxonomies, virtual reference services, and collaborative tools) and participate in professional associations.

Nancy Fawley is the reference librarian at Virginia Commonwealth University School of the Arts in Qatar. She received her MLIS from the University of Kentucky and was awarded the school's Melody Trosper Award for excellence in academics, leadership, and service. She has an undergraduate degree in journalism from Boston University.

E. Lorene Flanders is professor and director of university libraries at the University of West Georgia in Carrollton. She formerly served as associate university librarian at Georgia College & State University where she was appointed as instruction librarian in 1989. Prior to becoming an academic librarian, she worked in children's and young adult services in public libraries. She holds an MLN from the University of South Carolina and an MA in history from Georgia College.

Mary Jo P. Godwin was the librarian for the Metropolitan Club in Washington, D.C. She began her career as an administrator of a public library in North Carolina. She is the former editor of the *Wilson Library Bulletin* and worked as a marketing director for several reference and scholarly publishers.

Jenifer Grady was meant to be a librarian and earned her degree at the University of North Carolina at Chapel Hill's School of Information and Library Science. She has worked primarily in medical librarian positions and studied informatics and knowledge management, but also had positions in special and public libraries prior to completing an MBA at Case Western Reserve University in Cleveland, Ohio. All of this prepared her as well as it could to be the director of the ALA-APA: the Organization for the Advancement of Library Employees.

One of six librarians in her family, **Julie Harwell** worked in various academic libraries for more than thirteen years, serving in reference, interlibrary loan, and technical services. After receiving an MLIS in 1998, her first professional position was with SOLINET as a trainer for OCLC services, specializing in resource sharing. Julie joined EBSCO in 2002 as a training specialist and became manager of training resources in 2003. She is a member of the Alabama Library Association, ALA, the North American Serials Interest Group, and the American Society for Training and Development. She also serves as a member of the Library School Association, an advisory board for the University of Alabama School of Library and Information Studies.

Born and raised in Spokane, Washington, **Samantha Schmehl Hines** received a BA in political science from Linfield College in McMinnville, Oregon. She earned her MSLIS in 2003 from the University of Illinois at Urbana-Champaign. After graduation, she worked part-time as a cataloger at the National Czech & Slovak Museum in Cedar Rapids, Iowa, and as an adjunct reference librarian at Kirkwood Community College in Iowa City, until she was fortunate enough to land a full-time position back in the West. She now works as the social sciences librarian and outreach coordinator at the Mansfield Library of the University of Montana, Missoula. When not at work, she enjoys hiking, reading voraciously, and spending time with her family.

Jesse Holden is the ordering librarian and head of the Ordering Unit for the Stanford University Libraries. Previously he was the acquisitions librarian for the Robert Crown Law Library at Stanford Law School. He earned his MLIS from San José State University.

Alison Hopkins graduated with an MLIS from Dalhousie University in 1994, and started as an entry-level librarian at the Queens Borough Public Library that same year. After nine years of progressively more responsible positions, she accepted a management position in charge of circulation and technical services at the Brantford (Ontario) Public Library. After three years, she moved to her current position as territorial librarian for Canada's Northwest Territories.

Sarah Houghton-Jan is the former e-services librarian for the Marin County Free Library, the current information and Web services librarian for the San Mateo County Library, and a technology instructor for the Infopeople Project. She is a former president of the California Library Association's Information Technology Section, a member of CLA's assembly, and serves on LITA's Top Technology Trends Committee. She earned an MLIS from the University of Illinois at Urbana-Champaign and an MA in Irish literature from Washington State University. She runs a library technology blog, Librarian in Black (www.librarianinblack.net), and has been published in a dozen library publications. A native Chicagoan, she now resides in San Rafael, California.

Shelley Hourston graduated with an MLS in 1991 after working for four years as a library technician in a school library. She has worked as a technical/systems librarian and database editor/coordinator in special libraries, and as an information specialist in a private college. She has provided business research services as a consultant and published a current awareness newsletter for human resources professionals. For the past eight years, she has worked as a program director at the British Columbia Coalition of People with Disabilities in Vancouver; additionally, she works with librarians and information professionals who are interested in career change, work/life balance, and resilience issues. Through individual coaching and workshops, participants explore change using appreciative inquiry and life review techniques to rediscover their strengths and life goals. You can contact her through her Web site at www.shourstonandassociates.com.

Joy Huebert earned her MLS in 1981 from the University of British Columbia. She began her career as a children's librarian with the Calgary Public Library before moving into small public libraries as a consultant for a regional system in Grande Prairie, then managing libraries in Stony Plain, Spruce Grove, and Trail. She has held executive positions in the Library Association of Alberta, the West Kootenay Library Association, and the Association of British Columbia Public Library Directors. She has presented workshops at provincial conferences and has written many articles for library publications. She is an advanced Toastmaster who enjoys making speeches. Joy lives with her son and husband in the ski resort town of Rossland, British Columbia, and enjoys skiing all winter. She is a member of a writers' group and has won literary competitions. She also paints, draws, and likes to climb small mountains.

Jenna Innes is currently the youth librarian with the Edmonton Public Library in Alberta, Canada. She delights in discovering new ideas for connecting young people and their families with the world of reading.

Marie F. Jones has been a librarian since 1990 and extended campus services librarian at East Tennessee State University (Johnson City) since 2000. From 1990 to 2000, she was the reference and bibliographic instruction librarian at Muskingum College in New Concord, Ohio. She is the general editor of *Annotations: A Guide to the Independent Critical Press* (Alternative Press Center, 2004) and author of a number of articles on distance education librarianship.

Mylee Joseph joined Public Library Services, State Library of New South Wales (Australia) in 2005 after working as a library manager, outreach team leader, Internet trainer, children's librarian, reference librarian, and library assistant in a range of NSW public libraries. Her background includes organizing conferences and continuing professional development programs for library staff, Internet training, participation in the New Generation Policy Advisory Group of ALIA, Children's and Youth Services Group of ALIA, strategic planning, and library management. Mylee is the Public Library Services consultant for the Central West Zone of the Country Public Libraries Association and for the Metropolitan Public Libraries Association Central Region.

Laura Townsend Kane is assistant director for information services at the University of South Carolina School of Medicine Library, where she has been working for thirteen years. She earned her MLIS from USC's College of Library and Information Science in 1991. She also has a bachelor's degree in Spanish and is fluent in both Spanish and Italian. She is the author of *Straight from the Stacks: A Firsthand Guide to Careers in Library and Information Science* (ALA, 2003). She lives in Columbia, South Carolina, with her husband and two children.

Barbara Karp is the librarian at the Shulamith School for Girls in New York. She received her MLS from the University of Michigan in 1976 and has been migrating eastward ever since. Her first library position was in a college in Buffalo. She and her husband now live in Brooklyn. They have five grown children.

Rebekah Kilzer received her MLS from Drexel University in Philadelphia. She worked in technical services for several years before returning to Ohio to work as a metadata specialist at OCLC. She is currently systems librarian at the Ohio State University Libraries. She is an adjunct instructor for Drexel's College of Information Science and Technology, where she teaches the online cataloging course.

Douglas King currently works as special materials cataloger at the Thomas Cooper Library, University of South Carolina, where he has been employed since 2004. Prior to his current position, Doug held cataloging positions at Georgia Tech and the University of South Florida. He earned his MLIS in 2000 from the University of South Florida, and has a BS in English education, also from USF.

Lana Krolikowski is a knowledge management specialist for Comcast. She is a recent graduate of the University of Michigan's School of Information. She received her BS in physics from Hope College. In her spare time, she likes to run marathons, synchronized swim, garden, and do anything that gets her outside.

Helen Kwaka has worked in public libraries for over ten years in Adelaide, Australia. She held the position of librarian, client services for just over two years, and was then promoted to a comanagerial role with the same library service at the City of Tea Tree Gully Library. Previously, Helen worked in the area of children's and youth services, which is her ultimate passion.

Despite this specialty she always seemed to be involved in anything else that was going on, from Internet training to event management to library marketing. She loves overseas travel, especially visiting lighthouses and libraries, where she always purchases library bags.

Alexis Linoski received her MSLS from the University of North Texas in 2003. She has a business background and served as a solo librarian at a small career college prior to accepting her current position as the collection development librarian at the University of Central Arkansas. Librarianship is her third and, she hopes, last career.

Dallas Long was the visiting instructor in library and information science at Berzsenyi College in Hungary. He is now the director of the university housing libraries at the University of Illinois at Urbana-Champaign. He doesn't miss washing his clothes by hand, but he wishes he could find a bakery that makes really great *palacsinta*.

Michelle Mach has an MLIS from the University of Illinois at Urbana-Champaign and a BA in English literature from the University of California at Santa Cruz. Prior to her job as Web marketing coordinator at Interweave Press, she spent seven years as an academic librarian. Her work has appeared in *College & Research Libraries*, *Computers in Libraries*, and *The Successful Academic Librarian* (Information Today). She also developed the Job Title Generator Web site (www.michellemach.com/jobtitles) while in library school and continues to receive more e-mail about that project than anything else!

Betsy Van der Veer Martens holds an MLS and PhD in information transfer from the Syracuse University School of Information Studies. After four years as electronic marketing manager at Cornell University Press, she has become an assistant professor at the University of Oklahoma School of Library and Information Studies.

Michele McGinnis works as personal librarian to writer and cultural visionary Kevin Kelly. She holds an MSIS from the University of Tennessee, where she was awarded the Roger K. Summit Scholarship from the Dialog Corporation. She is a volunteer for Radical Reference, providing virtual reference services for activists and independent journalists. She resides in San Francisco.

Jo-Ann McQuillan has worked at the Institute of Communications and Advertising (ICA) since 2001, as director of information and communications and, more recently, as privacy officer. She previously worked in two theology libraries and the Inforum (University of Toronto's Faculty of Information Studies). Prior to completing her master of information studies in 2001, Jo-Ann worked as a rare book cataloger for an antiquarian bookstore and a fine art/antiquities appraiser for a local auction house. She also holds a specialist degree in English. Jo-Ann is an active volunteer, most recently completing a two-year term as editor of the SLA Toronto Chapter's newsletter, *The Courier*. She has also served as chair of SLA's Advertising and Marketing Division and Toronto Chapter Solos and sits on the board of directors for the Canadian Advertising Research Foundation. She lives in Toronto and has a perverse obsession for book collecting, urban exploration, and curiosities of all sorts.

Michelle S. Millet received her MLIS in 2001 from the University of South Florida. She works as the information literacy coordinator at Trinity University in San Antonio, Texas.

Jennifer Morrison lives in Aberdeen, Scotland, with her husband. She graduated from the University of Aberdeen with an MA (Hons) history and completed her MSc information and library studies from the Robert Gordon University, Aberdeen. She has worked in oil and gas industry libraries for the past several years, with three of those years in her current position as technical librarian and document controller.

Petter Næss is director of the Information Resource Center at the U.S. embassy in Oslo, Norway, where he has worked for twenty years. He was born in England of Norwegian parents, grew up in the United States, and has lived permanently in Norway since 1977. He has a BA in English from the University of Wisconsin–Madison and a degree in library science from the Norwegian College of Library and Information Sciences. He lives on a small farm west of Oslo with his wife and daughter. His interests include music, literature, public diplomacy, football (soccer), sheep, and other animals.

Robert R. Newlen has been with the Library of Congress, Congressional Research Service (CRS) for thirty years. He has been head of CRS's Legislative Relations Office since 1999. He is currently serving his second term as endowment trustee for the American Library Association and served on the ALA executive board from 1996 to 2000. He also serves on the ALA Council. He received an MLS from Catholic University of America, an MA in art history from American University, and a BA from Bridgewater College. The author of *Resume Writing and Interview Techniques That Work: A How-To-Do-It Manual for Librarians* (Neal-Schuman, 2006), he speaks frequently at state library conferences on résumé writing and interviewing.

Elaina Norlin is currently a senior program officer at the Institute of Museum and Library Services, a federal agency that provides over $280 million a year to support libraries and museums. Her program areas include recruitment, library education, and training. Elaina was also a tenured professor at the University of Arizona and is a published author of two books, several book chapters, and articles. Elaina has presented over thirty papers both nationally and internationally on several topics including strategic planning, marketing, assessment, and usability testing. Her first book, *Usability Testing for Library Websites,* has sold over two thousand copies. Currently she is coauthoring a new book, *E-learning and Business Plans: National and International Case Studie*s.

With previous experience supporting physical therapy rehabilitative programs, **Melody D. Parker** began her career at the Michigan Public Health Institute in 1999 working on the Traumatic Brain Injury Project in addition to the Michigan Local Public Health Accreditation Program. Currently, she coordinates the collaborative efforts of the accreditation program and provides support for Michigan's participation in the Robert Wood Johnson–funded Multi-State Learning Collaborative for Performance and Capacity Assessment or Accreditation of Public Health Departments.

Jim Pearson is the branch manager at both the Aldine Branch Library and High Meadows Branch Library in the Harris County Public Library system in Houston, Texas. He is a graduate of the Texas Library Association TALL Texans Leadership Institute class of 2006. He is a native of Michigan where at the age of eighteen he joined the army. A trained paramedic, Jim has served his country in Korea, Germany, and the United States. He is the father of three sons. He is currently enjoying changing the world, one library customer at a time.

Paula Pfoeffer graduated from the University of South Australia with a master's in library and information management in 1994. She worked in London, England, for two years as a school librarian and for five years as the children's and youth services librarian at Auburn Library and Stanton Library in Sydney, Australia. Most recently she worked as the school librarian at Cochabamba Cooperative School, Bolivia, for three years. She is currently helping public libraries in the cities of El Alto and Cochabamba create literacy programs and library spaces for children in these neighborhoods. Paula maintains a blog at www.paulasbigadventure.blogspot.com.

Sarah Pitkin is a librarian at the Program for the Blind and Disabled at the Utah State Library. She was born and raised in Utah and earned her bachelor's in English literature from Utah State

University and an MLS from Emporia State University. At the time of this writing, she has been a librarian for just over two years.

Kim M. Ricker is the GIS/data librarian in the Government Documents and Maps Department at the University of Maryland Libraries. She is a graduate of the College of Information Studies at the University of Maryland.

Officer **Tom Rink**, a twenty-three-year veteran of the Tulsa Police Department, completed his bachelor's in criminal justice/psychology from Michigan State University in 1982 and received his MLIS from the University of Oklahoma in 1992. For more than a decade Tom has been building (from scratch) and managing the library for the Tulsa Police Department. Tom is a member of Beta Phi Mu. He is active in the Special Libraries Association, was a recipient of SLA's President's Award in 2002, was named an SLA Fellow in 2005, and is the current president of the Oklahoma chapter. He was named one of *Library Journal*'s Movers and Shakers in 2005.

Elisabeth Rowan, MSLS, has been the medical librarian at Shriners Hospital for Children, Lexington, Kentucky, for over eight years. With a background in history, cataloging, archives, and computer use in libraries, the last thing she expected was to wind up as a solo librarian in a hospital. She has found it a unique opportunity for honing professional skills and immensely gratifying to see how her work supports the mission of family-centered care, the education of health professionals, and research that can help children in the future.

Michael Russell is a senior competitive intelligence analyst working in the health insurance industry. He is a graduate of Rutgers University School of Communication, Information and Library Studies. Michael has over twenty-five years of experience in the health care industry in a variety of roles prior to getting his MLS. He is studying for advanced degrees in business and psychology.

Michael Sauers was the Internet trainer for BCR's Member Services Division and part-time reference librarian for the Arapahoe County (Colorado) Library District. He is now the technology innovation librarian for the Nebraska State Library, where his duties are pretty much the same as they were at BCR. He is the author of eight books on libraries and technology. He maintains a blog at travelinlibrarian.info.

Dena Schoen holds an MLIS and MA in Russian literature from UC Berkeley. She has worked in the UC Berkeley Main Library and the library of the Hoover Institution at Stanford University, where she served as Slavic librarian. She also worked in the Open Society Archives in Budapest, Hungary, as samizdat curator. Eventually she joined the agent world as regional manager for YBP Library Services. Currently she is director of sales for North America for Otto Harrassowitz.

Laurie Selwyn received her MSL from Western Michigan University in 1980 and has been employed in a variety of positions ranging from audiovisual specialist and young adult services to reference and library administration in academic, public, and special libraries. A frequent reviewer for *Library Journal*, she has written audio, video, and reference reviews since the early 1980s and has been employed as a public law librarian in Texas since 2002.

Born and raised in Tennessee, **Tracy Shields** now lives in Westchester County, New York. She works as the assistant editor for The Medical Letter. She earned her bachelor's in biology from Vanderbilt University and master's in information sciences from the University of Tennessee, Knoxville. She spends most of her time curled up beside her black Labrador retriever with her nose in a good book.

Glennor Shirley works for the Maryland State Department of Education as the library coordinator for correctional education libraries. She previously managed public library branches in Maryland and Jamaica. She has written articles and created Web sites about prison libraries, and she also designed an innovative CD-ROM tutorial to teach prison inmates how to use the Internet. An active member of the Maryland Library Association, she has a BA from the University of the West Indies, an MAS from Johns Hopkins University, and an MLS from the University of Maryland.

Judith A. Siess is a recognized expert in one-person librarianship and interpersonal networking. She has drawn from her more than twenty years' experience and written seven books: *The SOLO Librarian's Sourcebook*; *The OPL Sourcebook: A Guide for Solo and Small Libraries*; *Time Management, Planning and Prioritization for Librarians*; *The Visible Librarian: Asserting Your Value with Marketing and Advocacy;* and *The Essential OPL, 1998–2004: The Best of Seven Years of The One-Person Library, A Newsletter for Librarians and Management; The New OPL Sourcebook: A Guide for Solo and Small Libraries;* and *Out Front with Stephen Abram: A Guide for Information Leaders.* Judith also has been the editor and publisher of *The One-Person Library: A Newsletter for Librarians and Management* since 1998 and is the author of numerous articles. An active member of SLA, she is very proud to have been the first chair of its Solo Librarians division.

Ann Snoeyenbos worked at the New York University Bobst Library in New York City for thirteen years. At NYU she was librarian for West European social science, a position that included reference, collection development, instruction, and departmental liaison activities. She started working as sales coordinator for international and special markets at Project MUSE in 2004.

Jenny Spadafora spends a freakish percentage of her waking hours online. She is an obsessive reader, a (very) amateur digital photographer, and because she lives in a major city, she can get around without a driver's license. Jenny invested quality time in pursuit of higher education, earning an undergraduate degree from Sarah Lawrence College, an MA in English from the University of Nebraska–Lincoln, and an MLS from Simmons College. She works as a community evangelist for Intuit's Innovation Lab. She can be contacted via her Web site, 12frogs.com.

Doug Stark has been the librarian at the United States Golf Association since 2002. He manages all aspects of the department, including acquisition, preservation, arrangement, and access. In addition, he assists with exhibitions and other large-scale projects. Prior to joining the USGA, he served as assistant curator and librarian/archivist at the Naismith Memorial Basketball Hall of Fame. Stark received his BA in American history and art history from Brandeis University, an MA in American history from New York University (including professional certification in archival management and museum studies), and an MBA with a concentration in nonprofit management from the University of Massachusetts at Amherst.

In early 1998 **Samantha Starmer** landed in the center of the dot-com bubble quite accidentally with a job at Amazon.com. She originally thought it would be a temporary diversion. Almost six years and a dozen big projects later, she realized that a lot of the work she had been doing actually had a name—information architecture. She decided to return to school at the University of Washington to get an MLIS and a more theoretical and historical understanding of information and its management. After a variety of experiences doing usability work, interaction design, and metadata management, she now uses all aspects of her degree and background as an intranet program manager at Microsoft. She is also pleased to serve on the boards for Content Management Professionals (www.cmprofessionals.org) and the Information Architecture Institute (iainstitute.org).

Beginning in 1995, **Christina Stoll** worked at the North Suburban Library System (NSLS) for five years. She is now a library consultant with the Metropolitan Library System. During her time at NSLS, she was the special library liaison and the knowledge manager, spearheading their Knowledge Management Initiative. Christina's expertise is with project management of the system's KM Initiative, organizational development, librarian recruitment, staff training, customer technical support, and professional development planning. She earned her MLIS from Dominican University in 2001. She has published and presented on several occasions about her work with knowledge management, including the article "Writing the Book on Knowledge Management" for *Association Management Magazine* (April 2004) and a presentation called "Expanding KM Outside the Enterprise" at APQC's (www.apqc.org) annual conference in 2005. Christina was most recently recognized in *Library Journal*'s 2006 Movers and Shakers issue.

Sarah Sutton began her career in librarianship at Texas A&M University–Corpus Christi in 2001. She has served as serials librarian and is currently serials/electronic resources librarian. Sarah is the recipient of the 2003 North American Serials Interest Group's Horizon Award for promising new serialists. She holds a bachelor's degree from Washington University in St. Louis, an MLS from Texas Woman's University, and is currently pursuing a PhD in library science from Texas Woman's University.

Ellen Symons has been a cataloging/training librarian at Queen's University since 2005. Prior to this, she worked at the Canadian Centre for Architecture in Montreal; Bishop's University in Lennoxville, Quebec; and OCLC Canada.

Vernon R. Totanes is a licensed librarian with an MLIS from the University of the Philippines and an undergraduate degree in management engineering from the Ateneo de Manila University. His experience as a freelance book producer contributed greatly to his decisions to become a librarian, set up the blog Filipino Librarian (filipinolibrarian.blogspot.com/), and pursue his PhD in book history and print culture at the University of Toronto..

Doris J. Van Kampen is systems librarian and assistant professor at Saint Leo University. She holds a doctorate of education from the University of Central Florida. Her research interests include library anxiety and the information search process, focused on graduate students and historians; information retrieval; copyright and intellectual property; and young adult and children's literature written in the 1940s, 1950s, and 1960s. She has been published in *College & Research Libraries*, the *Journal of Library & Information Services in Distance Learning*, *Women in Higher Education*, and *Florida Media Quarterly*.

Marc Vera is a self-diagnosed pop culture junkie. He sees over two hundred movies a year, owns over three thousand CDs, and reads way too much. He has taught about pop culture at the University of Michigan and presented a paper on the future of industrial music at the 2003 International Association for the Study of Popular Music Conference in Montreal. When not working for *Entertainment Weekly*'s EW.com, he writes for RewardTV.com, *Alternative Press* magazine, and works in his new modern boutique store, :nook.

Celia Waters (MA MCLIP) has spent the past fourteen years working in the library and information profession in the United Kingdom. Following a BA (Hons) degree in history from Southampton University, she took a one-year placement at the Science Museum Library in South Kensington, London, and then went on to complete her MA in librarianship at Sheffield University. Her first professional post was with the BBC's Engineering Research Department. From there she moved on to work for the Foreign and Commonwealth Office, the Civil Aviation Authority, DERA (the Defence Research and Evaluation Agency), and then QinetiQ when DERA was privatized. Since 2003, she has been with Dstl (Defence Science and Technology Laboratory), where she is responsible for setting up and running the library at their headquarters site in Farnborough, Hampshire.

Jessamyn West is a community technology educator in central Vermont, where she works with public librarians and seniors, helping them use technology to solve problems. Her first technology education position was in 1994, training journalists in Bucharest, Romania, how to use Pine and Gopher. She started her Web site (www.jessamyn.com) in 1995; she is also the editor of the Weblog librarian.net, where she examines the intersection of libraries, technology, and politics. She is a moderator of the online community MetaFilter (www.metafilter.com). Jessamyn can teach anyone how to use a computer and still types letters to friends on an Underwood-Olivetti Lettera 22. She will send you a letter if you send her a postcard.

When she wrote her chapter, **Cynthia I. Wilson** was a member support coordinator for PALINET; she has since been promoted to associate manager for support services. She started working in libraries while pursuing her bachelor's degree in communications at Beaver College (now Arcadia University). She worked her way up from being a student employee at the circulation desk to becoming a librarian after receiving her master's degree from Clarion University in 2004. Cynthia has experience in interlibrary loan, cataloging books and photographs, archives, special collections, serials check-in, circulation, shelf reading, and acquisitions. She is also a photographer who is trying to move the image of the librarian into the twenty-first century with her Web site, www.iamalibrarian.com.

Robert Wolfe started his library career in the Houghton Library as a stacks page, retrieving and reshelving rare printed books and manuscripts. Naturally, he fell in love with the printed word and sought to spend his entire career engaged in its care. After graduation he worked as an assistant bibliographer for the library and for a rare book dealer. He received his MLIS from Simmons College, where he discovered electronic and digital resources. While in library school he fell in with the "dot-bomb" crowd and had the good fortune to practice creating metadata (LOM and IMS-CP) for an educational publisher while still in school. He was laid off the same month that he received his degree. He worked at Genzyme, managing document delivery services for Infotrieve, while he waited for an opportunity as perfect as the Metadata Services Unit in the MIT Libraries. Robert is available via libraries.mit.edu/metadata.

Mary-Doug Wright is principal of Apex Information, a consulting firm in Vancouver, British Columbia. She brings to her clients extensive expertise and experience conducting environmental scans and comprehensive literature searches in all areas of health care for systematic reviews and critical appraisals. Her particular areas of concern include health services, policy, economics, and planning; health technology assessment; patient care planning; and therapeutics. Clients are in the public, nonprofit, and private sectors and include academic research centers, national and international consulting firms, decision makers, health care providers, independent researchers, and health information consumers. She is a member of the Association of Independent Information Professionals, the Canadian Health Libraries Association, and the Health Libraries Association of British Columbia. In her spare time, she reads, walks her dogs, and spends as much time as she can drawing and painting.

Since 1989, **Enid L. Zafran** has operated her own business, Indexing Partners. A graduate of Mount Holyoke College, she has a JD from Cleveland Marshall College of Law, an MLS from the University of Kentucky, and an LLM in labor law from Georgetown Law Center. She has worked at Banks-Baldwin Law Publishing in Cleveland, Ohio; Prentice Hall Law and Business in Paramus, New Jersey; and from 1990–2002 was director of indexing services at the Bureau of

National Affairs, Washington, D.C. She served as president of the American Society of Indexers as well as chair of the local D.C. chapter of the society. Enid has taught indexing classes at EEI Communications in Alexandria, Virginia, and given presentations and workshops at various publishing and librarian groups in the United States and Canada, including SLA and AALL. She has also written extensively on the subject of indexing.

Candy Zemon began her library career as a student worker in a preautomation small academic library. That training has been invaluable in her subsequent career, which deals exclusively with various tools to address variations, relatives, and descendents of the library problems she learned about in the mid-1960s. She received her AMLS from the University of Michigan, where she also gained experience working in larger academic libraries. Since 1980, Candy has worked for various library automation vendors, including a period as cofounder and president of Pigasus Software. Since 2001, she has served as senior product strategist for Polaris Library Systems.

About the Editors

Richard A. Murray is catalog librarian for Spanish and Portuguese languages at Duke University in Durham, North Carolina. Previously, he was a catalog librarian at Vanderbilt University and a paraprofessional cataloger at the University of North Carolina at Chapel Hill. Rich has written about library career issues for books, newsletters, and Web sites and is the assistant editor of LIScareer.com; he has also been actively involved with ALA's International Relations Committee and New Members Round Table. A native of Raleigh, North Carolina, Rich earned an MSLS and a BA in international studies (with concentrations in anthropology and Latin American studies) from the University of North Carolina at Chapel Hill.

Priscilla K. Shontz is the editor of *The Librarian's Career Guidebook* and author of *Jump Start Your Career in Library and Information Science*. She is also the founder, editor, and Webmaster of LIScareer.com. She currently works as a freelance writer in Houston, Texas, while staying home with her two young daughters. Over the past twenty years, Priscilla has worked as a student assistant, paraprofessional, and librarian in university, community college, medical, and public libraries. She is a past president of ALA's New Members Round Table. Priscilla earned a BS in communications from the University of Texas at Arlington and an MSLS from the University of North Texas.

About LIScareer.com

LIScareer.com offers career development resources for librarians, information professionals, and students. The goal of the site is to help new and prospective librarians and information professionals manage a successful and satisfying career. Though the site is primarily aimed at newer librarians and students, the resources may be helpful to a librarian at any stage of his or her career. The site includes practical advice contributed by information professionals, links to online resources, and information about print resources. LIScareer.com welcomes contributed articles and suggestions. Please visit www.liscareer.com for more information.